The Rinehart Reader

Jean Wyrick
Colorado State University

Beverly J. Slaughter
Brevard Community College

HARCOURT BRACE JOVANOVICH
College Publishers
*Fort Worth   Philadelphia   San Diego   New York   Orlando   Austin
San Antonio   Toronto   Montreal   London   Sydney   Tokyo*

COVER IMAGE:

Henri Matisse, "Poppies", c.1919, oil on canvas, 100.6 cm $\times$ 81.2 cm © The Detroit Institute of Arts, Bequest of Robert H. Tannahill.

Publisher: Ted Buchholz
Acquisitions Editor: Michael Rosenberg
Developmental Editors: Stacy Schoolfield and Camille Adkins
Senior Project Editor: Katherine Vardy Lincoln
Production Manager: Cynthia Young
Text & Cover Design: Terry Rasberry
Compositor: Impressions

Library of Congress Cataloging-in-Publication number 92-076693-1

Printed in the United States of America
2   3   4   090   9   8   7   6   5   4   3   2   1

ISBBN: 0-03-076693-1   88-9056
                                                           CIP

Harcourt Brace Jovanovich College Publishers
The Dryden Press
Saunders College Publishing

Preface

To some students the term "classic" suggests a certain accumulation of dust. This classic collection should dispose of that notion once and for all. The selections in *The Rinehart Reader* are classics in the sense of being established works by many of our best writers, works that instructors have turned to as models of eloquence and power again and again. But they are certainly not dusty. They are works that will challenge, inform, and stimulate student writers. In short, they are selections that fit Ezra Pound's wonderful definition of literature as "news that stays news."

Within that standard of quality, the selections provide ample variety. They range across the generations from the eighteenth century to the present. They vary in style from Thurber's whimsical touch to the fierce elegance of James Baldwin. They include multiple selections by several writers that illustrate the scope of individual style. And they range in method and intent across the traditional rhetorical categories.

In this second edition we were given the opportunity to offer some exciting new selections, based on information provided by teachers and students who had used the first edition. We are pleased to include such diverse writers as John Steinbeck, N. Scott Momaday, John Ciardi, Elizabeth Cady Stanton, Barry Lopez, and Garrison Keillor. In several cases we chose to present new selections by authors who appeared in the first edition; thus the splendid styles of writers such as Alice Walker, Annie Dillard, Ralph Ellison, Richard Rodriguez, and Lewis Thomas continue to be represented in this edition. Those who have taught from this textbook will be pleased to see that they may still introduce to their students the power of Maya Angelou, E. B. White, Jessica Mitford, Martin Luther King, Jr., and other favorites. Readers will discover twenty-four new selections added to the fifty-six essays most appreciated by users of the first edition.

This edition also features revised introductions to each rhetorical mode. Examples from the essays new to this edition are often used to illustrate the rhetorical modes.

To increase the usefulness of the selections, *The Rinehart Reader* opens with a unique two-part section. The first chapter, "Why Read?", offers a rationale for critical reading, followed by note-taking techniques that are

then demonstrated in detail in an annotated essay. Following this introduction are works by nine distinguished authors on the subject of reading.
These essays offer a variety of imaginative approaches to a task that some
students too often take for granted.

The second chapter, "The Writing Process," presents a clear, concise
guide to the methods most widely used in today's composition courses. Eight
essays on the subject of writing follow, many by authors experienced in
writing instruction. Other essays in this section offer a personal or inspirational look at what writing means to some of its finest practitioners.

This comprehensive introduction gives students more on the subject
of critical reading and the writing process than do most other college readers.
For many courses, it can eliminate the need for supplementary texts. After
completing the first two chapters, students will not only have an overview
of the reading-writing processes, they will also have their appetites whetted
for the classic essays to follow.

The essays themselves are grouped by chapter in the traditional rhetorical sequence, from narration to argumentation. Each chapter has a separate introduction that defines the rhetorical mode, shows how and when
it is commonly used, and describes it through brief examples. The introduction then provides students with step-by-step guidelines for developing
that particular rhetorical strategy in their own writing.

Each reading selection is preceded by a brief biography of the author,
most with photographs. A set of five review questions—one of them a writing
assignment—follows the reading. An additional set of writing assignments
concludes each chapter. These final assignments refer to the specific readings,
thus supporting what is, after all, the main purpose of the reader—to use
classic essays as working models for student writing.

Reference features include a glossary of rhetorical terms, a list of authors represented by more than one essay, an annotated table of contents,
and an alternate thematic table of contents. An excellent instructor's manual,
prepared by Kimberly Miller, is also available at no additional charge.

We hope this brief description has clarified what the second edition of
The Rinehart Reader is and what it isn't. We have not attempted to create a
reader with a "gimmick" or one with unusual or peripheral selections. What
The Rinehart Reader does provide is ample material on reading and the
writing process, the rhetorical organization that most instructors prefer, and
an excellent selection of essays that have demonstrated their value both as
literature and as models of effective writing. Our intention is to give you
what you need and expect from a traditional reader, developed to the very
highest editorial standards. We would be lax in pursuing that goal if we
failed to invite your comments and suggestions. Please direct them, along
with any requests for information or sample materials, to the English Editor;
Harcourt Brace Jovanovich Publishers; 301 Commerce Street, Suite 3700;
Fort Worth, Texas 76102.

Acknowledgments

We would like to thank the following people at HBJ for their work on this edition: Michael Rosenberg, English Acquisitions Editor, and Stacy Schoolfield, Development Editor, for their patience, advice, and many efforts to improve the manuscript in numerous ways; Katherine Lincoln, Senior Project Editor, for her careful guidance of the manuscript through production; and Barbara McGinnes, Photo/Permissions Editor, for securing photos, reprint rights and contracts. We would also like to express appreciation to Barbara Conner, copy editor, for an excellent job refining the text; Charles Naylor, for his meticulous care in the proofing of final pages; and Kimberly Miller, for her thorough work on the biographical sketches and the Instructor's Manual.

We are also indebted to the following colleagues who reviewed the text for this edition. Their comments were very helpful in our final selection of essays added to this edition: Tracey Baker, University of Alabama at Birmingham; James E. Barcus, Baylor University; Laura L. Burns, Bellevue Community College; Elizabeth T. Coffman, James H. Faulkner State Junior College; Diane Gould, Shoreline Community College; Paul Kleinpoppen, Florida Community College at Jacksonville; James Manis, Pennsylvania State University, Hazleton; and Linda S. Wilkins, Knoxville College.

To the Student

How do writers write? George Simenon would churn out whole novels in eleven-day frenzies, with a complete medical examination before and after. Flaubert would sit smoking a pipe from noon till four in the morning, often completing no more than a sentence. Proust wrote lying in bed. Hemingway wrote standing up. The lives and habits of writers offer endless anecdotes, but no useful rules.

Yet there are clearly problems and techniques that all writers share. This book is organized to reveal them. It groups diverse works according to essential rhetorical forms, allowing you to see, for example, how both Alice Walker and George Orwell develop a narration, how both Thomas Jefferson and Margaret Mead construct and close an argument. From such comparisons common elements emerge—not rules per se, but strategies, structures, methods, and tools.

These strategies may not be readily apparent in the essays themselves. In fact, the better the writing, the less exposed are its methods, the less obvious is the hard work that produced it. We may breeze through a piece by Thurber, but Thurber certainly didn't. Try stopping in the middle of one of his sentences. Then ask yourself how you would complete the sentence, the paragraph, or the entire essay. Suddenly, it's no breeze.

In this respect, the first chapters of the book are vital. They will show you how to read critically, think like a writer, and practice as you go. The same is true for the introductions to the mode and strategy that begin each chapter in Part 2. As you read the selections in each chapter, you should refer to the chapter's introduction often. Doing so will help you understand specific strategies of development you are studying. These introductions will also help you focus on the specific technique being considered. In the writing assignments that follow the selections, you will be asked to practice certain methods of organization and development.

Of course, any essay is more than just a neat stack of rhetorical techniques. This book offers a wealth of ideas, styles, voices, facts, punchlines, images, and philosophies, all of which are resources for your own writing. You can greatly expand these resources by using the book's Thematic Table of Contents for additional comparative readings and the list of multiple selections to examine the range of a single author's style. The Annotated Table of Contents is useful for the browser.

We hope that this book will be a part of a lively, informative course and a source of good reading long after graduation. We always enjoy hearing from students who use our texts. Any comments, questions, or suggestions may be sent to the English Editor; Harcourt Brace Jovanovich College Publishers; 301 Commerce Street, Suite 3700; Fort Worth, Texas 76102.

ABOUT THE TITLE OF THIS BOOK

STANLEY M. RINEHART, JR. (1897–1969), was a distinguished book publisher. In 1929, he, his brother Frederick, and editor John Farrar founded the publishing house of Farrar & Rinehart, which later became (in 1946) Rinehart & Company, and then (in 1960) Holt, Rinehart and Winston. As president of Rinehart & Company, Stanely Rinehart published such works as Norman Mailer's *The Naked and the Dead*, the "Nero Wolfe" detective novels of Rex Stout, and Rinehart Editions, a series of quality paperback editions of classic literature. The firm began its college department in 1934 and soon became a major publisher in the field, specializing in the humanities and social sciences. Today, Harcourt Brace Jovanovich College Publishers carries on this same tradition of publishing excellence through such noteworthy volumes as *The Rinehart Handbook for Writers, The Rinehart Guide to Grammar and Usage,* and *The Rinehart Reader.*

Contents

PART 1

Reading and Writing Essays

Chapter 1

**Why Read? How Can Reading These
Essays Help Me?**   3

WRITERS ON READING   13

Donald Murray, *Reading as a Reader*   15
Eudora Welty, *A Sweet Devouring*   31
Richard Wright, *Discovering Books*   35
Judith Viorst, *How Books Helped Shape My Life*   43
Donald Hall, *Four Kinds of Reading*   49
Lin Yutang, *The Art of Reading*   53
Robert MacNeil, *Wordstruck*   59
Lance Morrow, *The Best Refuge for Insomniacs*   65
Wendell Berry, *In Defense of Literacy*   68

Chapter 2

The Writing Process   73

WRITERS ON WRITING   90

Joan Didion, *Why I Write*   92
Annie Dillard, *Writing and Vision*   99
Henry D. Thoreau, *On Keeping a Private Journal*   104
Peter Elbow, *Freewriting*   106
Sheridan Baker, *What Shall I Write?*   109

Jacqueline Berke, *The Qualities of Good Writing*   115
William Zinsser, *Style*   122
Donald Murray, *The Maker's Eye: Revising Your Own Manuscripts*   127

PART 2

Essays for Reading and Analysis

Chapter 3

Narration   135

Langston Hughes, *Salvation*   139
Richard Selzer, *The Discus Thrower*   143
Maya Angelou, *Graduation in Stamps*   148
Martin Gansberg, *38 Who Saw Murder Didn't Call the Police*   160
Alice Walker, *Beauty: When the Other Dancer Is the Self*   165
George Orwell, *Shooting an Elephant*   174

Chapter 4

Description   183

John Steinbeck, *The Turtle*   188
Maxine Hong Kingston, *Portraits of My Parents*   192
N. Scott Momaday, *The Way To Rainy Mountain*   198
E. B. White, *Once More to the Lake*   205
Virginia Woolf, *If Shakespeare Had Had a Sister*   213
James Baldwin, *Stranger in the Village*   226

Chapter 5

Process   239

Carin Quinn, *The Jeaning of America*   242
Jessica Mitford, *The American Way of Death*   245
Garrison Keillor, *Attitude*   253
Martin Luther King, Jr., *Nonviolent Resistance*   258
Henry David Thoreau, *Economy*   264
Samuel H. Scudder, *Take This Fish and Look At It*   270

Chapter 6

Definition   277

Ellen Goodman, *It's Failure, Not Success*   282
John Ciardi, *What Is Happiness?*   285
Joan Didion, *On Self-Respect*   289
Richard Rodriguez, *Hispanic-American Culture*   295
Margaret Mead, *New Superstitions for Old*   301
Ralph Ellison, *Discrimination*   307

Chapter 7

Illustration   317

William F. Buckley, Jr., *Why Don't We Complain?*   321
Brent Staples, *Black Men and Public Space*   328
James Thurber, *University Days*   333
Barbara Tuchman, *Mankind's Better Moments*   340
Alice Walker, *In Search of Our Mothers' Gardens*   347
Loren Eiseley, *The Brown Wasps*   357

Chapter 8

Comparison and Contrast   367

Mark Twain, *Two Ways of Looking at the River*   372
Russell Baker, *The Two Ismo's*   376
Bruce Catton, *Grant and Lee: A Study in Contrasts*   380
Barry Lopez, *My Horse*   386
Lewis Thomas, *The Iks*   394
Toni Morrison, *A Slow Walk of Trees*   399

Chapter 9

Division and Classification   409

John Updike, *Three Boys*   414
Judith Viorst, *Friends, Good Friends, and Such Good Friends*   420
E.B. White, *Three New Yorks*   427
William Zinsser, *College Pressures*   430
William Golding, *Thinking as a Hobby*   439
Gilbert Highet, *The Face in the Mirror*   447

Chapter 10

Cause and Effect 455

Norman Cousins, *Pain Is Not the Ultimate Enemy* 460
E. M. Forster, *My Wood* 466
Barbara Tuchman, *"This Is The End of The World": The Black Death* 471
Alice Stewart Trillin, *Of Dragons and Garden Peas* 483
Marya Mannes, *How Do You Know It's Good?* 490
George Orwell, *Politics and the English Language* 498

Chapter 11

Persuasion and Argument 513

Rachel Carson, *The Obligation to Endure* 527
Martin Luther King, Jr., *I Have a Dream* 535
Lewis Thomas, *The Health-Care System* 541
Richard Rodriguez, *None of This Is Fair* 545
Gore Vidal, *Drugs* 551
Margaret Mead, *One Vote for This Age of Anxiety* 555
Flannery O'Connor, *Total Effect and the Eighth Grade* 561
Judy Brady, *I Want a Wife* 566
Thomas Jefferson, *Declaration of Independence* 570
Elizabeth Cady Stanton, *Declaration of Sentiments and Resolutions* 576
Virginia Woolf, *Professions for Women* 581
Jonathan Swift, *A Modest Proposal* 588

Glossary of Rhetorical Terms 599

Index 603

Annotated Contents

PART 1

Reading and Writing Essays

Chapter 1

Why Read? How Can Reading These Essays Help Me? 3

WRITERS ON READING 13

Donald Murray, *Reading as a Reader* 15
A practical approach to the craft of reading—"write to learn how to read and read to learn how to write"—is outlined by a Pulitzer Prize winning journalist and successful teacher of writing.

Eudora Welty, *A Sweet Devouring* 31
A respected novelist and short story writer recalls first falling in love with the printed page.

Richard Wright, *Discovering Books* 35
Through reading novels that he schemed to borrow, a writer discovered both point of view and a sense of himself.

Judith Viorst, *How Books Helped Shape My Life* 43
Influenced first by heroines who "went out and did," this popular writer found fictional models in each stage of her life that powerfully affected her intellectual and spiritual growth.

Donald Hall, *Four Kinds of Reading* 49
A noted poet and editor distinguishes "four kinds of reading, each with a characteristic manner and purpose."

Lin Yutang, *The Art of Reading* 53
The best reading, argues a Chinese scholar, leads us into the contemplative mood, "for our interests grow like a tree or flow like a river."

Robert MacNeil, *Wordstruck* 59
This award-winning commentator recalls how reading helped shape his imagination and led to the discovery that "words make another place, a place to escape to with your spirit alone."

Lance Morrow, *The Best Refuge for Insomniacs* 65
According to this respected essayist, books not only inspire us to recognize our possibilities in life, but they also provide comfort and help us survive our bleakest hours in difficult times.

Wendell Berry, *In Defense of Literacy* 68
"The mastery of language and the knowledge of books" is a necessity if the average American is to resist the media's premeditated language-as-weapon.

Chapter 2

The Writing Process 73

WRITERS ON WRITING 90

Joan Didion, *Why I Write* 92
For one of the most impressive observers of contemporary society, writing is a forceful way of turning the pictures in her head into important messages.

Annie Dillard, *Writing and Vision* 99
A famous naturalist draws a subtle analogy between chopping wood and the process by which writers discover their ideas, concluding with an answer to the question, "Who will teach me to write?"

Henry D. Thoreau, *On Keeping a Journal* 104
An important American thinker and writer explains the value of keeping a journal, not only to record good ideas but also to examine our thoughts, feelings, and character.

Peter Elbow, *Freewriting* 106
A proponent of "the teacherless class" describes a non-traditional way to begin writing: "Freewriting may seem crazy but actually it makes simple sense."

Sheridan Baker, *What Shall I Write?*   109
"The best subjects lie nearest at hand and nearest the heart," advises an expert on writing, who also advocates drafting essays with a clear "argumentative edge."

Jacqueline Berke, *The Qualities of Good Writing*   115
Economy, simplicity, and clarity are three of the several qualities that characterize all good writing, according to this teacher and writer who practices what she preaches in her straight-forward, clear essay.

William Zinsser, *Style*   122
A well-known expert on writing urges novice writers to listen to their own voice and resist the temptation to imitate others, "as if 'style' were something you could buy at a style store and drape onto your words in bright decorator colors."

Donald Murray, *The Maker's Eye: Revising Your Own Manuscripts*   127
A noted author and teacher who firmly believes revision is integral to the writing process offers practical advice to help writers become "their own best enemy" as they rework their drafts for clearer meaning.

PART 2

Essays for Reading and Analysis

Chapter 3

Narration   135

Langston Hughes, *Salvation*   139
An admired poet recalls how, as a boy of thirteen, he was pressured into feigning religious conversion.

Richard Selzer, *The Discus Thrower*   143
A sympathetic surgeon observes the last days of a terminally ill patient whose bitter humor reveals a man dying according to the advice of poet Dylan Thomas: "Do not go gentle into that good night."

Maya Angelou, *Graduation in Stamps*   148
A multitalented writer remembers her high school graduation ceremony with pride, despite the intrusion of a racist school official.

Martin Gansberg, *38 Who Saw Murder Didn't Call the Police*   160
This famous newspaper story, written by a New York journalist, narrates
the brutal murder of Kitty Genovese, a young woman repeatedly attacked
as 38 of her neighbors watched but refused to become involved.

Alice Walker, *Beauty: When the Other Dancer Is the Self*   165
Blinded in one eye by a childhood accident, this prize-winning novelist
struggles to see herself "beautiful, whole, and free."

George Orwell, *Shooting an Elephant*   174
When a young Englishman serving with the Burmese police confronts a
raging elephant, he discovers important insights into "the real nature of
imperialism" and his own character.

Chapter 4

Description   183

John Steinbeck, *The Turtle*   188
Excerpted from the classic novel *The Grapes of Wrath*, this description of a
lowly turtle illustrates Steinbeck's belief in the perseverance and dignity of
life.

Maxine Hong Kingston, *Portraits of My Parents*   192
A child of Chinese immigrants searches in old photographs for the
meaning of her parents' past.

N. Scott Momaday, *The Way to Rainy Mountain*   198
The landscape of Oklahoma and the legends of the Kiowa people inspire
this Native-American writer to recall the richness of his culture and the
love of his grandmother.

E. B. White, *Once More to the Lake*   205
Revisiting a Maine lake transports a prominent essayist to his childhood
and also reveals a glimpse of the future.

Virginia Woolf, *If Shakespeare Had Had a Sister*   213
Using the hypothetical figure "Judith Shakespeare," this British novelist
describes the formidable difficulties confronting the creative woman.

James Baldwin, *Stranger in the Village*   226
Experiences in a Swiss village lead a black writer to consider his status in
America and to conclude "the interracial drama acted out on the American
continent has not only created a new black man, it has created a new
white man as well."

Chapter 5

Process   239

Carin Quinn, *The Jeaning of America*   242
Creative thinking by a nineteenth-century peddler led to the invention of
blue jeans, an American symbol.

Jessica Mitford, *The American Way of Death*   245
An investigative journalist parts "the formaldehyde curtain" and vividly
describes the process of embalming and "casketing" Mr. Jones.

Garrison Keillor, *Attitude*   253
"Each player is responsible for his or her own attitude, and to a
considerable degree you can *create* a good attitude," declares this humorist
as he outlines the proper steps one must take to develop the right
character for slow-pitch baseball.

Martin Luther King, Jr., *Nonviolent Resistance*   258
Because "the old law of an eye for an eye leaves everybody blind," the
leader of the Civil Rights Movement advocates nonviolent resistance.

Henry David Thoreau, *Economy*   264
In the course of describing the construction of his cabin, an American
philosopher defines independence.

Samuel H. Scudder, *Take This Fish and Look at It*   270
By following the wise advice of his professor, a student of natural history
learns about the value of close, repeated observations and the relationship
between facts and general laws.

Chapter 6

Definition   277

Ellen Goodman, *It's Failure, Not Success*   282
The success extolled by popular self-help books lacks an ethical dimension,
claims this well-known newspaper columnist.

John Ciardi, *What Is Happiness?*   285
According to this American poet, the advertised version of happiness in
this country is false; true happiness, he argues, "is neither in having nor in
being, but in becoming."

Joan Didion, *On Self-Respect*   289
Self-respect derives from "the willingness to accept responsibility for one's own life" and is essential for mental health, says this contemporary writer.

Richard Rodriguez, *Hispanic-American Culture*   295
"Expect a marriage. We will change America even as we will be changed," advises this Hispanic-American writer, who believes that this country will profit greatly from an infusion of Latin American culture.

Margaret Mead, *New Superstitions for Old*   301
A famous anthropologist looks at the functions of superstition in the modern world.

Ralph Ellison, *Discrimination*   307
An acclaimed American writer recalls learning the meaning of discrimination as a boy by watching his family experience racial prejudice.

Chapter 7

Illustration   317

William F. Buckley, Jr., *Why Don't We Complain?*   321
By describing a series of humbling personal incidents, this well-known political commentator examines the puzzling hesitancy of Americans to complain and offers his explanation for our "increased sense of helplessness in an age of technology."

Brent Staples, *Black Men and Public Space*   328
A journalist discovers his "unwieldy inheritance" as a black man walking near-deserted urban streets at night: "the ability to alter public space in ugly ways."

James Thurber, *University Days*   333
The delightful comedy of undergraduate life is recollected by a famous humorist.

Barbara Tuchman, *Mankind's Better Moments*   340
To counterbalance prevailing modern pessimism, a noted historian cites examples of human achievement against overwhelming adversity.

Alice Walker, *In Search of Our Mothers' Gardens*   347
In this moving essay, a prize-winning novelist pays homage to the mothers and grandmothers who, even in the most hostile circumstances, handed down the creative spark that enabled their children to become the artists and poets of today.

Loren Eiseley, *The Brown Wasps*   357
A respected conservationist uses a series of natural images to illustrate
how, amidst a changing world, all life clings to a time and place.

Chapter 8

Comparison and Contrast   367

Mark Twain, *Two Ways of Looking at the River*   372
A one-time riverboat pilot uses his own experiences to show that in the
transition from romantic to pragmatist, more may be lost than gained.

Russell Baker, *The Two Ismo's*   376
According to a popular humorist, today's urban males conform to one of
two warring dogmas: machismo or "quichismo."

Bruce Catton, *Grant and Lee: A Study in Contrasts*   380
Although the two generals symbolized conflicting philosophies, a well-
known historian believes that their behavior at Appomatox made possible
"a peace of reconciliation."

Barry Lopez, *My Horse*   386
This contemporary writer draws an analogy between the horse proudly
ridden by the nineteenth-century Native-American warrior and his own
means of transportation, his dented but ever-faithful truck.

Lewis Thomas, *The Iks*   394
The repellent behavior of the members of a displaced Ugandan tribe
resembles the hostile behavior of cities and nations, charges a widely read
scientist.

Toni Morrison, *A Slow Walk of Trees*   399
By listening to her grandparents' widely disparate views on "the
possibilities of life for black people in this country," this highly regarded
novelist finds her own point of view.

Chapter 9

Division and Classification   409

John Updike, *Three Boys*   414
A prize-winning novelist remembers how three boys taught the author
about human nature and about himself.

Judith Viorst, *Friends, Good Friends, and Such Good Friends*   420
Each of the seven varieties of friendship described by a popular magazine writer is valuable in its own way.

E. B. White, *Three New Yorks*   427
A columnist's look at New York inhabitants shows that the city is distinctly different for commuters, natives, and settlers.

William Zinsser, *College Pressures*   430
Pressured by parents and peers, squeezed by economic constraints, and stressed by the demands they make on themselves, "the young are growing up old," argues this writer and teacher.

William Golding, *Thinking as a Hobby*   439
Statuettes in his headmaster's study lead this novelist to conclude that there are three grades of thinking.

Gilbert Highet, *The Face in the Mirror*   447
According to this scholar, everyone has at least one book inside him or her—an autobiography—and there are three different ways of telling the fascinating story of one's life.

Chapter 10

Cause and Effect   455

Norman Cousins, *Pain Is Not the Ultimate Enemy*   460
A respected editor proposes that pain-killers may be more hazardous to your health than the pain they are meant to treat.

E. M. Forster, *My Wood*   466
Buying a piece of land showed this writer how possession of property can affect one's character.

Barbara Tuchman, *"This Is the End of the World": The Black Death*   471
In this detailed, vivid account, a noted historian reveals the causes and the catastrophic effects of the bubonic plague as it spread across fourteenth-century Europe.

Alice Stewart Trillin, *Of Dragons and Garden Peas*   483
In a speech to medical students, later published in the *New England Journal of Medicine*, this writer and former cancer patient discusses the ways the fear of dying affects both the sick and the well.

Marya Mannes, *How Do You Know It's Good?* 490
What would we do if there were no critics offering their assessments of music, drama, art, or literature, asks this former *New York Times'* columnist, who argues that a knowledge of purpose and craftsmanship should govern our critical judgments.

George Orwell, *Politics and the English Language* 498
In this well-known essay, an acclaimed British novelist shows the relationship between corrupt language and foolish thinking.

Chapter 11

Persuasion and Argument 513

Rachel Carson, *The Obligation to Endure* 527
The public has a right to know all the facts about insecticides because "It is the public that is being asked to assume the risks that the insect controllers calculate," according to this well-known biologist.

Martin Luther King, Jr., *I Have a Dream* 535
The leader of the Civil Rights Movement urges his audience to use nonviolent protest to bring about the fulfillment of the American promise.

Lewis Thomas, *The Health-Care System* 541
According to this admired physician-writer, people today are obsessed with health issues, an obsession encouraged by the media that not only makes us insecure and apprehensive but that will also make any sort of health-care system unworkable.

Richard Rodriguez, *None of This Is Fair* 545
Affirmative action programs are unfair, decided this controversial Hispanic-American writer after he received—and declined—a flood of job offers.

Gore Vidal, *Drugs* 551
Addiction could be stopped, argues this contemporary novelist, if the profit were removed from the sale of illegal drugs and if the drugs were honestly labeled with the effects on the user.

Margaret Mead, *One Vote for This Age of Anxiety* 555
Modern anxiety may be a sign of hope, rather than despair, suggests this famous anthropologist.

Flannery O'Connor, *Total Effect and the Eighth Grade* 561
A modern fiction writer firmly believes that high schools should be
guiding students through the best writing of the past before assigning
them contemporary literature.

Judy Brady, *I Want a Wife* 566
Using irony and her own list of demands, the author points out the
incredible number of roles wives are often expected to fulfill.

Thomas Jefferson, *The Declaration of Independence* 570
The self-evident truths and tyrannies that led to the Revolution are clearly
presented by one of the Founding Fathers.

Elizabeth Cady Stanton, *Declaration of Sentiments and Resolutions* 576
In 1848, an advocate of women's rights presented a declaration of the
tyrannies against women and the resolutions to alleviate them, writing in a
style strikingly similar to that of another famous revolutionary, Thomas
Jefferson.

Virginia Woolf, *Professions for Women* 581
As she describes her experiences of becoming a writer, the author reveals
her murder of "The Angel of the House" and argues that for professional
women "there are many phantoms and obstacles" blocking the way.

Jonathan Swift, *A Modest Proposal* 588
In protest against the social conditions caused by the mistreatment of the
Irish in the eighteenth century, the author ironically proposes that the
children of the poor be used as food.

Thematic Contents

I. Self

Judith Viorst, *How Books Helped Shape My Life*   43
Joan Didion, *Why I Write*   92
Langston Hughes, *Salvation*   139
Alice Walker, *Beauty: When the Other Dancer Is the Self*   165
Joan Didion, *On Self-Respect*   289
Gilbert Highet, *The Face in the Mirror*   447
E. M. Forster, *My Wood*   466

II. Relationships: Family and Friends

Maxine Hong Kingston, *Portraits of My Parents*   192
E. B. White, *Once More to the Lake*   205
John Updike, *Three Boys*   414
Judith Viorst, *Friends, Good Friends, and Such Good Friends*   420
Judy Brady, *I Want a Wife*   566

III. On Women and Men

Judith Viorst, *How Books Helped Shape My Life*   43
Virginia Woolf, *If Shakespeare Had Had a Sister*   213
Brent Staples, *Black Men and Public Space*   328
Russell Baker, *The Two Ismo's*   376
Judith Viorst, *Friends, Good Friends, and Such Good Friends*   420
Judy Brady, *I Want a Wife*   566
Elizabeth Cady Stanton, *Declaration of Sentiments and Resolutions*   576
Virginia Woolf, *Professions for Women*   581

IV. Women's Issues

Alice Walker, *Beauty: When the Other Dancer Is the Self*   165
Maxine Hong Kingston, *Portraits of My Parents*   192
Virginia Woolf, *If Shakespeare Had Had a Sister*   213
Judith Viorst, *Friends, Good Friends, and Such Good Friends*   420
Judy Brady, *I Want a Wife*   566

Elizabeth Cady Stanton, *Declaration of Sentiments and Resolutions*   576
Virginia Woolf, *Professions for Women*   581

V. Cultural Identity

Richard Wright, *Discovering Books*   35
Maya Angelou, *Graduation in Stamps*   148
George Orwell, *Shooting an Elephant*   174
N. Scott Momaday, *The Way to Rainy Mountain*   198
James Baldwin, *Stranger in the Village*   226
Martin Luther King, Jr., *Nonviolent Resistance*   258
Richard Rodriguez, *Hispanic-American Culture*   295
Ralph Ellison, *Discrimination*   307
Brent Staples, *Black Men and Public Space*   328
Alice Walker, *In Search of Our Mothers' Gardens*   347
Martin Luther King, Jr., *I Have a Dream*   535
Richard Rodriguez, *None of This Is Fair*   545

VI. Education

William Zinsser, *College Pressures*   430
Maya Angelou, *Graduation in Stamps*   148
Samuel H. Scudder, *Take This Fish and Look At It*   270
James Thurber, *University Days*   333
William Golding, *Thinking as a Hobby*   439
Flannery O'Connor, *Total Effect and the Eighth Grade*   561

VII. Health and Medicine

Richard Selzer, *The Discus Thrower*   143
Jessica Mitford, *The American Way of Death*   245
Norman Cousins, *Pain Is Not the Ultimate Enemy*   460
Barbara Tuchman, *"This Is The End of the World": The Black Death*   471
Alice Stewart Trillin, *Of Dragons and Garden Peas*   483
Rachel Carson, *The Obligation to Endure*   527
Lewis Thomas, *The Health-Care System*   541
Gore Vidal, *Drugs*   551

VIII. Social Behavior

Martin Gansberg, *38 Who Saw Murder Didn't Call the Police*   160
Garrison Keillor, *Attitude*   253
Margaret Mead, *New Superstitions for Old*   301
William F. Buckley, Jr., *Why Don't We Complain?*   321
Brent Staples, *Black Men and Public Space*   328
Barbara Tuchman, *Mankind's Better Moments*   340
Loren Eiseley, *The Brown Wasps*   357

Lewis Thomas, *The Iks*   394
Marya Mannes, *How Do You Know It's Good?*   490
Margaret Mead, *One Vote for This Age of Anxiety*   555

IX. Ethical Choices

Langston Hughes, *Salvation*   139
Martin Gansberg, *38 Who Saw Murder Didn't Call the Police*   160
George Orwell, *Shooting an Elephant*   174
Martin Luther King, Jr., *Nonviolent Resistance*   258
Ellen Goodman, *It's Failure, Not Success*   282
John Ciardi, *What Is Happiness?*   285
Joan Didion, *On Self-Respect*   289
William F. Buckley, Jr., *Why Don't We Complain?*   321
Martin Luther King, Jr., *I Have a Dream*   535
Gore Vidal, *Drugs*   551

X. Power and Politics

George Orwell, *Shooting an Elephant*   174
Martin Luther King, Jr., *Nonviolent Resistance*   258
George Orwell, *Politics and the English Language*   498
Martin Luther King, *I Have a Dream*   535
Lewis Thomas, *The Health-Care System*   541
Richard Rodriguez, *None of This Is Fair*   545
Gore Vidal, *Drugs*   551
Thomas Jefferson, *Declaration of Independence*   570
Elizabeth Cady Stanton, *Declaration of Sentiments and Resolutions*   576
Jonathan Swift, *A Modest Proposal*   588

XI. A Sense of Time

Maxine Hong Kingston, *Portraits of My Parents*   192
N. Scott Momaday, *The Way To Rainy Mountain*   198
E. B. White, *Once More to the Lake*   205
Alice Walker, *In Search of Our Mothers' Gardens*   347
Loren Eiseley, *The Brown Wasps*   357
Mark Twain, *Two Ways of Looking at the River*   372

X. Nature and the Environment

Annie Dillard, *Writing and Vision*   99
John Steinbeck, *The Turtle*   188
Samuel H. Scudder, *Take This Fish and Look At It*   270
Mark Twain, *Two Ways of Looking at the River*   372
Barry Lopez, *My Horse*   386
Lewis Thomas, *The Iks*   394

E. M. Forster, *My Wood*   466
Rachel Carson, *The Obligation to Endure*   527

XII. Americana

E. B. White, *Once More to the Lake*   205
Carin Quinn, *The Jeaning of America*   242
Jessica Mitford, *The American Way of Death*   245
Garrison Keillor, *Attitude*   253
Henry David Thoreau, *Economy*   264
Bruce Catton, *Grant and Lee: A Study in Contrasts*   380
E. B. White, *Three New Yorks*   427
Thomas Jefferson, *Declaration of Independence*   570
Elizabeth Cady Stanton, *Declaration of Sentiments and Resolutions*   576

XIII. On Reading

Donald Murray, *Reading as a Reader*   15
Eudora Welty, *A Sweet Devouring*   31
Richard Wright, *Discovering Books*   35
Judith Viorst, *How Books Helped Shape My Life*   43
Donald Hall, *Four Kinds of Reading*   49
Lin Yutang, *The Art of Reading*   53
Robert MacNeil, *Wordstruck*   59
Lance Morrow, *The Best Refuge for Insomniacs*   65
Wendell Berry, *In Defense of Literacy*   68
Flannery O'Connor, *Total Effect and the Eighth Grade*   561

XIV. On Writing

Joan Didion, *Why I Write*   92
Annie Dillard, *Writing and Vision*   99
Henry D. Thoreau, *On Keeping a Private Journal*   104
Peter Elbow, *Freewriting*   106
Sheridan Baker, *What Shall I Write?*   109
Jacqueline Berke, *The Qualities of Good Writing*   115
William Zinsser, *Style*   122
Donald Murray, *The Maker's Eye: Revising Your Own Manuscripts*   127
George Orwell, *Politics and the English Language*   498

Authors Represented by Multiple Essays

Joan Didion,
Why I Write (Writers on Writing)   92
On Self-Respect (Definition)   289
Martin Luther King, Jr.,
I Have a Dream (Process)   535
Nonviolent Resistance (Persuasion and Argument)   258
Margaret Mead,
New Superstitions for Old (Definition)   301
One Vote for This Age of Anxiety (Persuasion and Argument)   555
Donald Murray,
Reading as a Reader (Writers on Reading)   15
The Maker's Eye: Revising Your Own Manuscripts (Writers on Writing)   127
George Orwell,
Politics and the English Language (Cause and Effect)   498
Shooting an Elephant (Narration)   174
Richard Rodriguez,
Hispanic-American Culture (Definition)   295
None of This Is Fair (Persuasion and Argument)   545
Lewis Thomas,
The Iks (Comparison and Contrast)   394
The Health-Care System (Persuasion and Argument)   541
Barbara Tuchman,
Mankind's Better Moments (Illustration)   340
"This Is the End of The World": The Black Death (Cause and Effect)   471
Henry David Thoreau,
On Keeping a Private Journal (Writers on Writing)   104
Economy (Process)   264
Judith Viorst,
Friends, Good Friends, and Such Good Friends (Division and Classification)   420
How Books Helped Shape My Life (Writers on Reading)   43
Alice Walker,
In Search of Our Mothers' Gardens (Illustration)   347
Beauty: When the Other Dancer Is the Self (Narration)   165
E. B. White,
Once More to the Lake (Description)   205
Three New Yorks (Division and Classification)   427
Virginia Woolf,
If Shakespeare Had Had a Sister (Description)   213
Professions for Women (Persuasion and Argument)   581

PART 1

Reading and Writing Essays

Chapter One

Why Read?
How Can Reading
These Essays Help Me?

Almost no student or professional ends a day without having read or written something: he or she has, in fact, most likely done both. Students read textbooks, research articles, study outlines, and lab manuals and must write tests, essays, term papers, critiques, summaries, reports, and eventually, letters of application. Professionals of all kinds face proposals, memos, committee minutes, reports, evaluations, computer printouts, and business letters. Because so much of life's important business (both personal and professional) is conducted by reading and writing, you can improve your chances of success if you improve your reading and writing skills now.

Reading and writing are intertwined skills; if you improve one, the other will also profit. Consequently, close study of the essays in this text should help you become a better writer in several ways.

First, you'll get to see what good writing looks like. Discovering the various ways that admired authors such as Mark Twain, George Orwell, and Maya Angelou organized and developed their material should give you some new ideas about selecting your own strategies, arranging your ideas, and clarifying your explanatory details. Familiarizing yourself with the effective stylistic devices and diction of great writers may also stimulate you to use language in ways you've never tried before. And while no one expects you to sound like James Thurber or Virginia Woolf at this point, why not study the best while you're working on your own prose style?

Second, reading and discussing the prose of others should make you more aware of the writing process itself. Each writer represented in this book faced a series of problems similar to those you face when you write; each had to make decisions regarding organization, development, coherence, sentence style, tone, and so forth, just as you do. By asking questions (Why did Ellen Goodman begin the essay this way? Why did Lewis Thomas compare this to that?), you will begin to see how the writer constructed the essay—and that knowledge in turn can help you build your essay.

Third, exposure to some of the interesting opinions and arguments expressed in this collection may help you discover some new insights of your own, ideas you may wish to write about now and think about for years.

Finally, discussing the ideas and rhetorical choices of these authors should also help you become more sensitive to the importance of revision. All good writers revise, and most revise as they write as well as between drafts. Reading the excellent prose in this text should encourage you to write and revise for readers, not just for yourself. As you revise, ask yourself questions such as: Can my reader see this as clearly as I could see Maxine Kingston's parents in "Portraits of My Parents" (Chapter 4)? Is my conclusion as emphatic as E. B. White's ("Once More to the Lake," Chapter 4)? Do I need to add details to make my prose as vivid as Jessica Mitford's ("The American Way of Death," Chapter 5)?

Thus, by becoming a critical reader of the essays in this text, you can improve the content, clarity, organization, and style of your own writing.

How to Become a Critical Reader

To become a critical reader, you need to understand not only the content but also the composition of the essay under study. Try practicing the process outlined below; while this process calls for a thorough reading, some rereading, marking of the text, and note taking, the benefits to you as both reader and writer will be worth the extra time.

I. Stage One: Prereading

Before you begin the essay, consider these questions:

1.   *Who is the author?* Is he or she an authority on this subject? What expectations do you have about his or her opinions? The author's reputation, previous works, occupation, political stance, or philosophy may help you prepare for the ideas ahead. (In this text, always read the biographical headnotes.) For instance, it may be helpful to know, before you begin her piece on the funeral industry, that Jessica Mitford is a well-known investigative reporter or that when Norman Cousins wrote "Pain Is Not the Ultimate Enemy," he was a respected editor who had just recovered from a nearly fatal disease.

2. *Who was the original audience?* Writers expand, delete, and shape their material according to the needs and attitudes of their readers. Martin Luther King, Jr., for instance, had to calm as well as inspire the audience listening to his "I Have a Dream" speech (Chapter 11). Seeing how other writers addressed their audiences will help you learn this skill yourself.

3. *Where and when was this essay published?* A selection from a scientific journal may have more credibility than one in a popular magazine, and it may demand more concentration from its readers, too. The date of publication might explain some of the unfamiliar references or slightly archaic language. If the essay is an older one, such as the classic "Politics and the English Language" (Chapter 10) you may find some examples drawn from the 1940's illustrating the author's still-relevant main point.

4. *What is the title?* Titles often announce the essay's subject matter ("The Jeaning of America," "College Pressures," or "Three New Yorks") or even state the writer's attitude toward the subject ("How Books Helped Shape My Life," or "Mankind's Better Moments," or "Why Don't We Complain?") or tell what the essay will do ("Two Ways of Looking at the River," "Grant and Lee: A Study in Contrasts," or "Once More to the Lake"). Titles also often set up the tone of the essay, and they frequently act like barkers outside of circus tents: they try to grab your attention and encourage you to go in. Studying the titles of professional essays can help you name your own work in an engaging way.

II. Stage Two: Reading for Purpose and Primary Strategy

1. First, read the essay through without marking anything. Then jot down a sentence or two summarizing your general impression. Consider what you think the author was trying to do (*purpose*) and how well he or she succeeded (a typical response might be "argued for a new work-study program—unconvincing, boring—too many confusing statistics").

2. Next, identify the *primary strategy of development*. Is the essay written in the form of a narrative or a description? An argument? An expository essay primarily developed by examples, process analysis, definition, comparison/contrast, causal analysis, or classification? Did the author select the best strategy for his or her purpose? Why or why not? For instance, would George Orwell have been more persuasive in an editorial on imperialism than in the narrative of "Shooting an Elephant" (Chapter 3)? Would Jessica Mitford in "The American Way of Death" (Chapter 5) have been more effective if she had merely argued against embalming rather than allowing readers to see the process?

III. Stage Three: Essay Analysis

Once you have a clear overview of the essay's purpose and form, go back to the beginning of the selection and begin to make notes on the essay's content, organization, and style. These notes will help show you how the author put his or her essay together, and they will also prepare you to discuss the essay in class. (A sample essay marked according to the advice below appears on pp. 8–12 for you to use as a model.)

1.   Look again at the *title* and at the *introduction*. Did they draw you into the essay? Did they set the appropriate tone?

2.   Frequently writers of expository and argumentative essays will present their main point *(thesis)* early in the essay; the thesis may be stated plainly in one or more sentences or it may be implied. Once you've located the main point, underline the sentence (or note the area in which it is most strongly implied) and write the word "thesis" or a capital "T" in the margin so that you can find it easily.

3.   As you read through the essay again, you may discover important statements that support the thesis. These statements are sometimes found in *topic sentences*, which often occur near the beginning or at the end of body paragraphs. So that you can quickly find each of these supporting points later, underline and number each one and place a key word or a short phrase in the margin by each number. (Hint: writers often use subheadings to announce a new point; watch for these and also for any italicized or underlined words.) Writing down these key words and ideas will also help you remember the *content* of the essay. You may also find it useful to underline or put a star by important or especially effective statements, to put a question mark by those passages you think are weak, exaggerated, or untrue. Use the top and bottom margins to jot brief responses, raise questions, or make note of new ideas (or possible essay topics). Don't be afraid to talk back or argue with the author. These markings and notes will help you assess the essay's effectiveness in your final evaluation.

4.   Each time you discover one of the essay's key points, ask yourself how the author *develops* that idea. For instance, does he or she try to support or prove the point by providing examples, statistics, or testimony; by comparing or contrasting it to something else; or by describing, classifying, or defining the subject? A writer can choose one method of development or any combination, but each major point in an essay should be presented clearly and logically with some sort of evidence. Underdeveloped ideas or ones supported only by generalizations, obviously biased sources, or emotional outpourings are not ultimately convincing.

5.   As you move through the essay, you will probably run across some words you don't know. Often you can guess the meanings of these words

from their context, the surrounding words and ideas. If, however, you find some unfamiliar words essential to the author's main points, you may wish to circle these, consult your dictionary, and jot their definition or a familiar synonym in the margin.

6.   Look closely at the essay's *conclusion*. Does it emphasize the author's thesis without being boring or repetitive? Does it call for action or suggest a solution? A good conclusion offers a pleasing sense of closure; readers should not feel they just stepped off the edge of a cliff.

7.   Consider the essay's *tone*, the writer's *voice*. Is it ironic, sarcastic, serious, informal, humorous, or something else? An inappropriate tone can undercut an author's intended effect on the reader. For instance, a flippant, overly informal tone may offend the reader who takes seriously the subject in question; a sarcastic tone may signal a writer who's too angry to be logical. On the other hand, a coolly rational tone can be convincing, and sometimes humor can be persuasive in a way that nothing else can. Creating the right tone is important.

8.   The author's *style* is important, too. Does he or she use figurative language (for example, similes, metaphors, personification) in an arresting way? Literary allusions? Specialized diction? Does he or she use any sentence patterns that are especially effective? Repetition of words or phrases? Writers use a variety of stylistic devices to make their prose vivid and memorable; you may want to study some of the devices you find so that you can try using them in your own essays.

9.   To help you structure your own essay, you may find it useful to note how the writer moved from one point to the next. Bracketing the *transition devices* that link the paragraphs or the ideas within paragraphs can make you aware of the ways a good writer subtly creates a smooth, easy-to-follow flow of thought. (You won't have time to do this throughout the essay, but you might try marking a few paragraphs.)

10.   Once you have completed the steps above, you're ready to make your final evaluation of the essay. Review your notes and markings; they should help you quickly locate the important parts of the essay and your impressions of those parts. Is the essay's thesis supported by enough logically developed, persuasive points? Is each point as clear, convincing, and well stated as it should be? Is the essay organized effectively? What strengths and weaknesses did you find after this critical reading? Has your original evaluation changed? If so, write a new assessment of the essay. Add any other comments you want to remember about this piece of writing.

Finally, after this critical reading of the essay, have you discovered any new ideas, strategies, or techniques you wish to incorporate into *your* writing?

Following is an essay marked and annotated according to the steps listed on these two pages.

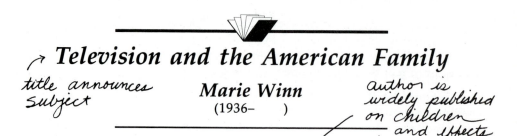

Television and the American Family

↗ title announces
subject

Marie Winn
(1936–   )

author is
widely published
on children
and effects
of television

Marie Winn is the author of twelve books for or about children and many articles for such publications as *The New York Times Magazine* and *The Village Voice.* An influential book, *Children Without Childhood* (1983), grew from her article, "What Became of Childhood Innocence?" and illustrates the changes in attitudes toward children since the 1960s. Her most recent book, *Unpluging the Plug-In Drug* (1987), continues a discussion begun in (1977) with the publication of her well-known study *The Plug-In Drug: Television, Children and the Family,* from which this excerpt is taken.

general audience
of readers concerned
about television's
relationship to
family

Over 10 years ago.
Dated?

1   Home and family life have changed in important ways since the advent of television. The peer group has become television-oriented, and much of the time children spend together is occupied by television viewing. Culture generally has been transformed by television. Therefore it is improper to assign to television the subsidiary role its many apologists (too often members of the television industry) insist it plays. Television is not merely one of a number of important influences upon today's child. Through the changes it has made in family life, television emerges as *the* important influence in children's lives today.

Introduction sets
up T.V. as
most important
influence

THE QUALITY OF FAMILY LIFE

2 [Television's] contribution to [family life] has been an (equivocal) one. For while it has, indeed,

having more than
one outcome

kept the members of the family from dispersing, it has not served to bring them *together*. By its domination of the time families spend together, it destroys the special quality that distinguishes one family from another, a quality that depends to a great extent on what a family *does*, what special rituals, games, recurrent jokes, familiar songs, and shared activities it accumulates.

Thesis: T.V.'s domination of family time destroys "specialness"

3   "Like the sorcerer of old," writes Urie Bronfenbrenner, "the television set casts its magic spell, freezing speech and action, turning the living into silent statues so long as the enchantment lasts. The primary danger of the television screen lies not so much in the behavior it produces—although there is danger there—as in the behavior it prevents: the talks, the games, the family festivities and arguments through which much of the child's learning takes place and through which his character is formed. Turning on the television set can turn off the process that transforms children into people."

* Supporting testimony

4   Yet parents have accepted a [television]-dominated [family life] so completely that they cannot see how the medium is involved in whatever problems they might be having. A first-grade teacher reports:

1. Acceptance by parents

← Quotation shows T.V. replacing mother-daughter conversation

5   "I have one child in the group who's an only child. I wanted to find out more about her family life because this little girl was quite isolated from the group, didn't make friends, so I talked to her mother. Well, they don't have time to do anything in the evening, the mother said. The parents come home after picking up the child at the babysitter's. Then the mother fixes dinner while the child watches TV. Then they have dinner and the child goes to bed. I said to this mother, 'Well, couldn't she help you fix dinner? That would be a nice time for the two of you to talk,' and the mother said, 'Oh, but I'd hate to have her miss 'Zoom.' It's such a good program!' "

6   Even when families make efforts to control television, too often its very presence counterbalances the positive features of family life. A writer and mother of two boys aged 3 and 7 described

2. Even "controlled" T.V. disrupts family life

her family's television schedule in *The New York Times:*

> We were in the midst of a full-scale War. Every day was a new battle and every program was a major skirmish. We agreed it was a bad scene all around and were ready to enter diplomatic negotiations. . . . In principle we have agreed on 2½ hours of TV a day, "Sesame Street," "Electric Company" (with dinner gobbled up in between) and two half-hour shows between 7 and 8:30 which enables the grown-ups to eat in peace and prevents the two boys from destroying one another. Their pre-bedtime choice is dreadful, because, as Josh recently admitted, "There's nothing much on I really like." So . . . it's "What's My Line" or "To Tell the Truth." . . . Clearly there is a need for first-rate children's shows at this time. . . .

More quoted testimony — shows that watching is all-important

7   Consider the ["family life"] described here: Presumably the father comes home from work during the "Sesame Street"–"Electric Company" stint. The children are either watching television, gobbling their dinner, or both. While the parents eat their dinner in peaceful privacy, the children watch another hour of television. Then there is only a half-hour left before bedtime, just enough time for baths, getting pajamas on, brushing teeth, and so on. The children's evening is regimented with an almost military precision. They watch their favorite programs, and when there is "nothing much on I really like," they watch whatever else is on—because *watching* is the important thing. Their mother does not see anything amiss with watching programs just for the sake of watching; she only wishes there were some first-rate children's shows on at those times.

and mother?

?

3. Better shows not the solution

8   Without conjuring up memories of the Victorian era with family games and long, leisurely meals, and large families, the question arises: isn't there a better family life available than this dismal, mechanized arrangement of children

Contrast to pre-television era

watching television for however long is allowed them, evening after evening?

9   Of course, families today still do *special* things together at times: go camping in the summer, go to the zoo on a nice Sunday, take various trips and expeditions. But their *ordinary* daily life together is diminished—that sitting around at the dinner table, that spontaneous taking up of an activity, those little games invented by children on the spur of the moment when there is nothing else to do, the scribbling, the chatting, and even the quarreling, all the things that form the fabric of a family, that define a childhood. Instead, the children have their regular schedule of television programs and bedtime, and the parents have their peaceful dinner together.

10   The author of the article in the *Times* notes that "keeping a family sane means mediating between the needs of both children and adults." But surely the needs of adults are being better met than the needs of the children, who are effectively shunted away and rendered untroublesome, while their parents enjoy a life as undemanding as that of any childless couple. In reality, it is those very demands that young children make upon a family that lead to growth, and it is the way parents accede to those demands that builds the relationships upon which the future of the family depends. If the family does not accumulate its backlog of shared experiences, shared *everyday* experiences that occur and recur and change and develop, then it is not likely to survive as anything other than a caretaking institution.

[Marginal annotations:]

4. T.V. diminishes ordinary life

← Gives examples of what's missed

5. T.V. keeps peace but prevents family growth

exaggerated?

Conclusion: calls for shared experiences & gives warning

First impression: Winn wants us to see that television is destroying the quality of family life. Several persuasive points show how T.V. replaces family activity, talking.

Primary strategy: causal analysis—the effects of T.V. on kids and family are clearly presented.

Final Evaluation : Winn is convincing.
It's not just violent T.V. that hurts
kids -- it's the time spent watching
instead of interacting with parents as
a family. I agree -- when I think of
good times with my family, we were
doing things together, not watching T.V.
(Possible essay topic : the importance
of last summer's family camping trip.)

Other Notes

1. Organization and development: good
   use of personal and professional
   testimony and real examples to
   support points. Should she have
   addressed times when the family
   watches together? And what about
   when the T.V. is on as background
   noise only?

2. Style/Voice - Winn is serious,
   straightforward, concerned. Note good
   use of question in ¶ 8. Uses
   italics for emphasis -- too often?
   Easy to read -- no jargon.

3. Transitions - ¶'s are connected by
   repeating key terms like "television",
   "family life." No problem following
   discussions in paragraphs.

Writers on Reading

In the following section, nine writers praise the diverse pleasures and benefits of reading. Some of these authors, such as Richard Wright and Eudora Welty, describe their first experiences with books; others, such as Judith Viorst, Lance Morrow, and Robert MacNeil, explain how reading has influenced their lives in numerous ways and at various times. Donald Murray suggests ways to best profit from one's reading, and Wendell Berry argues for the absolute necessity of reading skills in today's society. Certainly most of these authors would agree with booklover and editor Clifton Fadiman, who once wrote that when you study a classic, "you do not see more in the book than you did before; you see more in *you* than was there before." According to these writers, the art of reading is possibly the most essential part of your education not only because it aids you in becoming a better writer, but also because it helps you adapt to a changing world.

Donald Murray (© Courtesy Donald Murray)

Reading as a Reader

Donald Murray
(1924–   )

Donald M. Murray enjoys a national reputation as an authority on the writing process. He was until recently a Professor of English at the University of New Hampshire and has been a reporter for *The Boston Globe* and a contributing editor of *Time* magazine. He won the Pulitzer Prize for editorial writing and writes nonfiction books for both adults and children as well as magazine articles, novels, short stories, and poetry. In addition, he is the author of several widely adopted writing textbooks, including *The Craft of Revision* (1991). In "Reading as a Reader," which was first published as part of *Read to Write* (1986), he describes a useful process for reading both to understand what is going on in our world and to discover the craft writers use to convey information.

1   A nightmare. You are shoved into a huge room that has dozens of doors and windows along every wall. You go to an open door and see a party you want to join. The door slams shut. You can't open it. You run to a window across the room and see a street in a city you've never visited. There are stores, restaurants, a jazz band playing, and a crowd of shoppers laughing and talking with each other in a strange language. Suddenly shutters slam shut and you can't see anything but darkness.

2   You step to a door where a man and a woman sit in comfortable chairs by a fireplace. They are talking to each other, but most of all you notice the way they listen. It would be wonderful to be listened to that way. They spot you, smile, and invite you to join them. The door shuts. Out another door is space and a spacewalker tumbles down, twists around, and starts to point.

That door shuts. You start moving from window to door, catching a glimpse of surf rippling along an endless beach, a large book that seems to have important instructions, what looks like a movie but is far more real than that, and a formula that lies upon a laboratory table. Each door, each window slams shut. You move faster from door to window to door. You can see through each, but you can't escape the empty room. In a window, you see a newspaper with large headlines you can't understand; through a door someone beckons you to join a committee examining an accounting balance sheet; two couples dance a poem and wave as if they'd like to know you; a computer screen fills with green marks that don't make sense to you. Each window and every door shuts and you are left alone in the empty room.

3   That is the world of the person who can't read. Messages are delivered that can't be understood, opportunities are available that can't be taken, and, worst of all, there is a terrible loneliness, for the nonreader is isolated from the past, from what happens out of sight or off camera, from joining—and influencing—the members of those groups interested in business, the environment, religion, politics, sports, engineering, theatre, travel, art, music, and science, who communicate with each other by writing and reading.

4   The student in any field—medicine, public safety, language study, computer technology, environmental studies, sociology, biochemistry, political science, engineering, history, hotel management, law, business—finds it is essential to be an effective reader. Reading is increasingly important in a complex, global, technical society. We depend on the communication of an enormous amount of information and, in such a world, information, even more than money, means power. We may read books, memos, newspapers, or we may read a computer screen or printout, but read we must if we are to understand and participate in our world, to know and to influence what is going on. We also read to write, to learn the craft that not only allows us to receive information but also to discover what we know and share it.

IF YOU HAVE TROUBLE READING

5 Everybody has trouble reading. We all face texts that are incomprehensible to us. In some cases the material is extremely difficult; in some cases the author's style is difficult, and in many cases the writing is bad—we can't make the meaning come clear because there is no clear meaning. We cannot, of course, know whether the writer has anything of importance to say to us until we figure out what the writer has said. If we are reading just for recreation, then we can toss aside a book that is too difficult or has a style we don't enjoy. But on the job, as citizens, and in following our hobbies we have to read a lot of difficult writing and a lot of bad writing. Some of the worst writing unfortunately occurs in textbooks that students have to read to learn a subject or pass a course, or both. We all need to know what to do when we have trouble reading.

The Reader's Attitude

6 Our attitude about reading usually controls how we read as much as our attitude about writing, doing math, playing a sport, or having friends controls our effectiveness in those areas. If we approach a text believing that we are not readers, or that we can't read, that attitude may make it more difficult for us to understand the challenging text.

7 In some cases the attitude we have simply may not be appropriate. Most students who get to college can read moderately well, regardless of what teachers and newspapers say. What we have to do is to build on the skills we already have. Our attitude should be that we are in college to learn, and learning means being able to read a broad variety of texts more effectively. You are taking this course to learn how to read with greater skill and to learn how reading can help improve your writing.

8 Don't worry too much about television and film making your generation nonreaders. The myths about the past only make us guilty and they are often just myths. In the good old days when I was growing up, you were a wimp if you read, and I was a secret reader. Most people I knew did very little reading. But if you are to be educated—to make use of information from many fields and times and authorities—then you will have to improve your reading.

9 The best way is simply to read more. You learn to ride a bicycle by hopping aboard and pedaling until you get up enough speed. Reading is, at the beginning, a skill that takes frequent practice.

10 Also remember that the writer has some responsibility to go halfway or more to the reader. Writing that is hard to read is occasionally the product of a complicated and important mind; however, it is more likely the product of an arrogant and pretentious mind. Do not blame yourself for a writer's irresponsibility.

11 It is not helpful to feel inadequate, stupid, whipped by a text before you begin. It *is* helpful to have command of a variety of strategies which may help you decipher a text.

READING FOR EXPERIENCE

12 Humans are the animals that can live more lives than a cat, and many of them are lived through reading. As we read we go back and forth in time, pass across oceans and barriers of language, religion, and culture.

13 Yes, for many readers, reading is an escape. I used to hide the fact that I read to escape or, if discovered, apologize for fleeing to the make-believe world of adventure stories or mysteries as other people escape by reading science fiction, westerns, or romance novels—even though President Kennedy never apologized for using spy stories to escape the realities of international affairs, nor did President Eisenhower hide his affection for westerns. And, after my daughter Lee died suddenly when she was only twenty, I

learned an important lesson—one of many. Although I had been a lifetime compulsive reader, for weeks I could not read and, when I began to read again, it was only mystery and spy stories with a strong story line that could hold my interest. I escaped and I had good reason to escape, no apologies needed. Since then I keep a piece of escape reading nearby all the time, and when I travel or can't sleep or start thinking too compulsively about what can't be thought about, I escape into a story.

14   We should not, however, forget that reading for escape from our world may also mean that we escape into other worlds. Reading is the enemy of ignorance, provincialism, and parochialism.

15   It is important that we read our way out of our own world, our own times, our own skin and live the lives of other people to find out how they feel and think. The ability to distance ourselves from ourselves and become someone else is a significant way to learn.

16   We may read biography or autobiography and escape into another person's life. We can, through reading, escape into the mind of a philosopher, observe with a scientist, study with a scholar, analyze with a critic, and live through a novel or a play. Reading powerful texts provides us with experience that rivals real experience in our memory, and may, in fact, influence us more than what we learn from our actual living.

Learning to Be Uncritical

17 To read for experience we have to learn to suppress our critical faculties for the moment and enter into the story, allowing the author to carry us along so that we absorb the world the writer has created for us. It usually helps to read fast and let the language, the flow, the energy of the text carry us along.

18   Reading for experience is usually an emotional as well as an intellectual activity, and in many cases all our senses are involved. We see the world of the writer, smell it, taste it, touch it. In some cases it becomes more real to us than ordinary living, the way a dream has its own special intensity. We have to learn how not to fight the text, but to give ourselves up to it, and not worry too much if we miss something here or there. We shouldn't stop to argue with the text, but to listen to the text in this first reading. Later we may want to read the text again differently, critically, more slowly. And certainly we will want to stand back from the experience we have had, the way we stand back from a party, a game, or a job, and put the experience into context, evaluate it, judge it, try to figure out what we learned from it. But first we have to have the experience.

READING FOR INFORMATION

19 When we read for information we experience the text in a different way. Depending on the information we seek, we may not want to enter into the

story, and we do not much care how the writing is written, as long as the writing does not get in the way of the information we need. Our newspapers know we want information on stocks and football standings, and so they give us this information in the form of tables and listings. That writing is hardly "written" at all. Other times we need information that is hidden in a normal text of sentences and paragraphs. In that case we have to mine the text and extract the information we need. In this kind of reading we may choose to stand apart from the text, not to be involved in but simply to make use of what is said.

Scanning

20 To extract information from a text we need to scan, swooping over the text, looking for any clues that may help us find where the information is. We may turn first to an index or table of contents to see if it will tell us where the information we need is placed. In the case of an academic article we may read the abstract, a summary paragraph usually printed in small type at the beginning of the article to serve information gatherers and save them time.

Watching for Road Signs

21 If we think the text has the information we need, we should run through it, paying attention to chapter headings, crossheads (such as the one above, "Watching for Road Signs"), illustrations, diagrams, or other signals designed to help us get to the information we need. When we confront the text itself we should look for key words that will tell us that the information may be nearby. For example, if we are looking for information on the low salaries of women office workers, we may look for such words as "secretaries," "file clerks," "typists," "receptionists," "salaries," "wages," "compensation," "sexism," "prejudice," "women," "girls," "office workers," and so on. We can run through many pages of type easily, stopping only when we see something that tells us the information may be nearby.

Making Notes

22 In reading for information we usually have a notebook or note cards handy so that we can put down the information we find. If the information is to be quoted directly, we should put quotation marks around it so that we know when we come to use it that the note is precisely as the author presented it. If we are to put the information in our own words it's helpful to do that immediately. It's also important to note the context in which the information was presented. The context for the information on office workers might be a feminist political statement, a report by a male scholar, a study by a union that wants to organize office workers, a statement by a corpo-

ration, or a survey by a government agency. It is most important that the note include the precise reference so that it can be included in the text and so that you and your reader can go back and find the information. This means the title of the publication, the author, and all of the details about the publication itself.

READING FOR UNDERSTANDING

23   Our most important reading occurs when we read to comprehend everything that a text has to teach us. We read for the experience of the text and we read for the information we can mine from it—and more. Reading stocks our mind with information and connections between pieces of information—theories, ideas, concepts, principles—that grow and change as we grow and change, experiencing, integrating all that we take in from living and thinking. We read to learn, to stimulate our minds, and so we have to learn to read well enough to make intellectual use of a great variety of texts, including many which are not easy to read. Some of them are difficult because the subject matter is difficult and the author has not been able to—or is writing for a specialized audience and feels no need to—simplify it for a general reader. Other books are difficult because the author does not write well but still has brought together information and ideas that are significant.

24   All our lives we will be reading texts that are difficult for us to read. We will learn about a subject, read intensely in that area, get to know significant but difficult authors, and find it relatively easy to read what was once difficult; but, at the same time, we will continue to be learners, reading in new areas, and meeting new and challenging authors.

25   This process of lifelong education has become true for many people who have not considered themselves intellectuals or who did not imagine they would continue to learn—or have to continue to learn—after graduation. We live, however, in a society in which change seems to be the only constant. People advised me, for example, not to leave jobs with companies that no longer exist. Some security. The best security is an education that teaches you how to learn so you can adapt to the inevitable changes life will bring. Guess who laughed at writing on a word processor and found himself using one a few weeks later?

26   We all have difficult friends who are worth the effort, and you will have difficult authors to read whose articles, stories, poems, manuals, monographs, plays, and books—fiction and nonfiction—are worth the effort. We have to learn strategies for dealing with these texts. We do not need to use these strategies all the time, but we do need to have them on hand when we cannot understand what we are reading and so cannot even tell if the text is worth reading.

Who Are You?

27 The first step toward understanding is to know what you bring to the text as a reader. If a police officer, black or white, is assigned to a neighborhood, he or she must first know what prejudices, what stereotypes, what beliefs, what fears he or she wears with the badge. Each of us looks at the same neighborhood with significant differences, depending on our experience and our background. The same thing is true of a reader.

28 Expert readers know what they don't know and what they know as they approach a text. They know that their prejudices, preconceptions, personal background, and experiences affect the way they read the text. We all come to a book with a complicated inventory of information, ideas, and opinions that combine to make the text our own. We have begun to realize it is important to understand this. Every text is different for every reader. That doesn't mean that we can't agree on what the text says, because we can, in discussion, usually work out a common understanding. It does mean that we often get to that understanding in very different ways. And it certainly can include the fact that we may disagree about what the text says.

29 The text is not separate from the reader. As the reader reads the text becomes what is read. If you see, for example, a group of teenagers with different colored skins fighting, what each observer sees is powerfully colored, pun intended, by the observer's own background. Often there is not just one truth, but many truths. And we see through our own eyes, our own experiences, our own knowledge.

Who's the Author?

30 Once you know who you are—at least who you are in relation to this subject—then it may help to know who the writer is. Usually there are short biographies or an identifying sentence that tells who the writer is and what is the writer's authority to write this piece: "Norbert Morrison, now a Congressman from Iowa, has been practicing cannibalism since his Freshman year in college." If you think that the background of the author is vital to your understanding of the piece, then you can use the standard reference books, such as *Who's Who* and *Current Biography,* in the library to discover what you need to know about the writer.

What's the Form?

31 It may help to understand the piece we are reading if we know the genre or form in which it is written. This sounds obvious, but notice how many people use the term "novel," which means a fictional story, a work of the imagination, to describe nonfiction books of history or biography which are supposed to be based on documentable facts. It may help you understand the piece you are reading if you know it is a profile, a short biography written by someone other than the subject, or an autobiographical essay

in which the person is writing about himself or herself. Part of form is purpose. In an argument the author wants to persuade us, but in a personal essay about the same subject the author may simply want to entertain. In a news story about the same subject, the writer may simply want to deliver objective fact.

What's the Context?

32   It helps to know the context or the nature of the world in which the piece was written. Pieces that were written during the Vietnam War, when there was both strong opposition to the war and powerful support for the war, may be confusing to a young reader who did not experience the pressure from both sides.

33   The reader should know the point of view of the publication in which an article is published. Some political magazines, for example, have a conservative point of view. Others are liberal. The reader needs to know that context. It may help, for example, to know that the discussion of a nuclear plant is written in a context of concern for human safety, for the environment, or for the economy.

Reading the Front Matter

34   Clues to questions of the writer's authority and the context of the book or article may be found by reading the notes about authors in a magazine or the material published on the dust jacket of a book or on a title page. It is often a good idea, for example, to see where the book was published. It may be significant to know that a book about Vietnam was published first in France, a nation that suffered their Vietnam ahead of ours. It also may be important to know if the book was written in 1958, before we got deeply involved, in 1968, when we were heavily involved, or in 1978, when the war was over. The table of contents, the preface, bibliographical notes at the end, and the index are all clues that may help us unlock the meaning of the book.

Reading Uncritically

35   The more difficult the text, the more important it is that we read it *uncritically* first. This doesn't seem to make sense until you realize that if the subject matter, the form of the writing, and the author's style are all strange to the reader, then the reader may bog down in paying too close attention to each specific piece of information, each sentence, each word. If we pay too close attention the first time around, we have no idea of the whole, no feeling for the meaning or the purpose of the piece of writing. If we read it fast, uncritically, we will miss a lot, and at times even feel as if we were in a foreign country where we can't understand what anyone is saying. But we

do pick up more than we know and get a feeling for the piece of writing. Once we have an overall view of the territory we can go back and, working within that overall vision, pay close attention to the details that will give us a true understanding of the text. Remember the first time you went to a big game; you had to try to absorb the crowd, the teams, the whole atmosphere of what was going on. You probably didn't pay too much attention to the details of the game. But when you become a fan you understand the larger context and can focus your attention on a revealing detail, such as how a player moves away from the main action of the game. Reading uncritically is the first step toward reading critically.

Reading Carefully

36 When a text deserves close attention, then we keep repeating the pattern of looking from larger context to smaller and back. We need to know what each word means in context, and that cannot be known simply by knowing the meaning of each word. Most words have many meanings. Those meanings change, depending on all the other meanings into which they are built.

37   This diagram may help:

BOOK
    CHAPTER
        SECTION
            PARAGRAPH
                SENTENCE
                    PHRASE
                      WORD

38   It looks complicated, and it is. Reading is one of the most sophisticated, intellectual acts we perform. But remember that you bring an enormous background of experience to this task. Even if you are not a person who considers yourself a reader, you are reading other people all the time. You read your parents and your roommate, your teachers and your friends, and the strangers you meet on the street or in a bar. You read the place in which they exist—who sits behind the desk or comes around and sits beside you in a chair during an interview. You read dress—formal or casual—and whether it is appropriate to the situation and the person. We are often amused at the Freshman who tries to look middle-aged, and at the middle-aged professor who tries to look like a Freshman. You read what the person says and how he or she says it: "You look as if you're new around here, can I help you?" You read body language: the hands on hips or the arms folded across the chest, or the hand extended palm out for a shake. You come to a text bringing all these intellectual skills with you so you can apply them to written language.

39   The diagram shows what you already do, reading the detail (the hesitant step, the avoiding eye, the move that brings the person too close to you) and fitting it into a generalization (this guy doesn't trust people like me) that, in turn, causes you to read meaning into what seemed like insignificant details a moment before. The reader moves back and forth from concept to word and word to concept, with increasing understanding.

40   Some of the tricks of the careful reader's trade are:

Underline.   It may help to understand the text if you underline key words, facts, phrases, sentences, and, on occasion, paragraphs. The purpose of underlining, however, is to help you identify the points of greatest significance and make them clear by pulling them out of the text. We have all seen inexperienced students highlighting or underlining almost every word of the text, a sure clue that they do not understand the text and are learning little from it.

Marginal comments.   Reading is a private encounter between writer and reader. Writing in the margins allows the reader to talk back—or write back—to the writer. It is a helpful way for the reader to make the text his or her own. These comments can be abrupt, quick, or extensive, sometimes even extending to a card or a piece of paper that is taped to the page. In the margin the reader agrees and disagrees, extends the text and connects it with the reader's own experience, questions the text on the basis of the reader's experience, makes connections with other experiences, other evidence, other pieces of writing. You should train yourself to become more than a passive reader, to enter into the act of making meaning with the writer.

Connecting.   It's often helpful to use arrows or circles or squares or lines or numbers to connect significant facts, words, or lines in a text. Sometimes you can see the importance of a word that is repeated in a text in this way, or actually draw the map of the piece right over the text, revealing how a meaning has been woven through the text.

Outlining.   The skill of outlining may be even more important to a reader than a writer. If you outline—in whatever form is comfortable to you—what is being said in the text, you will strip the text down to its essentials, and you may be able to see the meaning that lies under the text and then be able to understand what the writer was doing in the text.

Precis.   This is an old-fashioned device that is extremely helpful in understanding a text. I grumped at Miss Leavitt—no Ms. in those days—who made us precis, precis, precis our way through the eleventh grade, and groaned again when I saw my English teacher for the twelfth grade—you guessed it: Miss Leavitt. I precised my way through the twelfth grade. But it taught me to read with a piercing eye, tracking down meaning and helping to teach me to write concise, disciplined prose.

41   To write a precis, say in a few paragraphs—preferably one paragraph—what is said in an entire article, chapter, or book, using your own words. The effort of compression squeezes out the nonessentials and forces you to discover the central meaning of the text.

42   Some of the key elements in the text that reveal meaning include:

43   1. *Title.* The title attempts to tell the reader what follows in a way that will attract the reader. Often it gives away the point of view or the tone of the piece of writing. I find titles extremely helpful as a way of planning writing. They often tell me how I feel as well as how I think about the subject, establish a point of view, and even set up limits for the piece of writing. The title of this book, for example, helped me focus on the fact that this text is designed to help the student read to improve the student's own writing.

44   2. *The lead.* The lead is a journalistic term for the introduction or beginning of a piece of writing. A formal introduction too often announces what will be in the writing, so that the piece of writing itself becomes repetitive, an expansion of what has already been said. The lead—the first sentence, the first paragraph, the first page of the text—attempts to lead the reader into the text. It is quick and direct, but it establishes the subject, the limits of the subject, and the tone of the piece. Good writers usually will not proceed until they have the lead right. I may write 50 or 60 leads to an article before I get one that is right. You will be wise to pay attention to leads, both as a reader and as a writer.

45   3. *The ending.* The ending is the reverse of the lead. It is the last line, the last paragraph, the last page, and it is vital, for the ending is what the reader remembers best about a piece of writing. In the formal conclusion there is usually too much repetition. It has been said, and is said again in the same way with the same evidence. Skillful writers conclude by implication, not so much summarizing as giving the reader a quotation, an anecdote, a piece of evidence that draws the piece to a close in the reader's mind. Again, a young writer should pay close attention to how effective endings are written, and the reader should pay close attention, because in the ending the author gives away what he or she thinks has been said. The end is the writer's destination, the point toward which the writer has been writing.

46   4. *Turning points.* The reader should look for turning points in the text. They are like marks blazed on a tree on a mountain trail, and more. They not only point the reader to where the reader should go, but they also quickly summarize where they think the reader has been. If you spot the turning points and understand what the writer believes has been said and intends to say next, you will begin to see how the piece is working.

47   5. *Documentation.* One of the most revealing elements in the text is the evidence the writer uses to persuade the reader to believe what is being said. The evidence is crucial, and it should be questioned by the reader. Remember that evidence is not only formal, footnoted, scholarly documentation, but the anecdotes, analogies, and metaphors the writer uses to connect the text to the reader's own experience.

48   6. *Voice.* The element more than any other that makes us read on, makes us believe—or disbelieve—the text, makes us think and care, is the writer's voice. When we read we listen to the text, and what we hear influences us. We should look closely at how the writer uses language to understand what the writer is saying. We should be aware of the denotation of words, the precise meaning; and the connotation, what they mean in context. We can, for example, use the word bread to mean food, and by changing the context have it mean money. To hear the voice—and the meaning—it is often essential to read aloud.

49   7. *Key words.* Every piece of writing has key words. We must try to see what they are and to make sure we understand them. Those words often carry a huge weight of meaning, and we must attempt to understand what meanings they have in the text. A journalist writing about freedom of the press in this country uses freedom to mean protection *from* government interference, but a Russian may use the word freedom to argue for freedom *by* government interference, a concept we find very hard to understand.

50   When we understand what the text says, then we can stand back and judge the entire text, evaluating what was said and how it was said.

READING FOR APPRECIATION

51 Another way to approach a text is for appreciation. Of course, to appreciate a text it must be experienced and understood but then the reader, knowing what is said, can consider *how* it is said.

52   You all have experience as critics in many fields. For example, think how you relate to "your" music. You listen to the latest in a particular tradition, usually understanding how that tradition has evolved and how it relates to other musical traditions. You notice how the songs that are popular today are different from yesterday. You notice what they say and how they say it. You study, often unconsciously, how the music itself is changing, and you not only evaluate a particular piece of music, but performers as well. You see them in a tradition and you see how they relate to each other. And you know that the more familiar you become with a kind of music, a particular song, a type of performer, or a particular performer, the better you understand and appreciate what is going on.

53   This is what readers do, and it is so much a part of what writers do that we will discuss much of this in greater detail before the end of the chapter. Experienced readers heighten the quality of their experience by an interest in esthetics, the "how" in writing.

Listening for the How

54 Readers who want to appreciate reading are good listeners. They listen for the music in the writing, the rise and fall of the voice of the writer, the rhythm, the pace, and the change in pace, the intensity. To hear the music it is a good idea to read aloud, and read with some feeling, letting yourself enter into the text, act out the text so you can hear the writer speaking. Expert readers hear what they are reading as much or more than they see it.

55   Sometimes a difficult text will come clear if it is read aloud. And, of course, the opposite can be true. Reading a text aloud can make the text self-destruct. The out-loud reading can reveal just how badly the writer writes.

Knowing the Tradition

56 As in music, each tradition of writing—poetry, fiction, nonfiction, drama— has its own historical flow. And so do the subgroups under each tradition. Nonfiction prose, for example, has divisions such as argument, whose roots pass back through the Romans to the ancient Greeks; and modern reportage isn't really so modern, it goes back at least to Addison, Steele, Thomas Paine, and others in the eighteenth century. The personal new journalism of the recent past was really a cyclical movement in which writers and editors relearned the lessons of earlier periods, when personalized journalism was popular. English professors spend a lifetime studying literary traditions, how they evolved, and how they are changing. You don't have to do that to appreciate writing. But the more you know about the history of a form in which you are interested, the deeper your appreciation will be.

Knowing What You Like and Knowing What There Is to Like

57 The great defense of ignorance is, "I don't know anything about painting (literature, plays, movies, music), but I know what I like." You should know what you like and don't like, but you should also grow in your appreciation of what you are hearing, reading, and seeing. You should start with the assumption that what is in front of you has been done on purpose. That doesn't mean that you will like it. The cook may have very carefully prepared liver. You may not appreciate the craft and art of the chef, but you should at least taste it.

58   Tasting it in the arts means more than looking. It means making an attempt to understand what the artist or writer or composer was doing, and why.

Don't have unrealistic expectations for a piece of writing. Each piece of work should be seen in its own tradition, for reading and the other arts are not just emotional experiences. They are esthetic experiences in which the emotion and the intellect combine. They are not accidental; they are purposeful. If you make a lifetime habit of trying to understand, you will find many more things that will give you appreciation—satisfaction, fulfillment, and joy. And, of course, you will find many things that you do not like, no matter what effort you make. I like liver, no reason you should.

59   You should know what you like but that knowing should keep growing, building on what you already appreciate. I like classical chamber music today. I came to it through an appreciation of small jazz combos. My understanding of what small jazz groups were trying to do allowed me to appreciate quintets, quartets, and trios, and the pleasing combat between the players. The more we know and appreciate, the more we see to know and appreciate. It keeps us forever young. Reading opens doors and windows so that we can decide what we want to learn and explore.

READING TO WRITE AND WRITING TO READ

60 Think of what you do as you read. It is an interesting and complex act. You look at the symbols on the page—the letters, the words—and take in what the writer has written. You experience the text, but that experience is mixed at the same time with all the other experiences you have had. The author's experience, and your experience, mix together as hot and cold water mix as they come out of the shower head. The text you are "reading" is no longer the author's text but a new text that has been composed by you as you read it.

61   We write as we read, and this experience of composing a text from our reading obviously helps us learn to write. We see the material that is around us. We see how each person shapes that material. Some of you may read in this book a text you have read a few years ago, or in high school, and find that you are a different reader now. Of course. We change and grow with our experiences in living, in writing, and in reading. And we learn not passively from a text that is given to us, but actively, interacting with the text, studying it as some people study the Bible, the Torah, or the Koran, putting into the text what we can and getting out of the text what we are able to receive.

62   We also read as we write. The text we expect to write is not the text we write. We pour our experience with life and language through that tap, and it is mixed with the evolving text. The words we choose limit and shape our meaning. The phrases and sentences with which we hook our words together carry us in directions we did not expect to go. The denotation—the precise meaning of the words—and the connotation—the meanings that hover around the words—teach us as we write.

63   The text on our page moves us forward toward meaning in the same way that speech does. We all need to talk things out with a friend, a counselor, a member of the clergy, sometimes a stranger. We need to talk, not so much to get advice, but to hear what we have to say about a crisis in our life, or a decision we have to make. What we say gives discipline and form and meaning to those thoughts and feelings that are vague until we speak. We write a text through speaking, and we read it through hearing.

64   What appears on the page has to be read quickly as it is written, the way a football player has to read the defense while attempting to run through it. The text is in motion; it is changing as we do it. And that's something that the writer finds exciting. Too many of us have the idea that you are supposed to know what you have to say before you say it. If that were true few writers would write. We write to find what we have to say, to read a text that is changing as we read it. We read what we have just written, and that influences what is being written and continually changes what may be written. Eventually we rewrite and revise and edit to clarify the meaning that we are reading.

65   Readers are writers whether they know it or not. And writers are always readers. There is no reasonable separation between the acts of reading and writing. Each activity is twin to the other, providing us with information and a disciplined way of finding meaning in that information, with the special bonus of being able to share that meaning with others, who, like you in reading my text, will compose your own text from it. I can no more control what you will find in your head in reading my words than I can control who my daughters may marry.

66   Write to learn how to read, and read to learn how to write.

Eudora Welty (© Nancy Crampton)

A Sweet Devouring

Eudora Welty
(1909–   )

Born and raised in Jackson, Mississippi, Eudora
Welty attended Mississippi State College for
Women and the University of Wisconsin. In
addition, she studied advertising at Columbia
University's school of business. Following her
graduate work, she returned to Mississippi where
she wrote for local newspapers and radio stations.
During the Depression she worked for the Works
Progress Administration, interviewing and
photographing residents of her area. In the 1930s,
she published stories in such magazines and
literary journals as *The Southern Review* and *The
Atlantic Monthly,* and she has continued to write
critically acclaimed fiction, including *The Optimist's
Daughter* (1972) that won the Pulitzer Prize. *One
Writer's Beginnings* (1984) is a written version of a
series of lectures she gave at Harvard University
describing her growth as a writer. *Photographs,* a
collection culled from Welty's decades-spanning
photographic record of the South, was published in
1989. In "A Sweet Devouring," first printed in her
collection of essays *The Eye of the Story* (1977), she
describes the pleasures of reading she discovered
as a young girl and her love of "the printed page."

1 Our library in those days was a big rotunda lined with shelves. A
copy of *V.V.'s Eyes* seemed to follow you wherever you went, even after
you'd read it. I didn't know what I liked, I just knew what there was a lot
of. After *Randy's Spring* there came *Randy's Summer, Randy's Fall* and *Randy's*

Winter. True, I didn't care very much myself for her spring, but it didn't occur to me that I might not care for her summer, and then her summer didn't prejudice me against her fall, and I still had hopes as I moved on to her winter. I was disappointed in her whole year, as it turned out, but a thing like that didn't keep me from wanting to read every word of it. The pleasures of reading itself—who doesn't remember?—were like those of a Christmas cake, a sweet devouring. The "Randy Books" failed chiefly in being so soon over. Four seasons doesn't make a series.

2   All that summer I used to put on a second petticoat (our librarian wouldn't let you past the front door if she could see through you), ride my bicycle up the hill and "through the Capitol" (shortcut) to the library with my two read books in the basket (two was the limit you could take out at one time when you were a child and also as long as you lived), and tiptoe in ("Silence") and exchange them for two more in two minutes. Selection was no object. I coasted the two new books home, jumped out of my petticoat, read (I suppose I ate and bathed and answered questions put to me), then in all hope put my petticoat back on and rode those two books back to the library to get my next two.

3   The librarian was the lady in town who wanted to be it. She called me by my full name and said, "Does your mother know where you are? You know good and well the fixed rule of this library: *Nobody is going to come running back here with any book on the same day they took it out.* Get both those things out of here and don't come back till tomorrow. And I can practically see through you."

4   My great-aunt in Virginia, who understood better about needing more to read than you *could* read, sent me a book so big it had to be read on the floor—a bound volume of six or eight issues of *St. Nicholas* from a previous year. In the very first pages a series began: *The Lucky Stone* by Abbie Farwell Brown. The illustrations were right down my alley: a heroine so poor she was ragged, a witch with an extremely pointed hat, a rich, crusty old gentleman in—better than a wheelchair—a runaway carriage; and I set to. I gobbled up installment after installment through the whole luxurious book, through the last one, and then came the words, turning me to *un*lucky stone: "To be concluded." The book had come to an end and *The Lucky Stone* wasn't finished! The witch had it! I couldn't believe this infidelity from my aunt. I still had my secret childhood feeling that if you hunted long enough in a book's pages, you could find what you were looking for, and long after I knew books better than that, I used to hunt again for the end of *The Lucky Stone.* It never occurred to me that the story had an existence anywhere else outside the pages of that single green-bound book. The last chapter was just something I would have to do without. Polly Pepper could do it. And then suddenly I tried something—I read it again, as much as I had of it. I was in love with books at least partly for what they looked like; I loved the printed page.

5   In my little circle books were almost never given for Christmas, they cost too much. But the year before, I'd been given a book and got a shock. It was from the same classmate who told me there was no Santa Claus. She gave me a book, all right—*Poems by Another Little Girl*. It looked like a real book, was printed like a real book—but it was *by her. Homemade* poems? Illusion-dispelling was her favorite game. She was in such a hurry, she had such a pile to get rid of—her mother's electric runabout was stacked to the bud vases with copies—that she hadn't even time to say "Merry Christmas!" With only the same raucous laugh with which she had told me, "Been filling my own stocking for years!" she shot me her book, received my Japanese pencil box with a moonlight scene on the lid and a sharpened pencil inside, jumped back into the car and was sped away by her mother. I stood right where they had left me, on the curb in my Little Nurse's uniform, and read that book, and I had no better way to prove when I got through than I had when I started that this was not a real book. But of course it wasn't. The printed page is not absolutely everything.

6   Then this Christmas was coming, and my grandfather in Ohio sent along in his box of presents an envelope with money in it for me to buy myself the book I wanted.

7   I went to Kress's. Not everybody knew Kress's sold books, but children just before Christmas know everything Kress's ever sold or will sell. My father had showed us the mirror he was giving my mother to hang above her desk, and Kress's is where my brother and I went to reproduce that by buying a mirror together to give her ourselves, and where our little brother then made us take him and he bought her one his size for fifteen cents. Kress's had also its version of the Series Books, called, exactly like another series, "The Camp Fire Girls," beginning with *The Camp Fire Girls in the Woods.*

8   I believe they were ten cents each and I had a dollar. But they weren't all that easy to buy, because the series stuck, and to buy some of it was like breaking into a loaf of French bread. Then after you got home, each single book was as hard to open as a box stuck in its varnish, and when it gave way it popped like a firecracker. The covers once prized apart would never close; those books once open stayed open and lay on their back helplessly fluttering their leaves like a turned-over June bug. They were as light as a matchbox. They were printed on yellowed paper with corners that crumbled, if you pinched on them too hard, like old graham crackers, and they smelled like attic trunks, caramelized glue, their own confinement with one another and, over all, the Kress's smell—bandanas, peanuts and sandalwood from the incense counter. Even without reading them I loved them. It was hard, that year, that Christmas is a day you can't read.

9   What could have happened to those books?—but I can tell you about the leading character. His name was Mr. Holmes. He was not a Camp Fire Girl: he wanted to catch one. Through every book of the series he gave chase.

He pursued Bessie and Zara—those were the Camp Fire Girls—and kept scooping them up in his touring car, while they just as regularly got away from him. Once Bessie escaped from the second floor of a strange inn by climbing down a gutter pipe. Once she escaped by driving away from Mr. Holmes in his own automobile, which she had learned to drive by watching him. What Mr. Holmes wanted with them—either Bessie or Zara would do—didn't give me pause; I was too young to be a Camp Fire Girl; I was just keeping up. I wasn't alarmed by Mr. Holmes—when I cared for a chill, I knew to go to Dr. Fu Manchu, who had his own series in the library. I wasn't fascinated either. There was one thing I wanted from those books, and that was for me to have ten to read at one blow.

10   Who in the world wrote those books? I knew all the time they were the false "Camp Fire Girls" and the ones in the library were the authorized. But book reviewers sometimes say of a book that if anyone else had written it, it might not have been this good, and I found it out as a child—their warning is justified. This was a proven case, although a case of the true not being as good as the false. In the true series the characters were either totally different or missing (Mr. Holmes was missing), and there was too much time given to teamwork. The Kress's Campers, besides getting into a more reliable kind of trouble than the Carnegie Campers, had adventures that even they themselves weren't aware of: the pages were in wrong. There were transposed pages, repeated pages, and whole sections in upside down. There was no way of telling if there was anything missing. But if you know your way in the woods at all, you could enjoy yourself tracking it down. I read the library "Camp Fire Girls," since that's what they were there for, but though they could be read by poorer light they were not as good.

11   And yet, in a way, the false Campers were no better either. I wonder whether I felt some flaw at the heart of things or whether I was just tired of not having any taste; but it seemed to me when I had finished that the last nine of those books weren't as good as the first one. And the same went for all Series Books. As long as they are keeping a series going, I was afraid, nothing can really happen. The whole thing is one grand prevention. For my greed, I might have unwittingly dealt with myself in the same way Maria Edgeworth dealt with the one who put her all into the purple jar—I had received word it was just colored water.

12   And then I went again to the home shelves and my lucky hand reached and found Mark Twain—twenty-four volumes, not a series, and good all the way through.

Discovering Books
Richard Wright
(1908–1960)

Richard Wright
(AP/Wide World)

Born near Natchez, Mississippi, Richard Wright had little formal education and after the age of 15 did not attend school. As a young adult, he moved to Chicago and worked as a post office clerk. Wright joined the Communist party in 1932 and published numerous short stories and poems in political journals. His individualistic outlook, however, caused conflicts with party members who insisted on strict adherence to the Marxist party line and in 1944 he officially left the party. As part of the Works Progress Administration Federal Writers' Project in New York and Chicago, he continued to write poetry and fiction, and in 1938 Wright won *Story* magazine's prize for his four long stories later published under the title *Uncle Tom's Children.* He first gained national recognition with his next book *Native Son* (1940). In 1946, Wright moved with his wife and children to Paris where he wrote many books including *White Man, Listen!* (1957) and *The Man Who Lived Underground,* published posthumously in 1971. In "Discovering Books" Wright explains why he saw reading as an essential part of preparing himself to become a writer.

1   One morning I arrived early at work and went into the bank lobby where the Negro porter was mopping. I stood at a counter and picked up the Memphis *Commercial Appeal* and began my free reading of the press. I came finally to the editorial page and saw an article dealing with one H. L. Mencken. I knew by hearsay that he was the editor of the *American Mercury,* but aside from that I knew nothing about him. The article was a furious denunciation of Mencken, concluding with one, hot, short sentence: Mencken is a fool.

2   I wondered what on earth this Mencken had done to call down upon him the scorn of the South. The only people I had ever heard denounced in the South were Negroes, and this man was not a Negro. Then what ideas did Mencken hold that made a newspaper like the *Commercial Appeal* castigate him publicly? Undoubtedly he must be advocating ideas that the South did not like. Were there, then, people other than Negroes who criticized the South? I knew that during the Civil War the South had hated northern whites, but I had not encountered such hate during my life. Knowing no more of Mencken than I did at that moment, I felt a vague sympathy for him. Had not the South, which had assigned me the role of a nonman, cast at him its hardest words?

3   Now, how could I find out about this Mencken? There was a huge library near the riverfront, but I knew that Negros were not allowed to patronize its shelves any more than they were the parks and playgrounds of the city. I had gone into the library several times to get books for the white men on the job. Which of them would now help me to get books? And how could I read them without causing concern to the white men with whom I worked? I had so far been successful in hiding my thoughts and feelings from them, but I knew that I would create hostility if I went about this business of reading in a clumsy way.

4   I weighed the personalities of the men on the job. There was Don, a Jew; but I distrusted him. His position was not much better than mine and I knew that he was uneasy and insecure; he had always treated me in an offhand, bantering way that barely concealed his contempt. I was afraid to ask him to help me to get books; his frantic desire to demonstrate a racial solidarity with the whites against Negroes might make him betray me.

5   Then how about the boss? No, he was a Baptist and I had the suspicion that he would not be quite able to comprehend why a black boy would want to read Mencken. There were other white men on the job whose attitudes showed clearly that they were Kluxers or sympathizers, and they were out of the question.

6   There remained only one man whose attitude did not fit into an anti-Negro category, for I had heard the white men refer to him as a "Pope lover." He was an Irish Catholic and was hated by the white Southerners. I knew that he read books, because I had got him volumes from the library several times. Since he, too, was an object of hatred, I felt that he might refuse me but would hardly betray me. I hesitated, weighing and balancing the imponderable realities.

7   One morning I paused before the Catholic fellow's desk.

8   "I want to ask you a favor," I whispered to him.

9   "What is it?"

10   "I want to read. I can't get books from the library. I wonder if you'd let me use your card?"

11   He looked at me suspiciously.

12 "My card is full most of the time," he said.

13 "I see," I said and waited, posing my question silently.

14 "You're not trying to get me into trouble, are you, boy?" he asked, staring at me.

15 "Oh, no, sir."

16 "What book do you want?"

17 "A book by H. L. Mencken."

18 "Which one?"

19 "I don't know. Has he written more than one?"

20 "He has written several."

21 "I didn't know that."

22 "What makes you want to read Mencken?"

23 "Oh, I just saw his name in the newspaper," I said.

24 "It's good of you to want to read," he said. "But you ought to read the right things."

25 I said nothing. Would he want to supervise my reading?

26 "Let me think," he said. "I'll figure out something."

27 I turned from him and he called me back. He stared at me quizzically.

28 "Richard, don't mention this to the other white men," he said.

29 "I understand," I said. "I won't say a word."

30 A few days later he called me to him.

31 "I've got a card in my wife's name," he said. "Here's mine."

32 "Thank you, sir."

33 "Do you think you can manage it?"

34 "I'll manage fine," I said.

35 "If they suspect you, you'll get in trouble," he said.

36 "I'll write the same kind of notes to the library that you wrote when you sent me for books," I told him. "I'll sign your name."

37 He laughed.

38 "Go ahead. Let me see what you get," he said.

39 That afternoon I addressed myself to forging a note. Now, what were the names of books written by H. L. Mencken? I did not know any of them. I finally wrote what I thought would be a foolproof note: *Dear Madam: Will you please let this nigger boy*—I used the word "nigger" to make the librarian feel that I could not possibly be the author of the note—*have some books by H. L. Mencken?* I forged the white man's name.

40 I entered the library as I had always done when on errands for whites, but I felt that I would somehow slip up and betray myself. I doffed my hat, stood a respectful distance from the desk, looked as unbookish as possible, and waited for the white patrons to be taken care of. When the desk was clear of people, I still waited. The white librarian looked at me.

41 "What do you want, boy?"

42 As though I did not possess the power of speech, I stepped forward and simply handed her the forged note, not parting my lips.

43   "What books by Mencken does he want?" she asked.

44   "I don't know, ma'am," I said, avoiding her eyes.

45   "Who gave you this card?"

46   "Mr. Falk," I said.

47   "Where is he?"

48   "He's at work, at the M———— Optical Company," I said. "I've been in here for him before."

49   "I remember," the woman said. "But he never wrote notes like this."

50   Oh, God, she's suspicious. Perhaps she would not let me have the books? If she had turned her back at that moment, I would have ducked out the door and never gone back. Then I thought of a bold idea.

51   "You can call him up, ma'am," I said, my heart pounding.

52   "You're not using these books, are you?" she asked pointedly.

53   "Oh, no, ma'am. I can't read."

54   "I don't know what he wants by Mencken," she said under her breath.

55   I knew now that I had won; she was thinking of other things and the race question had gone out of her mind. She went to the shelves. Once or twice she looked over her shoulder at me, as though she was still doubtful. Finally she came forward with two books in her hand.

56   "I'm sending him two books," she said. "But tell Mr. Falk to come in next time, or send me the names of the books he wants. I don't know what he wants to read."

57   I said nothing. She stamped the card and handed me the books. Not daring to glance at them, I went out of the library, fearing that the woman would call me back for further questioning. A block away from the library I opened one of the books and read a title: *A Book of Prefaces*. I was nearing my nineteenth birthday and I did not know how to pronounce the word *preface*. I thumbed the pages and saw strange words and strange names. I shook my head, disappointed. I looked at the other book; it was called *Prejudices*. I knew what that word meant; I had heard it all my life. And right off I was on guard against Mencken's books. Why would a man want to call a book *Prejudices?* The word was so stained with all my memories of racial hate that I could not conceive of anybody using it for a title. Perhaps I had made a mistake about Mencken? A man who had prejudices must be wrong.

58   When I showed the books to Mr. Falk, he looked at me and frowned.

59   "That librarian might telephone you," I warned him.

60   "That's all right," he said. "But when you're through reading those books, I want you to tell me what you get out of them."

61   That night in my rented room, while letting the hot water run over my can of pork and beans in the sink, I opened *A Book of Prefaces* and began to read. I was jarred and shocked by the style, the clear, clean, sweeping sentences. Why did he write like that? And how did one write like that? I pictured the man as a raging demon, slashing with his pen, consumed with hate, denouncing everything American, extolling everything European or

German, laughing at the weaknesses of people, mocking God, authority. What was this? I stood up, trying to realize what reality lay behind the meaning of the words. . . . Yes, this man was fighting, fighting with words. He was using words as a weapon, using them as one would use a club. Could words be weapons? Well, yes, for here they were. Then, maybe, perhaps, I could use them as a weapon? No. It frightened me. I read on and what amazed me was not what he said, but how on earth anybody had the courage to say it.

62   Occasionally I glanced up to reassure myself that I was alone in the room. Who were these men about whom Mencken was talking so passionately? Who was Anatole France? Joseph Conrad? Sinclair Lewis, Sherwood Anderson, Dostoevski, George Moore, Gustave Flaubert, Maupassant, Tolstoy, Frank Harris, Mark Twain, Thomas Hardy, Arnold Bennett, Stephen Crane, Zola, Norris, Gorky, Bergson, Ibsen, Balzac, Bernard Shaw, Dumas, Poe, Thomas Mann, O. Henry, Dreiser, H. G. Wells, Gogol, T. S. Eliot, Gide, Baudelaire, Edgar Lee Masters, Stendhal, Turgenev, Huneker, Nietzsche, and scores of others? Were these men real? Did they exist or had they existed? And how did one pronounce their names?

63   I ran across many words whose meanings I did not know, and I either looked them up in a dictionary or, before I had a chance to do that, encountered the word in a context that made its meaning clear. But what strange world was this? I concluded the book with the conviction that I had somehow overlooked something terribly important in life. I had once tried to write, had once reveled in feeling, had let my crude imagination roam, but the impulse to dream had been slowly beaten out of me by experience. Now it surged up again and I hungered for books, new ways of looking and seeing. It was not a matter of believing or disbelieving what I read, but of feeling something new, or being affected by something that made the look of the world different.

64   As dawn broke I ate my pork and beans, feeling dopey, sleepy. I went to work, but the mood of the book would not die; it lingered, coloring everything I saw, heard, did. I now felt that I knew what the white men were feeling. Merely because I had read a book that had spoken of how they lived and thought, I identified myself with that book. I felt vaguely guilty. Would I, filled with bookish notions, act in a manner that would make the whites dislike me?

65   I forged more notes and my trips to the library became more frequent. Reading grew into a passion. My first serious novel was Sinclair Lewis's *Main Street*. It made me see my boss, Mr. Gerald, and identify him as an American type. I would smile when I saw him lugging his golf bags into the office. I had always felt a vast distance separating me from the boss, and now I felt closer to him, though still distant. I felt now that I knew him, that I could feel the very limits of his narrow life. And this had happened because I had read a novel about a mythical man called George F. Babbitt.

66   The plots and stories in the novels did not interest me so much as the point of view revealed. I gave myself over to each novel without reserve, without trying to criticize it; it was enough for me to see and feel something different. And for me, everything was something different. Reading was like a drug, a dope. The novels created moods in which I lived for days. But I could not conquer my sense of guilt, my feeling that the white men around me knew that I was changing, that I had begun to regard them differently.

67   Whenever I brought a book to the job, I wrapped it in newspaper—a habit that was to persist for years in other cities and under other circumstances. But some of the white men pried into my packages when I was absent and they questioned me.

68   "Boy, what are you reading those books for?"

69   "Oh, I don't know, sir,"

70   "That's deep stuff you're reading, boy."

71   "I'm just killing time, sir."

72   "You'll addle your brains if you don't watch out."

73   I read Dreiser's *Jennie Gerhardt* and *Sister Carrie* and they revived in me a vivid sense of my mother's suffering; I was overwhelmed, I grew silent, wondering about the life around me. It would have been impossible for me to have told anyone what I derived from these novels, for it was nothing less than a sense of life itself. All my life had shaped me for the realism, the naturalism of the modern novel, and I could not read enough of them.

74   Steeped in new moods and ideas, I bought a ream of paper and tried to write; but nothing would come, or what did come was flat beyond telling. I discovered that more than desire and feeling were necessary to write and I dropped the idea. Yet I still wondered how it was possible to know people sufficiently to write about them? Could I ever learn about life and people? To me, with my vast ignorance, my Jim Crow station in life, it seemed a task impossible of achievement. I now knew what being a Negro meant. I could endure the hunger. I had learned to live with hate. But to feel that there were feelings denied me, that the very breath of life itself was beyond my reach, that more than anything else hurt, wounded me. I had a new hunger.

75   In buoying me up, reading also cast me down, made me see what was possible, what I had missed. My tension returned, new, terrible, bitter, surging, almost too great to be contained. I no longer *felt* that the world about me was hostile, killing; I *knew* it. A million times I asked myself what I could do to save myself, and there were no answers. I seemed forever condemned, ringed by walls.

76   I did not discuss my reading with Mr. Falk, who had lent me his library card; it would have meant talking about myself and that would have been too painful. I smiled each day, fighting desperately to maintain my old behavior, to keep my disposition seemingly sunny. But some of the white men discerned that I had begun to brood.

77   "Wake up there, boy!" Mr. Olin said one day.

78   "Sir!" I answered for the lack of a better word.

79   "You act like you've stolen something," he said.

80   I laughed in the way I knew he expected me to laugh, but I resolved to be more conscious of myself, to watch my every act, to guard and hide the new knowledge that was dawning within me.

81   If I went north, would it be possible for me to build a new life then? But how could a man build a life upon vague, unformed yearnings? I wanted to write and I did not even know the English language. I bought English grammars and found them dull. I felt that I was getting a better sense of the language from novels than grammars. I read hard, discarding a writer as soon as I felt that I had grasped his point of view. At night the printed page stood before my eyes in sleep.

82   Mrs. Moss, my landlady, asked me one Sunday morning:

83   "Son, what is this you keep on reading?"

84   "Oh, nothing. Just novels."

85   "What you get out of 'em?"

86   "I'm just killing time," I said.

87   "I hope you know your own mind," she said in a tone which implied that she doubted if I had a mind.

88   I knew of no Negroes who read the books I liked and I wondered if any Negroes ever thought of them. I knew that there were Negro doctors, lawyers, newspapermen, but I never saw any of them. When I read a Negro newspaper I never caught the faintest echo of my preoccupation in its pages. I felt trapped and occasionally, for a few days, I would stop reading. But a vague hunger would come over me for books, books that opened up new avenues of feeling and seeing, and again I would forge another note to the white librarian. Again I would read and wonder as only the naive and unlettered can read and wonder, feeling that I carried a secret, criminal burden about with me each day.

89   That winter my mother and brother came and we set up housekeeping, buying furniture on the installment plan, being cheated and yet knowing no way to avoid it. I began to eat warm food and to my surprise found the regular meals enabled me to read faster. I may have lived through many illnesses and survived them, never suspecting that I was ill. My brother obtained a job and we began to save toward the trip north, plotting our time, setting tentative dates for departure. I told none of the white men on the job that I was planning to go north; I knew that the moment they felt I was thinking of the North they would change toward me. It would have made them feel that I did not like the life I was living, and because my life was completely conditioned by what they said or did, it would have been tantamount to challenging them.

90   I could calculate my chances for life in the South as a Negro fairly clearly now.

91   I could fight the southern whites by organizing with other Negros, as my grandfather had done. But I knew that I could never win that way; there were many whites and there were but few blacks. They were strong and we were weak. Outright black rebellion could never win. If I fought openly I would die and I did not want to die. News of lynchings were frequent.

92   I could submit and live the life of a genial slave, but that was impossible. All of my life had shaped me to live by my own feelings and thoughts. I could make up to Bess and marry her and inherit the house. But that, too, would be the life of a slave; if I did that, I would crush to death something within me, and I would hate myself as much as I knew the whites already hated those who had submitted. Neither could I ever willingly present myself to be kicked, as Shorty had done. I would rather have died than do that.

93   I could drain off my restlessness by fighting with Shorty and Harrison. I had seen many Negroes solve the problem of being black by transferring their hatred of themselves to others with a black skin and fighting them. I would have to be cold to do that, and I was not cold and I could never be.

94   I could, of course, forget what I had read, thrust the whites out of my mind, forget them; and find release from anxiety and longing in sex and alcohol. But the memory of how my father had conducted himself made that course repugnant. If I did not want others to violate my life, how could I voluntarily violate it myself?

95   I had no hope whatever of being a professional man. Not only had I been so conditioned that I did not desire it, but the fulfillment of such an ambition was beyond my capabilities. Well-to-do Negroes lived in a world that was almost as alien to me as the world inhabited by whites.

96   What, then, was there? I held my life in my mind, in my consciousness each day, feeling at times that I would stumble and drop it, spill it forever. My reading had created a vast sense of distance between me and the world in which I lived and tried to make a living, and that sense of distance was increasing each day. My days and nights were one long, quiet, continuously contained dream of terror, tension, and anxiety. I wondered how long I could bear it.

How Books Helped Shape My Life

Judith Viorst
(1936–   )

Judith Viorst
(© David Morowitz)

A contributing editor to *Redbook* magazine, Judith Viorst was born in Newark, New Jersey, and educated at Rutgers University. Her poetic monologues written for the CBS special "Annie, the Woman in the Life of a Man" won an Emmy Award in 1970. She has published a collection of poems, *It's Hard to Be Hip Over Thirty, and Other Tragedies of Married Life* (1970), and a collection of prose, *Yes, Married: A Saga of Love and Complaint* (1972). She has collaborated with her husband, Milton, on a guide to Washington, D.C., restaurants and, in addition, writes children's books. More recent works include *Forever Fifty* (1989) and *Earrings!* (1990). In "How Books Shaped My Life," which was first published in *Redbook* magazine in 1960, Viorst explains the powerful influence fictional heroines have had on her emotional and intellectual development.

1   In books I've read since I was young I've searched for heroines who could serve as ideals, as models, as possibilities—some reflecting the secret self that dwelled inside me, others pointing to whole new ways that a woman (if only she dared!) might try to be. The person that I am today was shaped by Nancy Drew; by Jo March, Jane Eyre and Heathcliff's soul mate Cathy; and by other fictional females whose attractiveness or character or audacity for a time were the standards by which I measured myself.

2   I return to some of these books to see if I still understand the powerful hold that these heroines once had on me. I still understand.

3   Consider teen-aged Nancy Drew—beautiful, blond-haired, blue-eyed girl detective—who had the most terrific life that I as a ten-year-old could ever imagine. Motherless (in other words, quite free of maternal controls), she lived with her handsome indulgent lawyer father in a large brick house set back from the street with a winding tree-lined driveway on the outside and a faithful, nonintrusive housekeeper Hannah cooking yummy meals

on the inside. She also had a boy friend, a convertible, nice clothes and two close girl friends—not as perfect as she, but then it seemed to me that no one could possibly be as perfect as Nancy Drew, who in dozens and dozens of books *(The Hidden Staircase, The Whispering Statue, The Clue in the Diary, The Clue of the Tapping Heels)* was resourceful and brave and intelligent as she went around solving mysteries left and right, while remaining kind to the elderly and invariably polite and absolutely completely delightfully feminine.

4   I mean, what else *was* there?

5   I soon found out what else when I encountered the four March sisters of *Little Women,* a sentimental, old-fashioned book about girls growing up in Civil War time in New England. About spoiled, vain, pretty Amy. And sickly, saintly Beth. And womanly, decent Meg. And about—most important of all—gawky, bookworm Jo. Dear Jo, who wasn't as flawless as the golden Nancy Drew but who showed me that girls like her—like *us*—could be heroines. Even if we weren't much to look at. Even if we were clumsy and socially gauche. And even if the transition into young womanhood often appeared to our dubious eye to be difficult and scary and even unwelcome.

6   Jo got stains on her dress and laughed when she shouldn't and lost her temper and didn't display tact or patience or restraint. Jo brought a touch of irreverence to the cultural constraints of the world she lived in. And yet her instincts were good and her heart was pure and her headstrong ways led always to virtue. And furthermore Jo—as I yearned to be—was a writer!

7   In the book the years go by, Beth dies, Meg and Amy marry and Jo—her fierce heart somewhat tamed—is alone. " 'An old maid, that's what I'm to be. A literary spinster, with a pen for a spouse, a family of stories for children, and twenty years hence a morsel of fame, perhaps!' . . . Jo sighed, as if the prospect was not inviting."

8   This worried young reader concurred—not inviting at all!

9   And so I was happy to read of Jo's nice suitor, Mr. Bhaer, not handsome or rich or young or important or witty, but possessed of kindness and dignity and enough intelligence to understand that even a girl who wasn't especially pretty, who had no dazzling charms and who wanted to write might make a wonderful wife. And a wonderful mother. And live happily ever after.

10   What a relief!

11   What Jo and Nancy shared was active participation in life—they went out and *did;* they weren't simply done to—and they taught and promised me (at a time when mommies stayed home and there was no Women's Movement) that a girl could go out and do and still get a man. Jo added the notion that brusque, ungainly girls could go out and do and still get a man. And Jane of *Jane Eyre,* whose author once said, "I will show you a heroine as small and as plain as myself," added the further idea that such women were able to "feel just as men feel" and were capable of being just as passionate.

12   Orphaned Jane, a governess at stately Thornfield Hall, was a no-nonsense lady, cool and self-contained, whose lonely, painful childhood had ingrained in her an impressive firmness of character, an unwillingness to charm or curry favor and a sense of herself as the equal of any man. Said Jane to Mr. Rochester, the brooding, haughty, haunted master of Thornfield: "Do you think I am an automaton?—a machine without feelings? Do you think, because I am poor, obscure, plain, and little, I am soulless and heartless? You think wrong—I have as much soul as you, and full as much heart!"

13   I loved it that such hot fires burned inside so plain a Jane. I loved her for her unabashed intensity. And I loved her for being so pure that when she learned of Mr. Rochester's lunatic wife, she sacrificed romance for honor and left him immediately.

14   For I think it's important to note that Nancy and Jo and Jane, despite their independence, were basically as good as girls can be: honest, generous, kind, sincere, reliable, respectable, possessed of absolute integrity. They didn't defy convention. They didn't challenge the rules. They did what was right, although it might cause them pain. And their virtue was always rewarded— look at Jane, rich and married at last to her Mr. Rochester. Oh, how I identified with Jane!

15   But then I read *Wuthering Heights,* a novel of soul-consuming love on the Yorkshire moors, and Catherine Earnshaw totally captured me. And she captured me, not in spite of her dangerous, dark and violent spirit, but *because* of it.

16   Cathy was as wild as the moors. She lied and connived and deceived. She was insolent, selfish, manipulative and cruel. And by marrying meek, weak Edgar instead of Heathcliff, her destiny, she betrayed a love she described in throbbing, unforgettable prose as . . . elemental:

17   "My love for Heathcliff resembles the eternal rocks beneath—a source of little visible delight, but necessary. Nelly, I *am* Heathcliff—he's always, always in my mind—not as a pleasure, any more than I am always a pleasure to myself—but as my own being. . . ."

18   Now who, at the age of 16, could resist such quivering intensity? Who would settle for less than elemental? Must we untamed creatures of passion— I'd muse as I lay awake in my red flannel nightie—submit ourselves to conventional morality? Or could I actually choose not to be a good girl?

19   Cathy Earnshaw told me that I could. And so did Lady Brett, of *The Sun Also Rises.*

20   Brett Ashley was to me, at 18, free, modern, woman incarnate, and she dangled alluring new concepts before my eyes:

21   The value of style: "She wore a slipover jersey sweater and a tweed skirt, and her hair was brushed back like a boy's. She started all that."

22   The glamour of having a dark and tortured past: "Finally, when he got really bad, he used to tell her he'd kill her. . . . She hasn't had an absolutely happy life."

23   The excitement of nonconformity: "I've always done just what I wanted."

24   The importance of (understated) grace under pressure: "Brett was rather good. She's always rather good."

25   And the thrill of unrepressed sexuality: "Brett's had affairs with men before. She tells me all about everything."

26   Brett married lovelessly and drank too much and drifted too much and had an irresponsible fling with a bullfighter. But she also had class—and her own morality. She set her bullfighter free—"I'd have lived with him if I hadn't seen it was bad for him." And even though she was broke, she lied and "told him I had scads of it. . . . I couldn't take his money, you know."

27   Brett's wasn't the kind of morality that my mother was teaching me in suburban New Jersey. But maybe I wasn't meant for suburban life. Maybe— I would muse as I carefully lined my eyes with blue liner—maybe I'm meant for something more . . . emancipated.

28   I carried Brett's image with me when, after college, I lived for a while in Greenwich Village, in New York. But I couldn't achieve her desperate gallantry. And it struck me that Brett was too lonely and sad, and that Cathy had died too young (and that Scarlett O'Hara got Tara but lost her Rhett), and that maybe I ought to forget about unconventionality if the price was going to be so painfully high. Although I enjoyed my Village fling, I had no wish to live anguishedly ever after. I needed a heroine who, like me, wanted just a small taste of the wild before settling down into happy domesticity.

29   I found her in *War and Peace*. Her name was Natasha.

30   Natasha, the leading lady of this epic of Russian society during Napoleon's time, was "poetic .. charming . . . overflowing with life," an enchanting girl whose sweet eagerness and passionate impulsivity were tempered by historic and private tragedies. Betrothed to the handsome and excellent Prince Andrew, she fell in love with a heel named Anatole, and when she was warned that this foolish and dangerous passion would lead to her ruin, "I'll go to my ruin . . .," she said, "as soon as possible."

31   It ended badly with Anatole. Natasha tried suicide. Prince Andrew died. Natasha turned pale, thin, subdued. But unlike Brett and Cathy, her breach with convention was mended and, at long last, she married Pierre—a decent, substantial, loving man, the kind of man all our mothers want us to marry.

32   In marriage Natasha grew stouter and "the old fire very rarely kindled in her face now." She became an exemplary mother, an ideal wife. "She felt that her unity with her husband was maintained not by the poetic feelings that had attracted him to her but by something else—indefinite but firm as the bond between her own body and soul."

33   It sounded—if not elemental and doomed—awfully nice.

34   I identified with Natasha when, the following year, I married and left Greenwich Village. I too was ready for domesticity. And yet . . . her husband and children became "the subject which wholly engrossed Natasha's atten-

tion." She had lost herself—and I didn't want to lose me. What I needed next was a heroine who could reconcile all the warring wants of my nature—for fire and quiet, independence and oneness, ambition and love, and marriage and family.

35   But such reconciling heroines, in novels and real life, may not yet exist.

36   Nevertheless Natasha and Jane and Jo, Cathy, Nancy and Brett—each spoke to my heart and stirred me powerfully. On my journey into young womanhood I was fortunate to have them as my companions. They were, they will always remain, a part of me.

Donald Hall (© Gary Samson)

Four Kinds of Reading

Donald Hall
(1928–   )

Born in New Haven, Connecticut, Donald Hall
began writing poetry at age 14. He graduated from
Harvard and did graduate work at Oxford and
Stanford where he was named a Creative Writing
Fellow. Following his work at Stanford, he became
editor for the *Paris Review* and later he taught at
the University of Michigan. He has published
many books of prose, criticism, and poetry as well
as several writing and literature textbooks. His
most recent works include the poetry of *New Voices*
(1989) and *The One Day and Poems 1947–1990*
(1991). In addition, he has edited several
anthologies. Hall currently lives in Danbury, New
Hampshire, where he works full time at writing. In
"Four Kinds of Reading," which was originally
published in *The New York Times* on January 26,
1969, Hall suggests that there are at least four
different purposes for reading and that each
requires a different process.

1   Everywhere one meets the idea that reading is an activity desirable in
itself. It is understandable that publishers and librarians—and even writers—
should promote this assumption, but it is strange that the idea should have
general currency. People surround the idea of reading with piety and do
not take into account the purpose of reading or the value of what is being
read. Teachers and parents praise the child who reads, and praise themselves,
whether the text be the *Reader's Digest* or *Moby-Dick*. The advent of TV has
increased the false values ascribed to reading, since TV provides a vulgar
alternative. But this piety is silly; and most reading is no more cultural or
intellectual or imaginative than shooting pool or watching *What's My Line.*

2   It is worth asking how the act of reading became something to value in itself, as opposed for instance to the act of conversation or the act of taking a walk. Mass literacy is a recent phenomenon, and I suggest that the aura which decorates reading is a relic of the importance of reading to our great-great-grandparents. Literacy used to be a mark of a social distinction, separating a small portion of humanity from the rest. The farm laborer who was ambitious for his children did not daydream that they would become schoolteachers or doctors; he daydreamed that they would learn to read, and that a world would therefore open up to them in which they did not have to labor in the fields fourteen hours a day for six days a week in order to buy salt and cotton. On the next rank of society, ample time for reading meant that the reader was free from the necessity to spend most of his waking hours making a living of any kind. This sort of attitude shades into the contemporary man's boast of his wife's cultural activities. When he says that his wife is interested in books and music and pictures, he is not only enclosing the arts in a delicate female world; he is saying that he is rich enough to provide her with the leisure to do nothing. Reading is an inactivity, and therefore a badge of social class. Of course, these reasons for the piety attached to reading are never acknowledged. They show themselves in the shape of our attitudes toward books; reading gives off an air of gentility.

3   It seems to be possible to name four kinds of reading, each with a characteristic manner and purpose. The first is reading for information—reading to learn about a trade, or politics, or how to accomplish something. We read a newspaper this way, or most textbooks, or directions on how to assemble a bicycle. With most of this sort of material, the reader can learn to scan the page quickly, coming up with what he needs and ignoring what is irrelevant to him, like the rhythm of the sentence, or the play of metaphor. Courses in speed-reading can help us read for this purpose, training the eye to jump quickly across the page. If we read *The New York Times* with the attention we should give a novel or a poem, we will have time for nothing else, and our mind will be cluttered with clichés and dead metaphors. Quick eye-reading is a necessity to anyone who wants to keep up with what's happening or learn much of what has happened in the past. The amount of reflection, which interrupts and slows down the reading, depends on the material.

4   But it is not the same activity as reading literature. There ought to be another word. If we read a work of literature properly, we read slowly, and we hear all the words. If our lips do not actually move, it's only laziness. The muscles in our throats move and come together when we see the word "squeeze." We hear the sounds so accurately that if a syllable is missing in a line of poetry we hear the lack, though we may not know what we are lacking. In prose we accept the rhythms and hear the adjacent sounds. We also register a track of feeling through the metaphors and associations of words. Careless writing prevents this sort of attention, and becomes offen-

sive. But the great writers reward this attention. Only by the full exercise of our powers to receive language can we absorb their intelligence and their imagination. This kind of reading goes through the ear—though the eye takes in the print and decodes it into sound—to the throat and the understanding, and it can never be quick. It is slow and sensual, a deep pleasure that begins with touch and ends with the sort of comprehension that we associate with dream.

5   Too many intellectuals read in order to reduce images to abstractions. With a philosopher one reads slowly, as if it were literature, but much time must be spent with the eyes turned away from the pages, reflecting on the text. To read literature this way is to turn it into something it is not—to concepts clothed in character, or philosophy sugar-coated. I think that most literary intellectuals read this way, including the brighter Professors of English, with the result that they miss literature completely, and concern themselves with a minor discipline called the history of ideas. I remember a course in Chaucer at my university in which the final exam largely required the identification of a hundred or more fragments of Chaucer, none as long as a line. If you liked poetry and read Chaucer through a couple of times slowly, you found yourself knowing them all. If you were a literary intellectual, well-informed about the great chain of being, chances are you had a difficult time. To read literature is to be intimately involved with the words on the page and never to think of them as the embodiments of ideas which can be expressed in other terms. On the other hand, intellectual writing—closer to mathematics on a continuum that has at its opposite pole lyric poetry—requires intellectual reading, which is slow because it is reflective and because the reader must pause to evaluate concepts.

6   But most of the reading which is praised for itself is neither literary nor intellectual. It is narcotic. Novels, stories, and biographies—historical sagas, monthly regurgitations of book clubs, four- and five-thousand word daydreams of the magazines—these are the opium of the suburbs. The drug is not harmful except to the addict himself and is no more injurious to him than Johnny Carson or a bridge club, but it is nothing to be proud of. This reading is the automated daydream, the mild trip of the housewife and the tired businessman, interested not in experience and feeling but in turning off the possibilities of experience and feeling. Great literature, if we read it well, opens us up to the world, and makes us more sensitive to it, as if we acquired eyes that could see through things and ears that could hear smaller sounds. But by narcotic reading, one can reduce great literature to the level of *The Valley of the Dolls*. One can read *Anna Karenina* passively and inattentively, and float down the river of lethargy as if one were reading a confession magazine: "I Spurned My Husband for a Count."

7   I think that everyone reads for narcosis occasionally, and perhaps most consistently in late adolescence, when great readers are born. I remember reading to shut the world out, away at a school where I did not want to be;

I invented a word to name my disease: "bibliolepsy," on the analogy of narcolepsy. But after a while the books became a window on the world and not a screen against it. This change doesn't always happen. I think that late adolescent narcotic reading accounts for some of the badness of English departments. As a college student, the boy loves reading and majors in English because he would be reading anyway. Deciding on a career, he takes up English teaching for the same reason. Then in graduate school he is trained to be a scholar, which is painful and irrelevant, and finds he must write papers and publish them to be a Professor—and at about this time he no longer requires reading for narcosis, and he is left with nothing but a Ph.D. and the prospect of fifty years of teaching literature; and he does not even like literature.

8   Narcotic reading survives the impact of television, because this type of reading has even less reality than melodrama; that is, the reader is in control: once the characters reach into the reader's feelings, he is able to stop reading, or glance away, or superimpose his own daydreams. The trouble with television is that it writes its own script. Literature is often valued precisely because of its distance from the tangible. Some readers prefer looking into the text of a play to seeing it performed. Reading a play, it is possible to stage it oneself by an imaginative act; but it is also possible to remove it from real people. Here is Virginia Woolf, who was lavish in her praise of the act of reading, talking about reading a play rather than seeing it: "Certainly there is a good deal to be said for reading *Twelfth Night* in the book if the book can be read in a garden, with no sound but the thud of an apple falling to the earth, or of the wind ruffling the branches of the trees." She sets her own stage; the play is called *Virginia Woolf Reads Twelfth Night in a Garden*. Piety moves into narcissism, and the high metaphors of Shakespeare's lines dwindle into the flowers of an English garden; actors in ruffles wither, while the wind ruffles branches.

The Art of Reading

Lin Yutang
(1895–   )

*Lin Yutang
(AP/Wide World)*

Lin Yutang was born in Amoy, Fukien Province, China, and was sent to Christian schools where he learned English. As an adult, he left China with his wife and furthered his education at Leipzig, Jena, and Harvard. Lin later returned to China, having completed his Ph.D., and took a position as professor of English Philosophy at Peking National University. He has written many books; the two most widely read by English-speaking readers are *My Country and My People* (1935) and *The Importance of Living* (1937). In "The Art of Reading" Lin suggests that reading is not a grim obligation to be dutifully fulfilled but rather a joyful pursuit that should be "entirely spontaneous."

1   Reading or the enjoyment of books has always been regarded among the charms of a cultured life and is respected and envied by those who rarely give themselves that privilege. This is easy to understand when we compare the difference between the life of a man who does no reading and that of a man who does. The man who has not the habit of reading is imprisoned in his immediate world, in respect to time and space. His life falls into a set routine; he is limited to contact and conversation with a few friends and acquaintances, and he sees only what happens in his immediate neighborhood. From this prison there is no escape. But the moment he takes up a book, he immediately enters a different world, and if it is a good book, he is immediately put in touch with one of the best talkers of the world. This talker leads him on and carries him into a different country or a different age, or unburdens to him some of his personal regrets, or discusses with him some special line or aspect of life that the reader knows nothing about. An ancient author puts him in communion with a dead spirit of long ago, and as he reads along, he begins to imagine what that ancient author looked like and what type of person he was. Both Mencius and Ssema Ch'ien, China's greatest historian, have expressed the same idea. Now to be able

to live two hours out of twelve in a different world and take one's thoughts off the claims of the immediate present is, of course, a privilege to be envied by people shut up in their bodily prison. Such a change of environment is really similar to travel in its psychological effect.

2   But there is more to it than this. The reader is always carried away into a world of thought and reflection. Even if it is a book about physical events, there is a difference between seeing such events in person or living through them, and reading about them in books, for then the events always assume the quality of the spectacle and the reader becomes a detached spectator. The best reading is therefore that which leads us into this contemplative mood, and not that which is merely occupied with the report of events. The tremendous amount of time spent on newspapers I regard as not reading at all, for the average readers of papers are mainly concerned with getting reports about events and happenings without contemplative value.

3   The best formula for the object of reading, in my opinion, was stated by Huang Shanku, a Sung poet and friend of Su Tungp'o. He said, "A scholar who hasn't read anything for three days feels that *his talk has no flavor* (becomes insipid), *and his own face becomes hateful to look at* (in the mirror)." What he means, of course, is that reading gives a man a certain charm and flavor, which is the entire object of reading, and only reading with this object can be called an art. One doesn't read to "improve one's mind," because when one begins to think of improving his mind, all the pleasure of reading is gone. He is the type of person who says to himself: "I must read Shakespeare, and I must read Sophocles, and I must read the entire Five-foot Shelf of Dr. Eliot, so I can become an educated man." I'm sure that man will never become educated. He will force himself one evening to read Shakespeare's *Hamlet* and come away, as if from a bad dream, with no greater benefit than that he is able to say that he had "read" *Hamlet.* Anyone who reads a book with a sense of obligation does not understand the art of reading. This type of reading with a business purpose is in no way different from a senator's reading up on files and reports before he makes a speech. It is asking for business advice and information, and not reading at all.

4   Reading for the cultivation of personal charm of appearance and flavor in speech is then, according to Huang, the only admissible kind of reading. This charm of appearance must evidently be interpreted as something other than physical beauty. What Huang means by "hateful to look at" is not physical ugliness. There are ugly faces that have a fascinating charm and beautiful faces that are insipid to look at. I have among my Chinese friends one whose head is shaped like a bomb and yet who is nevertheless always a pleasure to see. The most beautiful face among Western authors, so far as I have seen them in pictures, was that of G. K. Chesterton. There was such a diabolical conglomeration of mustache, glasses, fairly bushy eyebrows and knitted lines where the eyebrows met. One felt there were a vast number of ideas playing about inside that forehead, ready at any time to burst out

from those quizzically penetrating eyes. That is what Huang would call a beautiful face, a face not made up by powder and rouge, but by the sheer force of thinking. As for flavor of speech, it all depends on one's way of reading. Whether one has "flavor" or not in his talk, depends on his method of reading. If a reader gets the flavor of books, he will show that flavor in his conversations, and if he has flavor in his conversations, he cannot help also having a flavor in his writing.

5   Hence I consider flavor or taste as the key to all reading. It necessarily follows that taste is selective and individual, like the taste for food. The most hygienic way of eating is, after all, eating what one likes, for then one is sure of his digestion. In reading as in eating, what is one man's meat may be another's poison. A teacher cannot force his pupils to like what he likes in reading, and a parent cannot expect his children to have the same tastes as himself. And if the reader has no taste for what he reads, all the time is wasted. As Yüan Chunglang says, "You can leave the books that you don't like alone, *and let other people read them.*"

6   There can be, therefore, no books that one absolutely must read. For our intellectual interests grow like a tree or flow like a river. So long as there is proper sap, the tree will grow anyhow, and so long as there is fresh current from the spring, the water will flow. When water strikes a granite cliff, it just goes around it; when it finds itself in a pleasant low valley, it stops and meanders there a while; when it finds itself in a deep mountain pond, it is content to stay there; when it finds itself traveling over rapids, it hurries forward. Thus, without any effort or determined aim, it is sure of reaching the sea some day. There are no books in this world that everybody must read, but only books that a person must read at a certain time in a given place under given circumstances and at a given period of his life. I rather think that reading, like matrimony, is determined by fate or *yinyüan.* Even if there is a certain book that everyone must read, like the Bible, there is a time for it. When one's thoughts and experience have not reached a certain point for reading a masterpiece, the masterpiece will leave only a bad flavor on his palate. Confucius said, "When one is fifty, one may read the *Book of Changes,*" which means that one should not read it at forty-five. The extremely mild flavor of Confucius' own sayings in the *Analects* and his mature wisdom cannot be appreciated until one becomes mature himself.

7   I regard the discovery of one's favorite author as the most critical event in one's intellectual development. There is such a thing as the affinity of spirits, and among the authors of ancient and modern times, one must try to find an author whose spirit is akin with his own. Only in this way can one get any real good out of reading. One has to be independent and search out his masters. Who is one's favorite author, no one can tell, probably not even the man himself. It is like love at first sight. The reader cannot be told to love this one or that one, but when he has found the author he loves, he knows it himself by a kind of instinct. We have such famous cases of

discoveries of authors. Scholars seem to have lived in different ages, separated by centuries, and yet their modes of thinking and feeling were so akin that their coming together across the pages of a book was like a person finding his own image. In Chinese phraseology, we speak of these kindred spirits as reincarnations of the same soul, as Su Tungp'o was said to be a reincarnation of Chuangtse or T'ao Yüanming, and Yüan Chunglang was said to be the reincarnation of Su Tungp'o. Su Tungp'o said that when he first read Chuangtse, he felt as if all the time since his childhood he had been thinking the same things and taking the same views himself. When Yüan Chunglang discovered one night Hsü Wench'ang, a contemporary unknown to him, in a small book of poems, he jumped out of bed and shouted to his friend, and his friend began to read it and shout in turn, and then they both read and shouted again until their servant was completely puzzled. George Eliot described her first reading of Rousseau as an electric shock. Nietzsche felt the same thing about Schopenhauer, but Schopenhauer was a peevish master and Nietzsche was a violent-tempered pupil, and it was natural that the pupil later rebelled against the teacher.

8   It is only this kind of reading, this discovery of one's favorite author, that will do one any good at all. Like a man falling in love with his sweetheart at first sight, everything is right. She is of the right height, has the right face, the right color of hair, the right quality of voice and the right way of speaking and smiling. This author is not something that a young man need be told about by his teacher. The author is just right for him; his style, his taste, his point of view, his mode of thinking, are all right. And then the reader proceeds to devour every word and every line that the author writes, and because there is a spiritual affinity, he absorbs and readily digests everything. The author has cast a spell over him, and he is glad to be under the spell, and in time his own voice and manner and way of smiling and way of talking become like the author's own. Thus he truly steeps himself in his literary lover and derives from these books sustenance for his soul. After a few years, the spell is over and he grows a little tired of this lover and seeks for new literary lovers, and after he has had three or four lovers and completely eaten them up, he emerges as an author himself. There are many readers who never fall in love, like many young men and women who flirt around and are incapable of forming a deep attachment to a particular person. They can read any and all authors, and they never amount to anything.

9   Such a conception of the art of reading completely precludes the idea of reading as a duty or as an obligation. In China, one often encourages students to "study bitterly." There was a famous scholar who studied bitterly and who stuck an awl in his calf when he fell asleep while studying at night. There was another scholar who had a maid stand by his side as he was studying at night, to wake him up every time he fell asleep. This was nonsensical. If one has a book lying before him and falls asleep while some wise ancient author is talking to him, he should just go to bed. No amount

of sticking an awl in his calf or of shaking him up by a maid will do him any good. Such a man has lost all sense of pleasure of reading. Scholars who are worth anything at all never know what is called "a hard grind" or what "bitter study" means. They merely love books and read on because they cannot help themselves.

10   What, then, is the true art of reading? The simple answer is to just take up a book and read when the mood comes. To be thoroughly enjoyed, reading must be entirely spontaneous.

Robert MacNeil © by Kate Kunz, Courtesy of MacNeil/Lehrer News Hour

Wordstruck

Robert MacNeil
(1931–   )

Born in Montreal, Robert MacNeil began his
broadcasting career in Canadian radio and
television in the early 1950s. He later served as a
national and foreign news correspondent for NBC,
receiving a 1974 Emmy Award for his coverage of
the Senate Watergate hearings. He is best known
for "The MacNeil/Lehrer News Hour," a weekly
show that first aired on PBS in 1975 and now has
over four million viewers each week. His books,
including *The People Machine: The Influence of
Television on American Politics* (1968) and the
autobiography *The Right Place at the Right Time*
(1982), capitalize on his broadcasting experience.
Admitting, however, that television broadcasts do
not replace his need to write, he published his first
novel, *Burden of Desire*, in 1992. In this excerpt
from a second autobiography, *Wordstruck* (1989),
MacNeil reveals his love of literature and his belief
that layers of "words and word patterns"
powerfully nourish each one of us.

1   Nova Scotia lies one time zone closer to England than most of North
America, but in the days of my childhood it was spiritually closer still.
Psychologically, the province I grew up in was still in large measure a British
colony. Halifax society was conditioned by the presence of generations of
well-born, sometimes aristocratic, British officers and showed it. The higher
up the social pecking order in that small but cosmopolitan seaport town,
the more people identified with England. We looked to England for the real
juice of our patriotism, our ideals of dress and manners, codes of honour,

military dash, and styles of drill, marmalade and gin, pipe tobacco and tweed. We drew spiritual values from the Church of England and humour from *Punch*. It was natural, therefore, that from that fountainhead of everything wise and wonderful came the books that shaped my imagination. When the magic of words first ensnared me, they were words for the most part written in England and intended for English ears: nursery rhymes, Beatrix Potter, *Winnie-the-Pooh*, *Peter Pan*, *The Water Babies*, and *The Wind in the Willows*.

2   Obviously I must have been steeped in British middle-class idiom. After all, Canadian boys didn't say *Oh, bother!* when something annoyed them, or wear *Wellingtons* or *mackintoshes*, as Christopher Robin did, yet I knew them well. They became as familiar as the rubber boots and raincoats we wore. In spite of all this concentrated exposure to English writing, I didn't pick up and use such expressions. They accumulated in a reserve store, a second vocabulary; my dictionary of vicarious literary experience.

3   What did consciously affect me was the literary landscape. I was, and remain today, highly susceptible to the physical setting described in books. Starting with the Milne stories, part of me began inhabiting or wishing to be in the places they depicted, both the landscape and the emotional climate.

4   With a few exceptional moments, my life was unclouded and serene. There was the row over the taxi window. At the age of five I was sitting on the curb throwing stones into the street. A taxi passed and one of my stones broke a window. The taxi stopped, the driver grabbed me and marched me up to the house. My mother reacted so strongly that he began pleading with her, "No, don't beat him. It's all right! It was just an accident."

5   Nothing like that ever happened to Christopher Robin. Nobody threw sand in his eyes, which happened once to me, followed by an agonizing session of having them flushed out with boric acid. Nobody required him to eat everything on the plate—the liver or the scrambled egg which had long gone cold and clammy—down to the last bite, because of the starving Chinese or my moral character. The emotional climate was irresistible, I suppose, because Christopher Robin seemed to be totally in command of his world, as I manifestly was not of mine. He seemed, from a child's perspective, free from arbitrary orders. He decided when to put on his Wellingtons and when to visit his friends. He seemed to live to please himself as long as he bore the tedium of being polite to his elders.

6   The backdrop to the serenity of this emotional landscape was a physical world which also drew me strongly. It was something else first experienced in these books. The land in a book is a magic land: the author may tell you that it is ugly and barren, devastated by storms or wars, but it will fascinate me as real landscapes often cannot. The mere fact that they form the setting for a story that draws you in, for characters you identify with, casts an enchantment over that place. So it was with the meadows, the woods, the brooks inhabited by Winnie-the-Pooh, Rabbit, Owl, Kanga, and Tigger.

7   This was my first experience of being drawn into the spell cast by a storyteller whose words spin gossamer bonds that tie your heart and hopes to him. It was the discovery that words make another place, a place to escape to with your spirit alone. Every child entranced by reading stumbles on that blissful experience sooner or later.

8   For this Canadian child in the thirties there was something more at work. Somehow the idea was planted in me that the English landscape had a spiritual legitimacy that our Canadian landscape did not, because it was always the English landscape we read about. England was where stories were set, where people had adventures; England became the land of story books for me.

9   English woods, meadows, lanes, and villages stirred feelings that ours did not, as did the words for features of the English landscape not encountered in Canada: *commons, dells, dingles, downs, moors, fells, tarns, burns,* and *becks*—the words were heavy with the promise of adventure.

10   That played subtly into other Anglophile influences working on me and I grew up putting a special value on things English. The forces drawing me there were irresistible, like a strong elastic band pulling me to the British Isles.

11   Lots of Americans feel that. For Canadians of my generation struggling, and often losing the struggle, for a national and psychic identity, England became more real than our own world, because of the books we lived in from childhood. It has taken another generation to throw off the vestiges of that psychic colonialism I grew up with, although there are a few shreds of it still left in the Canadian psyche. The seeds of my personal struggle, my personal strain of the virus, must have been planted by the words of Milne, Stevenson, Dickens, and Barrie.

12   In the garden of the small apartment house we lived in was a very big tree. One day, filled with visions of hollow trees that people could enter, even live in, I attacked the trunk of this tree. The power of imagination or wishful thinking was so strong that it by-passed any sense of physical reality. I actually believed I could cut rooms inside the tree; or, if I made a little effort, a staircase would magically appear. I would ascend the tree into an enchanted storybook world. Under my puny hatchet, the tree suffered no more than a few nicks and I retired very disappointed. I must have been thinking of Owl's tree with its curved steps in the Hundred Acre Wood or the hollow-tree entrances to the homes of the Lost Boys in *Peter Pan*.

13   That book made a strong impression at the age of four or five. *Peter Pan* was the first story that actually frightened me a little, just enough fear to make it pleasurable. The snatching of the Lost Boys by the pirates was a moment I could laugh off only when Captain Hook got it from the crocodile which had swallowed the alarm clock, but it left a shadow of anxiety. As for Peter, I never shared his desire not to grow up. I was less moved by the

pathetic need to have his shadow sewn back on than by the hard-to-define attractions I felt for Wendy, who did the sewing.

14   Wendy jumped into my psyche as though there had been a template for her already cut out: the sister I did not have; a subtle blend of comforting maternalism and other vaguely intuited but desirable feminine attributes.

15   (No sister, but by now I had a brother, Hugh, almost four years younger. He arrived home just before the Christmas on which we had one of the last trees with real lighted candles on the tips of its branches, as memorable for its warm wax smell as for the sight.)

16   In *Peter Pan* I do not recall being consciously aware of the language, just the stories and the characters. What surprises me now is to find how face-tious Barrie's style is, full of coy nudges and arch asides, which, if I had ever noticed them, were forgotten. Even more surprising is the level of the language:

> Next comes Nibs, the gay and debonair, followed by Slightly, who cuts whistles out of the trees and dances ecstatically to his own tunes.

17   *Debonair* and *ecstatically* are not nowadays considered vocabulary for chil-dren under ten. But then that is true of many of the books considered appropriate to read to us fifty years ago, and probably even truer fifty years before that.

18   Certainly, *Robinson Crusoe* and *Gulliver's Travels*, written for adults, make no concessions to twentieth-century children. This is Gulliver's scene setting for the naval attack by Blefuscu on Lilliput:

> . . . upon this notice of an intended invasion, I avoided appearing on that side of the coast, for fear of being discovered by some of the enemy's ships, who had received no intelligence of me, all intercourse between the two empires having been strictly forbidden during the war, upon pain of death, and an embargo laid by our Emperor upon all vessels whatsoever.

19   What happened when I heard words I did not understand? I may have asked occasionally, but I remember clearly never wanting to interrupt the story. Either I got the drift from the context or ignored the words I did not know until some later time. That is how I find myself dealing with foreign languages: asking for translations of some words, guessing at others, re-membering, forgetting, but, in net terms, the word command growing by the day.

20   Archaic language did not put me off. The stories had such compelling narrative ideas—Crusoe marooned alone, Gulliver in a land of people six inches tall—that I listened past the older words, listened harder. When I was aware of them they gave the stories a pleasant flavour, a little addi-tional mystery, part of the atmosphere, like the illustrations of period cos-

tumes and weapons. It did not discourage me that Robin Hood said *meth-inks* and *sooth*.

> "Ah, Little John, methinks care for thine own appetite hath a share in that speech, as well as care for me. But in sooth I care not to dine alone. I would have a stranger guest, some abbot or bishop or baron, who would pay us for our hospitality. I will not dine till a guest be found, and I leave it to you three to find him."

21   In the *Just So Stories* and *The Jungle Books*, which we read in the same years, Kipling pushed his language right in front of me; I couldn't ignore it, the exotic Indian words, like *Bandarlog* and *dhak* tree, that seemed to have a taste as well as a sound; the strong names for the characters like Tabaqui the jackal, Nag the cobra, and Rikki-Tikki-Tavi, the mongoose. There were also his rhetorical devices, borrowed from the oral storytellers, repetitions like *the great grey-green, greasy Limpopo River, all set about with fever trees*. They are funny to a child and they grow hypnotic like magic incantations. The repetitions, the sing-song rhythms, and the exotic vocabulary were so suggestive that I imagined I could smell things like the perfumed smoke from the dung fire or the mysterious odour of sandalwood.

22   Kipling would make me sense a world totally beyond my experience: the heat, the dust, the smells, the clamour, the cries and noises of men and animals. The dark natural forces, like the snakes, were never sentimentalized but in Kipling's hands became both more menacing and yet more tolerable because you were permitted to know their thoughts, too.

> Nag waved to and fro, and then Rikki-Tikki heard him drinking from the biggest water jar that was used to fill the bath. "That is good," said the snake. "Now, when Karait was killed, the big man had a stick. He may have that stick still, but when he comes to bathe in the morning he will not have a stick. I shall wait here till he comes." . . . Nag coiled himself down, coil by coil, round the bulge at the bottom of the water jar, and Rikki-Tikki stayed still as death.

23   Robinson Crusoe was my first full-blooded adult hero and his story enthralled me. I did not know until I got to college and heard about Defoe's place in the social history of England that what I absorbed so avidly was really an exemplar of right values—a model for the emerging British middle class—God-fearing, devout, honest, hard-working, sober, and obsessively protective of property. Something quite bourgeois in me must have responded, because I felt a deepening satisfaction and security as the poor devil retrieved each useful tool or cask of gunpowder from his wrecked ship.

24   Crusoe was another fictional character instantly congenial to me. I knew that I could cope with being the lone survivor of such a disaster. Crusoe

made his isolation so cosy that I envied his being alone to fend for himself so cheerfully.

25   All these stories were laying down little lessons in psychology, as well as language, and this material was not being laid down in an empty place. New pieces triggered responses from material that was already there, for example, the pleasure it gave me as Crusoe provisioned his cave.

26   *Laid down* is a term with many associations—the keel of a ship to be built; fruits preserved for the winter; wine laid down to age. It is the term they use in sound and videotape editing when one track or sequence has been recorded and others will be added and mixed together.

27   It must be with words as it is with music. Music heard early in life lays down a rich bed of memories against which you evaluate and absorb music encountered later. Each layer adds to the richness of your musical experience; it ingrains expectations that will govern your taste for future music and perhaps change your feelings about music you already know. Certain harmonic patterns embed themselves in your consciousness and create yearnings for repetition, so that you can relive that pleasurable disturbance of the soul. Gradually, your head becomes an unimaginably large juke box, with instantaneous recall and cross-referencing, far more sophisticated than anything man-made.

28   It is so with words and word patterns. They accumulate in layers, and as the layers thicken they govern all use and appreciation of language thenceforth. Like music, the patterns of melody, rhythm, and quality of voice become templates against which we judge the sweetness and justness of new patterns and rhythms; and the patterns laid down in our memories create expectations and hungers for fulfillment again. It is the same for the bookish person and for the illiterate. Each has a mind programmed with language—from prayers, hymns, verses, jokes, patriotic texts, proverbs, folk sayings, clichés, stories, movies, radio, and television.

I picture each of those layers of experience and language gradually accumulating and thickening to form a kind of living matrix, nourishing like a placenta, serving as a mini-thesaurus or dictionary of quotations, yet more retrievable and interactive and richer because it is so one's own, steeped in emotional colour and personal associations.

The Best Refuge for Insomniacs

Lance Morrow
(1939–   )

Lance Morrow
(© Neal Boenei)

Shortly after graduating from Harvard, Lance Morrow began a career as a writer for *Time* magazine that has spanned nearly thirty years. During this time he has garnered recognition for his essays, winning the 1981 National Magazine Award, in addition to writing numerous cover stories. Other works include *America: A Rediscovery* (1987), *Fishing in the Tiber* (1989), and *The Chief: A Memoir of Fathers and Sons* (1984), a chronicle of his relationship with his father, former *Saturday Evening Post* writer Hugh Morrow. In "The Best Refuge for Insomniacs," first published in *Time* in 1991, Morrow argues that books not only give readers "intellectual dignity and a higher sense of [their] possibilities," but that they also help us survive the bleakest hours of difficult times.

1   I know a woman whose son died by drowning on the night of his high school graduation. She told me she got through the weeks and months afterward by reading and rereading the works of Willa Cather. The calm and clarity of Cather's prose stabilized the woman and helped her through the time.

2   We have rafts that we cling to in bad weather—consolations, little solidarities, numbers we dial, people we wake up in the middle of the night.

3   Somehow it is not much fun to wake up the television set. The medium is a microwave: it makes reality taste wrong. Television transforms the world into a bright dust of electrons, noisy and occasionally toxic. Turn on the set and lingering dreams float out to mingle with CNN. Dreams are not an electronic medium.

4   During the war in the gulf, the escapist magician made urgent reality inescapable. Television became spookier than usual in its metaphysical way: the instant global connection that is informative and hypnotic and jumpy all at once—immediate and unreal. The sacramental anchormen dispensed their unctions and alarms. During the war, I found shelter in books in the

middle of the night. They are cozier. The global electronic collective, the knife of the news, could wait until the sun came up. The mind prefers to be private in its sleepless stretches.

5   Read what? I am not talking exactly about reading to escape. Nor about reading to edify and impress oneself. *Paradise Lost* is not much help at 3 in the morning, except of course as a heavy sleeping potion. I mean the kind of reading one does to keep sane, to touch other intelligences, to absorb a little grace. In Vietnam the soldiers said, "He is a man you can walk down the road with." They meant, a man you can trust when the road is very dangerous. Every reader knows there are certain books you can go down the road with.

6   Everyone has his or her own list—each list no doubt is peculiar, idiosyncratic. The books you keep for the middle of the night serve a deeply personal purpose, one of companionship. Your connection with them is a mystery of affinities. Each mind has its night weather, its topographies. I like certain books about fly fishing, for example, especially Norman Maclean's brilliant *A River Runs Through It*, which, like fishing itself, sometimes makes sudden, taut connections to divinity.

7   One man rereads the adventures of Sherlock Holmes. He cherishes their world, the fogs and bobbies, the rational wrapped in an ambient madness, the inexplicable each time yielding its secret in a concluding sunburst, a sharp clarity.

8   Television news, when it flies in raw and ragged, can be lacerating. The medium destroys sequence. Reading restores to the mind a stabilization of linear prose, a bit of the architecture of thought. First one sentence, then another, building paragraphs, whole pages, chapters, books, until eventually something like an attention span returns and perhaps a steadier regard for cause and effect. War (and television) shatters. Reading, thought reconstruct. The mind in reading is active, not passive-depressive.

9   There is no point in being too reverent about books. *Mein Kampf* was—is—a book. Still, some books have the virtue of being processed through an intelligence. Writers make universes. To enter that creation gives the reader some intellectual dignity and a higher sense of his possibilities. The dignity encourages relief and acceptance. The universe may be the splendid, twittish neverland of P. G. Wodehouse (escape maybe, but a steadying one) or Anthony Trollope's order, or Tolkien's. I know a married couple who got through a tragic time by reading Dickens to each other every night. Years ago, recovering from a heart operation, I read Shelby Foote's three-volume history of the American Civil War—a universe indeed, the fullest, most instructive tragedy of American history, all of the New World's Homer and Shakespeare enacted in four years. People find the books they need.

10   I like writers who have struggled with a dark side and persevered: Samuel Johnson, for example; his distinction and his majestic sanity both achieved the hard way. He emerged very human and funny and with astonishing

resources of kindness. I have been reading Henry James' letters in the middle of the night. If James' novels are sometimes tiresome, his letters, which he produced in amazing quantity, are endlessly intelligent and alive. To a friend named Grace Norton, who was much afflicted, he wrote, "Remember that every life is a special problem which is not yours but another's and content yourself with the terrible algebra of your own . . . We all live together, and those of us who love and know, live so most." He told her, "Even if we don't reach the sun, we shall at least have been up in a balloon."

11   Odd that 19th century writers should write a prose that seems so stabilizing in the late 20th. Ralph Waldo Emerson is good to have beside the bed between 3 and 6 in the morning. So is the book of *Job.* Poetry: Wallace Stevens for his strange visual clarities, Robert Frost for his sly moral clarities, Walt Whitman for his spaciousness and energy. Some early Hemingway. I read the memoirs of Nadezhda Mandelstam (*Hope Against Hope; Hope Abandoned),* the widow of Osip Mandelstam, a Soviet poet destroyed by Stalin. I look at *The Wind in the Willows* out of admiration for Mr. Toad and for what he has to teach about folly and resilience.

12   The contemplation of anything intelligent—it need not be writing—helps the mind through the black hours. Mozart, for example; music like bright ice water, or, say, the memory of the serene Palladian lines of Jefferson's Monticello. These things realign the mind and teach it not to be petty. All honest thought is a form of prayer. I read Samuel Johnson ("Despair is criminal") and go back to sleep.

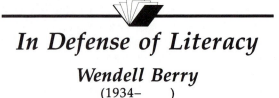

In Defense of Literacy

Wendell Berry
(1934–   )

Wendell Berry
(Thomas Victor)

Born in Henry County, Kentucky, Wendell Berry received his B.A. and M.A. degrees from the University of Kentucky where he later became a distinguished professor of English. He has published several novels as well as many volumes of poetry. His collections of essays include *The Long-Legged House* (1969), *The Hidden Wound* (1970), *The Unsettling of America* (1977), *The Gift of Good Land* (1981), and *Standing by Woods* (1985). More recent publications include *Harlan Hubbard* (1990). In the following essay, which comes from *A Continuous Harmony* (1972), Berry argues for the study of literature as a defense against the assault of "prepared public language" that addresses only the "practical" and "immediate" concerns of humankind.

1   In a country in which everybody goes to school, it may seem absurd to offer a defense of literacy, and yet I believe that such a defense is in order, and that the absurdity lies not in the defense, but in the necessity for it. The published illiteracies of the certified educated are on the increase. And the universities seem bent upon ratifying this state of things by declaring the acceptability, in their graduates, of adequate—that is to say, of mediocre—writing skills.

2   The schools, then, are following the general subservience to the "practical," as that term has been defined for us according to the benefit of corporations. By "practicality" most users of the term now mean whatever will most predictably and most quickly make a profit. Teachers of English and literature have either submitted, or are expected to submit, along with teachers of the more "practical" disciplines, to the doctrine that the purpose of education is the mass production of producers and consumers. This has forced our profession into a predicament that we will finally have to recognize as a perversion. As if awed by the ascendency of the "practical" in our society, many of us secretly fear, and some of us are apparently ready

to say, that if a student is not going to become a teacher of his language, he has no need to master it.

3   In other words, to keep pace with the specialization—and the dignity according to specialization—in other disciplines, we have begun to look upon and to teach our language and literature as specialties. But whereas specialization is of the nature of the applied sciences, it is a perversion of the disciplines of language and literature. When we understand and teach these as specialties, we submit willy-nilly to the assumption of the "practical men" of business, and also apparently of education, that literacy is no more than an ornament: when one has become an efficient integer of the economy, *then* it is permissible, even desirable, to be able to talk about the latest novels. After all, the disciples of "practicality" may someday find themselves stuck in conversation with an English teacher.

4   I may have oversimplified that line of thinking, but not much. There are two flaws in it. One is that, among the self-styled "practical men," the practical is synonymous with the immediate. The long-term effects of their values and their acts lie outside the boundaries of their interest. For such people a strip mine ceases to exist as soon as the coal has been extracted. Short-term practicality is long-term idiocy.

5   The other flaw is that language and literature are always *about* something else, and we have no way to predict or control what they may be about. They are about the world. We will understand the world, and preserve ourselves and our values in it, only insofar as we have a language that is alert and responsive to it, and careful of it. I mean that literally. When we give our plows such brand names as "Sod Blaster," we are imposing on their use conceptual limits which raise the likelihood that they will be used destructively. When we speak of man's "war against nature," or of a "peace offensive," we are accepting the limitations of a metaphor that suggests and even proposes, violent solutions. When students ask for the right of "participatory input" at the meetings of a faculty organization, they are thinking of democratic process, but they are *speaking* of a convocation of robots, and are thus devaluing the very traditions that they invoke.

6   Ignorance of books and the lack of a critical consciousness of language were safe enough in primitive societies with coherent oral traditions. In our society, which exists in an atmosphere of prepared, public language—language that is either written or being read—illiteracy is both a personal and a public danger. Think how constantly "the average American" is surrounded by premeditated language, in newspapers, and magazines, on signs and billboards, on TV and radio. He is forever being asked to buy or believe somebody else's line of goods. The line of goods is being sold, moreover, by men who are trained to make him buy it or believe it, whether or not he needs it or understands it or knows its value or wants it. This sort of selling is an honored profession among us. Parents who grow hysterical at the thought that their son might not cut his hair are *glad* to have him taught,

and later employed, to lie about the quality of an automobile or the ability of a candidate.

7   What is our defense against this sort of language—this language-as-weapon? There is only one. We must know a better language. We must speak, and teach our children to speak, a language precise and articulate and lively enough to tell the truth about the world as we know it. And to do this we must know something of the roots and resources of our language, we must know its literature. The only defense against the worst is a knowledge of the best. By their ignorance people enfranchise their exploiters.

8   But to appreciate fully the necessity for the best sort of literacy we must consider not just the environment of prepared language in which most of us now pass most of our lives, but also the utter transience of most of this language, which is meant to be merely glanced at, or heard only once, or read once and thrown away. Such language is by definition, and often by calculation, not memorable; it is language meant to be replaced by what will immediately follow it, like that of shallow conversation between strangers. It cannot be pondered or effectively criticized. For those reasons an unmixed diet of it is destructive of the informed, resilient, critical intelligence that the best of our traditions have sought to create and to maintain— an intelligence that Jefferson held to be indispensable to the health and longevity of freedom. Such intelligence does not grow by bloating upon the ephemeral information and misinformation of the public media. It grows by returning again and again to the landmarks of its cultural birthright, the works that have proved worthy of devoted attention.

9   "Read not the Times. Read the Eternities," Thoreau said. Ezra Pound wrote that "literature is news that STAYS news." In his lovely poem, "The Island," Edwin Muir spoke of man's inescapable cultural boundaries and of his consequent responsibility for his own sources and renewals:

> Men are made of what is made,
> The meat, the drink, the life, the corn,
> Laid up by them, in them reborn.
> And self-begotten cycles close
> About our way; indigenous art
> And simple spells make unafraid
> The haunted labyrinths of the heart . . . .

10   These men spoke of a truth that no society can afford to shirk for long: we are dependent, for understanding, and for consolation and hope, upon what we learn of ourselves from songs and stories. This has always been so, and it will not change.

11   I am saying, then, that literacy—the mastery of language and the knowledge of books—is not an ornament, but a necessity. It is impractical only

by the standards of quick profit and easy power. Longer perspective will show that it alone can preserve in us the possibility of an accurate judgment of ourselves, and the possibilities of correction and renewal. Without it, we are adrift in the present, in the wreckage of yesterday, in the nightmare of tomorrow.

Chapter Two

The Writing Process

The writing process too often begins with the prospective "author" staring blankly at an empty sheet of paper, wondering where to start. Undoubtedly, every student has, at one time, been in that position. Even for many professionals, writing is not always easy. The symptoms of "writer's woes" are often the same for everyone: groping for an idea, perhaps finding a few thoughts but drawing a blank after a few sentences, struggling with words, fighting frustration.

No, writing is not a job entered into lightly, but it is a job that is possible to master and even enjoy. Even though no one has invented a foolproof, step-by-step formula for good writing, there are some ways to approach writing to make the task less of a struggle. The trick is in knowing the "phases" of the writing process and progressing toward your writing goal through those phases. Once you master the process of writing, you will find yourself staring less frequently at that empty sheet of paper.

The three phases of the writing process are *planning, shaping,* and *structuring and revising.* In the planning phase (sometimes called the *prewriting* phase), you gather your thoughts and collect the information you will need to support or explain your ideas. When you move into the next phase, shaping, you will examine the form your information has taken as you begin to logically structure the writing. In the final phase, you will work on the formal structure of the essay and eventually refine your ideas into a finished product. It takes practice, practice, and more practice, but you will discover that with each time you move through the phases of writing, the process becomes easier. You will also discover your own version of the writing-process phases and ultimately find that all writing will be easier. Remember, you will need the skill of writing in every walk of life, not just the academic one. You may have resumés, business letters, memos, proposals, and other tasks ahead of you, so the more time you spend in honing your skills, the more those skills can work for you—now and in the future.

Phase One: Planning

Planning your essay simply means thinking about what you have to say and how you want to say it. Begin this phase by identifying the purpose of the writing. In writing a business letter, define the reason behind it. In answering an exam question, determine exactly what is being asked. In writing a letter to your best friend, think about what you have to say. The same principle is applied to writing an essay: first, determine the purpose of the writing.

For much of your college writing, you will be given assignments of some sort. In planning an essay to address such an assignment, start by making sure you understand precisely what you are being asked to do. If you have questions, do not hesitate to ask for clarification. Remember, before you *can* write, you must know *why* you're writing.

Once you understand just what the assignment is and what it asks of you, you can decide on an approach to the topic. Are you being asked to express personal feelings or attitudes? Is your goal to explain, define, describe, or persuade? All of these are important considerations in this pre-writing phase.

When your purpose is clear, you will find it easier to set the boundaries that will lead to shaping your material. One of the elements to consider is your *audience*. Although it may seem so, writing is not a solitary action. Whatever you put down on paper must be addressed to someone, and that person's knowledge, needs, and attitudes will influence what you write and how you write it. Even diary entries are addressed to "Dear Diary," that pseudonym for the writer's other self. You should tailor your subject, your word choice, your tone, and your support to the audience you are addressing.

Consider a discussion, for instance, on the need for better health insurance for people over age sixty-five. The audience being addressed would greatly influence the treatment of the subject. The content and emphasis of the topic would certainly be different for an audience of teenagers, for whom age 65 may seem an eternity away, than for people in their forties, who envision requiring coverage for their own eventual health needs or who now have relatives needing better coverage. Treatment of the topic would be still different if the discussion were addressed to people who are now over sixty-five and are presently needing better health-insurance coverage.

Many of your college essays will be addressed to a *general* audience. A general audience expects information and language that is clear and easily understood, not the jargon of a specific technical field or social group. Since your audience will most often be college-level, intelligent people who are interested in current issues and events, approach your subject with those characteristics in mind. On occasion, though, you might address a *specific* audience—such as clergy, doctors, attorneys, musicians, engineers, or scientists. With this group, you can use terminology unique to the profession, language that members of a specific audience would readily understand but a general audience might not. In other words, write on a level that corresponds to the characteristics that describe your reader. However, no matter who will receive the writing, your goal should be the same—to convince the reader that what you have to say is reasonable, intelligent, valid, and worthy of consideration.

Depending on the subject you are writing about, you may find that your own personal knowledge is not enough. When that is the case, gather the information you will need to support your ideas. Remember that you, the writer, should strive for clear and complete communication, and if that means researching a topic to provide sufficient and precise information or to enhance your own knowledge, do it. You will present yourself as a more credible source, and your reader will more readily accept your ideas.

What Do I Write about?

As a writer, your objective is to present clear, concise information to your reader. That job will be easier if the scope of your project is reasonable. Therefore, the first step in deciding what to write about is narrowing the subject into a workable topic. It would be impossible, for instance, to write a 500-word paper describing how the AIDS virus has affected the American health arena. However, you might explore the effect that the virus has had on one segment of the population, say preschool-aged hemophiliacs, and the acceptance of these children in the classroom. With a narrowed topic, you will be able to discuss intelligently the important aspects of your subject and truly enlighten your reader, not confuse him or her with vague generalities caused by attempting to discuss a complex subject in too little space.

The best way to narrow your subject to a workable topic is to see what topic ideas fall within the limits of the assignment you are addressing. For instance, if your assignment is an essay of 1,000 words, your subjects might be narrowed to topics like these:

Subject: Recent Supreme Court Decisions

Possible Topic: Your local district's reaction to a ruling
                  regulating the sale of "kiddie porn" magazines
                  in convenience stores

Subject: New Trends in Education

Possible Topic: The impact of year-round classes in the public
                    schools

What Do I Have to Say?

All right, you've decided on a topic. Now what? What are you going to say
about it? One of the best ways to discover what you have to say is through
brainstorming. In brainstorming you start by listing everything you can think
of about your topic. Jot down words, phrases, sentences—anything and
everything that comes to mind about the topic. Don't worry about relevance
or grammar—just write.

If you were going to write about the impact of year-round schooling, you
might start with a list of the effects of such a plan:

• flexible school/vacation schedules

• greater student success in music courses

• greater student success in foreign language courses

• scheduling problems for teachers who want to take summer courses

• better use of school equipment

• higher school attendance

• retention of knowledge

• higher test scores

• better use of school facilities

• fewer mischievous acts such as vandalism

• fewer criminal acts such as theft

• less student boredom

• greater opportunity for remediation

• greater opportunity for enhancements programs

• greater variety in curricula

• disrupted family vacations

• disrupted family summer schedules (with other children NOT in such a
  program)

• costly renovation to school not usually used during summer (e.g., air
  conditioning)

• increased supply costs

• increased need for building maintenance

• increased energy costs

Give yourself ten minutes to brainstorm. Remember, the object is not necessarily to compose or to organize—you will move into that phase later—but to get some ideas down onto paper.

Once you have something in front of you, you can begin to group those ideas into related clusters.

• flexible school/vacation schedule

• greater success in music courses
  (because of continuity of study)

• greater success in foreign language courses
  (because of continuity of study)

• better use of school equipment

• better use of school facilities

• greater retention of knowledge

• less vandalism

• less theft

• more activities/less boredom

• greater opportunity for remediation

• greater opportunity for cultural enrichment/
  enhancement

• greater variety in curricula

} advantages to
year-round school

• scheduling problems for teachers who
  want to take summer classes

• disrupted family vacations

• costly renovations

• increased supply costs

• increased need for building maintenance

• increased energy costs

} disadvantages to
year-round school

Clusters, then, are created when you group your ideas together around some common topic. As you cluster the effects of year-round schools, you may find that some items can fit into more than one cluster. That's fine. You might also find that some items do not fit very well with the common topic you have established. That's fine, too, because now is a good time to reexamine your list—adding items, deleting items, creating new clusters. You should also see that your ideas are taking on a rough organizational "shape" created by the clusters. For example, these clusters of advantages and disadvantages can be even further refined:

• greater student success in foreign
  language and music courses

• greater opportunity for remediation   advantages for
  or enhancement programs   children

• retention of knowledge

• higher test scores

• variety in curricula

• greater student success overall   advantages for
                                               teachers
• more activities/less boredom

• better use of facilities

• better use of equipment   advantages for
                                               school districts
• less vandalism/theft

• scheduling problems for teachers in
  their continuing education   disadvantage
                                               for teachers
• possible need to redesign units
  to fit new scheduling

• increased energy costs

• increased supply costs
                                               disadvantages for
• increased need for facilities maintenance   school districts

• costly renovation to schools not usually
  used during summer (e.g., air conditioning)

• disrupted family vacations

• disrupted family schedules
with other children NOT
in year-round school
(plans for summer camp or
after-school care)

} disadvantages to
children and families

Another way to narrow your subject and discover a method of rhetorical development at the same time is by asking yourself a series of questions about the topic. You will not be able to answer each question for every topic, of course, but if you can answer most of the questions beside the name of the pattern (or patterns) below, you may find not only a topic to write about but also one or more methods of rhetorical development to use in structuring your essay.

Narration: What happened?
                  When did it happen?
                  Where did it happen?
                  To whom did it happen?

Description: What does it look, smell, sound, or feel like?
                      That is, identify aspects such as size, shape, texture,
                      and the like.
                  How can it be characterized?

Exemplification: What are some examples of it?
                  What details typify it?

Process: How did it happen?
                  How does it work?
                  How is it made?

Cause and Effect: Why did it happen?
                  What caused it?
                  What are the results?

Division and   What are its parts?
Classification: Can its parts be separated, grouped, or subdivided?
                  Do its parts fit into a logical order?
                  Can its parts be categorized?
                  Into what categories can the parts be arranged?

Definition: What is it?
                  Are there other things like it?
                  How does it resemble the other things?
                  How does it differ from the other things?
                  What are its unique characteristics?

Comparison and   How is it similar to other things?
Contrast: How is it different from other things?

The benefit of using these questions is not only in obtaining a workable topic but also in discovering a preliminary method of organizing those ideas according to the rhetorical modes discussed later in this text.

Creating a Thesis

Once you have discovered what there is to say about a topic, you can decide how you want to say it. Your ideas will need a focus, a concentration, a *thesis.* Your thesis will be the central or main idea of your essay. It will tell your reader what point you plan to make about your topic.

As you look at the clusters examining the impact of year-round schooling, notice the organizational shape that is emerging. Since you noted both advantages and disadvantages of the system, you might start this part of the planning phase by deciding which aspect is stronger or which one you feel better equipped to write about. Here is a possibility: you notice that your list of advantages far outnumbers the list of disadvantages, so you decide to concentrate on the advantages. Now you discover it is possible to express your ideas in a sentence—a "working" thesis—that explains your assessment of the system:

> Year-round classes present many advantages to public schools.

Notice the path your ideas have taken:

Subject: Trends in Education

Possible Topic: The impact of year-round classes in public
                  schools

Thesis: Year-round classes present many advantages to
                  public schools.

The subject was narrowed to a more specific topic that in turn was narrowed still further to a more specific structure, the thesis.

Your thesis sentence will be the focal point of your essay, so you should take care in developing it. Consider these principles for a good thesis sentence:

1.   Structure: The thesis must be presented as a declarative sentence—not as a fragmented idea or as a question. Questions may be used to introduce your topic, but the thesis should be viewed as an answer to a question, not as a question itself.

2.   Content: Your thesis is best expressed as an opinion, a judgment, something that needs to be supported. Remember, your goal is to present

an idea to your reader and then show why your idea is valid, why it should be accepted. The thesis should be expressed as an idea that your reader *could* disagree with.

3. Style: The thesis statement is not a declaration of purpose, an announcement of intent, or a title for your work.

Declaration of Purpose:	In this paper I intend to show that year-round schooling can benefit everyone involved.
Announcement:	This paper will explore the advantages of year-round schooling.
Title:	Year-Round Schools—A Better Way to Learn

Notice that while each of these examples gives only a hint of what you intend to discuss in the essay, the thesis clearly shows the reader the central point you intend to make about your subject.

Remember, too, that any thesis you write at this point is a *working thesis*. That is, it's a thesis that will help you start thinking and writing, but it's not cast in stone. Revision occurs in every stage of the writing process, so you may find that your ideas and even your thesis may change as you plan, shape, and draft. Use the working thesis to help you think and unify your ideas.

You may find in some types of writing a thesis that is not stated explicitly but instead is strongly implied. For example, Toni Morrison does not state an explicit thesis in "A Slow Walk of Trees," but her main idea is clear: If African Americans are to improve their status and condition, *they* must do it themselves without seeking help from or succumbing to hindrances imposed by whites. Here, the *sense* of the thesis is present so the reader understands Morrison's focus and direction. Note, also, that a thesis is generally used in essay writing. On occasion you may be asked to write an objective *report* that stresses the presentation of solid, factual information. You will still need some central idea to structure the writing, but you will find that your purpose is to relate facts rather than to support (or validate) an idea. In such writing, your focus may be expressed as a declaration of purpose: "This report will outline the University's budget proposal for the new computer center."

Phase Two: Shaping

Once you have progressed through the planning phase of writing an essay, you will probably notice that your ideas are now loosely structured. Your essay is heading in a specific direction. It is taking shape.

In essence, you have already taken your first step into the next phase of writing: shaping your work. Here you will develop a definite form for your work, molded by the elements you will use to support your thesis. One method of shaping an essay is through outlining. You probably noticed that as you clustered your ideas in the planning stage, you actually created an informal outline.

Another method of organization uses a thesis *plan*. A plan suggests to the reader exactly how the thesis will be supported and to the writer exactly which elements need to be fully developed. As you look over your clusters on year-round classes, you see that the advantages you listed primarily affect the students, the teachers, and the school districts' budgets. Thus your plan might look like this:

> Plan: A year-round calendar would promote children's learning, increase teachers' effectiveness, and improve school districts' financial problems.

The plan above suggests the structure of the essay's body very much as an outline would. It gives the reader a glimpse of the topics the writer has chosen to use to support the thesis. Each benefit of the year-round plan would be explored separately.

It is also in the shaping phase that you can begin to look more closely at the rhetorical development you will use for the essay. Ideas can be formulated or reformulated to adhere to specific strategies (definition, classification, exemplification, and others). In many ways you will see that the shaping phase is a transitional phase, preparing you for the next phase of structuring and revising your essay.

Phase Three: Structuring and Revising

Now that you are equipped with a rough draft or sketch of your essay, it is time to formalize the essay's structure and refine the writing until you are satisfied that you have a finished product. Review what you already have. Perhaps you might start with your thesis. Are you satisfied that it presents your main idea? Have you thought of new material to include? Does the thesis allow for the new material? Does your plan need revision at this point? Next, check your support. Do you have enough evidence for the points you will cover? Perhaps now is a good time again to ask yourself the questions that suggest rhetorical organization. Or ask the traditional journalistic questions—who, what, when, where, and how. If you find that this first rendering is bursting with material, don't worry. You will pare it down in the next writing. And remember—it is much easier to write from abundance.

When you are sufficiently satisfied with what you have at this point, you can start to think in terms of a more formal structure for the essay.

Structuring the Essay

An essay's structure consists of three parts: the *introduction*, the *body*, and the *conclusion*. You will see that your writing is already loosely fitting into these basic parts. So one way to structure your essay is to take each part and refine it piece by piece. Of course, if you work better by looking at the whole, by all means approach this phase in that manner.

The *introduction* literally introduces your reader to your topic and to the position you will take in discussing it. Generally consisting of one or two paragraphs, the introduction sets the stage for your essay, so it is in the introduction that you must get your reader's attention, engage your reader's interest, make your reader curious enough to read on.

A good introduction usually starts with one or two *lead* or *introductory* sentences or paragraphs. These "leads" are used to get the reader's initial attention and to work your way into your topic. A lead may appear in the form of a question (or series of questions), a definition, an anecdote, a quotation, or even a construction resembling the thesis itself. From the lead you can work into the presentation of your thesis.

Judith Viorst, for example, in her essay, "Friends, Good Friends, and Such Good Friends," (Chapter 8) uses three lead paragraphs to introduce her ideas about friendship. She introduces her topic with ideas she once had about friendship and then moves toward her thesis (and loosely structured plan) expressed in ¶3:

> . . . I once would have said that a friend is a friend all the way, but now I believe that's a narrow point of view. For the friendships I have and the friendships I see are conducted at many levels of intensity, serve many different functions, meet many different needs and range from those as all-the-way as the friendship of soul sisters . . . to that of the most nonchalant and casual playmates.

The *body* of the essay, or middle section, is the "meat" of the work. Here your thesis is supported, expanded, explored. Here you present your reader with all the facts, details, statistics, examples, and descriptions needed to prove your thesis valid. Notice how Viorst develops her essay on the multiple types and facets of friendships. She takes the controlling idea and starts by organizing friends into types or "varieties." Then she discusses each variety according to the criteria of her thesis plan: the intensity of the relationship, the function of the relationship, and the needs met by the relationship.

As you examine and develop the body of your own essay, notice that the most prominent examples of the different rhetorical strategies appear here. Organizing the body of your essay is as important as structuring the essay as a whole.

Consider your paragraphs. Most paragraphs you use for support will be *unified* around a clear *topic sentence*. The topic sentence works very much like the thesis, but it governs the paragraph instead of the essay as the thesis does. When a paragraph is unified, all the material used as support is relevant to the topic sentence. Include nothing that does not directly relate to the topic sentence. Whether the topic sentence appears at the beginning, middle, or end of the paragraph, its inclusion in the paragraph is vital, whether it is explicitly stated or strongly implied.

The reader should also sense *coherence* in the paragraph bodies. There should be a sense of smoothness or fluency as the reader moves from sentence to sentence, thought to thought, with appropriate connections acting as bridges. You can achieve coherence in several ways:

1.   Use synonyms and pronouns to avoid monotonous repetition of key words.

William Golding's "Thinking as a Hobby" provides a good example of this:

. . . Some time later I learned about these statuettes . . . they symbolized . . . the whole of life. The naked lady was the Venus of Milo. She was Love. . . . She was just busy being beautiful. The leopard was Nature and he was being natural. The naked, muscular gentleman was . . . Rodin's Thinker an image of pure thought. . . .

2.   Use transitional words to show relationships between clauses and between paragraphs.

Addition: and
                 in addition
                 also
                 furthermore

Contrast: however
                 but
                 on the contrary
                 still
                 nevertheless

Comparison: likewise
                 similarly
                 in the same way

Cause/Effect: as a result
                        hence
                        otherwise
                        therefore
                        thus
                        then
                        consequently

Concession: even though
                        although
                        of course

Time: afterward
                        until
                        at length
                        immediately
                        presently
                        thereafter
                        meantime
                        soon

Example/   for example
Illustration: in fact
                        for instance
                        in other words
                        to illustrate
                        indeed
                        specifically

Notice Lewis Thomas' use of transitions to connect ideas in the paragraph taken from "The Iks" (Chapter 8):

Connects ideas to previous ¶.

But this may be too narrow a view. For one thing the Iks are extraordinary. They are absolutely astonishing, in fact The anthropologist has never seen people like them anywhere nor have I. You'd think, if they were simply examples of the common essence of mankind, they'd seem more recognizable. Instead they are bizarre, anomalous. I have known my share of peculiar, difficult, nervous, grabby people, but I've never encountered any genuinely, consistently detestable human beings in all my life. The Iks sound more like abnormalities, maladies.

3.   Use parallel grammatical structures in successive sentences to emphasize the relationship of the sentences to a single idea in the paragraph.

Look at one paragraph taken from Martin Luther King's speech "I Have a Dream" (Chapter 11):

> . . . We have also come to this hallowed spot to remind America of the fierce urgency of *now*. This is no time to engage in the luxury of cooling off or to take the tranquilizing drugs of gradualism. *Now* is the time to make real the promises of democracy. *Now* is the time to rise from the dark and desolate valley of segregation to the sunlit path of racial justice. *Now* is the time to open the doors of opportunity to all of God's children. *Now* is the time to lift our nation from the quicksands of racial injustice to the solid rock of brotherhood.

Another important consideration for your body paragraphs is their development. In order for a paragraph to be well developed you must use as much relevant detail or specific information as necessary. Examples should be clear; reasons should be logical; evidence should be persuasive. Remember, it is your duty to explain and support any general statement you make in a manner appropriate for your audience and your purpose in the writing.

Richard Rodriguez begins the first body paragraph of his essay about affirmative action, "None of This Is Fair" (Chapter 11) with a clear, focused topic sentence: "For me opportunities had been extravagant." He goes on to give concrete examples of those extravagant opportunities, citing "fellowships, summer research grants, teaching assistantships" along with invitations to conferences, offers of teaching positions, and travel opportunities. Each sentence pertains to the topic-sentence idea—extravagant opportunities.

Your essay's *conclusion* should be as carefully planned as its introduction and body paragraphs. Keep in mind that the conclusion is the last part your audience reads; thus it is the part that should reinforce your major ideas and give the reader a sense of completeness. Just as the introduction is generally one paragraph, the conclusion will probably be one paragraph long.

Your conclusion may take one of several forms:

1.   A *restatement* of the thesis.

Notice how Judith Viorst uses this technique in "How Books Helped Shape My Life" (Chapter 1):

Thesis:

> The person that I am today was shaped by Nancy Drew; by Jo March, Jane Eyre and Heathcliff's soul mate Cathy; and by other fictional females whose attractiveness or character or audacity for a time were the standards by which I measured myself.

Conclusion:

> Nevertheless Natasha and Jane and Jo, Cathy, Nancy and Brett—each one spoke to my heart and stirred me powerfully. On my journey into young womanhood I was fortunate to have them as my companions. They were, they will always remain, a part of me.

2. A *quotation* that relates to your thesis.

Barbara Tuchman ends " 'This Is the End of the World': The Black Death" (Chapter 10) with a quotation from St. John:

> . . . those who survived "repented not of the work of their hands. . . . Neither repented they of their murders, nor of their sorceries, nor of their fornication, nor of their thefts."

3. A *summary* of the main points of your essay.

John Ciardi uses this method in "What is Happiness?" (Chapter 6) when he sums up the central points of the essay with the last paragraph:

> By all means let the happiness-market sell us minor satisfactions and even minor follies so long as we keep them in scale and buy them out of spiritual change. I am no customer for either puritanism or asceticism. But drop any real spiritual capital at those bazaars, and what you come home to will be your own poorhouse.

4. A one- or two-sentence *clincher* that gives a sense of suspense, irony, surprise, or humor to the end of the essay.

Consider Brett Staples' "Black Men and Public Space" (Chapter 7). The essay relates incidents the author has had "as a night walker in an urban landscape." He speaks of the perception white people—especially white women—have of black men, particularly at night. Describing himself as "a softy who is scarcely able to take a knife to a raw chicken—let alone hold one to a person's throat—," he was "surprised, embarrassed, and dismayed" that a woman coincidentally walking the same dark street as he found him "indistinguishable from the muggers who occasionally seeped into the area from the surrounding ghetto." After several illustrations of similar experiences, Staples concludes the essay this way:

> And on late-evening constitutionals I employ what has proved to be an excellent tension-reducing measure: I whistle melodies from Beethoven and Vivaldi and the more popular classical composers. . . . Virtually everybody seems to sense that a mugger wouldn't be warbling bright, sunny selections from Vivaldi's *Four*

Seasons. It is my equivalent of the cowbell that hikers wear when they know they are in bear country.

Your conclusion should *not* take on these characteristics:

1.   a tone inconsistent with the rest of the essay

2.   an introduction of new material

3.   an apology for your writing style (I've tried to explain this idea as best I can . . .), for your lack of expertise (Of course I'm not an expert on the subject . . .), or for the stance you've taken in the essay (These are only my opinions, mind you . . .)

4.   a flat or exact restatement of thesis

Revising the Essay

Revising your essay is an essential part of the writing process. You have probably been revising your essay from the start—discovering and exploring new ideas as you clarified your purpose and position. You may have found that one area of your writing sparked an idea that suggested a better treatment or wording of something you expressed earlier—so you revised that earlier part. Or perhaps as you were writing, you discovered an additional idea pertinent to the topic, an idea that needed to be expressed (but one you somehow overlooked). In many ways, large and small, revision has been a part of your writing process all along. Rethinking, reshaping, reconsidering, and reconstructing all take place *within* each phase of the writing process—they make up important parts of the entire process.

After you examine your essay's formal structure, put the essay away for a while—a few hours, a day or two—giving yourself a cooling-off period. After you have been away from your work for a while, you will see that it is much easier to check for such things as organization, logic, coherence, development, and consistency of style. Also, as you reevaluate your work, you will probably begin to edit it—checking punctuation, correcting spelling errors, redesigning and rearranging sentences, deleting anything unnecessary and adding anything needed but absent from the prior draft.

If your instructor asks you to submit your first draft, you can also use your teacher's comments or comments from your peers (if peer evaluation is used) to help in reexamining your work and preparing the next draft. If you are not required to submit early drafts of your work, experiment with revision approaches until you find one that works well for you. Actually, you will probably discover that the more you write, the more methodical your revision becomes. Remember that professional writers continually revise their work. Revision is an essential part of good writing, so be prepared to revise your essay repeatedly.

Consider the guidelines below and incorporate the principles at some point in your revision methodology.

Review Content and Organization

Examine your thesis. Is it worded in a way that makes clear the point you intend to discuss in the paper? If you have used a thesis plan, does it delineate the particular points you intend to use to support the thesis?

Examine your support. Identify your main ideas. Are they clear? Do they relate directly to your thesis? Have you used enough evidence to support your points? Have you eliminated any material that is irrelevant to your discussion? Does your support reflect a clear pattern of development? Have you used support appropriate for the audience you are addressing?

Review Style and Mechanics

Examine your writing style. Is the tone of the essay appropriate for its purpose? For its intended audience? Have you maintained that tone throughout the writing? Have you varied your sentence structures to produce fresh, lively, smooth, effective prose? Have you used words that are clear? Is your language appropriate for the assignment and for the audience?

Examine grammar and punctuation. Is each sentence grammatically correct? Have you syntactically redesigned awkward sentences? Have you maintained consistent voice, mood, tense, and number? Are modifiers used correctly? Are subject and verbs, pronouns and antecedents in agreement? Is your use of commas, periods, semicolons, and other marks of punctuation consistent with standard rules of grammar? Have you used capitals, italics, abbreviations and numbers correctly? Have you corrected all misspelled words?

General Review

Is the organization of the essay logical? Does it clearly adhere to the rhetorical strategy you chose to develop your ideas? Does your introduction attract your reader? Is your conclusion strong? Will your reader feel a sense of satisfaction at the end of the essay, believing that the subject has been discussed thoroughly? Are *you* satisfied with the writing?

Once you have answered "yes" to all of the review questions, you are ready to submit your essay.

The writing process may seem exhausting at first, but you will see that becoming proficient in writing is akin to becoming proficient in any skill—you get better at it the more you do it—and you will also discover that the more you write, the easier it is to write and revise.

Writers on Writing

You may never have stopped to consider how or why writers write, but now, as you are beginning a composition course, is a good time to look at writing from a professional's viewpoint. The eight writers included in this section will share with you the "writing wisdom" they have discovered over the years. Joan Didion, for example, tries to explain why she writes, and Jacqueline Berke outlines the characteristics she believes all good writing displays. Veteran teacher-writers Peter Elbow, Sheridan Baker, and Donald Murray offer multiple suggestions for getting started and for clarifying ideas. As you read these writers and the others included here, think about your attitude toward writing while you ponder the questions these professionals ask: Why do I write? How do I write? How can I improve my writing?

Joan Didion (© Jack Manning/The New York Times)

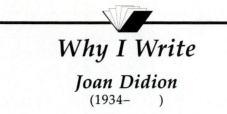

Why I Write

Joan Didion
(1934–   )

A native Californian, Joan Didion is a descendant of pioneers. Her great-great-great grandmother was one of the few who survived the trouble-ridden journey of the Donner party that crossed the mountains in 1846. Didion earned her bachelor's degree at the University of California at Berkeley and is best known for her perceptive essays, collected in several volumes including *Slouching Toward Bethlehem* (1969) and *The White Album* (1983). She has also written screenplays (in collaboration with her husband, John Gregory Dunne) and novels (*Play It As It Lays*, 1970, *Book of Common Prayer*, 1977 and *Democracy*, 1984). Didion's essays are praised for their realistic descriptions and their keen reflections on the events of her life. Didion admits that she "stole" the title of her essay from George Orwell, and, as he did, she explores the motivations and purposes behind the act of writing.

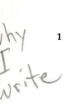

1   Of course I stole the title for this talk, from George Orwell. One reason I stole it was that I like the sound of the words: *Why I Write*. There you have three short unambiguous words that share a sound, and the sound they share is this:

I

I

I

2   In many ways writing is the act of saying *I*, of imposing oneself upon other people, of saying *listen to me, see it my way, change your mind*. It's an

aggressive, even a hostile act. You can disguise its aggressiveness all you want with veils of subordinate clauses and qualifiers and tentative subjunctives, with ellipses and evasions—with the whole manner of intimating rather than claiming, of alluding rather than stating—but there's no getting around the fact that setting words on paper is the tactic of a secret bully, an invasion, an imposition of the writer's sensibility on the reader's most private space.

3   I stole the title not only because the words sounded right but because they seemed to sum up, in a no-nonsense way, all I have to tell you. Like many writers I have only this one "subject," this one "area": the act of writing. I can bring you no reports from any other front. I may have other interests: I am "interested," for example, in marine biology, but I don't flatter myself that you would come out to hear me talk about it. I am not a scholar. I am not in the least an intellectual, which is not to say that when I hear the word "intellectual" I reach for my gun, but only to say that I do not think in abstracts. During the years when I was an undergraduate at Berkeley I tried, with a kind of hopeless late-adolescent energy, to buy some temporary visa into the world of ideas, to forge for myself a mind that could deal with the abstract.

4   In short I tried to think. I failed. My attention veered inexorably back to the specific, to the tangible, to what was generally considered, by everyone I knew then and for that matter have known since, the peripheral. I would try to contemplate the Hegelian dialectic and would find myself concentrating instead on a flowering pear tree outside my window and the particular way the petals fell on my floor. I would try to read linguistic theory and would find myself wondering instead if the lights were on in the bevatron up the hill. When I say that I was wondering if the lights were on in the bevatron you might immediately suspect, if you deal in ideas at all, that I was registering the bevatron as a political symbol, thinking in shorthand about the military-industrial complex and its role in the university community, but you would be wrong. I was only wondering if the lights were on in the bevatron, and how they looked. A physical fact.

5   I had trouble graduating from Berkeley, not because of this inability to deal with ideas—I was majoring in English, and I could locate the house-and-garden imagery in "The Portrait of a Lady" as well as the next person, "imagery" being by definition the kind of specific that got my attention—but simply because I had neglected to take a course in Milton. For reasons which now sound baroque I needed a degree by the end of that summer, and the English department finally agreed, if I would come down from Sacramento every Friday and talk about the cosmology of "Paradise Lost," to certify me proficient in Milton. I did this. Some Fridays I took the Greyhound bus, other Fridays I caught the Southern Pacific's City of San Francisco on the last leg of its transcontinental trip. I can no longer tell you whether Milton put the sun or the earth at the center of his universe in

← By Milton

"Paradise Lost," the central question of at least one century and a topic about which I wrote 10,000 words that summer, but I can still recall the exact rancidity of the butter in the City of San Francisco's dining car, and the way the tinted windows on the Greyhound bus cast the oil refineries around Carquinez Straits into a grayed and obscurely sinister light. In short my attention was always on the periphery, on what I could see and taste and touch, on the butter, and the Greyhound bus. During those years I was traveling on what I knew to be a very shaky passport, forged papers: I knew that I was no legitimate resident in any world of ideas. I knew I couldn't think. All I knew then was what I couldn't do. All I knew then was what I wasn't, and it took me some years to discover what I was.

6 Which was a writer.

7 By which I mean not a "good" writer or a "bad" writer but simply a writer, a person whose most absorbed and passionate hours are spent arranging words on pieces of paper. Had my credentials been in order I would never have become a writer. Had I been blessed with even limited access to my own mind there would have been no reason to write. I write entirely to find out what I'm thinking, what I'm looking at, what I see and what it means. What I want and what I fear. Why did the oil refineries around Carquinez Straits seem sinister to me in the summer of 1956? Why have the night lights in the bevatron burned in my mind for twenty years? *What is going on in these pictures in my mind?*

8 When I talk about pictures in my mind I am talking, quite specifically, about images that shimmer around the edges. There used to be an illustration in every elementary psychology book showing a cat drawn by a patient in varying stages of schizophrenia. This cat had a shimmer around it. You could see the molecular structure breaking down at the very edges of the cat: the cat became the background and the background the cat, everything interacting, exchanging ions. People on hallucinogens describe the same perception of objects. I'm not a schizophrenic, nor do I take hallucinogens, but certain images do shimmer for me. Look hard enough, and you can't miss the shimmer. It's there. You can't think too much about these pictures that shimmer. You just lie low and let them develop. You stay quiet. You don't talk to many people and you keep your nervous system from shorting out and you try to locate the cat in the shimmer, the grammar in the picture.

9 Just as I meant "shimmer" literally I mean "grammar" literally. Grammar is a piano I play by ear, since I seem to have been out of school the year the rules were mentioned. All I know about grammar is its infinite power. To shift the structure of a sentence alters the meaning of that sentence, as definitely and inflexibly as the position of a camera alters the meaning of the object photographed. Many people know about camera angles now, but not so many know about sentences. The arrangement of the words matters, and the arrangement you want can be found in the picture in your mind. The picture dictates the arrangement. The picture dictates whether this will

be a sentence with or without clauses, a sentence that ends hard or a dying-fall sentence, long or short, active or passive. The picture tells you how to arrange the words and the arrangement of the words tells you, or tells me, what's going on in the picture. *Nota bene:*

10   It tells you.

11   You don't tell it.

12   Let me show you what I mean by pictures in the mind. I began "Play It As It Lays" just as I have begun each of my novels, with no notion of "character" or "plot" or even "incident." I had only two pictures in my mind, more about which later, and a technical intention, which was to write a novel so elliptical and fast that it would be over before you noticed it, a novel so fast that it would scarcely exist on the page at all. About the pictures: the first was of white space. Empty space. This was clearly the picture that dictated the narrative intention of the book—a book in which anything that happened would happen off the page, a "white" book to which the reader would have to bring his or her own bad dreams—and yet this picture told me no "story," suggested no situation. The second picture did. This second picture was of something actually witnessed. A young woman with long hair and a short white halter dress walks through the casino at the Riviera in Las Vegas at one in the morning. She crosses the casino alone and picks up a house telephone. I watch her because I have heard her paged, and recognize her name: she is a minor actress I see around Los Angeles from time to time, in places like Jax and once in a gynecologist's office in the Beverly Hills Clinic, but have never met. I know nothing about her. Who is paging her? Why is she here to be paged? How exactly did she come to this? It was precisely this moment in Las Vegas that made "Play It As It Lays" begin to tell itself to me, but the moment appears in the novel only obliquely, in a chapter which begins:

13   "Maria made a list of things she would never do. She would never: walk through the Sands or Caesar's alone after midnight. She would never: ball at a party, do S-M unless she wanted to, borrow furs from Abe Lipsey, deal. She would never: carry a Yorkshire in Beverly Hills."

14   That is the beginning of the chapter and that is also the end of the chapter, which may suggest what I meant by "white space."

15   I recall having a number of pictures in my mind when I began the novel I just finished, "A Book of Common Prayer." As a matter of fact one of these pictures was of that bevatron I mentioned, although I would be hard put to tell you a story in which nuclear energy figures. Another was a newspaper photograph of a hijacked 707 burning on the desert in the Middle East. Another was the night view from a room in which I once spent a week with paratyphoid, a hotel room on the Colombian coast. My husband and I seemed to be on the Colombian coast representing the United States of America at a film festival (I recall invoking the name "Jack Valenti" a lot, as if its reiteration could make me well), and it was a bad place to have

fever, not only because my indisposition offended our hosts but because every night in this hotel the generator failed. The lights went out. The elevator stopped. My husband would go to the event of the evening and make excuses for me and I would stay alone in this hotel room, in the dark. I remember standing at the window trying to call Bogotá (the telephone seemed to work on the same principle as the generator) and watching the night wind come up and wondering what I was doing eleven degrees off the equator with a fever of 103. The view from that window definitely figures in "A Book of Common Prayer," as does the burning 707, and yet none of these pictures told me the story I needed.

16 The picture that did, the picture that shimmered and made these other images coalesce, was the Panama airport at 6 A.M. I was in this airport only once, on a plane to Bogotá that stopped for an hour to refuel, but the way it looked that morning remained superimposed on everything I saw until the day I finished "A Book of Common Prayer." I lived in that airport for several years. I can still feel the hot air when I step off the plane, can see the heat already rising off the tarmac at 6 A.M. I can feel my skirt damp and wrinkled on my legs. I can feel the asphalt stick to my sandals. I remember the big tail of a Pan American plane floating motionless down at the end of the tarmac. I remember the sound of a slot machine in the waiting room. I could tell you that I remember a particular woman in the airport, an American woman, a *norteamericana*, a thin *norteamericana* about 40 who bore a big square emerald in lieu of a wedding ring, but there was no such woman there.

17 I put this woman in the airport later. I made this woman up, just as I later made up a country to put the airport in, and a family to run the country. This woman in the airport is neither catching a plane nor meeting one. She is ordering tea in the airport coffee shop. In fact she is not simply "ordering" tea but insisting that the water be boiled, in front of her, for twenty minutes. Why is this woman in this airport? Why is she going nowhere, where has she been? Where did she get that big emerald? What derangement, or disassociation, makes her believe that her will to see the water boiled can possibly prevail?

18 "She had been going to one airport or another for four months, one could see it, looking at the visas on her passport. All those airports where Charlotte Douglass's passport had been stamped would have looked alike. Sometimes the sign on the tower would say 'Bienvenidos' and sometimes the sign on the tower would say 'Bienvenue,' some places were wet and hot and others dry and hot, but at each of these airports the pastel concrete walls would rust and stain and the swamp off the runway would be littered with the fuselages of cannibalized Fairchild F-227's and the water would need boiling.

19 "I knew why Charlotte went to the airport even if Victor did not.

20 "I knew about airports."

21   These lines appear about halfway through "A Book of Common Prayer," but I wrote them during the second week I worked on the book, long before I had any idea where Charlotte Douglas had been or why she went to airports. Until I wrote these lines I had no character called "Victor" in mind: the necessity for mentioning a name, and the name "Victor," occurred to me as I wrote the sentence. *I knew why Charlotte went to the airport* sounded incomplete. *I knew why Charlotte went to the airport even if Victor did not* carried a little more narrative drive. Most important of all, until I wrote these lines I did not know who "I" was, who was telling the story. I had intended until that moment that the "I" be no more than the voice of the author, a 19th-century omniscient narrator. But there it was:

22   "I knew why Charlotte went to the airport even if Victor did not.

23   "I knew about airports."

24   This "I" was the voice of no author in my house. This "I" was someone who not only knew why Charlotte went to the airport but also knew someone called "Victor." Who was Victor? Who was this narrator? Why was this narrator telling me this story? Let me tell you one thing about why writers write: had I known the answer to any of these questions I would never have needed to write a novel.

Annie Dillard (© Nancy Crampton)

Writing And Vision
Annie Dillard
(1945–   )

Born in Pittsburgh, Pennsylvania, Annie Dillard
received a B.A. and an M.A. degree from Hollins
College near Roanoke, Virginia. She lived for
nearly ten years in the Roanoke Valley, recording
observations about her surroundings that became
the basis for her Pulitzer Prize–winning book,
Pilgrim at Tinker Creek (1974). Acclaimed as an
essayist, poet, and literary critic, she has written a
column for *Living Wilderness* and served as a
contributing editor for *Harper's* magazine. Her
work has been published in *Atlantic, American
Scholar*, and *Cosmopolitan*. She has been teaching at
Wesleyan University in Middletown, Connecticut,
since 1979, and her books include *Living by Fiction*
(1982), *Encounters with Chinese Writers* (1984),
The Writing Life (1989), and *Living* (1992). One of
her best known works, *Teaching a Stone to Talk*
(1982) is the source for "Writing and Vision." In
this essay Dillard presents an analogy between the
seemingly disparate processes of cutting wood and
writing well: aim through the wood for the
chopping block.

1 Once, in order to finish a book I was writing and yet not live in the
same room with it, I begged a cabin to use as a study. I finished the book
there, wrote some other things, and learned to split wood. All this was on
a remote and sparsely populated island on Haro Strait, where I moved when
I left Virginia. The island was in northern Puget Sound, Washington State,
across the water from Canadian islands.

2 The cabin was a single small room near the water. Its walls were shrunken planks, not insulated; in January, February, and March, it was cold. There were two small metal beds in the room, two cupboards, some shelves over a little counter, a wood stove, and a table under a window, where I wrote. The window looked out on a bit of sandflat overgrown with thick, varicolored mosses; there were a few small firs where the sandflat met the cobble beach; and there was the water: Puget Sound, and all the sky over it and all the other wild islands in the distance under the sky. It was very grand. But you get used to it. I don't much care where I work. I don't notice things. The door used to blow open and startle me witless. I did, however, notice the cold.

3 I tried to heat the cabin with the wood stove and a kerosene heater, but I never was warm. I used to work wearing a wool cap, long wool tights, sweaters, a down jacket, and a scarf. I was too lazy to stick a damper in the wood stove chimney; I kept putting off the task for a warm day. Thoreau said that his firewood warmed him twice—because he labored to cut his own. Mine froze me twice, for the same reason. After I learned to split wood, in a manner I am shortly to relate—after I learned to split wood, I stepped out into the brute northeaster and split just enough alder to last me through working hours, which was not enough splitting to warm me. Then I came in and kindled a fire in the stove, all the heat of which vanished up the chimney.

4 At first, in the good old days, I did not know how to split wood. I set a chunk of alder on the chopping block and harassed it, at enormous exertion, into tiny wedges that flew all over the sandflat and lost themselves. What I did was less like splitting wood than chipping flints. After a few whacks my alder chunk still stood serene and unmoved, its base untouched, its tip a thorn. And then I actually tried to turn the sorry thing over and balance it on its wee head while I tried to chop its feet off before it fell over. God save us.

5 All this was a very warm process. I removed my down jacket, my wool hat and scarf. Alas, those early wood-splitting days, when I truly warmed myself, didn't last long. I lost the knack.

6 I did not know it at the time, but during those first weeks when I attacked my wood every morning, I was collecting a crowd—or what passed on the island for a crowd. At the sound of my ax, Doe and Bob—real islanders, proper, wood-splitting islanders—paused in their activities and mustered, unseen, across the sandflat, under the firs. They were watching me (oh, the idleness) try to split wood. It must have been a largely silent comedy. Later, when they confessed, and I railed at them, Bob said innocently that the single remark he had ever permitted himself had been, "I love to watch Annie split wood."

7 One night, while all this had been going on, I had a dream in which I was given to understand, by the powers that be, how to split wood. You

aim, said the dream—of course!—at the chopping block. It is true. You aim at the chopping block, not at the wood; then you split the wood, instead of chipping it. You cannot do the job cleanly unless you treat the wood as the transparent means to an end, by aiming past it. But then, alas, you easily split your day's wood in a few minutes, in the freezing cold, without working up any heat; then you utterly forfeit your only chance of getting warm.

8   The knack of splitting wood was the only useful thing I had ever learned from any dream, and my attitude toward the powers that be was not entirely grateful. The island comedy was over; everybody had to go back to work; and I never did get warm. . . .

9   Here is a fairly sober version of what happens in the small room between the writer and the work itself. It is similar to what happens between a painter and the canvas.

10   First you shape the vision of what the projected work of art will be. The vision, I stress, is no marvelous thing: It is the work's intellectual structure and aesthetic surface. It is a chip of mind, a pleasing intellectual object. It is a vision of the work, not of the world. It is a glowing thing, a blurred thing of beauty. Its structure is at once luminous and translucent; you can see the world through it. After you receive the initial charge of this imaginary object, you add to it at once several aspects, and incubate it most gingerly as it grows into itself.

11   Many aspects of the work are still uncertain, of course; you know that. You know that if you proceed you will change things and learn things, that the form will grow under your hands and develop new and richer lights. But that change will not alter the vision or its deep structures; it will only enrich it. You know that, and you are right.

12   But you are wrong if you think that in the actual writing, or in the actual painting, you are filling in the vision. You cannot fill in the vision. You cannot even bring the vision to light. You are wrong if you think that you can in any way take the vision and tame it to the page. The page is jealous and tyrannical; the page is made of time and matter; the page always wins. The vision is not so much destroyed, exactly, as it is, by the time you have finished, forgotten. It has been replaced by this changeling, this bastard, this opaque lightless chunky ruinous work.

13   Here is how it happens. The vision is, *sub specie aeternitatis*,[1] a set of mental relationships, a coherent series of formal possibilities. In the actual rooms of time, however, it is a page or two of legal paper filled with words and questions; it is a terrible diagram, a few books' names in a margin, an ambiguous doodle, a corner folded down in a library book. These are memos from the thinking brain to witless hope.

14   Nevertheless, ignoring the provisional and pathetic nature of these scraps, and bearing the vision itself in mind—having it before your sights like the

[1]Translation: "under the aspect of eternity." [Editors' note]

very Grail—you begin to scratch out the first faint marks on the canvas, on the page. You begin the work proper. Now you have gone and done it. Now the thing is no longer a vision: It is paper.

15   Words lead to other words and down the garden path. You adjust the paints' values and hues not to the world, not to the vision, but to the rest of the paint. The materials are stubborn and rigid; push is always coming to shove. You can fly—you can fly higher than you thought possible—but you can never get off the page. After every passage another passage follows, more sentences, more everything on drearily down. Time and materials hound the work; the vision recedes ever farther into the dim realms.

16   And so you continue the work, and finish it. Probably by now you have been forced to toss the most essential part of the vision. But this is a concern for mere nostalgia now: For before your eyes, and stealing your heart, is this fighting and frail finished product, entirely opaque. You can see nothing through it. It is only itself, a series of well-known passages, some colored paint. Its relationship to the vision that impelled it is the relationship between any energy and any work, anything unchanging to anything temporal.

17   The work is not the vision itself, certainly. It is not the vision filled in, as if it had been a coloring book. It is not the vision reproduced in time; that were impossible. It is rather a simulacrum and a replacement. It is a golem. You try—you try every time—to reproduce the vision, to let your light so shine before men. But you can only come along with your bushel and hide it.

18   Who will teach me to write? a reader wanted to know.

19   The page, the page, that eternal blankness, the blankness of eternity which you cover slowly, affirming time's scrawl as a right and your daring as necessity; the page, which you cover woodenly, ruining it, but asserting your freedom and power to act, acknowledging that you ruin everything you touch but touching it nevertheless, because acting is better than being here in mere opacity; the page, which you cover slowly with the crabbed thread of your gut; the page in the purity of its possibilities; the page of your death, against which you pit such flawed excellences as you can muster with all your life's strength: That page will teach you to write.

20   There is another way of saying this. Aim for the chopping block. If you aim for the wood, you will have nothing. Aim past the wood, aim through the wood; aim for the chopping block.

Henry David Thoreau (© Archive Photos)

On Keeping a Private Journal
Henry David Thoreau
(1817–1862)

Henry David Thoreau was a lifelong resident of
Concord, Massachusetts. He was educated at
Harvard University, and after graduation he
worked at a variety of jobs ranging from teaching
to house painting. A political activist, Thoreau once
chose to be jailed rather than to pay a poll tax
supporting a government that had failed to abolish
slavery and, in addition, made war with Mexico.
His essay "Civil Disobedience" (1849) makes a
powerful argument for the individual's right to
rebel against the laws of the state. When Thoreau
was twenty-eight years old, he built a cabin in the
woods near Walden Pond and went to live there,
hoping "to front only the essential facts of life."
The journals that he kept at Walden Pond were the
extension of a long-held habit; written when he
was eighteen years old, "On Keeping a Private
Journal" establishes the importance Thoreau placed
on the literary form that served as the basis for *A
Week on the Concord and Merrimack Rivers* (1849)
and *Walden* (1854).

1   As those pieces which the painter sketches for his own amusement
in his leisure hours are often superior to his most elaborate productions, so
it is that ideas often suggest themselves to us spontaneously, as it were, far
surpassing in beauty those which arise in the mind upon applying ourselves
to any particular subject. Hence, could a machine be invented which would
instantaneously arrange on paper each idea as it occurs to us, without any
exertion on our part, how extremely useful would it be considered! The

relation between this and the practice of keeping a journal is obvious. But yet, the preservation of our scattered thoughts is to be considered an object but of minor importance.

2   Every one can think, but comparatively few can write, can express their thoughts. Indeed, how often do we hear one complain of his inability to express what he feels! How many have occasion to make the following remark, "I am sensible that I understand this perfectly, but am not able to find words to convey my idea to others."

3   But if each one would employ a certain portion of each day in looking back upon the time which has passed, and in writing down his thoughts and feelings, in reckoning up his daily gains, that he may be able to detect whatever false coins have crept into his coffers, and, as it were, in settling accounts with his mind, not only would his daily experience be greatly increased, since his feelings and ideas would thus be more clearly defined, but he would be ready to turn over a new leaf, having carefully perused the preceding one, and would not continue to glance carelessly over the same page, without being able to distinguish it from a new one.

4   Most of us are apt to neglect the study of our own characters, thoughts, and feelings, and for the purpose of forming our own minds, look to others, who should merely be considered as different editions of the same great work. To be sure, it would be well for us to examine the various copies, that we might detect any errors, but yet, it would be foolish for one to borrow a work which he possessed himself, but had not perused.

5   In fine, if we endeavoured more to improve ourselves by reflection, by making a business of thinking, and giving our thoughts form and expression, we should be led to "read not to contradict and confute, nor to believe and take for granted, nor to find talk and discourse, but to weigh and consider."

Thinks everyone should write there thoughts. Not read them from others thoughts.

Freewriting

Peter Elbow
(1935–   )

Born in New York City, Peter Elbow was educated at Williams, Oxford, Harvard, and Brandeis. He has taught writing at many colleges and universities, including MIT, Franconia, Evergreen State College, and currently at The University of Massachusetts at Amherst. In 1975, he published *Oppositions in Chaucer* and he has written extensively on learning and teaching writing. His books on these topics include *Writing without Teachers* (1973), *Writing with Power* (1981), *Embracing Contraries: Explorations in Learning and Teaching* (1986), and *Sharing and Responding* (1989). In "Freewriting," first published as a chapter in *Writing without Teachers*, Elbow suggests a useful technique both for discovering ideas and for improving one's writing.

Peter Elbow
(Oxford University Press)

1   The most effective way I know to improve your writing is to do free-writing exercises regularly. At least three times a week. They are sometimes called "automatic writing," "babbling," or "jabbering" exercises. The idea is simply to write for ten minutes (later on, perhaps fifteen or twenty). Don't stop for anything. Go quickly without rushing. Never stop to look back, to cross something out, to wonder how to spell something, to wonder what word or thought to use, or to think about what you are doing. If you can't think of a word or a spelling, just use a squiggle or else write, "I can't think of it." Just put down something. The easiest thing is just to put down whatever is in your mind. If you get stuck it's fine to write "I can't think what to say, I can't think what to say" as many times as you want; or repeat the last word you wrote over and over again; or anything else. The only requirement is that you *never* stop.

2   What happens to a freewriting exercise is important. It must be a piece of writing which, even if someone reads it, doesn't send any ripples back to you. It is like writing something and putting it in a bottle in the sea. The teacherless class helps your writing by providing maximum feedback. Free-

writings help you by providing no feedback at all. When I assign one, I invite the writer to let me read it, but also tell him to keep it if he prefers. I read it quickly and make no comments at all and I do not speak with him about it. The main thing is that a freewriting must never be evaluated in any way; in fact there must be no discussion or comment at all.

3　　Here is an example of a fairly coherent exercise (sometimes they are very coherent, which is fine):

> I think I'll write what's on my mind, but the only thing on my mind right now is what to write for ten minutes. I've never done this before and I'm not prepared in any way—the sky is cloudy today, how's that? now I'm afraid I won't be able to think of what to write when I get to the end of the sentence—well, here I am at the end of the sentence—here I am again, again, again, again, at least I'm still writing—Now I ask is there some reason to be happy that I'm still writing—ah yes! Here comes the question again—What am I getting out of this? What point is there in it? It's almost obscene to always ask it but I seem to question everything that way and I was gonna say something else pertaining to that but I got so busy writing down the first part that I forgot what I was leading into. This is kind of fun oh don't stop writing—cars and trucks speeding by somewhere out the window, pens clittering across peoples' papers. The sky is still cloudy—is it symbolic that I should be mentioning it? Huh? I dunno. Maybe I should try colors, blue, red, dirty words—wait a minute—no can't do that, orange, yellow, arm tired, green pink violet magenta lavender red brown black green—now that I can't think of any more colors—just about done—relief? maybe.

4　　Freewriting may seem crazy but actually it makes simple sense. Think of the difference between speaking and writing. Writing has the advantage of permitting more editing. But that's its downfall too. Almost everybody interposes a massive and complicated series of editings between the time words start to be born into consciousness and when they finally come off the end of the pencil or typewriter onto the page. This is partly because schooling makes us obsessed with the "mistakes" we make in writing. Many people are constantly thinking about spelling and grammar as they try to write. I am always thinking about the awkwardness, wordiness, and general mushiness of my natural verbal product as I try to write down words.

5　　But it's not just "mistakes" or "bad writing" we edit as we write. We also edit unacceptable thoughts and feelings, as we do in speaking. In writing there is more time to do it so the editing is heavier: when speaking, there's someone right there waiting for a reply and he'll get bored or think we're crazy if we don't come out with *something*. Most of the time in speaking, we settle for the catch-as-catch-can way in which the words tumble out. In writing, however, there's a chance to try to get them right. But the opportunity to get them right is a terrible burden: you can work for two hours trying to get a paragraph "right" and discover it's not right at all. And then give up.

6   Editing, *in itself,* is not the problem. Editing is usually necessary if we want to end up with something satisfactory. The problem is that editing goes on *at the same time* as producing. The editor is, as it were, constantly looking over the shoulder of the producer and constantly fiddling with what he's doing while he's in the middle of trying to do it. No wonder the producer gets nervous, jumpy, inhibited, and finally can't be coherent. It's an unnecessary burden to try to think of words and also worry at the same time whether they're the right words.

7   The main thing about freewriting is that it is *nonediting.* It is an exercise in bringing together the process of producing words and putting them down on the page. Practiced regularly, it undoes the ingrained habit of editing at the same time you are trying to produce. It will make writing less blocked because words will come more easily. You will use up more paper, but chew up fewer pencils.

8   Next time you write, notice how often you stop yourself from writing down something you were going to write down. Or else cross it out after it's written. "Naturally," you say, "it wasn't any good." But think for a moment about the occasions when you spoke well. Seldom was it because you first got the beginning just right. Usually it was a matter of a halting or even garbled beginning, but you kept going and your speech finally became coherent and even powerful. There is a lesson here for writing: trying to get the beginning just right is a formula for failure—and probably a secret tactic to make yourself give up writing. Make some words, whatever they are, and then grab hold of that line and reel in as hard as you can. Afterwards you can throw away lousy beginnings and make new ones. This is the quickest way to get into good writing.

9   The habit of compulsive, premature editing doesn't just make writing hard. It also makes writing dead. Your voice is damped out by all the interruptions, changes, and hesitations between the consciousness and the page. In your natural way of producing words there is a sound, a texture, a rhythm—a voice—which is the main source of power in your writing. I don't know how it works, but this voice is the force that will make a reader listen to you, the energy that drives the meanings through his thick skull. Maybe you don't *like* your voice; maybe people have made fun of it. But it's the only voice you've got. It's your only source of power. You better get back into it, no matter what you think of it. If you keep writing in it, it may change into something you like better. But if you abandon it, you'll likely never have a voice and never be heard.

What Shall I Write?

Sheridan Baker
(1918–   )

Courtesy of Sheridan Baker

A respected editor of literary works, Sheridan Baker was for many years a professor of English at the University of Michigan. He has published two classic texts on writing: *The Practical Stylist* and *The Complete Stylist*. In this excerpt from *The Practical Stylist*, Baker offers useful advice for finding a subject and then defining a thesis that both reader and writer will regard as intriguing.

1   First you need a subject, and then you need a thesis. Yes, but *what shall I write?* That is the question, persisting from the first Christmas thank-you letter down to this very night. Here you are, an assignment due and the paper as blank as your mind. The Christmas letter may give us a clue. Your mother probably told you, as mine did, to write about what you had been doing. Almost anything would do—Cub Scouts, Brownies, the birthday party, skating—so long as you had been doing it. As you wrote, it grew interesting all over again. Finding a mature subject is no different: look for something you have experienced, or thought about. The more it matters to you, the more you can make it matter to your readers. It might be skiing. It might be clothes. It might be roommates, wives, husbands, the Peloponnesian War, running for office, a personal discovery of racial tensions, an experience on the job. But do not tackle a big philosophical abstraction, like Freedom, or a big subject, like the Supreme Court. They are too vast; your time and space and knowledge, all too small. You would probably manage no more than a collection of platitudes. Start rather with something specific, like apartment-hunting, and let the ideas of freedom and justice and responsibility arise from there. An abstract idea is a poor beginning. To be sure, as you move ahead through your course in writing, you will work

more directly with ideas, with problems posed by literature, with questions in the great civilizing debate about what we are doing in this strange world and universe. But again, look for something within your concern. The best subjects lie nearest at hand, and nearest the heart.

2   Suppose we start with Adulthood. That is certainly something close enough to all of us in prospect or achievement. It will illustrate conveniently how to generalize from personal experience, and how to narrow a subject down to manageable size. Your first impulse will be to describe your first realization that you were grown up, say, a recent test of responsibility: drugs, theft, speeding, sex. Written as autobiography, in the first person, "I," it would doubtless be interesting, even amusing or heartrending, as are most things human. But it would remain merely personal, a kind of confession, or hymn of self-praise. It would probably lack an important ingredient of intellectual maturity. You would still be working in that bright, self-centered spotlight of consciousness in which we live before we really begin to grow up and beyond which many of us never learn to step—where the child assumes that all his experiences are unique. If you shift from "me" to "the adult," however, you will be actually stepping into the perspective of maturity: acknowledging that others have gone through exactly the same thing, that your particular experiences have illustrated once again the general dilemma of responsibility versus the group at some perilous threshold to adulthood. So you will write not "I was afraid to say anything" but:

> The teen-ager fears going against the group more than death itself. When the speedometer hits 100, silence is the rule, though terror is screaming in every throat.

By *generalizing* your private feelings, you change your subject into a thesis by asserting something about it, by finding publicly valid reasons for your private convictions. You simply assume you are normal and fairly representative, and you then generalize with confidence, transposing your particular experiences, your particular thoughts and reactions, into statements about the general ways of the world. You might want to sharpen your statement a little more, as you turn your subject into a thesis, asserting something like: "The teen-ager's thrilling high-speed ride, if survived, can be a sobering lesson in the dynamics of the group and adult responsibility." Put your proposition into one sentence. This will get you focused. And now you are ready to begin.

WHERE ESSAYS FAIL

3 You can usually blame a bad essay on a bad beginning. If your essay falls apart, it probably has no primary idea to hold it together. "What's the big idea?" we used to ask. The phrase will serve as a reminder that you must

find the "big idea" behind your several smaller thoughts and musing before you start to write. In the beginning was the *logos*, says the Bible—the idea, the plan, caught in a flash as if in a single word. Find your *logos*, and you are ready to round out your essay and set it spinning.

4 The big idea behind our ride in the speeding car was that in adolescence, especially, the group can have a deadly influence on the individual. If you had not focused your big idea in a thesis, you might have begun by picking up thoughts at random, something like this:

> Everyone thinks he is a good driver. There are more accidents caused by young drivers than any other group. Driver education is a good beginning, but further practice is very necessary. People who object to driver education do not realize that modern society, with its suburban pattern of growth, is built around the automobile. The car becomes a way of life and a status symbol. When teenagers go too fast they are probably only copying their own parents, without any sense of responsibility.

5 A little reconsideration, aimed at a good thesis-sentence, could turn this into a reasonably good opening paragraph, with your thesis, your big idea, asserted at the end to focus your reader's attention:

> Modern society is built on the automobile. Children play with tiny cars; teenagers long to take out the car alone. Soon they are testing their skills at higher and higher speeds, especially with a group of friends along. One final test at extreme speeds usually suffices. It is usually a sobering experience, if survived, and can open one's eyes to the deadly dynamics of the group and the emerging sense of an adult responsibility for oneself and others.

6 Thus the central idea, or thesis, is your essay's life and spirit. If your thesis is sufficiently clear, it may tell you immediately how to organize your supporting material. But if you do not find a thesis, your essay will be a tour through the miscellaneous. Essays replete with scaffolds and catwalks—"We have just seen this; now let us turn to this"—are essays in which the inherent idea is weak or nonexistent. A purely expository and descriptive essay, one simply about "Cats," for instance, will have to rely on outer scaffolding alone (some orderly progression from Persia to Siam) since it really has no idea at all. It is all subject, all cats, instead of being based on an idea *about* cats, with a thesis *about* cats.

THE ARGUMENTATIVE EDGE

Find Your Thesis

7 The *about*-ness puts an argumentative edge on the subject. When you have something to say *about* cats, you have found your underlying idea. You have

something to defend, something to fight about: not just "Cats," but "The cat is really a person's best friend." Now the hackles on all dog people are rising, and you have an argument on your hands. You have something to prove. You have a thesis.

8   "What's the big idea, Mac?" Let the impudence in that time-honored demand remind you that the most dynamic thesis is a kind of affront to somebody. No one will be very much interested in listening to you expound the thesis "The dog is a person's best friend." Everyone knows that already. Even the dog lovers will be uninterested, convinced they know better than you. But the cat. . . .

9   So it is with any unpopular idea. The more unpopular the viewpoint and the stronger the push against convention, the stronger the thesis and the more energetic the essay. Compare the energy in "Democracy is good" with that in "Communism is good," for instance. The first is filled with platitudes, the second with plutonium. By the same token, if you can find the real energy in "Democracy is good," if you can get down through the sand to where the roots and water are, you will have a real essay, because the opposition against which you generate your energy is the heaviest in the world: boredom. Probably the most energetic thesis of all, the greatest inner organizer, is some tired old truth that you cause to spurt with new life, making the old ground green again.

10   To find a thesis and to put it into one sentence is to narrow and define your subject to a workable size. Under "Cats" you must deal with all felinity from the jungle up, carefully partitioning the eons and areas, the tigers and tabbies, the sizes and shapes. The minute you proclaim the cat the friend of humanity, you have pared away whole categories and chapters, and need only think up the arguments sufficient to overwhelm the opposition. So, put an argumentative edge on your subject—and you will have found your thesis.

11   Simple exposition, to be sure, has its uses. You may want to tell someone how to build a doghouse, how to can asparagus, how to follow the outlines of relativity, or even how to write an essay. Performing a few exercises in simple exposition will no doubt sharpen your insight into the problems of finding orderly sequences, of considering how best to lead your readers through the hoops of writing clearly and accurately. It will also illustrate how much finer and surer an argument is.

12   You will see that picking an argument immediately simplifies the problems so troublesome in straight exposition: the defining, the partitioning, the narrowing of the subject. Not that you must be constantly pugnacious or aggressive. I have overstated my point to make it stick. Actually, you can put an argumentative edge on the flattest of expository subjects. "How to build a doghouse" might become "Building a doghouse is a thorough introduction to the building trades, including architecture and mechanical engineering." "Canning asparagus" might become "An asparagus patch is a

Pick an arguement
That will find your thesis.

course in economics." "Relativity" might become "Relativity is not so inscrutable as many suppose." Literary subjects take an argumentative edge almost by nature. You simply assert what the essential point of a poem or play seems to be: "*Hamlet* is essentially about a world that has lost its values." You assume that your readers are in search of clarity, that you have a loyal opposition consisting of the interested but uninformed. You have given your subject its edge; you have limited and organized it at a single stroke. Pick an *argument*, then, and you will automatically be defining and narrowing your subject, and all the partitions you don't need will fold up. Instead of dealing with things, subjects, and pieces of subjects, you will be dealing with an idea and its consequences.

Sharpen Your Thesis

13 Come out with your subject pointed. Take a stand, make a judgment of value, make a *thesis.* Be reasonable, but don't be timid. It is helpful to think of your thesis, your main idea, as a debating question—"Resolved: Welfare payments must go"—taking out the "Resolved" when you actually write your thesis down. But your resolution will be even stronger, your essay clearer and tighter, if you can sharpen your thesis even further—"Resolved: Welfare payments must go because—." Fill in that blank, and your worries are practically over. The main idea is to put your whole argument into one sentence.

14 Try, for instance: "Welfare payments must go because they are making people irresponsible." I don't know at all if that is true, and neither will you until you write your way into it, considering probabilities and alternatives and objections, and especially the underlying assumptions. In fact, no one, no master sociologist or future historian, can tell absolutely if it is true, so multiplex are the causes in human affairs, so endless and tangled the consequences. The basic assumption—that irresponsibility is growing—might be entirely false. No one, I repeat, can tell absolutely. But by the same token, your guess may be as good as another's. At any rate, you are ready to write. You have found your *logos.*

15 Now put your well-pointed thesis-sentence on a scrap of paper to keep from drifting off target. But you will want to dress it for the public, to burnish it and make it comely. Suppose you try:

> Welfare payments, perhaps more than anything else, are eroding personal initiative.

But is this fully true? Perhaps you had better try something like:

> Despite their immediate benefits, welfare payments may actually be eroding personal initiative and depriving society of needed workers.

This is your full thesis; write that down on a scrap of paper too.

① *Find your Thesis*
Sharpen your Thesis

Jacqueline Berke (© Courtesy of Jacqueline Berke)

The Qualities of Good Writing

Jacqueline Berke

A professor at Drew University for more than thirty years, Jacqueline Berke was awarded the university's Scholar/Teacher of the Year award in 1986. With an undergraduate degree from New York University, an MA in Journalism from Columbia, and doctoral studies in literature at Rutgers, Berke currently teaches graduate courses in composition as well as "Literary Representations of the Holocaust," a course that educates students about the Nazi genocide of the Jews during World War II. Berke's current research and writing include a critical study of *The Diary of Anne Frank* which examines the work "in a more realistic way than the dramatic reputation suggests." In October 1991 she presented this perspective to the Modern Language Association in the paper *"The Diary of Anne Frank:* Widely Acclaimed but Doubly Betrayed." The author of the highly regarded writing text *Twenty Questions for the Writer,* Berke has also contributed to a number of anthologies. In the following excerpt from *Twenty Questions,* Berke discusses the necessary components of effective writing.

1   Even before you set out, you come prepared by instinct and intuition to make certain judgments about what is "good." Take the following familiar sentence, for example: "I know not what course others may take, but as for me, give me liberty or give me death." Do you suppose this thought of Patrick Henry's would have come ringing down through the centuries if

he had expressed this sentiment not in one tight, rhythmical sentence but as follows?

> It would be difficult, if not impossible, to predict on the basis of my limited information as to the predilections of the public, what the citizenry at large will regard as action commensurate with the present provocation, but after arduous consideration I personally feel so intensely and irrevocably committed to the position of social, political, and economic independence, that rather than submit to foreign and despotic control which is anathema to me, I will make the ultimate sacrifice of which humanity is capable—under the aegis of personal honor, ideological conviction, and existential commitment, I will sacrifice my own mortal existence.

2   How does this rambling, high-flown paraphrase measure up to the bold "Give me liberty or give me death"? Who will deny that something is "happening" in Patrick Henry's rousing challenge that not only fails to happen in the paraphrase but is actually negated there? Would you bear with this long-winded, pompous speaker to the end? If you were to judge this statement strictly on its rhetoric (its choice and arrangement of words), you might aptly call it more boring than brave. Perhaps a plainer version will work better:

> Liberty is a very important thing for a person to have. Most people—at least the people I've talked to or that other people have told me about—know this and therefore are very anxious to preserve their liberty. Of course I can't be absolutely sure about what other folks are going to do in this present crisis, what with all these threats and everything, but I've made up my mind that I'm going to fight because liberty is really a very important thing to me; at least that's the way I feel about it.

3   This flat, "homely" prose, weighted down with what the French author Gustave Flaubert called "fatty deposits," is grammatical enough. As in the pompous paraphrase, every verb agrees with its subject, every comma is in its proper place; nonetheless it lacks the qualities that make a statement—of one sentence or one hundred pages—pungent, vital, moving, and memorable.

4   Let us isolate these qualities and describe them briefly.

ECONOMY

5   The first quality of good writing is *economy*. In an appropriately slender volume entitled *The Elements of Style,* authors William Strunk Jr. and E. B. White state the case for economy concisely:

> A sentence should contain no unnecessary words, for the same reason that a drawing should have no unnecessary lines and a machine no unnecessary parts. This requires not that the writer make all his sentences short or that he avoid all detail . . . but that every word tell.

6   In other words, economical writing is *efficient* and *aesthetically satisfying.* While it makes a minimum demand on the energy and patience of readers, it returns to them a maximum of sharply compressed meaning. This is one of your basic responsibilities as a writer: to inflict no unnecessary words on your reader—just as a dentist inflicts no unnecessary pain, a lawyer no unnecessary risk. Economical writing avoids strain and at the same time promotes pleasure by producing a sense of form and right proportion, a sense of words that fit the ideas they embody. Economical writing contains no "deadwood" to dull the reader's attention, not an extra, useless phrase to clog the free flow of ideas, one following swiftly and clearly upon another.

SIMPLICITY

7 Another basic quality of good writing is *simplicity*. Here again this does not require that you make all your sentences primer-like or that you reduce complexities to the bare bone, but rather that you avoid embellishment and embroidery. A natural, unpretentious style is best. It signifies sincerity, for one thing: when people say what they *really mean*, they tend to say it with disarming simplicity. But paradoxically, simplicity or naturalness does not come naturally. By the time we are old enough to write, most of us have grown so self-conscious that we stiffen, sometimes to the point of rigidity, when we are called upon to make a statement in speech or in writing. It is easy to offer the kindly advice "Be yourself" but many people do not feel like themselves when they take a pencil in hand or sit down at a typewriter. During the early days of the Second World War, when air raids were feared in New York City and blackouts were instituted, an anonymous writer—probably a young civil service worker at City Hall—produced and distributed the following poster:

Illumination
Is Required
to be
Extinguished
on These Premises
After Nightfall

8   What this meant, of course, was simply "Lights Out After Dark." But apparently that direct imperative—clear and to the point—did not sound "official" enough, so the writer resorted to long Latinate words and involved syntax (note the awkward passives "*Is* Required" and "*to be* Extinguished")

to establish a tone of dignity and authority. In contrast, how beautifully simple are the words of the translators of the King James Version of the Bible, who felt no need for flourish, flamboyance, or grandiloquence. The Lord did not loftily or bombastically proclaim that universal illumination was required to be instantaneously installed. Simply but majestically "God said, Let there be light: and there was light. . . . And God called the light Day, and the darkness He called Night."

9   Most memorable declarations have been spare and direct. The French author Andre Maurois noted that Abraham Lincoln and John F. Kennedy seemed to "speak to each other across the span of a century," for both men embodied noble themes in eloquently simple terms. Said Lincoln in his second Inaugural Address "With malice toward none, with charity for all, with firmness in the right as God gives us to see the right, let us strive on to finish the work we are in. . . ." One hundred years later President Kennedy made his Inaugural dedication: "With a good conscience our only sure reward, with history the final judge of our deeds, let us go forth to lead the land we love. . . ."

CLARITY

10   A third fundamental element of good writing is *clarity*. Some people question whether it is always possible to be clear. After all, certain ideas are inherently complicated and inescapably difficult. True enough. But the responsible writer recognizes that writing should not add to the complications nor increase the difficulty: it should not set up an additional roadblock to understanding. If writers understand their own ideas and want to convey them to others, they are obliged to render those ideas in clear, orderly, readable, understandable prose—else why bother writing in the first place? Actually, obscure writers are usually confused themselves, uncertain of what they want to say or what they mean; they have not yet completed that process of thinking through and reasoning into the heart of the subject.

11   Whatever the topic, whatever the occasion, expository writing should be readable, informative, and, wherever possible, engaging. At its best it may even be poetic.

12   Even in technical writing, where the range of styles is necessarily limited, you must always be aware of "the reader over your shoulder." Take topics such as how to follow postal regulations for overseas mail, how to change oil in an engine, or how to produce aspirin from salicylic acid. Here are technical descriptions that defy a memorable turn of phrase. Such writing is of necessity cut and dried, dispassionate, and bloodless. But it need not be tedious or confusing to readers who want to find out about mailing letters, changing oil, or making aspirin. Readers who are looking for such information should have reasonably easy access to it. Written instructions should be clear, spare, direct, and, most of all, *human:* No matter how technical the

subject, all writing is done *for* human beings *by* human beings. Writing, like language itself, is a strictly human enterprise. Machines may stamp letters, measure oil, and convert acids, but only human beings talk and write about these procedures so that other human beings may better understand them. It is always appropriate, therefore, to be human in the way you write.

RHETORICAL STANCE

13 Part of this humanity must stem from your sense of who your readers are. You must assume a "rhetorical stance." Indeed this is a fundamental principle of rhetoric: *nothing should ever be written in a vacuum.* You should identify your audience, hypothetical or real, so that you may speak to them in an appropriate voice. A student, for example, should never "just write," without visualizing a definite group of readers—fellow students, perhaps, or the educated community at large (intelligent nonspecialists). Without such definite readers in mind, you cannot assume a suitable and appropriate relationship to your material, your purpose, and your audience. A proper rhetorical stance, in other words, requires that you have an active sense of the following:

1. Who you are as a writer

2. Who your readers are

3. Why you are addressing them and on what occasion

4. Your relationship to your subject matter

5. How you want your readers to relate to the subject matter

"COURTSHIP" DEVICES

14 In addition to a rhetorical stance, a writer should draw upon those personal and aesthetic effects that enhance a statement without distorting it and that delight—or at least sustain—a reader's attention. "One's case," said Aristotle, "should, in justice, be fought on the strength of the facts alone." This would be ideal: mind speaking to mind. The truth is, however, that people do not react solely on rational grounds, or, to quote Aristotle in a more cynical mood, "External matters do count much, because of the sorry nature of the audience." Facing reality then, you should try to "woo" the reader through a kind of "courtship." You should try, as Carl Rogers reminds us, to break down the natural barriers and fears that separate people, whether their encounters are face to face or on the printed page.

15 You must personalize your relationship with the reader by using those rhetorical devices that enable you to emerge from the page as a human being, with a distinctive voice and, in a broad sense, a personality. When

the writer and reader come together, the occasion should be special, marked by a common purpose and an element of pleasure.

16   Rhetoric provides a rich storehouse of courting devices, and we shall consider these in Part Three. For example, the pleasant rhythm of a balanced antithesis is evident in President Kennedy's immortal statement, ". . . ask not what your country can do for you; ask what you can do for your country." The lilting suspense of a periodic sentence (one that suspends its subject or predication until the end) appears in Edward Gibbon's delightful account of how he came to write the famous *Decline and Fall of the Roman Empire:*

> It was at Rome, on the 15th of October 1764, as I sat musing amidst the ruins of the Capitol, while the barefooted friars were singing vespers in the temple of Jupiter, that the idea of writing the decline and fall of the city first started to my mind.

17   Simeon Potter, a modern scholar, has observed that the word picture Gibbon draws, although brief, is "artistically perfect":

> The rhythm is stately and entirely satisfying. The reader is held in suspense to the end. Had he wished, and had he been less of an artist, Gibbon might have said exactly the same things in a different way, arranging them in their logical and grammatical order: "The idea of writing the decline and fall of the city first started to my mind as I sat musing amidst the ruins of the Capitol at Rome on the 15th of October 1764, while the barefooted friars were singing vespers in the temple of Jupiter." What has happened? It is not merely that a periodic sentence has been re-expressed as a loose one. The emphasis is now all wrong and the magnificent cadence of the original is quite marred. All is still grammatically correct, but "proper words" are no longer in "proper places." The passage has quite lost its harmonious rhythm.

18   In addition, then, to economy, simplicity, and clarity—the foundation of sound, dependable rhetoric—include this marvelous dimension of "harmonious rhythm," of proper words in proper places. If you are sensitive to these strategies, you will delight as well as inform your reader, and in delighting, reinforce your statement.

William Zinsser (© Thomas Victor)

Style

William Zinsser
(1922–   )

Born in New York, William Zinsser attended
Princeton University and after graduation worked
for *Life, Look,* and the *New York Herald Tribune.* In
1959, he left the *Tribune* to become a full-time
freelance writer. He became a member of the
English Department at Yale University in 1970
where he planned and taught the first nonfiction
writing course ever offered at Yale. In 1976 he
wrote his highly acclaimed book *On Writing Well:
An Informal Guide to Writing Nonfiction* based on
his own writing experiences as well as his
observations of his students' writing processes.
Zinsser continues to write for magazines and
newspapers, and in 1979 he became executive
editor of the Book-of-the-Month Club. He has
written several books, including *Pop Goes America*
(1966), *Writing with a Word Processor* (1982), *Paths
of Resistance: The Art and Craft of the Political Novel*
(1989), and *Worlds of Childhood: The Art and Craft
of Writing for Children* (1990). In the following
excerpt from *On Writing Well* Zinsser advises
writers to "believe in your own identity" and to
resist shopping around for a gaudy style.

1   So much for early warnings about the bloated monsters that lie in
ambush for the writer trying to put together a clean English sentence.

2   "But," you may say, "if I eliminate everything that you think is clutter
and strip every sentence to its barest bones, will there be anything left
of me?"

3   The question is a fair one and the fear entirely natural. Simplicity carried to its extreme might seem to point to a style where the sentences are little more sophisticated than "Dick likes Jane" and "See Spot run."

4   I'll answer the question first on the level of mere carpentry. Then I'll get to the larger issue of who the writer is and how to preserve his or her identity.

5   Few people realize how badly they write. Nobody has shown them how much excess or murkiness has crept into their style and how it obstructs what they are trying to say. If you give me an article that runs to eight pages and I tell you to cut it to four, you'll howl and say it can't be done. Then you will go home and do it, and it will be infinitely better. After that comes the hard part: cutting it to three.

6   The point is that you have to strip down your writing before you can build it back up. You must know what the essential tools are and what job they were designed to do. If I may labor the metaphor of carpentry, it is first necessary to be able to saw wood neatly and to drive nails. Later you can bevel the edges or add elegant finials, if that is your taste. But you can never forget that you are practicing a craft that is based on certain principles. If the nails are weak, your house will collapse. If your verbs are weak and your syntax is rickety, your sentences will fall apart.

7   I'll admit that various nonfiction writers like Tom Wolfe and Norman Mailer and Hunter Thompson have built some remarkable houses. But these are writers who spent years learning their craft, and when at last they raised their fanciful turrets and hanging gardens, to the surprise of all of us who never dreamed of such ornamentation, they knew what they were doing. Nobody becomes Tom Wolfe overnight, not even Tom Wolfe.

8   First, then, learn to hammer in the nails, and if what you build is sturdy and serviceable, take satisfaction in its plain strength.

9   But you will be impatient to find a "style"—to embellish the plain words so that readers will recognize you as someone special. You will reach for gaudy similes and tinseled adjectives, as if "style" were something you could buy at a style store and drape onto your words in bright decorator colors. (Decorator colors are the colors that decorators come in.) Resist this shopping expedition: there is no style store.

10   Style is organic to the person doing the writing, as much a part of him as his hair, or, if he is bald, his lack of it. Trying to add style is like adding a toupee. At first glance the formerly bald man looks young and even handsome. But at second glance—and with a toupee there is always a second glance—he doesn't look quite right. The problem is not that he doesn't look well groomed; he does, and we can only admire the wigmaker's almost perfect skill. The point is that he doesn't look like himself.

11   This is the problem of the writer who sets out deliberately to garnish his prose. You lose whatever it is that makes you unique. The reader will usually

notice if you are putting on airs. He wants the person who is talking to him to sound genuine. Therefore a fundamental rule is: be yourself.

12   No rule, however, is harder to follow. It requires the writer to do two things which by his metabolism are impossible. He must relax and he must have confidence.

13   Telling a writer to relax is like telling a man to relax while being prodded for a possible hernia, and, as for confidence, he is a bundle of anxieties. See how stiffly he sits at his typewriter, glaring at the paper that awaits his words, chewing the eraser on the pencil that is so sharp because he has sharpened it so many times. A writer will do anything to avoid the act of writing. I can testify from my newspaper days that the number of trips made to the water cooler per reporter-hour far exceeds the body's known need for fluids.

14   What can be done to put the writer out of these miseries? Unfortunately, no cure has yet been found. I can only offer the consoling thought that you are not alone. Some days will go better than others; some will go so badly that you will despair of ever writing again. We have all had many of these days and will have many more.

15   Still, it would be nice to keep the bad days to a minimum, which brings me back to the matter of trying to relax.

16   As I said earlier, the average writer sets out to commit an act of literature. He thinks that his article must be of a certain length or it won't seem important. He thinks how august it will look in print. He thinks of all the people who will read it. He thinks that it must have the solid weight of authority. He thinks that its style must dazzle. No wonder he tightens: he is so busy thinking of his awesome responsibility to the finished article that he can't even start. Yet he vows to be worthy of the task. He will do it—by God!—and, casting about for heavy phrases that would never occur to him if he weren't trying so hard to make an impression, he plunges in.

17   Paragraph 1 is a disaster—a tissue of ponderous generalities that seem to have come out of a machine. No *person* could have written them. Paragraph 2 is not much better. But Paragraph 3 begins to have a somewhat human quality, and by Paragraph 4 the writer begins to sound like himself. He has started to relax.

18   It is amazing how often an editor can simply throw away the first three or four paragraphs of an article and start with the paragraph where the writer begins to sound like himself. Not only are the first few paragraphs hopelessly impersonal and ornate; they also don't really say anything. They are a self-conscious attempt at a fancy introduction, and none is necessary.

19   A writer is obviously at his most natural and relaxed when he writes in the first person. Writing is, after all, a personal transaction between two people, even if it is conducted on paper, and the transaction will go well to the extent that it retains its humanity. Therefore I almost always urge people

to write in the first person—to use "I" and "me" and "we" and "us." They usually put up a fight.

20   "Who am I to say what *I* think?" they ask. "Or what *I* feel?"

21   "Who are you *not* to say what you think?" I reply. "There's only one you. Nobody else thinks or feels in exactly the same way."

22   "But no one cares about my opinions," they say. "It would make me feel conspicuous."

23   "They'll care if you tell them something interesting," I say, "and tell them in words that come naturally."

24   Nevertheless, getting writers to use "I" is seldom easy. They think they must somehow earn the right to reveal their emotions or their deepest thoughts. Or that it is egotistical. Or that it is undignified—a fear that hobbles the academic world. Hence the professorial use of "one" ("One finds oneself not wholly in accord with Dr. Maltby's view of the human condition") and of the impersonal "it is" ("It is to be hoped that Professor Felt's essay will find the wider audience that it most assuredly deserves"). These are arid constructions. "One" is a pedantic fellow—I've never wanted to meet him. I want a professor with a passion for his subject to tell me why it fascinates *him*.

25   I realize that there are vast regions of writing where "I" is not allowed. Newspapers don't want "I" in their news stories; many magazines don't want it in their articles and features; businesses and institutions don't want it in the annual reports and pamphlets that they send so profusely into the American home. Colleges don't want "I" in their term papers or dissertations, and English teachers in elementary and high schools have been taught to discourage any first-person pronoun except the literary "we" ("We see in Melville's symbolic use of the white whale . . .").

26   Many of these prohibitions are valid. Newspaper articles should consist of news, reported as objectively as possible. And I sympathize with schoolteachers who don't want to give students an easy escape into opinion—"I think Hamlet was stupid"—before the students have grappled with the discipline of assessing a work on its merits and on external sources. "I" can be a self-indulgence and a cop-out.

27   Still, we have become a society fearful of revealing who we are. We have evolved a national language of impersonality. The institutions that seek our support by sending us their brochures tend to sound remarkably alike, though surely all of them—hospitals, schools, libraries, museums—were founded and are still sustained by men and women with different dreams and visions. Where are these people? It is hard to glimpse them among all the passive sentences that say "initiatives were undertaken" and "priorities have been identified."

28   Even when "I" is not permitted, it's still possible to convey a sense of I-ness. James Reston and Red Smith, for instance, don't use "I" in their columns; yet I have a good idea of what kind of people they are, and I could

say the same of other essayists and reporters. Good writers are always visible just behind their words. If you aren't allowed to use "I," at least think "I" while you write, or write the first draft in the first person and then take the "I"s out. It will warm up your impersonal style.

29   Style, of course, is ultimately tied to the psyche, and writing has deep psychological roots. The reasons why we express ourselves as we do, or fail to express ourselves because of "writer's block," are buried partly in the subconscious mind. There are as many different kinds of writer's block as there are kinds of writers, and I have no intention of trying to untangle them here. This is a short book, and my name isn't Sigmund Freud.

30   But I'm struck by what seems to be a new reason for avoiding "I" that runs even deeper than what is not allowed or what is undignified. Americans are suddenly uncertain of what they think and unwilling to go out on a limb—an odd turn of events for a nation famous for the "rugged individualist." A generation ago our leaders told us where they stood and what they believed. Today they perform the most strenuous verbal feats to escape this fate. Watch them wriggle through *"Meet the Press"* or *"Face the Nation"* without committing themselves on a single issue.

31   President Ford, trying to assure a group of visiting businessmen that his fiscal policies would work, said: "We see nothing but increasingly brighter clouds every month." I took this to mean that the clouds were still fairly dark. Ford's sentence, however, was just misty enough to say nothing and still sedate his constituents.

32   But the true champ is Elliot Richardson, who held four major Cabinet positions in the 1970s—Attorney General and Secretary of Defense, Commerce and H.E.W. It's hard to know even where to begin picking from his vast trove of equivocal statements, but consider this one: "And yet, on balance, affirmative action has, I think, been a qualified success." A thirteen-word sentence with five hedging words. I give it first prize as the most wishy-washy sentence of the decade, though a close rival would be Richardson's analysis of how to ease boredom among assembly-line workers: "And so, at last, I come to the one firm conviction that I mentioned at the beginning: it is that the subject is too new for final judgments."

33   That's a firm conviction? Leaders who bob and weave like aging boxers don't inspire confidence—or deserve it. The same thing is true of writers. Sell yourself, and your subject will exert its own appeal. Believe in your own identity and your own opinions. Proceed with confidence, generating it, if necessary, by pure willpower. Writing is an act of ego and you might as well admit it. Use its energy to keep yourself going.

The Maker's Eye:
Revising Your Own Manuscripts

Donald Murray
(1924–   )

Donald Murray
(University of Wyoming)

Donald M. Murray enjoys a national reputation as an authority on the writing process. He was a Professor of English at the University of New Hampshire and a reporter for the *Boston Globe* as well as a contributing editor of *Time* magazine. He won the Pulitzer Prize for editorial writing and writes magazine articles, novels, short stories, and poetry as well as nonfiction books for both children and adults. In addition, he is the author of several widely adopted textbooks, including *The Craft of Revision* (1991). In "The Maker's Eye," Murray explains that revising is not a step that takes place only after a piece of writing is completed. Revising, he argues, is an integral part of every step in the writing process.

1   When students complete a first draft, they consider the job of writing done—and their teachers too often agree. When professional writers complete a first draft, they usually feel that they are at the start of the writing process. When a draft is completed, the job of writing can begin.

2   That difference in attitude is the difference between amateur and professional, inexperience and experience, journeyman and craftsman. Peter F. Drucker, the prolific business writer, calls his first draft "the zero draft"—after that he can start counting. Most writers share the feeling that the first draft, and all of those which follow, are opportunities to discover what they have to say and how best they can say it.

3   To produce a progression of drafts, each of which says more and says it more clearly, the writer has to develop a special kind of reading skill. In school we are taught to decode what appears on the page as finished writing. Writers, however, face a different category of possibility and responsibility when they read their own drafts. To them the words on the page are never finished. Each can be changed and rearranged, can set off a chain reaction

of confusion or clarified meaning. This is a different kind of reading which is possibly more difficult and certainly more exciting.

4   Writers must learn to be their own best enemy. They must accept the criticism of others and be suspicious of it; they must accept the praise of others and be even more suspicious of it. Writers cannot depend on others. They must detach themselves from their own pages so that they can apply both their caring and their craft to their own work.

5   Such detachment is not easy. Science fiction writer Ray Bradbury supposedly puts each manuscript away for a year to the day and then rereads it as a stranger. Not many writers have the discipline or the time to do this. We must read when our judgment may be at its worst, when we are close to the euphoric moment of creation.

6   Then the writer, counsels novelist Nancy Hale, "should be critical of everything that seems to him most delightful in his style. He should excise what he most admires, because he wouldn't thus admire it if he weren't . . . in a sense protecting it from criticism." John Ciardi, the poet, adds, "The last act of the writing must be to become one's own reader. It is, I suppose, a schizophrenic process, to begin passionately and to end critically, to begin hot and to end cold; and, more important, to be passion-hot and critic-cold at the same time."

7   Most people think that the principal problem is that writers are too proud of what they have written. Actually, a greater problem for most professional writers is one shared by the majority of students. They are overly critical, think everything is dreadful, tear up page after page, never complete a draft, see the task as hopeless.

8   The writer must learn to read critically but constructively, to cut what is bad, to reveal what is good. Eleanor Estes, the children's book author, explains: "The writer must survey his work critically, cooly, as though he were a stranger to it. He must be willing to prune, expertly and hard-heartedly. At the end of each revision, a manuscript may look . . . worked over, torn apart, pinned together, added to, deleted from, words changed and words changed back. Yet the book must maintain its original freshness and spontaneity."

9   Most readers underestimate the amount of rewriting it usually takes to produce spontaneous reading. This is a great disadvantage to the student writer, who sees only a finished product and never watches the craftsman who takes the necessary step back, studies the work carefully, returns to the task, steps back, returns, steps back, again and again. Anthony Burgess, one of the most prolific writers in the English-speaking world, admits, "I might revise a page twenty times." Roald Dahl, the popular children's writer, states, "By the time I'm nearing the end of a story, the first part will have been reread and altered and corrected at least 150 times. . . . Good writing is essentially rewriting. I am positive of this."

10   Rewriting isn't virtuous. It isn't something that ought to be done. It is simply something that most writers find they have to do to discover what they have to say and how to say it. It is a condition of the writer's life.

11   There are, however, a few writers who do little formal rewriting, primarily because they have the capacity and experience to create and review a large number of invisible drafts in their minds before they approach the page. And some writers slowly produce finished pages, performing all the tasks of revision simultaneously, page by page, rather than draft by draft. But it is still possible to see the sequence followed by most writers most of the time in rereading their own work.

12   Most writers scan their drafts first, reading as quickly as possible to catch the larger problems of subject and form, then move in closer and closer as they read and write, reread and rewrite.

13   The first thing writers look for in their drafts is *information*. They know that a good piece of writing is built from specific, accurate, and interesting information. The writer must have an abundance of information from which to construct a readable piece of writing.

14   Next writers look for *meaning* in the information. The specifics must build to a pattern of significance. Each piece of specific information must carry the reader toward meaning.

15   Writers reading their own drafts are aware of *audience*. They put themselves in the reader's situation and make sure that they deliver information which a reader wants to know or needs to know in a manner which is easily digested. Writers try to be sure that they anticipate and answer the questions a critical reader will ask when reading the piece of writing.

16   Writers make sure that the *form* is appropriate to the subject and the audience. Form, or genre, is the vehicle which carries meaning to the reader, but form cannot be selected until the writer has adequate information to discover its significance and an audience which needs or wants that meaning.

17   Once writers are sure the form is appropriate, they must then look at the *structure*, the order of what they have written. Good writing is built on a solid framework of logic, argument, narrative, or motivation which runs through the entire piece of writing and holds it together. This is the time when many writers find it most effective to outline as a way of visualizing the hidden spine by which the piece of writing is supported.

18   The element on which writers may spend a majority of their time is *development*. Each section of a piece of writing must be adequately developed. It must give readers enough information so that they are satisfied. How much information is enough? That's as difficult as asking how much garlic belongs in a salad. It must be done to taste, but most beginning writers underdevelop, underestimating the reader's hunger for information.

19   As writers solve development problems, they often have to consider questions of *dimension*. There must be a pleasing and effective proportion among

all the parts of the piece of writing. There is a continual process of subtracting and adding to keep the piece of writing in balance.

20   Finally, writers have to listen to their own voices. *Voice* is the force which drives a piece of writing forward. It is an expression of the writer's authority and concern. It is what is between the words on the page, what glues the piece of writing together. A good piece of writing is always marked by a consistent, individual voice.

21   As writers read and reread, write and rewrite, they move closer and closer to the page until they are doing line-by-line editing. Writers read their own pages with infinite care. Each sentence, each line, each clause, each phrase, each word, each mark of punctuation, each section of white space between the type has to contribute to the clarification of meaning.

22   Slowly the writer moves from word to word, looking through language to see the subject. As a word is changed, cut, or added, as a construction is rearranged, all the words used before that moment and all those that follow that moment must be considered and reconsidered.

23   Writers often read aloud at this stage of the editing process, muttering or whispering to themselves, calling on the ear's experience with language. Does this sound right—or that? Writers edit, shifting back and forth from eye to page to ear to page. I find I must do this careful editing in short runs, no more than fifteen or twenty minutes at a stretch, or I become too kind with myself. I begin to see what I hope is on the page, not what actually is on the page.

24   This sounds tedious if you haven't done it, but actually it is fun. Making something right is immensely satisfying, for writers begin to learn what they are writing about by writing. Language leads them to meaning, and there is the joy of discovery, of understanding, of making meaning clear as the writer employs the technical skills of language.

25   Words have double meanings, even triple and quadruple meanings. Each word has its own potential for connotation and denotation. And when writers rub one word against the other, they are often rewarded with a sudden insight, an unexpected clarification.

26   The maker's eye moves back and forth from word to phrase to sentence to paragraph to sentence to phrase to word. The maker's eye sees the need for variety and balance, for a firmer structure, for a more appropriate form. It peers into the interior of the paragraph, looking for coherence, unity, and emphasis, which make meaning clear.

27   I learned something about this process when my first bifocals were prescribed. I had ordered a larger section of the reading portion of the glass because of my work, but even so, I could not contain my eyes within this new limit of vision. And I still find myself taking off my glasses and bending my nose towards the page, for my eyes unconsciously flick back and forth across the page, back to another page, forward to still another, as I try to see each evolving line in relation to every other line.

28 When does this process end? Most writers agree with the great Russian writer Tolstoy, who said, "I scarcely ever reread my published writings; if by chance I come across a page, it always strikes me: all this must be rewritten; this is how I should have written it."

29 The maker's eye is never satisfied, for each word has the potential to ignite new meaning. This article has been twice written all the way through the writing process, and it was published four years ago. Now it is to be republished in a book. The editors made a few small suggestions, and then I read it with my maker's eye. Now it has been re-edited, re-revised, re-read, re-re-edited, for each piece of writing to the writer is full of potential and alternatives.

30 A piece of writing is never finished. It is delivered to a deadline, torn out of the typewriter on demand, sent off with a sense of accomplishment and shame and pride and frustration. If only there were a couple more days, time for just another run at it, perhaps then. . . .

PART 2

Essays for Reading and Analysis

Chapter Three

Narration

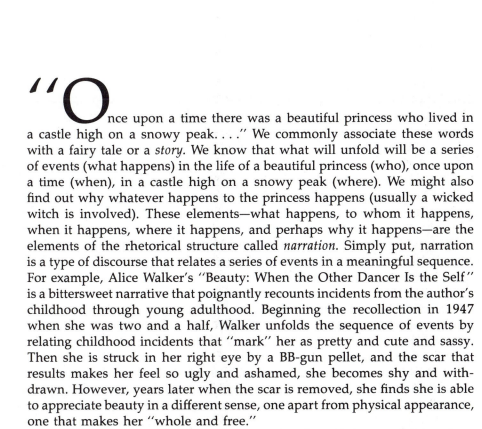

"Once upon a time there was a beautiful princess who lived in a castle high on a snowy peak. . . ." We commonly associate these words with a fairy tale or a *story*. We know that what will unfold will be a series of events (what happens) in the life of a beautiful princess (who), once upon a time (when), in a castle high on a snowy peak (where). We might also find out why whatever happens to the princess happens (usually a wicked witch is involved). These elements—what happens, to whom it happens, when it happens, where it happens, and perhaps why it happens—are the elements of the rhetorical structure called *narration*. Simply put, narration is a type of discourse that relates a series of events in a meaningful sequence. For example, Alice Walker's "Beauty: When the Other Dancer Is the Self" is a bittersweet narrative that poignantly recounts incidents from the author's childhood through young adulthood. Beginning the recollection in 1947 when she was two and a half, Walker unfolds the sequence of events by relating childhood incidents that "mark" her as pretty and cute and sassy. Then she is struck in her right eye by a BB-gun pellet, and the scar that results makes her feel so ugly and ashamed, she becomes shy and withdrawn. However, years later when the scar is removed, she finds she is able to appreciate beauty in a different sense, one apart from physical appearance, one that makes her "whole and free."

Another example to examine is Langston Hughes' "Salvation." Taken from his 1940 autobiography *The Big Sea*, the selection humorously recounts the events that led to the author's fraudulent salvation at a revival meeting.

He begins the narrative by telling us when the revival meeting takes place (he was 13), where it takes place (at his Aunt Reed's church), and, of course, who is involved (the children).

The narrative is probably the most natural of the rhetorical structures and is widely used in combination with other structures. Minutes of a business meeting often appear as incidents. An essay on the men who fought in Operation Desert Storm could be introduced with a brief story about one soldier. Using narration with other rhetorical structures, such as illustration (Chapter 7) or definition (Chapter 6) can add to the richness of the discussion and can also clarify difficult issues or principles by presenting them in a story with which the reader can identify.

Writing the Narrative

Remember that the key to writing a good narrative is arranging your material into a sequence of events that is logical, clear, and effective. The following tips will help you prepare your narrative:

  1. *Concentrate on what's important.*

Remember your purpose and avoid spending too much space on elements that are secondary to your purpose. For example, if you are writing a story that illustrates the virtue of honesty, it may not be necessary to give elaborate details of the narrative's setting.

  2. *Use details to create a vivid picture.*

Regardless of the narrative's purpose, your goal is to create a scene so vivid that the reader will experience the lesson, know the character, or understand the experience. The use of well-placed, colorful language in your writing will do much to evoke a feeling or mood, produce a mental picture, or induce a particular emotion. As you choose your words, be aware of their connotation and denotation. Colorful words can easily become emotionally charged words containing positive or negative associations. Certainly, you may choose to use such words deliberately for one purpose or another; just remember to keep your audience in mind, and make sure your language is appropriate for your reader.

  3. *Keep the narrative perspective consistent.*

Obviously your narrative will need a "voice" to tell it. A first-person narrator will recount the events in personal terms, using first-person pronouns (I, we, us). A third-person narrator may also be used, referring to characters as he, she, they. Whatever the case, be sure to maintain a consistent voice throughout the narration.

Once you have established the narrative perspective, do maintain the "character" of that perspective. If your narrator is a tough, rough-and-tumble sort of fellow, his language should reflect that personality trait. Don't have him speaking the language of "the street" in some places and switch to that of an intellectual sophisticate in others.

4. *Select an appropriate and logical time sequence.*

The time framework of your narrative should enhance its purpose. You may use straight chronology (relating the events as they happen) or retrospective—flashback—(momentarily leaving the present, reaching into a time before the main action of the narrative) to develop the writing. Whatever sequencing technique you use, though, should complement the overall effect and purpose of the narrative.

5. *Create and maintain smoothness in the narrative.*

A sense of coherence is as important in narrative writing as it is in any other. You should, however, avoid connections of excessive coordinations—that is, stringing your sentences together with *and* or *and then*. Instead, vary your sentence structures and use synonyms and pronouns to add freshness to your writing. Deliberate, but careful (and sparse) repetition can also create emphasis.

Writing a good narrative takes practice, of course, but the time spent in honing the skill will be well worth your effort.

Langston Hughes (© Archive Photos)

Salvation

Langston Hughes
(1902–1967)

After a year at Columbia University in 1921, Langston Hughes left school to travel and to work at whatever jobs he could find. While he was working as a busboy in Washington, D.C., he asked poet Vachel Lindsay to read some of his poems. Lindsay was deeply impressed by what he read and helped Hughes to publish his work. After the publication of his first book of poems, *The Weary Blues* (1925), Hughes was recognized as a prominent figure in the Harlem Renaissance literary movement. He entered Lincoln University in Pennsylvania, graduated in 1929, and continued to pursue a career as a writer focusing on the lives of African Americans in America. Although his writings include novels, plays, and a series of newspaper sketches, he is best known for his innovative poetry that introduced the patterns of African-American dialect and the rhythms of jazz. In "Salvation," first published as part of his autobiography *The Big Sea* (1940), Hughes demonstrates his gift for humor and for poignant insight into the human experience.

1   I was saved from sin when I was going on thirteen. But not really saved. It happened like this. There was a big revival at my Auntie Reed's church. Every night for weeks there had been much preaching, singing, praying, and shouting, and some very hardened sinners had been brought to Christ, and the membership of the church had grown by leaps and bounds. Then just before the revival ended, they held a special meeting for children, "to

bring the young lambs to the fold." My aunt spoke of it for days ahead. That night I was escorted to the front row and placed on the mourners' bench with all the other young sinners, who had not yet been brought to Jesus.

2   My aunt told me that when you were saved you saw a light, and something happened to you inside! And Jesus came into your life! And God was with you from then on! She said you could see and hear and feel Jesus in your soul. I believed her. I had heard a great many old people say the same thing and it seemed to me they ought to know. So I sat there calmly in the hot, crowded church, waiting for Jesus to come to me.

3   The preacher preached a wonderful rhythmical sermon, all moans and shouts and lonely cries and dire pictures of hell, and then he sang a song about the ninety and nine safe in the fold, but one little lamb was left out in the cold. Then he said: "Won't you come? Won't you come to Jesus? Young lambs, won't you come?" And he held out his arms to all us young sinners there on the mourners' bench. And the little girls cried. And some of them jumped up and went to Jesus right away. But most of us just sat there.

4   A great many old people came and knelt around us and prayed, old women with jet-black faces and braided hair, old men with work-gnarled hands. And the church sang a song about the lower lights are burning, some poor sinners to be saved. And the whole building rocked with prayer and song.

5   Still I kept waiting to *see* Jesus.

6   Finally all the young people had gone to the altar and were saved, but one boy and me. He was a rounder's son named Westley. Westley and I were surrounded by sisters and deacons praying. It was very hot in the church, and getting late now. Finally Westley said to me in a whisper: "God damn! I'm tired o' sitting here. Let's get up and be saved." So he got up and was saved.

7   Then I was left all alone on the mourners' bench. My aunt came and knelt at my knees and cried, while prayers and song swirled all around me in the little church. The whole congregation prayed for me alone, in a mighty wail of moans and voices. And I kept waiting serenely for Jesus, waiting, waiting— but he didn't come. I wanted to see him, but nothing happened to me. Nothing! I wanted something to happen to me, but nothing happened.

8   I heard the songs and the minister saying: "Why don't you come? My dear child, why don't you come to Jesus? Jesus is waiting for you. He wants you. Why don't you come? Sister Reed, what is this child's name?"

9   "Langston," my aunt sobbed.

10   "Langston, why don't you come? Why don't you come and be saved? Oh, Lamb of God! Why don't you come?"

11   Now it was really getting late. I began to be ashamed of myself, holding everything up so long. I began to wonder what God thought about Westley, who certainly hadn't seen Jesus either, but who was now sitting proudly on

the platform, swinging his knickerbockered legs and grinning down at me, surrounded by deacons and old women on their knees praying. God had not struck Westley dead for taking his name in vain or for lying in the temple. So I decided that maybe to save further trouble, I'd better lie, too, and say that Jesus had come, and get up and be saved.

12   So I got up.

13   Suddenly the whole room broke into a sea of shouting, as they saw me rise. Waves of rejoicing swept the place. Women leaped in the air. My aunt threw her arms around me. The minister took me by the hand and led me to the platform.

14   When things quieted down, in a hushed silence, punctuated by a few ecstatic "Amens," all the new young lambs were blessed in the name of God. Then joyous singing filled the room.

15   That night, for the last time in my life but one—for I was a big boy twelve years old—I cried. I cried, in bed alone, and couldn't stop. I buried my head under the quilts, but my aunt heard me. She woke up and told my uncle I was crying because the Holy Ghost had come into my life, and because I had seen Jesus. But I was really crying because I couldn't bear to tell her that I had lied, that I had deceived everybody in the church, that I hadn't seen Jesus, and that now I didn't believe there was a Jesus any more, since he didn't come to help me.

Topics for Writing and Discussion

1.   While he is at the revival meeting, Hughes experiences pressure to "be saved" from many different sources. List these sources and explain how Hughes reacts to each. Which source finally convinces him to get up and join the ranks of those who have attained salvation?

2.   What did Hughes' aunt tell him about the experience of being saved? How did her description compare to Hughes' observations and feelings while he was at the service?

3.   Narratives frequently use dialogue (directly recorded conversation). Hughes uses dialogue sparingly, only occasionally interspersing a comment with his own observations of the scene. Which individuals speak directly? What effect does Hughes' use of dialogue have? How does the dialogue suggest the essay's thesis?

4.   How does Hughes use imagery and figurative language to heighten the sense of conflict he feels? Notice, for example, that the entire congregation breaks "into a sea of shouting" as Hughes finally rises and walks toward the altar.

5.   Write a narrative describing a conflict you faced, the pressures brought to bear on your decision, and the choice you made. As did Hughes, try to use dialogue and strong imagery.

Richard Selzer (© Nancy Crampton)

The Discus Thrower

Richard Selzer
(1928–   )

His experiences as a practicing surgeon and as a
professor of surgery at Yale Medical School are the
inspiration for Richard Selzer's insights into
humanity. He has published two collections of
short stories and four collections of essays,
including *Mortal Lessons* (1977), *Confessions of a
Knife* (1979) and *Taking the World in for Repairs*
(1986). His writings have been widely published in
popular magazines; "The Discus Thrower" was
first published in *Harper's*. In this essay, Selzer
crafts a thought-provoking portrait of human
resistance to mortality.

1   I spy on my patients. Ought not a doctor to observe his patients by any
means and from any stance, that he might the more fully assemble evidence?
So I stand in the doorways of hospital rooms and gaze. Oh, it is not all that
furtive an act. Those in bed need only look up to discover me. But they
never do.

2   From the doorway of Room 542 the man in the bed seems deeply tanned.
Blue eyes and close-cropped white hair give him the appearance of vigor
and good health. But I know that his skin is not brown from the sun. It is
rusted, rather, in the last stage of containing the vile repose within. And the
blue eyes are frosted, looking inward like the windows of a snowbound
cottage. This man is blind. This man is also legless—the right leg missing
from midthigh down, the left from just below the knee. It gives him the
look of a bonsai, roots and branches pruned into the dwarfed facsimile of
a great tree.

3   Propped on pillows, he cups his right thigh in both hands. Now and then
he shakes his head as though acknowledging the intensity of his suffering.
In all of this he makes no sound. Is he mute as well as blind?

4   The room in which he dwells is empty of all possessions—no get-well
cards, small, private caches of food, day-old flowers, slippers, all the usual

kickshaws of the sickroom. There is only the bed, a chair, a nightstand, and a tray on wheels that can be swung across his lap for meals.

5   "What time is it?" he asks.

"Three o'clock."

"Morning or afternoon?"

"Afternoon."

He is silent. There is nothing else he wants to know.

10   "How are you?" I say.

"Who is it?" he asks.

"It's the doctor. How do you feel?"

He does not answer right away.

"Feel?" he says.

15   "I hope you feel better," I say.

I press the button at the side of the bed.

"Down you go," I say.

"Yes, down," he says.

He falls back upon the bed awkwardly. His stumps, unweighted by legs and feet, rise in the air, presenting themselves. I unwrap the bandages from the stumps, and begin to cut away the black scabs and the dead, glazed fat with scissors and forceps. A shard of white bone comes loose. I pick it away. I wash the wounds with disinfectant and redress the stumps. All this while, he does not speak. What is he thinking behind those lids that do not blink? Is he remembering a time when he was whole? Does he dream of feet? Of when his body was not a rotting log?

20   He lies solid and inert. In spite of everything, he remains impressive, as though he were a sailor standing athwart a slanting deck.

"Anything more I can do for you?" I ask.

For a long moment he is silent.

"Yes," he says at last and without the least irony. "You can bring me a pair of shoes."

In the corridor, the head nurse is waiting for me.

25   "We have to do something about him," she says. "Every morning he orders scrambled eggs for breakfast, and, instead of eating them, he picks up the plate and throws it against the wall."

"Throws his plate?"

"Nasty. That's what he is. No wonder his family doesn't come to visit. They probably can't stand him any more than we can."

She is waiting for me to do something.

"Well?"

30   "We'll see," I say.

The next morning I am waiting in the corridor when the kitchen delivers his breakfast. I watch the aide place the tray on the stand and swing it across his lap. She presses the button to raise the head of the bed. Then she leaves.

In time the man reaches to find the rim of the tray, then on to find the dome of the covered dish. He lifts off the cover and places it on the stand. He fingers across the plate until he probes the eggs. He lifts the plate in both hands, sets it on the palm of his right hand, centers it, balances it. He hefts it up and down slightly, getting the feel of it. Abruptly, he draws back his right arm as far as he can.

There is the crack of the plate breaking against the wall at the foot of his bed and the small wet sound of the scrambled eggs dropping to the floor.

And then he laughs. It is a sound you have never heard. It is something new under the sun. It could cure cancer.

35   Out in the corridor, the eyes of the head nurse narrow.

"Laughed, did he?"

She writes something down on her clipboard.

A second aide arrives, brings a second breakfast tray, puts it on the nightstand, out of his reach. She looks over at me shaking her head and making her mouth go. I see that we are to be accomplices.

"I've got to feed you," she says to the man.

40   "Oh, no you don't," the man says.

"Oh, yes I do," the aide says, "after the way you just did. Nurse says so."

"Get me my shoes," the man says.

"Here's oatmeal," the aide says. "Open." And she touches the spoon to his lower lip.

"I ordered scrambled eggs," says the man.

45   "That's right," the aide says.

I step forward.

"Is there anything I can do?" I say.

"Who are you?" the man asks.

In the evening I go once more to that ward to make my rounds. The head nurse reports to me that Room 542 is deceased. She has discovered this quite by accident, she says. No, there had been no sound. Nothing. It's a blessing, she says.

50   I go into his room, a spy looking for secrets. He is still there in his bed. His face is relaxed, grave, dignified. After a while, I turn to leave. My gaze sweeps the wall at the foot of the bed, and I see the place where it has been repeatedly washed, where the wall looks very clean and very white.

Topics for Writing and Discussion

1. Describe the attitude of this patient toward his situation. Why is he called "the discus thrower"? Why is such a name ironic? Why does he repeatedly call for his shoes?

2.   What is Selzer's attitude toward this patient? How does his view of this man compare to that of the head nurse? What was Selzer's point in narrating this patient's last days?

3.   Analyze several of the many metaphors and similes that appear in this essay. What do each of these add to the vividness of the descriptions? What does dialogue add to our understanding of the people in these scenes?

4.   Selzer's subtitle for this essay was "Do Not Go Gentle," a reference to a well-known poem by Dylan Thomas. In the poem Thomas addresses his dying father and urges him to fight against death, to rage against "the dying of the light." Why do you think Selzer wanted his readers to think about the Thomas poem as they read his essay?

5.   Write an essay narrating a time you spent with a sick person, making clear that patient's response to his or her illness. Did your observation of this person's attitude change you in any way? Consider using figurative language and dialogue to make clear your story of the patient and your feelings.

Maya Angelou (© Nancy Crampton)

Graduation in Stamps

Maya Angelou
(1928–   )

Maya Angelou was born Marguerite Johnson; she grew up with her brother, Bailey, and her grandmother (called "Momma") in Stamps, Arkansas. A talented singer, actress, poet, and playwright, she is best known for her autobiographical series: *I Know Why the Caged Bird Sings* (1970), *Gather Together in My Name* (1974), *Singin' and Swingin' and Gettin' Merry Like Christmas* (1976), and *The Heart of a Woman* (1981). A more recent work, *I Shall Not Be Moved*, was published in 1990. Her writing often focuses on significant moments in her life—watching Momma confront a racist dentist; being hired as a streetcar conductor; and listening to the unforgettable speech delivered by the valedictorian, class of 1940, at Lafayette County Training School. The narrative essay "Graduation" describes the events leading up to that speech. As Angelou looks back on Henry Reed's words, she explains the extraordinary power they held for her and for other members of the black community.

1   The children in Stamps trembled visibly with anticipation. Some adults were excited too, but to be certain the whole young population had come down with graduation epidemic. Large classes were graduating from both the grammar school and the high school. Even those who were years removed from their own day of glorious release were anxious to help with preparations as a kind of dry run. The junior students who were moving into the vacating classes' chairs were tradition-bound to show their talents

for leadership and management. They strutted through the school and around the campus exerting pressure on the lower grades. Their authority was so new that occasionally if they pressed a little too hard it had to be overlooked. After all, next term was coming, and it never hurt a sixth grader to have a play sister in the eighth grade, or a tenth-year student to be able to call a twelfth grader Bubba. So all was endured in a spirit of shared understanding. But the graduating classes themselves were the nobility. Like travelers with exotic destinations on their minds, the graduates were remarkably forgetful. They came to school without their books, or tablets or even pencils. Volunteers fell over themselves to secure replacements for the missing equipment. When accepted, the willing workers might or might not be thanked, and it was of no importance to the pre-graduation rites. Even teachers were respectful of the now quiet and aging seniors, and tended to speak to them, if not as equals, as beings only slightly lower than themselves. After tests were returned and grades given, the student body, which acted like an extended family, knew who did well, who excelled, and what piteous ones had failed.

2   Unlike the white high school, Lafayette County Training School distinguished itself by having neither lawn, nor hedges, nor tennis court, nor climbing ivy. Its two buildings (main classrooms, the grade school and home economics) were set on a dirt hill with no fence to limit either its boundaries or those of bordering farms. There was a large expanse to the left of the school which was used alternately as a baseball diamond or a basketball court. Rusty hoops on the swaying poles represented the permanent recreational equipment, although bats and balls could be borrowed from the P.E. teacher if the borrower was qualified and if the diamond wasn't occupied.

3   Over this rocky area relieved by a few shady tall persimmon trees the graduating class walked. The girls often held hands and no longer bothered to speak to the lower students. There was a sadness about them, as if this old world was not their home and they were bound for higher ground. The boys, on the other hand, had become more friendly, more outgoing. A decided change from the closed attitude they projected while studying for finals. Now they seemed not ready to give up the old school, the familiar paths and classrooms. Only a small percentage would be continuing on to college—one of the South's A & M (agricultural and mechanical) schools, which trained Negro youths to be carpenters, farmers, handymen, masons, maids, cooks and baby nurses. Their future rode heavily on their shoulders, and blinded them to the collective joy that had pervaded the lives of the boys and girls in the grammar school graduating class.

4   Parents who could afford it had ordered new shoes and ready-made clothes for themselves from Sears and Roebuck or Montgomery Ward. They also engaged the best seamstresses to make the floating graduating dresses

and to cut down secondhand pants which would be pressed to a military slickness for the important event.

5   Oh, it was important, all right. Whitefolks would attend the ceremony, and two or three would speak of God and home, and the Southern way of life, and Mrs. Parsons, the principal's wife, would play the graduation march while the lower-grade graduates paraded down the aisles and took their seats below the platform. The high school seniors would wait in empty classrooms to make their dramatic entrance.

6   In the Store I was the person of the moment. The birthday girl. The center. Bailey had graduated the year before, although to do so he had had to forfeit all pleasures to make up for his time lost in Baton Rouge.

7   My class was wearing butter-yellow piqué dresses, and Momma launched out on mine. She smocked the yoke into tiny crisscrossing puckers, then shirred the rest of the bodice. Her dark fingers ducked in and out of the lemony cloth as she embroidered raised daisies around the hem. Before she considered herself finished she had added a crocheted cuff on the puff sleeves, and a pointy crocheted collar.

8   I was going to be lovely. A walking model of all the various styles of fine hand sewing and it didn't worry me that I was only twelve years old and merely graduating from the eighth grade. Besides, many teachers in Arkansas Negro schools had only that diploma and were licensed to impart wisdom.

9   The days had become longer and more noticeable. The faded beige of former times had been replaced with strong and sure colors. I began to see my classmate's clothes, their skin tones, and the dust that waved off pussy willows. Clouds that lazed across the sky were objects of great concern to me. Their shiftier shapes might have held a message that in my new happiness and with a little bit of time I'd soon decipher. During that period I looked at the arch of heaven so religiously my neck kept a steady ache. I had taken to smiling more often, and my jaws hurt from the unaccustomed activity. Between the two physical sore spots, I suppose I could have been uncomfortable, but that was not the case. As a member of the winning team (the graduating class of 1940) I had outdistanced unpleasant sensations by miles. I was headed for the freedom of open fields.

10   Youth and social approval allied themselves with me and we trammeled memories of slights and insults. The wind of our swift passage remodeled my features. Lost tears were pounded to mud and then to dust. Years of withdrawal were brushed aside and left behind, as hanging ropes of parasitic moss.

11   My work alone had awarded me a top place and I was going to be one of the first called in the graduating ceremonies. On the classroom blackboard, as well as on the bulletin board in the auditorium, there were blue stars and white stars and red stars. No absences, no tardinesses, and my academic work was among the best of the year. I could say the preamble to the Constitution even faster than Bailey. We timed ourselves often:

"WethepeopleoftheUnitedStatesinordertoformamoreperfectunion . . ." I had memorized the Presidents of the United States from Washington to Roosevelt in chronological as well as alphabetical order.

12   My hair pleased me too. Gradually the black mass had lengthened and thickened, so that it kept at last to its braided pattern, and I didn't have to yank my scalp off when I tried to comb it.

13   Louise and I had rehearsed the exercises until we tired out ourselves. Henry Reed was class valedictorian. He was a small, very black boy with hooded eyes, a long, broad nose and an oddly shaped head. I had admired him for years because each term he and I vied for the best grades in our class. Most often he bested me, but instead of being disappointed, I was pleased that we shared top places between us. Like many Southern black children, he lived with his grandmother, who was as strict as Momma and as kind as she knew how to be. He was courteous, respectful and soft-spoken to elders, but on the playground he chose to play the roughest games. I admired him. Anyone, I reckoned, sufficiently afraid or sufficiently dull could be polite. But to be able to operate at a top level with both adults and children was admirable.

14   His valedictory speech was entitled "To Be or Not to Be." The rigid tenth-grade teacher had helped him write it. He'd been working on the dramatic stresses for months.

15   The weeks until graduation were filled with heady activities. A group of small children were to be presented in a play about buttercups and daisies and bunny rabbits. They could be heard throughout the building practicing their hops and their little songs that sounded like silver bells. The older girls (non-graduates, of course) were assigned the task of making refreshments for the night's festivities. A tangy scent of ginger, cinnamon, nutmeg and chocolate wafted around the home economics building as the budding cooks made samples for themselves and their teachers.

16   In every corner of the workshop, axes and saws split fresh timber as the woodshop boys made sets and stage scenery. Only the graduates were left out of the general bustle. We were free to sit in the library at the back of the building or look in quite detachedly, naturally, on the measures being taken for our event.

17   Even the minister preached on graduation the Sunday before. His subject was, "Let your light so shine that men will see your good works and praise your Father, Who is in Heaven." Although the sermon was purported to be addressed to us, he used the occasion to speak to backsliders, gamblers and general ne'er-do-wells. But since he had called our names at the beginning of the service we were mollified.

18   Among Negroes the tradition was to give presents to children going only from one grade to another. How much more important this was when the person was graduating at the top of the class. Uncle Willie and Momma had sent away for a Mickey Mouse watch like Bailey's. Louise gave me four

embroidered handkerchiefs. (I gave her three crocheted doilies.) Mrs. Sneed, the minister's wife, made me an underskirt to wear for graduation, and nearly every customer gave me a nickel or maybe even a dime with the instruction "Keep on moving to higher ground," or some such encouragement.

19   Amazingly the great day finally dawned and I was out of bed before I knew it. I threw open the back door to see it more clearly, but Momma said, "Sister, come away from that door and put your robe on."

20   I hoped the memory of that morning would never leave me. Sunlight was itself still young, and the day had none of the insistence maturity would bring it in a few hours. In my robe and barefoot in the backyard, under cover of going to see about my new beans, I gave myself up to the gentle warmth and thanked God that no matter what evil I had done in my life He had allowed me to live to see this day. Somewhere in my fatalism I had expected to die, accidentally, and never have the chance to walk up the stairs in the auditorium and gracefully receive my hard-earned diploma. Out of God's merciful bosom I had won reprieve.

21   Bailey came out in his robe and gave me a box wrapped in Christmas paper. He said he had saved his money for months to pay for it. It felt like a box of chocolates, but I knew Bailey wouldn't save money to buy candy when we had all we could want under our noses.

22   He was as proud of the gifts as I. It was a soft-leather-bound copy of a collection of poems by Edgar Allan Poe, or, as Bailey and I called him, "Eap." I turned to "Annabel Lee" and we walked up and down the garden rows, the cool dirt between our toes, reciting the beautifully sad lines.

23   Momma made a Sunday breakfast although it was only Friday. After we finished the blessing, I opened my eyes to find the watch on my plate. It was a dream of a day. Everything went smoothly and to my credit. I didn't have to be reminded or scolded for anything. Near evening I was too jittery to attend to chores, so Bailey volunteered to do all before his bath.

24   Days before, we had made a sign for the Store, and as we turned out the lights Momma hung the cardboard over the doorknob. It read clearly: CLOSED. GRADUATION.

25   My dress fitted perfectly and everyone said that I looked like a sunbeam in it. On the hill, going toward the school, Bailey walked behind with Uncle Willie, who muttered, "Go on, Ju." He wanted him to walk ahead with us because it embarrassed him to have to walk so slowly. Bailey said he'd let the ladies walk together, and the men would bring up the rear. We all laughed, nicely.

26   Little children dashed by out of the dark like fireflies. Their crepe paper dresses and butterfly wings were not made for running and we heard more than one rip, dryly, and the regretful "uh uh" that followed.

27   The school blazed without gaiety. The windows seemed cold and un-friendly from the lower hill. A sense of ill-fated timing crept over me, and if Momma hadn't reached for my hand I would have drifted back to Bailey

and Uncle Willie, and possibly beyond. She made a few slow jokes about my feet getting cold, and tugged me along to the now-strange building.

28   Around the front steps, assurance came back. There were my fellow "greats," the graduating class. Hair brushed back, legs oiled, new dresses and pressed pleats, fresh pocket handkerchiefs and little handbags, all home-sewn. Oh, we were up to snuff, all right. I joined my comrades and didn't even see my family go in to find seats in the crowded auditorium.

29   The school band struck up a march and all classes filed in as had been rehearsed. We stood in front of our seats, as assigned, and on a signal from the choir director, we sat. No sooner had this been accomplished than the band started to play the national anthem. We rose again and sang the song, after which we recited the pledge of allegiance. We remained standing for a brief minute before the choir director and the principal signaled to us, rather desperately I thought, to take our seats. The command was so unusual that our carefully rehearsed and smooth-running machine was thrown off. For a full minute we fumbled for our chairs and bumped into each other awkwardly. Habits change or solidify under pressure, so in our state of nervous tension we had been ready to follow our usual assembly pattern: the American national anthem, then the pledge of allegiance, then the song every Black person I knew called the Negro National Anthem. All done in the same key, with the same passion and most often standing on the same foot.

30   Finding my seat at last, I was overcome with a presentiment of worse things to come. Something unrehearsed, unplanned, was going to happen, and we were going to be made to look bad. I distinctly remember being explicit in the choice of pronoun. It was "we," the graduating class, the unit, that concerned me then.

31   The principal welcomed "parents and friends" and asked the Baptist min-ister to lead us in prayer. His invocation was brief and punchy, and for a second I thought we were getting back on the high road to right action. When the principal came back to the dais, however, his voice had changed. Sounds always affected me profoundly and the principal's voice was one of my favorites. During assembly it melted and lowed weakly into the audience. It had not been in my plan to listen to him, but my curiosity was piqued and I straightened up to give him my attention.

32   He was talking about Booker T. Washington, our "late great leader," who said we can be as close as the fingers on the hand, etc. . . . Then he said a few vague things about friendship and the friendship of kindly people to those less fortunate than themselves. With that his voice nearly faded, thin, away. Like a river diminishing to a stream and then to a trickle. But he cleared his throat and said, "Our speaker tonight, who is also our friend, came from Texarkana to deliver the commencement address, but due to the irregularity of the train schedule, he's going to, as they say, 'speak and run.' " He said that we understood and wanted the man to know that we were

most grateful for the time he was able to give us and then something about how we were willing always to adjust to another's program, and without more ado—"I give you Mr. Edward Donleavy."

33   Not one but two white men came through the door offstage. The shorter one walked to the speaker's platform, and the tall one moved over to the center seat and sat down. But that was our principal's seat, and already occupied. The dislodged gentleman bounced around for a long breath or two before the Baptist minister gave him his chair, then with more dignity than the situation deserved, the minister walked off the stage.

34   Donleavy looked at the audience once (on reflection, I'm sure that he wanted only to reassure himself that we were really there), adjusted his glasses and began to read from a sheaf of papers.

35   He was glad "to be here and to see the work going on just as it was in the other schools."

36   At the first "Amen" from the audience I willed the offender to immediate death by choking on the word. But Amens and Yes, sir's began to fall around the room like rain through a ragged umbrella.

37   He told us of the wonderful changes we children in Stamps had in store. The Central School (naturally, the white school was Central) had already been granted improvements that would be in use in the fall. A well-known artist was coming from Little Rock to teach art to them. They were going to have the newest microscopes and chemistry equipment for their laboratory. Mr. Donleavy didn't leave us long in the dark over who made these improvements available to Central High. Nor were we to be ignored in the general betterment scheme he had in mind.

38   He said that he had pointed out to people at a very high level that one of the first-line football tacklers at Arkansas Agricultural and Mechanical College had graduated from good old Lafayette County Training School. Here fewer Amen's were heard. Those few that did break through lay dully in the air with the heaviness of habit.

39   He went on to praise us. He went on to say how he had bragged that "one of the best basketball players at Fisk sank his first ball right here at Lafayette County Training School."

40   The white kids were going to have a chance to become Galileos and Madame Curies and Edisons and Gauguins, and our boys (the girls weren't even in on it) would try to be Jesse Owenses and Joe Louises.

41   Owens and the Brown Bomber were great heroes in our world, but what school official in the white-goddom of Little Rock had the right to decide that those two men must be our only heroes? Who decided that for Henry Reed to become a scientist he had to work like George Washington Carver, as a bootblack, to buy a lousy microscope? Bailey was obviously always going to be too small to be an athlete, so which concrete angel glued to what country seat had decided that if my brother wanted to become a lawyer

he had to first pay penance for his skin by picking cotton and hoeing corn and studying correspondence books at night for twenty years?

42   The man's dead words fell like bricks around the auditorium and too many settled in my belly. Constrained by hard-learned manners I couldn't look behind me, but to my left and right the proud graduating class of 1940 had dropped their heads. Every girl in my row had found something new to do with her handkerchief. Some folded the tiny squares into love knots, some into triangles, but most were wadding them, then pressing them flat on their yellow laps.

43   On the dais, the ancient tragedy was being replayed. Professor Parsons sat, a sculptor's reject, rigid. His large, heavy body seemed devoid of will or willingness, and his eyes said he was no longer with us. The other teachers examined the flag (which was draped stage right) or their notes, or the windows which opened on our now-famous playing diamond.

44   Graduation, the hush-hush magic time of frills and gifts and congratulations and diplomas, was finished for me before my name was called. The accomplishment was nothing. The meticulous maps, drawn in three colors of ink, learning and spelling decasyllabic words, memorizing the whole of *The Rape of Lucrece*—it was for nothing. Donleavy had exposed us.

45   We were maids and farmers, handymen and washerwomen, and anything higher that we aspired to was farcical and presumptuous.

46   Then I wished that Gabriel Prosser and Nat Turner had killed all white-folks in their beds and that Abraham Lincoln had been assassinated before the signing of the Emancipation Proclamation, and that Harriet Tubman had been killed by that blow on her head and Christopher Columbus had drowned in the *Santa Maria*.

47   It was awful to be Negro and have no control over my life. It was brutal to be young and already trained to sit quietly and listen to charges brought against my color with no chance of defense. We should all be dead. I thought I should like to see us all dead, one on top of the other. A pyramid of flesh with the whitefolks on the bottom, as the broad base, then the Indians with their silly tomahawks and tepees and wigwams and treaties, the Negroes with their mops and recipes and cotton sacks and spirituals sticking out of their mouths. The Dutch children should all stumble in their wooden shoes and break their necks. The French should choke to death on the Louisiana Purchase (1803) while silkworms ate all the Chinese with their stupid pigtails. As a species, we were an abomination. All of us.

48   Donleavy was running for election, and assured our parents that if he won we could count on having the only colored paved playing field in that part of Arkansas. Also—he never looked up to acknowledge the grunts of acceptance—also, we were bound to get some new equipment for the home economics building and the workshop.

49   He finished, and since there was no need to give any more than the most perfunctory thank-you's, he nodded to the men on the stage, and the tall

white man who was never introduced joined him at the door. They left with the attitude that now they were off to something really important. (The graduation ceremonies at Lafayette County Training School had been a mere preliminary.)

50 The ugliness they left was palpable. An uninvited guest who wouldn't leave. The choir was summoned and sang a modern arrangement of "Onward, Christian Soldiers," with new words pertaining to graduates seeking their place in the world. But it didn't work. Elouise, the daughter of the Baptist minister, recited "Invictus," and I could have cried at the impertinence of "I am the master of my fate, I am the captain of my soul."

51 My name had lost its ring of familiarity and I had to be nudged to go and receive my diploma. All my preparations had fled. I neither marched up to the stage like a conquering Amazon, nor did I look in the audience for Bailey's nod of approval. Marguerite Johnson, I heard the name again, my honors were read, there were noises in the audience of appreciation, and I took my place on the stage as rehearsed.

52 I thought about colors I hated: ecru, puce, lavender, beige and black.

53 There was shuffling and rustling around me, then Henry Reed was giving his valedictory address, "To Be or Not to Be." Hadn't he heard the whitefolks? We couldn't *be*, so the question was a waste of time. Henry's voice came clear and strong. I feared to look at him. Hadn't he got the message? There was no "nobler in the mind" for Negroes because the world didn't think we had minds, and they let us know it. "Outrageous fortune"? Now, that was a joke. When the ceremony was over I had to tell Henry Reed some things. That is, if I still cared. Not "rub," Henry, "erase." "Ah, there's the erase." Us.

54 Henry had been a good student in elocution. His voice rose on tides of promise and fell on waves of warnings. The English teacher had helped him to create a sermon winging through Hamlet's soliloquy. To be a man, a doer, a builder, a leader, or to be a tool, an unfunny joke, a crusher of funky toadstools. I marveled that Henry could go through the speech as if we had a choice.

55 I had been listening and silently rebutting each sentence with my eyes closed; then there was a hush, which in an audience warns that something unplanned is happening. I looked up and saw Henry Reed, the conservative, the proper, the A student, turn his back to the audience and turn to us (the proud graduating class of 1940) and sing, nearly speaking,

> Lift ev'ry voice and sing
> Till earth and heaven ring
> Ring with the harmonies of Liberty . . .[1]

[1]"Lift Ev'ry Voice and Sing"—words by James Weldon Johnson and music by J. Rosamond Johnson. Copyright by Edward B. Marks Music Corporation. Used by permission.

It was the poem written by James Weldon Johnson. It was the music composed by J. Rosamond Johnson. It was the Negro national anthem. Out of habit we were singing it.

56 Our mothers and fathers stood in the dark hall and joined the hymn of encouragement. A kindergarten teacher led the small children onto the stage and the buttercups and daisies and bunny rabbits marked time and tried to follow:

> Stony the road we trod
> Bitter the chastening rod
> Felt in the days when hope, unborn, had died.
> Yet with a steady beat
> Have not our weary feet
> Come to the place for which our fathers sighed?

57 Every child I knew had learned that song with his ABC's and along with "Jesus Loves Me This I Know." But I personally had never heard it before. Never heard the words, despite the thousands of times I had sung them. Never thought they had anything to do with me.

58 On the other hand, the words of Patrick Henry had made such an impression on me that I had been able to stretch myself tall and trembling and say, "I know not what course others may take, but as for me, give me liberty or give me death."

59 And now I heard, really for the first time:

> We have come over a way that with tears has been watered,
> We have come, treading our path through the blood of the slaughtered.

60 While echoes of the song shivered in the air, Henry Reed bowed his head, said "Thank you," and returned to his place in the line. The tears that slipped down many faces were not wiped away in shame.

61 We were on top again. As always, again. We survived. The depths had been icy and dark, but now a bright sun spoke to our souls. I was no longer simply a member of the proud graduating class of 1940; I was a proud member of the wonderful beautiful Negro race.

Topics for Writing and Discussion

1. What is the title of Henry Reed's speech? How does the title become increasingly significant—and ironic—as Mr. Donleavy speaks and as Henry responds to that speech?

2. How does Marguerite respond when her name is called to receive her diploma? How does her response differ from the way she had imagined

herself at that moment? What caused the change between the expectation and the reality?

3.   The essay is titled "Graduation in Stamps," but the first half describes preparation for the ceremony rather than the event itself. Why does Angelou spend so much time explaining her own anticipation and the deep involvement of the community in the eighth-grade commencement? Look carefully at the incidents she describes in the first part of the narrative. How do they contribute to the significance of the events at the graduation?

4.   In narrative writing, authors usually arrange events in chronological order as they build toward the significant point of their essay. Notice the words and phrases Angelou uses to give us the sense of time passing. How does the time structure contribute to the tone of building excitement?

5.   The narrator, Marguerite, is profoundly changed by her experience at graduation. Describe an event that changed the way you think about yourself (or about others). Keep the essay "Graduation in Stamps" in mind as you write; develop a narrative that will show both the details of the event and the way they affected you.

Martin Gansberg (NYT Pictures)

38 Who Saw Murder Didn't Call the Police

Martin Gansberg
(1920–   )

After a career with the *New York Times* spanning four decades, Martin Gansberg retired in 1985. He began at the *Times* in 1942 as a copy boy and over the following years held a variety of positions, ranging from reporter to copy editor and editorial assistant. Gansberg's writing has also been featured in numerous magazines. "38 Who Saw Murder Didn't Call the Police," his coverage of the highly publicized murder of Kitty Genovese in 1964, is widely acclaimed as a powerful journalistic portrait of citizens who witnessed a crime but "didn't want to get involved."

1   For more than half an hour 38 respectable, law-abiding citizens in Queens watched a killer stalk and stab a woman in three separate attacks in Kew Gardens.

2   Twice the sound of their voices and the sudden glow of their bedroom lights interrupted him and frightened him off. Each time he returned, sought her out and stabbed her again. Not one person telephoned the police during the assault; one witness called after the woman was dead.

3   That was two weeks ago today. But Assistant Chief Inspector Frederick M. Lussen, in charge of the borough's detectives and a veteran of 25 years of homicide investigations, is still shocked.

4   He can give a matter-of-fact recitation of many murders. But the Kew Gardens slaying baffles him—not because it is a murder, but because the "good people" failed to call the police.

5   "As we have reconstructed the crime," he said, "the assailant had three chances to kill this woman during a 35-minute period. He returned twice

to complete the job. If we had been called when he first attacked, the woman might not be dead now."

6   This is what the police say happened beginning at 3:20 A.M. in the staid, middle-class, tree-lined Austin Street area:

7   Twenty-eight-year-old Catherine Genovese, who was called Kitty by almost everyone in the neighborhood, was returning home from her job as manager of a bar in Hollis. She parked her red Fiat in a lot adjacent to the Kew Gardens Long Island Rail Road Station, facing Mowbray Place. Like many residents of the neighborhood, she had parked there day after day since her arrival from Connecticut a year ago, although the railroad frowns on the practice.

8   She turned off the lights of her car, locked the door and started to walk the 100 feet to the entrance of her apartment at 82–70 Austin Street, which is in a Tudor building, with stores on the first floor and apartments on the second.

9   The entrance to the apartment is in the rear of the building because the front is rented to retail stores. At night the quiet neighborhood is shrouded in the slumbering darkness that marks most residential areas.

10   Miss Genovese noticed a man at the far end of the lot, near a seven-story apartment house at 82–40 Austin Street. She halted. Then, nervously, she headed up Austin Street toward Lefferts Boulevard, where there is a call box to the 102nd Police Precinct in nearby Richmond Hill.

"HE STABBED ME"

11   She got as far as a street light in front of a bookstore before the man grabbed her. She screamed. Lights went on in the 10-story apartment house at 82–67 Austin Street, which faces the bookstore. Windows slid open and voices punctuated the early-morning stillness.

12   Miss Genovese screamed: "Oh, my God, he stabbed me! Please help me! Please help me!"

13   From one of the upper windows in the apartment house, a man called down: "Let that girl alone!"

14   The assailant looked up at him, shrugged and walked down Austin Street toward a white sedan parked a short distance away. Miss Genovese struggled to her feet.

15   Lights went out. The killer returned to Miss Genovese, now trying to make her way around the side of the building by the parking lot to get to her apartment. The assailant stabbed her again.

16   "I'm dying!" she shrieked. "I'm dying!"

A CITY BUS PASSED

17   Windows were opened again, and lights went on in many apartments. The assailant got into his car and drove away. Miss Genovese staggered to her

feet. A city bus, Q-10, the Lefferts Boulevard line to Kennedy International Airport, passed. It was 3:35 A.M.

18 The assailant returned. By then, Miss Genovese had crawled to the back of the building, where the freshly painted brown doors to the apartment house held out hope of safety. The killer tried the first door; she wasn't there. At the second door, 82–62 Austin Street, he saw her slumped on the floor at the foot of the stairs. He stabbed her a third time–fatally.

19 It was 3:50 by the time the police received their first call, from a man who was a neighbor of Miss Genovese. In two minutes they were at the scene. The neighbor, a 70-year-old woman and another woman were the only persons on the street. Nobody else came forward.

20 The man explained that he had called the police after much deliberation. He had phoned a friend in Nassau County for advice and then he had crossed the roof of the building to the apartment of the elderly woman to get her to make the call.

21 "I didn't want to get involved," he sheepishly told the police.

SUSPECT IS ARRESTED

22 Six days later, the police arrested Winston Moseley, a 29-year-old business-machine operator, and charged him with homicide. Moseley had no previous record. He is married, has two children and owns a home at 133–19 Sutter Avenue, South Ozone Park, Queens. On Wednesday, a court committed him to Kings County Hospital for psychiatric observation.

23 When questioned by the police, Moseley also said that he had slain Mrs. Annie May Johnson, 24, of 146–12 133d Avenue, Jamaica, on Feb. 29 and Barbara Kralik, 15, of 174–17 140th Avenue, Springfield Gardens, last July. In the Kralik case, the police are holding Alvin L. Mitchell, who is said to have confessed that slaying.

24 The police stressed how simple it would have been to have gotten in touch with them. "A phone call," said one of the detectives, "would have done it." The police may be reached by dialing "O" for operator or SPring 7–3100. . . .

25 Today witnesses from the neighborhood, which is made up of one-family homes in the $35,000 to $60,000 range with the exception of the two apartment houses near the railroad station, find it difficult to explain why they didn't call the police. . . .

26 A housewife, knowingly if quite casually, said, "We thought it was a lover's quarrel." A husband and wife both said, "Frankly, we were afraid." They seemed aware of the fact that events might have been different. A distraught woman, wiping her hands in her apron, said, "I didn't want my husband to get involved."

27 One couple, now willing to talk about that night, said they heard the first screams. The husband looked thoughtfully at the bookstore where the killer first grabbed Miss Genovese.

28   "We went to the window to see what was happening," he said, "but the light from our bedroom made it difficult to see the street." The wife, still apprehensive, added: "I put out the light and we were able to see better."

29   Asked why they hadn't called the police, she shrugged and replied: "I don't know."

30   A man peeked out from a slight opening in the doorway to his apartment and rattled off an account of the killer's second attack. Why hadn't he called the police at the time? "I was tired," he said without emotion. "I went back to bed."

31   It was 4:25 A.M. when the ambulance arrived to take the body of Miss Genovese. It drove off. "Then," a solemn police detective said, "the people came out."

Topics for Writing and Discussion

1.   How does Gansberg realistically recreate the murder scene? Cite some examples of details that help readers see the people and events of this narrative.

2.   Does Gansberg remain consistently objective in his reporting? What was Gansberg's purpose in telling this story the way he did?

3.   Evaluate the first and last paragraphs of this narrative. What effects is Gansberg trying to achieve? Is he successful? What does his use of dialogue add to this story?

4.   This selection originally appeared in a newspaper. In what ways does this news story differ from an essay? Do you think this story would have been as powerful had it been written as an editorial?

5.   Have you ever been a victim of or a witness to a crime? Write a narrative that describes the crime and your reaction to it. If you were the victim, did others come to your aid? If you were a bystander, did you become involved? Do you, in retrospect, believe you made the right decision? Consider directing your essay to others who may someday find themselves in your position.

Alice Walker (Jeff Reinking/Picture Group)

Beauty: When the Other Dancer Is the Self

Alice Walker
(1944–   )

Alice Walker was the youngest of the eight
children born to Willie Lee and Minnie Grant
Walker. The Walkers worked as sharecroppers in
Georgia, and the author's early years inform both
her fiction and nonfiction. Following her
graduation from Sarah Lawrence College in New
York, Walker worked for civil rights, teaching in
Head Start programs and registering black voters.
A poet, essayist, and scholar, she has achieved
recognition for her work as editor of an anthology
of Zora Neale Hurston's writings (*I Love Myself
When I Am Laughing,* 1979) and as a contributing
editor to *Ms.* magazine. She is best known for her
fiction, particularly her novel *The Color Purple,*
which won the Pulitzer Prize in 1982 and was later
made into a popular film. Her most recent novel,
The Temple of My Familiar, was published in 1989,
and in 1991 she published a collection of poetry,
*Her Blue Body Everything We Know: Earthling Poems,
1965–1990.*

1   It is a bright summer day in 1947. My father, a fat, funny man with
beautiful eyes and a subversive wit, is trying to decide which of his eight
children he will take with him to the county fair. My mother, of course, will
not go. She is knocked out from getting most of us ready: I hold my neck
stiff against the pressure of her knuckles as she hastily completes the braiding
and then beribboning of my hair.

2   My father is the driver for the rich old white lady up the road. Her name is Miss Mey. She owns all the land for miles around, as well as the house in which we live. All I remember about her is that she once offered to pay my mother thirty-five cents for cleaning her house, raking up piles of her magnolia leaves, and washing her family's clothes, and that my mother— she of no money, eight children, and a chronic earache—refused it. But I do not think of this in 1947. I am two and a half years old. I want to go everywhere my daddy goes. I am excited at the prospect of riding in a car. Someone has told me fairs are fun. That there is room in the car for only three of us doesn't faze me at all. Whirling happily in my starchy frock, showing off my biscuit-polished patent-leather shoes and lavender socks, tossing my head in a way that makes my ribbons bounce, I stand, hands on hips, before my father. "Take me, Daddy," I say with assurance: "I'm the prettiest!"

3   Later, it does not surprise me to find myself in Miss Mey's shiny black car, sharing the back seat with the other lucky ones. Does not surprise me that I thoroughly enjoy the fair. At home that night I tell the unlucky ones all I can remember about the merry-go-round, the man who eats live chickens, and the teddy bears, until they say: that's enough, baby Alice. Shut up now, and go to sleep.

4   It is Easter Sunday, 1950. I am dressed in a green, flocked, scalloped-hem dress (handmade by my adoring sister, Ruth) that has its own smooth satin petticoat and tiny hot-pink roses tucked into each scallop. My shoes, new T-strap patent leather, again highly biscuit-polished. I am six years old and have learned one of the longest Easter speeches to be heard that day, totally unlike the speech I said when I was two: "Easter lilies / pure and white / blossom in / the morning light." When I rise to give my speech I do so on a great wave of love and pride and expectation. People in the church stop rustling their new crinolines. They seem to hold their breath. I can tell they admire my dress, but it is my spirit, bordering on sassiness (womanishness), they secretly applaud.

5   "That girl's a little *mess*," they whisper to each other, pleased.

6   Naturally I say my speech without stammer or pause, unlike those who stutter, stammer, or, worst of all, forget. This is before the word "beautiful" exists in people's vocabulary, but "Oh, isn't she the *cutest* thing!" frequently floats my way. "And got so much sense!" they gratefully add . . . for which thoughtful addition I thank them to this day.

7   *It was great fun being cute. But then, one day, it ended.*

8   I am eight years old and a tomboy. I have a cowboy hat, cowboy boots, checkered shirt and pants, all red. My playmates are my brothers, two and four years older than I. Their colors are black and green, the only difference

in the way we are dressed. On Saturday nights we all go to the picture show, even my mother; Westerns are her favorite kind of movie. Back home, "on the ranch," we pretend we are Tom Mix, Hopalong Cassidy, Lash LaRue (we've even named one of our dogs Lash LaRue); we chase each other for hours rustling cattle, being outlaws, delivering damsels from distress. Then my parents decide to buy my brothers guns. These are not "real" guns. They shoot "BBs," copper pellets my brothers say will kill birds. Because I am a girl, I do not get a gun. Instantly I am relegated to the position of Indian. Now there appears a great distance between us. They shoot and shoot at everything with their new guns. I try to keep up with my bow and arrows.

9   One day while I am standing on top of our makeshift "garage"—pieces of tin nailed across some poles—holding my bow and arrow and looking out toward the fields, I feel an incredible blow in my right eye. I look down just in time to see my brother lower his gun.

10   Both brothers rush to my side. My eye stings, and I cover it with my hand. "If you tell," they say, "we will get a whipping. You don't want that to happen, do you?" I do not. "Here is a piece of wire," says the older brother, picking it up from the roof; "say you stepped on one end of it and the other flew up and hit you." The pain is beginning to start. "Yes," I say. "Yes, I will say that is what happened." If I do not say this is what happened, I know my brothers will find ways to make me wish I had. But now I will say anything that gets me to my mother.

11   Confronted by our parents we stick to the lie agreed upon. They place me on a bench on the porch and I close my left eye while they examine the right. There is a tree growing from underneath the porch that climbs past the railing to the roof. It is the last thing my right eye sees. I watch as its trunk, its branches, and then its leaves are blotted out by the rising blood.

12   I am in shock. First there is intense fever, which my father tries to break using lily leaves bound around my head. Then there are chills: my mother tries to get me to eat soup. Eventually, I do not know how, my parents learn what has happened. A week after the "accident" they take me to see a doctor. "Why did you wait so long to come?" he asks, looking into my eye and shaking his head. "Eyes are sympathetic," he says. "If one is blind, the other will likely become blind too."

13   This comment of the doctor's terrifies me. But it is really how I look that bothers me most. Where the BB pellet struck there is glob of whitish scar tissue, a hideous cataract, on my eye. Now when I stare at people—a favorite pastime, up to now—they will stare back. Not at the "cute" little girl, but at her scar. For six years I do not stare at anyone, because I do not raise my head.

14 Years later, in the throes of a mid-life crisis, I ask my mother and sister whether I changed after the "accident." "No," they say, puzzled. "What do you mean?"

15   *What do I mean?*

16   I am eight, and, for the first time, doing poorly in school, where I have been something of a whiz since I was four. We have just moved to the place where the "accident" occurred. We do not know any of the people around us because this is a different county. The only time I see the friends I knew is when we go back to our old church. The new school is the former state penitentiary. It is a large stone building, cold and drafty, crammed to overflowing with boisterous, ill-disciplined children. On the third floor there is a huge circular imprint of some partition that has been torn out.

17   "What used to be here?" I ask a sullen girl next to me on our way past it to lunch.

18   "The electric chair," says she.

19   At night I have nightmares about the electric chair, and about all the people reputedly "fried" in it. I am afraid of the school, where all the students seem to be budding criminals.

20   "What's the matter with your eye?" they ask, critically.

21   When I don't answer (I cannot decide whether it was an "accident" or not), they shove me, insist on a fight.

22   My brother, the one who created the story about the wire, comes to my rescue. But then brags so much about "protecting" me, I become sick.

23   After months of torture at the school, my parents decide to send me back to our old community, to my old school. I live with my grandparents and the teacher they board. But there is no room for Phoebe, my cat. By the time my grandparents decide there *is* room, and I ask for my cat, she cannot be found. Miss Yarborough, the boarding teacher, takes me under her wing, and begins to teach me to play the piano. But soon she marries an African— a "prince," she says—and is whisked away to his continent.

24   At my old school there is at least one teacher who loves me. She is the teacher who "knew me before I was born" and bought my first baby clothes. It is she who makes life bearable. It is her presence that finally helps me turn on the one child at the school who continually calls me "one-eyed bitch." One day I simply grab him by his coat and beat him until I am satisfied. It is my teacher who tells me my mother is ill.

25 My mother is lying in bed in the middle of the day, something I have never seen. She is in too much pain to speak. She has an abscess in her ear. I stand looking down on her, knowing that if she dies, I cannot live. She is being treated with warm oils and hot bricks held against her cheek. Finally a doctor comes. But I must go back to my grandparents' house. The weeks pass but I am hardly aware of it. All I know is that my mother might die, my father is not so jolly, my brothers still have their guns, and I am the one sent away from home.

26   "You did not change," they say.

27   *Did I imagine the anguish of never looking up?*

28 I am twelve. When relatives come to visit I hide in my room. My cousin Brenda, just my age, whose father works in the post office and whose mother is a nurse, comes to find me. "Hello," she says. And then she asks, looking at my recent school picture, which I did not want taken, and on which the "glob," as I think of it, is clearly visible. "You still can't see out of that eye?"

29 "No," I say, and flop back on the bed over my book.

30 That night, as I do almost every night, I abuse my eye. I rant and rave at it, in front of the mirror. I plead with it to clear up before morning. I tell it I hate and despise it. I do not pray for sight. I pray for beauty.

31 "You did not change," they say.

32 I am fourteen and baby-sitting for my brother Bill, who lives in Boston. He is my favorite brother and there is a strong bond between us. Understanding my feelings of shame and ugliness he and his wife take me to a local hospital, where the "glob" is removed by a doctor named O. Henry. There is still a small bluish crater where the scar tissue was, but the ugly white stuff is gone. Almost immediately I become a different person from the girl who does not raise her head. Or so I think. Now that I've raised my head I win the boyfriend of my dreams. Now that I've raised my head I have plenty of friends. Now that I've raised my head classwork comes from my lips as faultlessly as Easter speeches did, and I leave high school as valedictorian, most popular student, and *queen*, hardly believing my luck. Ironically, the girl who was voted most beautiful in our class (and was) was later shot twice through the chest by a male companion, using a "real" gun, while she was pregnant. But that's another story in itself. Or is it?

33 "You did not change," they say.

34 It is now thirty years since the "accident." A beautiful journalist comes to visit and to interview me. She is going to write a cover story for her magazine that focuses on my latest book. "Decide how you want to look on the cover," she says. "Glamorous, or whatever."

35 Never mind "glamorous," it is the "whatever" that I hear. Suddenly all I can think of is whether I will get enough sleep the night before the photography session: if I don't, my eye will be tired and wander, as blind eyes will.

36 At night in bed with my lover I think up reasons why I should not appear on the cover of a magazine. "My meanest critics will say I've sold out," I say. "My family will now realize I write scandalous books."

37 "But what's the real reason you don't want to do this?" he asks.

38 "Because in all probability," I say in a rush, "my eye won't be straight."

39 "It will be straight enough," he says. Then, "Besides, I thought you'd made your peace with that."

40 And I suddenly remember that I have.

41 *I remember:*

42   I am talking to my brother Jimmy, asking if he remembers anything unusual about the day I was shot. He does not know I consider that day the last time my father, with his sweet home remedy of cool lily leaves, chose me, and that I suffered and raged inside because of this. "Well," he says, "all I remember is standing by the side of the highway with Daddy, trying to flag down a car. A white man stopped, but when Daddy said he needed somebody to take his little girl to the doctor, he drove off."

43   *I remember:*

44   I am in the desert for the first time. I fall totally in love with it. I am so overwhelmed by its beauty, I confront for the first time, consciously, the meaning of the doctor's words years ago: "Eyes are sympathetic. If one is blind, the other will likely become blind too." I realize I have dashed about the world madly, looking at that, storing up images against the fading of the light. *But I might have missed seeing the desert!* The shock of that possibility—and gratitude for over twenty-five years of sight—sends me literally to my knees. Poem after poem comes—which is perhaps how poets pray.

On Sight

I am so thankful I have seen
The Desert
And the creatures in the desert
And the desert Itself.

The desert has its own moon
Which I have seen
With my own eye.

There is no flag on it.

Trees of the desert have arms
All of which are always up
That is because the moon is up
The sun is up
Also the sky
The stars
Clouds
None with flags.

If there *were* flags, I doubt
the trees would point.
Would you?

45   *But mostly, I remember this:*

46   I am twenty-seven, and my baby daughter is almost three. Since her birth, I have worried about her discovery that her mother's eyes are different from other people's. Will she be embarrassed? I think. What will she say? Every

day she watches a television program called "Big Blue Marble." It begins with a picture of the earth as it appears from the moon. It is bluish, a little battered-looking, but full of light, with whitish clouds swirling around it. Every time I see it I weep with love, as if it is a picture of Grandma's house. One day when I am putting Rebecca down for her nap, she suddenly focuses on my eye. Something inside me cringes, gets ready to try to protect myself. All children are cruel about physical differences, I know from experience, and that they don't always mean to be is another matter. I assume Rebecca will be the same.

47   But no-o-o-o. She studies my face intently as we stand, her inside and me outside her crib. She even holds my face maternally between her dimpled little hands. Then, looking every bit as serious and lawyerlike as her father, she says, as if it may just possibly have slipped my attention: "Mommy, there's a *world* in your eye." (As in, "Don't be alarmed, or do anything crazy.") And then, gently, but with great interest: "Mommy, where did you *get* that world in your eye?"

48   For the most part, the pain left then. (So what, if my brothers grew up to buy even more powerful pellet guns for their sons and to carry real guns themselves. So what, if a young "Morehouse man" once nearly fell off the steps of Trevos Arnett Library because he thought my eyes were blue.) Crying and laughing I ran to the bathroom, while Rebecca mumbled and sang herself off to sleep. Yes indeed, I realized, looking into the mirror. There *was* a world in my eye. And I saw that it was possible to love it: that in fact, for all it had taught me of shame and anger and inner vision, I *did* love it. Even to see it drifting out of orbit in boredom, or rolling up out of fatigue, not to mention floating back at attention in excitement (bearing witness, a friend has called it), deeply suitable to my personality, and even characteristic of me.

49   That night I dream I am dancing to Stevie Wonder's song "Always" (the name of the song is really "As," but I hear it as "Always"). As I dance, whirling and joyous, happier than I've ever been in my life, another bright-faced dancer joins me. We dance and kiss each other and hold each other through the night. The other dancer has obviously come through all right, as I have done. She is beautiful, whole and free. And she is also me.

Topics for Writing and Discussion

1.   In this essay, Walker uses a series of short narratives to describe the path she took as she moved toward realizing her own worth. List the narratives, noting particularly the people who are central to each story. How does each person cause Walker to question or to affirm herself?

2.   Near the end of the essay, Walker's daughter Rebecca says, "Mommy, there's a *world* in your eye." What does she mean? What meanings does

Walker derive from her daughter's comment? How does this episode suggest the thesis of the essay?

3. A common structure for a narrative essay is straight chronological order, but Walker tells her story with many sudden jumps backward and forward in time. Identify these flashbacks and leaps ahead and explain how they affect the essay's meaning. Notice especially how this complicated time structure relates to the concluding paragraphs where Walker introduces a final series of memories with the repeated phrase, "I remember."

4. Read the next-to-last paragraph carefully and discuss how it helps to explain the relationship of the title to Walker's thesis.

5. Write a narrative essay focusing on a frightening event in your childhood. You may want to experiment with Walker's technique of moving back and forth from far past, to present, to more recent past, and back to present. Be sure to provide clear transitions, as Walker does, to show how the parts of your essay are related.

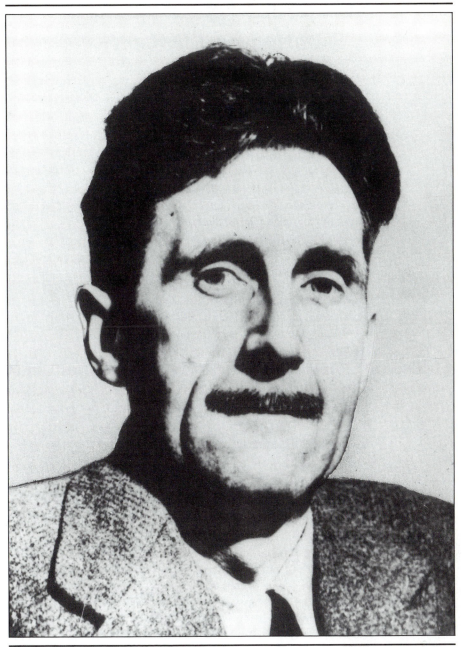

George Orwell (© Archive Photos)

Shooting an Elephant

George Orwell
(1903–1950)

George Orwell (a pen name for Eric Blair) served with the Indian imperial police in Burma after finishing his school years at Eton in England. His first novel, *Burmese Days,* reflects his experiences as a police official. When he left Burma in 1927, he returned to England and conducted a three-year study of poverty in London's East End. He recorded his observations in *Down and Out in Paris and London* (1933). In 1936, responding to his growing interest in socialism, he fought with the Loyalists in Spain. He is best known for *Animal Farm* (1945) and *1984* (1949), works that reflect his hatred of tyranny, his commitment to independence, and his sympathy for the oppressed. In "Shooting an Elephant" Orwell writes a narrative that raises profound questions about the relationship between those who hold authority and those over whom they have power.

1   In Moulmein, in lower Burma, I was hated by large numbers of people—the only time in my life that I have been important enough for this to happen to me. I was subdivisional police officer of the town, and in an aimless, petty kind of way anti-European feeling was very bitter. No one had the guts to raise a riot, but if a European woman went through the bazaars alone somebody would probably spit betel juice over her dress. As a police officer I was an obvious target and was baited whenever it seemed safe to do so. When a nimble Burman tripped me up on the football field and the referee (another Burman) looked the other way, the crowd yelled with hideous laughter. This happened more than once. In the end the sneering yellow

faces of young men that met me everywhere, the insults hooted after me when I was at a safe distance, got badly on my nerves. The young Buddhist priests were the worst of all. There were several thousands of them in the town and none of them seemed to have anything to do except stand on street corners and jeer at Europeans.

2   All this was perplexing and upsetting. For at that time I had already made up my mind that imperialism was an evil thing and the sooner I chucked up my job and got out of there the better. Theoretically—and secretly, of course—I was all for the Burmese and all against their oppressors, the British. As for the job I was doing, I hated it more bitterly than I can perhaps make clear. In a job like that you see the dirty work of Empire at close quarters. The wretched prisoners huddling in the stinking cages of the lock-ups, the gray, cowed faces of the long-term convicts, the scarred buttocks of the men who had been flogged with bamboos—all these oppressed me with an intolerable sense of guilt. But I could get nothing into perspective. I was young and ill educated and I had had to think out my problems in the utter silence that is imposed on every Englishman in the East. I did not even know that the British Empire is dying, still less did I know that it is a great deal better than the younger empires that are going to supplant it. All I knew was that I was stuck between my hatred of the empire I served and my rage against the evil-spirited little beasts who tried to make my job impossible. With one part of my mind I thought of the British Raj as an unbreakable tyranny, as something clamped down, in *saecula saeculorum,* upon the will of prostrate peoples; with another part I thought that the greatest joy in the world would be to drive a bayonet into a Buddhist priest's guts. Feelings like these are the normal by-products of imperialism; ask any Anglo-Indian official, if you can catch him off duty.

3   One day something happened which in a roundabout way was enlightening. It was a tiny incident in itself; but it gave me a better glimpse than I had had before of the real nature of imperialism—the real motives for which despotic governments act. Early one morning the sub-inspector at a police station the other end of the town rang me up on the 'phone and said that an elephant was ravaging the bazaar. Would I please come and do something about it? I did not know what I could do, but I wanted to see what was happening and I got on to a pony and started out. I took my rifle, an old .44 Winchester and much too small to kill an elephant, but I thought the noise might be useful *in terrorem.* Various Burmans stopped me on the way and told me about the elephant's doings. It was not, of course, a wild elephant, but a tame one which had gone "must." It had been chained up, as tame elephants always are when their attack of "must" is due, but on the previous night it had broken its chain and escaped. Its mahout, the only person who could manage it when it was in that state, had set out in pursuit, but had taken the wrong direction and was now twelve hours' journey away, and in the morning the elephant had suddenly reappeared in town. The

Burmese population had no weapons and were quite helpless against it. It had already destroyed somebody's bamboo hut, killed a cow and raided some fruit-stalls and devoured the stock; also it had met the municipal rubbish van and, when the driver jumped out and took to his heels, had turned the van over and inflicted violences upon it.

4   The Burmese sub-inspector and some Indian constables were waiting for me in the quarter where the elephant had been seen. It was a very poor quarter, a labyrinth of squalid bamboo huts, thatched with palm-leaf, winding all over a steep hillside. I remember that it was a cloudy, stuffy morning at the beginning of the rains. We began questioning the people as to where the elephant had gone and, as usual, failed to get any definite information. That is invariably the case in the East; a story always sounds clear enough at a distance, but the nearer you get to the scene of events the vaguer it becomes. Some of the people said that the elephant had gone in one direction, some said that he had gone in another, some professed not even to have heard of any elephant. I had almost made up my mind that the whole story was a pack of lies, when we heard yells a little distance away. There was a loud, scandalized cry of "Go away, child! Go away this instant!" and an old woman with a switch in her hand came round the corner of a hut, violently shooing away a crowd of naked children. Some more women followed, clicking their tongues and exclaiming; evidently there was something that the children ought not to have seen. I rounded the hut and saw a man's dead body sprawling in the mud. He was an Indian, a black Dravidian coolie, almost naked, and he could not have been dead many minutes. The people said that the elephant had come suddenly upon him round the corner of the hut, caught him with its trunk, put its foot on his back and ground him into the earth. This was the rainy season and the ground was soft, and his face had scored a trench a foot deep and a couple of yards long. He was lying on his belly with arms crucified and head sharply twisted to one side. His face was coated with mud, the eyes wide open, the teeth bared and grinning with an expression of unendurable agony. (Never tell me, by the way, that the dead look peaceful. Most of the corpses I have seen looked devilish.) The friction of the great beast's foot had stripped the skin from his back as neatly as one skins a rabbit. As soon as I saw the dead man I sent an orderly to a friend's house nearby to borrow an elephant rifle. I had already sent back the pony, not wanting it to go mad with fright and throw me if it smelt the elephant.

5   The orderly came back in a few minutes with a rifle and five cartridges, and meanwhile some Burmans had arrived and told us that the elephant was in the paddy fields below, only a few hundred yards away. As I started forward practically the whole population of the quarter flocked out of the houses and followed me. They had seen the rifle and were all shouting excitedly that I was going to shoot the elephant. They had not shown much interest in the elephant when he was merely ravaging their homes, but it

was different now that he was going to be shot. It was a bit of fun to them, as it would be to an English crowd; besides they wanted the meat. It made me vaguely uneasy. I had no intention of shooting the elephant—I had merely sent for the rifle to defend myself if necessary—and it is always unnerving to have a crowd following you. I marched down the hill, looking and feeling a fool, with the rifle over my shoulder and an ever-growing army of people jostling at my heels. At the bottom, when you got away from the huts, there was a metalled road and beyond that a miry waste of paddy fields a thousand yards across, not yet ploughed but soggy from the first rains and dotted with coarse grass. The elephant was standing eight yards from the road, his left side toward us. He took not the slightest notice of the crowd's approach. He was tearing up bunches of grass, beating them against his knees to clean them, and stuffing them into his mouth.

6   I had halted on the road. As soon as I saw the elephant I knew with perfect certainty that I ought not to shoot him. It is a serious matter to shoot a working elephant—it is comparable to destroying a huge and costly piece of machinery—and obviously one ought not to do it if it can possibly be avoided. And at that distance, peacefully eating, the elephant looked no more dangerous than a cow. I thought then and I think now that his attack of "must" was already passing off; in which case he would merely wander harmlessly about until the mahout came back and caught him. Moreover, I did not in the least want to shoot him. I decided that I would watch him for a little while to make sure that he did not turn savage again, and then go home.

7   But at that moment I glanced round at the crowd that had followed me. It was an immense crowd, two thousand at the least and growing every minute. It blocked the road for a long distance on either side. I looked at the sea of yellow faces above the garish clothes—faces all happy and excited over this bit of fun, all certain that the elephant was going to be shot. They were watching me as they would watch a conjurer about to perform a trick. They did not like me, but with the magical rifle in my hands I was momentarily worth watching. And suddenly I realized that I should have to shoot the elephant after all. The people expected it of me and I had got to do it; I could feel their two thousand wills pressing me forward, irresistibly. And it was at this moment, as I stood there with the rifle in my hands, that I first grasped the hollowness, the futility of the white man's dominion in the East. Here was I, the white man with his gun, standing in front of the unarmed native crowd—seemingly the leading actor of the piece; but in reality I was only an absurd puppet pushed to and fro by the will of those yellow faces behind. I perceived in this moment that when the white man turns tyrant it is his own freedom that he destroys. He becomes a sort of hollow, posing dummy, the conventionalized figure of a sahib. For it is the condition of his rule that he shall spend his life in trying to impress the "natives," and so in every crisis he has got to do what the "natives" expect

of him. He wears a mask, and his face grows to fit it. I had got to shoot the elephant. I had committed myself to doing it when I sent for the rifle. A sahib has got to act like a sahib; he has got to appear resolute, to know his own mind and do definite things. To come all that way, rifle in hand, with two thousand people marching at my heels, and then to trail feebly away, having done nothing—no, that was impossible. The crowd would laugh at me. And my whole life, every white man's life in the East, was one long struggle not to be laughed at.

8   But I did not want to shoot the elephant. I watched him beating his bunch of grass against his knees with that preoccupied grandmotherly air that elephants have. It seemed to me that it would be murder to shoot him. At that age I was not squeamish about killing animals, but I had never shot an elephant and never wanted to. (Somehow it always seems worse to kill a *large* animal.) Besides, there was the beast's owner to be considered. Alive, the elephant was worth at least a hundred pounds; dead, he would only be worth the value of his tusks, five pounds, possibly. But I had got to act quickly. I turned to some experienced-looking Burmans who had been there when we arrived, and asked them how the elephant had been behaving. They all said the same thing: he took no notice of you if you left him alone, but he might charge if you went too close to him.

9   It was perfectly clear to me what I ought to do. I ought to walk up to within, say, twenty-five yards of the elephant and test his behavior. If he charged, I could shoot; if he took no notice of me, it would be safe to leave him until the mahout came back. But also I knew that I was going to do no such thing. I was a poor shot with a rifle and the ground was soft mud into which one would sink at every step. If the elephant charged and I missed him, I should have about as much chance as a toad under a steamroller. But even then I was not thinking particularly of my own skin, only of the watchful yellow faces behind. For at that moment, with the crowd watching me, I was not afraid in the ordinary sense, as I would have been if I had been alone. A white man mustn't be frightened in front of "natives"; and so, in general, he isn't frightened. The sole thought in my mind was that if anything went wrong those two thousand Burmans would see me pursued, caught, trampled on, and reduced to a grinning corpse like that Indian up the hill. And if that happened it was quite probable that some of them would laugh. That would never do. There was only one alternative. I shoved the cartridges into the magazine and lay down on the road to get a better aim.

10   The crowd grew very still, and a deep, low, happy sigh, as of people who see the theater curtain go up at last, breathed from innumerable throats. They were going to have their bit of fun after all. The rifle was a beautiful German thing with cross-hair sights. I did not then know that in shooting an elephant one would shoot to cut an imaginary bar running from ear-hole to ear-hole. I ought, therefore, as the elephant was sideways on, to have

aimed straight at his ear-hole; actually I aimed several inches in front of this, thinking the brain would be further forward.

11   When I pulled the trigger I did not hear the bang or feel the kick—one never does when a shot goes home—but I heard the devilish roar of glee that went up from the crowd. In that instant, in too short a time, one would have thought, even for the bullet to get there, a mysterious, terrible change had come over the elephant. He neither stirred, nor fell, but every line of his body had altered. He looked suddenly stricken, shrunken, immensely old, as though the frightful impact of the bullet had paralyzed him without knocking him down. At last, after what seemed a long time—it might have been five seconds, I dare say—he sagged flabbily to his knees. His mouth slobbered. An enormous senility seemed to have settled upon him. One could have imagined him thousands of years old. I fired again into the same spot. At the second shot he did not collapse but climbed with desperate slowness to his feet and stood weakly upright, with legs sagging and head drooping. I fired a third time. That was the shot that did for him. You could see the agony of it jolt his whole body and knock the last remnant of strength from his legs. But in falling he seemed for a moment to rise, for as his hind legs collapsed beneath him he seemed to tower upward like a huge rock toppling, his trunk reaching skyward like a tree. He trumpeted, for the first and only time. And then down he came, his belly toward me, with a crash that seemed to shake the ground even where I lay.

12   I got up. The Burmans were already racing past me across the mud. It was obvious that the elephant would never rise again, but he was not dead. He was breathing very rhythmically with long rattling gasps, his great mound of a side painfully rising and falling. His mouth was wide open—I could see far down into caverns of pale pink throat. I waited a long time for him to die, but his breathing did not weaken. Finally I fired my two remaining shots into the spot where I thought his heart must be. The thick blood welled out of him like red velvet, but still he did not die. His body did not even jerk when the shots hit him, the tortured breathing continued without a pause. He was dying, very slowly and in great agony, but in some world remote from me where not even a bullet could damage him further. I felt that I had got to put an end to that dreadful noise. It seemed dreadful to see the great beast lying there, powerless to move and yet powerless to die, and not even to be able to finish him. I sent back for my small rifle and poured shot after shot into his heart and down his throat. They seemed to make no impression. The tortured gasps continued as steadily as the ticking of a clock.

13   In the end I could not stand it any longer and went away. I heard later that it took him half an hour to die. Burmans were bringing dahs and baskets even before I left, and I was told they had stripped his body almost to the bones by the afternoon.

14   Afterward, of course, there were endless discussions about the shooting of the elephant. The owner was furious, but he was only an Indian and could do nothing. Besides, legally I had done the right thing, for a mad elephant has to be killed, like a mad dog, if its owner fails to control it. Among the Europeans opinion was divided. The older men said I was right, the younger men said it was a damn shame to shoot an elephant for killing a coolie, because an elephant was worth more than any damn Coringhee coolie. And afterward I was very glad that the coolie had been killed; it put me legally in the right and it gave me a sufficient pretext for shooting the elephant. I often wondered whether any of the others grasped that I had done it solely to avoid looking a fool.

Topics for Writing and Discussion

1.   In the first sentence the narrator says he "was hated by large numbers of people." What evidence does he provide to support his contention? Do you find his examples convincing? Explain.

2.   At the end of the second paragraph, the narrator explains his ambivalence toward his job, the British Raj (sovereignty), and the Burmese people. How does the story of shooting the elephant explain his mixed feelings? After reading the narrative about the elephant do you understand his emotions more clearly? Do you have more sympathy for his situation?

3.   This narrative contrasts two deaths, the coolie's and the elephant's. Compare the descriptions of the two deaths. Which is given fuller treatment? What does the final paragraph contribute to the comparison?

4.   The narrator tells us that the events surrounding the shooting of the elephant were "enlightening." What exactly does he learn? Is this "lesson" the central idea of the essay? Or is Orwell's main point something else?

5.   The narrator describes the events in the essay as an older person looking back on an incident that happened earlier in his life. Choose an event that happened at least five years ago and write a narrative that shows both your actions and feelings at the time and your assessment of the incident now, as you view it retrospectively.

Writing Assignments for Chapter Three
Narration

1. In "Salvation" and "Shooting an Elephant" Langston Hughes and George Orwell tell about incidents in which they felt pressured to perform regrettable actions in an attempt to live up to the expectations of others—in Hughes' case, his aunt, and in Orwell's, the locals of Moulmein, Burma. Remember a time when you allowed yourself to be pressured by someone (a relative or friend, perhaps) into doing something that your conscience or better judgment rebelled against. You might think of this person as part of your audience and write a narrative explaining now what really happened then, making clear how you felt both during the event and afterward.

2. Think of a time when you did *not* give in to peer or family pressure. Tell the story of your determination and how you overcame the temptation to compromise your principles or beliefs.

3. In "The Discus Thrower" Richard Selzer narrates a series of descriptive episodes about his dying patient. These episodes appear almost as snapshots that, together, form a collage, a larger work that reveals the nature of the character Selzer is recreating. Think of an event or complex episode in your life and imitate Selzer's technique by narrating three or more short scenes that together capture the essence of the time or person you are presenting. Consider, for example, some of the important or even traumatic episodes of your life: a graduation, a move, a marriage or divorce, a competition or sporting event, or a serious illness. Remember that the narrative as a whole should be clearly unified through the scenes you are creating for the reader.

4. In "Graduation in Stamps" Maya Angelou narrates an incident that at first fills her with anger and bitterness but that ultimately gives her insight and pride. Recount an episode in your life that made you angry or upset before you finally realized an important lesson or value. Make your narrative as vivid as Angelou's by using clear, specific details that will help your readers see your responses to the event and its characters.

5. In "38 Who Saw Murder Didn't Call the Police" Martin Gansberg reports what happened to Kitty Genovese, but, in reality, he has another more important purpose: he exposes what *didn't* happen as a result of people's fear of involvement. Become an investigative reporter yourself and write an essay exposing the real nature of some crime in your community.

You might wish to read newspaper clippings or interview police officers or witnesses if available. Or, if you prefer, take another look at a crime that made national news that you feel needs additional scrutiny or more publicity. Such a crime could be an older one (Lizzie Borden and her infamous axe?) or a more recent one, such as the 1991 mass killing by a deranged man in a crowded cafeteria in Killeen, Texas. Have a clear purpose to your reporting as Gansberg did. (For example, a look at the well-publicized 1987 Lisa Steinberg case might permit you to say something about illegal adoption and its relationship to child abuse.)

6.   Almost all of us, at one time or another, have enormously disliked or even felt ashamed of some part of our body. This problematic feature may have been something we were born with or perhaps it was a result of an illness or of an accident, as in the case of Alice Walker's eye. In "Beauty: When the Other Dancer Is the Self" Walker eloquently explains how she came to terms with her problem, how she realized that she had "obviously come through all right." Narrate the story of how you (or perhaps a friend with a disability) came to a similar conclusion and accepted yourself, as did Walker, as someone who is "beautiful, whole and free." (If you wish, you might imagine as your audience someone who shares your problem and is looking to you for guidance.)

7.   In Orwell's essay "Shooting an Elephant" and Maya Angelou's "Graduation in Stamps" we see clear examples of racial prejudice at work. In Arkansas, young black students are lectured on their inferiority; in Burma, the British oppress the Burmese, with some of the Europeans believing that "an elephant was worth more than any damn Coringhee coolie." Narrate an incident of racial, ethnic, or gender-based prejudice you have experienced or witnessed, making clear to your readers the effect of this episode on you. Were you changed in any way after this incident?

Chapter Four

Description

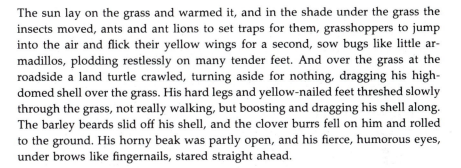

The sun lay on the grass and warmed it, and in the shade under the grass the insects moved, ants and ant lions to set traps for them, grasshoppers to jump into the air and flick their yellow wings for a second, sow bugs like little armadillos, plodding restlessly on many tender feet. And over the grass at the roadside a land turtle crawled, turning aside for nothing, dragging his high-domed shell over the grass. His hard legs and yellow-nailed feet threshed slowly through the grass, not really walking, but boosting and dragging his shell along. The barley beards slid off his shell, and the clover burrs fell on him and rolled to the ground. His horny beak was partly open, and his fierce, humorous eyes, under brows like fingernails, stared straight ahead.

The passage from John Steinbeck's *The Grapes of Wrath* illustrates a rhetorical structure called *description*. Description is used to tell how something looks, smells, sounds, feels, tastes, or behaves. It presents an impression or it indicates a mood, helping readers to visualize or understand ideas or concepts. In short, description relies on specific details sequenced carefully to produce a dominant impression. Steinbeck's well-known description of a turtle crossing a highway, "turning aside for nothing," presents a clear picture of determination, a slow but fierce tenacity.

Description is seldom used as an independent form of writing. Instead, it is usually combined with other rhetorical strategies to illustrate a point or to make an abstract idea more understandable. As you read Maxine Hong Kingston's "Portraits of My Parents," for example, you will see her masterful weaving of objective and subjective description, which combine to communicate the cultural differences of China and America.

Types of Description

Description can be classified as *objective* or *subjective*, though in your own writing you will probably use a combination of the two. Objective description is simply that, objective. It is factual, unaffected by the feelings or beliefs of the writer. The words used to portray something or someone objectively described are chosen for their denotations rather than their connotations. James Baldwin's description in "Stranger in the Village" contains many objective details:

> The village is very high, but it is only four hours from Milan and three from Lausanne. It is true that it is virtually unknown. Few people making plans for a holiday would elect to come here. On the other hand, the villagers are able, presumably, to come and go as they please—which they do: to another town at the foot of the mountain, with a population of approximately five thousand, the nearest place to see a movie or go to a bank. In the village there is no movie house, no bank, no library, no theater; very few radios, one jeep, one station wagon; and, at the moment one typewriter, mine, an invention which the woman next door to me here had never seen.

Though later in the essay his description moves to the subjective, the opening lines clearly and precisely describe the appearance of the village. However, a factual description need not be a sterile description. On the contrary, it could be quite vivid, graphic, as the Baldwin passage illustrates. If it stirs the emotions, however, it will do so solely because of the design of the sentences, not because of the connotations attached to the words of the sentences.

Subjective (or *impressionistic*) description, as the term implies, presents the impressions of the author. The words used may be suggestive, implicative. Subjective description relies on the creation of a *dominant impression*. Here, the selection of detail is crucial. The impression created is often the focal point of the writing. As you read the E. B. White essay "Once More to the Lake," you should notice that your attention is immediately drawn to the description of the camp. The opening paragraph also sets the *mood* of the description, and as the essay progresses, so does the suggestion of time and memory as they pertain to the camp on the lake.

Writing the Descriptive Essay

Though description is seldom used alone as a rhetorical structure, it can be used as a writing objective. The following advice should help you prepare an essay whose main purpose is to use description to make a point, illustrate a concept, or clarify an idea.

1. *Determine the purpose of the description.*
    Scientific papers, business reports, and proposals often include objective description. On the other hand, most personal or informal writing benefits from subjective description. The key is to determine which kind of language is appropriate for the writing task and audience.

2. *Carefully select details that will create a dominant impression.*
    Choose details that will focus the reader's attention on a particular impression or create for the reader a vivid general image; then use further details to expand the impression or image. Avoid, however, description that is too "busy," that is, one that contains too many different images. Omit details that could detract from your impression. Your goal should be to communicate a specific mood or feeling and hold the reader's attention there.

3. *Use a logical ordering of details.*
    If your description is a visual one, order the details in a manner in which the eye would most naturally view them. If you are describing a person, you might order your details from head to toe or vice versa, or you might begin with a dominant feature and work from there. A description of a room in a house might begin with items farthest away and work inward, from floor to ceiling, from ceiling to floor, from nearest to farthest, or from a focal point outward. Notice how N. Scott Momaday used spatial ordering in "The Way to Rainy Mountain":

    > Yellowstone, it seemed to me, was at the top of the world, a region of deep lakes and dark timber, canyons and waterfalls. . . . The skyline in all directions is close at hand, the high wall of the woods and deep cleavages of shade. . . . Descending eastward, the highland meadows are a stairway to the plain. . . . Clusters of trees, and animals grazing far in the distance, cause the vision to reach away and wonder to build upon the mind . . . Farther down, in the land of the Crows and the Blackfeet, the plain is yellow. . . .

Momaday begins with a panoramic view of Yellowstone and then narrows the description as he moves down from the "top of the world" to the yellow plains. From this spatial ordering, it is easy to get a specific visual image.

4. *Use figurative language to create vivid images.*
    Figures of speech such as similes, metaphors, personification, and oxymoron can be effective in creating images. A *simile* is a figure of speech that compares two dissimilar items, frequently to clarify an unclear, unknown, or abstract item or feeling. It is commonly expressed using the terms *like* or *as.* When Virginia Woolf describes fiction (in "If Shakespeare Had Had a Sister") as being "like a spider's web, attached ever lightly perhaps, but still attached to life at all four corners," she uses

simile. Similarly, John Steinbeck (in "The Turtle") uses similes to describe the turtle's encounter with a light truck: the front wheel of the vehicle "flipped the turtle like a tiddly-wink, spun it like a coin, and rolled it off the highway."

A figure of speech similar to a simile is a *metaphor*. Here, however, the comparison of dissimilar things is made without prepositions or connectives such as *like* or *as*. When Woolf examines the composite being created by the paradox of literature and reality, she describes the creation (woman) as "an odd monster that one made up by reading the historians first and the poets afterwards—a worm winged like an eagle [note the simile]; the spirit of life and beauty in a kitchen chopping up suet." Woolf actually goes on to *extend* the metaphor by making the entire essay a comparison of the perception of women's abilities and the reality of their abilities.

The key to the effective use of similes and metaphors is in avoiding overused expressions such as "blind as a bat" or "dead as a doornail." Also, you should avoid "mixing" more than one metaphor, for the image you create can be confusing: "The senators refuse to bite the bullet that is now an albatross around their necks."

Another figure of speech that writers use to create an impression is *personification*. In personification, human characteristics (actions, personality, speech, or emotions) are given to nonhuman entities. N. Scott Momaday tells a Native American legend and includes personification: ". . . The sisters were terrified; they ran, and the bear after them. They came to the stump of a great tree, and the tree spoke to them. It bade them climb upon it, . . ."

Still another device you might consider is *oxymoron*, the pairing of opposites to create an image or effect. For example, an uneasy quiet has been described as "deafening silence."

Simile, metaphor, personification, and oxymoron can be effective descriptive tools when used properly, but care should be taken to use fresh, vivid figures to create fresh, vivid impressions.

John Steinbeck (© Archive Photos/AM Stock)

The Turtle

John Steinbeck
(1902–1968)

Born in Salinas, California—the inspiration and
setting for many of his novels and short stories—
Nobel Prize recipient John Steinbeck gained
growing critical recognition for his fiction with the
1937 publication of *Of Mice and Men*. The Pulitzer
Prize–winning novel *The Grapes of Wrath* (1939)
confirmed his stature as a powerful voice in
American literature. Other major works include
Cannery Row (1945), *East of Eden* (1952), and *The
Winter of Our Discontent* (1961). In his often-quoted
acceptance speech for the 1962 Nobel Prize for
Literature, Steinbeck described the duty of the
writer as "to celebrate man's proven capacity for
greatness of heart and spirit—for gallantry in
defeat—for courage, compassion and love." In "The
Turtle," an early chapter from *The Grapes of Wrath*,
Steinbeck presents an allegory illustrating this
capacity for courage and persistence.

1   The concrete highway was edged with a mat of tangled, broken, dry
grass, and the grass heads were heavy with oat beards to catch on a dog's
coat, and foxtails to tangle in a horse's fetlocks, and clover burrs to fasten
in sheep's wool; sleeping life waiting to be spread and dispersed, every seed
armed with an appliance of dispersal, twisting darts and parachutes for the
wind, little spears and balls of tiny thorns, and all waiting for animals and
for the wind, for a man's trouser cuff or the hem of a woman's skirt, all
passive but armed with appliances of activity, still, but each possessed of
the anlage of movement.

2   The sun lay on the grass and warmed it, and in the shade under the grass
the insects moved, ants and ant lions to set traps for them, grasshoppers to

jump into the air and flick their yellow wings for a second, sow bugs like little armadillos, plodding restlessly on many tender feet. And over the grass at the roadside a land turtle crawled, turning aside for nothing, dragging his high-domed shell over the grass. His hard legs and yellow-nailed feet threshed slowly through the grass, not really walking, but boosting and dragging his shell along. The barley beards slid off his shell, and the clover burrs fell on him and rolled to the ground. His horny beak was partly open, and his fierce, humorous eyes, under brows like fingernails, stared straight ahead. He came over the grass leaving a beaten trail behind him, and the hill, which was the highway embankment, reared up ahead of him. For a moment he stopped, his head held high. He blinked and looked up and down. At last he started to climb the embankment. Front clawed feet reached forward but did not touch. The hind feet kicked his shell along, and it scraped on the grass, and on the gravel. As the embankment grew steeper and steeper, the more frantic were the efforts of the land turtle. Pushing hind legs strained and slipped, boosting the shell along, and the horny head protruded as far as the neck could stretch. Little by little the shell slid up the embankment until at last a parapet cut straight across its line of march, the shoulder of the road, a concrete wall four inches high. As though they worked independently the hind legs pushed the shell against the wall. The head upraised and peered over the wall to the broad smooth plain of cement. Now the hands, braced on top of the wall, strained and lifted, and the shell came slowly up and rested its front end on the wall. For a moment the turtle rested. A red ant ran into the shell, into the soft skin inside the shell, and suddenly head and legs snapped in, and the armored tail clamped in sideways. The red ant was crushed between body and legs. And one head of wild oats was clamped into the shell by a front leg. For a long moment the turtle lay still, and then the neck crept out and the old humorous frowning eyes looked about and the legs and tail came out. The back legs went to work, straining like elephant legs, and the shell tipped to an angle so that the front legs could not reach the level cement plain. But higher and higher the hind legs boosted it, until at last the center of balance was reached, the front tipped down, the front legs scratched at the pavement, and it was up. But the head of wild oats was held by its stem around the front legs.

3   Now the going was easy, and all the legs worked, and the shell boosted along, waggling from side to side. A sedan driven by a forty-year old woman approached. She saw the turtle and swung to the right, off the highway, the wheels screamed and a cloud of dust boiled up. Two wheels lifted for a moment and then settled. The car skidded back onto the road, and went on, but more slowly. The turtle had jerked into its shell, but now it hurried on, for the highway was burning hot.

4   And now a light truck approached, and as it came near, the driver saw the turtle and swerved to hit it. His front wheel struck the edge of the shell,

flipped the turtle like a tiddly-wink, spun it like a coin, and rolled it off the highway. The truck went back to its course along the right side. Lying on its back, the turtle was tight in its shell for a long time. But at last its legs waved in the air, reaching for something to pull it over. Its front foot caught a piece of quartz and little by little the shell pulled over and flopped upright. The wild oat head fell out and three of the spearhead seeds stuck in the ground. And as the turtle crawled on down the embankment, its shell dragged dirt over the seeds. The turtle entered a dust road and jerked itself along, drawing a wavy shallow trench in the dust with its shell. The old humorous eyes looked ahead, and the horny beak opened a little. His yellow toe nails slipped a fraction in the dust.

Topics for Writing and Discussion

1.   Does Steinbeck use objective or subjective description in this selection? Support your answer with references to the text.

2.   What dominant impression does Steinbeck create as he describes the turtle and its journey? Again, select some details and images that support your answer.

3.   Choose three examples of vivid figurative language that appear in this selection. Explain why you think these particular similes or metaphors are the most powerful ones in the description. What do they do for the scene that ordinary language would not?

4.   Why do you think Steinbeck included this scene in a novel about poor migrant workers in the Depression? What symbolic role might the description of the wild oats play in this story?

5.   Go to a crowded location, one that is bustling with people and activities, such as your student center, a cafeteria, or a shopping mall. Record as many sensory details as you can in a twenty-minute period: what you see, hear, smell, and so on. Review your list later and use selected details to write a description of the place that presents a unified dominant impression. Make your description a vivid and convincing picture for someone who has never seen the place.

Maxine Hong Kingston (© Nancy Crampton)

Portraits of My Parents

Maxine Hong Kingston
(1940–   )

In addition to her highly praised books of non-fiction, *The Woman Warrior* (1976) and *China Men* (1980), Maxine Hong Kingston has published an important article, "Cultural Misreading by American Reviewers," in *Asian and Western Writers in Dialogue: New Cultural Identities* (1982). Her writings combine memories of growing up in a Chinese-American community in Stockton, California, with her reflections on Chinese culture and history. Recent publications include the novel *Tripmaster Monkey* (1989). Following her graduation from the University of California at Berkeley, she married actor Earl Kingston. In 1967 she moved to Hawaii where she first taught high-school English and mathematics and, later, creative writing at the University of Honolulu. She now teaches at the University of California, Berkeley. In "Portraits of My Parents" she describes pictures of her parents. These old photographs suggest to Kingston her parents' strengths and weaknesses as well as the cultural differences they encountered in their move from China to America.

1   Once in a long while, four times so far for me, my mother brings out the metal tube that holds her medical diploma. On the tube are gold circles crossed with seven red lines each—"joy" ideographs in abstract. There are also little flowers that look like gears for a gold machine. According to the scraps of labels with Chinese and American addresses, stamps, and post-

marks, the family airmailed the can from Hong Kong in 1950. It got crushed
in the middle, and whoever tried to peel the labels off stopped because the
red and gold paint came off too, leaving silver scratches that rust. Somebody
tried to pry the end off before discovering that the tube pulls apart. When
I open it, the smell of China flies out, a thousand-year-old bat flying heavy-
headed out of the Chinese caverns where bats are as white as dust, a smell
that comes from long ago, far back in the brain. Crates from Canton, Hong
Kong, Singapore, and Taiwan have that smell too, only stronger because
they are more recently come from the Chinese.

2   Inside the can are three scrolls, one inside another. The largest says that
in the twenty-third year of the National Republic, the To Keung School of
Midwifery, where she has had two years of instruction and Hospital Practice,
awards its Diploma to my mother, who has shown through oral and written
examination her Proficiency in Midwifery, Pediatrics, Gynecology, "Me-
decine," "Surgary," Therapeutics, Ophthalmology, Bacteriology, Dermatol-
ogy, Nursing and Bandage. This document has eight stamps on it: one, the
school's English and Chinese names embossed together in a circle; one, as
the Chinese enumerate, a stork and a big baby in lavender ink; one, the
school's Chinese seal; one, an orangish paper stamp pasted in the border
design; one, the red seal of Dr. Wu Pak-liang, M.D., Lyon, Berlin, president
and "Ex-assistant étranger à la clinique chirurgicale et d'accouchement de
l'université de Lyon"; one, the red seal of Dean Woo Yin-kam, M.D.; one,
my mother's seal, her chop mark larger than the president's and the dean's;
and one, the number 1279 on the back. Dean Woo's signature is followed
by "(Hackett)." I read in a history book that Hackett Medical College for
Women at Canton was founded in the nineteenth century by European
women doctors.

3   The school seal has been pressed over a photograph of my mother at the
age of thirty-seven. The diploma gives her age as twenty-seven. She looks
younger than I do, her eyebrows are thicker, her lips fuller. Her naturally
curly hair is parted on the left, one wavy wisp tendrilling off to the right.
She wears a scholar's white gown, and she is not thinking about her appearance. She stares straight ahead as if she could see me and past me to
her grandchildren and grandchildren's grandchildren. She has spacy eyes,
as all people recently from Asia have. Her eyes do not focus on the camera.
My mother is not smiling; Chinese do not smile for photographs. Their faces
command relatives in foreign lands—"Send money"—and posterity forever—
"Put food in front of this picture." My mother does not understand Chinese-
American snapshots. "What are you laughing at?" she asks.

4   The second scroll is a long narrow photograph of the graduating class
with the school officials seated in front. I picked out my mother immediately.
Her face is exactly her own, though forty years younger. She is so familiar,
I can only tell whether or not she is pretty or happy or smart by comparing
her to the other women. For this formal group picture she straightened her

hair with oil to make a chinlength bob like the others'. On the other women, strangers, I can recognize a curled lip, a sidelong glance, pinched shoulders. My mother is not soft; the girl with the small nose and dimpled underlip is soft. My mother is not humorous, not like the girl at the end who lifts her mocking chin to pose like Girl Graduate. My mother does not have smiling eyes; the old woman teacher (Dean Woo?) in front crinkles happily, and the one faculty member in the western suit smiles westernly. Most of the graduates are girls whose faces have not yet formed; my mother's face will not change anymore, except to age. She is intelligent, alert, pretty. I can't tell if she's happy.

5   The graduates seem to have been looking elsewhere when they pinned the rose, zinnia, or chrysanthemum on their precise black dresses. One thin girl wears hers in the middle of her chest. A few have a flower over a left or a right nipple. My mother put hers, a chrysanthemum, below her left breast. Chinese dresses at that time were dartless, cut as if women did not have breasts; these young doctors, unaccustomed to decorations, may have seen their chests as black expanses with no reference points for flowers. Perhaps they couldn't shorten that far gaze that lasts only a few years after a Chinese emigrates. In this picture too my mother's eyes are big with what they held—reaches of oceans beyond China, land beyond oceans. Most emigrants learn the barbarians' directness—how to gather themselves and stare rudely into talking faces as if trying to catch lies. In America my mother has eyes as strong as boulders, never once skittering off a face, but she has not learned to place decorations and phonograph needles, nor has she stopped seeing land on the other side of the oceans. Now her eyes include the relatives in China, as they once included my father smiling and smiling in his many western outfits, a different one for each photograph that he sent from America.

6   He and his friends took pictures of one another in bathing suits at Coney Island beach, the salt wind from the Atlantic blowing their hair. He's the one in the middle with his arms about the necks of his buddies. They pose in the cockpit of a biplane, on a motorcycle, and on a lawn beside the "Keep Off the Grass" sign. They are always laughing. My father, white shirt sleeves rolled up, smiles in front of a wall of clean laundry. In the spring he wears a new straw hat, cocked at a Fred Astaire angle. He steps out, dancing down the stairs, one foot forward, one back, a hand in his pocket. He wrote to her about the American custom of stomping on straw hats come fall. "If you want to save your hat for next year," he said, "you have to put it away early, or else when you're riding the subway or walking along Fifth Avenue, any stranger can snatch it off your head and put his foot through it. That's the way they celebrate the change of seasons here." In the winter he wears a gray felt hat with his gray overcoat. He is sitting on a rock in Central Park. In one snapshot he is not smiling; someone took it when he was studying, blurred in the glare of the desk lamp.

7   There are no snapshots of my mother. In two small portraits, however, there is a black thumbprint on her forehead, as if someone had inked in bangs, as if someone had marked her.

8   "Mother, did bangs come into fashion after you had the picture taken?" One time she said yes. Another time when I asked, "Why do you have fingerprints on your forehead?" she said, "Your First Uncle did that." I disliked the unsureness in her voice.

9   The last scroll has columns of Chinese words. The only English is "Department of Health, Canton," imprinted on my mother's face, the same photograph as on the diploma. I keep looking to see whether she was afraid. Year after year my father did not come home or send for her. Their two children had been dead for ten years. If he did not return soon, there would be no more children. ("They were three and two years old, a boy and a girl. They could talk already.") My father did send money regularly, though, and she had nobody to spend it on but herself. She bought good clothes and shoes. Then she decided to use the money for becoming a doctor. She did not leave for Canton immediately after the children died. In China there was time to complete feelings. As my father had done, my mother left the village by ship. There was a sea bird painted on the ship to protect it against shipwreck and winds. She was in luck. The following ship was boarded by river pirates, who kidnapped every passenger, even old ladies. "Sixty dollars for an old lady" was what the bandits used to say. "I sailed alone," she says, "to the capital of the entire province." She took a brown leather suitcase and a seabag stuffed with two quilts.

Topics for Writing and Discussion

1. In the first paragraph, Kingston describes the metal tube that holds her mother's medical diploma. How do the details Kingston chooses to explain the significance of the tube relate to her character sketch of her mother?

2. The metal tube contains three scrolls. Summarize briefly the contents of each scroll. What does each scroll reveal about the mother's education and about her hopes and expectations?

3. Kingston describes several photographs of her mother and of her father. How do these photographs suggest the differences between her mother and her father? How do they suggest the difference between life in China and life in America at the time the pictures were taken?

4. Why does Kingston believe that "Chinese do not smile for photographs"? Consider details from this essay that would support her contention.

5.   Write a description of a photograph (from an old family album, a published book of photographs, or a collection in a museum). Explain the details of the picture and speculate on their significance.

M. Scott Momaday in his office at the University of Arizona, Tucson (Arizona Daily Star)

The Way to Rainy Mountain

N. Scott Momaday
(1934–   )

For writer, artist, and teacher N. Scott Momaday, his Kiowa heritage is central to his work. Raised in Oklahoma, he earned degrees from the University of New Mexico and Stanford; he has taught at both Stanford and the University of Arizona. In 1969 he was awarded the Pulitzer Prize for fiction for *House Made of Dawn*, the same year *The Way to Rainy Mountain* was published. Other works include *The Names: A Memoir* (1976) and more recently *The Ancient Child* (1989). In the following excerpt from *The Way to Rainy Mountain*, Momaday reflects on the passing of a culture and people he once described as "deeply involved in their traditional life, in the memories of their blood." He notes, "I like to celebrate that involvement in my writing."

1   A single knoll rises out of the plain in Oklahoma, north and west of the Wichita Range. For my people, the Kiowas, it is an old landmark, and they gave it the name Rainy Mountain. The hardest weather in the world is there. Winter brings blizzards, hot tornadic winds arise in the spring, and in summer the prairie is an anvil's edge. The grass turns brittle and brown, and it cracks beneath your feet. There are green belts along the rivers and creeks, linear groves of hickory and pecan, willow and witch hazel. At a distance in July or August the steaming foliage seems almost to writhe in fire. Great green and yellow grasshoppers are everywhere in the tall grass, popping up like corn to sting the flesh, and tortoises crawl about on the red earth, going nowhere in the plenty of time. Loneliness is an aspect of the land. All things in the plain are isolate; there is no confusion of objects in

the eye, but *one* hill or *one* tree or *one* man. To look upon that landscape in the early morning, with the sun at your back, is to lose the sense of proportion. Your imagination comes to life, and this, you think, is where Creation was begun.

2   I returned to Rainy Mountain in July. My grandmother had died in the spring, and I wanted to be at her grave. She had lived to be very old and at last infirm. Her only living daughter was with her when she died, and I was told that in death her face was that of a child.

3   I like to think of her as a child. When she was born, the Kiowas were living the last great moment of their history. For more than a hundred years they had controlled the open range from the Smoky Hill River to the Red, from the headwaters of the Canadian to the fork of the Arkansas and Cimarron. In alliance with the Comanches, they had ruled the whole of the southern Plains. War was their sacred business, and they were among the finest horsemen the world has ever known. But warfare for the Kiowas was preeminently a matter of disposition rather than of survival, and they never understood the grim, unrelenting advance of the U.S. Cavalry. When at last, divided and ill-provisioned, they were driven onto the Staked Plains in the cold rains of autumn, they fell into panic. In Palo Duro Canyon they abandoned their crucial stores to pillage and had nothing then but their lives. In order to save themselves, they surrendered to the soldiers at Fort Sill and were imprisoned in the old stone corral that now stands as a military museum. My grandmother was spared the humiliation of those high gray walls by eight or ten years, but she must have known from birth the affliction of defeat, the dark brooding of old warriors.

4   Her name was Aho, and she belonged to the last culture to evolve in North America. Her forebears came down from the high country in western Montana nearly three centuries ago. They were a mountain people, a mysterious tribe of hunters whose language has never been positively classified in any major group. In the late seventeenth century they began a long migration to the south and east. It was a journey toward the dawn, and it led to a golden age. Along the way the Kiowas were befriended by the Crows, who gave them the culture and religion of the Plains. They acquired horses, and their ancient nomadic spirit was suddenly free of the ground. They acquired Tai-me, the sacred Sun Dance doll, from that moment the object and symbol of their worship, and so shared in the divinity of the sun. Not least, they acquired the sense of destiny, therefore courage and pride. When they entered upon the southern Plains they had been transformed. No longer were they slaves to the simple necessity of survival; they were a lordly and dangerous society of fighters and thieves, hunters and priests of the sun. According to their origin myth, they entered the world through a hollow log. From one point of view, their migration was the fruit of an old prophecy, for indeed they emerged from a sunless world.

5   Although my grandmother lived out her long life in the shadow of Rainy Mountain, the immense landscape of the continental interior lay like memory in her blood. She could tell of the Crows, whom she had never seen, and of the Black Hills, where she had never been. I wanted to see in reality what she had seen more perfectly in the mind's eye, and traveled fifteen hundred miles to begin my pilgrimage.

6   Yellowstone, it seemed to me, was the top of the world, a region of deep lakes and dark timber, canyons and waterfalls. But, beautiful as it is, one might have the sense of confinement there. The skyline in all directions is close at hand, the high wall of the woods and deep cleavages of shade. There is a perfect freedom in the mountains, but it belongs to the eagle and the elk, the badger and the bear. The Kiowas reckoned their stature by the distance they could see, and they were bent and blind in the wilderness.

7   Descending eastward, the highland meadows are a stairway to the plain. In July the inland slope of the Rockies is luxuriant with flax and the buckwheat, stonecrop and larkspur. The earth unfolds and the limit of the land recedes. Clusters of trees, and animals grazing far in the distance, cause the vision to reach away and wonder to build upon the mind. The sun follows a longer course in the day, and the sky is immense beyond all comparison. The great billowing clouds that sail upon it are shadows that move upon the grain like water, dividing light. Farther down, in the land of the Crows and Blackfeet, the plain is yellow. Sweet clover takes hold of the hills and bends upon itself to cover and seal the soil. There the Kiowas paused on their way; they had come to the place where they must change their lives. The sun is at home on the plains. Precisely there does it have the certain character of a god. When the Kiowas came to the land of the Crows, they could see the dark lees of the hills at dawn across the Bighorn River, the profusion of light on the grain shelves, the oldest deity ranging after the solstices. Not yet would they veer southward to the caldron of the land that lay below; they must wean their blood from the northern winter and hold the mountains a while longer in their view. They bore Tai-me in procession to the east.

8   A dark mist lay over the Black Hills, and the land was like iron. At the top of a ridge I caught sight of Devil's Tower upthrust against the gray sky as if in the birth of time the core of the earth had broken through its crust and the motion of the world was begun. There are things in nature that engender an awful quiet in the heart of man; Devil's Tower is one of them. Two centuries ago, because they could not do otherwise, the Kiowas made a legend at the base of the rock. My grandmother said:

> *Eight children were there at play, seven sisters and their brother. Suddenly the boy was struck dumb; he trembled and began to run upon his hands and feet. His fingers became claws, and his body was covered with fur. Directly there was a bear where the boy had been. The sisters were terrified; they ran, and the bear after them. They*

came to the stump of a great tree, and the tree spoke to them. It bade them climb upon it, and as they did so it began to rise into the air. The bear came to kill them, but they were just beyond its reach. It reared against the tree and scored the bark all around with its claws. The seven sisters were borne into the sky, and they became the stars of the Big Dipper.

From that moment, and so long as the legend lives, the Kiowas have kinsmen in the night sky. Whatever they were in the mountains, they could be no more. However tenuous their well-being, however much they had suffered and would suffer again, they had found a way out of the wilderness.

9 My grandmother had a reverence for the sun, a holy regard that now is all but gone out of mankind. There was a wariness in her, and an ancient awe. She was a Christian in her later years, but she had come a long way about, and she never forgot her birthright. As a child she had been to the Sun Dances; she had taken part in those annual rites, and by them she had learned the restoration of her people in the presence of Tai-me. She was about seven when the last Kiowa Sun Dance was held in 1887 on the Washita River above Rainy Mountain Creek. The buffalo were gone. In order to consummate the ancient sacrifice—to impale the head of a buffalo bull upon the medicine tree—a delegation of old men journeyed into Texas, there to beg and barter for an animal from the Goodnight herd. She was ten when the Kiowas came together for the last time as a living Sun Dance culture. They could find no buffalo; they had to hang an old hide from the sacred tree. Before the dance could begin, a company of soldiers rode out from Fort Sill under orders to disperse the tribe. Forbidden without cause the essential act of their faith, having seen the wild herds slaughtered and left to rot upon the ground, the Kiowas backed away forever from the medicine tree. That was July 20, 1890, at the great bend of the Washita. My grandmother was there. Without bitterness, and for as long as she lived, she bore a vision of deicide.

10 Now that I can have her only in memory, I see my grandmother in the several postures that were peculiar to her: standing at the wood stove on a winter morning and turning meat in a great iron skillet; sitting at the south window, bent above her beadwork, and afterwards, when her vision failed, looking down for a long time into the fold of her hands; going out upon a cane, very slowly as she did when the weight of age came upon her; praying. I remember her most often at prayer. She made long, rambling prayers out of suffering and hope, having seen many things. I was never sure that I had the right to hear, so exclusive were they of all mere custom and company. The last time I saw her she prayed standing by the side of her bed at night, naked to the waist, the light of a kerosene lamp moving upon her dark skin. Her long, black hair, always drawn and braided in the day, lay upon her shoulders and against her breasts like a shawl. I do not speak Kiowa, and I never understood her prayers, but there was something inherently sad in

the sound, some merest hesitation upon the syllables of sorrow. She began in a high and descending pitch, exhausting her breath to silence; then again and again—and always the same intensity of effort, of something that is, and is not, like urgency in the human voice. Transported so in the dancing light among the shadows of her room, she seemed beyond the reach of time. But that was illusion; I think I knew then that I should not see her again.

11   Houses are like sentinels in the plain, old keepers of the weather watch. There, in a very little while, wood takes on the appearance of great age. All colors wear soon away in the wind and rain, and then the wood is burned gray and the grain appears and the nails turn red with rust. The window-panes are black and opaque; you imagine there is nothing within, and indeed there are many ghosts, bones given up to the land. They stand here and there against the sky, and you approach them for a longer time than you expect. They belong in the distance; it is their domain.

12   Once there was a lot of sound in my grandmother's house, a lot of coming and going, feasting and talk. The summers there were full of excitement and reunion. The Kiowas are a summer people; they abide the cold and keep to themselves, but when the season turns and the land becomes warm and vital they cannot hold still; an old love of going returns upon them. The aged visitors who came to my grandmother's house when I was a child were made of lean and leather, and they bore themselves upright. They wore great black hats and bright ample shirts that shook in the wind. They rubbed fat upon their hair and wound their braids with strips of colored cloth. Some of them painted their faces and carried the scars of old and cherished enmities. They were an old council of warlords, come to remind and be reminded of who they were. Their wives and daughters served them well. The women might indulge themselves; gossip was at once the mark and compensation of their servitude. They made loud and elaborate talk among themselves, full of jest and gesture, fright and false alarm. They went abroad in fringed and flowered shawls, bright beadwork and German silver. They were at home in the kitchen, and they prepared meals that were banquets.

13   There were frequent prayer meetings, and great nocturnal feasts. When I was a child I played with my cousins outside, where the lamplight fell upon the ground and the singing of the old people rose up around us and carried away into the darkness. There were a lot of good things to eat, a lot of laughter and surprise. And afterwards, when the quiet returned, I lay down with my grandmother and could hear the frogs away by the river and feel the motion of the air.

14   Now there is a funeral silence in the rooms, the endless wake of some final word. The walls have closed in upon my grandmother's house. When I returned to it in mourning, I saw for the first time in my life how small it was. It was late at night, and there was a white moon, nearly full. I sat for a long time on the stone steps by the kitchen door. From there I could see out across the land; I could see the long row of trees by the creek, the low

light upon the rolling plains, and the stars of the Big Dipper. Once I looked at the moon and caught sight of a strange thing. A cricket had perched upon the handrail, only a few inches away from me. My line of vision was such that the creature filled the moon like a fossil. It had gone there, I thought, to live and die, for there, of all places, was its small definition made whole and eternal. A warm wind rose up and purled like the longing within me.

15   The next morning I awoke at dawn and went out on the dirt road to Rainy Mountain. It was already hot, and the grasshoppers began to fill the air. Still, it was early in the morning, and the birds sang out of the shadows. The long yellow grass on the mountain shone in the bright light, and a scissortail hied above the land. There, where it ought to be, at the end of a long and legendary way, was my grandmother's grave. Here and there on the dark stones were ancestral names. Looking back once, I saw the mountain and came away.

Topics for Writing and Discussion

1. Why does Momaday use his grandmother as the central image of this essay? What does she represent to him in terms of his heritage?

2. For what purpose does the author take his readers on this trip to Rainy Mountain? To whom is this essay written?

3. Select three or four images that appeal to the readers' senses of sight, sound, smell, or touch. What do these images add to the descriptions of people or places?

4. How does Momaday structure his essay so that the reader realizes the end of both a literal and symbolic journey? What does Momaday mean when he describes his grandmother's grave "where it ought to be, at the end of a long and legendary way"?

5. Consider your own ethnic or cultural background. Is there one person or place that symbolizes your heritage for you? Write an essay describing this person or place, using distinctive detail (and historical information where necessary) to make your choice clear to readers who would appreciate knowing more about your culture.

E. B. White writing in his "office" boathouse at home in Brookline, Maine. (© 1988 by Jill Krementz)

Once More to the Lake

E. B. White
(1899–1985)

Elwyn Brooks White was educated at Cornell University where he studied with William Strunk, Jr. Years later, White revised Strunk's classic textbook *The Little Book* and renamed it *The Elements of Style* (1959). In 1927, White joined the staff of the *New Yorker* magazine. From 1938 to 1943 he contributed a column, "One Man's Meat," to *Harper's* magazine. Noted for his essays, editorials, poetry, and feature articles, he also won acclaim for his children's books, including *Charlotte's Web* and *Stuart Little* (1945). Although he lived for many years in New York City, White felt a deep connection to Maine and from 1930 until his death made his home on a saltwater farm there. His essay "Once More to the Lake" describes his poignant memories of vacations in Maine, both as a child and as a grown man returning to the lake with his son.

1   One summer, along about 1904, my father rented a camp on a lake in Maine and took us all there for the month of August. We all got ringworm from some kittens and had to rub Pond's Extract on our arms and legs night and morning, and my father rolled over in a canoe with all his clothes on; but outside of that the vacation was a success and from then on none of us ever thought there was any place in the world like that lake in Maine. We returned summer after summer—always on August 1 for one month. I have since become a salt-water man, but sometimes in summer there are days when the restlessness of the tides and the fearful cold of the sea water and the incessant wind that blows across the afternoon and into the evening make me wish for the placidity of a lake in the woods. A few weeks ago

this feeling got so strong I bought myself a couple of bass hooks and a spinner and returned to the lake where we used to go, for a week's fishing and to revisit old haunts.

2   I took along my son, who had never had any fresh water up his nose and who had seen lily pads only from train windows. On the journey over to the lake I began to wonder what it would be like. I wondered how time would have marred this unique, this holy spot—the coves and streams, the hills that the sun set behind, the camps and the paths behind the camps. I was sure that the tarred road would have found it out, and I wondered in what other ways it would be desolated. It is strange how much you can remember about places like that once you allow your mind to return into the grooves that lead back. You remember one thing, and that suddenly reminds you of another thing. I guess I remembered clearest of all the early mornings, when the lake was cool and motionless, remembered how the bedroom smelled of the lumber it was made of and of the wet woods whose scent entered through the screen. The partitions in the camp were thin and did not extend clear to the top of the rooms, and as I was always the first up I would dress softly so as not to wake the others, and sneak out into the sweet outdoors and start out in the canoe, keeping close along the shore in the long shadows of the pines. I remembered being very careful never to rub my paddle against the gunwale for fear of disturbing the stillness of the cathedral.

3   The lake had never been what you would call a wild lake. There were cottages sprinkled around the shores, and it was in farming country although the shores of the lake were quite heavily wooded. Some of the cottages were owned by nearby farmers, and you would live at the shore and eat your meals at the farmhouse. That's what our family did. But although it wasn't wild, it was a fairly large and undisturbed lake and there were places in it that, to a child at least, seemed infinitely remote and primeval.

4   I was right about the tar: it led to within half a mile of the shore. But when I got back there, with my boy, and we settled into a camp near a farmhouse and into the kind of summertime I had known, I could tell that it was going to be pretty much the same as it had been before—I knew it, lying in bed the first morning, smelling the bedroom and hearing the boy sneak quietly out and go off along the shore in a boat. I began to sustain the illusion that he was I, and therefore, by simple transposition, that I was my father. This sensation persisted, kept cropping up all the time we were there. It was not an entirely new feeling, but in this setting it grew much stronger. I seemed to be living a dual existence. I would be in the middle of some simple act, I would be picking up a bait box or laying down a table fork, or I would be saying something, and suddenly it would be not I but my father who was saying the words or making the gesture. It gave me a creepy sensation.

5   We went fishing the first morning. I felt the same damp moss covering the worms in the bait can, and saw the dragonfly alight on the tip of my rod as it hovered a few inches from the surface of the water. It was the arrival of this fly that convinced me beyond any doubt that everything was as it always had been, that the years were a mirage and that there had been no years. The small waves were the same, chucking the rowboat under the chin as we fished at anchor, and the boat was the same boat, the same color green and the ribs broken in the same places, and under the floorboards the same fresh-water leavings and débris—the dead helgramite, the wisps of moss, the rusty discarded fishhook, the dried blood from yesterday's catch. We stared silently at the tips of our rods, at the dragonflies that came and went. I lowered the tip of mine into the water, tentatively, pensively dislodging the fly, which darted two feet away, poised, darted two feet back, and came to rest again a little farther up the rod. There had been no years between the ducking of this dragonfly and the other one—the one that was part of memory. I looked at the boy, who was silently watching his fly, and it was my hands that held his rod, my eyes watching. I felt dizzy and didn't know which rod I was at the end of.

6   We caught two bass, hauling them in briskly as though they were mackerel, pulling them over the side of the boat in a businesslike manner without any landing net, and stunning them with a blow on the back of the head. When we got back for a swim before lunch, the lake was exactly where we had left it, the same number of inches from the dock, and there was only the merest suggestion of a breeze. This seemed an utterly enchanted sea, this lake you could leave to its own devices for a few hours and come back to, and find that it had not stirred, this constant and trustworthy body of water. In the shallows, the dark, water-soaked sticks and twigs, smooth and old, were undulating in clusters on the bottom against the clean ribbed sand, and the track of the mussel was plain. A school of minnows swam by, each minnow with its small individual shadow, doubling the attendance, so clear and sharp in the sunlight. Some of the other campers were in swimming, along the shore, one of them with a cake of soap, and the water felt thin and clear and unsubstantial. Over the years there had been this person with the cake of soap, this cultist, and here he was. There had been no years.

7   Up to the farmhouse to dinner through the teeming, dusty field, the road under our sneakers was only a two-track road. The middle track was missing, the one with the marks of the hooves and the splotches of dried, flaky manure. There had always been three tracks to choose from in choosing which track to walk in; now the choice was narrowed down to two. For a moment I missed terribly the middle alternative. But the way led past the tennis court, and something about the way it lay there in the sun reassured me; the tape had loosened along the backline, the alleys were green with plantains and other weeds, and the net (installed in June and removed in September) sagged in the dry noon, and the whole place steamed with

midday heat and hunger and emptiness. There was a choice of pie for dessert, and one was blueberry and one was apple, and the waitresses were the same country girls, there having been no passage of time, only the illusion of it as in a dropped curtain—the waitresses were still fifteen; their hair had been washed, that was the only difference—they had been to the movies and seen the pretty girls with the clean hair.

8   Summertime, oh, summertime, pattern of life indelible, the fade-proof lake, the woods unshatterable, the pasture with the sweetfern and the juniper forever and ever, summer without end; this was the background, and the life along the shore was the design, their tiny docks with the flagpole and the American flag floating against the white clouds in the blue sky, the little paths over the roots of the trees leading from camp to camp and the paths leading back to the outhouses and the can of lime for sprinkling, and at the souvenir counters at the store the miniature birchbark canoes and the post-cards that showed things looking a little better than they looked. This was the American family at play, escaping the city heat, wondering whether the newcomers in the camp at the head of the cover were "common" or "nice," wondering whether it was true that the people who drove up for Sunday dinner at the farmhouse were turned away because there wasn't enough chicken.

9   It seemed to me, as I kept remembering all this, that those times and those summers had been infinitely precious and worth saving. There had been jollity and peace and goodness. The arriving (at the beginning of August) had been so big a business in itself, at the railway station the farm wagon drawn up, the first smell of the pine-laden air, the first glimpse of the smiling farmer, and the great importance of the trunks and your father's enormous authority in such matters, and the feel of the wagon under you for the long ten-mile haul, and at the top of the last long hill catching the first view of the lake after eleven months of not seeing this cherished body of water. The shouts and cries of the other campers when they saw you, and the trunks to be unpacked, to give up their rich burden. (Arriving was less exciting nowadays, when you sneaked up in your car and parked it under a tree near the camp and took out the bags and in five minutes it was all over, no fuss, no loud wonderful fuss about trunks.)

10   Peace and goodness and jollity. The only thing that was wrong now, really, was the sound of the place, an unfamiliar nervous sound of the outboard motors. This was the note that jarred, the one thing that would sometimes break the illusion and set the years moving. In those other summertimes all motors were inboard; and when they were at a little distance, the noise they made was a sedative, an ingredient of summer sleep. They were one-cylinder and two-cylinder engines, and some were make-and-break and some were jump-spark, but they all made a sleepy sound across the lake. The one-lungers throbbed and fluttered, and the twin-cylinder ones purred and purred, and that was a quiet sound, too. But now the campers all had out-

boards. In the daytime, in the hot mornings, these motors made a petulant, irritable sound; at night, in the still evening when the afterglow lit the water, they whined about one's ears like mosquitoes. My boy loved our rented outboard, and his great desire was to achieve single-handed mastery over it, and authority, and he soon learned the trick of choking it a little (but not too much), and the adjustment of the needle valve. Watching him I would remember the things you could do with the old one-cylinder engine with the heavy flywheel, how you could have it eating out of your hand if you got really close to it spiritually. Motorboats in those days didn't have clutches, and you would make a landing by shutting off the motor at the proper time and coasting in with a dead rudder. But there was a way of reversing them, if you learned the trick, by cutting the switch and putting it on again exactly on the final dying revolution of the flywheel, so that it would kick back against compression and begin reversing. Approaching a dock in a strong following breeze, it was difficult to slow up sufficiently by the ordinary coasting method, and if a boy felt he had complete mastery over his motor, he was tempted to keep it running beyond its time and then reverse it a few feet from the dock. It took a cool nerve, because if you threw the switch a twentieth of a second too soon you would catch the flywheel when it still had speed enough to go up past center, and the boat would leap ahead, charging bull-fashion at the dock.

11   We had a good week at the camp. The bass were biting well and the sun shone endlessly, day after day. We would be tired at night and lie down in the accumulated heat of the little bedrooms after the long hot day and the breeze would stir almost imperceptibly outside and the smell of the swamp drift in through the rusty screens. Sleep would come easily and in the morning the red squirrel would be on the roof, tapping out his gay routine. I kept remembering everything, lying in bed in the mornings—the small steamboat that had a long rounded stern like the lip of a Ubangi, and how quietly she ran on the moonlight sails, when the older boys played their mandolins and the girls sang and we ate doughnuts dipped in sugar, and how sweet the music was on the water in the shining night, and what it had felt like to think about girls then. After breakfast we would go up to the store and the things were in the same place—the minnows in a bottle, the plugs and spinners disarranged and pawed over by the youngsters from the boys' camp, the Fig Newtons and the Beeman's gum. Outside, the road was tarred and cars stood in front of the store. Inside, all was just as it had always been, except there was more Coca-Cola, and not so much Moxie and root beer and birch beer and sarsaparilla. We would walk out with the bottle of pop apiece and sometimes the pop would backfire up our noses and hurt. We explored the streams, quietly, where the turtles slid off the sunny logs and dug their way into the soft bottom; and we lay on the town wharf and fed worms to the tame bass. Everywhere we went I had trouble making out which was I, the one walking at my side, the one walking in my pants.

12   One afternoon while we were there at that lake a thunderstorm came up. It was like the revival of an old melodrama that I had seen long ago with childish awe. The second-act climax of the drama of the electrical disturbance over a lake in America had not changed in any important respect. This was the big scene, still the big scene. The whole thing was so familiar, the first feeling of oppression and heat and a general air around camp of not wanting to go very far away. In mid-afternoon (it was all the same) a curious darkening of the sky, and a lull in everything that had made life tick; and then the way the boats suddenly swung the other way at their moorings with the coming of a breeze out of the new quarter, and the premonitory rumble. Then the kettle drum, then the snare, then the bass drum and cymbals, then crackling light against the dark, and the gods grinning and licking their chops in the hills. Afterward the calm, the rain steadily rustling in the calm lake, the return of light and hope and spirits, and the campers running out in joy and relief to go swimming in the rain, their bright cries perpetuating the deathless joke about how they were getting simply drenched, and the children screaming with delight at the new sensation of bathing in the rain, and the joke about getting drenched linking the generations in a strong indestructible chain. And the comedian who waded in carrying an umbrella.

13   When the others went swimming, my son said he was going in, too. He pulled his dripping trunks from the line where they had hung all through the shower and wrung them out. Languidly, and with no thought of going in, I watched him, his hard little body, skinny and bare, saw him wince slightly as he pulled up around his vitals the small, soggy, icy garment. As he buckled the swollen belt, suddenly my groin felt the chill of death.

Topics for Writing and Discussion

1. Make a list of six changes White observes when he takes his son to the lake. Then make a list of six things that have stayed the same. What do these differences and similarities suggest about the nature of his vacations at the lake as compared to his son's vacation?

2. White says that while he was at the lake he seemed to be living a "dual existence." What does he mean by this? How does his sense of the distortion of time relate to his "dual existence"?

3. Analyze the rhythm of the language in paragraph 8 (beginning "Summertime, oh, summertime"). What does the rhythm contribute to the images? What tone is created by the combination of rhythm and images?

4. The final paragraph describes White watching his son pull on a wet bathing suit and feeling in his own groin "the chill of death." Why does he feel this premonition? How is this image connected to the images in the rest of the essay? Has anything in the essay prepared the reader for the sense of mortality White describes in the conclusion?

5. Think of a favorite childhood vacation place and describe making a return visit now, bringing with you a younger brother, sister, son, daughter, or friend. The return visit may be either real or imagined, but be sure to describe the differences you observe and to comment on their significance both to you and to the person you have brought with you.

Virginia Woolf (© 1935 Man Ray)

If Shakespeare Had Had a Sister

Virginia Woolf
(1882–1941)

The daughter of a respected biographer and scholar
Sir Leslie Stephen, Virginia Woolf read widely in
her father's library and thus attained a thorough,
although informal, education. Her older sister,
Vanessa, married art critic Clive Bell and soon
after, in 1912, Virginia Stephen married author and
publisher Leonard Woolf. The Bells and Woolfs,
together with economist John Maynard Keynes,
painter Roger Fry, biographer Lytton Strachey, and
novelist E. M. Forster, comprised the "Bloomsbury
Group." The members of this group were
committed to excellence in literature and art and
rebelled against the traditional norms of the
Victorians. Virginia and Leonard Woolf founded
the Hogarth Press and published the innovative
novels that established Virginia Woolf as a major
literary figure. She is particularly acclaimed for her
striking use of stream-of-consciousness writing and
for her experimental approach to point of view.
From her first published book, *The Voyage Out*
(1915), it was clear that her work demonstrated her
considerable intelligence. It was the novel *Mrs.
Dalloway* (1925), however, that first indicated her
break from previous literary tradition and her
fascination with the limitations and possibilities of
time and space. In her long essay, *A Room of One's
Own* (1929), she explored the questions and
pressures faced by women. "If Shakespeare Had
Had a Sister" is taken from that work. Here, Woolf
describes the frustrations and pitfalls a talented
female writer might have encountered in sixteenth-

century England and suggests comparisons
between that Elizabethan woman and all creative
women in the centuries that followed.

---

1   It was disappointing not to have brought back in the evening some important statement, some authentic fact. Women are poorer than men because—this or that. Perhaps now it would be better to give up seeking for the truth, and receiving on one's head an avalanche of opinion hot as lava, discoloured as dish-water. It would be better to draw the curtains; to shut out distractions; to light the lamp; to narrow the enquiry and to ask the historian, who records not opinions but facts, to describe under what conditions women lived, not throughout the ages, but in England, say in the time of Elizabeth.

2   For it is a perennial puzzle why no woman wrote a word of that extraordinary literature when every other man, it seemed, was capable of song or sonnet. What were the conditions in which women lived, I asked myself; for fiction, imaginative work that is, is not dropped like a pebble upon the ground, as science may be; fiction is like a spider's web, attached ever so lightly perhaps, but still attached to life at all four corners. Often the attachment is scarcely perceptible; Shakespeare's plays, for instance, seem to hang there complete by themselves. But when the web is pulled askew, hooked up at the edge, torn in the middle, one remembers that these webs are not spun in midair by incorporeal creatures, but are the work of suffering human beings, and are attached to grossly material things, like health and money and the houses we live in.

3   I went, therefore, to the shelf where the histories stand and took down one of the latest, Professor Trevelyan's *History of England*. Once more I looked up Women, found "position of," and turned to the pages indicated. "Wife-beating," I read, "was a recognised right of man, and was practised without shame by high as well as low. . . . Similarly," the historian goes on, "the daughter who refused to marry the gentleman of her parents' choice was liable to be locked up, beaten and flung about the room, without any shock being inflicted on public opinion. Marriage was not an affair of personal affection, but of family avarice, particularly in the 'chivalrous' upper classes. . . . Betrothal often took place while one or both of the parties was in the cradle, and marriage when they were scarcely out of the nurses' charge." That was about 1470, soon after Chaucer's time. The next reference to the position of women is some two hundred years later, in the time of

the Stuarts. "It was still the exception for women of the upper and middle class to choose their own husbands, and when the husband had been assigned, he was lord and master, so far at least as law and custom could make him. Yet even so," Professor Trevelyan concludes, "neither Shakespeare's women nor those of authentic seventeenth-century memoirs, like the Verneys and the Hutchinsons, seem wanting in personality and character." Certainly, if we consider it, Cleopatra must have had a way with her; Lady Macbeth, one would suppose, had a will of her own; Rosalind, one might conclude, was an attractive girl. Professor Trevelyan is speaking no more than the truth when he remarks that Shakespeare's women do not seem wanting in personality and character. Not being a historian, one might go even further and say that women have burnt like beacons in all the works of all the poets from the beginning of time—Clytemnestra, Antigone, Cleopatra, Lady Macbeth, Phèdre, Cressida, Rosalind, Desdemona, the Duchess of Malfi, among the dramatists; then among the prose writers: Millamant, Clarissa, Becky Sharp, Anna Karenina, Emma Bovary, Madame de Guermantes—the names flock to mind, nor do they recall women "lacking in personality and character." Indeed, if woman had no existence save in the fiction written by men, one would imagine her a person of the utmost importance; very various; heroic and mean; splendid and sordid; infinitely beautiful and hideous in the extreme; as great as a man, some think even greater. But this is woman in fiction. In fact, as Professor Trevelyan points out, she was locked up, beaten and flung about the room.

4   A very queer, composite being thus emerges. Imaginatively she is of the highest importance; practically she is completely insignificant. She pervades poetry from cover to cover; she is all but absent from history. She dominates the lives of kings and conquerors in fiction; in fact she was the slave of any boy whose parents forced a ring upon her finger. Some of the most inspired words, some of the most profound thoughts in literature fall from her lips; in real life she could hardly read, could scarcely spell, and was the property of her husband.

5   It was certainly an odd monster that one made up by reading the historians first and the poets afterwards—a worm winged like an eagle; the spirit of life and beauty in a kitchen chopping up suet. But these monsters, however amusing to the imagination, have no existence in fact. What one must do to bring her to life was to think poetically and prosaically at one and the same moment, thus keeping in touch with fact—that she is Mrs. Martin, aged thirty-six, dressed in blue, wearing a black hat and brown shoes; but not losing sight of fiction either—that she is a vessel in which all sorts of spirits and forces are coursing and flashing perpetually. The moment, however, that one tries this method with the Elizabethan woman, one branch of illumination fails; one is held up by the scarcity of facts. One knows nothing detailed, nothing perfectly true and substantial about her. History scarcely mentions her. And I turned to Professor Trevelyan again to see what

history meant to him. I found by looking at his chapter headings that it meant—

6   "The Manor Court and the Methods of Open-field Agriculture . . . The Cistercians and Sheep-farming . . . The Crusades . . . The University . . . The House of Commons . . . The Hundred Years' War . . . The Wars of the Roses . . . The Renaissance Scholars . . . The Dissolution of the Monasteries . . . Agrarian and Religious Strife . . . The Origin of English Seapower . . . The Armada . . ." and so on. Occasionally an individual woman is mentioned, an Elizabeth, or a Mary; a queen or a great lady. But by no possible means could middle-class women with nothing but brains and character at their command have taken part in any one of the great movements which, brought together, constitute the historian's view of the past. Nor shall we find her in any collection of anecdotes. Aubrey hardly mentions her. She never writes her own life and scarcely keeps a diary; there are only a handful of her letters in existence. She left no plays or poems by which we can judge her. What one wants, I thought—and why does not some brilliant student at Newnham or Girton supply it?—is a mass of information; at what age did she marry; how many children had she as a rule; what was her house like; had she a room to herself; did she do the cooking; would she be likely to have a servant? All these facts lie somewhere, presumably, in parish registers and account books; the life of the average Elizabethan woman must be scattered about somewhere, could one collect it and make a book of it. It would be ambitious beyond my daring, I thought, looking about the shelves for books that were not there, to suggest to the students of those famous colleges that they should re-write history, though I own that it often seems a little queer as it is, unreal, lopsided; but why should they not add a supplement to history? calling it, of course, by some inconspicuous name so that women might figure there without impropriety? For one often catches a glimpse of them in the lives of the great, whisking away into the background, concealing, I sometimes think, a wink, a laugh, perhaps a tear. And, after all, we have lives enough of Jane Austen; it scarcely seems necessary to consider again the influence of the tragedies of Joanna Baillie upon the poetry of Edgar Allan Poe; as for myself, I should not mind if the homes and haunts of Mary Russell Mitford were closed to the public for a century at least. But what I find deplorable, I continued, looking about the bookshelves again, is that nothing is known about women before the eighteenth century. I have no model in my mind to turn about this way and that. Here I am asking why women did not write poetry in the Elizabethan age, and I am not sure how they were educated; whether they were taught to write; whether they had sitting-rooms to themselves; how many women had children before they were twenty-one; what, in short, they did from eight in the morning till eight at night. They had no money evidently; according to Professor Trevelyan they were married whether they liked it or not before they were out of the nursery, at fifteen or sixteen very likely. It would have

been extremely odd, even upon this showing, had one of them suddenly written the plays of Shakespeare, I concluded, and I thought of that old gentleman, who is dead now, but was a bishop, I think, who declared that it was impossible for any woman, past, present, or to come, to have the genius of Shakespeare. He wrote to the papers about it. He also told a lady who applied to him for information that cats do not as a matter of fact go to heaven, though they have, he added, souls of a sort. How much thinking those old gentlemen used to save one! How the borders of ignorance shrank back at their approach! Cats do not go to heaven. Women cannot write the plays of Shakespeare.

7   Be that as it may, I could not help thinking, as I looked at the works of Shakespeare on the shelf, that the bishop was right at least in this; it would have been impossible, completely and entirely, for any woman to have written the plays of Shakespeare in the age of Shakespeare. Let me imagine, since facts are so hard to come by, what would have happened had Shakespeare had a wonderfully gifted sister, called Judith, let us say. Shakespeare himself went, very probably—his mother was an heiress—to the grammar school, where he may have learnt Latin—Ovid, Virgil and Horace—and the elements of grammar and logic. He was, it is well known, a wild boy who poached rabbits, perhaps shot a deer, and had, rather sooner than he should have done, to marry a woman in the neighbourhood, who bore him a child rather quicker than was right. That escapade sent him to seek his fortune in London. He had, it seemed, a taste for the theatre; he began by holding horses at the stage door. Very soon he got work in the theatre, became a successful actor, and lived at the hub of the universe, meeting everybody, knowing everybody, practising his art on the boards, exercising his wits in the streets, and even getting access to the palace of the queen. Meanwhile his extraordinarily gifted sister, let us suppose, remained at home. She was as adventurous, as imaginative, as agog to see the world as he was. But she was not sent to school. She had no chance of learning grammar and logic, let alone of reading Horace and Virgil. She picked up a book now and then, one of her brother's perhaps, and read a few pages. But then her parents came in and told her to mend the stockings or mind the stew and not moon about with books and papers. They would have spoken sharply but kindly, for they were substantial people who knew the conditions of life for a woman and loved their daughter—indeed, more likely than not she was the apple of her father's eye. Perhaps she scribbled some pages up in an apple loft on the sly, but was careful to hide them or set fire to them. Soon, however, before she was out of her teens, she was to be betrothed to the son of a neighbouring wool-stapler. She cried out that marriage was hateful to her, and for that she was severely beaten by her father. Then he ceased to scold her. He begged her instead not to hurt him, not to shame him in this matter of her marriage. He would give her a chain of beads or a fine petticoat, he said; and there were tears in his eyes. How could she disobey him? How

could she break his heart? The force of her own gift alone drove her to it. She made up a small parcel of her belongings, let herself down by a rope one summer's night and took the road to London. She was not seventeen. The birds that sang in the hedge were not more musical than she was. She had the quickest fancy, a gift like her brother's, for the tune of words. Like him, she had a taste for the theatre. She stood at the stage door; she wanted to act, she said. Men laughed in her face. The manager—a fat, loose-lipped man—guffawed. He bellowed something about poodles dancing and women acting—no woman, he said, could possibly be an actress. He hinted—you can imagine what. She could get no training in her craft. Could she even seek her dinner in a tavern or roam the streets at midnight? Yet her genius was for fiction and lusted to feed abundantly upon the lives of men and women and the study of their ways. At last—for she was very young, oddly like Shakespeare the poet in her face, with the same grey eyes and rounded brows—at last Nick Greene the actor-manager took pity on her; she found herself with child by that gentleman and so—who shall measure the heat and violence of the poet's heart when caught and tangled in a woman's body?—killed herself one winter's night and lies buried at some cross-roads where the omnibuses now stop outside the Elephant and Castle.

8   That, more or less, is how the story would run, I think, if a woman in Shakespeare's day had had Shakespeare's genius. But for my part, I agree with the deceased bishop, if such he was—it is unthinkable that any woman in Shakespeare's day should have had Shakespeare's genius. For genius like Shakespeare's is not born among labouring, uneducated, servile people. It was not born in England among the Saxons and the Britons. It is not born today among the working classes. How, then, could it have been born among women whose work began, according to Professor Trevelyan, almost before they were out of the nursery, who were forced to it by their parents and held to it by all the power of law and custom? Yet genius of a sort must have existed among women as it must have existed among the working classes. Now and again an Emily Brontë or a Robert Burns blazes out and proves its presence. But certainly it never got itself on to paper. When, however, one reads of a witch being ducked, of a woman possessed by devils, of a wise woman selling herbs, or even of a very remarkable man who had a mother, then I think we are on the track of a lost novelist, a suppressed poet, of some mute and inglorious Jane Austen, some Emily Brontë who dashed her brains out on the moor or mopped and mowed about the highways crazed with the torture that her gift had put her to. Indeed, I would venture to guess that Anon, who wrote so many poems without signing them, was often a woman. It was a woman Edward Fitzgerald, I think, suggested who made the ballads and the folk-songs, crooning them to her children, beguiling her spinning with them, or the length of the winter's night.

9   This may be true or it may be false—who can say?—but what is true in
it, so it seemed to me, reviewing the story of Shakespeare's sister as I had
made it, is that any woman born with a great gift in the sixteenth century
would certainly have gone crazed, shot herself, or ended her days in some
lonely cottage outside the village, half witch, half wizard, feared and mocked
at. For it needs little skill in psychology to be sure that a highly gifted girl
who had tried to use her gift for poetry would have been so thwarted and
hindered by other people, so tortured and pulled asunder by her own contrary instincts, that she must have lost her health and sanity to a certainty.
No girl could have walked to London and stood at a stage door and forced
her way into the presence of actor-managers without doing herself a violence
and suffering an anguish which may have been irrational—for chastity may
be a fetish invented by certain societies for unknown reasons—but were
none the less inevitable. Chastity had then, it has even now, a religious
importance in a woman's life, and has so wrapped itself round with nerves
and instincts that to cut it free and bring it to the light of day demands
courage of the rarest. To have lived a free life in London in the sixteenth
century would have meant for a woman who was poet and playwright a
nervous stress and dilemma which might well have killed her. Had she
survived, whatever she had written would have been twisted and deformed,
issuing from a strained and morbid imagination. And undoubtedly, I
thought, looking at the shelf where there are no plays by women, her work
would have gone unsigned. That refuge she would have sought certainly.
It was the relic of the sense of chastity that dictated anonymity to women
even so late as the nineteenth century. Currer Bell, George Eliot, George
Sand, all the victims of inner strife as their writings prove, sought ineffec-
tively to veil themselves by using the name of a man. Thus they did homage
to the convention, which if not implanted by the other sex was liberally
encouraged by them (the chief glory of a woman is not to be talked of, said
Pericles, himself a much-talked-of man), that publicity in women is detestable. Anonymity runs in their blood. The desire to be veiled still possesses
them. They are not even now as concerned about the health of their fame
as men are, and, speaking generally, will pass a tombstone or a signpost
without feeling an irresistible desire to cut their names on it, as Alf, Bert or
Chas must do in obedience to their instinct, which murmurs if it sees a fine
woman go by, or even a dog, *Ce chien est à moi*. And, of course, it may not
be a dog, I thought, remembering Parliament Square, the Sieges Allee and
other avenues; it may be a piece of land or a man with curly black hair. It
is one of the great advantages of being a woman that one can pass even a
very fine negress without wishing to make an Englishwoman of her.

10   That woman, then, who was born with a gift of poetry in the sixteenth
century, was an unhappy woman, a woman at strife against herself. All the
conditions of her life, all her own instincts, were hostile to the state of mind
which is needed to set free whatever is in the brain. But what is the state

of mind that is most propitious to the act of creation, I asked. Can one come by any notion of the state that furthers and makes possible that strange activity? Here I opened the volume containing the Tragedies of Shakespeare. What was Shakespeare's state of mind, for instance, when he wrote *Lear* and *Antony and Cleopatra?* It was certainly the state of mind most favourable to poetry that there has ever existed. But Shakespeare himself said nothing about it. We only know casually and by chance that he "never blotted a line." Nothing indeed was ever said by the artist himself about his state of mind until the eighteenth century perhaps. Rousseau perhaps began it. At any rate, by the nineteenth century self-consciousness had developed so far that it was the habit for men of letters to describe their minds in confessions and autobiographies. Their lives also were written, and their letters were printed after their deaths. Thus, though we do not know what Shakespeare went through when he wrote *Lear,* we do know what Carlyle went through when he wrote the *French Revolution;* what Flaubert went through when he wrote *Madame Bovary;* what Keats was going through when he tried to write poetry against the coming of death and the indifference of the world.

11   And one gathers from this enormous modern literature of confession and self-analysis that to write a work of genius is almost always a feat of prodigious difficulty. Everything is against the likelihood that it will come from the writer's mind whole and entire. Generally material circumstances are against it. Dogs will bark; people will interrupt; money must be made; health will break down. Further, accentuating all these difficulties and making them harder to bear is the world's notorious indifference. It does not ask people to write poems and novels and histories; it does not need them. It does not care whether Flaubert finds the right word or whether Carlyle scrupulously verifies this or that fact. Naturally, it will not pay for what it does not want. And so the writer, Keats, Flaubert, Carlyle, suffers, especially in the creative years of youth, every form of distraction and discouragement. A curse, a cry of agony rises from those books of analysis and confession. "Mighty poets in their misery dead"—that is the burden of their song. If anything comes through in spite of all this, it is a miracle, and probably no book is born entire and uncrippled as it was conceived.

12   But for women, I thought, looking at the empty shelves, these difficulties were infinitely more formidable. In the first place, to have a room of her own, let alone a quiet room or a sound-proof room, was out of the question, unless her parents were exceptionally rich or very noble, even up to the beginning of the nineteenth century. Since her pin money, which depended on the good will of her father, was only enough to keep her clothed, she was debarred from such alleviations as came even to Keats or Tennyson or Carlyle, all poor men, from a walking tour, a little journey to France, from the separate lodging which, even if it were miserable enough, sheltered them from the claims and tyrannies of their families. Such material difficulties were formidable; but much worse were the immaterial. The indifference of

the world which Keats and Flaubert and other men of genius have found so hard to bear was in her case not indifference but hostility. The world did not say to her as it said to them, Write if you choose; it makes no difference to me. The world said with a guffaw, Write? What's the good of your writing? Here the psychologists of Newnham and Girton might come to our help, I thought, looking again at the blank spaces on the shelves. For surely it is time that the effect of discouragement upon the mind of the artist should be measured, as I have seen a dairy company measure the effect of ordinary milk and Grade A milk upon the body of the rat. They set two rats in cages side by side, and of the two one was furtive, timid and small, and the other was glossy, bold and big. Now what food do we feed women as artists upon? I asked, remembering, I suppose, that dinner of prunes and custard. To answer that question I had only to open the evening paper and to read that Lord Birkenhead is of opinion—but really I am not going to trouble to copy out Lord Birkenhead's opinion upon the writing of women. What Dean Inge says I will leave in peace. The Harley Street specialist may be allowed to rouse the echoes of Harley Street with his vociferations without raising a hair on my head. I will quote, however, Mr. Oscar Browning, because Mr. Oscar Browning was a great figure in Cambridge at one time, and used to examine the students at Girton and Newnham. Mr. Oscar Browning was wont to declare "that the impression left on his mind, after looking over any set of examination papers, was that, irrespective of the marks he might give, the best woman was intellectually the inferior of the worst man." After saying that Mr. Browning went back to his rooms—and it is this sequel that endears him and makes him a human figure of some bulk and majesty—he went back to his rooms and found a stable-boy lying on the sofa—"a mere skeleton, his cheeks were cavernous and sallow, his teeth were black, and he did not appear to have the full use of his limbs. . . . 'That's Arthur' [said Mr. Browning]. 'He's a dear boy really and most highminded.' " The two pictures always seem to me to complete each other. And happily in this age of biography the two pictures often do complete each other, so that we are able to interpret the opinions of great men not only by what they say, but by what they do.

13   But though this is possible now, such opinions coming from the lips of important people must have been formidable enough even fifty years ago. Let us suppose that a father from the highest motives did not wish his daughter to leave home and become a writer, painter or scholar. "See what Mr. Oscar Browning says," he would say; and there was not only Mr. Oscar Browning; there was the *Saturday Review*; there was Mr. Greg—the "essentials of a woman's being," said Mr. Greg emphatically, "are that *they are supported by, and they minister to, men*"—there was an enormous body of masculine opinion to the effect that nothing could be expected of women intellectually. Even if her father did not read out loud these opinions, any girl could read them for herself; and the reading, even in the nineteenth

century, must have lowered her vitality, and told profoundly upon her work. There would always have been that assertion—you cannot do this, you are incapable of doing that—to protest against, to overcome. Probably for a novelist this germ is no longer of much effect; for there have been women novelists of merit. But for painters it must still have some sting in it; and for musicians, I imagine, is even now active and poisonous in the extreme. The woman composer stands where the actress stood in the time of Shakespeare. Nick Greene, I thought, remembering the story I had made about Shakespeare's sister, said that a woman acting put him in mind of a dog dancing. Johnson repeated the phrase two hundred years later of women preaching. And here, I said, opening a book about music, we have the very words used again in this year of grace, 1928, of women who try to write music. "Of Mlle. Germaine Tailleferre one can only repeat Dr. Johnson's dictum concerning a woman preacher, transposed into terms of music. 'Sir, a woman's composing is like a dog's walking on his hind legs. It is not done well, but you are surprised to find it done at all.' " So accurately does history repeat itself.

14   Thus, I concluded, shutting Mr. Oscar Browning's life and pushing away the rest, it is fairly evident that even in the nineteenth century a woman was not encouraged to be an artist. On the contrary, she was snubbed, slapped, lectured and exhorted. Her mind must have been strained and her vitality lowered by the need of opposing this, of disproving that. For here again we come within range of that very interesting and obscure masculine complex which has had so much influence upon the woman's movement; that deep-seated desire, not so much that *she* shall be inferior as that *he* shall be superior, which plants him wherever one looks, not only in front of the arts, but barring the way to politics too, even when the risk to himself seems infinitesimal and the suppliant humble and devoted. Even Lady Bessborough, I remembered, with all her passion for politics, must humbly bow herself and write to Lord Granville Leveson-Gower: ". . . notwithstanding all my violence in politicks and talking so much on that subject, I perfectly agree with you that no woman has any business to meddle with that or any other serious business, further than giving her opinion (if she is ask'd)." And so she goes on to spend her enthusiasm where it meets with no obstacle whatsoever upon that immensely important subject, Lord Granville's maiden speech in the House of Commons. The spectacle is certainly a strange one, I thought. The history of men's opposition to women's emancipation is more interesting perhaps than the story of that emancipation itself. An amusing book might be made of it if some young student at Girton or Newnham would collect examples and deduce a theory—but she would need thick gloves on her hands, and bars to protect her of solid gold.

15   But what is amusing now, I recollected, shutting Lady Bessborough, had to be taken in desperate earnest once. Opinions that one now pastes in a book labelled cock-a-doodle-dum and keeps for reading to select audiences

on summer nights once drew tears, I can assure you. Among your grand-mothers and great-grandmothers there were many that wept their eyes out. Florence Nightingale shrieked aloud in her agony. Moreover, it is all very well for you, who have got yourselves to college and enjoy sitting-rooms—or is it only bed-sitting-rooms?—of your own to say that genius should disregard such opinions; that genius should be above caring what is said of it. Unfortunately, it is precisely the men or women of genius who mind most what is said of them. Remember Keats. Remember the words he had cut on his tombstone. Think of Tennyson; think—but I need hardly multiply instances of the undeniable, if very unfortunate, fact that it is the nature of the artist to mind excessively what is said about him. Literature is strewn with the wreckage of men who have minded beyond reason the opinions of others.

16   And this susceptibility of theirs is doubly unfortunate, I thought, returning again to my original enquiry into what state of mind is most propitious for creative work, because the mind of an artist, in order to achieve the pro-digious effort of freeing whole and entire the work that is in him, must be incandescent, like Shakespeare's mind, I conjectured, looking at the book which lay open at *Antony and Cleopatra*. There must be no obstacle in it, no foreign matter unconsumed.

17   For though we say that we know nothing about Shakespeare's state of mind, even as we say that, we are saying something about Shakespeare's state of mind. The reason perhaps why we know so little of Shakespeare—compared with Donne or Ben Jonson or Milton—is that his grudges and spites and antipathies are hidden from us. We are not held up by some "revelation" which reminds us of the writer. All desire to protest, to preach, to proclaim an injury, to pay off a score, to make the world the witness of some hardship or grievance was fired out of him and consumed. Therefore his poetry flows from him free and unimpeded. If ever a human being got his work expressed completely, it was Shakespeare. If ever a mind was incandescent, unimpeded, I thought, turning again to the bookcase, it was Shakespeare's mind.

Topics for Writing and Discussion

1.   In the larger essay from which this section is taken, Woolf says that in order to write, a woman must have a small independent income and "a room of one's own." In what ways does the example of Shakespeare's sister support that assertion? Why does Woolf think the sister would have failed to write immortal dramas as did her brother Shakespeare? Notice particularly the details of the Elizabethan woman's life as Woolf found it described in Trevelyan's *History of England*.

2.   Woolf imagines various ways in which gifted women in the past ex-pressed their talents. List several of the outlets she describes and explain

whether you find her projections plausible. Do modern women with literary, artistic, and musical genius still resort to any of these outlets or do most of them find the same means of expression as do men with similar talents?

3. Notice the choice of words, the point of view, and the way Woolf addresses her audience. What tone is established? Formal? Informal? Pleading? Demanding? Sarcastic? Despairing? Hopeful? Or something else? Indicate specific passages to support your analysis.

4. What does Woolf mean when she says (near the end of the essay) that if a young woman were to write the history of men's opposition to women's emancipation "she would need thick gloves on her hands, and bars to protect her of solid gold." What kind of protection would thick gloves offer? Why would the bars be made of gold?

5. Describe a woman you know personally (or one about whom you have read or studied) who has become successful in a previously male-dominated field. Some famous choices might include Amelia Earhart, Margaret Mead, Golda Meir, Sally Ride, or Sandra Day O'Connor. Focus your description on one outstanding quality that helped your choice succeed.

James Baldwin at his home in Saint Paul de Vence, March 17, 1981 (Y. Coatsaliou/ Sygma)

Stranger in the Village

James Baldwin
(1924–1987)

Born in Harlem, James Baldwin became a lay
preacher at age 14 but soon left religious life,
determined to become a writer. After winning a
Eugene Saxon Fellowship, he moved to Paris
where he lived and wrote from 1948 to 1956.
While in France, he wrote both fiction and
nonfiction, including two of his best-known works,
the novel *Go Tell It on the Mountain* (1953) and the
collection of essays *Notes of a Native Son* (1956).
Always deeply committed to human-rights issues,
Baldwin returned to the United States in 1957 and
became actively involved in the struggle for civil
liberty. His nonfiction books such as *The Fire Next
Time* (1963) and *No Name Street* (1972) reflect his
experiences, thoughts, and feelings as a tireless
worker for equality. "Stranger in the Village"
describes his stay in a small Swiss village where he
was the first black man ever to visit. His
observations lead him to analyze black-white
relations in the United States and to express his
profound concern about the conflicts he sees.

1 From all available evidence no black man had ever set foot in this tiny
Swiss village before I came. I was told before arriving that I would probably
be a "sight" for the village; I took this to mean that people of my complexion
were rarely seen in Switzerland, and also that city people are always something of a "sight" outside of the city. It did not occur to me—possibly because
I am an American—that there could be people anywhere who had never
seen a Negro.

2   It is a fact that cannot be explained on the basis of the inaccessibility of the village. The village is very high, but it is only four hours from Milan and three hours from Lausanne. It is true that it is virtually unknown. Few people making plans for a holiday would elect to come here. On the other hand, the villagers are able, presumably, to come and go as they please— which they do: to another town at the foot of the mountain, with a population of approximately five thousand, the nearest place to see a movie or go to the bank. In the village there is no movie house, no bank, no library, no theater; very few radios, one jeep, one station wagon; and, at the moment, one typewriter, mine, an invention which the woman next door to me here had never seen. There are about six hundred people living here, all Catholic— I conclude this from the fact that the Catholic church is open all year round, whereas the Protestant chapel, set off on a hill a little removed from the village, is open only in the summertime when the tourists arrive. There are four or five hotels, all closed now, and four or five *bistros*, of which, however, only two do any business during the winter. These two do not do a great deal, for life in the village seems to end around nine or ten o'clock. There are a few stores, butcher, baker, *épicerie*, a hardware store, and a money-changer—who cannot change travelers' checks, but must send them down to the bank, an operation which takes two or three days. There is something called the *Ballet Haus*, closed in the winter and used for God knows what, certainly not ballet, during the summer. There seems to be only one school-house in the village, and this for the quite young children; I suppose this to mean that their older brothers and sisters at some point descend from these mountains in order to complete their education—possibly, again, to the town just below. The landscape is absolutely forbidding, mountains towering on all four sides, ice and snow as far as the eye can reach. In this white wilderness, men and women and children move all day, carrying washing, wood, buckets of milk or water, sometimes skiing on Sunday after-noons. All week long boys and young men are to be seen shoveling snow off the rooftops, or dragging wood down from the forest in sleds.

3   The village's only real attraction, which explains the tourist season, is the hot spring water. A disquietingly high proportion of these tourists are crip-ples, or semi-cripples, who come year after year—from other parts of Switz-erland, usually—to take the waters. This lends the village, at the height of the season, a rather terrifying air of sanctity, as though it were a lesser Lourdes. There is often something beautiful, there is always something aw-ful, in the spectacle of a person who has lost one of his faculties, a faculty he never questioned until it was gone, and who struggles to recover it. Yet people remain people, on crutches or indeed on deathbeds; and wherever I passed, the first summer I was here, among the native villagers or among the lame, a wind passed with me—of astonishment, curiosity, amusement, and outrage. That first summer I stayed two weeks and never intended to return. But I did return in the winter, to work; the village offers, obviously,

no distractions whatever and has the further advantage of being extremely cheap. Now it is winter again, a year later, and I am here again. Everyone in the village knows my name, though they scarcely ever use it, knows that I come from America—though, this, apparently, they will never really believe: black men come from Africa—and everyone knows that I am the friend of the son of a woman who was born here, and that I am staying in their chalet. But I remain as much a stranger today as I was the first day I arrived, and the children shout *Neger! Neger!* as I walk along the streets.

4　　It must be admitted that in the beginning I was far too shocked to have any real reaction. In so far as I reacted at all, I reacted by trying to be pleasant—it being a great part of the American Negro's education (long before he goes to school) that he must make people "like" him. This smile-and-the-world-smiles-with-you routine worked about as well in this situation as it had in the situation for which it was designed, which is to say that it did not work at all. No one, after all, can be liked whose human weight and complexity cannot be, or has not been, admitted. My smile was simply another unheard-of phenomenon which allowed them to see my teeth—they did not, really, see my smile and I began to think that, should I take to snarling, no one would notice any difference. All of the physical characteristics of the Negro which had caused me, in America, a very different and almost forgotten pain were nothing less than miraculous—or infernal—in the eyes of the village people. Some thought my hair was the color of tar, that it had the texture of wire, or the texture of cotton. It was jocularly suggested that I might let it all grow long and make myself a winter coat. If I sat in the sun for more than five minutes some daring creature was certain to come along and gingerly put his fingers on my hair, as though he were afraid of an electric shock, or put his hand on my hand, astonished that the color did not rub off. In all of this, in which it must be conceded there was the charm of genuine wonder and in which there was certainly no element of intentional unkindness, there was yet no suggestion that I was human: I was simply a living wonder.

5　　I knew that they did not mean to be unkind, and I know it now; it is necessary, nevertheless, for me to repeat this to myself each time I walk out of the chalet. The children who shout *Neger!* have no way of knowing the echoes this sound raises in me. They are brimming with good humor and the more daring swell with pride when I stop to speak with them. Just the same, there are days when I cannot pause and smile, when I have no heart to play with them; when, indeed, I mutter sourly to myself, exactly as I muttered on the streets of a city these children have never seen, when I was no bigger than these children are now: *Your* mother *was a nigger.* Joyce is right about history being a nightmare—but it may be the nightmare from which no one *can* awaken. People are trapped in history and history is trapped in them.

6   There is a custom in the village—I am told it is repeated in many villages—of "buying" African natives for the purpose of converting them to Christianity. There stands in the church all year round a small box with a slot for money, decorated with a black figurine, and into this box the villagers drop their francs. During the *carnaval* which precedes Lent, two village children have their faces blackened—out of which bloodless darkness their blue eyes shine like ice—and fantastic horsehair wigs are placed on their blond heads; thus disguised, they solicit among the villagers for money for the missionaries in Africa. Between the box in the church and the blackened children, the village "bought" last year six or eight African natives. This was reported to me with pride by the wife of one of the *bistro* owners and I was careful to express astonishment and pleasure at the solicitude shown by the village for the souls of black folk. The *bistro* owner's wife beamed with a pleasure far more genuine than my own and seemed to feel that I might now breathe more easily concerning the souls of at least six of my kinsmen.

7   I tried not to think of these so lately baptized kinsmen, of the price paid for them, or the peculiar price they themselves would pay, and said nothing about my father, who having taken his own conversion too literally never, at bottom, forgave the white world (which he described as heathen) for having saddled him with a Christ in whom, to judge at least from their treatment of him, they themselves no longer believed. I thought of white men arriving for the first time in an African village, strangers there, as I am a stranger here, and tried to imagine the astounded populace touching their hair and marveling at the color of their skin. But there is a great difference between being the first white man to be seen by Africans and being the first black man to be seen by whites. The white man takes the astonishment as tribute, for he arrives to conquer and to convert the natives, whose inferiority in relation to himself is not even to be questioned; whereas I, without a thought of conquest, find myself among a people whose culture controls me, has even, in a sense, created me, people who have cost me more in anguish and rage than they will ever know, who yet do not even know of my existence. The astonishment with which I might have greeted them, should they have stumbled into my African village a few hundred years ago, might have rejoiced their hearts. But the astonishment with which they greet me today can only poison mine.

8   And this is so despite everything I may do to feel differently, despite my friendly conversations with the *bistro* owner's wife, despite their three-year-old son who has at last become my friend, despite the *saluts* and *bonsoirs* which I exchange with people as I walk, despite the fact that I know that no individual can be taken to task for what history is doing, or has done. I say that the culture of these people controls me—but they can scarcely be held responsible for European culture. America comes out of Europe, but these people have never seen America, nor have most of them seen more

of Europe than the hamlet at the foot of their mountain. Yet they move with an authority which I shall never have; and they regard me, quite rightly, not only as a stranger in their village but as a suspect latecomer, bearing no credentials, to everything they have—however unconsciously—inherited.

9   For this village, even were it incomparably more remote and incredibly more primitive, is the West, the West onto which I have been so strangely grafted. These people cannot be, from the point of view of power, strangers anywhere in the world; they have made the modern world, in effect, even if they do not know it. The most illiterate among them is related, in a way that I am not, to Dante, Shakespeare, Michelangelo, Aeschylus, Da Vinci, Rembrandt, and Racine; the cathedral at Chartres says something to them which it cannot say to me, as indeed would New York's Empire State Building, should anyone here ever see it. Out of their hymns and dances come Beethoven and Bach. Go back a few centuries and they are in their full glory—but I am in Africa, watching the conquerors arrive.

10   The rage of the disesteemed is personally fruitless, but it is also absolutely inevitable; this rage, so generally discounted, so little understood even among the people whose daily bread it is, is one of the things that makes history. Rage can only with difficulty, and never entirely, be brought under the domination of the intelligence and is therefore not susceptible to any arguments whatever. This is a fact which ordinary representatives of the *Herrenvolk*, having never felt this rage and being unable to imagine it, quite fail to understand. Also, rage cannot be hidden, it can only be dissembled. This dissembling deludes the thoughtless, and strengthens rage and adds, to rage, contempt. There are, no doubt, as many ways of coping with the resulting complex of tensions as there are black men in the world, but no black man can hope ever to be entirely liberated from this internal warfare— rage, dissembling, and contempt having inevitably accompanied his first realization of the power of white men. What is crucial here is that, since white men represent in the black man's world so heavy a weight, white men have for black men a reality which is far from being reciprocal; and hence all black men have toward all white men an attitude which is designed, really, either to rob the white man of the jewel of his naïveté, or else to make it cost him dear.

11   The black man insists, by whatever means he finds at his disposal, that the white man cease to regard him as an exotic rarity and recognize him as a human being. This is a very charged and difficult moment, for there is a great deal of will power involved in the white man's naïveté. Most people are not naturally reflective any more than they are naturally malicious, and the white man prefers to keep the black man at a certain human remove because it is easier for him thus to preserve his simplicity and avoid being called to account for crimes committed by his forefathers, or his neighbors. He is inescapably aware, nevertheless, that he is in a better position in the world than black men are, nor can he quite put to death the suspicion that

he is hated by black men therefore. He does not wish to be hated, neither does he wish to change places, and at this point in his uneasiness he can scarcely avoid having recourse to those legends which white men have created about black men, the most usual effect of which is that the white man finds himself enmeshed, so to speak, in his own language which describes hell, as well as the attributes which lead one to hell, as being as black as night.

12   Every legend, moreover, contains its residuum of truth, and the root function of language is to control the universe by describing it. It is of quite considerable significance that black men remain, in the imagination, and in overwhelming numbers in fact, beyond the disciplines of salvation; and this despite the fact that the West has been "buying" African natives for centuries. There is, I should hazard, an instantaneous necessity to be divorced from this so visibly unsaved stranger, in whose heart, moreover, one cannot guess what dreams of vengeance are being nourished; and, at the same time, there are few things on earth more attractive than the idea of the unspeakable liberty which is allowed the unredeemed. When, beneath the black mask, a human being begins to make himself felt one cannot escape a certain awful wonder as to what kind of human being it is. What one's imagination makes of other people is dictated, of course, by the laws of one's own personality and it is one of the ironies of black-white relations that, by means of what the white man imagines the black man to be, the black man is enabled to know who the white man is.

13   I have said, for example, that I am as much a stranger in this village today as I was the first summer I arrived, but this is not quite true. The villagers wonder less about the texture of my hair than they did then, and wonder rather more about me. And the fact that their wonder now exists on another level is reflected in their attitudes and in their eyes. There are the children who make those delightful, hilarious, sometimes astonishing grave overtures of friendship in the unpredictable fashion of children; other children, having been taught that the devil is a black man, scream in genuine anguish as I approach. Some of the older women never pass without a friendly greeting, never pass, indeed, if it seems that they will be able to engage me in conversation; other women look down or look away or rather contemptuously smirk. Some of the men drink with me and suggest that I learn how to ski—partly, I gather, because they cannot imagine what I would look like on skis—and want to know if I am married, and ask questions about my *métier*. But some of the men have accused *le sale nègre*—behind my back—of stealing wood and there is already in the eyes of some of them that peculiar intent, paranoiac malevolence which one sometimes surprises in the eyes of American white men when, out walking with their Sunday girl, they see a Negro male approach.

14   There is a dreadful abyss between the streets of this village and the streets of the city in which I was born, between the children who shout *Neger!*

today and those who shouted *Nigger!* yesterday—the abyss is experience, the American experience. The syllable hurled behind me today expresses, above all, wonder: I am a stranger here. But I am not a stranger in America and the same syllable riding on the American air expresses the war my presence has occasioned in the American soul.

15   For this village brings home to me this fact: that there was a day, and not really a very distant day, when Americans were scarcely Americans at all but discontented Europeans, facing a great unconquered continent and strolling, say, into a marketplace and seeing black men for the first time. The shock this spectacle afforded is suggested, surely, by the promptness with which they decided that these black men were not really men but cattle. It is true that the necessity on the part of the settlers of the New World of reconciling their moral assumptions with the fact—and the necessity—of slavery enhanced immensely the charm of this idea, and it is also true that this idea expresses, with a truly American bluntness, the attitude which to varying extents all masters have had toward all slaves.

16   But between all former slaves and slave-owners and the drama which begins for Americans over three hundred years ago at Jamestown, there are at least two differences to be observed. The American Negro slave could not suppose, for one thing, as slaves in past epochs had supposed and often done, that he would ever be able to wrest the power from his master's hands. This was a supposition which the modern era, which was to bring about such vast changes in the aims and dimensions of power, put to death; it only begins, in unprecedented fashion, and with dreadful implications, to be resurrected today. But even had this supposition persisted with undiminished force, the American Negro slave could not have used it to lend his condition dignity, for the reason that this supposition rests on another: that the slave in exile yet remains related to his past, has some means—if only in memory—of revering and sustaining the forms of his former life, is able, in short, to maintain his identity.

17   This was not the case with the American Negro slave. He is unique among the black men of the world in that his past was taken from him, almost literally, at one blow. One wonders what on earth the first slave found to say to the first dark child he bore. I am told that there are Haitians able to trace their ancestry back to African kings, but any American Negro wishing to go back so far will find his journey through time abruptly arrested by the signature on the bill of sale which served as the entrance paper for his ancestor. At the time—to say nothing of the circumstances—of the enslavement of the captive black man who was to become the American Negro, there was not the remotest possibility that he would ever take power from his master's hands. There was no reason to suppose that his situation would ever change, nor was there, shortly, anything to indicate that his situation had ever been different. It was his necessity, in the words of E. Franklin Frazier, to find a "motive" for living under American culture or die." The

identity of the American Negro comes out of this extreme situation, and the evolution of this identity was a source of the most intolerable anxiety in the minds and the lives of his masters.

18   For the history of the American Negro is unique also in this: that the question of his humanity, and of his rights therefore as a human being, became a burning one for several generations of Americans, so burning a question that it ultimately became one of those used to divide the nation. It is out of this argument that the venom of the epithet *Nigger!* is derived. It is an argument which Europe has never had, and hence Europe quite sincerely fails to understand how or why the argument arose in the first place, why its effects are so frequently disastrous and always so unpredictable, why it refuses until today to be entirely settled. Europe's black possessions remained—and do remain—in Europe's colonies, at which remove they represented no threat to European identity. If they posed any problem at all for the European conscience, it was a problem which remained comfortingly abstract: in effect, the black man, *as a man*, did not exist for Europe. But in America, even as a slave, he was an inescapable part of the general social fabric and no American could escape having an attitude toward him. Americans attempt until today to make an abstraction of the Negro, but the very nature of these abstractions reveals the tremendous effects the presence of the Negro has had on the American character.

19   When one considers the history of the Negro in America it is of the greatest importance to recognize that the moral beliefs of a person, or a people, are never really as tenuous as life—which is not moral—very often causes them to appear; these create for them a frame of reference and a necessary hope, the hope being that when life has done its worst they will be enabled to rise above themselves and to triumph over life. Life would scarcely be bearable if this hope did not exist. Again, even when the worst has been said, to betray a belief is not by any means to have put oneself beyond its power; the betrayal of a belief is not the same thing as ceasing to believe. If this were not so there would be no moral standards in the world at all. Yet one must also recognize that morality is based on ideas and that all ideas are dangerous—dangerous because ideas can only lead to action and where the action leads no man can say. And dangerous in this respect: that confronted with the impossibility of remaining faithful to one's beliefs, and the equal impossibility of becoming free of them, one can be driven to the most inhuman excesses. The ideas on which American beliefs are based are not, though Americans often seem to think so, ideas which originated in America. They came out of Europe. And the establishment of democracy on the American continent was scarcely as radical a break with the past as was the necessity, which Americans faced, of broadening this concept to include black men.

20   This was, literally, a hard necessity. It was impossible, for one thing, for Americans to abandon their beliefs, not only because these beliefs alone

seemed able to justify the sacrifices they had endured and the blood that they had spilled, but also because these beliefs afforded them their only bulwark against a moral chaos as absolute as the physical chaos of the continent it was their destiny to conquer. But in the situation in which Americans found themselves, these beliefs threatened an idea which, whether or not one likes to think so, is the very warp and woof of the heritage of the West, the idea of white supremacy.

21   Americans have made themselves notorious by the shrillness and the brutality with which they have insisted on this idea, but they did not invent it; and it has escaped the world's notice that those very excesses of which Americans have been guilty imply a certain, unprecedented uneasiness over the idea's life and power, if not, indeed, the idea's validity. The idea of white supremacy rests simply on the fact that white men are the creators of civilization (the present civilization, which is the only one that matters; all previous civilizations are simply "contributions" to our own) and are therefore civilization's guardians and defenders. Thus it was impossible for Americans to accept the black man as one of themselves, for to do so was to jeopardize their status as white men. But not so to accept him was to deny his human reality, his human weight and complexity, and the strain of denying the overwhelmingly undeniable forced Americans into rationalizations so fantastic that they approached the pathological.

22   At the root of the American Negro problem is the necessity of the American white man to find a way of living with the Negro in order to be able to live with himself. And the history of this problem can be reduced to the means used by Americans—lynch law and law, segregation and legal acceptance, terrorization and concession—either to come to terms with this necessity, or to find a way around it, or (most usually) to find a way of doing both these things at once. The resulting spectacle, at once foolish and dreadful, led someone to make the quite accurate observation that "the Negro-in-America is a form of insanity which overtakes white men."

23   In this long battle, a battle by no means finished, the unforeseeable effects of which will be felt by many future generations, the white man's motive was the protection of his identity; the black man was motivated by the need to establish an identity. And despite the terrorization which the Negro in America endured and endures sporadically until today, despite the cruel and totally inescapable ambivalence of his status in his country, the battle for his identity has long ago been won. He is not a visitor to the West, but a citizen there, an American; as American as the Americans who despise him, the Americans who fear him, the Americans who love him—the Americans who became less than themselves, or rose to be greater than themselves by virtue of the fact that the challenge he represented was inescapable. He is perhaps the only black man in the world whose relationship to white men is more terrible, more subtle, and more meaningful than the relationship of bitter possessed to uncertain possessor. His survival depended, and his de-

velopment depends, on his ability to turn his peculiar status in the Western world to his own advantage and, it may be, to the very great advantage of that world. It remains for him to fashion out of his experience that which will give him sustenance, and a voice.

24 The cathedral of Chartres, I have said, says something to the people of this village which it cannot say to me; but it is important to understand that this cathedral says something to me which it cannot say to them. Perhaps they are struck by the power of the spires, the glory of the windows; but they have known God, after all, longer than I have known him, and in a different way, and I am terrified by the slippery bottomless well to be found in the crypt, down which heretics were hurled to death, and by the obscene, inescapable gargoyles jutting out of the stone and seeming to say that God and the devil can never be divorced. I doubt that the villagers think of the devil when they face a cathedral because they have never been identified with the devil. But I must accept the status which myth, if nothing else, gives me in the West before I can hope to change the myth.

25 Yet, if the American Negro has arrived at his identity by virtue of the absoluteness of his estrangement from his past, American white men still nourish the illusion that there is some means of recovering the European innocence, of returning to a state in which black men do not exist. This is one of the greatest errors Americans can make. The identity they fought so hard to protect has, by virtue of that battle, undergone a change: Americans are as unlike any other white people in the world as it is possible to be. I do not think, for example, that it is too much to suggest that the American vision of the world—which allows so little reality, generally speaking, for any of the darker forces in human life, which tends until today to paint moral issues in glaring black and white—owes a great deal to the battle waged by Americans to maintain between themselves and black men a human separation which could not be bridged. It is only now beginning to be borne in on us—very faintly, it must be admitted, very slowly, and very much against our will—that this vision of the world is dangerously inaccurate, and perfectly useless. For it protects our moral high-mindedness at the terrible expense of weakening our grasp of reality. People who shut their eyes to reality simply invite their own destruction, and anyone who insists on remaining in a state of innocence long after that innocence is dead turns himself into a monster.

26 The time has come to realize that the interracial drama acted out on the American continent has not only created a new black man, it has created a new white man, too. No road whatever will lead Americans back to the simplicity of this European village where white men still have the luxury of looking on me as a stranger. I am not, really, a stranger any longer for any American alive. One of the things that distinguishes Americans from other people is that no other people has ever been so deeply involved in the lives of black men, and vice versa. This fact faced, with all its impli-

cations, it can be seen that the history of the American Negro problem is not merely shameful, it is also something of an achievement. For even when the worst has been said, it must also be added that the perpetual challenge posed by this problem was always, somehow, perpetually met. It is precisely this black-white experience which may prove of indispensable value to us in the world we face today. This world is white no longer, and it will never be white again.

Topics for Writing and Discussion

1. Explain the differences Baldwin sees between the experience of a black man visiting a white village and the experience of a white man visiting an African village. What significance does Baldwin attach to these distinctions?

2. Why do the Swiss villagers have the custom of "buying" African natives? How do the villagers feel about the custom? What is their intent in telling Baldwin about this tradition? How does Baldwin react? How does this incident relate to the central idea of the essay?

3. Read the first and last paragraph of the essay. Notice the sentence in the final paragraph that reflects an idea expressed in the opening paragraph. How does this device serve to unite the complex examples and comparisons Baldwin develops in "Stranger in the Village"?

4. Near the end of the essay, Baldwin says, "The cathedral at Chartres . . . says something to the people of this village which it cannot say to me; but it is important to understand that this cathedral says something to me which it cannot say to them." What does the cathedral "say" to the Swiss villagers? To Baldwin? How does the cathedral serve as a symbol for the conflict Baldwin describes between black and white Americans?

5. Write a description of a place in which you have felt isolated or alienated. Keep Baldwin's essay in mind and include descriptions of people, objects, landscapes, dwellings—anything that will make clear your role as "stranger." What discoveries did you make about yourself or your culture?

Writing Assignments for Chapter Four

Description

1. In John Steinbeck's novel *The Grapes of Wrath*, from which "The Turtle" was taken, some readers see the slow, determined animal as a symbol of the beleaguered but enduring farm workers of the story. Try writing your own symbolic description of another animal, making clear to your readers through your use of language the person, group of people, or philosophy the animal represents.

2. Describe objectively one creature or object in nature you can study closely, one that you can repeatedly observe in person or through a microscope, telescope, binoculars, or camera eye. Select a logical pattern of organization for your description, and avoid making your description bland by using numerous clear details rather than generalities. (Hint: You might find it helpful to read an essay that arose from a similar assignment, "Take This Fish and Look at It," on pp. 272–275.)

3. In "Portraits of my Parents" Maxine Hong Kingston describes pictures of her mother and father in such a clear way that readers can not only visualize her parents but also understand how they differed from each other. Write a description of two influential people in your life (your parents, grandparents, siblings, teachers, mentors) that reveals their physical characteristics, their personalities, and possibly their differences.

4. In "The Way to Rainy Mountain" Scott Momaday describes a journey. Think of a journey you have taken, a trip in which you discovered something important about yourself or your family. Was it a pilgrimage of some sort, as Momaday describes his journey? A retracing of steps taken at an earlier time by you or an ancestor? A trip home or a new adventure? Focus on some significant part of your journey and describe what you saw and experienced, revealing its importance to the reader. (Perhaps your memory will be triggered by a scene of an important person, just as Momaday most vividly recalls a picture of his grandmother at her prayers.)

5. After E. B. White returned to his childhood vacation site with his son, he wrote about the experience (and his feelings of mortality) in the essay "Once More to the Lake." Think of an important place in your life (a room, a house, a hideaway) and describe it vividly so that your feelings toward the place are clear to your readers. You may wish, as did White,

to use your last sentence to emphasize the deeper significance of the place you have chosen.

6. Virginia Woolf uses her imagination in "If Shakespeare Had Had a Sister" to draw a picture of what might have happened to a talented Elizabethan woman with aspirations similar to those of Shakespeare. Using your own imagination, describe the fate of a modern brother and sister who also wish to pursue similar goals, professional training, or careers. Do young women today still face any of the problems Woolf imagined for Judith Shakespeare?

7. In "Stranger in the Village" James Baldwin wrote that prior to 1953 white Americans had tried unsuccessfully to "maintain between themselves and black men a human separation which could not be bridged." He saw in the early 1950s, however, a faint recognition by some Americans that such a relationship could not continue. Has the relationship between black and white Americans improved since Baldwin wrote his essay? Write an essay describing one or two important changes you see today. In what ways are blacks and whites no longer strangers to each other?

Chapter Five

Process

Whenever you tell how something works or how something happens or how something can be accomplished, you explain a *process*. If you were to purchase an unassembled file cabinet, you would probably need step-by-step instructions to guide you to the completion of the finished product. Similarly, if you wanted to know how diet and exercise are related to weight gain, weight loss, or weight maintenance, a nutritionist could demonstrate the relationship between calorie intake and physical activity to weight control by explaining the process of calorie burning. In both situations you would get the information you want by understanding carefully prescribed, sequenced steps or stages that lead to the desired end. Thus, to explain a process, a writer must clearly present the steps or stages of the process and the order in which those steps or stages appear.

Types of Processes

There are two kinds of process essays: *directional* and *informative*.

A *directional process* tells readers how to do or make something; in other words, it gives "how to" instructions. For instance, if you wanted to tell a friend how to get to your house, you would write clear, logical directions to your home. Or if you wanted to tell someone how to assemble a bookcase, you would write clear, logically ordered, step-by-step directions that would enable him or her to complete the project. Examples of directional processes can be found throughout your home and workplace: cookbooks (how to make chili), first-aid kits (how to treat a burn), telephone books (how to call person-to-person), car repair manuals (how to change the oil), copy machine instructions (how to reduce a page of print). Most often, a directional process essay teaches the reader to create, fix, or do something, which explains why this kind of essay is also known as *instructional* or *how to* process.

A second type of process is *informative*. In this kind of essay, the process is analyzed in order to explain and to inform readers about the steps of the process. *Informative process* differs from directional process in that the emphasis is not on completing a procedure or performing a task, but on understanding how or why a process works. Informative processes are not meant to be duplicated by the reader; the writer's purpose is to inform through analysis rather than to give "how to" directions. For instance, Carin Quinn wrote "The Jeaning of America" not to tell readers how to make blue jeans but to reveal the steps in the creation of a uniquely American product. In "The American Way of Death" Jessica Mitford's intention is not for her readers to embalm their friends and relatives; rather, she presents her analysis to enlighten her readers about a little-known but common procedure that she feels may not be necessary or desirable.

Organizing the Process Essay

Like other essays, the process essay—whether it is directional or informative—should consist of three parts: the introduction, the body, and the conclusion. The *introduction* is particularly important because it will contain the thesis statement or give the objective you wish to accomplish. You might also include any background information the reader may need to understand the process fully, a list of materials needed to complete the task, or any other information that will be needed to set the process in motion.

The *body* of the essay will develop the thesis or unfold the directions. Steps that contain many or complex details might be grouped together in stages in the process. Each stage should be sequenced in a logical, chronological order. As you construct the process essay, rely on the other rhetorical structures to help clarify steps: use description, narration, definition, or illustration to simplify complex principles or directions. Strive for a smooth writing style by using clear transitions. Numerical transitions (*first, second, third,* and so on) may be precise but can be boring. Try more creative sequencing techniques with transitions such as *begin by* (or, perhaps, verbal forms like *beginning with* or *to begin* . . .), *continue by, go on to, when you have finished,* and so on.

Your *conclusion* may tell the significance of the completed process or explain other important uses. Or, if appropriate, you might leave the reader with a thought or image that sums up or emphasizes the essay's purpose, as Jessica Mitford does in "The American Way of Death" when she concludes her satirical attack on the embalming process by describing a scene of a corpse holding an "open house" from 10 A.M. to 9 P.M. While your choice of conclusions may depend upon your purpose, don't abruptly stop your essay after the last step and don't end with a dry rewording of your thesis. Leave the reader with a feeling of having satisfactorily completed an interesting procedure.

Writing the Process Essay

Whether you are constructing a directional or an informative process, consider the following advice to help you produce a clear essay:

1. *Present your process essay's objective or purpose in a thesis statement.*
   In "The American Way of Death" Jessica Mitford explains the "purpose of embalming is to make the corpse presentable for viewing in a suitably costly container," and her essay goes on to explain the process of embalming and at the same time raises the question of the appropriateness of the practice. Carin Quinn first announces that blue jeans are an "American symbol," and her essay then shows how jeans became such a national tradition.

2. *Consider your audience.*
   Are you addressing a novice or an expert? How much detail will your reader need to follow your directions or to understand your information? Do you need to describe any essential equipment or to define any technical terms? Remember that you are the specialist explaining a process to people who are interested but unfamiliar with its steps, stages, or parts.

3. *Explain each step clearly in sufficient detail and in logical order.*
   Skipping a step in a process may mean that your readers cannot follow or complete the directions; fuzzy, unclear, or haphazard descriptions may mean that readers will misunderstand your instructions or will miss the point of your analysis. Notice that in "Attitude" Garrison Keillor carefully and methodically (and humorously) explains the steps involved in creating a good attitude on the baseball field. In "The American Way of Death" Jessica Mitford vividly moves through each stage of the embalming process using an abundance of sensory details so that the reader clearly understands the entire process and Mitford's view of it. The steps in the process are ordered chronologically and are smoothly connected with transitional devices for easy comprehension.

4. *Maintain a consistent tense and point of view throughout the essay.*
   Most often, directional process essays are written in the present tense and are directed at "you," a reader who wishes to follow the "how to" instructions. Informational essays may be written in the present or past tense and are generally presented from a third-person point of view (he, she, it, or they are doing something). If a writer is retelling a personal series of events, the first person "I" can be used to present the information.

Learning to write a clear process essay is a valuable skill because in today's complex society people frequently need to understand new procedures or products.

The Jeaning of America

Carin Quinn

Carin C. Quinn is an essayist who received her
Master's degree in American Studies from
California State University at Los Angeles in 1976.
In "The Jeaning of America—and the World,"
which was first published in *American Heritage*
magazine in 1978, she describes the significance of
blue jeans to the American way of life and traces
the growth of their popularity both in the United
States and abroad.

1   This is the story of a sturdy American symbol which has now spread
throughout most of the world. The symbol is not the dollar. It is not even
Coca-Cola. It is a simple pair of pants called blue jeans, and what the pants
symbolize is what Alexis de Tocqueville called "a manly and legitimate
passion for equality. . . ." Blue jeans are favored equally by bureaucrats and
cowboys; bankers and deadbeats; fashion designers and beer drinkers. They
draw no distinctions and recognize no classes; they are merely American.
Yet they are sought after almost everywhere in the world—including Russia,
where authorities recently broke up a teen-aged gang that was selling them
on the black market for two hundred dollars a pair. They have been around
for a long time, and it seems likely that they will outlive even the necktie.

2   This ubiquitous American symbol was the invention of a Bavarian-born
Jew. His name was Levi Strauss.

3   He was born in Bad Ocheim, Germany, in 1829, and during the European
political turmoil of 1848 decided to take his chances in New York, to which
his two brothers already had emigrated. Upon arrival, Levi soon found that
his two brothers had exaggerated their tales of an easy life in the land of
the main chance. They were landowners, they had told him; instead, he
found them pushing needles, thread, pots, pans, ribbons, yarn, scissors, and
buttons to housewives. For two years he was a lowly peddler, hauling some
180 pounds of sundries door-to-door to eke out a marginal living. When a

married sister in San Francisco offered to pay his way West in 1850, he jumped at the opportunity, taking with him bolts of canvas he hoped to sell for tenting.

4   It was the wrong kind of canvas for that purpose, but while talking with a miner down from the mother lode, he learned that pants—sturdy pants that would stand up to the rigors of the digging—were almost impossible to find. Opportunity beckoned. On the spot, Strauss measured the man's girth and inseam with a piece of string and, for six dollars in gold dust, had [the canvas] tailored into a pair of stiff but rugged pants. The miner was delighted with the result, word got around about "those pants of Levi's," and Strauss was in business. The company has been in business ever since.

5   When Strauss ran out of canvas, he wrote his two brothers to send more. He received instead a tough, brown cotton cloth made in Nîmes, France—called *serge de Nîmes* and swiftly shortened to "denim" (the word "jeans" derives from Gênes, the French word for Genoa, where a similar cloth was produced). Almost from the first, Strauss had his cloth dyed the distinctive indigo that gave blue jeans their name, but it was not until the 1870s that he added the copper rivets which have long since become a company trademark. The rivets were the idea of a Virginia City, Nevada, tailor, Jacob W. Davis, who added them to pacify a mean-tempered miner called Alkali Ike. Alkali, the story goes, complained that the pockets of his jeans always tore when he stuffed them with ore samples and demanded that Davis do something about it. As a kind of joke, Davis took the pants to a blacksmith and had the pockets riveted; once again, the idea worked so well that word got around; in 1873 Strauss appropriated and patented the gimmick—and hired Davis as a regional manager.

6   By this time, Strauss had taken both his brothers and two brothers-in-law into the company and was ready for his third San Francisco store. Over the ensuing years the company prospered locally, and by the time of his death in 1902, Strauss had become a man of prominence in California. For three decades thereafter the business remained profitable though small, with sales largely confined to the working people of the West—cowboys, lumberjacks, railroad workers, and the like. Levi's jeans were first introduced to the East, apparently, during the dude-ranch craze of the 1930s, when vacationing Easterners returned and spread the word about the wonderful pants with rivets. Another boost came in World War II, when blue jeans were declared an essential commodity and were sold only to people engaged in defense work. From a company with fifteen salespeople, two plants, and almost no business east of the Mississippi in 1946, the organization grew in thirty years to include a sales force of more than twenty-two thousand, with fifty plants and offices in thirty-five countries. Each year, more than 250,000,000 items of Levi's clothing are sold—including more than 83,000,000 pairs of riveted blue jeans. They have become, through marketing, word of mouth, and demonstrable reliability, the common pants of America. They can be pur-

chased pre-washed, pre-faded, and pre-shrunk for the suitably proletarian look. They adapt themselves to any sort of idiosyncratic use; women slit them at the inseams and convert them into long skirts, men chop them off above the knees and turn them into something to be worn while challenging the surf. Decorations and ornamentations abound.

7   The pants have become a tradition, and along the way have acquired a history of their own—so much so that the company has opened a museum in San Francisco. There was, for example, the turn-of-the-century trainman who replaced a faulty coupling with a pair of jeans; the Wyoming man who used his jeans as a towrope to haul his car out of a ditch; the Californian who found several pairs in an abandoned mine, wore them, then discovered they were sixty-three years old and still as good as new and turned them over to the Smithsonian as a tribute to their toughness. And then there is the particularly terrifying story of the careless construction worker who dangled fifty-two stories above the street until rescued, his sole support the Levi's belt loop through which his rope was hooked.

Topics for Writing and Discussion

1.   Why are blue jeans a symbol of the American way of life? What qualities do they represent that are uniquely American?

2.   How did a series of errors and practical jokes contribute to the development of jeans? How does this process further reinforce blue jeans as an American symbol? As you answer this question, keep in mind frontier tall tales and folk heroes.

3.   Quinn's use of parallel structure contributes to her lively writing style. Find examples of parallel structure and explain how Quinn's use of this pattern contributes to the pace and tone of the essay.

4.   Quinn traces the history of blue jeans up to 1978 (the year the essay was first published). What details and examples would you include if you were to bring her essay up to date? How have jeans—and people's response to them—changed in the past decade?

5.   Just as America can claim blue jeans as a symbol, so too can most cities, states, or regions identify an object or event that has become almost synonymous with their names. Write an essay describing such a symbol and explain the process by which it came to symbolize a particular city, state, or region. Quinn's essay shows that she researched her topic extensively; you may need to follow her example as you gather data about the symbol you choose.

The American Way of Death

Jessica Mitford
(1917–   )

Jessica Mitford
(© Courtesy Jessica Mitford)

Jessica Mitford was the sixth of seven children born to Lord and Lady Redesdale. She was educated, along with her five sisters, by her mother at their family home. The notorious and eccentric activities of her family have been the subject of several novels written by her sister Nancy Mitford and of her own autobiography *Daughter and Rebels* (1960). More recently the family trials and triumphs served as inspiration for a public broadcasting television series. Mitford first came to the United States in 1939 and worked as a bartender and a sales representative. She later became an investigator for the Office of Price Administration in Washington and in her late thirties began her career as an investigative journalist. Among her best-known studies of American institutions, businesses, and governmental policies are *The Trial of Dr. Spock* (1969), which describes the trial of the famous pediatrician who assisted draft resisters during the Vietnam conflict, and *Kind and Usual Punishment: The Prison Business* (1973), which critiques the American penal system. In "The American Way of Death," an excerpt from the book of the same title (1963), Mitford uses a detailed description of the embalming process to launch a bitingly satiric attack on the American funeral industry.

1   The drama begins to unfold with the arrival of the corpse at the mortuary.

2   Alas, poor Yorick! How surprised he would be to see how his counterpart of today is whisked off to a funeral parlor and is in short order sprayed, sliced, pierced, pickled, trussed, trimmed, creamed, waxed, painted, roughed,

and neatly dressed—transformed from a common corpse into a Beautiful Memory Picture. This process is known in the trade as embalming and restorative art, and is so universally employed in the United States and Canada that the funeral director does it routinely, without consulting corpse or kin. He regards as eccentric those few who are hardy enough to suggest that it might be dispensed with. Yet no law requires embalming, no religious doctrine commends it, nor is it dictated by considerations of health, sanitation, or even of personal daintiness. In no part of the world but in Northern America is it widely used. The purpose of embalming is to make the corpse presentable for viewing in a suitably costly container; and here too the funeral director routinely, without first consulting the family, prepares the body for public display.

3   Is all this legal? The processes to which a dead body may be subjected are after all to some extent circumscribed by law. In most states, for instance, the signature of next of kin must be obtained before an autopsy may be performed, before the deceased may be cremated, before the body may be turned over to a medical school for research purposes; or such provision must be made in the decedent's will. In the case of embalming, no such permission is required nor is it ever sought. A textbook, *The Principles and Practices of Embalming*, comments on this: "There is some question regarding the legality of much that is done within the preparation room." The author points out that it would be most unusual for a responsible member of a bereaved family to instruct the mortician, in so many words, to "*embalm*" the body of a deceased relative. The very term "embalming" is so seldom used that the mortician must rely upon custom in the matter. The author concludes that unless the family specifies otherwise, the act of entrusting the body to the care of a funeral establishment carries with it an implied permission to go ahead and embalm.

4   Embalming is indeed a most extraordinary procedure, and one must wonder at the docility of Americans who each year pay hundreds of millions of dollars for its perpetuation, blissfully ignorant of what it is all about, what is done, how it is done. Not one in ten thousand has any idea of what actually takes place. Books on the subject are extremely hard to come by. They are not to be found in most libraries or bookshops.

5   In an era when huge television audiences watch surgical operations in the comfort of their living rooms, when, thanks to the animated cartoon, the geography of the digestive system has become familiar territory even to the nursery school set, in a land where the satisfaction of curiosity about almost all matters is a national pastime, the secrecy surrounding embalming can, surely, hardly be attributed to the inherent gruesomeness of the subject. Custom in this regard has within this century suffered a complete reversal. In the early days of American embalming, when it was performed in the home of the deceased, it was almost mandatory for some relative to stay by the embalmer's side and witness the procedure. Today, family members

who might wish to be in attendance would certainly be dissuaded by the funeral director. All others, except apprentices, are excluded by law from the preparation room.

6   A close look at what does actually take place may explain in large measure the undertaker's intractable reticence concerning a procedure that has become his major *raison d'être*. It is possible he fears the public information about embalming might lead patrons to wonder if they really want this service? If the funeral men are loath to discuss the subject outside the trade, the reader may, understandably, be equally loath to go on reading at this point. For those who have the stomach for it, let us part the formaldehyde curtain. . . .

7   The body is first laid out in the undertaker's morgue—or rather, Mr. Jones is reposing in the preparation room—to be readied to bid the world farewell.

8   The preparation room in any of the better funeral establishments has the tiled and sterile look of a surgery, and indeed the embalmer-restorative artist who does his chores there is beginning to adopt the term "dermasurgeon" (appropriately corrupted by some mortician-writers as "demisurgeon") to describe his calling. His equipment, consisting of scalpels, scissors, augurs, forceps, clamps, needles, pumps, tubes, bowls and basins, is crudely imitative of the surgeon's, as is his technique, acquired in a nine- or twelve-month post-high-school course in an embalming school. He is supplied by an advanced chemical industry with a bewildering array of fluids, sprays, pastes, oils, powders, creams, to fix or soften tissue, shrink or distend it as needed, dry it here, restore the moisture there. There are cosmetics, waxes and paints to fill and cover features, even plaster of Paris to replace entire limbs. There are ingenious aids to prop and stabilize the cadaver: a Vari-Pose Head Rest, the Edwards Arm and Hand Positioner, the Repose Block (to support the shoulders during the embalming), and the Throop Foot Positioner, which resembles an old-fashioned stocks.

9   Mr. John H. Eckels, president of the Eckels College of Mortuary Science, thus describes the first part of the embalming procedure: "In the hands of a skilled practitioner, this work may be done in a comparatively short time and without mutilating the body other than by slight incision—so slight that it scarcely would cause serious inconvenience if made upon a living person. It is necessary to remove the blood, and doing this not only helps in the disinfecting, but removes the principal cause of disfigurements due to discoloration."

10   Another textbook discusses the all-important time element: "The earlier this is done, the better, for every hour that elapses between death and embalming will add to the problems and complications encountered. . . ." Just how soon should one get going on the embalming? The author tells us, "On the basis of such scanty information made available to this profession through its rudimentary and haphazard system of technical research, we must conclude that the best results are to be obtained if the subject is em-

balmed before life is completely extinct—that is, before cellular death has occurred. In the average case, this would mean within an hour after somatic death." For those who feel that there is something a little rudimentary, not to say haphazard, about this advice, a comforting thought is offered by another writer. Speaking of fears entertained in early days of premature burial, he points out, "One of the effects of embalming by chemical injection, however, has been to dispel fears of live burial." How true; once blood is removed, chances of live burial are indeed remote.

11 To return to Mr. Jones, the blood is drained out through the veins and replaced by embalming fluid pumped in through the arteries. As noted in *The Principles and Practices of Embalming*, "every operator has a favorite injection and drainage point—a fact which becomes a handicap only if he fails or refuses to forsake his favorites when conditions demand it." Typical favorites are the carotid artery, femoral artery, jugular vein, subclavian vein. There are various choices of embalming fluid. If Flextone is used, it will produce a "mild, flexible rigidity. The skin retains a velvety softness, the tissues are rubbery and pliable. Ideal for women and children." It may be blended with B. and G. Products Company's Lyf-Lyk tint, which is guaranteed to reproduce "nature's own skin texture . . . the velvety appearance of living tissue." Suntone comes in three separate tints: Suntan; Special Cosmetic Tint, a pink shade "especially indicated for young female subjects"; and Regular Cosmetic Tint, moderately pink.

12 About three to six gallons of a dyed and perfumed solution of formaldehyde, glycerin, borax, phenol, alcohol, and water is soon circulating through Mr. Jones, whose mouth has been sewn together with a "needle directed upward between the upper lip and gum and brought out through the left nostril," with the corners raised slightly "for a more pleasant expression." If he should be bucktoothed, his teeth are cleaned with Bon Ami and coated with colorless nail polish. His eyes, meanwhile, are closed with flesh-tinted eye caps and eye cement.

13 The next step is to have at Mr. Jones with a thing called a trocar. This is a long, hollow needle attached to a tube. It is jabbed into the abdomen, poked around the entrails and chest cavity, the contents of which are pumped out and replaced with "cavity fluid." This done, and the hole in the abdomen sewn up, Mr. Jones's face is heavily creamed (to protect the skin from burns which may be caused by leakage of the chemicals), and he is covered with a sheet and left unmolested for a while. But not for long— there is more, much more, in store for him. He has been embalmed, but not yet restored, and the best time to start the restorative work is eight to ten hours after embalming, when the tissues have become firm and dry.

14 The object of all this attention to the corpse, it must be remembered, is to make it presentable for viewing in an attitude of healthy repose. "Our customs require the presentation of our dead in the semblance of normality . . . unmarred by the ravages of illness, disease or mutilation," says Mr. J.

Sheridan Mayer in his *Restorative Art.* This is rather a large order since few people die in the full bloom of health, unravaged by illness and unmarked by some disfigurement. The funeral industry is equal to the challenge: "In some cases the gruesome appearance of a mutilated or disease-ridden subject may be quite discouraging. The task of restoration may seem impossible and shake the confidence of the embalmer. This is the time for intestinal fortitude and determination. Once the formative work is begun and affected tissues are cleaned or removed, all doubts of success vanish. It is surprising and gratifying to discover the results which may be obtained."

15   The embalmer, having allowed an appropriate interval to elapse, returns to the attack, but now he brings into play the skill and equipment of sculptor and cosmetician. Is a hand missing? Casting one in plaster of Paris is a simple matter. "For replacement purposes, only a cast of the back of the hand is necessary; this is within the ability of the average operator and is quite adequate." If a lip or two, a nose or an ear should be missing, the embalmer has at hand a variety of restorative waxes with which to model replacements. Pores and skin texture are simulated by stippling with a little brush, and over this cosmetics are laid on. Head off? Decapitation cases are rather routinely handled. Ragged edges are trimmed, and head joined to torso with a series of splints, wires and sutures. It is a good idea to have a little something at the neck—a scarf or high collar—when time for viewing comes. Swollen mouth? Cut out tissue as needed from inside the lips. If too much is removed, the surface contour can easily be restored by padding with cotton. Swollen necks and cheeks are reduced by removing tissue through vertical incisions made down each side of the neck. "When the deceased is casketed, the pillow will hide the suture incisions . . . as an extra precaution against leakage, the suture may be painted with liquid sealer."

16   The opposite condition is more likely to present itself—that of emaciation. His hypodermic syringe now loaded with massage cream, the embalmer seeks out and fills the hollowed and sunken areas by injection. In this pro-cedure the backs of the hands and fingers and the under-chin area should not be neglected.

17   Positioning the lips is a problem that recurrently challenges the ingenuity of the embalmer. Closed too tightly they tend to give a stern, even disap-proving expression. Ideally, embalmers feel, the lips should give the impres-sion of being ever so slightly parted, the upper lip protruding slightly for a more youthful appearance. This takes some engineering, however, as the lips tend to drift apart. Lip drift can sometimes be remedied by pushing one or two straight pins through the inner margin of the lower lip and then inserting them between the two front upper teeth. If Mr. Jones happens to have no teeth, the pins can just as easily be anchored in his Armstrong Face Former and Denture Replacer. Another method to maintain lip closure is to dislocate the lower jaw, which is then held in its new position by a wire run through holes which have been drilled through the upper and lower

jaws at the midline. As the French are fond of saying, *il faut souffrir pour être belle.*[1]

18   If Mr. Jones has died of jaundice, the embalming fluid will very likely turn him green. Does this deter the embalmer? Not if he has intestinal fortitude. Masking pastes and cosmetics are heavily laid on, burial garments and casket interiors are color-correlated with particular care, and Jones is displayed beneath rose-colored lights. Friends will say, "How *well* he looks." Death by carbon monoxide, on the other hand, can be rather a good thing from the embalmer's viewpoint: "One advantage is the fact that this type of discoloration is an exaggerated form of a natural pink coloration." This is nice because the healthy glow is already present and needs but little attention.

19   The patching and filling completed, Mr. Jones is now shaved, washed and dressed. Cream-based cosmetic, available in pink, flesh, suntan, brunette, and blond, is applied to his hands and face, his hair is shampooed and combed (and, in the case of Mrs. Jones, set), his hands manicured. For the horny-handed son of toil special care must be taken; cream should be applied to remove ingrained grime, and the nails cleaned. "If he were not in the habit of having them manicured in life, trimming and shaping is advised for better appearance—never questioned by kin."

20   Jones is now ready for casketing (this is the present participle of the verb "to casket"). In this operation his right shoulder should be depressed slightly "to turn the body a bit to the right and soften the appearance of lying flat on the back." Positioning the hands is a matter of importance, and special rubber positioning blocks may be used. The hands should be cupped slightly for a more lifelike, relaxed appearance. Proper placement of the body requires a delicate sense of balance. It should lie as high as possible in the casket, yet not so high that the lid, when lowered, will hit the nose. On the other hand, we are cautioned, placing the body too low "creates the impression that the body is in a box."

21   Jones is next wheeled into the appointed slumber room where a few last touches may be added—his favorite pipe placed in his hand or, if he was a great reader, a book propped into position. (In the case of little Master Jones a Teddy bear may be clutched.) Here he will hold open house for a few days, visiting hours 10 A.M. to 9 P.M.

Topics for Writing and Discussion

1.   Why, according to Mitford, are embalming and restoration nearly universally practiced in the United States and Canada? What are the benefits of these procedures? What are the disadvantages?

---

[1]"One must suffer to be beautiful." [Ed.'s note.]

2.   Why does Mitford explain the processes of embalming and restoration in such detail? What was your response to her descriptions? Why does she quote extensively from textbooks and trade journals used by funeral directors?

3.   How does Mitford inject humor into her discussion? What is the purpose of the humor? Does it support her thesis? Or do you find the humor distracting and inappropriate?

4.   Mitford calls the body she uses as an example "Mr. Jones" and in the concluding paragraph refers to "little Master Jones" clutching a favorite Teddy bear. Why does she give her example a name? How would the essay change if she simply referred to "the body" or "the corpse"?

5.   Write an essay describing a funeral or memorial service that either supports or refutes Mitford's point of view.

Garrison Keillor. (© Mario Ruiz / Picture Group)

Attitude

Garrison Keillor
(1942–   )

A self-proclaimed "shy person" heralded as a
savior of the radio theater genre and one of
America's master storytellers, Garrison Keillor
began his broadcasting career in 1963 as an
announcer in Minnesota. In 1974 "A Prairie Home
Companion," an old-time radio variety show with
a blend of storytelling, music, and humor that
would make Keillor famous, began its long run on
National Public Radio stations. The show, which
continued until 1987, introduced listeners to the
town of Lake Wobegon, Minnesota—the mythical
setting that is the heart of many of Keillor's tales
on the air and in print. His books include *Lake
Wobegon Days* (1985), *Leaving Home* (1987), and *We
Are Still Married* (1989) and *WLT: A Radio Romance*
(1991). In 1990 Keillor returned to the public radio
airwaves with another variety show, the
"American Radio Company." "Attitude" was
published in a 1982 collection of essays, *Happy to
Be Here*.

1   Long ago I passed the point in life when major-league ballplayers begin
to be younger than yourself. Now all of them are, except for a few aging
trigenarians and a couple of quadros who don't get around on the fastball
as well as they used to and who sit out the second games of doubleheaders.
However, despite my age (thirty-nine), I am still active and have a lot of
interests. One of them is slow-pitch softball, a game that lets me go through
the motions of baseball without getting beaned or having to run too hard.
I play on a pretty casual team, one that drinks beer on the bench and

substitutes freely. If a player's wife or girlfriend wants to play, we give her a glove and send her out to right field, no questions asked, and if she lets a pop fly drop six feet in front of her, nobody agonizes over it.

2   Except me. This year. For the first time in my life, just as I am entering the dark twilight of my slow-pitch career, I find myself taking the game seriously. It isn't the bonehead play that bothers me especially—the pop fly that drops untouched, the slow roller juggled and the ball then heaved ten feet over the first baseman's head and into the next diamond, the routine singles that go through outfielders' legs for doubles and triples with gloves flung after them. No, it isn't our stone-glove fielding or pussyfoot base-running or limp-wristed hitting that gives me fits, though these have put us on the short end of some mighty ridiculous scores this summer. It's our attitude.

3   Bottom of the ninth, down 18–3, two outs, a man on first and a woman on third, and our third baseman strikes out. *Strikes out!* In slow-pitch, not even your grandmother strikes out, but this guy does, and after his third strike—a wild swing at a ball that bounces on the plate—he topples over in the dirt and lies flat on his back, laughing. *Laughing!*

4   Same game, earlier. They have the bases loaded. A weak grounder is hit toward our second baseperson. The runners are running. She picks up the ball, and she looks at them. She looks at first, at second, at home. We yell, "Throw it! Throw it!" and she throws it, underhand, at the pitcher, who has turned and run to back up the catcher. The ball rolls across the third-base line and under the bench. Three runs score. The batter, a fatso, chugs into second. The other team hoots and hollers, and what does she do? She shrugs and smiles ("Oh, silly me"); after all, it's only a game. Like the aforementioned strikeout artist, she treats her error as a joke. They have forgiven themselves instantly, which is unforgivable. It is *we* who should forgive them, who can say, "It's all right, it's only a game." They are supposed to throw up their hands and kick the dirt and hang their heads, as if this boner, even if it is their sixteenth of the afternoon—*this* is the one that really and truly breaks their hearts.

5   That attitude sweetens the game for everyone. The sinner feels sweet remorse. The fatso feels some sense of accomplishment; this is no bunch of rumdums he forced into an error but a team with some class. We, the sinner's teammates, feel momentary anger at her—dumb! dumb play!—but then, seeing her grief, we sympathize with her in our hearts (any one of us might have made that mistake or one worse), and we yell encouragement, including the shortstop, who, moments before, dropped an easy throw for a force at second. "That's all right! Come on! We got 'em!" we yell. "Shake it off! These turkeys can't hit!" This makes us all feel good, even though the turkeys now lead us by ten runs. We're getting clobbered, but we have a winning attitude.

6   Let me say this about attitude: Each player is responsible for his or her own attitude, and to a considerable degree you can *create* a good attitude by doing certain little things on the field. These are certain little things that ballplayers do in the Bigs, and we ought to be doing them in the Slows.

1.   When going up to bat, don't step right into the batter's box as if it were an elevator. The box is your turf, your stage. Take possession of it slowly and deliberately, starting with a lot of back-bending, knee-stretching, and torso-revolving in the on-deck circle. Then, approaching the box, stop outside it and tap the dirt off your spikes with your bat. You don't have spikes, you have sneakers, of course, but the significance of the tapping is the same. Then, upon entering the box, spit on the ground. It's a way of saying, "This here is mine. This is where I get my hits."

2.   Spit frequently. Spit at all crucial moments. Spit correctly. Spit should be *blown*, not ptuied weakly with the lips, which often results in dribble. Spitting should convey forcefulness of purpose, concentration, pride. Spit down, not in the direction of others. Spit in the glove and on the fingers, especially after making a real knucklehead play; it's a way of saying, "I dropped the ball because my glove was dry."

3.   At bat and in the field, pick up dirt. Rub dirt in the fingers (especially after spitting on them). Toss dirt, as if testing the wind for velocity and direction. Smooth the dirt. Be involved with dirt. If no dirt is available (e.g., in the outfield), pluck tufts of grass. Fielders should be grooming their areas constantly between plays, flicking away tiny sticks and bits of gravel.

4.   Take your time. Tie your laces. Confer with your teammates about possible situations that may arise and conceivable options in dealing with them. Extend the game. Three errors on three consecutive plays can be humiliating if the plays occur within the space of a couple of minutes, but if each error is separated from the next by extensive conferences on the mound, lace-tying, glove adjustments, and arguing close calls (if any), the effect on morale is minimized.

5.   Talk. Not just an occasional "Let's get a hit now" but continuous rhythmic chatter, a flow of syllables: "Hey babe hey babe c'mon babe good stick now hey babe long tater take him downtown babe . . . hey good eye good eye."

Infield chatter is harder to maintain. Since the slow-pitch pitch is required to be a soft underhand lob, infielders hesitate to say, "Smoke him babe hey low heat hey throw it on the black babe chuck it in there back him up babe no hit no hit." Say it anyway.

6.   One final rule, perhaps the most important of all: When your team is up and has made the third out, the batter and the players who were left on base do not come back to the bench for their gloves. *They remain on the field, and their teammates bring their gloves out to them.* This requires some

organization and discipline, but it pays off big in morale. It says, "Although we're getting our pants knocked off, still we must conserve our energy."

7   Imagine that you have bobbled two fly balls in this rout and now you have just tried to stretch a single into a double and have been easily thrown out sliding into second base, where the base runner ahead of you had stopped. It was the third out and a dumb play, and your opponents smirk at you as they run off the field. You are the goat, a lonely and tragic figure sitting in the dirt. You curse yourself, jerking your head sharply forward. You stand up and kick the base. How miserable! How degrading! Your utter shame, though brief, bears silent testimony to the worthiness of your team-mates, whom you have let down, and they appreciate it. They call out to you now as they take the field, and as the second baseman runs to his position he says, "Let's get 'em now," and tosses you your glove. Lowering your head, you trot slowly out to right. There you do some deep knee bends. You pick grass. You find a pebble and fling it into foul territory. As the first batter comes to the plate, you check the sun. You get set in your stance, poised to fly. Feet spread, hands on hips, you bend slightly at the waist and spit the expert spit of a veteran ballplayer—a player who has known the agony of defeat but who always bounces back, a player who has lost a stride on the base paths but can still make the big play.

8   This is *ball*, ladies and gentlemen. This is what it's all about.

Topics for Writing and Discussion

1. What process is Keillor explaining in this essay? Is it directional or informative?

2. What is Keillor's purpose in writing this essay? Is his thesis confined to the playing of softball? How, according to this author, are attitude and performance related?

3. Describe the tone of this essay. How does Keillor produce this tone? What role do personal anecdotes play in this essay?

4. Why does Keillor take five paragraphs before introducing the steps in his process? Would the essay be more successful had he begun his list earlier? Why or why not?

5. Think of a time when you or someone you know did *not* conduct himself or herself with the right attitude during or following a difficult situation. Use this person's response to illustrate an essay showing others how to avoid the damage that can result from a negative or inappropriate attitude.

Martin Luther King (© 1966 Ernst Haas / © 1966 Magnum Photos)

Nonviolent Resistance

Martin Luther King, Jr.
(1929–1968)

Martin Luther King, Jr., was the son of a Baptist minister and at age 18 was himself ordained. He later studied at Morehouse College, Crozer Theological Seminary, Boston University, and Chicago Theological Seminary. Soon after his ordination in 1947, he became involved in civil-rights actions, and in 1955 he became an acknowledged leader of the movement against segregation when he organized a successful boycott against the Montgomery, Alabama, bus system. In 1957 he founded the Southern Christian Leadership Conference and served as its first president. While holding this office, he continued to support and promote his belief in nonviolent resistance to civil-rights violations, and in 1964 King was awarded the Nobel Peace Prize. In 1968 he was assassinated in Memphis, Tennessee. Widely acclaimed for his powerful use of the English language, King's writing includes *Letter from Birmingham Jail* (1963), *Why We Can't Wait* (1964), and *Where Do We Go from Here: Chaos or Community?* (1967). In "Nonviolent Resistance," which first appeared in 1958 as part of King's book *Stride toward Freedom*, he describes the processes oppressed people follow as they confront their situation.

1   Oppressed people deal with their oppression in three characteristic ways. One way is acquiescence: the oppressed resign themselves to their

doom. They tacitly adjust themselves to oppression, and thereby become conditioned to it. In every movement toward freedom some of the oppressed prefer to remain oppressed. Almost 2800 years ago Moses set out to lead the children of Israel from the slavery of Egypt to the freedom of the promised land. He soon discovered that slaves do not always welcome their deliverers. They become accustomed to being slaves. They would rather bear those ills they have, as Shakespeare pointed out, than flee to others that they know not of. They prefer the "fleshpots of Egypt" to the ordeals of emancipation.

2   There is such a thing as the freedom of exhaustion. Some people are so worn down by the yoke of oppression that they give up. A few years ago in the slum areas of Atlanta, a Negro guitarist used to sing almost daily: "Ben down so long that down don't bother me." This is the type of negative freedom and resignation that often engulfs the life of the oppressed.

3   But this is not the way out. To accept passively an unjust system is to coöperate with that system; thereby the oppressed become as evil as the oppressor. Noncoöperation with evil is as much a moral obligation as is coöperation with good. The oppressed must never allow the conscience of the oppressor to slumber. Religion reminds every man that he is his brother's keeper. To accept injustice or segregation passively is to say to the oppressor that his actions are morally right. It is a way of allowing his conscience to fall asleep. At this moment the oppressed fails to be his brother's keeper. So acquiescence—while often the easier way—is not the moral way. It is the way of the coward. The Negro cannot win the respect of his oppressor by acquiescing; he merely increases the oppressor's arrogance and contempt. Acquiescence is interpreted as proof of the Negro's inferiority. The Negro cannot win the respect of the white people of the South or the peoples of the world if he is willing to sell the future of his children for his personal and immediate comfort and safety.

4   A second way that oppressed people sometimes deal with oppression is to resort to physical violence and corroding hatred. Violence often brings about momentary results. Nations have frequently won their independence in battle. But in spite of temporary victories, violence never brings permanent peace. It solves no social problem; it merely creates new and more complicated ones.

5   Violence as a way of achieving racial justice is both impractical and immoral. It is impractical because it is a descending spiral ending in destruction for all. The old law of an eye for an eye leaves everybody blind. It is immoral because it seeks to humiliate the opponent rather than win his understanding; it seeks to annihilate rather than to convert. Violence is immoral because it thrives on hatred rather than love. It destroys community and makes brotherhood impossible. It leaves society in monologue rather than dialogue. Violence ends by defeating itself. It creates bitterness in the survivors and brutality in the destroyers. A voice echoes through time saying to every

potential Peter, "Put up your sword." History is cluttered with the wreckage of nations that failed to follow his command.

6   If the American Negro and other victims of oppression succumb to the temptation of using violence in the struggle for freedom, future generations will be the recipients of a desolate night of bitterness, and our chief legacy to them will be an endless reign of meaningless chaos. Violence is not the way.

7   The third way open to oppressed people in their quest for freedom is the Read way of nonviolent resistance. Like the synthesis in Hegelian philosophy, the principle of nonviolent resistance seeks to reconcile the truths of two opposites—acquiescence and violence—while avoiding the extremes and immoralities of both. The nonviolent resister agrees with the person who acquiesces that one should not be physically aggressive toward his opponent; but he balances the equation by agreeing with the person of violence that evil must be resisted. He avoids the nonresistance of the former and the violent resistance of the latter. With nonviolent resistance, no individual or group need submit to any wrong, nor need anyone resort to violence in order to right a wrong.

8   It seems to me that this is the method that must guide the actions of the Negro in the present crisis in race relations. Through nonviolent resistance the Negro will be able to rise to the noble height of opposing the unjust system while loving the perpetrators of the system. The Negro must work passionately and unrelentingly for full stature as a citizen, but he must not use inferior methods to gain it. He must never come to terms with falsehood, malice, hate, or destruction.

9   Nonviolent resistance makes it possible for the Negro to remain in the South and struggle for his rights. The Negro's problem will not be solved by running away. He cannot listen to the glib suggestion of those who would urge him to migrate en masse to other sections of the country. By grasping his great opportunity in the South he can make a lasting contribution to the moral strength of the nation and set a sublime example of courage for generations yet unborn.

10   By nonviolent resistance, the Negro can also enlist all men of good will in his struggle for equality. The problem is not a purely racial one, with Negroes set against whites. In the end, it is not a struggle between people at all, but a tension between justice and injustice. Nonviolent resistance is not aimed against oppressors but against oppression. Under its banner consciences, not racial groups, are enlisted.

11   If the Negro is to achieve the goal of integration, he must organize himself into a militant and nonviolent mass movement. All three elements are indispensable. The movement for equality and justice can only be a success if it has both a mass and militant character; the barriers to be overcome require both. Nonviolence is an imperative in order to bring about ultimate community.

12   A mass movement of militant quality that is not at the same time committed to nonviolence tends to generate conflict, which in turn breeds anarchy. The support of the participants and the sympathy of the uncommitted
are both inhibited by the threat that bloodshed will engulf the community.
This reaction in turn encourages the opposition to threaten and resort to
force. When, however, the mass movement repudiates violence while moving resolutely toward its goal, its opponents are revealed as the instigators
and practitioners of violence if it occurs. Then public support is magnetically
attracted to the advocates of nonviolence, while those who employ violence
are literally disarmed by overwhelming sentiment against their stand.

13   Only through a nonviolent approach can the fears of the white community
be mitigated. A guilt-ridden white minority lives in fear that if the Negro
should ever attain power, he would act without restraint or pity to revenge
the injustices and brutality of the years. It is something like a parent who
continually mistreats a son. One day that parent raises his hand to strike
the son, only to discover that the son is now as tall as he is. The parent is
suddenly afraid—fearful that the son will use his new physical power to
repay his parent for all the blows of the past.

14   The Negro, once a helpless child, has now grown up politically, culturally,
and economically. Many white men fear retaliation. The job of the Negro
is to show them that they have nothing to fear, that the Negro understands
and forgives and is ready to forget the past. He must convince the white
man that all he seeks is justice, *for both himself and the white man.* A mass
movement exercising nonviolence is an object lesson in power under discipline, a demonstration to the white community that if such a movement
attained a degree of strength, it would use its power creatively and not
vengefully.

15   Nonviolence can touch men where the law cannot reach them. When the
law regulates behavior it plays an indirect part in molding public sentiment.
The enforcement of the law is itself a form of peaceful persuasion. But the
law needs help. The courts can order desegregation of the public schools.
But what can be done to mitigate the fears, to disperse the hatred, violence,
and irrationality gathered around school integration, to take the initiative
out of the hands of racial demagogues, to release respect for the law? In the
end, for laws to be obeyed, men must believe they are right.

16   Here nonviolence comes in as the ultimate form of persuasion. It is the
method which seeks to implement the just law by appealing to the conscience of the great decent majority who through blindness, fear, pride, or
irrationality have allowed their consciences to sleep.

17   The nonviolent resisters can summarize their message in the following
simple terms: We will take direct action against injustice without waiting for
other agencies to act. We will not obey unjust laws or submit to unjust
practices. We will do this peacefully, openly, cheerfully because our aim is
to persuade. We adopt the means of nonviolence because our end is a com-

munity at peace with itself. We will try to persuade with our words, but if our words fail, we will try to persuade with our acts. We will always be willing to talk and seek fair compromise, but we are ready to suffer when necessary and even risk our lives to become witnesses to the truth as we see it.

18   The way of nonviolence means a willingness to suffer and sacrifice. It may mean going to jail. If such is the case the resister must be willing to fill the jail houses of the South. It may even mean physical death. But if physical death is the price that a man must pay to free his children and his white brethren from a permanent death of the spirit, then nothing could be more redemptive.

Topics for Writing and Discussion

1. What are the three ways oppressed people deal with their situation? How do the examples and the words King chooses to describe the first two processes let readers know that he opposes those choices?

2. Why does King believe that nonviolent resistance is the right method for black people to choose as they strive for freedom? What three elements must be part of the process of nonviolent resistance?

3. Who are King's intended readers? How does he appeal to those readers? How might other readers react to his proposals?

4. Read "Graduation" (Maya Angelou), "Stranger in the Village" (James Baldwin), "Discrimination" (Ralph Ellison), and "I Have a Dream" (Martin Luther King, Jr.). Then create a dialogue among these people as they discuss the best process for facing oppression.

5. Research an important act of nonviolent resistance in the fight for civil rights, such as Rosa Park's famous bus ride or the Freedom Riders' Mississippi sit-ins, and recreate the stages of the event as they occurred for a reader who has heard of the subject but never knew exactly what happened.

Henry David Thoreau. (The Bettmann Archive)

Economy

Henry David Thoreau
(1817–1862)

Henry David Thoreau was a lifelong resident of
Concord, Massachusetts. He was educated at
Harvard University, and after graduation he
worked at a variety of jobs ranging from teaching
to house painting. A political activist, Thoreau once
chose to be jailed rather than to pay a poll tax
supporting a government that had failed to abolish
slavery and, in addition, made war with Mexico.
His essay "Civil Disobedience" (1849) makes a
powerful argument for the individual's right to
rebel against the laws of the state. When Thoreau
was 28 years old, he built a cabin in the woods
near Walden Pond and went to live there, hoping
"to front only the essential facts of life." In the
following selection taken from *Walden*, the book he
wrote about his life in the woods, he describes the
construction of his cabin while demonstrating his
concern with the principles of economy and
self-reliance.

1   Near the end of March, 1845, I borrowed an axe and went down to
the woods by Walden Pond, nearest to where I intended to build my house,
and began to cut down some tall arrowy white pines, still in their youth,
for timber. It is difficult to begin without borrowing, but perhaps it is the
most generous course thus to permit your fellow-men to have an interest
in your enterprise. The owner of the axe, as he released his hold on it, said
that it was the apple of his eye; but I returned it sharper than I received it.
It was a pleasant hillside where I worked, covered with pine woods, through
which I looked out on the pond, and a small open field in the woods where

pines and hickories were springing up. The ice in the pond was not yet
dissolved, though there were some open spaces, and it was all dark colored
and saturated with water. There were some slight flurries of snow during
the days that I worked there; but for the most part when I came out on to
the railroad, on my way home, its yellow sand heap stretched away gleaming
in the hazy atmosphere, and the rails shone in the spring sun, and I heard
the lark and pewee and other birds already come to commence another year
with us. They were pleasant spring days, in which the winter of man's
discontent was thawing as well as the earth, and the life that had lain torpid
began to stretch itself. One day, when my axe had come off and I had cut
a green hickory for a wedge, driving it with a stone, and had placed the
whole to soak in a pond hole in order to swell the wood, I saw a striped
snake run into the water, and he lay on the bottom, apparently without
inconvenience, as long as I stayed there, or more than a quarter of an hour;
perhaps because he had not yet fairly come out of the torpid state. It appeared
to me that for a like reason men remain in their present low and primitive
condition; but if they should feel the influence of the spring of springs
arousing them, they would of necessity rise to a higher and more ethereal
life. I had previously seen the snakes in frosty mornings in my path with
portions of their bodies still numb and inflexible, waiting for the sun to thaw
them. On the 1st of April it rained and melted the ice, and in the early part
of the day, which was very foggy, I heard a stray goose groping about over
the pond and cackling as if lost, or like the spirit of the fog.

2   So I went on for some days cutting and hewing timber, and also studs
and rafters, all with my narrow axe, not having many communicable or
scholar-like thoughts, singing to myself.

> Men say they know many things;
> But lo! they have taken wings,—
> The arts and sciences,
> And a thousand appliances;
> The wind that blows
> Is all that any body knows.

I hewed the main timber six inches square, most of the studs on two sides
only, and the rafters and floor timbers on one side, leaving the rest of the
bark on, so that they were just as straight and much stronger than sawed
ones. Each stick was carefully mortised or tenoned by its stump, for I had
borrowed other tools by this time. My days in the woods were not very
long ones; yet I usually carried my dinner of bread and butter, and read the
newspaper in which it was wrapped, at noon, sitting amid the green pine
boughs which I had cut off, and to my bread was imparted some of their
fragrance, for my hands were covered with a thick coat of pitch. Before I
had done I was more the friend than the foe of the pine tree, though I had
cut down some of them, having become better acquainted with it. Sometimes

a rambler in the wood was attracted by the sound of my axe, and we chatted pleasantly over the chips which I had made.

3   By the middle of April, for I made no haste in my work, but rather made the most of it, my house was framed and ready for the raising. I had already bought the shanty of James Collins, an Irishman who worked on the Fitchburg Railroad, for boards. James Collins' shanty was considered an uncommonly fine one. When I called to see it he was not at home, I walked about the outside, at first unobserved from within, the window was so deep and high. It was of small dimensions, with a peaked cottage roof, and not much else to be seen, the dirt being raised five feet all around as if it were a compost heap. The roof was the soundest part, though a good deal warped and made brittle by the sun. Doorsill there was none, but a perennial passage for the hens under the door board. Mrs. C. came to the door and asked me to view it from the inside. The hens were driven in by my approach. It was dark, and had a dirt floor for the most part, dank, clammy, and aguish, only here a board and there a board which would not bear removal. She lighted a lamp to show me the inside of the roof and the walls, and also that the board floor extended under the bed, warning me not to step into the cellar, a sort of dust hole two feet deep. In her own words, they were "good boards overhead, good boards all around, and a good window"—of two whole squares originally, only the cat had passed out that way lately. There was a stove, a bed, and a place to sit, an infant in the house where it was born, a silk parasol, gilt-framed looking-glass, and a patent new coffee-mill nailed to an oak sapling, all told. The bargain was soon concluded, for James had in the mean while returned. I to pay four dollars and twenty-five cents tonight, he to vacate at five tomorrow morning, selling to nobody else meanwhile: I to take possession at six. It were well, he said, to be there early, and anticipate certain indistinct but wholly unjust claims on the score of ground rent and fuel. This he assured me was the only encumbrance. At six I passed him and his family on the road. One large bundle held their all—bed, coffee-mill, looking-glass, hens—all but the cat; she took to the woods and became a wild cat and, as I learned afterward, trod in a trap set for woodchucks, and so became a dead cat at last.

4   I took down this dwelling the same morning, drawing the nails, and removed it to the pond side by small cartloads, spreading the boards on the grass there to bleach and warp back again in the sun. One early thrush gave me a note or two as I drove along the woodland path. I was informed treacherously by a young Patrick that neighbor Seeley, an Irishman, in the intervals of the carting, transferred the still tolerable, straight, and drivable nails, staples, and spikes to his pocket, and then stood when I came back to pass the time of day, and look freshly up, unconcerned, with spring thoughts, at the devastation; there being a dearth of work, as he said. He was there to represent spectatordom, and help make this seemingly insignificant event one with the removal of the gods of Troy.

5   I dug my cellar in the side of a hill sloping to the south, where a woodchuck had formerly dug his burrow, down through sumach and blackberry roots, and the lowest stain of vegetation, six feet square by seven deep, to a fine sand where potatoes would not freeze in any winter. The sides were left shelving, and not stoned; but the sun having never shone on them, the sand still keeps its place. It was but two hours' work. I took particular pleasure in this breaking of ground, for in almost all latitudes men dig into the earth for an equable temperature. Under the most splendid house in the city is still to be found the cellar where they store their roots as of old, and long after the superstructure had disappeared posterity remark its dent in the earth. The house is still but a sort of porch at the entrance of a burrow.

6   At length, in the beginning of May, with the help of some of my acquaintances, rather to improve so good an occasion for neighborliness than from any necessity, I set up the frame of my house. No man was ever more honored in the character of his raisers than I. They are destined, I trust, to assist at the raising of loftier structures one day. I began to occupy my house on the 4th of July, as soon as it was boarded and roofed, for the boards were carefully feather-edged and lapped, so that it was perfectly impervious to rain, but before boarding I laid the foundation of a chimney at one end, bringing two cartloads of stones up the hill from the pond in my arms. I built the chimney after my hoeing in the fall, before a fire became necessary for warmth, doing my cooking in the meanwhile out of doors on the ground, early in the morning: which mode I still think is in some respects more convenient and agreeable than the usual one. When it stormed before my bread was baked, I fixed a few boards over the fire, and sat under them to watch my loaf, and passed some pleasant hours in that way. In those days, when my hands were much employed, I read but little, but the least scraps of paper which lay on the ground, my holder, or tablecloth, afforded me as much entertainment, in fact answered the same purpose as the Iliad.

Topics for Writing and Discussion

1.   In the first paragraph, Thoreau makes an analogy between a snake's behavior and human behavior. What principle does he illustrate with this comparison?

2.   Thoreau says that "James Collins' shanty was considered an uncommonly fine one." After considering carefully the description of the shanty, explain why you agree or disagree with the common opinion of the Collins' dwelling. For what purpose might it be "uncommonly fine"?

3.   How does Thoreau's description of building his cabin suggest his concern for and connection with nature? How do his observations on the

plants and animals of the woods contrast with his observations on humans and on domestic animals?

4. This selection from *Walden* is titled "Economy." What details illustrate Thoreau's beliefs about economy? After noting Thoreau's examples, describe what you believe to be his economic principles.

5. Write an essay explaining how you came to possess, to create, or to build something you wanted very much—just as Thoreau wanted his house in the woods. Make clear your reason for obtaining this important possession.

Samuel Scudder (Museum of Comparative Zoology, Harvard University, © President and Fellows of Harvard University)

Take This Fish and Look at It

Samuel H. Scudder
(1837–1911)

American entomologist Samuel H. Scudder's
scholarly work included a comprehensive
cataloguing of the scientific serials published
between 1633 and 1876 in the natural and physical
sciences as well as mathematics. The development
of the close observational skills necessary for the
compilation of this 1879 catalogue actually began
years earlier under the instruction of acclaimed
naturalist Louis Agassiz. In "Take This Fish and
Look at It," the Harvard-trained Scudder recalls his
discovery that only through intense, repeated
observation was he able "to see how little I saw
before."

1   It was more than fifteen years ago that I entered the laboratory of Professor Agassiz, and told him I had enrolled my name in the Scientific School as a student of natural history. He asked me a few questions about my object in coming, my antecedents generally, the mode in which I afterwards proposed to use the knowledge I might acquire, and, finally, whether I wished to study any special branch. To the latter I replied that, while I wished to be well grounded in all departments of zoology, I purposed to devote myself specially to insects.

2   "When do you wish to begin?" he asked.

3   "Now," I replied.

4   This seemed to please him, and with an energetic "Very well!" he reached from a shelf a huge jar of specimens in yellow alcohol. "Take this fish," he said, "and look at it; we call it a haemulon; by and by I will ask what you have seen."

5   With that he left me, but in a moment returned with explicit instructions as to the care of the object entrusted to me.

6 "No man is fit to be a naturalist," said he, "who does not know how to take care of specimens."

7 I was to keep the fish before me in a tin tray, and occasionally moisten the surface with alcohol from the jar, always taking care to replace the stopper tightly. Those were not the days of ground-glass stoppers and elegantly shaped exhibition jars; all the old students will recall the huge neckless glass bottles with their leaky, wax-besmeared corks, half eaten by insects, and begrimed with cellar dust. Entomology was a cleaner science than ichthyology, but the example of the Professor, who had unhesitatingly plunged to the bottom of the jar to produce the fish, was infectious; and though this alcohol had a "very ancient and fishlike smell," I really dared not show any aversion within these sacred precincts, and treated the alcohol as though it were pure water. Still I was conscious of a passing feeling of disappointment, for gazing at a fish did not commend itself to an ardent entomologist. My friends at home, too, were annoyed when they discovered that no amount of eau-de-Cologne would drown the perfume which haunted me like a shadow.

8 In ten minutes I had seen all that could be seen in that fish, and started in search of the Professor—who had, however, left the Museum; and when I returned, after lingering over some of the odd animals stored in the upper apartment, my specimen was dry all over. I dashed the fluid over the fish as if to resuscitate the beast from a fainting fit, and looked with anxiety for a return of the normal sloppy appearance. This little excitement over, nothing was to be done but to return to a steadfast gaze at my mute companion. Half an hour passed—an hour—another hour; the fish began to look loathsome. I turned it over and around; looked it in the face—ghastly; from behind, beneath, above, sideways, at three-quarters' view—just as ghastly. I was in despair; at an early hour I concluded that lunch was necessary; so, with infinite relief, the fish was carefully replaced in the jar, and for an hour I was free.

9 On my return, I learned that Professor Agassiz had been at the Museum, but had gone, and would not return for several hours. My fellow-students were too busy to be disturbed by continued conversation. Slowly I drew forth that hideous fish, and with a feeling of desperation again looked at it. I might not use a magnifying-glass; instruments of all kinds were interdicted. My two hands, my two eyes, and the fish: it seemed a most limited field. I pushed my finger down its throat to feel how sharp the teeth were. I began to count the scales in the different rows, until I was convinced that was nonsense. At last a happy thought struck me—I would draw the fish; and now with surprise I began to discover new features in the creature. Just then the Professor returned.

10 That is right," said he; "a pencil is one of the best of eyes. I am glad to notice, too, that you keep your specimen wet, and your bottle corked."

11   With these encouraging words, he added: "Well, what is it like?"

12   He listened attentively to my brief rehearsal of the structure of parts whose names were still unknown to me: the fringed gill-arches and movable operculum; the pores of the head, fleshy lips and lidless eyes; the lateral line, the spinous fins and forked tail; the compressed and arched body. When I finished, he waited as if expecting more, and then, with an air of disappointment:

13   "You have not looked very carefully; why," he continued more earnestly, "you haven't even seen one of the most conspicuous features of the animal, which is plainly before your eyes as the fish itself; look again, look again!" and he left me to my misery.

14   I was piqued; I was mortified. Still more of that wretched fish! But now I set myself to my task with a will, and discovered one new thing after another, until I saw how just the Professor's criticism had been. The afternoon passed quickly; and when, towards its close, the Professor inquired:

15   "Do you see it yet?"

16   "No," I replied, "I am certain I do not, but I see how little I saw before."

17   "That is next best," said he, earnestly, "but I won't hear you now; put away your fish and go home; perhaps you will be ready with a better answer in the morning. I will examine you before you look at the fish."

18   This was disconcerting. Not only must I think of my fish all night, studying, without the object before me, what this unknown but most visible feature might be; but also, without reviewing my discoveries, I must give an exact account of them the next day. I had a bad memory; so I walked home by Charles River in a distracted state, with my two perplexities.

19   The cordial greeting from the Professor the next morning was reassuring; here was a man who seemed to be quite as anxious as I that I should see for myself what he saw.

20   "Do you perhaps mean," I asked, "that the fish has symmetrical sides with paired organs?"

21   His thoroughly pleased "Of course! of course!" repaid the wakeful hours of the previous night. After he had discoursed most happily and enthusiastically—as he always did—upon the importance of this point, I ventured to ask what I should do next.

22   "Oh, look at your fish!" he said, and left me again to my own devices. In a little more than an hour he returned, and heard my new catalogue.

23   "That is good, that is good!" he repeated; "but that is not all; go on"; and so for three long days he placed that fish before my eyes, forbidding me to look at anything else, or to use any artificial aid. "Look, look, look," was his repeated injunction.

24   This was the best entomological lesson I ever had—a lesson whose influence has extended to the details of every subsequent study; a legacy the Professor had left to me, as he has left it to so many others, of inestimable value, which we could not buy, with which we cannot part.

25   A year afterward, some of us were amusing ourselves with chalking outlandish beasts on the Museum blackboard. We drew prancing starfishes; frogs in mortal combat; hydra-headed worms; stately crawfishes, standing on their tails, bearing aloft umbrellas; and grotesque fishes with gaping mouths and staring eyes. The Professor came in shortly after, and was as amused as any at our experiments. He looked at the fishes.

26   "Haemulons, every one of them," he said; "Mr. ———— drew them."

27   True; and to this day, if I attempt a fish, I can draw nothing but haemulons.

28   The fourth day, a second fish of the same group was placed beside the first, and I was bidden to point out the resemblances and differences between the two; another and another followed, until the entire family lay before me, and a whole legion of jars covered the table and surrounding shelves; the odor had become a pleasant perfume; and even now, the sight of an old, six-inch worm-eaten cork brings fragrant memories.

29   The whole group of haemulons was thus brought in review; and, whether engaged upon the dissection of the internal organs, the preparation and examination of the bony framework, or the description of the various parts, Agassiz's training in the method of observing facts and their orderly arrangement was ever accompanied by the urgent exhortation not to be content with them.

30   "Facts are stupid things," he would say, "until brought into connection with some general law."

31   At the end of eight months, it was almost with reluctance that I left these friends and turned to insects; but what I had gained by this outside experience has been of greater value than years of later investigation in my favorite groups.

Topics for Writing and Discussion

1.   What was Professor Agassiz's purpose in demanding that Scudder repeatedly look at the fish?

2.   Scudder claims that Professor Agassiz's process taught him a lesson "of inestimable value." What was this lesson? What does Agassiz mean when he says, "Facts are stupid things until brought into connection with some general law"?

3.   Why does Scudder use a narrative approach to tell about the process he learned from Agassiz? Why not simply present an essay that lists the steps one should take to become a good observer?

4.   Consider your own academic or professional life. How might the process of observation Scudder praises here be successfully applied to a subject you are studying? How might it be applied to the draft of an essay you are currently revising?

5. Select and read an essay of your choice in this text—and then follow Professor Agassiz's good advice: look at it again. And again. Take notes on its purpose and craft after each reading. Write an essay that explains what you learned from this process. What did you see in later readings that you missed the first time through? How might your essay help other students improve their reading skills?

Writing Assignments for Chapter Five

Process

1. Research a popular product and write a general-interest article about its creation and history, as Carin C. Quinn did in "The Jeaning of America." For instance, consider the frisbee, the skateboard, Muzak, the microwave, panty hose, or men's ties. Or, select a product that is important in your field of study and describe its discovery or production. Consider as your audience the readers of a magazine or journal in your area of study, who are familiar with this product but not its history.

2. In "The American Way of Death," Jessica Mitford describes the custom of embalming. Select another American or family ritual, such as a wedding, a graduation, a twenty-first birthday party, Thanksgiving dinner, family reunion, or New Year's Eve, and describe the process as it occurs in your family or circle of friends. Make your attitude toward the process clear to the reader.

3. In "Attitude" humorist Garrison Keillor explains how to develop the proper frame of mind for slow-pitch baseball by going through a series of steps on the field. Write an essay for real or imagined teammates or friends that describes the acquisition of the proper attitude for participation in some group activity. Don't feel limited to a sport, however. You might, for instance, create the steps for adopting the right demeanor in the great art of mall walking, bar lounging, apartment renting, or library browsing. How does one create an aura of having the "right stuff" at the big job interview? On a blind date? Your essay might be humorous or serious, depending on your purpose and audience.

4. Select a problem on your campus and describe the steps you would urge your fellow students to take to resolve it. You may also wish to mention the responses that will not work, as Martin Luther King, Jr., did in his essay "Nonviolent Resistance." Your essay should be directed

either to the person(s) in charge of the problem (a certain administrator, for example) or to those you wish to participate in your solution (students boycotting the dorm cafeteria, for instance).

5. Henry David Thoreau went to the woods near Walden Pond to experience a simpler life because, in part, he felt that most people "lead lives of quiet desperation." In a clear essay addressed to a friend who is feeling overly stressed, describe a process that helps you deal with some of the anxieties of modern life.

6. Professor Louis Agassiz did more for Samuel Scudder than merely teach him how to "Take This Fish and Look at It." Recall a time in your own life when a teacher, relative, or friend showed you a method of doing something that taught you more than you expected to learn. Write about this experience in a way that presents your step-by-step discovery of the significance of your study. What did this experience teach you that was, to use Scudder's words, of "inestimable value"?

7. Professor Agassiz was fond of saying, "Facts are stupid things until brought into connection with some general law." Write an essay that illustrates the process of some discovery you have made that illustrates or refutes this saying. Or, if you prefer, select a theory or controversy from your field of study and present the logical steps that lead some professionals to adopt a particular theory or "general law." For instance, what logical progression of "facts" leads some scientists to accept the astroid theory explaining the disappearance of the dinosaurs?

Chapter Six

Definition

Have you found yourself faced with an essay exam assignment that asked you to "Explain (or fully discuss) . . ."? For example, in a literature course you might see an assignment like this: "Explain Flannery O'Connor's concept of 'moment of grace'" or "Explore Ursula LeGuin's short story 'The Ones Who Walk Away from Omelas' as an example of anti-utopian fiction." Suppose your psychology or sociology professor asked you to "Discuss the question of ethics surrounding surrogate parenting." How would you start such assignments? What approach would you take? Perhaps the best place to start would be with a definition of "moment of grace" or anti-utopian fiction or surrogate parenting.

The rhetorical structure called *definition* is a handy one indeed, for it will allow you to analyze a concept as fully as you can as you look for a broader understanding of the concept. Typically, there are three types of definitions. The *formal* definition is the one you might call the "dictionary meaning." This type of definition has three parts: *term* (the thing or idea itself), *class* (the general class to which the thing or idea belongs), and the *differentiation* (how the thing or idea differs from other things or ideas in the same class).

TERM	CLASS	DIFFERENTIATION
sonata	an instrumental composition	generally consisting of three or four related movements
sombrero	a broad-brimmed, tall-crowned hat	worn in Mexico and the Southwest
sonnet	a form of poetry	consisting of 14 lines in a fixed verse and rhyme scheme

277

Another type of definition is the *restrictive* definition, which defines a term by limiting it, thus allowing a writer to use a term in a specific manner for a particular discussion. For example, "moment of grace" is a term that can be specifically applied to discussions of Flannery O'Connor's fiction, for it was coined by the author herself. Many slang terms, professional jargon, and family idiolects are examples of restrictive definitions. Terms like "chill out" (slang for calm down) or "cream puff" (real estate jargon for a meticulously maintained home) or a term that has special meaning only for your immediate family may be meaningless outside a particular context.

The third type of definition is the one you are most likely to use—the *extended* definition. This type will allow you to delve into a subject more deeply, to analyze a concept more fully in order to make it clearer to the reader. Often the extended definition begins with a formal definition, may include a restrictive definition, and then uses other rhetorical structures to develop it. Generally speaking, the scope of your extended definition will be determined by the word or idea being defined, the purpose of the definition, and your audience.

Return to the assignment regarding O'Connor's concept of "moment of grace." You might begin your response with a formal definition:

> "Moment of grace" is the spiritual act of accepting or rejecting the gift of salvation.

Then you might restrict the definition:

> It is a concept created and used by the Southern writer Flannery O'Connor to identify the climax of her fictional works.

From this point you would probably explore the subject more fully (*extending* the definition) by providing examples of the "moment of grace" in several of the author's works, by describing typical scenes illustrating the "moment of grace," by analyzing the process by which the "moment of grace" occurs, by comparing or contrasting O'Connor's concept to the climactic scenes written by other writers, or by providing a narrative summary of the plot leading to the "moment of grace."

The essence of a successful definition essay is clarity. The purpose of a definition essay is to give your readers clearly presented, precise information that will allow them to understand better a principle, idea, or object.

Writing the Definition

As you prepare your definition, consider the following suggestions to clarify your presentation:

1. *Use a synonym.*

   Using other, more familiar words or phrases that have similar meanings may help clarify the concept you are defining. For example, in "What Is Happiness?" John Ciardi argues that happiness is neither in "having" nor in "being" but in "becoming." In her definition essay, Joan Didion claims that people who have self-respect have "the courage of their mistakes."

2. *Use examples.*

   Frequently a term or abstract concept is best understood when the writer offers examples to illustrate its nature or use. Ralph Ellison's essay "Discrimination" presents several detailed scenes that show the racial prejudice his family encountered. Richard Rodriguez presents numerous examples to illustrate the emerging presence of a "Hispanic-American culture."

3. *Use a description.*

   Sometimes it is helpful to describe what a term looks like, how its parts fit together, or how it functions or acts. Margaret Mead in "New Superstitions for Old," for example, describes one of the uses of superstitions as helping people deal with their feelings of helplessness in difficult situations. John Ciardi reminds us that happiness is always partial and that "effort is the gist of it."

4. *Use comparison or contrast.*

   An idea or word may be made clearer by pointing out how it is similar to something else or by pointing out how it differs from another similar concept. Throughout his essay, Richard Rodriguez compares and contrasts symbols of American culture to those of Hispanic origins to show the benefits of a new Hispanic-American culture. Margaret Mead contrasts old and new superstitions in her essay as well as people's attitudes towards them.

5. *Use division and classification.*

   On occasion it is useful to clarify a complex topic by discussing its types, kinds, classes, or categories. For instance, if you were writing a humorous essay defining "nerds," you might organize your discussion by categorizing the types of nerds you see on campus whose collective qualities contribute to the larger definition of the word.

6. *Use negation*

   Telling what a word or idea is *not* often clarifies it for the reader. In "It's Failure, Not Success," Ellen Goodman uses this technique to explain that her definition of success differs greatly from that of many authors of self-help books.

By using *definition*, you can clarify difficult or unfamiliar terms, ideas, or principles; analyze seemingly simple terms to expose deeper meanings; explain controversial concepts; or reveal new meanings. The strategy of definition may be incorporated in essays of all kinds, whenever readers would profit from a clearer understanding of the ideas under discussion.

Ellen Goodman, (© William Huber)

It's Failure, Not Success

Ellen Goodman
(1941–   )

After graduating from Radcliffe, Ellen Goodman
became a reporter for *Newsweek.* She has also
worked as a feature writer for the *Detroit Free Press*
and for the *Boston Globe.* Her popular columns,
originally written for the *Globe,* have been
syndicated by the Washington Post Writers Group
since 1976. In 1980, she received a Pulitzer Prize
for distinguished commentary. In addition, she has
won praise for her work as a commentator on
television and radio. Her astute personal essays
have been collected in *Close to Home* (1979), *At
Large* (1980), *Keeping in Touch* (1985) and *Making
Sense* (1989). In "It's Failure, Not Success,"
Goodman challenges a definition established by
the author of a popular self-help book.

1   I knew a man who went into therapy about three years ago because, as
he put it, he couldn't live with himself any longer. I didn't blame him. The
guy was a bigot, a tyrant and a creep.

2   In any case, I ran into him again after he'd finished therapy. He was still
a bigot, a tyrant and a creep, *but . . .* he had learned to live with himself.

3   Now, I suppose this was an accomplishment of sorts. I mean, nobody else
could live with him. But it seems to me that there are an awful lot of people
running around and writing around these days encouraging us to feel good
about what we should feel terrible about, and to accept in ourselves what
we should change.

4   The only thing they seem to disapprove of is disapproval. The only judgment they make is against being judgmental, and they assure us that we

have nothing to feel guilty about except guilt itself. It seems to me that they are all intent on proving that I'm OK and You're OK, when in fact, I may be perfectly dreadful and you may be unforgivably dreary, and it may be—gasp!—*wrong*.

5 What brings on my sudden attack of judgmentitis is success, or rather, *Success!*—the latest in a series of exclamation-point books all concerned with How to Make it.

6 In this one, Michael Korda is writing a recipe book for success. Like the other authors, he leapfrogs right over the "Shoulds" and into the "Hows." He eliminates value judgments and edits out moral questions as if he were Fanny Farmer and the subject was the making of a blueberry pie.

7 It's not that I have any reason to doubt Mr. Korda's advice on the way to achieve success. It may very well be that successful men wear handkerchiefs stuffed neatly in their breast pockets, and that successful single women should carry suitcases to the office on Fridays whether or not they are going away for the weekend.

8 He may be realistic when he says that "successful people generally have very low expectations of others." And he may be only slightly cynical when he writes: "One of the best ways to ensure success is to develop expensive tastes or marry someone who has them."

9 And he may be helpful with his handy hints on how to sit next to someone you are about to overpower.

10 But he simply finesses the issues of right and wrong—silly words, embarrassing words that have been excised like warts from the shiny surface of the new how-to books. To Korda, guilt is not a prod, but an enemy that he slays on page four. Right off the bat, he tells the would-be successful reader that:

• It's OK to be greedy.

• It's OK to look out for Number One.

• It's OK to be Machiavellian (if you can get away with it).

• It's OK to recognize that honesty is not always the best policy (provided you don't go around saying so).

• And it's always OK to be rich.

11 Well, in fact, it's not OK. It's not OK to be greedy, Machiavellian, dishonest. It's not always OK to be rich. There is a qualitative difference between succeeding by making napalm or by making penicillin. There is a difference between climbing the ladder of success, and macheteing a path to the top.

12 Only someone with the moral perspective of a mushroom could assure us that this was all OK. It seems to me that most Americans harbor ambivalence toward success, not for neurotic reasons, but out of a realistic perception of what it demands.

13   Success is expensive in terms of time and energy and altered behavior—the sort of behavior he describes in the grossest of terms: "If you can undermine your boss and replace him, fine, do so, but never express anything but respect and loyalty for him while you're doing it."

14   This author—whose *Power!* topped the best-seller list last year—is intent on helping rid us of that ambivalence which is a signal from our conscience. He is like the other "Win!" "Me First!" writers, who try to make us comfortable when we should be uncomfortable.

15   They are all Doctor Feelgoods, offering us placebo prescriptions instead of strong medicine. They give us a way to live with ourselves, perhaps, but not a way to live with each other. They teach us a whole lot more about "Failure!" than about success.

Topics for Writing and Discussion

1.   In paragraphs 1 and 2, Goodman describes the characteristics of a man she knows. How does the man change? Why does he change? Does Goodman see the change as positive or negative? Why?

2.   How does Goodman use the opening example to lead to the generalization that is the thesis of her essay? State the thesis in your own words.

3.   What is Goodman's main objection to Korda's book? How does she use Korda's definition of *success* to support and explain her objection?

4.   What does Goodman mean when she calls Korda, and authors like him, "Doctor Feelgoods, offering us placebo prescriptions instead of strong medicine"? How does she use this metaphor to support her thesis?

5.   In this essay Goodman contrasts her definition of *success* to that of some popular "me first" authors. Write an essay that explains your idea of success or failure in the 1990s. You might include some illustrations drawn from your experience that show how your definition differs from those of others. According to Goodman, only "someone with the moral perspective of a mushroom" could approve of success without ethics. Where does your definition stand on the issues of dishonesty, greed, and selfishness?

What Is Happiness?

John Ciardi
(1916–1986)

John Ciardi
(Michael Mardikes,
Courtesy of the University
of Arkansas Press)

Literary critic and poet John Ciardi left teaching in 1961, after holding positions at Harvard, Rutgers, and the University of Kansas City, to pursue a full-time literary career. A poetry editor for the *Saturday Review* (1956–1972), he believed poetry should be accessible to a mass audience, rather than only a select academic elite. Ciardi translated the works of Dante Alighieri over a span of 16 years; his translations of *Inferno* (1954), *Purgatorio* (1961), and *Paradiso* (1970) have been widely acknowledged as classics. Other works include a poetry collection, *Homeward to America* (1940), and the text, *How Does a Poem Mean?* (1960). Following his death in 1986, there have been a number of posthumous publications including *Echoes: Poems Left Behind* (1989). A writer who once said of himself, "I'm not a complicated man, and I don't have any gripping internal problems," Ciardi addresses the nature of happiness in the following essay.

1   The right to pursue happiness is issued to Americans with their birth certificates, but no one seems quite sure which way it ran. It may be we are issued a hunting license but offered no game. Jonathan Swift seemed to think so when he attacked the idea of happiness as "the possession of being well-deceived," the felicity of being "a fool among knaves." For Swift saw society as Vanity Fair, the land of false goals.

2   It is, of course, un-American to think in terms of fools and knaves. We do, however, seem to be dedicated to the idea of buying our way to happiness. We shall all have made it to Heaven when we possess enough.

3   And at the same time the forces of American commercialism are hugely dedicated to making us deliberately unhappy. Advertising is one of our major industries, and advertising exists not to satisfy desires but to create them—and to create them faster than any man's budget can satisfy them. For that

matter, our whole economy is based on a dedicated insatiability. We are taught that to possess is to be happy, and then we are made to want. We are even told it is our duty to want. It was only a few years ago, to cite a single example, that car dealers across the country were flying banners that read "You Auto Buy Now." They were calling upon Americans, as an act approaching patriotism, to buy at once, with money they did not have, automobiles they did not really need, and which they would be required to grow tired of by the time the next year's models were released.

4   Or look at any of the women's magazines. There, as Bernard DeVoto once pointed out, advertising begins as poetry in the front pages and ends as pharmacopoeia and therapy in the back pages. The poetry of the front matter is the dream of perfect beauty. This is the baby skin that must be hers. These, the flawless teeth. This, the perfumed breath she must exhale. This, the sixteen-year-old figure she must display at forty, at fifty, at sixty, and forever.

5   Once past the vaguely uplifting fiction and feature articles, the reader finds the other face of the dream in the back matter. This is the harness into which Mother must strap herself in order to display that perfect figure. These, the chin straps she must sleep in. This is the salve that restores all, this is her laxative, these are the tablets that melt away fat, these are the hormones of perpetual youth, these are the stockings that hide varicose veins.

6   Obviously no half-sane person can be completely persuaded either by such poetry or by such pharmacopoeia and orthopedics. Yet someone is obviously trying to buy the dream as offered and spending billions every year in the attempt. Clearly the happiness-market is not running out of customers, but what is it trying to buy?

7   The idea "happiness," to be sure, will not sit still for easy definition: the best one can do is to try to set some extremes to the idea and then work in toward the middle. To think of happiness as acquisitive and competitive will do to set the materialistic extreme. To think of it as the idea one senses in, say, a holy man of India will do to set the spiritual extreme. That holy man's idea of happiness is in needing nothing from outside himself. In wanting nothing, he lacks nothing. He sits immobile, rapt in contemplation, free even of his own body. Or nearly free of it. If devout admirers bring him food he eats it; if not, he starves indifferently. Why be concerned? What is physical is an illusion to him. Contemplation is his joy and he achieves it through a fantastically demanding discipline, the accomplishment of which is itself a joy within him.

8   Is he a happy man? Perhaps his happiness is only another sort of illusion. But who can take it from him? And who will dare say it is more illusory than happiness on the installment plan?

9   But, perhaps because I am Western, I doubt such catatonic happiness, as I doubt the dreams of the happiness-market. What is certain is that his way of happiness would be torture to almost any Western man. Yet these extremes will still serve to frame the area within which all of us must find some sort

of balance. Thoreau—a creature of both Eastern and Western thought—had his own firm sense of that balance. His aim was to save on the low levels in order to spend on the high.

10   Possession for its own sake or in competition with the rest of the neighborhood would have been Thoreau's idea of the low levels. The active discipline of heightening one's perception of what is enduring in nature would have been his idea of the high. What he saved from the low was time and effort he could spend on the high. Thoreau certainly disapproved of starvation, but he would put into feeding himself only as much effort as would keep him functioning for more important efforts.

11   Effort is the gist of it. There is no happiness except as we take on life-engaging difficulties. Short of the impossible, as Yeats put it, the satisfactions we get from a lifetime depend on how high we choose our difficulties. Robert Frost was thinking in something like the same terms when he spoke of "The pleasure of taking pains." The mortal flaw in the advertised version of happiness is in the fact that it purports to be effortless.

12   We demand difficulty even in our games. We demand it because without difficulty there can be no game. A game is a way of making something hard for the fun of it. The rules of the game are an arbitrary imposition of difficulty. When the spoilsport ruins the fun, he always does so by refusing to play by the rules. It is easier to win at chess if you are free, at your pleasure, to change the wholly arbitrary rules, but the fun is in winning within the rules. No difficulty, no fun.

13   The buyers and sellers at the happiness-market seem too often to have lost their sense of the pleasure of difficulty. Heaven knows what they are playing, but it seems a dull game. And the Indian holy man seems dull to us, I suppose, because he seems to be refusing to play anything at all. The Western weakness may be in the illusion that happiness can be bought. Perhaps the Eastern weakness is in the idea that there is such a thing as perfect (and therefore static) happiness.

14   Happiness is never more than partial. There are no pure states of mankind. Whatever else happiness may be, it is neither in having nor in being, but in becoming. What the Founding Fathers declared for us as an inherent right, we should do well to remember, was not happiness but the *pursuit* of happiness. What they might have underlined, could they have foreseen the happiness-market, is the cardinal fact that happiness is in the pursuit itself, in the meaningful pursuit of what is life-engaging and life-revealing, which is to say, in the idea of *becoming*. A nation is not measured by what it possesses or wants to possess, but by what it wants to become.

15   By all means let the happiness-market sell us minor satisfactions and even minor follies so long as we keep them in scale and buy them out of spiritual change. I am no customer for either puritanism or asceticism. But drop any real spiritual capital at those bazaars, and what you come home to will be your own poorhouse.

Topics for Writing and Discussion

1. In defining "happiness" Ciardi presents the conflicts between Eastern and Western perceptions. What emerges as his own definition of happiness? Does he believe happiness is fully attainable? Why or why not?

2. What methods (such as comparison, contrast, illustration) does Ciardi use to define "happiness"? Cite some examples.

3. Consider Ciardi's comments regarding the role of advertising and consumerism in prescribing what "happiness" should be for the American public. What other terms (beauty? success?) are defined for us by mass media advertising's exhortations to "buy!"? Choose two terms and explain how the media helps define them for us.

4. Ciardi's discussion of happiness suggests that some definitions may be culturally influenced. Consider various types of cultural or social groups (ethnic, racial, religious, political, economic, age, gender, and so on) that you know well. What other terms might be defined in very different ways by such groups? Choose one term and give a brief definition from the perspective of two cultures or social groups.

5. Present an extended definition of the term chosen for question 4 in an essay that might employ examples, description, comparison or contrast, division and classification, negation, or other techniques. Examine the term being defined from the perspective of one of the cultures chosen previously.

On Self-Respect

Joan Didion
(1934–   )

*Joan Didion
(Jack Manning/
NYT Pictures)*

A native Californian, Joan Didion is a descendent of pioneers. Her great-great-great grandmother was one of the few who survived the trouble-ridden journey of the Donner party that crossed the mountains in 1846. Didion earned her bachelor's degree at the University of California at Berkeley and is best known for her perceptive essays, collected in several volumes, including *Slouching toward Bethlehem* (1969) and *The White Album* (1983). She has also written screen plays (in collaboration with her husband, John Gregory Dunne) and novels (*Play It As It Lays*, 1970; *Democracy*, 1984; *Book of Common Prayer*, 1977 and *After Henry* (1992). Didion's essays are praised for their realistic descriptions and their keen reflections on the events of her life. In this selection, she examines her failure to be elected to Phi Beta Kappa and in doing so creates a definition for self-respect.

1   Once, in a dry season, I wrote in large letters across two pages of a notebook that innocence ends when one is stripped of the delusion that one likes oneself. Although now, some years later, I marvel that a mind on the outs with itself should have nonetheless made painstaking record of its every tremor, I recall with embarrassing clarity the flavor of those particular ashes. It was a matter of misplaced self-respect.

2   I had not been elected to Phi Beta Kappa. This failure could scarcely have been more predictable or less ambiguous (I simply did not have the grades), but I was unnerved by it; I had somehow thought myself a kind of academic Raskolnikov, curiously exempt from the cause–effect relationships which hampered others. Although even the humorless nineteen-year-old that I was must have recognized that the situation lacked real tragic stature, the day that I did not make Phi Beta Kappa nonetheless marked the end of some-thing, and innocence may well be the word for it. I lost the conviction that

lights would always turn green for me, the pleasant certainty that those rather passive virtues which had won me approval as a child automatically guaranteed me not only Phi Beta Kappa keys but happiness, honor, and the love of a good man; lost a certain touching faith in the totem power of good manners, clean hair, and proven competence on the Stanford-Binet scale. To such doubtful amulets had my self-respect been pinned, and I faced myself that day with the nonplused apprehension of someone who has come across a vampire and has no crucifix at hand.

3   Although to be driven back upon oneself is an uneasy affair at best, rather like trying to cross a border with borrowed credentials, it seems to me now the one condition necessary to the beginnings of real self-respect. Most of our platitudes notwithstanding, self-deception remains the most difficult deception. The tricks that work on others count for nothing in that very well-lit back alley where one keeps assignations with oneself: no winning smiles will do here, no prettily drawn lists of good intentions. One shuffles flashily but in vain through one's marked cards—the kindness done for the wrong reason, the apparent triumph which involved no real effort, the seemingly heroic act into which one had been shamed. The dismal fact is that self-respect has nothing to do with the approval of others—who are, after all, deceived easily enough; has nothing to do with reputation, which, as Rhett Butler told Scarlett O'Hara, is something people with courage can do without.

4   To do without self-respect, on the other hand, is to be an unwilling audience of one to an interminable documentary that details one's failings, both real and imagined, with fresh footage spliced in for every screening. *There's the glass you broke in anger, there's the hurt on X's face; watch now, this next scene, the night Y came back from Houston, see how you muff this one.* To live without self-respect is to lie awake some night, beyond the reach of warm milk, phenobarbital, and the sleeping hand on the coverlet, counting up the sins of commission and omission, the trusts betrayed, the promises subtly broken, the gifts irrevocably wasted through sloth or cowardice or carelessness. However long we postpone it, we eventually lie down alone in that notoriously uncomfortable bed, the one we make ourselves. Whether or not we sleep in it depends, of course, on whether or not we respect ourselves.

5   To protest that some fairly improbable people, some people who *could not possibly respect themselves,* seem to sleep easily enough is to miss the point entirely, as surely as those people miss it who think that self-respect has necessarily to do with not having safety pins in one's underwear. There is a common superstition that "self-respect" is a kind of charm against snakes, something that keeps those who have it locked in some unblighted Eden, out of strange beds, ambivalent conversations, and trouble in general. It does not at all. It has nothing to do with the face of things, but concerns instead a separate peace, a private reconciliation. Although the careless,

suicidal Julian English in *Appointment in Samarra* and the careless, incurably dishonest Jordan Baker in *The Great Gatsby* seem equally improbable candidates for self-respect, Jordan Baker had it, Julian English did not. With that genius for accommodation more often seen in women than in men, Jordan took her own measure, made her own peace, avoided threats to that peace: "I hate careless people," she told Nick Carraway. "It takes two to make an accident."

6   Like Jordan Baker, people with self-respect have the courage of their mistakes. They know the price of things. If they choose to commit adultery, they do not then go running, in an access of bad conscience, to receive absolution from the wronged parties; nor do they complain unduly of the unfairness, the undeserved embarrassment, of being named corespondent. In brief, people with self-respect exhibit a certain toughness, a kind of moral nerve; they display what was once called *character*, a quality which, although approved in the abstract, sometimes loses ground to other, more instantly negotiable virtues. The measure of its slipping prestige is that one tends to think of it only in connection with homely children and United States senators who have been defeated, preferably in the primary, for reelection. Nonetheless, character—the willingness to accept responsibility for one's own life—is the source from which self-respect springs.

7   Self-respect is something that our grandparents, whether or not they had it, knew all about. They had instilled in them, young, a certain discipline, the sense that one lives by doing things one does not particularly want to do, by putting fears and doubts to one side, by weighing immediate comforts against the possibility of larger, even intangible, comforts. It seemed to the nineteenth century admirable, but not remarkable, that Chinese Gordon put on a clean white suit and held Khartoum against the Mahdi; it did not seem unjust that the way to free land in California involved death and difficulty and dirt. In a diary kept during the winter of 1846, an emigrating twelve-year-old named Narcissa Cornwall noted coolly: "Father was busy reading and did not notice that the house was being filled with strange Indians until Mother spoke about it." Even lacking any clue as to what Mother said, one can scarcely fail to be impressed by the entire incident: the father reading, the Indians filing in, the mother choosing the words that would not alarm, the child duly recording the event and noting further that those particular Indians were not, "fortunately for us," hostile. Indians were simply part of the *donnée*.

8   In one guise or another, Indians always are. Again, it is a question of recognizing that anything worth having has its price. People who respect themselves are willing to accept the risk that the Indians will be hostile, that the venture will go bankrupt, that the liaison may not turn out to be one in which *every day is a holiday because you're married to me*. They are willing to invest something of themselves; they may not play at all, but when they do play, they know the odds.

9   That kind of self-respect is a discipline, a habit of mind that can never be faked but can be developed, trained, coaxed forth. It was once suggested to me that, as an antidote to crying, I put my head in a paper bag. As it happens, there is a sound physiological reason, something to do with oxygen, for doing exactly that, but the psychological effect alone is incalculable: it is difficult in the extreme to continue fancying oneself Cathy in *Wuthering Heights* with one's head in a Food Fair bag. There is a similar case for all the small disciplines, unimportant in themselves; imagine maintaining any kind of swoon, commiserative or carnal, in a cold shower.

10   But those small disciplines are available only insofar as they represent larger ones. To say that Waterloo was won on the playing fields of Eton is not to say that Napoleon might have been saved by a crash program in cricket; to give formal dinners in the rain forest would be pointless did not the candlelight flickering on the liana call forth deeper, stronger disciplines, values instilled long before. It is a kind of ritual, helping us to remember who and what we are. In order to remember it, one must have known it.

11   To have that sense of one's intrinsic worth which constitutes self-respect is potentially to have everything: the ability to discriminate, to love and to remain indifferent. To lack it is to be locked within oneself, paradoxically incapable of either love or indifference. If we do not respect ourselves, we are on the one hand forced to despise those who have so few resources as to consort with us, so little perception as to remain blind to our fatal weaknesses. On the other, we are peculiarly in thrall to everyone we see, curiously determined to live out—since our self-image is untenable—their false notions of us. We flatter ourselves by thinking this compulsion to please others an attractive trait: a gist for imaginative empathy, evidence of our willingness to give. Of *course* I will play Francesca to your Paolo, Helen Keller to anyone's Annie Sullivan: no expectation is too misplaced, no role too ludicrous. At the mercy of those we cannot but hold in contempt, we play roles doomed to failure before they are begun, each defeat generating fresh despair at the urgency of divining and meeting the next demand made upon us.

12   It is the phenomenon sometimes called "alienation from self." In its advanced stages, we no longer answer the telephone, because someone might want something; that we could say *no* without drowning in self-reproach is an idea alien to this game. Every encounter demands too much, tears the nerves, drains the will, and the specter of something as small as an unanswered letter arouses such disproportionate guilt that answering it becomes out of the question. To assign unanswered letters their proper weight, to free us from the expectations of others, to give us back to ourselves—there lies the great, the singular power of self-respect. Without it, one eventually discovers the final turn of the screw: one runs away to find oneself, and finds no one at home.

Topics for Writing and Discussion

1. Why was Didion upset that she was not elected to Phi Beta Kappa? How did this failure initially change the way she looked at herself? What examples does she provide in paragraph 2 to explain her altered view of herself and her future?

2. At the beginning of paragraph 5, Didion anticipates an objection some readers might make to her comments on self-respect. Explain the protest Didion expects and her response to that protest. Do you find her ideas convincing? Why or why not?

3. Didion uses several different methods as she develops her definition. One particularly effective method is the use of examples. Beginning with paragraph 2, notice the pattern she follows for presenting examples. Do you find this pattern effective? Why?

4. Didion cites many authorities and makes many literary and historical allusions. What do these citations and allusions suggest about Didion's view of her audience? Would the essay be difficult to understand for the reader who did not recognize the sources or the meaning of the allusions?

5. Choose a concept such as honesty, loyalty, pride, bravery, or self-doubt, and write an essay that builds a definition of the concept through the use of anecdotes, examples, allusions, and references to authorities.

Richard Rodriguez. (© Robert Messick)

Hispanic-American Culture
Richard Rodriguez
(1944–   )

Richard Rodriguez is a journalist who has written
for many publications, including *Time, Harper's,*
and *Mother Jones.* He was born in San Francisco
the son of Mexican-American immigrants and was
raised speaking only Spanish until, at the age of
five, he started school. Rodriguez reacted strongly
to his early school experiences and for a while
refused to speak Spanish at all, learning most of
what he knows of his parents' native tongue from
studying Spanish as a "foreign" language in high
school. He continued his education at the
University of California at Berkeley where he
received the Ph.D. degree in English. In 1982,
*Hunger of Memory: The Education of Richard
Rodriguez* was published; his most recent book is
Mexico's Children (1990). "Hispanic-American
Culture" examines Rodriguez' belief that a true
marriage of culture is yet to occur in a United
States still wary of full assimilation of its many
ethnic and racial groups. When this union does
happen, Rodriguez argues, the New World will
finally fulfill its potential as a society of genuine
cultural blending.

1 hat is culture?

2   The immigrant shrugs. Latin American immigrants come to the United
States with only the things they need in mind—not abstractions like culture.
Money. They need dollars. They need food. Maybe they need to get out of
the way of bullets.

3　　Most of us who concern ourselves with Hispanic-American culture, as painters, musicians, writers—or as sons and daughters—are the children of immigrants. We have grown up on this side of the border, in the land of Elvis Presley and Thomas Edison; our lives are prescribed by the mall, by the DMV and the Chinese restaurant. Our imaginations yet vascillate between an Edenic Latin America (the blue door)—which nevertheless betrayed our parents—and the repellent plate glass of a real American city—which has been good to us.

4　　Hispanic-American culture is where the past meets the future. Hispanic-American culture is not an Hispanic milestone only, not simply a celebration at the crossroads. America transforms into pleasure what America cannot avoid. Is it any coincidence that at a time when Americans are troubled by the encroachment of the Mexican desert, Americans discover a chic in cactus, in the decorator colors of the Southwest? In sand?

5　　Hispanic-American culture of the sort that is now showing (the teen movie, the rock song) may exist in an hourglass; may in fact be irrelevant to the epic. The U.S. Border Patrol works through the night to arrest the flow of illegal immigrants over the border, even as Americans wait in line to get into "La Bamba." Even as Americans vote to declare, once and for all, that English shall be the official language of the United States, Madonna starts recording in Spanish.

6　　But then so is Bill Cosby's show irrelevant to the 10 o'clock news, where families huddle together in fear on porches, pointing at the body of the slain boy bagged in tarpoline. Which is not to say that Bill Cosby or Michael Jackson are irrelevant to the future or without neo-Platonic influence. Like players within the play, they prefigure, they resolve. They make black and white audiences aware of a bond that may not yet exist.

7　　Before a national TV audience, Rita Moreno tells Geraldo Rivera that her dream as an actress is to play a character rather like herself: "I speak English perfectly well . . . I'm not dying from poverty . . . I want to play *that* kind of Hispanic woman, which is to say, an American citizen." This is an actress talking, these are show-biz pieties. But Moreno expresses as well the general Hispanic-American predicament. Hispanics want to belong to America without betraying the past.

8　　Hispanics fear losing ground in any negotiation with the American city. We come from an expansive, an intimate culture that has been judged second-rate by the United States of America. For reasons of pride, therefore, as much as of affection, we are reluctant to give up our past. Hispanics often express a fear of "losing" culture. Our fame in the United States has been our resistance to assimilation.

9　　The symbol of Hispanic culture has been the tongue of flame—Spanish. But the remarkable legacy Hispanics carry from Latin America is not language—an inflatable skin—but breath itself, capacity of soul, an inclination to live. The genius of Latin America is the habit of synthesis.

10   We assimilate. Just over the border there is the example of Mexico, the country from which the majority of U.S. Hispanics come. Mexico is mestizo—Indian and Spanish. Within a single family, Mexicans are light-skinned and dark. It is impossible for the Mexican to say, in the scheme of things, where the Indian begins and the Spaniard surrenders.

11   In culture as in blood, Latin America was formed by a rape that became a marriage. Due to the absorbing generosity of the Indian, European culture took on new soil. What Latin America knows is that people create one another as they marry. In the music of Latin America you will hear the litany of bloodlines—the African drum, the German accordian, the cry from the minaret.

12   The United States stands as the opposing New World experiment. In North America the Indian and the European stood apace. Whereas Latin America was formed by a medieval Catholic dream of one world—of meltdown conversion—the United States was built up from Protestant individualism. The American melting pot washes away only embarrassment; it is the necessary initiation into public life. The American faith is that our national strength derives from separateness, from "diversity." The glamour of the United States is a carnival promise: You can lose weight, get rich as Rockefeller, tough up your roots, get a divorce.

13   Immigrants still come for the promise. But the United States wavers in its faith. As long as there was space enough, sky enough, as long as economic success validated individualism, loneliness was not too high a price to pay. (The cabin on the prairie or the Sony Walkman.)

14   As we near the end of the American century, two alternative cultures beckon the American imagination—both highly communal cultures—the Asian and the Latin American. The United States is a literal culture. Americans devour what we might otherwise fear to become. Sushi will make us corporate warriors. Combination Plate #3, smothered in mestizo gravy, will burn a hole in our hearts.

15   Latin America offers passion. Latin America has a life—I mean *life*—big clouds, unambiguous themes, death, birth, faith, that the United States, for all its quality of life, seems without now. Latin America offers communal riches: an undistressed leisure, a kitchen table, even a full sorrow. Such is the solitude of America, such is the urgency of American need, Americans reach right past a fledgling, homegrown Hispanic-American culture for the real thing—the darker bottle of Mexican beer; the denser novel of a Latin American master.

16   For a long time, Hispanics in the United States withheld from the United States our Latin American gift. We denied the value of assimilation. But as our presence is judged less foreign in America, we will produce a more generous art, less timid, less parochial. Carlos Santana, Luis Valdez, Linda Ronstadt—Hispanic Americans do not have a "pure" Latin American art to offer. Expect bastard themes, expect ironies, comic conclusions. For we live

on this side of the border, where Kraft manufactures bricks of "Mexican style" Velveeta, and where Jack in the Box serves "Fajita Pita."

17   *The flame-red Chevy floats a song down the Pan American Highway: From a rolled-down window, the grizzled voice of Willie Nelson rises in disembodied harmony with the voice of Julio Iglesias. Gabby Hayes and Cisco are thus resolved.*

18   Expect marriage. We will change America even as we will be changed. We will disappear with you into a new miscegenation.

19   Along the border, real conflicts remain. But the ancient tear separating Europe from itself—the Catholic Mediterranean from the Protestant north— may yet heal itself in the New World. For generations, Latin America has been the place—the bed—of a confluence of so many races and cultures that Protestant North America shuddered to imagine it.

Imagine it.

Topics for Writing and Discussion

1.   How does Rodriguez define Hispanic-American culture? In his view, what are the current conflicts between this culture and the general culture of the United States?

2.   Does Rodriguez believe that cultures can remain pure? Why or why not? Do you think he believes that they should? What is the result of assimilation? Do you agree with his perspective?

3.   Is it possible for an individual to be part of more than one culture? Write your own definition of culture, and then, using that definition as your guide, list the different cultures to which you may belong.

4.   Rodriguez writes that Americans "reach right past a fledgling, home-grown Hispanic-American culture for the real thing—the darker bottle of Mexican beer; the denser novel of a Latin American master." Is this true of American attitudes toward other cultures assimilated within the United States? Describe one such culture whose "Americanized" branch may be ignored while its origins are romanticized or celebrated. Or describe a culture that, although "Americanized," receives a great deal of popular attention.

5.   Review Rodriguez' forecast, "Expect marriage. We will change America even as we will be changed," and compare it to his earlier statement that "The American faith is that our national strength derives from separateness." Do you believe that some of the many ethnic and regional cultures that comprise America have remained largely separate? Have there already been cultures, now mostly assimilated, who have changed America even as they were changed? Choosing a specific cultural group

as your focus, write an essay showing how this group has maintained—by choice or pressure—its "separateness" or how it has changed, and, in turn, been changed through its assimilation.

Margaret Mead at the Museum of Natural History in New York City. (© John Laundis / Black Star)

New Superstitions for Old

Margaret Mead
(1901–1978)

Noted anthropologist Margaret Mead attended
Barnard College and Columbia University. In 1925
she went to live in the Samoan Islands where she
began her fieldwork living with and studying the
mores and customs of the people. Following her
years in Asia and the Pacific, she published three
books reporting and evaluating her experiences,
Coming of Age in Samoa (1928), *Growing Up in New
Guinea* (1930), and *Sex and Temperament in Three
Primitive Societies* (1935). In her later years she
turned to the study of contemporary Western
society and published works such as *The School in
American Culture* and *Culture and Commitment, a
Study of the Generation Gap* (1970). In addition, she
wrote a series of essays for *Redbook* magazine,
including "New Superstitions for Old." In this
essay, she examines the concept of superstition and
develops a detailed definition for this common, but
often misunderstood, term.

1   Once in a while there is a day when everything seems to run smoothly
and even the riskiest venture comes out exactly right. You exclaim, "This is
my lucky day!" Then as an afterthought you say, "Knock on wood!" Of
course, you do not really believe that knocking on wood will ward off danger.
Still, boasting about your own good luck gives you a slightly uneasy feeling—
and you carry out the little protective ritual. If someone challenged you at
that moment, you would probably say, "Oh, that's nothing. Just an old
superstition."

2   But when you come to think about it, what is a superstition?

3   In the contemporary world most people treat old folk beliefs as super-stitions—the belief, for instance, that there are lucky and unlucky days or numbers, that future events can be read from omens, that there are protective charms or that what happens can be influenced by casting spells. We have excluded magic from our current world view, for we know that natural events have natural causes.

4   In a religious context, where truths cannot be demonstrated, we accept them as a matter of faith. Superstitions, however, belong to the category of beliefs, practices and ways of thinking that have been discarded because they are inconsistent with scientific knowledge. It is easy to say that other people are superstitious because they believe what we regard to be untrue. "Superstition" used in that sense is a derogatory term for the beliefs of other people that we do not share. But there is more to it than that. For superstitions lead a kind of half life in a twilight world where, sometimes, we partly suspend our disbelief and act as if magic worked.

5   Actually, almost every day, even in the most sophisticated home, some-thing is likely to happen that evokes the memory of some old folk belief. The salt spills. A knife falls to the floor. Your nose tickles. Then perhaps, with a slightly embarrassed smile, the person who spilled the salt tosses a pinch over his left shoulder. Or someone recites the old rhyme, "Knife falls, gentleman calls." Or as you rub your nose you think, That means a letter. I wonder who's writing? No one takes these small responses very seriously or gives them more than a passing thought. Sometimes people will preface one of these ritual acts—walking around instead of under a ladder or hastily closing an umbrella that has been opened inside a house—with such a remark as "I remember my great-aunt used to . . ." or "Germans used to say you ought not . . ." And then, having placed the belief at some distance away in time or space, they carry out the ritual.

6   Everyone also remembers a few of the observances of childhood—wishing on the first star; looking at the new moon over the right shoulder; avoiding the cracks in the sidewalk on the way to school while chanting, "Step on a crack, break your mother's back"; wishing on white horses, on loads of hay, on covered bridges, on red cars; saying quickly, "Bread-and-butter" when a post or a tree separated you from the friend you were walking with. The adult may not actually recite the formula "Star light, star bright . . ." and may not quite turn to look at the new moon, but his mood is tempered by a little of the old thrill that came when the observance was still freighted with magic.

7   Superstition can also be used with another meaning. When I discuss the religious beliefs of other peoples, especially primitive peoples, I am often asked, "Do they really have a religion, or is it all just superstition?" The point of contrast here is not between a scientific and a magical view of the world but between the clear, theologically defensible religious beliefs of members of civilized societies and what we regard as the false and childish

views of the heathen who "bow down to wood and stone." Within the civilized religions, however, where membership includes believers who are educated and urbane and others who are ignorant and simple, one always finds traditions and practices that the more sophisticated will dismiss offhand as "just superstition" but that guide the steps of those who live by older ways. Mostly these are very ancient beliefs, some handed on from one religion to another and carried from country to country around the world.

8   Very commonly, people associate superstition with the past, with very old ways of thinking that have been supplanted by modern knowledge. But new superstitions are continually coming into being and flourishing in our society. Listening to mothers in the park in the 1930's, one heard them say, "Now, don't you run out into the sun, or Polio will get you." In the 1940's elderly people explained to one another in tones of resignation, "It was the Virus that got him down." And every year the cosmetics industry offers us new magic—cures for baldness, lotions that will give every woman radiant skin, hair coloring that will restore to the middle-aged the charm and ro-mance of youth—results that are promised if we will just follow the simple directions. Families and individuals also have their cherished, private su-perstitions. You must leave by the back door when you are going on a journey, or you must wear a green dress when you are taking an exami-nation. It is a kind of joke, of course, but it makes you feel safe.

9   These old half-beliefs and new half-beliefs reflect the keenness of our wish to have something come true or to prevent something bad from hap-pening. We do not always recognize new superstitions for what they are, and we still follow the old ones because someone's faith long ago matches our contemporary hopes and fears. In the past people "knew" that a black cat crossing one's path was a bad omen, and they turned back home. Today we are fearful of taking a journey and would give anything to turn back—and then we notice a black cat running across the road in front of us.

10   Child psychologists recognize the value of the toy a child holds in his hand at bedtime. It is different from his thumb, with which he can close himself in from the rest of the world, and it is different from the real world, to which he is learning to relate himself. Psychologists call these toys—these furry animals and old, cozy baby blankets—"transitional objects"; that is, objects that help the child move back and forth between the exactions of everyday life and the world of wish and dream.

11   Superstitions have some of the qualities of these transitional objects. They help people pass between the areas of life where what happens has to be accepted without proof and the areas where sequences of events are ex-plicable in terms of cause and effect, based on knowledge. Bacteria and viruses that cause sickness have been identified; the cause of symptoms can be diagnosed and a rational course of treatment prescribed. Magical charms no longer are needed to treat the sick; modern medicine has brought the whole sequence of events into the secular world. But people often act as if

this change had not taken place. Laymen still treat germs as if they were invisible, malign spirits, and physicians sometimes prescribe antibiotics as if they were magic substances.

12   Over time, more and more of life has become subject to the controls of knowledge. However, this is never a one-way process. Scientific investigation is continually increasing our knowledge. But if we are to make good use of this knowledge, we must not only rid our minds of old, superseded beliefs and fragments of magical practice, but also recognize new superstitions for what they are. Both are generated by our wishes, our fears and our feeling of helplessness in difficult situations.

13   Civilized peoples are not alone in having grasped the idea of superstitions—beliefs and practices that are superseded but that still may evoke compliance. The idea is one that is familiar to every people, however primitive, that I have ever known. Every society has a core of transcendent beliefs—beliefs about the nature of the universe, the world and man—that no one doubts or questions. Every society also has a fund of knowledge related to practical life—about the succession of day and night and of the seasons; about correct ways of planting seeds so that they will germinate and grow; about the process involved in making dyes or the steps necessary to remove the deadly poison from manioc roots so they become edible. Island peoples know how the winds shift and they know the star toward which they must point the prow of the canoe exactly so that as the sun rises they will see the first fringing palms on the shore toward which they are sailing.

14   This knowledge, based on repeated observations of reliable sequences, leads to ideas and hypotheses of the kind that underlie scientific thinking. And gradually as scientific knowledge, once developed without conscious plan, has become a great self-corrective system and the foundation for rational planning and action, old magical beliefs and observances have had to be discarded.

15   But it takes time for new ways of thinking to take hold, and often the transition is only partial. Older, more direct beliefs live on in the hearts and minds of elderly people. And they are learned by children who, generation after generation, start out life as hopefully and fearfully as their forebears did. Taking their first steps away from home, children use the old rituals and invent new ones to protect themselves against the strangeness of the world into which they are venturing.

16   So whatever has been rejected as no longer true, as limited, provincial and idolatrous, still leads a half life. People may say, "It's just a superstition," but they continue to invoke the ritual's protection or potency. In this transitional, twilight state such beliefs come to resemble dreaming. In the dream world a thing can be either good or bad; a cause can be an effect and an effect can be a cause. Do warts come from touching toads, or does touching a toad cure the wart? Is sneezing a good omen or a bad omen? You can have

it either way—or both ways at once. In the same sense, the half-acceptance and half-denial accorded superstitions give us the best of both worlds.

17   Superstitions are sometimes smiled at and sometimes frowned upon as observances characteristic of the old-fashioned, the unenlightened, children, peasants, servants, immigrants, foreigners or backwoods people. Nevertheless, they give all of us ways of moving back and forth among the different worlds in which we live—the sacred, the secular and the scientific. They allow us to keep a private world also, where, smiling a little, we can banish danger with a gesture and summon luck with a rhyme, make the sun shine in spite of storm clouds, force the stranger to do our bidding, keep an enemy at bay and straighten the paths of those we love.

Topics for Writing and Discussion

1.   In spite of our growing body of scientific knowledge, superstitions continue to play a role in our lives. How does Mead explain this apparently contradictory circumstance?

2.   To develop her definition, Mead contrasts superstition with religion. After reading paragraphs 4 and 7 carefully, explain how she distinguishes superstition from religion. Note that *religion* has a different meaning in the two paragraphs.

3.   Mead tells us both what superstition *is* and what it *is not*. Make a list of the things she says superstition is not and then analyze how she uses these negative examples to establish her definition.

4.   Does Mead see superstitions as entirely positive? Entirely negative? Give examples from the essay to support your response.

5.   In paragraph 8, Mead says "individuals also have their cherished, private superstitions." Develop a definition of "private superstitions" by explaining both what they *are* and what they *are not*. Use examples from your own observations and experiences to support the generalizations you make. Consider concluding your essay with a commentary on the positive and negative aspects of private superstitions.

Ralph Ellison (Woodfin Camp, Inc.)

Discrimination

Ralph Ellison
(1914–   )

Born in Oklahoma City, Ralph Waldo Ellison was
named after nineteenth-century poet and essayist
Ralph Waldo Emerson. Ellison studied music at
Tuskegee Institute and in 1936 moved to New York
City where he met author Richard Wright.
Encouraged by Wright, he began writing in 1939
and in 1953 received the National Book Award for
his novel *Invisible Man* (1952), now regarded as a
contemporary classic. He has taught and lectured
at many colleges including Bard, Rutgers, Yale, and
the University of Chicago. "Discrimination," a
1989 essay first published as part of a *New York
Times* supplement focusing on ethnocentrism and
racism, recreates pivotal childhood moments as
Ellison confronts and recognizes prejudice.

1   It got to you first at the age of six, and through your own curiosity. With
kindergarten completed and the first grade ahead, you were eagerly antic-
ipating your first day of public school. For months you had been imagining
your new experience and the children, known and unknown, with whom
you would study and play. But the physical framework of your imagining,
an elementary school in the process of construction, lay close at hand on
the block-square site across the street from your home. For over a year you
had watched it rise and spread in the air to become a handsome structure
of brick and stone, then seen its broad encircling grounds arrayed with
seesaws, swings, and baseball diamonds. You had imagined this picture-
book setting as the scene of your new experience, and when enrollment day
arrived, with its grounds astir with bright colors and voices of kids like
yourself, it did, indeed, become the site of your very first lesson in public

schooling—though not within its classrooms, as you had imagined, but well outside its walls. For while located within a fairly mixed neighborhood this new public school was exclusively for whites.

2   It was then you learned that you would attend a school located far to the south of your neighborhood, and that reaching it involved a journey which took you over, either directly or by way of a viaduct which arched head-spinning high above, a broad expanse of railroad tracks along which a constant traffic of freight-cars, switch engines, and passenger trains made it dangerous for a child to cross. And that once the tracks were safely negotiated you continued past warehouses, factories, and loading docks, and then through a notorious red-light district where black prostitutes in brightly colored housecoats and Mary Jane shoes supplied the fantasies and needs of a white clientele. Considering the fact that you couldn't attend school with white kids this made for a confusion that was further confounded by the giggling jokes which older boys whispered about the district's peculiar form of integration. For you it was a grown-up's mystery, but streets being no less schools than routes to schools, the district would soon add a few forbidden words to your vocabulary.

3   It took a bit of time to forget the sense of incongruity aroused by your having to walk *past* a school to get *to* a school, but soon you came to like your school, your teachers, and most of your schoolmates. Indeed, you soon enjoyed the long walks and anticipated the sights you might see, the adventures you might encounter, and the many things not taught in school that could be learned along the way. Your school was not nearly so fine as that which faced your home but it had its attractions. Among them its nearness to a park, now abandoned by whites, in which you picnicked and played. And there were the two tall cylindrical fire-escapes on either wing of its main building down which it was a joy to lie full-length and slide, spiraling down and around three stories to the ground—providing no outraged teacher was waiting to strap your legs once you sailed out of its chute like a shot off a fireman's shovel. Besides, in your childish way you were learning that it was better to take self-selected risks and pay the price than be denied the joy or pain of risk-taking by those who begrudged your existence.

4   Beginning when you were four or five you had known the joy of trips to the city's zoo, but one day you would ask your mother to take you there and have her sigh and explain that it was now against the law for Negro kids to view the animals. Had someone done something bad to the animals? No. Had someone tried to steal them or feed them poison? No. Could white kids still go? Yes! So why? Quit asking questions, it's the law and only because some white folks are out to turn this state into a part of the South.

5   This sudden and puzzling denial of a Saturday's pleasure was disappointing and so angered your mother that later, after the zoo was moved north of the city, she decided to do something about it. Thus one warm Saturday

afternoon with you and your baby brother dressed in your best she took you on a long streetcar ride which ended at a strange lakeside park, in which you found a crowd of noisy white people. Having assumed that you were on your way to the integrated cemetery where at the age of three you had been horrified beyond all tears or forgetting when you saw your father's coffin placed in the ground, you were bewildered. But now as your mother herded you and your brother in to the park you discovered that you'd come to the zoo and were so delighted that soon you were laughing and babbling as excitedly as the kids around you.

6   Your mother was pleased and as you moved through the crowd of white parents and children she held your brother's hand and allowed as much time for staring at the cages of rare animals as either of you desired. But once your brother began to tire she herded you out of the park and toward the streetcar line. And then it happened.

7   Just as you reached the gate through which crowds of whites were coming and going you had a memorable lesson in the strange ways of segregated-democracy as instructed by a guard in civilian clothes. He was a white man dressed in a black suit and a white straw hat, and when he looked at the fashion in which your mother was dressed, then down to you and your brother, he stiffened, turned red in the face, and stared as though at something dangerous.

8   "Girl," he shouted, "where are your *white* folks!"

9   "*White* folks," your mother said, "What white folks? I don't *have* any white folks, I'm a Negro!"

10   "Now don't you get smart with me, colored gal," the white man said, "I mean where are the white folks you come *out* here with!"

11   "But I just told you that I didn't come here with any white people," your mother said, "I came here with my boys . . ."

12   "Then what are you doing in this park," the white man said.

13   And now when your mother answered you could hear the familiar sound of anger in her voice.

14   "I'm here," she said, "because I'm a *taxpayer*, and I thought it was about time that my boys have a look at those animals. And for that I didn't *need* any *white* folks to show me the way!"

15   "Well," the white man said, "*I'm* here to tell you that you're breaking the law! So now you'll have to leave. Both you and your chillun too. The rule says no niggers is allowed in the zoo. That's the law and I'm enforcing it!"

16   "Very well," your mother said, "we've seen the animals anyway and were on our way to the streetcar line when you stopped us."

17   "That's fine," the white man said, "and when that car comes you be sure that you get on it, you hear? You and your chillun too!"

18   So it was quite a day. You had enjoyed the animals with your baby brother and had another lesson in the sudden ways good times could be turned into bad when white people looked at your color instead of *you*. But better still,

you had learned something of your mother's courage and were proud that she had broken an unfair law and stood up for her right to do so. For while the white man kept staring until the streetcar arrived she ignored him and answered your brother's questions about the various animals. Then the car came with its crowd of white parents and children, and when you were entrained and rumbling home past the fine lawns and houses your mother gave way to a gale of laughter; in which, hesitantly at first, and then with assurance and pride, you joined. And from that day the incident became the source of a family joke that was sparked by accidents, faux pas, or obvious lies. Then one of you was sure to frown and say, "Well, I think you'll have to go now, both you and your chillun too!" And the family would laugh hilariously. Discrimination teaches one to discriminate between discriminators while countering absurdity with black (Negro? Afro-American? African-American?) comedy.

19   When you were eight you would move to one of the white sections through which you often passed on the way to your father's grave and your truly last trip to the zoo. For now your mother was the custodian of several apartments located in a building which housed on its street floor a drug store, a tailor shop, a Piggly Wiggly market, and a branch post office. Built on a downward slope, the building had at its rear a long driveway which led from the side street past an empty lot to a group of garages in which the apartments' tenants stored their cars. Built at an angle with wings facing north and east, the structure supported a servant's quarters which sat above its angle like a mock watchtower atop a battlement, and it was there that you now lived.

20   Reached by a flight of outside stairs, it consisted of four small rooms, a bath, and a kitchen. Windows on three of its sides provided a view across the empty frontage to the street, of the back yards behind it, and of the back wall and windows of the building in which your mother worked. It was quite comfortable but you secretly disliked the idea of your mother living in service and missed your friends who now lived far away. Nevertheless, the neighborhood was pleasant, served by a sub-station of the streetcar line, and marked by a variety of activities which challenged your curiosity. Even its affluent alleys were more exciting to explore than those of your old neighborhood, and the one white friend you were to acquire in the area lived nearby.

21   This friend was a brilliant but sickly boy who was tutored at home, and with him you shared your new interest in building radios, a hobby at which he was quite skilled. Your friendship eased your loneliness and helped dispel some of the mystery and resentment imposed by segregation. Through access to his family, headed by an important Episcopalian minister, you learned more about whites and thus about yourself. With him you could make comparisons that were not so distorted by the racial myths which obstructed your thrust toward self-perception; compare their differences in taste, dis-

cipline, and manners with those of Negro families of comparable status and income; observe variations between your friend's boyish lore and your own, and measure his intelligence, knowledge, and ambitions against your own. For you this was a most important experience and a rare privilege, because up to now the prevailing separation of the races had made it impossible to learn how you and your Negro friends compared with boys who lived on the white side of the color line. It was said by word of mouth, proclaimed in newsprint, and dramatized by acts of discriminatory law that you were inferior. You were barred from vying with them in sports and games, competing in the classroom or the world of art. Yet what you saw, heard, and smelled of them left irrepressible doubts. So you ached for objective proof, for a fair field of testing.

22   Even your school's proud marching band was denied participation in the statewide music contests so popular at the time, as though so airy and earth-transcending an art as music would be contaminated if performed by musicians of different races.

23   Which was especially disturbing because after the father of a friend who lived next door in your old neighborhood had taught you the beginner's techniques required to play valved instruments you had decided to become a musician. Then shortly before moving among whites your mother had given you a brass cornet, which in the isolation of the servant's quarters you practiced hours on end. But you yearned to play with other musicians and found none available. Now you lived less than a block from a white school with a famous band, but there was no one in the neighborhood with whom to explore the mysteries of the horn. You could hear the school band's music and watch their marching, but joining in making the thrilling sounds was impossible. Nor did it help that you owned the scores to a few of their marches and could play with a certain facility and fairly good tone. So there, surrounded by sounds but unable to share a sound, you went it alone. You turned yourself into a one-man band.

24   You played along as best you could with the phonograph, read the score to *The Carnival of Venice* while listening to Del Steigers executing triple-tongue variations on its themes; played the trumpet parts of your bandbook's marches while humming in your head the supporting voices of horns and reeds. And since your city was a seedbed of Southwestern jazz you played Kansas City riffs, bugle calls, and wha-wha-muted imitations of blues singers' pleas. But none of this made up for your lack of fellow musicians. And then, late one Saturday afternoon when your mother and brother were away, and when you had dozed off while reading, you awoke to the nearby sound of live music. At first you thought you were dreaming, and then that you were listening to the high school band, but that couldn't be the source because, instead of floating over building tops and bouncing off wall and windowpane, the sounds you heard rose up, somewhat muffled, from below.

25   With that you ran to a window which faced the driveway, and looking down through the high windowpane of the lighted post office you could see the metal glint of instruments. Then you were on your feet and down the stairs, keeping to the shadows as you drew close and peeped below. And there you looked down upon a room full of men and women postal workers who were playing away at a familiar march. It was like the answer to a silent prayer because you could tell by the sound that they were beginners like yourself and the covers of the thicket of bandbooks revealed that they were of the same set as yours. For a while you listened and hummed along, unseen but shaking with excitement in the dimming twilight. And then, hardly before the idea formed in your head, you were skipping up the stairs to grab your cornet, lyre, and bandbook and hurtling down again to the drive.

26   For a while you listened, hearing the music come to a pause and the sound of the conductor's voice. Then came a rap on a music stand and once again the music. And now turning to the march by the light from the window, you snapped score to lyre, raised horn to lip, and began to play; at first silently tonguing the notes through the mouthpiece and then, carried away with the thrill of stealing a part of the music, you tensed your diaphragm and blew. And as you played, keeping time with your foot on the concrete drive, you realized that you were a better cornetist than some in the band and grew bold in the pride of your sound. Now in your mind you were marching along a downtown street to the flying of flags, the tramping of feet, and the cheering of excited crowds. For at last by an isolated act of brassy cunning you had become a member of the band.

27   Yes, but unfortunately you then let yourself become so carried away that you forgot to listen for the conductor's instructions which you were too high and hidden to see. Suddenly the music faded and you opened your ears to the fact that you were now rendering a lonely solo in the startled quietness. And before you could fully return to reality there came the sound of table legs across a floor and a rustle of movement ending in the appearance of a white startled face in the opened window. Then you heard a man's voice exclaim, "I'll be damn, it's a little nigger!" whereupon you took off like quail at the sound of sudden shotgun fire.

28   Next thing you knew, you were up the stairs and on your bed, crying away in the dark your guilt and embarrassment. You cried and cried, asking yourself how could you have been so lacking in pride as to shame yourself and your entire race by butting in where you weren't wanted. And this just to make some amateur music. To this you had no answers but then and there you made a vow that it would never happen again. And then, slowly, slowly, as you lay in the dark, your earlier lessons in the absurd nature of racial relations came to your aid. And suddenly you found yourself laughing, both at the way you'd run away and the shock you'd caused by joining unasked in the music.

29   Then you could hear yourself intoning in youreight-year-old's imitation of a white Southern accent. "Well boy, you broke the law, so you have to go, and that means you and your chillun too!"

Topics for Writing and Discussion

1.   What is Ellison's purpose in writing this essay? What is his definition of "discrimination"?

2.   What is the primary strategy of development used to present this definition? What details make this essay vivid?

3.   What is the effect of Ellison's use of second person ("you") to present his narrative? Does this give an indication of his intended audience?

4.   In what way does Ellison's chronological structuring of the essay, as well as the amount of time covered, comment on how discrimination is defined for an individual? Consider Ellison's use of the refrain, "Well, I think you'll have to go now, both you and your chillun too!" How does it affect tone, structure, and theme?

5.   There is an ongoing debate over allocating college scholarships to students who belong to certain groups (women, ethnic and racial groups; low-income families; first-generation college students) rather than awarding scholarships based solely on academic strengths. By your own definition, does this constitute discrimination? Is discrimination ever justified? If so, under what conditions? Defend your views in an essay.

Writing Assignments for Chapter Six
Definition

1.   As Ellen Goodman notes in "It's Failure, Not Success," people sometimes define words differently. Select an abstract word or phrase used frequently today and compare your definition to that of your parents or grandparents. Consider such words as *success, power, patriotism, prejudice, cultural diversity,* or *feminism.* To what degree does your definition differ from that of your parents or the previous generation? (You might wish to consider your parents or grandparents as your audience.)

2.   Poet John Ciardi presents a number of provocative thoughts about the nature of "happiness." Select one of the following statements from

"What Is Happiness?" and use it as a basis for your own essay in which you define "happiness" as you have experienced it or hope to experience it in your own life:

Effort is the gist of it. There is no happiness except as we take on life-engaging difficulties.

Happiness is never more than partial.

Happiness . . . is neither in having nor in being, but in becoming.

A nation is not measured by what it possesses or wants to possess, but by what it wants to become.

3. In her essay, "On Self-Respect," Joan Didion writes of a time "in a dry season" when she had lost her sense of self-worth. In contrast, she describes people with self-respect as those who are willing "to accept responsibility for one's own life" and "to recognize that anything worth having has its price." Think of several incidents in which you, or others you have seen, have shown the kind of respect Didion describes; use these as illustrations to clarify and make concrete your own definition of "self-respect."

4. Richard Rodriguez presents a picture of a "marriage" in his essay "His-panic-American Culture," a blending that will offer change and diversity to both our country and to Hispanic Americans themselves. Consider some aspect of American culture (or popular culture, such as music, movies, fashions, or fads) that has already been greatly influenced by another culture; write an essay defining your subject and explaining its influences. What might we have lost had we not enjoyed such diversity of cultures?

5. Superstitions, according to the late anthropologist Margaret Mead, help us move back and forth among the secular, scientific, and religious realms in which we live. Explain a superstition that you or your family maintains. Define the belief or ritual in such a way that your readers understand clearly its origin, purpose, and effects.

6. Some people may consider aromatherapy, channeling, astrology, crystal healing, reflexology, tarot-card reading, and other nonscientific practices as new superstitions "generated by our wishes, our fears, and our feel-ings of helplessness in difficult situations." Others defend them as non-traditional ways to improve our lives. Define a popular mystical or su-

pernatural belief or alternative technique according to your point of view. Try to convince a skeptical audience that your view is valid.

7. In his essay "Discrimination," Ralph Ellison presents a series of encounters to show how a child learns the meaning of racial injustice ("It got to you first at the age of six . . . "). In an essay of your own, use Ellison's narrative method to show your reader how you first learned the definition of some sort of racial, ethnic, or gender prejudice or about some important value, such as honesty, responsibility, or generosity.

Chapter Seven

Illustration

Whenever you state an opinion or a judgment, whenever you want to make a point, or explain something, you use some kind of specific detail to support your ideas, to give credibility to your position. Often, that specific support appears in the form of *illustrations* or *examples*. In many cases, well-chosen examples can explain a principle or concept far better than any other method. In her essay "Mankind's Better Moments" Barbara Tuchman uses extensive examples drawn from history to illustrate her belief in "the positive and even admirable capacities of the human race." Brent Staples helps readers to understand and accept his point about black men and public space by retelling several incidents he and his friends have experienced. And James Thurber captures the spirit of his youth through a selection of humorous events illustrating life during his "University Days."

Illustration is also frequently used in combination with other rhetorical strategies. In "Discrimination" (Chapter 6) writer Ralph Ellison defines the term for his readers by presenting examples of his family's encounters with racial prejudice. Judith Viorst, in "How Books Helped Shape My Life" (Chapter 1), offers examples of specific heroines to show how her life has been changed in its various stages by her reading. Almost all arguments profit from examples to persuade their readers; neither Thomas Jefferson nor Elizabeth Cady Stanton would have been half as convincing in their "Declarations" (Chapter 11) had they not presented examples of their grievances.

Illustration, then, has many functions:

1. *Illustration may be used to clarify.*

Examples may be used to clarify complex, confusing, or controversial ideas; they may also be used to make abstract ideas more concrete and accessible. For example, when Alice Walker ("In Search of Our Mothers' Gardens") makes her point about ancestors passing down a creative spirit, she uses real people, such as her own mother, to illustrate what she means.

2. *Illustrations may be used to interest.*

Lively, vivid examples not only clarify, but they give readers great pleasure as well. Generalities can be monotonous, pretentious, or boring without clear examples to catch and hold the readers' attention. William Buckley's essay "Why Don't We Complain?" is transformed from a potential lecture on our lack of assertiveness into sly commentary on human nature largely because of the humorous examples Buckley interjects to illustrate our—and his own—helplessness.

3. *Illustrations may be used to persuade.*

The use of illustration can add validity to a thesis or central idea, urging the reader to accept the ideas because they have been tested, proven, or found to exist elsewhere. In "Mankind's Better Moments" Barbara Tuchman presents a convincing argument that humankind has many "positive and even admirable capacities," even though such positive images are often obscured.

Writing an Illustration Essay

When you decide to support a thesis primarily by using examples, you should keep several principles in mind:

1. *Choose accurate examples.*

Certainly nothing can ruin a discussion more than conclusions based on incorrect or faulty information. When you use an example to illustrate a point, make sure that the example is accurate.

2. *Select examples that are relevant and appropriate to the situation.*

The examples you use should *specifically* support your general statements. Examples that only remotely illustrate your point will only confuse your reader, not clarify your ideas.

3. *Use a sufficient number of examples, but resist "overkill."*

Consider how many examples are enough to illustrate your point adequately. If your thesis is that travel abroad is particularly dangerous for Americans, more than one example of a dangerous or tragic situation would

Illustration   319

be needed to support your assessment. However, be careful not to give too many examples. Choose only those that best serve your purpose. Overuse of examples could be interpreted as padding, which gives your reader the impression that you are merely filling space.

4. *Decide if an* extended *illustration would best serve your purpose.*

An *extended* illustration could be used when one *in-depth* example is enough to support your thesis. Alice Walker uses this method to illustrate what she believes it meant for a black woman to be an artist two or three generations ago. In "In Search of Our Mothers' Gardens," Walker uses Phillis Wheatley, a slave in the 1700s, as an example of a woman with enormous poetic talent who, shackled by slavery, suffered from "malnutrition and neglect and who knows what mental agonies. . . ."

William F. Buckley (© Marilynn K. Yoe / NYT Pictures)

Why Don't We Complain?
William F. Buckley, Jr.
(1925–   )

One of America's best-known proponents of
political conservatism, William F. Buckley, Jr., was
born in New York City in 1925 and received his
B.A. with honors from Yale in 1950. His first major
work, *God and Man at Yale: The Superstitions of
"Academic Freedom"* (1951), accused Yale University
of restricting the political freedoms of conservative
students. In 1955 he founded the *National Review*
magazine, a forum for conservative views. He has
been a widely syndicated newspaper columnist
since 1962, and has hosted a weekly television
show of political debate, "Firing Line." Buckley has
also authored a number of successful novels,
including *Marco Polo, If You Can* (1982) and
Mongoose, RIP (1987). When once asked whether
fiction or non-fiction is "easier" to write, Buckley
noted that fiction is "only easier because research
is less intensive. There are advantages to
improvising our own facts, as politicians teach us."

1   It was the very last coach and the only empty seat on the entire train,
so there was no turning back. The problem was to breathe. Outside, the
temperature was below freezing. Inside the railroad car the temperature must
have been about 85 degrees. I took off my overcoat, and a few minutes later
my jacket, and noticed that the car was flecked with the white shirts of the
passengers. I soon found my hand moving to loosen my tie. From one end
of the car to the other, as we rattled through Westchester County, we
sweated; but we did not moan.

2   I watched the train conductor appear at the head of the car. "Tickets, all
tickets, please!" In a more virile age, I thought, the passengers would seize

the conductor and strap him down on a seat over the radiator to share the fate of his patrons. He shuffled down the aisle, picking up tickets, punching commutation cards. *No one addressed a word to him.* He approached my seat, and I drew a deep breath of resolution. "Conductor," I began with a considerable edge to my voice. . . . Instantly the doleful eyes of my seatmate turned tiredly from his newspaper to fix me with a resentful stare: What question could be so important as to justify my sibilant intrusion into his stupor? I was shaken by those eyes. I am incapable of making a discreet fuss, so I mumbled a question about what time we were due in Stamford (I didn't even ask whether it would be before or after dehydration could be expected to set in), got my reply, and went back to my newspaper and to wiping my brow.

3   The conductor had nonchalantly walked down the gauntlet of eighty sweating American freemen, and not one of them had asked him to explain why the passengers in that car had been consigned to suffer. There is nothing to be done when the temperature *outdoors* is 85 degrees, and indoors the air conditioner has broken down; obviously when that happens there is nothing to do, except perhaps curse the day that one was born. But when the temperature outdoors is below freezing, it takes a positive act of will on somebody's part to set the temperature *indoors* at 85. Somewhere a valve was turned too far, a furnace overstocked, a thermostat maladjusted: something that could easily be remedied by turning off the heat and allowing the great outdoors to come indoors. All this is so obvious. What is not obvious is what has happened to the American people.

4   It isn't just the commuters, whom we have come to visualize as a supine breed who have got on to the trick of suspending their sensory faculties twice a day while they submit to the creeping dissolution of the railroad industry. It isn't just they who have given up trying to rectify irrational vexations. It is the American people everywhere.

5   A few weeks ago at a large movie theater I turned to my wife and said, "The picture is out of focus." "Be quiet," she answered. I obeyed. But a few minutes later I raised the point again, with mounting impatience. "It will be all right in a minute," she said apprehensively. (She would rather lose her eyesight than be around when I make one of my infrequent scenes.) I waited. It was *just* out of focus—not glaringly out, but out. My vision is 20–20, and I assume that is the vision, adjusted, of most people in the movie house. So, after hectoring my wife throughout the first reel, I finally prevailed upon her to admit that it *was* off, and very annoying. We then settled down, coming to rest on the presumption that: a) someone connected with the management of the theater must soon notice the blur and make the correction; or b) that someone seated near the rear of the house would make the complaint in behalf of those of us up front; or c) that—any minute now— the entire house would explode into catcalls and foot stamping, calling dramatic attention to the irksome distortion.

6   What happened was nothing. The movie ended, as it had begun *just* out of focus, and as we trooped out, we stretched our faces in a variety of contortions to accustom the eye to the shock of normal focus.

7   I think it is safe to say that everybody suffered on that occasion. And I think it is safe to assume that everyone was expecting someone else to take the initiative in going back to speak to the manager. And it is probably true even that if we had supposed the movie would run right through the blurred image, someone surely would have summoned up the purposive indignation to get up out of his seat and file his complaint.

8   But notice that no one did. And the reason no one did is because we are all increasingly anxious in America to be unobtrusive, we are reluctant to make our voices heard, hesitant about claiming our rights; we are afraid that our cause is unjust, or that if it is not unjust, that it is ambiguous; or if not even that, that it is too trivial to justify the horrors of a confrontation with Authority; we will sit in an oven or endure a racking headache before undertaking a head-on, I'm-here-to-tell-you complaint. That tendency to passive compliance, to a heedless endurance, is something to keep one's eyes on—in sharp focus.

9   I myself can occasionally summon the courage to complain, but I cannot, as I have intimated, complain softly. My own instinct is so strong to let the thing ride, to forget about it—to expect that someone will take the matter up, when the grievance is collective, in my behalf—that it is only when the provocation is at a very special key, whose vibrations touch simultaneously a complexus of nerves, allergies, and passions, that I catch fire and find the reserves of courage and assertiveness to speak up. When that happens, I get quite carried away. My blood gets hot, my brow wet, I become unbearably and unconscionably sarcastic and bellicose; I am girded for a total showdown.

10   Why should that be? Why could not I (or anyone else) on that railroad coach have said simply to the conductor, "Sir"—I take that back: that sounds sarcastic—"Conductor, would you be good enough to turn down the heat? I am extremely hot. In fact, I tend to get hot every time the temperature reaches 85 degr———." Strike that last sentence. Just end it with the simple statement that you are extremely hot, and let the conductor infer the cause.

11   Every New Year's Eve I resolve to do something about the Milquetoast in me and vow to speak up, calmly, for my rights, and for the betterment of our society, on every appropriate occasion. Entering last New Year's Eve I was fortified in my resolve because that morning at breakfast I had had to ask the waitress three times for a glass of milk. She finally brought it— after I had finished my eggs, which is when I don't want it any more. I did not have the manliness to order her to take the milk back, but settled instead for a cowardly sulk, and ostentatiously refused to drink the milk—though I later paid for it—rather than state plainly to the hostess, as I should have, why I had not drunk it, and would not pay for it.

12　So by the time the New Year ushered out the Old, riding in on my morning's indignation and stimulated by the gastric juices of resolution that flow so faithfully on New Year's Eve, I rendered my vow. Henceforward I would conquer my shyness, my despicable disposition to supineness. I would speak out like a man against the unnecessary annoyances of our time.

13　Forty-eight hours later, I was standing in line at the ski repair store in Pico Peak, Vermont. All I needed, to get on with my skiing, was the loan, for one minute, of a small screwdriver, to tighten a loose binding. Behind the counter in the workshop were two men. One was industriously engaged in servicing the complicated requirements of a young lady at the head of the line, and obviously he would be tied up for quite a while. The other—"Jiggs," his workmate called him—was a middle-aged man, who sat in a chair puffing a pipe, exchanging small talk with his working partner. My pulse began its telltale acceleration. The minutes ticked on. I stared at the idle shopkeeper, hoping to shame him into action, but he was impervious to my telepathic reproof and continued his small talk with his friend, brazenly insensitive to the nervous demands of six good men who were raring to ski.

14　Suddenly my New Year's Eve resolution struck me. It was now or never. I broke from my place in line and marched to the counter. I was going to control myself. I dug my nails into my palms. My effort was only partially successful.

15　"If you are not too busy," I said icily, "would you mind handing me a screwdriver?"

16　Work stopped and everyone turned his eyes on me, and I experienced that mortification I always feel when I am the center of centripetal shafts of curiosity, resentment, perplexity.

17　But the worst was yet to come. "I am sorry, sir," said Jiggs deferentially, moving the pipe from his mouth. "I am not supposed to move. I have just had a heart attack." That was the signal for a great whirring noise that descended from heaven. We looked, stricken, out the window, and it appeared as though a cyclone had suddenly focused on the snowy courtyard between the shop and the ski lift. Suddenly a gigantic army helicopter materialized, and hovered down to a landing. Two men jumped out of the plane carrying a stretcher, tore into the ski shop, and lifted the shopkeeper onto the stretcher. Jiggs bade his companion good-bye, was whisked out the door, into the plane, up to the heavens, down—we learned—to a nearby army hospital. I looked up manfully—into a score of man-eating eyes. I put the experience down as a reversal.

18　As I write this, on an airplane, I have run out of paper and need to reach into my briefcase under my legs for more. I cannot do this until my empty lunch tray is removed from my lap. I arrested the stewardess as she passed empty-handed down the aisle on the way to the kitchen to fetch the lunch trays for the passengers up forward who haven't been served yet. "Would you please take my tray?" "Just a *moment, sir!"* she said, and marched on sternly. Shall I tell her that since she is headed for the kitchen *anyway,* it could not delay the feeding of the other passengers by more than two seconds necessary to stash away my empty tray? Or remind her that not fifteen minutes ago she spoke unctuously into the loudspeaker the words undoubtedly devised by the airline's highly paid public relations counselor: "If there is anything I or Miss French can do for you to make your trip more enjoyable, *please* let us—" I have run out of paper.

19   I think the observable reluctance of the majority of Americans to assert themselves in minor matters is related to our increased sense of helplessness in an age of technology and centralized political and economic power. For generations, Americans who were too hot, or too cold, got up and did something about it. Now we call the plumber, or the electrician, or the furnace man. The habit of looking after our own needs obviously had something to do with the assertiveness that characterized the American family familiar to readers of American literature. With the technification of life goes our direct responsibility for our material environment, and we are conditioned to adopt a position of helplessness not only as regards the broken air conditioner, but as regards the overheated train. It takes an expert to fix the former, but not the latter; yet these distinctions, as we withdraw into helplessness, tend to fade away.

20   Our notorious political apathy is a related phenomenon. Every year, whether the Republican or the Democratic Party is in office, more and more power drains away from the individual to feed vast reservoirs in far-off places; and we have less and less say about the shape of events which shape our future. From this alienation of personal power comes the sense of resignation with which we accept the political dispensations of a powerful government whose hold upon us continues to increase.

21   An editor of a national weekly news magazine told me a few years ago that as few as a dozen letters of protest against an editorial stance of his magazine was enough to convene a plenipotentiary meeting of the board of editors to review policy. "So few people complain, or make their voices heard," he explained to me, "that we assume a dozen letters represent the inarticulate views of thousands of readers." In the past ten years, he said, the volume of mail has noticeably decreased, even though the circulation of his magazine has risen.

22   When our voices are finally mute, when we have finally suppressed the natural instinct to complain, whether the vexation is trivial or grave, we shall have become automatons, incapable of feeling. When Premier Khrushchev first came to this country late in 1959 he was primed, we are informed, to experience the bitter resentment of the American people against his tyranny, against his persecutions, against the movement which is responsible for the great number of American deaths in Korea, for billions in taxes every year, and for life everlasting on the brink of disaster; but Khrushchev was

pleasantly surprised, and reported back to the Russian people that he had been met with overwhelming cordiality (read: apathy), except, to be sure, for "a few fascists who followed me around with their wretched posters, and should be horsewhipped."

23   I may be crazy, but I say there would have been lots more posters in a society where train temperatures in the dead of winter are not allowed to climb to 85 degrees without complaint.

Topics for Writing and Discussion

1.   What point is Buckley making about modern Americans? Where is this view most clearly stated? Do you agree with his position?

2.   Do Buckley's examples adequately support his point? Select two that best illustrate his claims and explain why you chose them.

3.   Characterize the tone of this essay. Is it consistent throughout the essay or does it vary according to the point Buckley is making? Is the tone effective? Why or why not?

4.   Do you agree with Buckley's claim that the "reluctance of the majority of Americans to assert themselves in minor manners is related to our increased helplessness in an age of technology and centralized political and economic power"? Cite some examples that support or refute this claim. (Your response to this question might also provide the basis for an interesting essay.)

5.   Complaints sometimes work—they do bring about necessary changes. Write an essay illustrating a time when someone (you?) lodged a legitimate complaint and caused an important change in behavior, beliefs, or policy.

Brent Staples in his office at The New York Times (© Nancy Crampton)

Black Men and Public Space

Brent Staples
(1951–   )

Born in Chester, Pennsylvania, journalist and
editor Brent Staples has written for numerous
publications including the *Chicago Sun Times,
Harper's,* and *Down Beat* magazine. In 1985 he
joined the *New York Times,* where he is currently
on the editorial board, and in 1991 he published
Parallel Time: A Memoir. "Black Men and Public
Space" was first published in *Ms.* magazine in
1986.

1   **M**y first victim was a woman—white, well dressed, probably in her
late twenties. I came upon her late one evening on a deserted street in Hyde
Park, a relatively affluent neighborhood in an otherwise mean, impoverished
section of Chicago. As I swung onto the avenue behind her, there seemed
to be a discreet, uninflammatory distance between us. Not so. She cast back
a worried glance. To her, the youngish black man—a broad six feet two
inches with a beard and billowing hair, both hands shoved into the pockets
of a bulky military jacket—seemed menacingly close. After a few more quick
glimpses, she picked up her pace and was soon running in earnest. Within
seconds she disappeared into a cross street.

2   That was more than a decade ago. I was twenty-two years old, a graduate
student newly arrived at the University of Chicago. It was in the echo of
that terrified woman's footfalls that I first began to know the unwieldy
inheritance I'd come into—the ability to alter public space in ugly ways. It
was clear that she thought herself the quarry of a mugger, a rapist, or worse.
Suffering a bout of insomnia, however, I was stalking sleep, not defenseless
wayfarers. As a softy who is scarcely able to take a knife to a raw chicken—
let alone hold one to a person's throat—I was surprised, embarrassed, and
dismayed all at once. Her flight made me feel like an accomplice in tyranny.

It also made it clear that I was indistinguishable from the muggers who occasionally seeped into the area from the surrounding ghetto. That first encounter, and those that followed, signified that a vast, unnerving gulf lay between nighttime pedestrians—particularly women—and me. And I soon gathered that being perceived as dangerous is a hazard in itself. I only needed to turn a corner into a dicey situation, or crowd some frightened, armed person in a foyer somewhere, or make an errant move after being pulled over by a policeman. Where fear and weapons meet—and they often do in urban America—there is always the possibility of death.

3   In that first year, my first away from my hometown, I was to become thoroughly familiar with the language of fear. At dark, shadowy intersections, I could cross in front of a car stopped at a traffic light and elicit the *thunk, thunk, thunk, thunk* of the driver—black, white, male, or female— hammering down the door locks. On less traveled streets after dark, I grew accustomed to but never comfortable with people crossing to the other side of the street rather than pass me. Then there were the standard unpleas- antries with policemen, doormen, bouncers, cabdrivers, and others whose business it is to screen out troublesome individuals *before* there is any nastiness.

4   I moved to New York nearly two years ago and I have remained an avid night walker. In central Manhattan, the near-constant crowd cover minimizes tense one-on-one street encounters. Elsewhere—in SoHo, for example, where sidewalks are narrow and tightly spaced buildings shut out the sky—things can get very taut indeed.

5   After dark, on the warrenlike streets of Brooklyn where I live, I often see women who fear the worst from me. They seem to have set their faces on neutral, and with their purse straps strung across their chests bandolier- style, they forge ahead as though bracing themselves against being tackled. I understand, of course, that the danger they perceive is not a hallucination. Women are particularly vulnerable to street violence, and young black males are drastically overrepresented among the perpetrators of that violence. Yet these truths are no solace against the kind of alienation that comes of being ever the suspect, a fearsome entity with whom pedestrians avoid making eye contact.

6   It is not altogether clear to me how I reached the ripe old age of twenty- two without being conscious of the lethality nighttime pedestrians attributed to me. Perhaps it was because in Chester, Pennsylvania, the small, angry industrial town where I came of age in the 1960s, I was scarcely noticeable against a backdrop of gang warfare, street knifings, and murders. I grew up one of the good boys, had perhaps a half-dozen fistfights. In retrospect, my shyness of combat has clear sources.

7   As a boy, I saw countless tough guys locked away; I have since buried several, too. They were babies, really—a teenage cousin, a brother of twenty- two, a childhood friend in his mid-twenties—all gone down in episodes of

bravado played out in the streets. I came to doubt the virtues of intimidation early on. I chose, perhaps unconsciously, to remain a shadow—timid, but a survivor.

8   The fearsomeness mistakenly attributed to me in public places often has a perilous flavor. The most frightening of these confusions occurred in the late 1970s and early 1980s, when I worked as a journalist in Chicago. One day, rushing into the office of a magazine I was writing for with a deadline story in hand, I was mistaken for a burglar. The office manager called security and, with an ad hoc posse, pursued me through the labyrinthine halls, nearly to my editor's door. I had no way of proving who I was. I could only move briskly toward the company of someone who knew me.

9   Another time I was on assignment for a local paper and killing time before an interview. I entered a jewelry store on the city's affluent Near North Side. The proprietor excused herself and returned with an enormous red Doberman pinscher straining at the end of a leash. She stood, the dog extended toward me, silent to my questions, her eyes bulging nearly out of her head. I took a cursory look around, nodded, and bade her good night.

10   Relatively speaking, however, I never fared as badly as another black male journalist. He went to nearby Waukegan, Illinois, a couple of summers ago to work on a story about a murderer who was born there. Mistaking the reporter for the killer, police officers hauled him from his car at gunpoint and but for his press credentials would probably have tried to book him. Such episodes are not uncommon. Black men trade tales like this all the time.

11   Over the years, I learned to smother the rage I felt at so often being taken for a criminal. Not to do so would surely have led to madness. I now take precautions to make myself less threatening. I move about with care, particularly late in the evening. I give a wide berth to nervous people on subway platforms during the wee hours, particularly when I have exchanged business clothes for jeans. If I happen to be entering a building behind some people who appear skittish, I may walk by, letting them clear the lobby before I return, so as not to seem to be following them. I have been calm and extremely congenial on those rare occasions when I've been pulled over by the police.

12   And on late-evening constitutionals I employ what has proved to be an excellent tension-reducing measure: I whistle melodies from Beethoven and Vivaldi and the more popular classical composers. Even steely New Yorkers hunching toward nighttime destinations seem to relax, and occasionally they even join in the tune. Virtually everybody seems to sense that a mugger wouldn't be warbling bright, sunny selections from Vivaldi's *Four Seasons*. It is my equivalent of the cowbell that hikers wear when they know they are in bear country.

Topics for Writing and Discussion

1. Why does Staples refer to his "first victim" in his opening paragraph? What effect on the reader is such language intended to have? Who else, according to Staples, is victimized by faulty perceptions?

2. What is Staples' attitude toward "the ability to alter public space in ugly ways"? What is his purpose in writing this essay?

3. Why does Staples retell so many personal experiences? Why include the story of a colleague's experience in Waukegan, Illinois? What details add to the realism of these scenes?

4. What stereotypes does Staples criticize in this essay? Why does he refer to family members and friends, "all gone down in episodes of bravado played out in the streets"?

5. Write an essay exposing a current stereotype of a particular kind of person, using examples drawn from your own experience, from the media, or from advertising. Your exposé might illustrate racial, ethnic, or gender-based prejudice, or perhaps the more subtle stereotyping of a particular class of people (the homeless, the mentally ill, "dumb blondes") or people in certain occupations (the homemaker, the accountant, the athlete).

James Thurber, photographed with his wife returning on the ship Acadia *from Les Revenants, their winter home in Bermuda. (AP/Wide World Photos)*

University Days

James Thurber
(1894–1961)

James Thurber began his career as a journalist for the Columbus, Ohio, *Dispatch* and later worked in Paris as a reporter for the *Chicago Tribune.* When he returned from Paris in 1926, he began a lifelong association with the *New Yorker* magazine. As a contributor, he delighted readers with his satiric essays and hilarious cartoons drawn with the quick and biting wit for which he is now famous. As Thurber grew older, his eyesight became increasingly worse, and he began to draw less and write more. His first book, coauthored by E. B. White and titled *Is Sex Necessary?* (1929), is a delightful parody of the self-help book. Few targets escaped Thurber's sharp pen, and the essay "University Days" reveals the frustrations, incompetence, and inefficiency that comprised his experience as a student at Ohio State University.

1 I passed all the other courses that I took at my university, but I could never pass botany. This was because all botany students had to spend several hours a week in a laboratory looking through a microscope at plant cells, and I could never see through a microscope. I never once saw a cell through a microscope. This used to enrage my instructor. He would wander around the laboratory pleased with the progress all the students were making in drawing the involved and, so I am told, interesting structure of flower cells, until he came to me. I would just be standing there. "I can't see anything," I would say. He would begin patiently enough, explaining how anybody can see through a microscope, but he would always end up in a fury, claiming that I could *too* see through a microscope but just pretended that I couldn't.

"It takes away from the beauty of flowers anyway," I used to tell him. "We are not concerned with beauty in this course," he would say. "We are concerned solely with what I may call the *mechanics* of flars." "Well," I'd say, "I can't see anything." "Try it just once again," he'd say, and I would put my eye to the microscope and see nothing at all, except now and again a nebulous milky substance—a phenomenon of maladjustment. You were supposed to see a vivid, restless clockwork of sharply defined plant cells. "I see what looks like a lot of milk," I would tell him. This, he claimed, was the result of my not having adjusted the microscope properly, so he would readjust it for me, or rather, for himself. And I would look again and see milk.

2   I finally took a deferred pass, as they called it, and waited a year and tried again. (You had to pass one of the biological sciences or you couldn't graduate.) The professor had come back from vacation brown as a berry, bright-eyed, and eager to explain cell-structure again to his classes. "Well," he said to me, cheerily, when we met in the first laboratory hour of the semester, "we're going to see cells this time, aren't we?" "Yes, sir," I said. Students to right of me and to left of me and in front of me were seeing cells; what's more, they were quietly drawing pictures of them in their notebooks. Of course, I didn't see anything.

3   "We'll try it," the professor said to me grimly, "with every adjustment of the microscope known to man. As God is my witness, I'll arrange this glass so that you see cells through it or I'll give up teaching. In twenty-two years of botany, I—" He cut off abruptly for he was beginning to quiver all over, like Lionel Barrymore, and he genuinely wished to hold onto his temper; his scenes with me had taken a great deal out of him.

4   So we tried it with every adjustment of the microscope known to man. With only one of them did I see anything but blackness or the familiar lacteal opacity, and that time I saw, to my pleasure and amazement, a variegated constellation of flecks, specks, and dots. These I hastily drew. The instructor, noting my activity, came back from an adjoining desk, a smile on his lips and his eyebrows high in hope. He looked at my cell drawing. "What's that?" he demanded, with a hint of a squeal in his voice. "That's what I saw," I said. "You didn't, you didn't, you *didn't*!" he screamed, losing control of his temper instantly, and he bent over and squinted into the microscope. His head snapped up. "That's your eye!" he shouted. "You've fixed the lens so that it reflects! You've drawn your eye!"

5   Another course that I didn't like, but somehow managed to pass, was economics. I went to that class straight from the botany class, which didn't help me any in understanding either subject. I used to get them mixed up. But not as mixed up as another student in my economics class who came there direct from a physics laboratory. He was a tackle on the football team, named Bolenciecwcz. At that time Ohio State University had one of the best football teams in the country, and Bolenciecwcz was one of its outstanding

stars. In order to be eligible to play it was necessary for him to keep up in his studies, a very difficult matter, for while he was not dumber than an ox he was not any smarter. Most of his professors were lenient and helped him along. None gave him more hints in answering questions or asked him simpler ones than the economics professor, a thin, timid man named Bassum. One day when we were on the subject of transportation and distribution, it came Bolenciecwcz's turn to answer a question. "Name one means of transportation," the professor said to him. No light came into the big tackle's eyes. "Just any means of transportation," said the professor. Bolenciecwcz sat staring at him. "That is," pursued the professor, "any medium, agency, or method of going from one place to another." Bolenciecwcz had the look of a man who is being led into a trap. "You may choose among steam, horse-drawn, or electrically propelled vehicles," said the instructor. "I might suggest the one which we commonly take in making long journeys across land." There was a profound silence in which everybody stirred uneasily, including Bolenciecwcz and Mr. Bassum. Mr. Bassum abruptly broke this silence in an amazing manner. "Choo-choo-choo," he said, in a low voice, and turned instantly scarlet. He glanced appealingly around the room. All of us, of course, shared Mr. Bassum's desire that Bolenciecwcz should stay abreast of the class in economics, for the Illinois game, one of the hardest and most important of the season, was only a week off. "Toot, toot, too-tooooooot!" some student with a deep voice moaned, and we all looked encouragingly at Bolenciecwcz. Somebody else gave a fine imitation of a locomotive letting off steam. Mr. Bassum himself rounded off the little show. "Ding, dong, ding, dong," he said hopefully. Bolenciecwcz was staring at the floor now, trying to think, his great brow furrowed, his huge hands rubbing together, his face red.

6   "How did you come to college this year, Mr. Bolenciecwcz?" asked the professor. "*Chuffa* chuffa, *chuffa* chuffa."

7   "M'father sent me," said the football player.

8   "What on?" asked Bassum.

9   "I git an 'lowance," said the tackle, in a low, husky voice, obviously embarrassed.

10   "No, no," said Bassum. "Name a means of transportation. What did you *ride* here on?"

11   "Train," said Bolenciecwcz.

12   "Quite right," said the professor. "Now, Mr. Nugent, will you tell us—"

13   If I went through anguish in botany and economics—for different reasons— gymnasium work was even worse. I don't even like to think about it. They wouldn't let you play games or join in the exercises with your glasses on and I couldn't see with mine off. I bumped into professors, horizontal bars, agricultural students, and swinging iron rings. Not being able to see, I could take it but I couldn't dish it out. Also, in order to pass gymnasium (and you had to pass it to graduate) you had to learn to swim if you didn't know

how. I didn't like the swimming pool, I didn't like swimming, and I didn't like the swimming instructor, and after all these years I still don't. I never swam but I passed my gym work anyway, by having another student give my gymnasium number (978) and swim across the pool in my place. He was a quiet, amiable blond youth, number 473, and he would have seen through a microscope for me if we could have got away with it, but we couldn't get away with it. Another thing I didn't like about gymnasium work was that they made you strip the day you registered. It is impossible for me to be happy when I am stripped and being asked a lot of questions. Still, I did better than a lanky agricultural student who was cross-examined just before I was. They asked each student what college he was in—that is, whether Arts, Engineering, Commerce, or Agriculture. "What college are you in?" the instructor snapped at the youth in front of me. "Ohio State University," he said promptly.

14   It wasn't that agricultural student but it was another a whole lot like him who decided to take up journalism, possibly on the ground that when farming went to hell he could fall back on newspaper work. He didn't realize, of course, that that would be very much like falling back full-length on a kit of carpenter's tools. Haskins didn't seem cut out for journalism, being too embarrassed to talk to anybody and unable to use a typewriter, but the editor of the college paper assigned him to the cow barns, the sheep house, the horse pavilion, and the animal husbandry department generally. This was a genuinely big "beat," for it took up five times as much ground and got ten times as great a legislative appropriation as the College of Liberal Arts. The agricultural student knew animals, but nevertheless his stories were dull and colorlessly written. He took all afternoon on each of them, on account of having to hunt for each letter on the typewriter. Once in a while he had to ask somebody to help him hunt. "C" and "L," in particular, were hard letters for him to find. His editor finally got pretty much annoyed at the farmer-journalist because his pieces were so uninteresting. "See here, Haskins," he snapped at him one day, "why is it we never have anything hot from you on the horse pavilion? Here we have two hundred head of horses on this campus—more than any other university in the Western Conference except Purdue—and yet you never get any real lowdown on them. Now shoot over to the horse barns and dig up something lively." Haskins shambled out and came back in about an hour; he said he had something. "Well, start it off snappily," said the editor. "Something people will read." Haskins set to work and in a couple of hours brought a sheet of typewritten paper to the desk; it was a two-hundred-word story about some disease that had broken out among the horses. Its opening sentence was simple but arresting. It read: "Who has noticed the sores on the tops of the horses in the animal husbandry building?"

15   Ohio State was a land grant university and therefore two years of military drill was compulsory. We drilled with old Springfield rifles and studied the

tactics of the Civil War even though the World War was going on at the time. At 11 o'clock each morning thousands of freshmen and sophomores used to deploy over the campus, moodily creeping up on the old chemistry building. It was good training for the kind of warfare that was waged at Shiloh but it had no connection with what was going on in Europe. Some people used to think there was German money behind it, but they didn't dare say so or they would have been thrown in jail as German spies. It was a period of muddy thought and marked, I believe, the decline of higher education in the Middle West.

16   As a soldier I was never any good at all. Most of the cadets were glumly indifferent soldiers, but I was no good at all. Once General Littlefield, who was commandant of the cadet corps, popped up in front of me during regimental drill and snapped, "You are the main trouble with this university!" I think he meant that my type was the main trouble with the university but he may have meant me individually. I was mediocre at drill, certainly—that is, until my senior year. By that time I had drilled longer than anybody else in the Western Conference, having failed at military at the end of each preceding year so that I had to do it all over again. I was the only senior still in uniform. The uniform which, when new, had made me look like an interurban railway conductor, now that it had become faded and too tight made me look like Bert Williams in his bellboy act. This had a definitely bad effect on my morale. Even so, I had become by sheer practice little short of wonderful at squad maneuvers.

17   One day General Littlefield picked our company out of the whole regiment and tried to get it mixed up by putting it through one movement after another as fast as we could execute them: squads right, squads left, squads on right into line, squads right about, squads left front into line, etc. In about three minutes one hundred and nine men were marching in one direction and I was marching away from them at an angle of forty degrees, all alone. "Company, halt!" shouted General Littlefield. "That man is the only man who has it right!" I was made a corporal for my achievement.

18   The next day General Littlefield summoned me to his office. He was swatting flies when I went in. I was silent and he was silent too, for a long time. I don't think he remembered me or why he had sent for me, but he didn't want to admit it. He swatted some more flies, keeping his eyes on them narrowly before he let go with the swatter. "Button up your coat!" he snapped. Looking back on it now I can see that he meant me although he was looking at a fly, but I just stood there. Another fly came to rest on a paper in front of the general and began rubbing its hind legs together. The general lifted the swatter cautiously. I moved restlessly and the fly flew away. "You startled him!" barked General Littlefield, looking at me severely. I said I was sorry. "That won't help the situation!" snapped the General, with cold military logic. I didn't see what I could do except offer to chase some more flies toward his desk, but I didn't say anything. He stared out

the window at the faraway figures of co-eds crossing the campus toward the library. Finally, he told me I could go. So I went. He either didn't know which cadet I was or else he forgot what he wanted to see me about. It may have been that he wished to apologize for having called me the main trouble with the university; or maybe he had decided to compliment me on my brilliant drilling of the day before and then at the last minute decided not to. I don't know. I don't think about it much any more.

Topics for Writing and Discussion

1. Why was Thurber unable to pass botany? What two stories does he tell to illustrate his difficulty? Does he explain how he was able to fulfill his requirement in the biological sciences?

2. What two meanings does Thurber suggest for General Littlefield's observation, "You are the main trouble with the university!"? After reading the incidents describing Thurber's performance as a cadet and his various encounters with the general, which interpretation do you think is more plausible?

3. "University Days" includes several short stories, each designed to illustrate some aspect of Thurber's college experience. Look carefully at the sentences that begin paragraphs 5, 13, and 14; then analyze how Thurber connects his stories to form a coherent whole. Note also the beginning of paragraph 15 that introduces the section on military drill. Is this section clearly related to the others?

4. Thurber's essay has no introductory paragraph, no thesis statement, and no concluding paragraph. What would be gained or lost by the addition of a standard opening and closing? How would you state the thesis of the essay?

5. Campus life has changed a great deal since Thurber attended college. Write an updated "University Days," using a series of examples that illustrate your own difficulties as you pursue higher education.

Barbara Tuchman (Steve Miller / NYT Pictures)

Mankind's Better Moments

Barbara Tuchman
(1912–1989)

After graduating from Radcliffe in 1933, Barbara
Tuchman worked for the Institute for Public
Relations. She began her career as a journalist
writing for the *Nation* and *The New Statesman*
magazines. During the Spanish Civil War and
during World War II, she served as a correspondent
for the *Nation* (London Office). Her historical
writings have been highly praised for both their
narrative power and their careful scholarship. Two
of her books have been awarded the Pulitzer Prize:
The Guns of August (1962) and *Stillwell and the
American Experiment in China* (1971). Tuchman was
a frequent contributor to such magazines as
Atlantic, American Scholar, Foreign Affairs, and
Harper's. In 1981, she collected many of her essays
and speeches, including "Mankind's Better
Moments," in the highly regarded *Practicing
History.* In this optimistic essay, Tuchman offers a
series of historical examples intended to counteract
the negative self-image she sees as characteristic of
the twentieth-century person.

1   **F**or a change from prevailing pessimism, I should like to recall some of
the positive and even admirable capacities of the human race. We hear very
little of them lately. Ours is not a time of self-esteem or self-confidence—as
was, for instance, the nineteenth century, when self-esteem may be seen
oozing from its portraits. Victorians, especially the men, pictured themselves
as erect, noble, and splendidly handsome. Our self-image looks more like
Woody Allen or a character from Samuel Beckett. Amid a mass of worldwide

troubles and a poor record for the twentieth century, we see our species—
with cause—as functioning very badly, as blunderers when not knaves, as
violent, ignoble, corrupt, inept, incapable of mastering the forces that
threaten us, weakly subject to our worst instincts; in short, decadent.

2   The catalogue is familiar and valid, but it is growing tiresome. A study
of history reminds one that mankind has its ups and downs and during the
ups has accomplished many brave and beautiful things, exerted stupendous
endeavors, explored and conquered oceans and wilderness, achieved marvels of beauty in the creative arts and marvels of science and social progress;
has loved liberty with a passion that throughout history has led men to fight
and die for it over and over again; has pursued knowledge, exercised reason,
enjoyed laughter and pleasures, played games with zest, shown courage,
heroism, altruism, honor, and decency; experienced love; known comfort,
contentment, and occasionally happiness. All these qualities have been part
of human experience, and if they have not had as important notice as the
negatives nor exerted as wide and persistent an influence as the evils we
do, they nevertheless deserve attention, for they are currently all but
forgotten.

3   Among the great endeavors, we have in our own time carried men to the
moon and brought them back safely—surely one of the most remarkable
achievements in history. Some may disapprove of the effort as unproductive,
too costly, and a wrong choice of priorities in relation to greater needs, all
of which may be true but does not, as I see it, diminish the achievement.
If you look carefully, all positives have a negative underside—sometimes
more, sometimes less—and not all admirable endeavors have admirable motives. Some have sad consequences. Although most signs presently point
from bad to worse, human capacities are probably what they have always
been. If primitive man could discover how to transform grain into bread,
and reeds growing by the riverbank into baskets; if his successors could
invent the wheel, harness the insubstantial air to turn a millstone, transform
sheep's wool, flax, and worms' cocoons into fabric—we, I imagine, will find
a way to manage the energy problem.

4   Consider how the Dutch accomplished the miracle of making land out of
sea. By progressive enclosure of the Zuider Zee over the last sixty years,
they have added half a million acres to their country, enlarging its area by
eight percent and providing homes, farms, and towns for close to a quarter
of a million people. The will to do the impossible, the spirit of can-do that
overtakes our species now and then, was never more manifest than in this
earth-altering act by the smallest of the major European nations.

5   A low-lying, windswept, waterlogged land, partly below sea level, pitted
with marshes, rivers, lakes, and inlets, sliding all along its outer edge into
the stormy North Sea with only fragile sand dunes as nature's barrier against
the waves, Holland, in spite of physical disadvantages, has made itself into
one of the most densely populated, orderly, prosperous, and, at one stage

of its history, dominant nations of the West. For centuries, ever since the first inhabitants, fleeing enemy tribes, settled in the bogs where no one cared to bother them, the Dutch struggled against water and learned how to live with it: building on mounds, constructing and reconstructing seawalls of clay mixed with straw, carrying mud in an endless train of baskets, laying willow mattresses weighted with stones, repairing each spring the winter's damage, draining marshes, channeling streams, building ramps to their attics to save the cattle in times of flood, gaining dike-enclosed land from the waves in one place and losing as much to the revengeful ocean somewhere else, progressively developing methods to cope with their eternal antagonist.

6   The Zuider Zee was a tidal gulf penetrating eighty miles into the land over an area ten to thirty miles wide. The plan to close off the sea by a dam across the entire mouth of the gulf had long been contemplated but never adopted, for fear of the cost, until a massive flood in 1916, which left salt-water standing on all the farmlands north of Amsterdam, forced the issue. The act for enclosure was passed unanimously by both houses of Parliament in 1918. As large in ambition as the country was small, the plan called for a twenty-mile dike from shore to shore, rising twenty feet above sea level, wide enough at the top to carry an auto road and housing for the hydraulic works, and as much as six hundred feet wide on the sea bottom. The first cartload of gravel was dumped in 1920.

7   The dike was but part of the task. The inland sea it formed had to be drained of its saltwater and transformed from salt to fresh by the inflow from lower branches of the Rhine. Four polders, or areas rising from the shallows, would be lifted by the draining process from under water into the open air. Secondary dikes, pumping stations, sluices, drainage ditches to control the inflow, as well as locks and inland ports for navigation, had to be built, the polder lands restored to fertility, trees planted, roads, bridges, and rural and urban housing constructed, the whole scheduled for completion in sixty years.

8   The best-laid plans of engineers met errors and hazards. During construction, gravel that had been painstakingly dumped within sunken frameworks would be washed away in a night by heavy currents or a capricious storm. Means proved vulnerable, methods sometimes unworkable. Yet slowly the dike advanced from each shore toward the center. As the gap narrowed, the pressure of the tidal current rushing through increased daily in force, carrying away material at the base, undermining the structure, and threatening to prevent a final closing. In the last days a herd of floating derricks, dredges, barges, and every piece of available equipment was mustered at the spot, and fill was desperately poured in before the next return of the tide, due in twelve hours. At this point, gale winds were reported moving in. The check dam to protect the last gap showed signs of giving way; operations were hurriedly moved thirty yards inward. Suspense was now extreme. Roaring and foaming with sand, the tide threw itself upon the narrowing passage;

the machines closed in, filled the last space in the dike, and it held. Men stood that day in 1932 where the North Sea's waves had held dominion for seven hundred years.

9 As the dry land appeared, the first comers to take possession were the birds. Gradually, decade by decade, crops, homes, and civilization followed, and unhappily, too, man's destructive intervention. In World War II the retreating Germans blew up a section of the dike, completely flooding the western polder, but by the end of the year the Dutch had pumped it dry, resowed the fields in the spring, and over the next seven years restored the polder's farms and villages. Weather, however, is never conquered. The disastrous floods of 1953 laid most of coastal Holland under water. The Dutch dried themselves out and, while the work at Zuider Zee continued, applied its lessons elsewhere and lent their hydraulic skills to other countries. Today the *Afsluitdijk,* or Zuider Zee road, is a normal thoroughfare. To drive across it between the sullen ocean on one side and new land on the other is for that moment to feel optimism for the human race.

10 Great endeavor requires vision and some kind of compelling impulse, not necessarily practical as in the case of the Dutch, but sometimes less definable, more exalted, as in the case of the Gothic cathedrals of the Middle Ages. The architectural explosion that produced this multitude of soaring vaults— arched, ribbed, pierced with jeweled light, studded with thousands of figures of the stone-carvers' art—represents in size, splendor, and numbers one of the great, permanent artistic achievements of human hands. What accounts for it? Not religious fervor alone but the zeal of a dynamic age, a desire to outdo, an ambition for the biggest and the best. Only the general will, shared by nobles, merchants, guilds, artisans, and commoners, could command the resources and labor to sustain so great an undertaking. Each group contributed donations, especially the magnates of commerce, who felt relieved thereby from the guilt of money-making. Voluntary work programs involved all classes. "Who has ever seen or heard tell in times past," wrote an observer, "that powerful princes of the world, that men brought up in honors and wealth, that nobles—men and women—have bent their haughty necks to the harness of carts and, like beasts of burden, have dragged to the abode of Christ these wagons loaded with wines, grains, oil, stones, timber and all that is necessary for the construction of the church?"

11 Abbot Suger, whose renovation of St. Denis is considered the start of Gothic architecture, embodied the spirit of the builders. Determined to create the most splendid basilica in Christendom, he supervised every aspect of the work from fund-raising to decoration, and caused his name to be inscribed for immortality on keystones and capitals. He lay awake worrying, as he tells us, where to find trees large enough for the beams, and went personally with his carpenters to the forest to question the woodcutters under oath. When they swore that nothing of the kind he wanted could be found

in the area, he insisted on searching for them himself and, after nine hours of scrambling through thorns and thickets succeeded in locating and marking twelve trees of the necessary size.

12   Mainly the compelling impulse lay in the towns, where, in those years, economic and political strengths and wealth were accumulating. Amiens, the thriving capital of Picardy, decided to build the largest church in France, "higher than all the saints, higher than all the kings." For the necessary space, the hospital and bishop's palace had to be relocated and the city walls moved back. At the same time Beauvais, a neighbor town, raised a vault over the crossing of transept and nave to an unprecedented height of 158 feet, the apogee of architects' daring in its day. It proved too daring, for the height of the columns and spread of the supports caused the vault to collapse after twelve years. Repaired with undaunted purpose, it was defiantly topped by a spire rising 492 feet above ground, the tallest in France. Beauvais, having used up its resources, never built the nave, leaving a structure foreshortened but glorious. The interior is a fantasy of soaring space; to enter is to stand dazed in wonder, breathless in admiration.

13   The higher and lighter grew the buildings and the slenderer the columns, the more new expedients and techniques had to be devised to hold them up. Buttresses flew like angels' wings against the exteriors. This was a period of innovation and audacity, and a limitless spirit of excelsior. In a single century, from 1170 to 1270, six hundred cathedrals and major churches were built in France alone. In England in that period, the cathedral of Salisbury, with the tallest spire in the country, was completed in thirty-eight years. The spire of Freiburg in Germany was constructed entirely of filigree in stone as if spun by some supernatural spider. In the St. Chapelle in Paris the fifteen miraculous windows swallow the walls; they have become the whole.

14   Embellishment was integral to the construction. Reims is populated by five thousand statues of saints, prophets, kings and cardinals, bishops, knights, ladies, craftsmen and commoners, devils, animals and birds. Every type of leaf known in northern France is said to appear in the decoration. In carving, stained glass, and sculpture the cathedrals displayed the art of medieval hands, and the marvel of these buildings is permanent even when they no longer play a central role in everyday life. Rodin said he could feel the beauty and presence of Reims even at night when he could not see it. "Its power," he wrote, "transcends the senses so that the eye sees what it sees not."

15   Explanations for the extraordinary burst that produced the cathedrals are several. Art historians will tell you that it was the invention of the ribbed vault. Religious historians will say it was the product of an age of faith which believed that with God's favor anything was possible, in fact it was not a period of untroubled faith, but of heresies and Inquisition. Rather, one can only say that conditions were right. Social order under monarchy and the

towns was replacing the anarchy of the barons, so that existence was no longer merely a struggle to stay alive but allowed a surplus of goods and energies and greater opportunity for mutual effort. Banking and commerce were producing capital, roads were making possible wheeled transport, universities nourishing ideas and communication. It was one of history's high tides, an age of vigor, confidence, and forces converging to quicken the blood.

16 Even when the historical tide is low, a particular group of doers may emerge in exploits that inspire awe. Shrouded in the mists of the eighth century, long before the cathedrals, Viking seamanship was a wonder of daring, stamina, and skill. Pushing relentlessly outward in open boats, the Vikings sailed south, around Spain to North Africa and Arabia, north to the top of the world, west across uncharted seas to American coasts. They hauled their boats overland from the Baltic to make their way down Russian rivers to the Black Sea. Why? We do not know what engine drove them, only that it was part of the human endowment.

17 What of the founding of our own country, America? We take the *Mayflower* for granted—yet think of the boldness, the enterprise, the determined independence, the sheer grit it took to leave the known and set out across the sea for the unknown where no houses or food, no stores, no cleared land, no crops or livestock, none of the equipment or settlement of organized living awaited.

18 Equally bold was the enterprise of the French in the northern forests of the American continent, who throughout the seventeenth century explored and opened the land from the St. Lawrence to the Mississippi, from the Great Lakes to the Gulf of Mexico. They came not for liberty like the Pilgrims, but for gain and dominion, whether in spiritual empire for the Jesuits or in land, glory, and riches for the agents of the King; and rarely in history have men willingly embraced such hardship, such daunting adventure, and persisted with such tenacity and endurance. They met hunger, exhaustion, frostbite, capture and torture by Indians, wounds and disease, dangerous rapids, swarms of insects, long portages, bitter weather, and hardly ever did those who suffered the experience fail to return, reenter the menacing but bountiful forest, and pit themselves once more against danger, pain, and death.

19 Above all others, the perseverance of La Salle in his search for the mouth of the Mississippi was unsurpassed. While preparing in Quebec, he mastered eight Indian languages. From then on he suffered accidents, betrayals, desertions, losses of men and provisions, fever and snow blindness, the hostility and intrigues of rivals who incited the Indians against him and plotted to ambush or poison him. He was truly pursued, as Francis Parkman wrote, by "a demon of havoc." Paddling through heavy waves in a storm over Lake Ontario, he waded through freezing surf to beach the canoes each night, and lost guns and baggage when a canoe was swamped and sank. To lay the foundations of a fort above Niagara, frozen ground had to be

thawed by boiling water. When the fort was at last built, La Salle christened it Crèvecoeur—that is, Heartbreak. It earned the name when in his absence it was plundered and deserted by its half-starved mutinous garrison. Farther on, a friendly Indian village, intended as a destination, was found laid waste by the Iroquois with only charred stakes stuck with skulls standing among the ashes, while wolves and buzzards prowled through the remains.

20   When at last, after four months' hazardous journey down the Great River, La Salle reached the sea, he formally took possession in the name of Louis XIV of all the country from the river's mouth to its source and of its tributaries—that is, of the vast basin of the Mississippi from the Rockies to the Appalachians—and named it Louisiana. The validity of the claim, which seems so hollow to us (though successful in its own time), is not the point. What counts is the conquest of fearful adversity by one man's extraordinary exertions and inflexible will.

Topics for Writing and Discussion

1.   In the first paragraph, Tuchman gives a list of reasons for the "prevailing pessimism" of the twentieth century. What is her attitude toward these examples of poor performance? How does the rest of the essay respond to this list of negative qualities?

2.   What examples from ancient and recent history does Tuchman use to support her belief that we will discover a way to solve the energy crisis? Why does she explain one of her examples in great detail?

3.   Tuchman offers several examples to support her premise that the Gothic cathedrals of the Middle Ages represented extraordinary achievement. List several of these examples and explain what positive quality Tuchman ascribes to each.

4.   What common activity unites Tuchman's final series of examples? Does that activity have any relevance today? Who might Tuchman add to her final series as representative of the twentieth century?

5.   Tuchman uses a series of examples to refute a widely held view. Write a similar essay that refutes a common attitude you find "familiar and valid, but . . . tiresome." For instance, you might argue against the idea that college students are primarily interested in making money. Or you might refute the view that nontraditional families do not provide a stable support system for their members.

In Search of Our Mothers' Gardens

Alice Walker

(1944–   )

Alice Walker
(© 1991 F. Capri/Saga 1991)

Alice Walker was the youngest of the eight children born to Willie Lee and Minnie Grant Walker. The Walkers worked as sharecroppers in Georgia, and the author's early years inform both her fiction and nonfiction. Following her graduation from Sarah Lawrence College in New York, Walker worked for civil rights, teaching in Head Start programs and registering black voters. A poet, essayist, and scholar, she has achieved particular recognition for her work as editor of an anthology of Zora Neale Hurston's writings (*I Love Myself When I Am Laughing,* 1979) and as a contributing editor to *Ms.* magazine. She is best known for her fiction, particularly her novel *The Color Purple,* which won the Pulitzer Prize in 1982 and was later made into a popular film. Her most recent novels are *The Temple of My Familiar* (1989) and *Possessing the Secret of Joy* (1992), and in 1991 she published a collection of poetry, *Her Blue Body Everything We Know: Earthling Poems, 1965–1990.* "In Search of Our Mothers' Gardens," from the 1983 essay collection of the same name, examines "the far-reaching world of the creative black woman," a world oppressed by a history of slavery and racism.

I described her own nature and temperament. Told how they needed a larger life for their expression. . . . I pointed out that in lieu of proper channels, her emotions had overflowed into paths that dissipated them. I talked, beautifully I thought, about an art that would be born, an art that would open the way for women the likes of her. I asked her to hope, and build up an inner life against the coming of that day. . . . I sang, with a strange quiver in my voice, a promise song.

—"Avey," Jean Toomer, *Cane*
(The poet speaking to a prostitute who falls asleep while he's talking)

1   Wh
hen the poet Jean Toomer walked through the South in the early
twenties, he discovered a curious thing: black women whose spirituality was
so intense, so deep, so *unconscious*, they were themselves unaware of the
richness they held. They stumbled blindly through their lives: creatures so
abused and mutilated in body, so dimmed and confused by pain, that they
considered themselves unworthy even of hope. In the selfless abstractions
their bodies became to the men who used them, they became more than
"sexual objects," more even than mere women: they became "Saints." Instead of being perceived as whole persons, their bodies became shrines:
what was thought to be their minds became temples suitable for worship. These crazy Saints stared out at the world, wildly, like lunatics—or
quietly, like suicides; and the "God" that was in their gaze was as mute as
a great stone.

2   Who were these Saints? These crazy, loony, pitiful women?

3   Some of them, without a doubt, were our mothers and grandmothers.

4   In the still heat of the post-Reconstruction South, this is how they seemed
to Jean Toomer: exquisite butterflies trapped in an evil honey, toiling away
their lives in an era, a century, that did not acknowledge them, except as
"the *mule* of the world." They dreamed dreams that no one knew—not even
themselves, in any coherent fashion—and saw visions no one could understand. They wandered or sat about the countryside crooning lullabies to
ghosts, and drawing the mother of Christ in charcoal on courthouse walls.

5   They forced their minds to desert their bodies and their striving spirits
sought to rise, like frail whirlwinds from the hard red clay. And when those
frail whirlwinds fell, in scattered particles, upon the ground, no one
mourned. Instead, men lit candles to celebrate the emptiness that remained,
as people do who enter a beautiful but vacant space to resurrect a God.

6   Our mothers and grandmothers, some of them: moving to music not yet
written. And they waited.

7   They waited for a day when the unknown thing that was in them would
be made known; but guessed, somehow in their darkness, that on the day
of their revelation they would be long dead. Therefore to Toomer they
walked, and even ran, in slow motion. For they were going nowhere immediate, and the future was not yet within their grasp. And men took our
mothers and grandmothers, "but got no pleasure from it." So complex was
their passion and their calm.

8   To Toomer, they lay vacant and fallow as autumn fields, with harvest time
never in sight: and he saw them enter loveless marriages, without joy; and
become prostitutes, without resistance; and become mothers of children,
without fulfillment.

9   For these grandmothers and mothers of ours were not Saints, but Artists;
driven to a numb and bleeding madness by the springs of creativity in them
for which there was no release. They were Creators, who lived lives of

spiritual waste, because they were so rich in spirituality—which is the basis of Art—that the strain of enduring their unused and unwanted talent drove them insane. Throwing away this spirituality was their pathetic attempt to lighten the soul to a weight their work-worn, sexually abused bodies could bear.

10   What did it mean for a black woman to be an artist in our grandmothers' time? In our great-grandmothers' day? It is a question with an answer cruel enough to stop the blood.

11   Did you have a genius of a great-great-grandmother who died under some ignorant and depraved white overseer's lash? Or was she required to bake biscuits for a lazy backwater tramp, when she cried out in her soul to paint watercolors of sunsets, or the rain falling on the green and peaceful pasturelands? Or was her body broken and forced to bear children (who were more often than not sold away from her)—eight, ten, fifteen, twenty children—when her one joy was the thought of modeling heroic figures of rebellion, in stone or clay?

12   How was the creativity of the black woman kept alive, year after year and century after century, when for most of the years black people have been in America, it was a punishable crime for a black person to read or write? And the freedom to paint, to sculpt, to expand the mind with action did not exist. Consider, if you can bear to imagine it, what might have been the result if singing, too, had been forbidden by law. Listen to the voices of Bessie Smith, Billie Holiday, Nina Simone, Roberta Flack, and Aretha Franklin, among others, and imagine these voices muzzled for life. Then you may begin to comprehend the lives of our "crazy," "Sainted" mothers and grandmothers. The agony of the lives of women who might have been Poets, Novelists, Essayists, and Short-Story Writers (over a period of centuries), who died with their real gifts stifled within them.

13   And, if this were the end of the story, we would have cause to cry out in my paraphrase of Okot p'Bitek's great poem:

> O, my clanswomen
> Let us all cry together!
> Come,
> Let us mourn the death of our mother,
> The death of a Queen
> The ash that was produced
> By a great fire!
> O, this homestead is utterly dead
> Close the gates
> With *lacari* thorns,
> For our mother
> The creator of the Stool is lost!
> And all the young men

Have perished in the wilderness!

14   But this is not the end of the story, for all the young women—our mothers and grandmothers, *ourselves*—have not perished in the wilderness. And if we ask ourselves why, and search for and find the answer, we will know beyond all efforts to erase it from our minds, just exactly who, and of what, we black American women are.

15   One example, perhaps the most pathetic, most misunderstood one, can provide a backdrop for our mothers' work: Phillis Wheatley, a slave in the 1700s.

16   Virginia Woolf, in her book *A Room of One's Own*, wrote that in order for a woman to write fiction she must have two things, certainly: a room of her own (with key and lock) and enough money to support herself.

17   What then are we to make of Phillis Wheatley, a slave, who owned not even herself? This sickly, frail black girl who required a servant of her own at times—her health was so precarious—and who, had she been white, would have been easily considered the intellectual superior of all the women and most of the men in the society of her day.

18   Virginia Woolf wrote further, speaking of course not of our Phillis, that "any woman born with a great gift in the sixteenth century [insert "eighteenth century," insert "black woman," insert "born or made a slave"] would certainly have gone crazed, shot herself, or ended her days in some lonely cottage outside the village, half witch, half wizard [insert "Saint"], feared and mocked at. For it needs little skill and psychology to be sure that a highly gifted girl who had tried to use her gift of poetry would have been so thwarted and hindered by contrary instincts [add "chains, guns, the lash, the ownership of one's body by someone else, submission to an alien religion"], that she must have lost her health and sanity to a certainty."

19   The key words, as they relate to Phillis, are "contrary instincts." For when we read the poetry of Phillis Wheatley—as when we read the novels of Nella Larsen or the oddly false-sounding autobiography of that freest of all black women writers, Zora Hurston—evidence of "country instincts" is everywhere. Her loyalties were completely divided, as was, without question, her mind.

20   But how could this be otherwise? Captured at seven, a slave of wealthy, doting whites who instilled in her the "savagery" of the Africa they "rescued" her from . . . one wonders if she was even able to remember her homeland as she had known it, or as it really was.

21   Yet, because she did try to use her gift for poetry in a world that made her a slave, she was "so thwarted and hindered by . . . contrary instincts, that she . . . lost her health. . . ." In the last years of her brief life, burdened not only with the need to express her gift but also with a penniless, friendless "freedom" and several small children for whom she was forced to do strenuous work to feed, she lost her health, certainly. Suffering from malnutrition and neglect and who knows what mental agonies, Phillis Wheatley died.

22   So torn by "contrary instincts" was black, kidnapped, enslaved Phillis that her description of "the Goddess"—as she poetically called the Liberty she did not have—is ironically, cruelly humorous. And, in fact, has held Phillis up to ridicule for more than a century. It is usually read prior to hanging Phillis's memory as that of a fool. She wrote:

> The Goddess comes, she moves divinely fair,
>   Olive and laurel binds her *golden* hair.
> Wherever shines this native of the skies,
> Unnumber'd charms and recent graces rise. [My italics]

23   It is obvious that Phillis, the slave, combed the "Goddess's" hair every morning; prior, perhaps, to bringing in the milk, or fixing her mistress's lunch. She took her imagery from the one thing she saw elevated above all others.

24   With the benefit of hindsight we ask, "How could she?"

25   But at last, Phillis, we understand. No more snickering when your stiff, struggling, ambivalent lines are forced on us. We know now that you were not an idiot or a traitor; only a sickly little black girl, snatched from your home and country and made a slave; a woman who still struggled to sing the song that was your gift, although in a land of barbarians who praised you for your bewildered tongue. It is not so much what you sang, as that you kept alive, in so many of our ancestors, *the notion of song.*

26   Black women are called, in the folklore that so aptly identifies one's status in society, "the *mule* of the world," because we have been handed the burdens that everyone else—*everyone* else—refused to carry. We have also been called "Matriarchs," "Superwomen," and "Mean and Evil Bitches." Not to mention "Castraters" and "Sapphire's Mama." When we have pleaded for understanding, our character has been distorted; when we have asked for simple caring, we have been handed empty inspirational appellations, then stuck in the farthest corner. When we have asked for love, we have been given children. In short, even our plainer gifts, our labors of fidelity and love, have been knocked down our throats. To be an artist and a black woman, even today, lowers our status in many respects, rather than raises it: and yet, artists we will be.

27   Therefore we must fearlessly pull out of ourselves and look at and identify with our lives the living creativity some of our great-grandmothers were not allowed to know. I stress *some* of them because it is well known that the majority of our great-grandmothers knew, even without "knowing" it, the reality of their spirituality, even if they didn't recognize it beyond what happened in the singing at church—and they never had any intention of giving it up.

28   How they did it—those millions of black women who were not Phillis Wheatley, or Lucy Terry or Frances Harper or Zora Hurston or Nella Larsen

or Bessie Smith; or Elizabeth Catlett, or Katherine Dunham, either—brings me to the title of this essay, "In Search of Our Mothers' Gardens," which is a personal account that is yet shared, in its theme and its meaning, by all of us. I found, while thinking about the far-reaching world of the creative black woman, that often the truest answer to a question that really matters can be found very close.

29   In the late 1920s my mother ran away from home to marry my father. Marriage, if not running away, was expected of seventeen-year-old girls. By the time she was twenty, she had two children and was pregnant with a third. Five children later, I was born. And this is how I came to know my mother: she seemed a large, soft, loving-eyed woman who was rarely impatient in our home. Her quick, violent temper was on view only a few times a year, when she battled with the white landlord who had the misfortune to suggest to her that her children did not need to go to school.

30   She made all the clothes we wore, even my brothers' overalls. She made all the towels and sheets we used. She spent the summers canning vegetables and fruits. She spent the winter evenings making quilts enough to cover all our beds.

31   During the "working" day, she labored beside—not behind—my father in the fields. Her day began before sunup, and did not end until late at night. There was never a moment for her to sit down, undisturbed, to unravel her own private thoughts; never a time free from interruption—by work or the noisy inquiries of her many children. And yet, it is to my mother—and all our mothers who were not famous—that I went in search of the secret of what has fed that muzzled and often mutilated, but vibrant, creative spirit that the black woman has inherited, and that pops out in wild and unlikely places to this day.

32   But when, you will ask, did my overworked mother have time to know or care about feeding the creative spirit?

33   The answer is so simple that many of us have spent years discovering it. We have constantly looked high, when we should have looked high—and low.

34   For example: in the Smithsonian Institute in Washington, D.C., there hangs a quilt unlike any other in the world. In fanciful, inspired, and yet simple and identifiable figures, it portrays the story of the Crucifixion. It is considered rare, beyond price. Though it follows no known pattern of quilt-making, and though it is made of bits and pieces of worthless rags, it is obviously the work of a person of powerful imagination and deep spiritual feeling. Below this quilt I saw a note that says it was made by "an anonymous Black woman in Alabama, a hundred years ago."

35   If we could locate this "anonymous" black woman from Alabama, she would turn out to be one of our grandmothers—an artist who left her mark in the only materials she could afford, and in the only medium her position in society allowed her to use.

36   As Virginia Woolf wrote further, in *A Room of One's Own:*

> Yet genius of a sort must have existed among women as it must have existed
> among the working class. [Change this to "slaves" and "the wives and daughters
> of sharecroppers."] Now and again an Emily Brontë or a Robert Burns [change
> this to "a Zora Hurston or a Richard Wright"] blazes out and proves its presence.
> But certainly it never got itself on to paper. When, however, one reads of a witch
> being ducked, of a woman possessed by devils [or "Sainthood"], of a wise woman
> selling herbs [our root workers], or even a very remarkable man who had a
> mother, then I think we are on the track of a lost novelist, a suppressed
> poet, or some mute and inglorious Jane Austen. . . . Indeed, I would venture to
> guess that Anon, who wrote so many poems without signing them, was often
> a woman. . . .

37   And so our mothers and grandmothers have, more often than not anonymously, handed on the creative spark, the seed of the flower they themselves never hoped to see: or like a sealed letter they could not plainly read.

38   And so it is, certainly, with my own mother. Unlike "Ma" Rainey's songs,
which retained their creator's name even while blasting forth from Bessie
Smith's mouth, no song or poem will bear my mother's name. Yet so many
of the stories that I write, that we all write, are my mother's stories. Only
recently did I fully realize this: that through years of listening to my mother's
stories of her life, I have absorbed not only the stories themselves, but
something of the manner in which she spoke, something of the urgency
that involves the knowledge that her stories—like her life—must be recorded.
It is probably for this reason that so much of what I have written is about
characters whose counterparts in real life are so much older than I am.

39   But the telling of these stories, which came from my mother's lips as
naturally as breathing, was not the only way my mother showed herself as
an artist. For stories, too, were subject to being distracted, to dying without
conclusion. Dinners must be started, and cotton must be gathered before
the big rains. The artist that was and is my mother showed itself to me only
after many years. This is what I finally noticed:

40   Like Mem, a character in *The Third Life of Grange Copeland,* my mother
adorned with flowers whatever shabby house we were forced to live in.
And not just your typical straggly country stand of zinnias, either. She
planted ambitious gardens—and still does—with over fifty different varieties
of plants that bloom profusely from early March until late November. Before
she left home for the fields, she watered her flowers, chopped up the grass,
and laid out new beds. When she returned from the fields she might divide
clumps of bulbs, dig a cold pit, uproot and replant roses, or prune branches
from her taller bushes or trees—until night came and it was too dark to see.

41   Whatever she planted grew as if by magic, and her fame as a grower of flowers spread over three counties. Because of her creativity with her flowers, even my memories of poverty are seen through a screen of blooms—sunflowers, petunias, roses, dahlias, forsythia, spirea, delphiniums, verbena . . . and on and on.

42   And I remember people coming to my mother's yard to be given cuttings from her flowers; I hear again the praise showered on her because whatever rocky soil she landed on, she turned into a garden. A garden so brilliant with colors, so original in its design, so magnificent with life and creativity, that to this day people drive by our house in Georgia—perfect strangers and imperfect strangers—and ask to stand or walk among my mother's art.

43   I notice that it is only when my mother is working in her flowers that she is radiant, almost to the point of being invisible—except as Creator: hand and eye. She is involved in work her soul must have. Ordering the universe in the image of her personal conception of Beauty.

44   Her face, as she prepares the Art that is her gift, is a legacy of respect she leaves to me, for all that illuminates and cherishes life. She has handed down respect for the possibilities—and the will to grasp them.

45   For her, so hindered and intruded upon in so many ways, being an artist has still been a daily part of her life. This ability to hold on, even in very simple ways, is work black women have done for a very long time.

46   This poem is not enough, but it is something, for the woman who literally covered the holes in our walls with sunflowers:

> They were women then
> My mama's generation
> Husky of voice—Stout of
> Step
> With fists as well as
> Hands
> How they battered down
> Doors
> And ironed
> Starched white
> Shirts
> How they led
> Armies
> Headragged Generals
> Across mined
> Fields
> Booby-trapped
> Kitchens
> To discover books
> Desks

> A place for us
> How they knew what we
> *Must* know
> Without knowing a page
> Of it
> Themselves.

47　Guided by my heritage of a love of beauty and a respect for strength—in search of my mother's garden, I found my own.

48　And perhaps in Africa over two hundred years ago, there was just such a mother; perhaps she painted vivid and daring decorations in oranges and yellows and greens on the walls of her hut; perhaps she sang—in a voice like Roberta Flack's—*sweetly* over the compounds of her village; perhaps she wove the most stunning mats or told the most ingenious stories of all the village storytellers. Perhaps she was herself a poet—though only her daughter's name is signed to the poems that we know.

49　Perhaps Phillis Wheatley's mother was also an artist.

50　Perhaps in more than Phillis Wheatley's biological life is her mother's signature made clear.

Topics for Writing and Discussion

1.　In a symbolic sense, what are the "gardens" Walker speaks of in the essay title?

2.　Why, according to Walker, were the "Saints" described by Jean Toomer driven to staring "out at the world wildly, like lunatics—or quietly, like suicides"?

3.　For whom is Walker writing this essay? What is her purpose and how do the examples she gives illustrate the dominant idea of the piece?

4.　How does Walker's theme transcend the plight of the black woman and speak to the situation of women in general? What problems do black women face that are not shared by their white counterparts? As part of your response, consider Walker's references to Virginia Woolf's views.

5.　Walker's essay describes the tragedy of a group denied expression of self. What other groups, current or past, have lost their "voices" through oppression? Present the plight of one such group in a fully developed, illustrative essay. Did this group lose its "voice" but pass on its spirit?

Loren Eiseley in his office at the University Museum, Philadelphia (Bernie Cleff)

The Brown Wasps

Loren Eiseley
(1907–1977)

A highly respected naturalist and conservationist, Loren Eiseley was a professor of anthropology and the history of science at the University of Pennsylvania. In addition to being a gifted scientist, Eiseley was also a fine writer who contributed articles to professional journals such as *Scientific Monthly* and *American Anthropologist* as well as to popular magazines such as *Harper's, Holiday,* and *Ladies' Home Journal.* His books include *The Immense Journey* (1957), *The Mind as Nature* (1962), and *The Unexpected Universe* (1969). In "The Brown Wasps," taken from *The Night Country* (1971), Eiseley uses a series of images to explain the drive of all living creatures—including humans—to the places that have defined them and given them a sense of belonging.

1　　There is a corner in the waiting room of one of the great Eastern stations where women never sit. It is always in the shadow and overhung by rows of lockers. It is, however, always frequented—not so much by genuine travelers as by the dying. It is here that a certain element of the abandoned poor seeks a refuge out of the weather, clinging for a few hours longer to the city that has fathered them. In a precisely similar manner I have seen, on a sunny day in midwinter, a few old brown wasps creep slowly over an abandoned wasp nest in a thicket. Numbed and forgetful and frost-blackened, the hum of the spring hive still resounded faintly in their sodden tissues. Then the temperature would fall and they would drop away into the white oblivion of the snow. Here in the station it is in no way different save the city is busy in its snows. But the old ones cling to their seats as though these were symbolic and could not be given up. Now and then they sleep, their gray old heads resting with painful awkwardness on the backs of the benches.

2   Also they are not at rest. For an hour they may sleep in the gasping exhaustion of the ill-nourished and aged who have to walk in the night. Then a policeman comes by on his round and nudges them upright.

3   "You can't sleep here," he growls.

4   A strange ritual then begins. An old man is difficult to waken. After a muttered conversation the policeman presses a coin into his hand and passes fiercely along the benches prodding and gesturing toward the door. In his wake, like birds rising and settling behind the passage of a farmer through a cornfield, the men totter up, move a few paces and subside once more upon the benches.

5   One man, after a slight, apologetic lurch, does not move at all. Tubercularly thin, he sleeps on steadily. The policeman does not look back. To him, too, this has become a ritual. He will not have to notice it again officially for another hour.

6   Once in a while one of the sleepers will not awaken. Like the brown wasps, he will have had his wish to die in the great droning center of the hive rather than in some lonely room. It is not so bad here with the shuffle of footsteps and the knowledge that there are others who share the bad luck of the world. There are also the whistles and the sounds of everyone, everyone in the world, starting on journeys. Amidst so many journeys somebody is bound to come out all right. Somebody.

7   Maybe it was on a like thought that the brown wasps fell away from the old paper nest in the thicket. You hold till the last, even if it is only to a public seat in a railroad station. You want your place in the hive more than you want a room or a place where the aged can be eased gently out of the way. It is the place that matters, the place at the heart of things. It is life that you want, that bruises your gray old head with the hard chairs; a man has a right to his place.

8   But sometimes the place is lost in the years behind us. Or sometimes it is a thing of air, a kind of vaporous distortion above a heap of rubble. We cling to a time and place because without them man is lost, not only man but life. This is why the voices, real or unreal, which speak from the floating trumpets at spiritualist seances are so unnerving. They are voices out of nowhere whose only reality lies in their ability to stir the memory of a living person with some fragment of the past. Before the medium's cabinet both the dead and the living revolve endlessly about an episode, a place, an event that has already been engulfed by time.

9   This feeling runs deep in life; it brings stray cats running over endless miles, and birds homing from the ends of the earth. It is as though all living creatures, and particularly the more intelligent, can survive only by fixing or transforming a bit of time into space or by securing a bit of space with

its objects immortalized and made permanent in time. For example, I once saw, on a flower pot in my own living room, the efforts of a field mouse to build a remembered field. I have lived to see this episode repeated in a thousand guises, and since I have spent a large portion of my life in the shade of a nonexistent tree, I think I am entitled to speak for the field mouse.

10 One day as I cut across the field, which at that time extended on one side of our suburban shopping center, I found a giant slug feeding from a runnel of pink ice cream in an abandoned Dixie cup. I could see his eyes telescope and protrude in a kind of dim, uncertain ecstasy as his dark body bunched and elongated in the curve of the cup. Then, as I stood there at the edge of the concrete, contemplating the slug, I began to realize it was like standing on a shore where a different type of life creeps up and fumbles tentatively among the rocks and sea wrack. It knows its place and will only creep so far until something changes. Little by little as I stood there, I began to see more of this shore that surrounds the place of man. I looked with sudden care and attention at things I had been running over thoughtlessly for years. I even waded out a short way into the grass and the wild-rose thickets to see more. A huge black-belted bee went droning by and there were some indistinct scurryings in the underbrush.

11 Then I came to a sign which informed me that this field was to be the site of a new Wanamaker suburban store. Thousands of obscure lives were about to perish, the spores of puffballs would go smoking off to new fields, and the bodies of little white-footed mice would be crunched under the inexorable wheels of the bulldozers. Life disappears or modifies its appearances so fast that everything takes on an aspect of illusion—a momentary fizzing and boiling with smoke rings, like pouring dissident chemicals into a retort. Here man was advancing, but in a few years his plaster and bricks would be disappearing once more into the insatiable maw of the clover. Being of an archaeological cast of mind, I thought of this fact with an obscure sense of satisfaction and waded back through the rose thickets to the concrete parking lot. As I did so, a mouse scurried ahead of me, frightened of my steps if not of that ominous Wanamaker sign. I saw him vanish in the general direction of my apartment house, his little body quivering with fear in the great open sun on the blazing concrete. Blinded and confused, he was running straight away from his field. In another week scores would follow him.

12 I forgot the episode then and went home to the quiet of my living room. It was not until a week later, letting myself into the apartment, that I realized I had a visitor. I am fond of plants and had several ferns standing on the floor in pots to avoid the noon glare by the south window.

13 As I snapped on the light and glanced carelessly around the room, I saw a little heap of earth on the carpet and a scrabble of pebbles that had been kicked merrily over the edge of one of the flower pots. To my astonishment I discovered a full-fledged burrow delving downward among the fern roots. I waited silently. The creature who had made the burrow did not appear. I

remembered the wild field then, and the flight of the mice. No house mouse, no *Mus domesticus,* had kicked up this little heap of earth or sought refuge under a fern root in a flower pot. I thought of the desperate little creature I had seen fleeing from the wild-rose thicket. Through intricacies of pipes and attics, he, or one of his fellows, had climbed to this high green solitary room. I could visualize what had occurred. He had an image in his head, a world of seed pods and quiet, of green sheltering leaves in the dim light among the weed stems. It was the only world he knew and it was gone.

14   Somehow in his flight he had found his way to this room with drawn shades where no one would come till nightfall. And here he had smelled green leaves and run quickly up the flower pot to dabble his paws in common earth. He had even struggled half the afternoon to carry his burrow deeper and had failed. I examined the hole, but no whiskered twitching face appeared. He was gone. I gathered up the earth and refilled the burrow. I did not expect to find traces of him again.

15   Yet for three nights thereafter I came home to the darkened room and my ferns to find the dirt kicked gaily about the rug and the burrow reopened, though I was never able to catch the field mouse within it. I dropped a little food about the mouth of the burrow, but it was never touched. I looked under beds or sat reading with one ear cocked for rustlings in the ferns. It was all in vain; I never saw him. Probably he ended in a trap in some other tenant's room.

16   But before he disappeared, I had come to look hopefully for his evening burrow. About my ferns there had begun to linger the insubstantial vapor of an autumn field, the distilled essence, as it were, of a mouse brain in exile from its home. It was a small dream, like our dreams, carried a long and weary journey along pipes and through spider webs, past holes over which loomed the shadows of waiting cats, and finally, desperately, into this room where he had played in the shuttered daylight for an hour among the green ferns on the floor. Every day these invisible dreams pass us on the street, or rise from beneath our feet, or look out upon us from beneath a bush.

17   Some years ago the old elevated railway in Philadelphia was torn down and replaced by a subway system. This ancient El with its barnlike stations containing nut-vending machines and scattered food scraps had, for generations, been the favorite feeding ground of flocks of pigeons, generally one flock to a station along the route of the El. Hundreds of pigeons were dependent upon the system. They flapped in and out of its stanchions and steel work or gathered in watchful little audiences about the feet of anyone who rattled the peanut-vending machines. They even watched people who jingled change in their hands, and prospected for food under the feet of the crowds who gathered between trains. Probably very few among the waiting people who tossed a crumb to an eager pigeon realized that this El was like a food-bearing river, and that the life which haunted its banks was dependent upon the running of the trains with their human freight.

18   I saw the river stop.

19   The time came when the underground tubes were ready; the traffic was transferred to a realm unreachable by pigeons. It was like a great river subsiding suddenly into desert sands. For a day, for two days, pigeons continued to circle over the El or stand close to the red vending machines. They were patient birds, and surely this great river which had flowed through the lives of unnumbered generations was merely suffering from some momentary drought.

20   They listened for the familiar vibrations that had always heralded an approaching train; they flapped hopefully about the head of an occasional workman walking along the steel runways. They passed from one empty station to another, all the while growing hungrier. Finally, they flew away.

21   I thought I had seen the last of them about the El, but there was a revival and it provided a curious instance of the memory of living things for a way of life or a locality that has long been cherished. Some weeks after the El was abandoned, workmen began to tear it down. I went to work every morning by one particular station, and the time came when the demolition crews reached this spot. Acetylene torches showered passersby with sparks, pneumatic drills hammered at the base of the structure, and a blind man who, like the pigeons, had clung with his cup to a stairway leading to the change booth, was forced to give up his place.

22   It was then, strangely, momentarily, one morning that I witnessed the return of a little band of the familiar pigeons. I even recognized one or two members of the flock that had lived around this particular station before they were dispersed into the streets. They flew bravely in and out among the sparks and the hammers and the shouting workmen. They had returned—and they had returned because the hubbub of the wreckers had convinced them that the river was about to flow once more. For several hours they flapped in and out through the empty windows, nodding their heads and watching the fall of girders with attentive little eyes. By the following morning the station was reduced to some burned-off stanchions in the street. My bird friends had gone. It was plain, however, that they retained a memory for an insubstantial structure now compounded of air and time. Even the blind man clung to it. Someone had provided him with a chair, and he sat at the same corner staring sightlessly at an invisible stairway where, so far as he was concerned, the crowds were still ascending to the trains.

23   I have said my life has been passed in the shade of a nonexistent tree, so that such sights do not offend me. Prematurely I am one of the brown wasps and I often sit with them in the great droning hive of the station, dreaming sometimes of a certain tree. It was planted sixty years ago by a boy with a bucket and a toy spade in a little Nebraska town. That boy was myself. It was a cottonwood sapling and the boy remembered it because of some words spoken by his father and because everyone died or moved away who was

supposed to wait and grow old under its shade. The boy was passed from hand to hand, but the tree for some intangible reason had taken root in his mind. It was under its branches that he sheltered; it was from this tree that his memories, which are my memories, led away into the world.

24   After sixty years the mood of the brown wasps grows heavier upon one. During a long inward struggle I thought it would do me good to go and look upon that actual tree. I found a rational excuse in which to clothe this madness. I purchased a ticket and at the end of two thousand miles I walked another mile to an address that was still the same. The house had not been altered.

25   I came close to the white picket fence and reluctantly, with great effort, looked down the long vista of the yard. There was nothing there to see. For sixty years that cottonwood had been growing in my mind. Season by season its seeds had been floating farther on the hot prairie winds. We had planted it lovingly there, my father and I, because he had a great hunger for soil and live things growing, and because none of these things had long been ours to protect. We had planted the little sapling and watered it faithfully, and I remembered that I had run out with my small bucket to drench its roots the day we moved away. And all the years since, it had been growing in my mind, a huge tree that somehow stood for my father and the love I bore him. I took a grasp on the picket fence and forced myself to look again.

26   A boy with the hard bird eye of youth pedaled a tricycle slowly beside me.

27   "What'cha lookin' at?" he asked curiously.

28   "A tree," I said.

29   "What for?" he said.

30   "It isn't there," I said, to myself mostly, and began to walk away at a pace just slow enough not to seem to be running.

31   "What isn't there?" the boy asked. I didn't answer. It was obvious I was attached by a thread to a thing that had never been there, or certainly not for long. Something that had to be held in the air, or sustained in the mind, because it was part of my orientation in the universe and I could not survive without it. There was more than an animal's attachment to a place. There was something else, the attachment of the spirit to a grouping of events in time; it was part of our morality.

32   So I had come home at last, driven by a memory in the brain as surely as the field mouse who had delved long ago into my flower pot or the pigeons flying forever amidst the rattle of nut-vending machines. These, the burrow under the greenery in my living room and the red-bellied bowls of peanuts now hovering in midair in the minds of pigeons, were all part of an elusive world that existed nowhere and yet everywhere. I looked once at the real world about me while the persistent boy pedaled at my heels.

It was without meaning, though my feet took a remembered path. In sixty years the house and street had rotted out of my mind. But the tree, the tree

Illustration 363

that no longer was, that had perished in its first season, bloomed on in my individual mind, unblemished as my father's words. "We'll plant a tree here, son, and we're not going to move any more. And when you're an old, old man you can sit under it and think how we planted it here, you and me, together."

34   I began to outpace the boy on the tricycle.

35   "Do you live here, Mister?" he shouted after me suspiciously. I took a firm grasp on airy nothing—to be precise, on the bole of a great tree. "I do," I said. I spoke for myself, one field mouse, and several pigeons. We were all out of touch but somehow permanent. It was the world that had changed.

Topics for Writing and Discussion

1. In the first paragraph, Eiseley compares the old men to brown wasps in an abandoned thicket. How does he develop the analogy and use it to lead to his thesis? What is his thesis? How does his reference to the brown wasps in paragraph 24 relate to the opening example?

2. Read paragraph 11 carefully, noticing particularly the examples Eiseley gives of the changes that will occur when the Wanamaker's store is built. What is his attitude toward the construction of the store? What does he believe will be the ultimate fate of the store and its builders?

3. Why does Eiseley leave food for the field mouse who burrows in his house plants? What does the mouse represent for him? What is the connection between the mouse's actions and human dreams, according to Eiseley?

4. How does Eiseley's story of the tree, and of his return to his old home, relate to the illustrations of the slug, the mouse, and the pigeons?

5. Write an essay in which you describe a change (or changes) in a place familiar to you. Use specific examples to illustrate your response to those changes.

Writing Assignments for Chapter Seven

Illustration

1. To address William F. Buckley's complaint that no one complains anymore, write a letter to a company owner or supervisor or to a depart-

ment/division head and register your complaint about a product or service. Consider, for example, some of the services provided on your campus. Are there problems associated with the bookstore, the student center, the dorms, the cafeterias? With your school's advising or registration systems or financial aid office? Try to imagine the person to whom you are addressing your complaint; remember that your letter will only be taken seriously if you use the appropriate tone and enough detailed examples to illustrate the nature of your complaint thoroughly and persuasively. After you have completed this assignment, send the letter and wait for a response. Is the response as effectively written as your original letter? (If you prefer, instead of a letter of complaint, send a letter complimenting some service or product. Such letters are rarely received and are always greatly appreciated.)

2. Brent Staples' essay "Black Men and Public Space" discusses the dangers of stereotyping and the many kinds of victims it produces. Have you ever been the victim of discrimination? Of someone's preconceived beliefs about you, your family, or your friends? Or have you ever held prejudices that caused you to behave in irrational or even shameful ways? Perhaps you silently participated in acts of discrimination by failing to speak up? Or did you confront prejudice? Write an essay that illustrates your role in one of these situations, making clear how you felt then and how you feel now about the way you or others acted. Did the experience change you in any way? Might your essay change others?

3. Assume that your younger brother or sister is preparing to enter your high school (or your college) and has asked you your opinion of that school. Offer several short incidents, as James Thurber did in "University Days," or one extended example that illustrates your attitude toward your school. For instance, was your school a playpen for adolescents? A prison? A genuinely challenging educational experience? A haven for the athletically endowed? Your essay may be serious or humorous, and you may discover that using some dialogue will help make your essay vivid and persuasive.

4. In the moving essay "In Search of Our Mothers' Gardens," Alice Walker uses her own mother as the example of black women who, prevented from becoming recognized artists themselves, passed down creativity, strength of character, and a love of beauty to their daughters and granddaughters. Think of someone you admire—an influential teacher, an older relative, or a close family friend—who was also an unrecognized or under-appreciated artist. Write about this person, using him or her to illustrate Walker's points about handing down "respect for the possibilities—and the will to grasp them."

Illustration 365

5. In her essay, Barbara Tuchman describes some of history's "better moments." Recollect some of your own "better moments" and accomplishments. What was extraordinary about them? What did they teach you? What could they teach others? Focus your answers into a thesis and use your successes as illustrations supporting your claim about the value of your better moments.

6. Select some important enterprise or discovery that people have successfully accomplished in the past five years. Use this accomplishment as an illustration of people's determination, hard work, independence, or daring. Why should this feat be regarded as one of our "better moments"?

7. In "The Brown Wasps," Loren Eiseley suggests that in an everchanging world, people need a place to cling to, even if this place exists only in memory. Remember a place that offers you mental or emotional refuge, such as Eiseley's tree planted with his father. In an essay, cite several reasons for your choice, supporting each of these with examples that make the nature of your attachment clear.

Chapter Eight

Comparison and Contrast

Comparing and contrasting is a natural human behavior that you perform so often you may not even be aware of it. When you stroll down the aisle of the supermarket, pick up two packages of chocolate chip cookies and determine which looks better, you are using your natural talent of contrasting, for you are looking at the differences in the products (number of cookies, size of each cookie, number of chips per cookie, price of package, and so on). Or if you look into your dresser drawer full of unmatched socks hoping to locate a pair to wear to class, you begin to compare socks because you want to find two that are alike rather than different. So, simply put, *comparing* means to look for *similarities,* while *contrasting* means to look for *differences.* Often you may discover that you use the two together, considering both the similarities *and* the differences of things being examined. For example, if you are contemplating the purchase of a new sports car, you might begin your research by comparing similar models, like a Mitsubishi 3000GT and a Dodge Stealth. Then you might go on to contrast those models with one very different, like a Porsche or a Ferrari.

A special type of comparison is the *analogy.* Here similarities are found between two seemingly dissimilar things. By comparing a herd of stampeding horses to drivers in rush-hour traffic, you can illustrate the wild and dangerous place a highway becomes at five o'clock. Beware the extent to which you carry the analogy, though. Eventually the comparisons do break down, so the point you want to make could be lost.

As you use the principles of comparison and contrast, you will find that they are valuable tools in analysis and evaluation.

367

Writing and Organizing the Comparison/ Contrast Essay

The first step in any writing is selecting a topic, and in writing a comparison or contrast essay that selection is especially important. You should focus your reader's attention on something significant. As you choose your subject, avoid the obvious or the "so what" topic. Unless you can present a truly informative or unusual approach to the topic, an essay such as contrasting attending high school with attending college could be boring. Consider the reader: once you have chosen a topic, ask yourself, "Would *I* enjoy reading about this? Would I learn something from this?" If your answers are "No," presume that would also be your reader's response and select another topic.

The following will provide additional help in developing, organizing, and writing a comparison or contrast essay:

1. *Clearly establish the basis of the comparison or contrast.*

Identify the purpose of the writing in a clearly stated (or strongly implied) thesis statement. Russell Baker establishes the basis of his contrast early on in "The Two Ismo's" as "two violently opposed doctrines of social conduct" in American life. The remainder of the essay explains the differences between the two "ismo's." Bruce Catton, however, takes more space to establish the basis of his contrast between the personalities of Lee and Grant. But by providing an appropriate "setting" in the opening two paragraphs, Catton moves smoothly and logically to the essay's thesis in paragraph 3. So, whether your introduction is one paragraph long or more, the reader should be prepared for the discussion that will follow.

2. *Carefully select the points you intend to discuss.*

As you review your thesis statement, determine the best way to emphasize the point of your discussion. Should you focus on similarities, differences, or both? If, for example, the purpose of your essay is to analyze the manner in which William Faulkner and Flannery O'Connor portray the South in their literary works, you might first determine which points you will examine. After some thought, you might select points such as *theme, characters,* and *locale.* Then after further thought, you may determine that there are few similarities between the two writers on these points, so your essay should be developed by *contrasting* their stories' themes, development of characters, and use of locale. Furthermore, since both writers have an extensive number of works to consider, you should also select the ones that would best illustrate the point of your thesis.

Lewis Thomas reveals his points of discussion in the second paragraph of "The Iks":

... the Iks have transformed themselves into an irreversibly disagreeable collection of unattached, brutish creatures, totally selfish and loveless, in response to the dismantling of their traditional culture.

Thomas then presents the thesis statement of the essay and proceeds to develop it according to the points he established earlier.

3.   *Decide if a point-by-point or a subject-by-subject method of development is better for your purpose.*

In the *point-by-point* method, you support your thesis by comparing or contrasting your two subjects first on point one, then on point two, then point three, and so on.

In the *subject-by-subject* method, you would make your comparison or contrast by *fully* discussing one subject before moving on to another. The key to the comparison or the contrast is in using the same basis of comparison for each subject.

The two methods of organization follow these plans:

POINT-BY-POINT METHOD	SUBJECT-BY-SUBJECT METHOD
(Type A)	(Type B)
Introduction	Introduction
I. Point 1	I. Subject A
A. Subject A	A. Point 1
B. Subject B	B. Point 2
II. Point 2	C. Point 3
A. Subject A	II. Subject B
B. Subject B	A. Point 1
III. Point 3	B. Point 2
A. Subject A	C. Point 3
B. Subject B	Conclusion
Conclusion	

Your purpose and your subject will determine which of the two systems is better for your essay, but consider the advantages and disadvantages of both. The advantage of the point-by-point system is that it allows you to present your ideas side by side. Russell Baker uses this method in "The Two Ismo's," alternating the characteristics of machismo and quichismo. The disadvantage of this approach is the possible back-and-forth "tennis ball" effect it may present to the reader. A variety of smooth transitions will help move the reader from subject to subject.

On the other hand, the subject-by-subject method will allow you to present your ideas as a unit, a whole. This approach is especially effective if only two or three points are being presented. You can, in essence, completely discuss one point and then move on to give a similarly thorough treatment to the other point. Notice how well this approach works in Mark Twain's "Two Ways of Looking at the River." Twain first describes his earlier, emotional response to the beauties of the Mississippi River and then gives a later view from his perspective of a trained river-boat pilot.

A problem with this subject-by-subject method can arise: if there is too much material offered about either of the subjects without adequate reference to the other subject, the essay may begin to resemble two separate essays stuck together in the middle rather than a whole comparison or contrast essay. To avoid this problem, writers can subtly remind their readers of their purpose by adding connecting phrases ("Unlike the Prohibition legislation of the Roaring Twenties, the new anti-drug laws are aimed at the sellers not the users.") and by repeating key terms or images from the first discussion in the second. Twain does a good job of carrying images from the first "block" of his essay into the second, contrasting, portion: " 'This sun means that we are going to have wind tomorrow; that floating log means the river is rising.' . . ."

4.   *Describe your subjects clearly and vividly.*

To understand a difference or similarity between two subjects, readers must be able to "see" them as you do. Consequently, use as many details and illustrations as you can to describe both your subjects. Beware a tendency to elaborate on one subject and skimp on the other, especially in a paper that asserts "X" is better than or preferable to "Y." Give each subject a reasonable treatment, as Bruce Catton does in "Grant and Lee: A Study in Contrasts."

5.   *Use transitions that indicate comparison or contrast to provide coherence in the development of your essay.*

Transitions such as "however," "on the other hand," "but," "whereas," and "unlike" will show a contrasting of ideas. Words such as "similarly," "also," "in addition to," "both," and "like" will show a comparing of ideas.

As you read the essays that follow, pay close attention to the ways the writers establish the bases of their comparison or contrast, organize their points of discussion, use clear details to focus each point of discussion, and provide transitions for coherence within and between the paragraphs.

Author Mark Twain, also known as Samuel Clemens (© Archive Photos)

Two Ways of Looking at the River

Mark Twain
(1835–1910)

Samuel Clemens was born in Florida, Missouri,
and grew up in the river town of Hannibal,
Missouri. As a young man, he worked on a
riverboat and took his pen name, Mark Twain,
from the cry of the riverboat captain as he
announced the safe navigating depth. Twain also
worked as a printer and as a frontier journalist. He
used his experiences and observations, both
humorous and pessimistic, when he wrote such
American classics as *The Adventures of Tom Sawyer*
(1876) and *The Adventures of Huckleberry Finn*
(1885). Other well-known works include *Innocents
Abroad* (1896) and *A Connecticut Yankee at King
Arthur's Court* (1889). "Two Ways of Looking at the
River" is a selection from his autobiography, *Life
on the Mississippi* (1883), in which he describes his
life as a riverboat pilot.

1   Now when I had mastered the language of this water and had come
to know every trifling feature that bordered the great river as familiarly as
I knew the letters of the alphabet, I had made a valuable acquisition. But I
had lost something, too. I had lost something which could never be restored
to me while I lived. All the grace, the beauty, the poetry, had gone out of
the majestic river! I still kept in mind a certain wonderful sunset which I
witnessed when steamboating was new to me. A broad expanse of the river
was turned to blood; in the middle distance the red hue brightened into
gold, through which a solitary log came floating, black and conspicuous; in
one place a long, slanting mark lay sparkling upon the water; in another
the surface was broken by boiling, tumbling rings, that were as many-tinted

as an opal; where the ruddy flush was faintest, was a smooth spot that was covered with graceful circles and radiating lines, ever so delicately traced; the shore on our left was densely wooded and the somber shadow that fell from this forest was broken in one place by a long, ruffled trail that shone like silver; and high above the forest wall a clean-stemmed dead tree waved a single leafy bough that glowed like a flame in the unobstructed splendor that was flowing from the sun. There were graceful curves, reflected images, woody heights, soft distances, and over the whole scene, far and near, the dissolving lights drifted steadily, enriching it every passing moment with new marvels of coloring.

2   I stood like one bewitched. I drank it in, in a speechless rapture. The world was new to me and I had never seen anything like this at home. But as I have said, a day came when I began to cease from noting the glories and the charms which the moon and the sun and the twilight wrought upon the river's face; another day came when I ceased altogether to note them. Then, if that sunset scene had been repeated, I should have looked upon it without rapture, and should have commented upon it inwardly after this fashion: "This sun means that we are going to have wind to-morrow; that floating log means that the river is rising, small thanks to it; that slanting mark on the water refers to a bluff reef which is going to kill somebody's steamboat one of these nights, if it keeps on stretching out like that; those tumbling 'boils' show a dissolving bar and a changing channel there; the lines and circles in the slick water over yonder are a warning that that troublesome place is shoaling up dangerously; that silver streak in the shadow of the forest is the 'break' from a new snag and he has located himself in the very best place he could have found to fish for steamboats; that tall dead tree, with a single living branch, is not going to last long, and then how is a body ever going to get through this blind place at night without the friendly old landmark?"

3   No, the romance and beauty were all gone from the river. All the value any feature of it had for me now was the amount of usefulness it could furnish toward compassing the safe piloting of a steamboat. Since those days, I have pitied doctors from my heart. What does the lovely flush in a beauty's cheek mean to a doctor but a "break" that ripples above some deadly disease? Are not all her visible charms sown thick with what are to him the signs and symbols of hidden decay? Does he ever see her beauty at all, or doesn't he simply view her professionally and comment upon her unwholesome condition all to himself? And doesn't he sometimes wonder whether he has gained most or lost most by learning his trade?

Topics for Writing and Discussion

1.   What two views of the river does Twain describe? Can you think of one word or one phrase that would characterize each of these views?

2.   What point is Twain making about the two different ways he has looked at the river? What is his thesis? How does his conclusion suggest the way of seeing nature he considers more desirable?

3.   In the third paragraph Twain poses a series of questions. Does he expect the reader to answer these questions? How do you think Twain might respond to his own queries? Would his responses differ from or agree with your own?

4.   How does Twain make smooth transitions from his first view of the river to the second and from the second view to the conclusion?

5.   Write an essay contrasting the way you looked at an object, a location, or a process before you learned the scientific, mechanical, or practical "truth" about it. For example, you might describe how you viewed the rainbows that form in puddles before and after you learned that they were caused by leaking oil from motor vehicles. Or you might describe your reaction to a magic trick before and after you learned the magician's secret.

Russell Baker in his office at The New York Times *in Washington, D.C. (Alan Mac-Weeney/Archive Pictures)*

The Two Ismo's

Russell Baker
(1925–   )

Russell Baker began his writing career as a
journalist with the *Baltimore Sun* in 1947. In 1954
he left the *Sun* to become a reporter for the *New
York Times.* At the *Times* he wrote his "Observer"
column for over twenty years. Baker was awarded
the George Polk Award for Distinguished
Commentary in 1972, and in 1979 he won
journalism's highest honor, his first Pulitzer Prize.
His columns have been collected in several books,
including *All Things Considered* (1965), *So This Is
Depravity* (1983), and *The Good Times* (1989). He
won a second Pulitzer Prize for *Growing Up* (1982),
a chronicle of his childhood in the Depression. In
"The Two Ismo's" Baker uses his famous wit to
make a satiric comparison between two kinds of
social conduct in American cities.

1   **A**merican city life is now torn by two violently opposed doctrines of
social conduct. One is machismo. Its adherents pride themselves on being
"machos." The opposing dogma is quichismo (pronounced "key shizmo"),
and its practitioners call themselves quiche-o's (pronounced "key shows").

2   A good study of a quichismo victory over machismo in an urban war zone
can be found in Philip Lopate's "Quiche Blitz on Columbus Avenue," included in his recent book, "Bachelorhood." Curiously, however, Mr. Lopate
refers to the quichismo doctrine by its French name, *quichisme.*

3   In doing so he unwittingly reveals that he is himself a quiche-o of the
highest order, for no macho would dream of using a French word when
discussing philosophy, and even the average quiche-o would avoid a word
as difficult to pronounce as *quichisme* for fear of getting it wrong and being
sneered at as unquiche-o.

4   For practitioners of quichismo there is no defense against being sneered at, and they live in dread of it. The machismo adherent, on the other hand, positively enjoys being sneered at since it entitles him to punch the sneerer in the nose, a ritual act ceremonially confirming that he is truly macho.

5   When a quiche-o is sneered at, his only recourse is to jog until he achieves a higher sense of total fulfillment. This is one reason behind the machismo slogan, "Machos have more fun."

6   Maybe so, quiche-o's say, but machos don't have French dry cleaning or white bucks. Machos prefer no dry cleaning at all though they sometimes get their clothes pressed if they've slept in them all week and want to impress females during the weekend.

7   Machos impress females by taking them to bars after opening the top four buttons on their shirts to show off the hair on their chests. Quiche-o women impress males by inviting them to dinner and serving salad from the carry-out gourmet shop, followed by a kiwi fruit. There are no macho women. If there were they would serve pigs' feet and beer because machos believe that real people don't eat salad, kiwi fruit or anything else that comes from gourmet shops.

8   Quiche-o people buy Swedish toothpaste at gourmet drugstores, Italian loafers at gourmet shoe shops, newspapers at gourmet newsstands and dogs at gourmet pet centers. Afterwards they have them wormed by gourmet veterinarians. They also go to the islands for a month or two, especially Bermuda, St. Bart's, Barbados and Trinidad. Machos also go to the islands— Coney and Long—usually for a Sunday afternoon. To primp for these vacations, machos first go to the barber.

9   No quiche-o has set foot in a barber shop for the last 20 years. He goes to a gourmet hairdresser for a styling, then, before jetting off to the islands, goes to the gourmet luggage shop for suitcases covered with the initials of gourmet designers. The macho packs a change of underwear and a drip-dry shirt in a zippered plastic briefcase his uncle brought back from a 1977 convention of T-shirt salesmen.

10   Quiche-o's are always redecorating. Machos are always repainting the room that has the TV set in it. When a macho's couch and chairs are finally ruined he goes to a department store and buys "a suit of furniture." Quiche-o furniture is never ruined, but it goes out of style every two years, and when it does the quiche-o goes to an environmental systems boutique and buys a new environment.

11   No quiche-o would ever take a walk in his undershirt unless it had something amusing printed on it, like *"Ou sont les neiges d'antan?"* No macho would ever appear on the beach in a male bikini. No quiche-o would ever wear black U.S. Keds with white soles and laces. No macho would ever walk into a hardware store and ask for a wok spatula.

12   Machos don't see anything funny about New Jersey. Quiche-o's never laugh at people who drive Volvos, people who pay $5.50 for a hamburger

or quiche jokes, unless they're told by another quiche-o. Quiche-o's like a lot of butcher block and stainless steel. Machos like a lot of children.

13   Machos never bake carrot cake and don't go out with women who do. Quiche-o's are proud of their cholesterol levels and never belch in public and never go out with women who do since they recognize them instantly as unquiche-o and unlikely ever to serve them a salad dinner followed with a kiwi fruit.

Topics for Writing and Discussion

1. Briefly explain the primary differences between machismo and quichismo. Cite three examples for each group to explain the differences you have defined.

2. How does Baker structure his contrast? What other patterns might he have used? What advantages does his arrangement have? Disadvantages?

3. What criticisms does Baker imply? How seriously are we, as readers, meant to take these criticisms? Does Baker seem to favor one group over the other? Do you find the behavior of one group (as described by Baker) more admirable or defensible than the other group?

4. In describing quiche-o people, Baker repeatedly uses the word "gourmet." Check the definition of "gourmet" and then notice the contexts in which Baker uses it. How does the repetition of this word add to the humor of the essay?

5. Using Russell Baker's humorous essay "The Two Ismo's" as a guide, write a lighthearted essay that contrasts two groups of people who love to hate each other: smokers versus nonsmokers, liberals versus conservatives, feminists versus chauvinists, exercisers versus couch potatoes. As you present your two groups, make a point about the strengths and weaknesses of extreme positions.

Bruce Catton (The Bettmann Archive)

Grant and Lee: A Study in Contrasts

Bruce Catton
(1899–1978)

A Civil War historian, Bruce Catton received both the Pulitzer Prize for historical work and the National Book Award in 1954. He worked as a reporter for various newspapers and served as director of information for the United States Department of Commerce. Later he became an editor and writer for *American Heritage* magazine. His highly respected books include *Mr. Lincoln's Army* (1951), *A Stillness at Appomattox* (1953), *Never Call Retreat* (1966), *Waiting for the Morning Train: An American Boyhood* (an autobiography, 1972), and *The Final Fury* (1974). "Grant and Lee: A Study in Contrasts" was published first in *The American Story* (1956), a collection of historical essays. In this selection, Catton recounts historical facts but goes beyond a simple description of the memorable surrender. By arranging his material thoughtfully and carefully, he builds a striking contrast not only between the leader of the Northern armies and his Southern counterpart, but also between two sharply divergent ways of life. The essay concludes with a discussion of Grant and Lee's similarities, perhaps suggesting that the ways of life they represented may also share common values.

1   When Ulysses S. Grant and Robert E. Lee met in the parlor of a modest house at Appomattox Court House, Virginia, on April 9, 1865, to work out the terms for the surrender of Lee's Army of Northern Virginia,

a great chapter in American life came to a close, and a great new chapter began.

2   These men were bringing the Civil War to its virtual finish. To be sure, other armies had yet to surrender, and for a few days the fugitive Confederate government would struggle desperately and vainly, trying to find some way to go on living now that its chief support was gone. But in effect it was all over when Grant and Lee signed the papers. And the little room where they wrote out the terms was the scene of one of the poignant, dramatic contrasts in American History.

3   They were two strong men these oddly different generals, and they represented the strengths of two conflicting currents that, through them, had come into final collision.

4   Back of Robert E. Lee was the notion that the old aristocratic concept might somehow survive and be dominant in American life.

5   Lee was tidewater Virginia, and in his background were family, culture, and tradition . . . the age of chivalry transplanted to a New World which was making its own legends and its own myths. He embodied a way of life that had come down through the age of knighthood and the English country squire. America was a land that was beginning all over again, dedicated to nothing much more complicated than the rather hazy belief that all men had equal rights and should have an equal chance in the world. In such a land Lee stood for the feeling that it was somehow of advantage to human society to have a pronounced inequality in the social structure. There should be a leisure class, backed by ownership of land; in turn, society itself should be keyed to the land as the chief source of wealth and influence. It would bring forth (according to this ideal) a class of men with a strong sense of obligation to the community; men who lived not to gain advantage for themselves, but to meet the solemn obligations which had been laid on them by the very fact that they were privileged. From them the country would get its leadership; to them it could look for the higher values—of thought, of conduct, or personal deportment—to give it strength and virtue.

6   Lee embodied the noblest elements of this aristocratic ideal. Through him, the landed nobility justified itself. For four years, the Southern states had fought a desperate war to uphold the ideals for which Lee stood. In the end, it almost seemed as if the Confederacy fought for Lee; as if he himself was the Confederacy . . . the best thing that the way of life for which the Confederacy stood could ever have to offer. He had passed into legend before Appomattox. Thousands of tired, underfed, poorly clothed Confederate soldiers, long since past the simple enthusiasm of the early days of the struggle, somehow considered Lee the symbol of everything for which they had been willing to die. But they could not quite put this feeling into words. If the Lost Cause, sanctified by so much heroism and so many deaths, had a living justification, its justification was General Lee.

7   Grant, the son of a tanner on the Western frontier, was everything Lee was not. He had come up the hard way and embodied nothing in particular except the eternal toughness and sinewy fiber of the men who grew up beyond the mountains. He was one of a body of men who owed reverence and obeisance to no one, who were self-reliant to a fault, who cared hardly anything for the past but who had a sharp eye for the future.

8   These frontier men were the precise opposites of the tidewater aristocrats. Back of them, in the great surge that had taken people over the Alleghenies and into the opening Western country, there was a deep, implicit dissatisfaction with a past that had settled into grooves. They stood for democracy, not from any reasoned conclusion about the proper ordering of human society, but simply because they had grown up in the middle of democracy and knew how it worked. Their society might have privileges, but they would be privileges each man had won for himself. Forms and patterns meant nothing. No man was born to anything, except perhaps to a chance to show how far he could rise. Life was competition.

9   Yet along with this feeling had come a deep sense of belonging to a national community. The Westerner who developed a farm, opened a shop, or set up in business as a trader could hope to prosper only as his own community prospered—and this community ran from the Atlantic to the Pacific and from Canada down to Mexico. If the land was settled, with towns and highways and accessible markets, he could better himself. He saw his fate in terms of the nation's own destiny. As its horizons expanded, so did his. He had, in other words, an acute dollars-and-cents stake in the continued growth and development of his country.

10   And that, perhaps, is where the contrast between Grant and Lee becomes most striking. The Virginia aristocrat, inevitably, saw himself in relation to his own region. He lived in a static society which could endure almost anything except change. Instinctively, his first loyalty would go to the locality in which that society existed. He would fight to the limit of endurance to defend it, because in defending it he was defending everything that gave his own life its deepest meaning.

11   The Westerner, on the other hand, would fight with an equal tenacity for the broader concept of society. He fought so because everything he lived by was tied to growth, expansion, and a constantly widening horizon. What he lived by would survive or fall with the nation itself. He could not possibly stand by unmoved in the face of an attempt to destroy the Union. He would combat it with everything he had, because he could only see it as an effort to cut the ground out from under his feet.

12   So Grant and Lee were in complete contrast, representing two diametrically opposed elements in American life. Grant was the modern man emerging; beyond him, ready to come on the stage, was the great age of steel and machinery, of crowded cities and a restless burgeoning vitality. Lee might have ridden down from the old age of chivalry, lance in hand, silken banner

fluttering over his head. Each man was the perfect champion of his cause, drawing both his strengths and his weaknesses from the people he led.

13   Yet it was not all contrast, after all. Different as they were—in background, in personality, in underlying aspiration—these two great soldiers had much in common. Under everything else, they were marvelous fighters. Furthermore, their fighting qualities were really very much alike.

14   Each man had, to begin with, the great virtue of utter tenacity and fidelity. Grant fought his way down the Mississippi Valley in spite of acute personal discouragement and profound military handicaps. Lee hung on in the trenches at Petersburg after hope itself had died. In each man there was an indomitable quality . . . the born fighter's refusal to give up as long as he can still remain on his feet and lift his two fists.

15   Daring and resourcefulness they had, too: the ability to think faster and move faster than the enemy. These were the qualities which gave Lee the dazzling campaigns of Second Manassas and Chancellorsville and won Vicksburg for Grant.

16   Lastly, and perhaps greatest of all, there was the ability, at the end, to turn quickly from war to peace once the fighting was over. Out of the way these two men behaved at Appomattox came the possibility of a peace of reconciliation. It was a possibility not wholly realized, in the years to come, but which did, in the end, help the two sections to become one nation again . . . after a war whose bitterness might have seemed to make such a reunion wholly impossible. No part of either man's life became him more than the part he played in their brief meeting in the McLean house at Appomattox. Their behavior there put all succeeding generations of Americans in their debt. Two great Americans, Grant and Lee—very different, yet under everything very much alike. Their encounter at Appomattox was one of the great moments of American history.

Topics for Writing and Discussion

1.   What qualities and values did Lee and Grant each represent? How did their personal appearance and behavior reflect these qualities and values?

2.   Does Catton's essay encourage more admiration for one of the generals than the other? Which details most effectively characterize these two men?

3.   Catton's essay is rich in figurative language. Reread paragraphs 1, 3, 5, 7, 8, 9, 10, and 11, noticing the metaphors he uses. How does he use these comparisons to describe the generals and the way of life each represents?

4.   Sketch an outline of the essay and use the outline to analyze the structure Catton uses to contrast Grant and Lee. Note the two one-sentence par-

agraphs, 3 and 4. What do these paragraphs add to the essay? Could they be omitted? Combined with other paragraphs? What would be lost or gained through such changes?

5. While Grant and Lee embodied different ideals, Catton points out that they were also alike in a number of their virtues. Think of two people you admire for some sort of "greatness." In an essay of comparison, show how these two people are similar, even though they may be in different fields or in pursuit of different goals.

Barry Lopez (© Nancy Crampton)

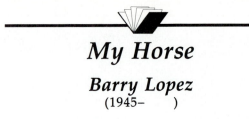

My Horse

Barry Lopez
(1945–   )

Widely acclaimed as a writer on environmental and
natural history issues, Barry Lopez' work reflects
his concern for the land and its inhabitants. His
books include *Desert Notes: Reflections in the Eye of
the Raven* (1976), *Of Wolves and Men* (1978), *Arctic
Dreams: Imagination and Desire in a Northern
Landscape* (1986), *Crossing Open Ground* (1988) and
Crow and Weasel (1990). He has received the Award
in Literature from the American Academy and
Institute of Arts and Letters for the body of his
work. In "My Horse," published in the *North
American Review*, Lopez ponders the link between
modern-day American road warriors and their
Native American predecessors.

1   It is curious that Indian warriors on the northern plains in the nineteenth
century, who were almost entirely dependent on the horse for mobility and
status, never gave their horses names. If you borrowed a man's horse and
went off raiding for other horses, however, or if you lost your mount in
battle and then jumped on mine and counted coup on an enemy—well, those
horses would have to be shared with the man whose horse you borrowed,
and that coup would be mine, not yours. Because even if I gave him no
name, he was my horse.

2   If you were a Crow warrior and I a young Teton Sioux out after a warrior's
identity and we came over a small hill somewhere in the Montana prairie and surprised each other, I could tell a lot about you by looking at
your horse.

3   Your horse might have feathers tied in his mane, or in his tail, or a medicine
bag tied around his neck. If I knew enough about the Crow, and had looked

at you closely, I might make some sense of the decoration, even guess who you were if you were well-known. If you had painted your horse I could tell even more, because we both decorated our horses with signs that meant the same things. Your white handprints high on his flanks would tell me you had killed an enemy in a hand-to-hand fight. Small horizontal lines stacked on your horse's foreleg, or across his nose, would tell me how many times you had counted coup. Horse hoof marks on your horse's rump, or three-sided boxes, would tell me how many times you had stolen horses. If there was a bright red square on your horse's neck I would know you were leading a war party and that there were probably others out there in the coulees behind you.

4   You might be painted all over as blue as the sky and covered with white dots, with your horse painted the same way. Maybe hailstorms were your power—or if I chased you a hailstorm might come down and hide you. There might be lightning bolts on the horse's legs and flanks, and I would wonder if you had lightning power, or a slow horse. There might be white circles around your horse's eyes to help him see better.

5   Or you might be like Crazy Horse, with no decoration, no marks on your horse to tell me anything, only a small lightning bolt on your cheek, a piece of turquoise tied behind your ear.

6   You might have scalps dangling from your rein.

7   I could tell something about you by your horse. All this would come to me in a few seconds. I might decide this was my moment and shout my war cry—*Hoka hey!* Or I might decide you were like the grizzly bear: I would raise my weapon to you in salute and go my way, to see you again when I was older.

8   I do not own a horse. I am attached to a truck, however, and I have come to think of it in a similar way. It has no name; it never occurred to me to give it a name. It has little decoration; neither of us is partial to decoration. I have a piece of turquoise in the truck because I had heard once that some of the southwestern tribes tied a small piece of turquoise in a horse's hock to keep him from stumbling. I like the idea. I also hang sage in the truck when I go on a long trip. But inside, the truck doesn't look much different from others that look just like it on the outside. I like it that way. Because I like my privacy.

9   For two years in Wyoming I worked on a ranch wrangling horses. The horse I rode when I had to have a good horse was a quarter horse and his name was Coke High. The name came with him. At first I thought he'd been named for the soft drink. I'd known stranger names given to horses by whites. Years later I wondered if some deviate Wyoming cowboy wise to cocaine had not named him. Now I think he was probably named after a rancher, an historical figure of the region. I never asked the people who owned him for fear of spoiling the spirit of my inquiry.

10   We were running over a hundred horses on this ranch. They all had names. After a few weeks I knew all the horses and the names too. You had to. No one knew how to talk about the animals or put them in order or tell the wranglers what to do unless they were using the names—Princess, Big Red, Shoshone, Clay.

11   My truck is named Dodge. The name came with it. I don't know if it was named after the town or the verb or the man who invented it. I like it for a name. Perfectly anonymous, like Rex for a dog, or Old Paint. You can't tell anything with a name like that.

12   The truck is a van. I call it a truck because it's not a car and because "van" is a suburban sort of consumer word, like "oxford loafer," and I don't like the sound of it. On the outside it looks like any other Dodge Sportsman 300. It's a dirty tan color. There are a few body dents, but it's never been in a wreck. I tore the antenna off against a tree on a pinched mountain road. A boy in Midland, Texas, rocked one of my rear view mirrors off. A logging truck in Oregon squeeze-fired a piece of debris off the road and shattered my windshield. The oil pan and gas tank are pug-faced from high-centering on bad roads. (I remember a horse I rode for a while named Targhee whose hocks were scarred from tangles in barbed wire when he was a colt and who spooked a lot in high grass, but these were not like "dents." They were more like bad tires.)

13   I like to travel. I go mostly in the winter and mostly on two-lane roads. I've driven the truck from Key West to Vancouver, British Columbia, and from Yuma to Long Island over the past four years. I used to ride Coke High only about five miles every morning when we were rounding up horses. Hard miles of twisting and turning. About six hundred miles a year. Then I'd turn him out and ride another horse for the rest of the day. That's what was nice about having a remuda. You could do all you had to do and not take it all out on your best horse. Three car family.

14   My truck came with a lot of seats in it and I've never really known what to do with them. Sometimes I put the seats in and go somewhere with a lot of people, but most of the time I leave them out. I like riding around with that empty cavern of space behind my head. I know it's something with a history to it, that there's truth in it, because I always rode a horse the same way—with empty saddle bags. In case I found something. The possibility of finding something is half the reason for being on the road.

15   The value of anything comes to me in its use. If I am not using something it is of no value to me and I give it away. I wasn't always that way. I used to keep everything I owned—just in case. I feel good about the truck because it gets used. A lot. To haul hay and firewood and lumber and rocks and garbage and animals. Other people have used it to haul furniture and freezers and dirt and recycled newspapers. And to move from one house to another. When I lend it for things like that I don't look to get anything back but

some gas (if we're going to be friends). But if you go way out in the country to a dump and pick up the things you can still find out there (once a load of cedar shingles we sold for $175 to an architect) I expect you to leave some of those things around my place when you come back—if I need them.

16 When I think back, maybe the nicest thing I ever put in that truck was timber wolves. It was a long night's drive from Oregon up into British Columbia. We were all very quiet about it; it was like moving clouds across the desert.

17 Sometimes something won't fit in the truck and I think about improving it—building a different door system, for example. I am forever going to add better gauges on the dash and a pair of driving lamps and a sunroof, but I never get around to doing any of it. I remember I wanted to improve Coke High once too, especially the way he bolted like a greyhound through patches of cottonwood on a river flat. But all I could do with him was to try to rein him out of it. Or hug his back.

18 Sometimes, road-stoned in a blur of country like southwestern Wyoming or North Dakota, I talk to the truck. It's like wandering on the high plains under a summer sun, on plains where, George Catlin wrote, you were "out of sight of land." I say what I am thinking out loud, or point at things along the road. It's a crazy, sun-stroked sort of activity, a sure sign it's time to pull over, to go for a walk, to make a fire and have some tea, to lie in the shade of the truck.

19 I've always wanted to pat the truck. It's basic to the relationship. But it never works.

20 I remember when I was on the ranch, just at sunrise, after I'd saddled Coke High, I'd be huddled down in my jacket smoking a cigarette and looking down into the valley, along the river where the other horses had spent the night. I'd turn to Coke and run my hand down his neck and slap-pat him on the shoulder to say I was coming up. It made a bond, an agreement we started the day with.

21 I've thought about that a lot with the truck, because we've gone out together at sunrise on so many mornings. I've even fumbled around trying to do it. But metal won't give.

22 The truck's personality is mostly an expression of two ideas: "with-you" and "alone." When Coke High was "with-you" he and I were the same animal. We could have cut a rooster out of a flock of chickens, we were so in tune. It's the same with the truck: rolling through Kentucky on a hilly two-lane road, three in the morning under a full moon and no traffic. Picture it. You roll like water.

23 There are other times when you are with each other but there's no connection at all. Coke got that way when he was bored and we'd fight each other about which way to go around a tree. When the truck gets like that—"alone"—it's because it feels its Detroit fat-ass design dragging at its heart and making a fool out of it.

24   I can think back over more than a hundred nights I've slept in the truck, sat in it with a lamp burning, bundled up in a parka, reading a book. It was always comfortable. A good place to wait out a storm. Like sleeping inside a buffalo.

25   The truck will go past 100,000 miles soon. I'll rebuild the engine and put a different transmission in it. I can tell from magazine advertisements that I'll never get another one like it. Because every year they take more of the heart out of them. One thing that makes a farmer or a rancher go sour is a truck that isn't worth a shit. The reason you see so many old pickups in ranch country is because these are the only ones with any heart. You can count on them. The weekend rancher runs around in a new pickup with too much engine and not enough transmission and with the wrong sort of tires because he can afford anything, even the worst. A lot of them have names for their pickups too.

26   My truck has broken down, in out of the way places at the worst of times. I've walked away and screamed the foulness out of my system and gotten the tools out. I had to fix a water pump in a blizzard in the Panamint Mountains in California once. It took all day with the Coleman stove burning under the engine block to keep my hands from freezing. We drifted into Beatty, Nevada, that night with it jury-rigged together with—I swear—baling wire, and we were melting snow as we went and pouring it in to compensate for the leaks.

27   There is a dent next to the door on the driver's side I put there one sweltering night in Miami. I had gone to the airport to meet my wife, whom I hadn't seen in a month. My hands were so swollen with poison ivy blisters I had to drive with my wrists. I had shut the door and was locking it when the window fell off its runners and slid down inside the door. I couldn't leave the truck unlocked because I had too much inside I didn't want to lose. So I just kicked the truck a blow in the side and went to work on the window. I hate to admit kicking the truck. It's like kicking a dog, which I've never done.

28   Coke High and I had an accident once. We hit a badger hole at a full gallop. I landed on my back and blacked out. When I came to, Coke High was about a hundred yards away. He stayed a hundred yards away for six miles, all the way back to the ranch.

29   I want to tell you about carrying those wolves, because it was a fine thing. There were ten of them. We had four in the truck with us in crates and six in a trailer. It was a five hundred mile trip. We went at night for the cool air and because there wouldn't be as much traffic. I could feel from the way the truck rolled along that its heart was in the trip. It liked the wolves inside it, the sweet odor that came from the crates. I could feel that same tireless wolf-lope developing in its wheels; it was like you might never have to stop for gas, ever again.

30   The truck gets very self-focused when it works like this; its heart is strong and it's good to be around it. It's good to be *with* it. You get the same feeling when you pull someone out of a ditch. Coke High and I pulled a Volkswagen out of the mud once, but Coke didn't like doing it very much. Speed, not strength, was his center. When the guy who owned the car thanked us and tried to pat Coke, the horse snorted and swung away, trying to preserve his distance, which is something a horse spends a lot of time on.

31   So does the truck.

32   Being distant lets the truck get its heart up. The truck has been cold and alone in Montana at 38 below zero. It's climbed horrible, eroded roads in Idaho. It's been burdened beyond overloading, and made it anyway. I've asked it to do these things because they build heart, and without heart all you have is a machine. You have nothing. I don't think people in Detroit know anything at all about heart. That's why everything they build dies so young.

33   One time in Arizona the truck and I came through one of the worst storms I've ever been in, an outrageous, angry blizzard. But we went down the road, right through it. You couldn't explain our getting through by the sort of tires I had on the truck, or the fact that I had chains on, or was a good driver, or had a lot of weight over my drive wheels or a good engine, because it was more than this. It was a contest between the truck and the blizzard—and the truck wouldn't quit. I could have gone to sleep and the truck would have just torn a road down Interstate 40 on its own. It scared the hell out of me; but it gave me heart, too.

34   We came off the Mogollon Rim that night and out of the storm and headed south for Phoenix. I pulled off the road to sleep for a few hours, but before I did I got out of the truck. It was raining. Warm rain. I tied a short piece of red avalanche cord into the grill. I left it there for a long time, like an eagle feather on a horse's tail. It flapped and spun in the wind. I could hear it ticking against the grill when I drove.

35   When I have to leave that truck I will just raise up my left arm—*Hoka hey!*—and walk away.

Topics for Writing and Discussion

1.   What analogy is Lopez drawing in this essay? What similarities does he see? Differences?

2.   How does Lopez make the comparison clear to the reader? What techniques are most persuasive? Why?

3.   How does Lopez' use of first-person point of view affect the reader's response to the essay?

4. Consider the essay's structure: is it formal or informal? How does his mention of transporting the wolves (paragraphs 16 and 29) affect essay unity? How does the essay's conclusion help tie the essay together?

5. Using Lopez' essay as a guide, write an essay comparing or contrasting a living creature to a mechanical object. Make the point of your essay clear to the reader—why is it important to see your subject in this way?

Lewis Thomas (© Nancy Crampton)

The Iks

Lewis Thomas
(1913–   )

Lewis Thomas was educated at Princeton
University and Harvard Medical School and is a
former president of the Memorial Sloan-Kettering
Cancer Center. His early writing on pathology
appeared in numerous scientific journals, and in
1971 he began contributing a regular column,
"Notes of a Biology Watcher," to the *New England
Journal of Medicine*. More recent work includes *Late
Night Thoughts on Listening to Mahler's Ninth
Symphony* (1983) and *Et Cetera, Et Cetera: Notes of a
Word-watcher* (1990). Thomas won the National
Book Award for Arts and Letters for his collection
of essays, *The Lives of A Cell: Notes of a Biology-
watcher* (1974). "The Iks," which appears in the
same collection, suggests both similarities and
differences between a tribe of displaced nomads
and groups in our own society.

1   The small tribe of Iks, formerly nomadic hunters and gatherers in the
mountain valleys of northern Uganda, have become celebrities, literary symbols for the ultimate fate of disheartened, heartless mankind at large. Two
disastrously conclusive things happened to them: the government decided
to have a national park, so they were compelled by law to give up hunting
in the valleys and become farmers on poor hillside soil, and then they were
visited for two years by an anthropologist who detested them and wrote a
book about them.

2   The message of the book is that the Iks have transformed themselves into
an irreversibly disagreeable collection of unattached, brutish creatures, totally selfish and loveless, in response to the dismantling of their traditional

culture. Moreover, this is what the rest of us are like in our inner selves, and we will all turn into Iks when the structure of our society comes all unhinged.

3   The argument rests, of course, on certain assumptions about the core of human beings, and is necessarily speculative. You have to agree in advance that man is fundamentally a bad lot, out for himself alone, displaying such graces as affection and compassion only as learned habits. If you take this view, the story of the Iks can be used to confirm it. These people seem to be living together, clustered in small, dense villages, but they are really solitary, unrelated individuals with no evident use for each other. They talk, but only to make ill-tempered demands and cold refusals. They share nothing. They never sing. They turn the children out to forage as soon as they can walk, and desert the elders to starve whenever they can, and the foraging children snatch food from the mouths of the helpless elders. It is a mean society.

4   They breed without love or even casual regard. They defecate on each other's doorsteps. They watch their neighbors for signs of misfortune, and only then do they laugh. In the book they do a lot of laughing, having so much bad luck. Several times they even laughed at the anthropologist, who found this especially repellent (one senses, between the lines, that the scholar is not himself the world's luckiest man). Worse, they took him into the family, snatched his food, defecated on his doorstep, and hooted dislike at him. They gave him two bad years.

5   It is a depressing book. If, as he suggests, there is only Ikness at the center of each of us, our sole hope for hanging onto the name of humanity will be in endlessly mending the structure of our society, and it is changing so quickly and completely that we may never find the threads in time. Meanwhile, left to ourselves alone, solitary, we will become the same joyless, zestless, untouching lone animals.

6   But this may be too narrow a view. For one thing, the Iks are extraordinary. They are absolutely astonishing, in fact. The anthropologist has never seen people like them anywhere, nor have I. You'd think, if they were simply examples of the common essence of mankind, they'd seem more recognizable. Instead, they are bizarre, anomalous. I have known my share of peculiar, difficult, nervous, grabby people, but I've never encountered any genuinely, consistently detestable human beings in all my life. The Iks sound more like abnormalities, maladies.

7   I cannot accept it. I do not believe that the Iks are representative of isolated, revealed man, unobscured by social habits. I believe their behavior is something extra, something laid on. This unremitting, compulsive repellence is a kind of complicated ritual. They must have learned to act this way; they copied it, somehow.

8   I have a theory, then. The Iks have gone crazy.

9   The solitary Ik, isolated in the ruins of an exploded culture, has built a new defense for himself. If you live in an unworkable society you can make up one of your own, and this is what the Iks have done. Each Ik has become a group, a one-man tribe on its own, a constituency.

10   Now everything falls into place. This is why they do seem, after all, vaguely familiar to all of us. We've seen them before. This is precisely the way groups of one size or another, ranging from committees to nations, behave. It is, of course, this aspect of humanity that has lagged behind the rest of evolution, and this is why the Ik seems so primitive. In his absolute selfishness, his incapacity to give anything away, no matter what, he is a successful committee. When he stands at the door of his hut, shouting insults at his neighbors in a loud harangue, he is a city addressing another city.

11   Cities have all the Ik characteristics. They defecate on doorsteps, in rivers and lakes, their own or anyone else's. They leave rubbish. They detest all neighboring cities, give nothing away. They even build institutions for deserting elders out of sight.

12   Nations are the most Iklike of all. No wonder the Iks seem familiar. For total greed, rapacity, heartlessness, and irresponsibility there is nothing to match a nation. Nations, by law, are solitary, self-centered, withdrawn into themselves. There is no such thing as affection between nations, and certainly no nation ever loved another. They bawl insults from their doorsteps, defecate into whole oceans, snatch all the food, survive by detestation, take joy in the bad luck of others, celebrate the death of others, live for the death of others.

13   That's it, and I shall stop worrying about the book. It does not signify that man is a sparse, inhuman thing at his center. He's all right. It only says what we've always known and never had enough time to worry about, that we haven't yet learned how to stay human when assembled in masses. The Ik, in his despair, is acting out this failure, and perhaps we should pay closer attention. Nations have themselves become too frightening to think about, but we might learn some things by watching these people.

Topics for Writing and Discussion

1.   In the first part of "The Iks," Thomas explains the premise of a book written about them by an anthropologist "who detested them." What comparison does Thomas identify as the central premise of the anthropologist's book? What details did the anthropologist use to support his comparison?

2.   Thomas's own explanation of the Iks' behavior contrasts with the anthropologist's. Describe the contrast and cite several examples offered by Thomas to support his refutation of the anthropologist's premise.

3. As Thomas argues against the anthropologist's view of humans as individuals, he offers his own view of humans as members of groups or institutions. Which view do you find more convincing? Do you agree or disagree completely with either view? If you agree, explain why. If you disagree, offer a third explanation of the Iks and their behavior.

4. Compare Thomas's view of humanity as explained in "The Iks" to his comments on a society obsessed with illness and death in "The Health Care System" (Chapter 11). Do the opinions expressed in both essays contradict or complement each other? Do you find one view more pessimistic than the other?

5. Thomas claims that humans behave differently as individuals and as members of groups. Develop your own examples to refute or agree with his premise. For example, you might compare and contrast your own behavior when you are acting as an individual with your behavior when you are a member of a committee, a club, a team, or a class.

Toni Morrison in her home along the Hudson River (© Sara Krulwich/The New York Times Pictures)

A Slow Walk of Trees

Toni Morrison
(1931–   )

Toni Morrison was born Chloe Anthony Wofford in Lorain, Ohio, a small town near Cleveland. She earned her B.A. from Howard University and her M.A. from Cornell. In 1964 she moved to New York City where she became an editor for Random House publishing company, helping to shape such books as the autobiographies of civil-rights activist Angela Davis and boxer Muhammad Ali. She has written six novels, all of which have won critical acclaim. *Sula* (1973) received a nomination for the National Book Award in 1975, while *Song of Solomon* (1977) received the National Book Critics Circle Award for fiction. Her most recent novels are *Tar Baby* (1981), *Beloved* (1986), also nominated for the National Book Award, and *Jazz* (1992). In "A Slow Walk of Trees," which was first published in the July 4, 1976, *New York Times Magazine,* she contrasts the way her grandfather and grandmother viewed the history of black people in America.

1   His name was John Solomon Willis, and when at age 5 he heard from the old folks that "the Emancipation Proclamation was coming," he crawled under the bed. It was his earliest recollection of what was to be his habitual response to the promise of white people: horror and an instinctive yearning for safety. He was my grandfather, a musician who managed to hold on to his violin but not his land. He lost all 88 acres of his Indian mother's inheritance to legal predators who built their fortunes on the likes of him. He was an unreconstructed black pessimist who, in spite of or be-

cause of emancipation, was convinced for 85 years that there was no hope whatever for black people in this country. His rancor was legitimate, for he, John Solomon, was not only an artist but a first-rate carpenter and farmer, reduced to sending home to his family money he made playing the violin because he was not able to find work. And this during the years when almost half the black male population were skilled craftsmen who lost their jobs to white ex-convicts and immigrant farmers.

2   His wife, however, was of a quite different frame of mind and believed that all things could be improved by faith in Jesus and an effort of the will. So it was she, Ardelia Willis, who sneaked her seven children out of the back window into the darkness, rather than permit the patron of their share-cropper's existence to become their executioner as well, and headed north in 1912, when 99.2 percent of all black people in the U.S. were native-born and only 60 percent of white Americans were. And it was Ardelia who told her husband that they could not stay in the Kentucky town they ended up in because the teacher didn't know long division.

3   They have been dead now for 30 years and more and I still don't know which of them came closer to the truth about the possibilities of life for black people in this country. One of their grandchildren is a tenured pro-fessor at Princeton. Another, who suffered from what the Peruvian poet called "anger that breaks a man into children," was picked up just as he entered his teens and emotionally lobotomized by the reformatories and mental institutions specifically designed to serve him. Neither John Solomon nor Ardelia lived long enough to despair over one or swell with pride over the other. But if they were alive today each would have selected and col-lected enough evidence to support the accuracy of the other's original point of view. And it would be difficult to convince either one that the other was right.

4   Some of the monstrous events that took place in John Solomon's America have been duplicated in alarming detail in my own America. There was the public murder of a President in a theater in 1865 and the public murder of another President on television in 1963. The Civil War of 1861 had its encore as the civil-rights movement of 1960. The torture and mutilation of a black West Point Cadet (Cadet Johnson Whittaker) in 1880 had its rerun with the 1970's murders of students at Jackson State College, Texas Southern and Southern University in Baton Rouge. And in 1976 we watch for what must be the thousandth time a pitched battle between the children of slaves and the children of immigrants—only this time, it is not the New York draft riots of 1863, but the busing turmoil in Paul Revere's home town, Boston.

5   Hopeless, he'd said. Hopeless. For he was certain that white people of every political, religious, geographical and economic background would band together against black people everywhere when they felt the threat of our progress. And a hundred years after he sought safety from the white man's "promise," somebody put a bullet in Martin Luther King's brain. And

not long before that some excellent samples of the master race demonstrated their courage and virility by dynamiting some little black girls to death. If he were here now, my grandfather, he would shake his head, close his eyes and pull out his violin—too polite to say, "I told you so." And his wife would pay attention to the music but not to the sadness in her husband's eyes, for she would see what she expected to see—not the occasional historical repetition, but, *like the slow walk of certain species of trees from the flatlands up into the mountains,* she would see the signs of irrevocable and permanent change. She, who pulled her girls out of an inadequate school in the Cumberland Mountains, knew all along that the gentlemen from Alabama who had killed the little girls would be rounded up. And it wouldn't surprise her in the least to know that the number of black college graduates jumped 12 percent in the last three years: 47 percent in 20 years. That there are 140 black mayors in this country; 14 black judges in the District Circuit, 4 in the Courts of Appeals and one on the Supreme Court. That there are 17 blacks in Congress, one in the Senate; 276 in state legislatures—223 in state houses, 53 in state senates. That there are 112 elected black police chiefs and sheriffs, 1 Pulitzer Prize winner; 1 winner of the Prix de Rome; a dozen or so winners of the Guggenheim; 4 deans of predominantly white colleges. . . . Oh, her list would go on and on. But so would John Solomon's sweet sad music.

6   While my grandparents held opposite views on whether the fortunes of black people were improving, my own parents struck similarly opposed postures, but from another slant. They differed about whether the moral fiber of white people would ever improve. Quite a different argument. The old folks argued about how and if black people could improve themselves, who could be counted on to help us, who would hinder us and so on. My parents took issue over the question of whether it was possible for white people to improve. They assumed that black people were the humans of the globe, but had serious doubts about the quality and existence of white humanity. Thus my father, distrusting every word and every gesture of every white man on earth, assumed that the white man who crept up the stairs one afternoon had come to molest his daughters and threw him down the stairs and then our tricycle after him. (I think my father was wrong, but considering what I have seen since, it may have been very healthy for me to have witnessed that as my first black-white encounter.) My mother, however, *believed* in them—their possibilities. So when the meal we got on relief was bug-ridden, she wrote a long letter to Franklin Delano Roosevelt. And when white bill collectors came to our door, it was she who received them civilly and explained in a sweet voice that we were people of honor and that the debt would be taken care of. Her message to Roosevelt got through—our meal improved. Her message to the bill collectors did not always get through and there was occasional violence when my father (self-exiled to the bedroom for fear he could not hold his temper) would hear that her

reasonableness had failed. My mother was always wounded by these scenes, for she thought the bill collector knew that she loved good credit more than life and that being in arrears on a payment horrified her probably more than it did him. So she thought he was rude because he was white. For years she walked to utility companies and department stores to pay bills in person and even now she does not seem convinced that checks are legal tender. My father loved excellence, worked hard (he held three jobs at once for 17 years) and was so outraged by the suggestion of personal slackness that he could explain it to himself only in terms of racism. He was a fastidious worker who was frightened of one thing: unemployment. I can remember now the doomsday-cum-graveyard sound of "laid off" and how the minute school was out he asked us, "Where you workin'?" Both my parents believed that all succor and aid came from themselves and their neighborhood, since "they"—white people in charge and those not in charge but in obstructionist positions—were in some way fundamentally, genetically corrupt.

7   So I grew up in a basically racist household with more than a child's share of contempt for white people. And for each white friend I acquired who made a small crack in that contempt, there was another who repaired it. For each one who related to me as a person, there was one who in my presence at least, became actively "white." And like most black people of my generation, I suffer from racial vertigo that can be cured only by taking what one needs from one's ancestors. John Solomon's cynicism and his deployment of his art as both weapon and solace, Ardelia's faith in the magic that can be wrought by sheer effort of the will; my mother's open-mindedness in each new encounter and her habit of trying reasonableness first; my father's temper, his impatience and his efforts to keep "them" (throw them) out of his life. And it is out of these learned and selected attitudes that I look at the quality of life for my people in this country now. These widely disparate and sometimes conflicting views, I suspect, were held not only by me, but by most black people. Some I know are clearer in their positions, have not sullied their anger with optimism or dirtied their hope with despair. But most of us are plagued by a sense of being worn shell-thin by constant repression and hostility as well as the impression of being buoyed by visible testimony of tremendous strides. There *is* repetition of the grotesque in our history. And there *is* the miraculous walk of trees. The question is whether our walk is progress or merely movement. O. J. Simpson leaning on a Hertz car *is* better than the Gold Dust Twins on the back of a soap box. But is "Good Times" better than Stepin Fetchit? Has the first order of business been taken care of? Does the law of the land work for us?

8   Are white people who murder black people punished with at least the same dispatch that sends black teen-age truants to Coxsackie? Can we relax now and discuss "The Jeffersons" instead of genocide? Or is the difference between the two only the difference between a greedy pointless white lifestyle and a messy pointless black death? Now that Mr. Poitier and Mr.

Belafonte have shot up all the racists in "Buck and the Preacher," have they all gone away? Can we really move into better neighborhoods and not be set on fire? Is there anybody who will lay me a $5 bet on it?

9   The past decade is a fairly good index of the odds at which you lay your money down.

10   Ten years ago in Queens, as black people like me moved into a neighborhood 20 minutes away from the Triborough Bridge, "for sale" signs shot up in front of white folks' houses like dandelions after a hot spring rain. And the black people smiled. "Goody, goody," said my neighbor. "Maybe we can push them on out to sea. You think?"

11   Now I live in another neighborhood, 20 minutes away from the George Washington Bridge, and again the "for sale" signs are pushing up out of the ground. Fewer, perhaps, and for different reasons, perhaps. Still the Haitian lady and I smile at each other. "My, my," she says "they goin' on up to the hills? Seem like they just come from there." "The woods," I say. "They like to live in the woods." She nods with infinite understanding, then shrugs. The Haitians have already arranged for one mass in the church to be said in French, already have their own newspaper, stores, community center. That's not movement. That's progress.

12   But the decade has other revelations. Ten years ago, young, bright, energetic blacks were sought out, pursued and hired into major corporations, major networks, and onto the staffs of newspapers and national magazines. *Many survived that courtship, some even with their souls intact.* Newscasters, corporate lawyers, marketing specialists, journalists, production managers, plant foremen, college deans. But many more spend a lot of time on the telephone these days, or at the typewriter preparing résumés, which they send out (mostly to friends now) with little notes attached: "Is there anything you know of?" Or they think there is a good book in the story of what happened to them, the great hoax that was played on them. They are right, of course, about the hoax, for many of them were given elegant executive jobs with the work drained out. Work minus power. Work minus decision-making. Work minus dominion. Affirmative Action Make Believe that a lot of black people *did* believe because they also believed that the white people in those nice offices were not like the ones in the general store or in the plumbers' union—that they were fundamentally kind, or fair, or something. Anything but the desperate prisoners of economics they turned out to be, holding on to their dominion with a tenacity and sang-froid that can only be described as Nixonian. So the bright and the black (architects, reporters, vice-presidents in charge of public relations) walk the streets right along with that astounding 38 percent of the black teen-aged female work force that does not have and never has had a job. So the black female college graduate earns two-thirds of what a white male high-school dropout earns. So the black people who put everything into community-action programs

supported by Government funds have found themselves bereft of action, bereft of funds and all but bereft of community.

13   This decade has been rife with disappointment in practically every place where we thought we saw permanent change: Hostos, CUNY, and the black-studies departments that erupted like minivolcanoes on campuses all over the nation; easy integrations of public-school systems; acceleration of promotion in factories and businesses. But now when we describe what has happened we cannot do it without using the verbs of upheaval and destruction: Open admission *closes;* minority-student quotas *fall* or *discontinue;* salary gaps between blacks and whites *widen;* black-studies departments *merge.* And the only growth black people can count on is in the prison population and the unemployment line. Even busing, which used to be a plain, if emotional, term at best, has now taken on an adjective normally reserved for rape and burglary—it is now called "forced" busing.

14   All of that counts, but I'm not sure that in the long haul it matters. Maybe Ardelia Willis had the best idea. One sees signs of her vision and the fruits of her prophecy in spite of the dread-lock statistics. The trees *are* walking, albeit slowly and quietly and without the fanfare of a cross-country run. It seems that at last black people have abandoned our foolish dependency on the Government to do the work that we once thought all of its citizenry would be delighted to do. Our love affair with the Federal Government is over. We misjudged the ardor of its attention. We thought its majority constituency would *prefer* having their children grow up among happy, progressive, industrious, contented black children rather than among angry, disenchanted and dangerous ones. That the profit motive of industry alone would keep us employed and therefore spending, and that our poverty was bad for business. We thought landlords wanted us to have a share in our neighborhoods and therefore love and care for them. That city governments wanted us to control our schools and therefore preserve them.

15   We were wrong. And now, having been eliminated from the lists of urgent national priorities, from TV documentaries and the platitudes of editorials, black people have chosen, or been forced to seek safety from the white man's promise, but happily not under a bed. More and more, there is the return to Ardelia's ways: the exercise of the will, the recognition of obstacles as only that—obstacles, not fixed stars. Black judges are fixing appropriate rather than punitive bail for black "offenders" and letting the rest of the community of jurisprudence scream. Young black women are leaving plush Northern jobs to sit in their living rooms and teach black children, work among factory women and spend months finding money to finance the college education of young blacks. Groups of blacks are buying huge tracts of land in the South and cutting off entirely the dependency of whole communities on grocery chains. For the first time, significant numbers of black people are returning or migrating to the South to focus on the acquisition

of land, the transferral of crafts and skills, and the sharing of resources, the rebuilding of neighborhoods.

16   In the shambles of closing admissions, falling quotas, widening salary gaps and merging black-studies departments, builders and healers are working quietly among us. They are not like the heroes of old, the leaders we followed blindly and upon whom we depended for everything, or the blacks who had accumulated wealth for its own sake, fame, medals or some public acknowledgment of success. These are the people whose work is real and pointed and clear in its application to the race. Some are old and have been at work for a long time in and out of the public eye. Some are new and just finding out what their work is. But they are unmistakably the natural aristocrats of the race. The ones who refuse to imitate, to compromise, and who are indifferent to public accolade. Whose work is free or priceless. They take huge risks economically and personally. They are not always popular, even among black people, but they are the ones whose work black people respect. They are the healers. Some are nowhere near the public eye: Ben Chavis, preacher and political activist languishing now in North Carolina prisons; Robert Moses, a pioneering activist; Sterling Brown, poet and teacher; Father Al McKnight, land reformer; Rudy Lombard, urban sociologist; Lerone Bennett, historian; C.L.R. James, scholar; Alyce Gullattee, psychologist and organizer. Others are public legends: Judge Crockett, Judge Bruce Wright, Stevie Wonder, Ishmael Reed, Miles Davis, Richard Pryor, Muhammad Ali, Fannie Lou Hamer, Eubie Blake, Angela Davis, Bill Russell. . . .

17   But a complete roll-call is neither fitting nor necessary. They know who they are and so do we. They clarify our past, make livable our present and are certain to shape our future. And since the future is where our immortality as a race lies, no overview of the state of black people at this time can ignore some speculation on the only ones certain to live it—the children.

18   They are both exhilarating and frightening, those black children, and a source of wonderment to me. Although statistics about black teen-age crime and the "failure" of the courts to gut them are regularly printed and regularly received with outrage and fear, the children I know and see, those born after 1960, do not make such great copy. They are those who have grown up with nothing to prove to white people, whose perceptions of themselves are so new, so different, so focused they appear to me to be either magnificent hybrids or throwbacks to the time when our ancestors were called "royal." They are the baby sisters of the sit-in generation, the sons of the neighborhood blockbusters, the nephews of jailed revolutionaries, and a huge number who have had college graduates in their families for three and four generations. I thought we had left them nothing to love and nothing to want to know. I thought that those who exhibited some excitement about their future had long ago looked into the eyes of their teachers and were either saddened or outraged by the death of possibility they found there. I thought that those who were interested in the past had looked into the faces of their

parents and seen betrayal. I thought the state had deprived them of a land and the landlords and banks had deprived them of a turf. So how is it that, with nothing to love, nothing they need to know, landless, turfless, minus a future and a past, these black children look us dead in the eye? They seem not to know how to apologize. And even when they are wrong they do not ask for forgiveness. It is as though they are waiting for us to apologize to them, to beg their pardon, to seek their approval. What species of black is this that not only does not choose to grovel, but doesn't know how? How will they keep jobs? How will they live? Won't they be killed before they reproduce? But they are unafraid. Is it because they refuse to see the world as we did? Is it because they have rejected both land and turf to seek instead a world? Maybe they finally got the message that we had been shouting into their faces; that they *live* here, *belong* here on this planet earth and that it is *theirs*. So they watch us with the eyes of poets and carpenters and musicians and scholars and other people who know who they are because they have invented themselves and know where they are going because they have envisioned it. All of which would please Ardelia—and John Solomon, too, I think. After all, he did hold on to his violin.

Topics for Writing and Discussion

1. How did Morrison's grandfather view the future of African Americans in the United States? How did her grandmother view that same future? List five details from the essay that could be used to support her grandfather's view and five details that could be used to support her grandmother's.

2. What is Morrison's main idea in this essay? Does she ever directly state her thesis? With whose ideas does she seem to identify most closely, those of her grandmother or of her grandfather?

3. Read the section of the essay comparing the situations of African Americans ten years before the essay was written to the situations of African Americans living at the time Morrison was writing. How does that comparison relate to the main comparison of the essay?

4. What kind of details, reasons, and examples does Morrison use to develop her ideas? Note, for instance, her use of statistics as well as her use of personal anecdotes.

5. Morrison uses the analogy of "the slow walk of certain species of trees from the flatlands up into the mountains" to describe the way her grandmother saw the progress of African Americans. Develop your own analogy to describe the way you see changes in the course of your own life. Then contrast your view with the view someone else might take of the same changes.

Writing Assignments for Chapter Eight
Comparison and Contrast

1. In "Two Ways of Looking at the River" Samuel Clemens describes the differences in his point of view before and after he became a riverboat pilot. Write an essay in which you contrast an earlier view of a scene with a later view. For instance, you might think of a visit to a childhood haunt or family vacation spot or even your room at home since you've been away at college. Has the place itself changed or has only your perception of it altered?

2. After reading Russell Baker's "The Two Ismo's," write a serious essay that contrasts two groups of people you see on your campus whose beliefs and activities seem totally opposed to one another. As you present your two groups, make a point about a particular kind of social value or controversy you see emerging today.

3. In "Grant and Lee: A Study in Contrasts" Bruce Catton contrasts two famous Civil War antagonists. Select two famous rivals from your field of study or from current politics, sports, or some social controversy. Familiarize yourself with each person's beliefs and present your readers with a clear contrast. You may either take a position that argues support for one person over the other, or you may make your essay an objective look at both parties that will allow your readers to decide a preference for themselves.

4. Analogies between a disagreeable tribe and our modern communities surface in Lewis Thomas's essay "The Iks." Nations and cities, claims Thomas, amass rubbish, foul the water, remain isolated and quarrelsome, and even have institutions for hiding away their old people—just like the Iks. Write an essay in which you compare yourself (or some group of people you know) to a particular place; what do you and this location have in common? Be sure to select a place that will enable you to make a clear point about your nature (or that of the people you're writing about), and use enough specific points of comparison so that the analogy seems convincing.

5. Contrast two towns (or two specific parts of a large city) you know well for an out-of-state friend who's considering a short visit to each. Is one place more Ik-like than the other? You might consider giving each place a personality to help you develop your contrast for your reader.

6. In "My Horse" Barry Lopez praises his truck, even though it is old, worn, and dented. According to Lopez, his truck has "heart" and gives this quality to its owner too. Car manufacturers in Detroit, says Lopez, know nothing about heart: "That's why everything they build dies so young." Think about an older possession, product, or service that you believe is far superior to its current or modern version. Is the older product better because it is more reliable, durable, or even more aesthetically pleasing? For example, are cars better today? Do you secretly prefer records to CDs? Is television programming less entertaining now than in its Golden Age? Are visits to movie theaters as pleasant as they used to be? Write an essay defending your choice of old-over-new, making your standards for judgment clear to your readers.

7. In "A Slow Walk of Trees" Toni Morrison contrasts her grandparents' views "on the possibilities of life for black people in this country." That contrast, in turn, helps her clarify her own point of view. Select an important social or political belief and make your attitude toward this subject clear by contrasting your opinion with that of your parents, brothers or sisters, grandparents, or close friends.

Chapter Nine

Division and Classification

To make large or complex subjects easier to comprehend, we frequently apply the principles of *division* and *classification.*

Division

Division is the act of separating one thing into its component parts so that the thing may be better understood or used by the reader. For example, consider a complex subject such as the national budget. Perhaps you have seen a picture on television or in the newspaper of the budget represented by a circle or a pie that has been divided into parts and labeled: a certain percentage or "slice" of the budget for military spending, a certain amount designated for social services, another for education, and so on. By studying the budget after it has been divided into its parts, taxpayers may have a better sense of how their money is being spent.

As a student, you see division in action in many of your college courses. Your anthropology teacher, for instance, might lecture on the Mesa Verde Indian Era by dividing it into its important time periods—Basket Maker (A.D. 1–450), Modified Basket Maker (A.D. 450–750), and Pueblo (A.D. 750–1300)—so that your class can clearly understand the characteristics of the era. Your chemistry lab-instructor may ask you to break down a substance into its components to learn how the parts interact to form the chemical. Even this textbook is divided into chapters to make it easier for you to use. When you think of *division*, then, think of dividing or separating one subject (often a large or complex or unfamiliar one) into its parts to help people understand it more easily.

Classification

While the principle of division calls for separating one thing into its parts, *classification* systematically groups a number of things into categories to make the information easier to grasp. Without some sort of imposed system of order, a body of information can be a jumble of facts and figures. For example, at some point you've probably turned to the classified ads in the newspaper; if the ads were not classified into categories such as "houses to rent," "cars for sale," and "help wanted," you would have to search through countless ads to find the service or item you needed.

Classification occurs everywhere around you. As a student, you may be classified as a freshman, sophomore, junior, or senior; you may also be classified by your major. If you vote, you may be categorized as a Democrat, Republican, Socialist, or something else; if you attend religious services, you may be classified as Baptist, Methodist, Catholic, Jewish, and so on. The books you buy may be grouped and shelved by the bookstore into "mysteries," "westerns," "biographies," "adventure stories," and other categories; the movies you see have already been typed as "G," "PG," "PG-13," "R," "X," or "NC-17." Professionals classify almost every kind of knowledge: ornithologists classify birds; etymologists classify words by origins; botanists classify plants; zoologists classify animals.

Remember that *classification* differs from division in that it sorts and organizes *many* things into appropriate groups, types, kinds, or categories. *Division* begins with *one* thing and separates it into its parts.

Uses of Division and Classification

Writers use division and classification to explain, to organize, and to clarify. William Zinsser in "College Pressures," for example, classifies into four types the pressures he sees weighing on today's college students. In "Friends, Good Friends, and Such Good Friends," Judith Viorst classifies her friends into a variety of categories to show the roles they play in her life. Sometimes authors divide or classify to give us a new way of looking at something. E. B. White, for instance, maintains in his essay "Three New Yorks" that there are really three cities rather than one. Many classification or division essays, especially those that appear in popular magazines and newspapers, often wish to entertain or evaluate as well as to inform, hence such articles as "Blind Dates to Avoid," "The Three Best Restaurants in Chicago," "The Four Biggest Mistakes in Buying a Used Car."

Writing the Division or Classification Essay

Once you have determined that your topic should be developed using division or classification, you may need some guidelines to help in planning your essay. The following hints should be useful.

1. *Select one principle of classification or division and apply it consistently.*

If you are classifying all the students at your school by major, for instance, don't suddenly switch to classification by college: French, economics, psychology, *arts and sciences*, math, and chemistry. A similar error occurs in this classification of dogs by breeds because it includes a physical characteristic: spaniels, terriers, *long-haired*, hounds, and retrievers. Decide on what basis you will classify or divide your subject and then be consistent throughout your essay.

2. *Make the purpose of your division or classification clear to your audience.*

Don't just announce that "There are four kinds of 'X'" or that "'Z' has three important parts." Why does your particular audience need this information? Consider these sample thesis statements:

> By recognizing the three kinds of poisonous snakes in this area, campers and backpackers may be able to take the proper medical steps if they are bitten.
>
> Knowing the four types of spinning reels will enable novice fishermen to purchase the equipment best suited to their needs.
>
> While karate has become a popular form of exercise as well as of self-defense, few people know what the six levels of achievement—or "belts" as they are called—actually stand for.

Organize your material for a particular purpose and then explain to your readers what that purpose is.

3. *After you have selected the principle you will use to divide or classify your topic, decide how you will discuss the parts or categories.*

A classification or division essay is not a mechanical list; each category or part should contain enough specific details to make it clearly recognizable and interesting. To present each category or part you may draw upon the methods of development you already know, such as illustration, description, comparison and contrast, and definition. Try to use the same techniques in each category so that no one category or part of your essay seems underdeveloped or unclear.

4. *Make sure that the categories you establish are mutually exclusive.*

For example, if you were classifying college students into groups, you might use undergraduates, graduate students, and postgraduate students, but you could not include commuter students and resident students because the latter two types probably also belong to one of the former groups. Similarly, in a classification of soft drinks by flavor, to include sugar-free with cola, root beer, orange, grape, and so on, is misleading because sugar-free drinks come in many different flavors. In other words, make each category distinct.

5.   *Account for all the parts in your division or classification.*

Don't, for instance, claim to classify all the trees native to your hometown and then leave out one or more species. For a short essay, narrow your ruling principle rather than omit categories. You couldn't, for instance, classify all the architectural styles in America in a short paper, but you might be able to discuss the major styles on your campus. In the same manner, the enormous task of classifying all types of mental illness might be narrowed to the most common forms of schizophrenia in American children under twelve.

As you read the essays that follow, carefully examine the authors' use of division or classification and note the ways that their use of the strategy helps to clarify, organize, or give insight into their subjects.

John Updike in his publisher's office (© Nancy Crampton)

Three Boys

John Updike
(1932–   )

John Updike grew up in Shillington, Pennsylvania,
where his father taught in the local high school.
Updike describes his typical middle-class American
boyhood in "Three Boys," an essay that first
appeared in *Five Boyhoods,* a collection of short
autobiographies. Updike graduated from Harvard
in 1954 and immediately began his career as a
writer, contributing poems, essays, and short
stories to national publications including the *New
Yorker.* Some of his best-known novels include
Rabbit, Run (1961), *Rabbit Redux* (1971), and *Rabbit
Is Rich* (1981). In 1990, Updike completed the
Rabbit series with the publication of *Rabbit at Rest.*
In "Three Boys" Updike categorizes his childhood
acquaintances. His tightly woven description shows
us each boy's unique qualities and explains the
effect he had on the young Updike.

1 **A**, B, and C, I'll say, in case they care. A lived next door; he *loomed*
next door, rather. He seemed immense—a great wallowing fatso stuffed with
possessions; he was the son of a full-fashioned knitter. He seemed to have
a beer-belly; after several generations beer-bellies may become congenital.
Also his face had no features. It was just a blank ball on his shoulders. He
used to call me "Ostrich," after Disney's Ollie Ostrich. My neck was not
very long; the name seemed horribly unfair; it was its injustice that made
me cry. But nothing I could say, or scream, would make him stop, and I
still, now and then—in reading, say, a book review by one of the apple-
cheeked savants of the quarterlies or one of the pious gremlins who manufacture puns for *Time*—get the old sensations: my ears close up, my eyes

go warm, my chest feels thin as an eggshell, my voice churns silently in my stomach. From A I received my first impression of the smug, chinkless, irresistible *power* of stupidity; it is the most powerful force on earth. It says "Ostrich" often enough, and the universe crumbles.

2   A was more than a boy, he was a force-field that could manifest itself in many forms, that could take the wiry, disconsolate shape of wide-mouthed, tiny-eared boys who would now and then beat me up on the way back from school. I did not greatly mind being beaten up, though I resisted it. For one thing, it firmly involved me, at least during the beating, with the circumambient humanity that so often seemed evasive. Also, the boys who applied the beating were misfits, periodic flunkers, who wore corduroy knickers with threadbare knees and men's shirts with the top button buttoned—this last an infallible sign of deep poverty. So that I felt there was some justice, some condonable revenge, being applied with their fists to this little teacher's son. And then there was the delicious alarm of my mother and grandmother when I returned home bloody, bruised, and torn. My father took the attitude that it was making a boy of me, an attitude I dimly shared. He and I both were afraid of me becoming a sissy—he perhaps more afraid than I.

3   When I was eleven or so I met B. It was summer and I was down at the playground. He was pushing a little tank with moving rubber treads up and down the hills in the sandbox. It was a fine little toy, mottled with camouflage green; patriotic manufacturers produced throughout the war millions of such authentic miniatures which we maneuvered with authentic, if miniature, militance. Attracted by the toy, I spoke to him; though taller and a little older than I, he had my dull straight brown hair and a look of being also alone. We became fast friends. He lived just up the street—toward the poorhouse, the east part of the street, from which the little winds of tragedy blew. He had just moved from the Midwest, and his mother was a widow. Beside wage war, we did many things together. We played marbles for days at a time, until one of us had won the other's entire coffee-canful. With jigsaws we cut out of plywood animals copied from comic books. We made movies by tearing the pages from Big Little Books and coloring the drawings and pasting them in a strip and winding them on toilet-paper spools, and making a cardboard carton a theatre. We rigged up telephones, and racing wagons, and cities of the future, using orange crates and cigar boxes and peanut-butter jars and such potent debris. We loved Smokey Stover and were always saying "Foo." We had an intense spell of Monopoly. He called me "Uppy"—the only person who ever did. I remember once, knowing he was coming down that afternoon to my house to play Monopoly, in order to show my joy I set up the board elaborately, with the Chance and Community Chest cards fanned painstakingly, like spiral staircases. He came into the room, groaned, "Uppy, what are you doing?" and impatiently scrabbled the cards together in a sensible pile. The older we got, the more the year between us told, and the more my friendship embarrassed him. We fought.

Once, to my horror, I heard myself taunting him with the fact that he had no father. The unmentionable, the unforgivable. I suppose we patched things up, children do, but the fabric had been torn. He had a long, pale, serious face, with buckteeth, and is probably an electronics engineer somewhere now, doing secret government work.

4   So through B I first experienced the pattern of friendship. There are three stages. First, acquaintance: we are new to each other, make each other laugh in surprise, and demand nothing beyond politeness. The death of the one would startle the other, no more. It is a pleasant stage, a stable stage; on austere rations of exposure it can live a lifetime, and the two parties to it always feel a slight gratification upon meeting, will feel vaguely confirmed in their human state. Then comes intimacy: now we laugh before two words of the joke are out of the other's mouth, because we know what he will say. Our two beings seem marvelously joined, from our toes to our heads, along tingling points of agreement; everything we venture is right, everything we put forth lodges in a corresponding socket in the frame of the other. The death of one would grieve the other. To be together is to enjoy a mounting excitement, a constant echo and amplification. It is an ecstatic and unstable stage, bound of its own agitation to tip into the third: revulsion. One or the other makes a misjudgment; presumes; puts forth that which does not meet agreement. Sometimes there is an explosion; more often the moment is swallowed in silence, and months pass before its nature dawns. Instead of dissolving, it grows. The mind, the throat, are clogged; forgiveness, forgetfulness, that have arrived so often, fail. Now everything jars and is distasteful. The betrayal, perhaps a tiny fraction in itself, has inverted the tingling column of agreement, made all pluses minuses. Everything about the other is hateful, despicable; yet he cannot be dismissed. We have confided in him too many minutes, too many words; he has those minutes and words as hostages, and his confidences are embedded in us where they cannot be scraped away, and even rivers of time cannot erode them completely, for there are indelible stains. Now—though the friends may continue to meet, and smile, as if they had never trespassed beyond acquaintance—the death of the one would please the other.

5   An unhappy pattern to which C is an exception. He was my friend before kindergarten, he is my friend still. I go to his home now, and he and his wife serve me and my wife with alcoholic drinks and slices of excellent cheese on crisp crackers, just as twenty years ago he served me with treats from his mother's refrigerator. He was a born host, and I a born guest. Also he was intelligent. If my childhood's brain, when I look back at it, seems a primitive mammal, a lemur or shrew, his brain was an angel whose visitation was widely hailed as wonderful. When in school he stood to recite, his cool rectangular forehead glowed. He tucked his right hand into his left armpit and with his left hand mechanically tapped a pencil against his thigh. His answers were always correct. He beat me at spelling bees and, in another

sort of competition, when we both collected Big Little Books, he outbid me for my supreme find (in the attic of a third boy), the first Mickey Mouse. I can still see that book, I wanted it so badly, in paper tan with age and its drawings done in Disney's primitive style, when Mickey's black chest is naked like a child's and his eyes are two nicked oblongs. Losing it was perhaps a lucky blow; it helped wean me away from hope of ever having possessions.

6   C was fearless. He deliberately set fields on fire. He engaged in rock-throwing duels with tough boys. One afternoon he persisted in playing quoits with me although—as the hospital discovered that night—his appendix was nearly bursting. He was enterprising. He peddled magazine subscriptions door-to-door; he mowed neighbors' lawns; he struck financial bargains with his father. He collected stamps so well his collection blossomed into a stamp company that filled his room with steel cabinets and mimeograph machinery. He collected money—every time I went over to his house he would get out a little tin box and count the money in it for me: $27.50 one week, $29.95 the next, $30.90 the next—all changed into new bills nicely folded together. It was a strange ritual, whose meaning for me was: since he was doing it, I didn't have to. His money made me richer. We read Ellery Queen and played chess and invented board games and discussed infinity together. In later adolescence, he collected records. He liked the Goodman quintets but loved Fats Waller. Sitting there in that room so familiar to me, where the machinery of the Shilco Stamp Company still crowded the walls and for that matter the tin box of money might still be stashed, while my thin friend grunted softly along with that dead dark angel on "You're Not the Only Oyster in the Stew," I felt, in the best sense, patronized: the perfect guest of the perfect host. What made it perfect was that we had both spent our entire lives in Shillington.

Topics for Writing and Discussion

1. Describe A and explain what Updike means when he says that "A was more than a boy, he was a force-field that could manifest itself in many forms. . . ." What group of individuals does he represent to Updike?

2. Updike divides his friendship with B into three stages. What are those stages? Do you agree with this definition of friendship?

3. How does Updike's attitude toward owning things change as he comes to know A, B, and C? What does he learn from C that neither A nor B could teach him? How does C teach Updike this lesson?

4. Compare Updike's attitude toward and definition of friendship with Judith Viorst's attitude and definition in "Friends, Good Friends, and Such Good Friends." Do you agree with one or the other? Why?

5. Write an essay tracing the growth of a friendship. Divide your life into a series of time periods that will help the reader see how the relationship developed.

Judith Viorst. (© 1991 by Jill Krementz)

Friends, Good Friends, and Such Good Friends

Judith Viorst
(1936–   )

A contributing editor to *Redbook* magazine, Judith Viorst was born in Newark, New Jersey, and educated at Rutgers University. Her poetic monologues written for the CBS special "Annie, the Woman in the Life of a Man" won an Emmy Award in 1970. She has published a collection of poems, *It's Hard to Be Hip over Thirty, and Other Tragedies of Married Life* (1970), and a collection of prose, *Yes, Married: A Saga of Love and Complaint* (1972). She also writes children's books, including the classic *Alexander and the Terrible, Horrible, No Good, Very Bad Day* (1972). More recent works are *Forever Fifty and Other Negotiations* (1989) and *Earrings!* (1990). "Friends, Good Friends, and Such Good Friends" first appeared in *Redbook* in 1977. In this essay, Viorst establishes categories to describe her friends, past and present, and to explain her changing beliefs about the nature of friendship.

1   Women are friends, I once would have said, when they totally love and support and trust each other, and bare to each other the secrets of their souls, and run—no questions asked—to help each other, and tell harsh truths to each other (no, you can't wear that dress unless you lose ten pounds first) when harsh truths must be told.

2   Women are friends, I once would have said, when they share the same affection for Ingmar Bergman, plus train rides, cats, warm rain, charades,

Camus, and hate with equal ardor Newark and Brussels sprouts and Lawrence Welk and camping.

3   In other words, I once would have said that a friend is a friend all the way, but now I believe that's a narrow point of view. For the friendships I have and the friendships I see are conducted at many levels of intensity, serve many different functions, meet different needs and range from those as all-the-way as the friendship of the soul sisters mentioned above to that of the most nonchalant and casual playmates.

4   Consider these varieties of friendship:

5   1. Convenience friends. These are the women with whom, if our paths weren't crossing all the time, we'd have no particular reason to be friends: a next-door neighbor, a woman in our car pool, the mother of one of our children's closest friends or maybe some mommy with whom we serve juice and cookies each week at the Glenwood Co-op Nursery.

6   Convenience friends are convenient indeed. They'll lend us their cups and silverware for a party. They'll drive our kids to soccer when we're sick. They'll take us to pick up our car when we need a lift to the garage. They'll even take our cats when we go on vacation. As we will for them.

7   But we don't, with convenience friends, ever come too close or tell too much; we maintain our public face and emotional distance. "Which means," says Elaine, "that I'll talk about being overweight but not about being depressed. Which means I'll admit being mad but not blind with rage. Which means I might say that we're pinched this month but never that I'm worried sick over money."

8   But which doesn't mean that there isn't sufficient value to be found in these friendships of mutual aid, in convenience friends.

9   2. Special-interest friends. These friendships aren't intimate, and they needn't involve kids or silverware or cats. Their value lies in some interest jointly shared. And so we may have an office friend or a yoga friend or a tennis friend or a friend from the Women's Democratic Club.

10   "I've got one woman friend," says Joyce, "who likes, as I do, to take psychology courses. Which makes it nice for me—and nice for her. It's fun to go with someone you know and it's fun to discuss what you've learned, driving back from the classes." And for the most part, she says, that's all they discuss.

11   "I'd say that what we're doing is *doing* together, not being together," Suzanne says of her Tuesday-doubles friends. "It's mainly a tennis relationship, but we play together well. And I guess we all need to have a couple of playmates."

12   I agree.

13   *My* playmate is a shopping friend, a woman of marvelous taste, a woman who knows exactly *where* to buy *what*, and furthermore is a woman who always knows beyond a doubt what one ought to be buying. I don't have the time to keep up with what's new in eyeshadow, hemlines and shoes

and whether the smock look is in or finished already. But since (oh, shame!) I care a lot about eyeshadow, hemlines and shoes, and since I don't *want* to wear smocks if the smock look is finished, I'm very glad to have a shopping friend.

14   3. Historical friends. We all have a friend who knew us when . . . maybe way back in Miss Meltzer's second grade, when our family lived in that three-room flat in Brooklyn, when our dad was out of work for seven months, when our brother Allie got in that fight where they had to call the police, when our sister married the endodontist from Yonkers and when, the morning after we lost our virginity, she was the first, the only, friend we told.

15   The years have gone by and we've gone separate ways and we've little in common now, but we're still an intimate part of each other's past. And so whenever we go to Detroit we always go to visit this friend of our girlhood. Who knows how we looked before our teeth were straightened. Who knows how we talked before our voice got un-Brooklyned. Who knows what we ate before we learned about artichokes. And who, by her presence, puts us in touch with an earlier part of ourself, a part of ourself it's important never to lose.

16   "What this friend means to me and what I mean to her," says Grace, "is having a sister without sibling rivalry. We know the texture of each other's lives. She remembers my grandmother's cabbage soup. I remember the way her uncle played the piano. There's simply no other friend who remembers those things."

17   4. Crossroads friends. Like historical friends, our crossroads friends are important for *what was*—for the friendship we shared at a crucial, now past, time of life. A time, perhaps, when we roomed in college together; or worked as eager young singles in the Big City together; or went together, as my friend Elizabeth and I did through pregnancy, birth and that scary first year of new motherhood.

18   Crossroads friends forge powerful links, links strong enough to endure with not much more contact than once-a-year letters at Christmas. And out of respect for those crossroads years, for those dramas and dreams we once shared, we will always be friends.

19   5. Cross-generational friends. Historical friends and crossroads friends seem to maintain a special kind of intimacy—dormant but always ready to be revived—and though we may rarely meet, whenever we do connect, it's personal and intense. Another kind of intimacy exists in the friendships that form across generations in what one woman calls her daughter-mother and her mother-daughter relationships.

20   Evelyn's friend is her mother's age—"but I share so much more than I ever could with my mother"—a woman she talks to of music, of books and of life. "What I get from her is the benefit of her experience. What she gets—and enjoys—from me is a youthful perspective. It's a pleasure for both of us."

21   I have in my own life a precious friend, a woman of 65 who has lived very hard, who is wise, who listens well; who has been where I am and can help me understand it; and who represents not only an ultimate ideal mother to me but also the person I'd like to be when I grow up.

22   In our daughter role we tend to do more than our share of self-revelation; in our mother role we tend to receive what's revealed. It's another kind of pleasure—playing wise mother to a questing younger person. It's another very lovely kind of friendship.

23   6. Part-of-a-couple friends. Some of the women we call our friends we never see alone—we see them as part of a couple at couples' parties. And though we share interests in many things and respect each other's views, we aren't moved to deepen the relationship. Whatever the reason, a lack of time or—and this is more likely—a lack of chemistry, our friendship remains in the context of a group. But the fact that our feeling on seeing each other is always, "I'm so glad she's here" and the fact that we spend half the evening talking together says that this too, in its own way, counts as a friendship.

24   (Other part-of-a-couple friends are the friends that came with the marriage, and some of these are friends we could live without. But sometimes, alas, she married our husband's best friend; and sometimes, alas, she *is* our husband's best friend. And so we find ourself dealing with her, somewhat against our will, in a spirit of what I'll call *reluctant* friendship.)

25   7. Men who are friends. I wanted to write just of women friends, but the women I've talked to won't let me—they say I must mention man-woman friendships too. For these friendships can be just as close and as dear as those that we form with women. Listen to Lucy's description of one such friendship:

26   "We've found we have things to talk about that are different from what he talks about with my husband and different from what I talk about with his wife. So sometimes we call on the phone or meet for lunch. There are similar intellectual interests—we always pass on to each other the books that we love—but there's also something tender and caring too."

27   In a couple of crises, Lucy says, "he offered himself, for talking and for helping. And when someone died in his family he wanted me there. The sexual, flirty part of our friendship is very small, but *some*—just enough to make it fun and different." She thinks—and I agree—that the sexual part, though small is always *some*, is always there when a man and a woman are friends.

28   It's only in the past few years that I've made friends with men, in the sense of a friendship that's *mine*, not just part of two couples. And achieving with them the ease and the trust I've found with women friends has value indeed. Under the dryer at home last week, putting on mascara and rouge, I comfortably sat and talked with a fellow named Peter. Peter, I finally

decided, could handle the shock of me minus mascara under the dryer. Because we care for each other. Because we're friends.

29   8. There are medium friends, and pretty good friends, and very good friends indeed, and these friendships are defined by their level of intimacy. And what we'll reveal at each of these levels of intimacy is calibrated with care. We might tell a medium friend, for example, that yesterday we had a fight with our husband. And we might tell a pretty good friend that this fight with our husband made us so mad that we slept on the couch. And we might tell a very good friend that the reason we got so mad in that fight that we slept on the couch had something to do with that girl who works in his office. But it's only to our very best friends that we're willing to tell all, to tell what's going on with that girl in his office.

30   The best of friends, I still believe, totally love and support and trust each other, and bare to each other the secrets of their souls, and run—no questions asked—to help each other, and tell harsh truths to each other when they must be told.

31   But we needn't agree about everything (only 12-year-old girl friends agree about *everything*) to tolerate each other's point of view. To accept without judgment. To give and to take without ever keeping score. And to *be* there, as I am for them and as they are for me, to comfort our sorrows, to celebrate our joys.

Topics for Writing and Discussion

1.   How does Viorst describe her earlier views of women's friendships? What single sentence sums up those views? How do those earlier views serve as an introduction to her thesis? What single sentence states that thesis?

2.   What are the categories of friends Viorst describes? Do your own friendships fall neatly into these categories? If you were writing about your own friendships, would you eliminate some of Viorst's groups? Would you add some of your own?

3.   Viorst originally published this essay in *Redbook* magazine, which defines its readers as primarily women between the ages of 25 and 35. What elements of the essay reflect Viorst's sensitivity to this audience? Would she need to revise the essay if she were submitting it to *Esquire* magazine, which has a primarily male audience? What if she were submitting it to a magazine read mainly by older Americans, both male and female?

4.   Are Viorst's categories distinct and clearly presented? Does Viorst use enough examples and details to explain each category? Support your answer with reference to the essay.

5. Write an essay classifying into categories the people at your place of work or the people who are members of a club or organization to which you belong. In your essay, explain how the people in each of these categories contribute to your attitude toward your job or your club or organization.

E. B. White at his home in Brookline, Maine. (© 1991 Jill Krementz)

Three New Yorks

E. B. White
(1899–1985)

Elwyn Brooks White was educated at Cornell University where he studied with William Strunk, Jr. Years later, White revised Strunk's classic textbook, *The Little Book,* and renamed it *The Elements of Style* (1952). In 1927, White joined the staff of the *New Yorker* magazine. From 1938 to 1943 he contributed a column, "One Man's Meat," to *Harper's* magazine. Noted for his essays, editorials, poetry, and feature articles, he also won acclaim for his children's books, which include *Charlotte's Web* (1952) and *Stuart Little* (1945). Although he felt a deep connection to the state of Maine and from 1930 until the end of his life made his home on a saltwater farm there, he lived and worked in New York City for many years. In "Three New Yorks," an excerpt from his book, *Here Is New York* (1949), he maintains that the city is really three cities, viewed distinctly by the natives, the settlers, and the commuters.

1 There are roughly three New Yorks. There is, first, the New York of the man or woman who was born here, who takes the city for granted and accepts its size and its turbulence as natural and inevitable. Second, there is the New York of the commuter—the city that is devoured by locusts each day and spat out each night. Third, there is the New York of the person who was born somewhere else and came to New York in quest of something. Of these three trembling cities the greatest is the last—the city of final destination, the city that is a goal. It is this third city that accounts for New York's high-strung disposition, its poetical deportment, its dedication to the

arts, and its incomparable achievements. Commuters give the city its tidal restlessness; natives give it solidity and continuity; but the settlers give it passion. And whether it is a farmer arriving from Italy to set up a small grocery store in a slum, or a young girl arriving from a small town in Mississippi to escape the indignity of being observed by her neighbors, or a boy arriving from the Corn Belt with a manuscript in his suitcase and a pain in his heart, it makes no difference; each embraces New York with the intense excitement of first love, each absorbs New York with the fresh eyes of an adventurer, each generates heat and light to dwarf the Consolidated Edison Company.

2   The commuter is the queerest bird of all. The suburb he inhabits has no essential vitality of its own and is a mere roost where he comes at day's end to go to sleep. Except in rare cases, the man who lives in Mamaroneck or Little Neck or Teaneck, and works in New York, discovers nothing much about the city except the time of arrival and departure of trains and buses, and the path to a quick lunch. He is desk-bound, and has never, idly roaming in the gloaming, stumbled suddenly on Belvedere Tower in the Park, seen the ramparts rise sheer from the water of the pond, and the boys along the shore fishing for minnows, girls stretched out negligently on the shelves of the rocks; he has never come suddenly on anything at all in New York as a loiterer, because he has had no time between trains. He has fished in Manhattan's wallet and dug out coins, but has never listened to Manhattan's breathing, never awakened to its morning, never dropped off to sleep in its night. About 400,000 men and women come charging onto the Island each week-day morning, out of the mouths of tubes and tunnels. Not many among them have ever spent a drowsy afternoon in the great rustling oaken silence of the reading room of the Public Library, with the book elevator (like an old water wheel) spewing out books onto the trays. They tend their furnaces in Westchester and in Jersey, but have never seen the furnaces of the Bowery, the fires that burn in oil drums on zero winter nights. They may work in the financial district downtown and never see the extravagant plantings of Rockefeller Center—the daffodils and grape hyacinths and birches of the flags trimmed to the wind on a fine morning in spring. Or they may work in a midtown office and may let a whole year swing round without sighting Governor's Island from the sea wall. The commuter dies with tremendous mileage to his credit, but he is no rover. His entrances and exits are more devious than those in a prairie-dog village; and he calmly plays bridge while his train is buried in the mud at the bottom of the East River. The Long Island Rail Road alone carried forty million commuters last year; but many of them were the same fellow retracing his steps.

3   The terrain of New York is such that a resident sometimes travels farther, in the end, than a commuter. The journey of the composer Irving Berlin from Cherry Street in the lower East Side to an apartment uptown was

through an alley and was only three or four miles in length; but it was like going three times around the world.

Topics for Writing and Discussion

1. Give a brief description of each of the three New Yorks and the New Yorkers who people them. Does White seem to favor any one of the three places (or three kinds of people)? Cite specific phrases, sentences, and images to explain your response.

2. What does each of the three types of people give to New York? What does the city give to them? Does any group take more than it gives? Does the city fulfill its promises to each group? Do you agree with White's opinions on these groups of people? Are his generalizations well supported?

3. Although White spends a great deal of time discussing commuters (who are, of course, not residents of New York), he ignores another category of nonresidents—tourists. What do tourists give to and take from New York? What does New York give to and take from tourists? How would White's picture of New York be changed if he added this group?

4. Read the concluding paragraph carefully. What is its literal meaning? What is its figurative meaning? How do both the literal and figurative meanings suggest White's thesis?

5. Write an essay describing a town or city you know well. Create categories of people to explain the unique qualities of that town or city.

College Pressures

William Zinsser
(1922–   )

William Zinsser
(© Nancy Crampton)

Born in New York, William Zinsser attended Princeton University and after graduation worked for *Life, Look,* and the *New York Herald Tribune.* In 1959, he left the *Tribune* to become a full-time freelance writer. He became a member of the English Department at Yale University in 1970 where he planned and taught the first nonfiction writing course ever offered at Yale. In 1976 he wrote his highly acclaimed book *On Writing Well: An Informal Guide to Writing Nonfiction* based on his own writing experiences as well as his observations of his students' writing processes. Zinsser continues to write for magazines and newspapers, and in 1979 he became executive editor of the Book-of-the-Month Club. He has written several books, including *Pop Goes America* (1966), and *Writing with a Word Processor* (1982). More recent works include *Paths of Resistance: The Art and Craft of the Political Novel* (1989), and *Worlds of Childhood: The Art and Craft of Writing for Children* (1990). In "College Pressures," which first appeared in the April 1979 issue of *Country Journal*, Zinsser groups pressures faced by college students into several categories and then analyzes their impact both on individuals and on the college community.

1   Dear Carlos: *I desperately need a dean's excuse for my chem midterm which will begin in about 1 hour. All I can say is that I totally blew it this week. I've fallen incredibly, inconceivably behind.*

2   Carlos: *Help! I'm anxious to hear from you. I'll be in my room and won't leave it until I hear from you. Tomorrow is the last day for . . .*

3 Carlos: *I left town because I started bugging out again. I stayed up all night to finish a take home make-up exam & am typing it to hand in on the 10th. It was due on the 5th. P.S. I'm going to the dentist. Pain is pretty bad.*

4 Carlos: *Probably by Friday I'll be able to get back to my studies. Right now I'm going to take a long walk. This whole thing has taken a lot out of me.*

5 Carlos: *I'm really up the proverbial creek. The problem is I really* bombed *the history final. Since I need that course for my major . . .*

6 Carlos: *Here follows a tale of woe. I went home this weekend, had to help my Mom, & caught a fever so didn't have much time to study. My professor . . .*

7 Carlos: *Aargh! Nothing original but everything's piling up at once. To be brief, my job interview . . .*

8 *Hey Carlos, good news! I've got mononucleosis.*

9 Who are these wretched supplicants, scribbling notes so laden with anxiety, seeking such miracles of postponement and balm? They are men and women who belong to Branford College, one of the twelve residential colleges at Yale University, and the messages are just a few of the hundreds that they left for their dean, Carlos Hortas—often slipped under his door at 4 A.M.—last year.

10 But students like the ones who wrote those notes can also be found on campuses from coast to coast—especially in New England and at many other private colleges across the country that have high academic standards and highly motivated students. Nobody could doubt that the notes are real. In their urgency and their gallows humor they are authentic voices of a generation that is panicky to succeed.

11 My own connection with the message writers is that I am master of Branford College. I live in its Gothic quadrangle and know the students well. (We have 485 of them.) I am privy to their hopes and fears—and also to their stereo music and their piercing cries in the dead of night ("Does anybody *ca-a-are?*"). If they went to Carlos to ask how to get through tomorrow, they come to me to ask how to get through the rest of their lives.

12 Mainly I try to remind them that the road ahead is a long one and that it will have more unexpected turns than they think. There will be plenty of time to change jobs, change careers, change whole attitudes and approaches. They don't want to hear such liberating news. They want a map—right now—that they can follow unswervingly to career security, financial security, Social Security and, presumably, a prepaid grave.

13 What I wish for all students is some release from the clammy grip of the future. I wish them a chance to savor each segment of their education as an experience in itself and not as a grim preparation for the next step. I wish

them the right to experiment, to trip and fall, to learn that defeat is as instructive as victory and is not the end of the world.

14   My wish, of course, is naive. One of the few rights that America does not proclaim is the right to fail. Achievement is the national god, venerated in our media—the million-dollar athlete, the wealthy executive—and glorified in our praise of possessions. In the presence of such a potent state religion, the young are growing up old.

15   I see four kinds of pressure working on college students today: economic pressure, parental pressure, peer pressure, and self-induced pressure. It is easy to look around for villains—to blame the colleges for charging too much money, the professors for assigning too much work, the parents for pushing their children too far, the students for driving themselves too hard. But there are no villains; only victims.

16   "In the late 1960s," one dean told me, "the typical question that I got from students was 'Why is there so much suffering in the world?' or 'How can I make a contribution?' Today it's 'Do you think it would look better for getting into law school if I did a double major in history and political science, or just majored in one of them?' " Many other deans confirmed this pattern. One said "They're trying to find an edge—the intangible something that will look better on paper if two students are about equal."

17   Note the emphasis on looking better. The transcript has become a sacred document, the passport to security. How one appears on paper is more important than how one appears in person. *A* is for Admirable and *B* is for Borderline, even though, in Yale's official system of grading, *A* means "excellent" and *B* means "very good." Today, looking very good is no longer good enough, especially for students who hope to go on to law school or medical school. They know that entrance into the better schools will be an entrance into the better law firms and better medical practices where they will make a lot of money. They also know that the odds are harsh. Yale Law School, for instance, matriculates 170 students from an applicant pool of 3,700; Harvard enrolls 550 from a pool of 7,000.

18   It's all very well for those of us who write letters of recommendation for our students to stress the qualities of humanity that will make them good lawyers or doctors. And it's nice to think that admission officers are really reading our letters and looking for the extra dimension of commitment or concern. Still, it would be hard for a student not to visualize these officers shuffling so many transcripts studded with *A*s that they regard a *B* as positively shameful.

19   The pressure is almost as heavy on students who just want to graduate and get a job. Long gone are the days of the "gentleman's *C*," when students journeyed through college with a certain relaxation, sampling a wide variety of courses—music, art, philosophy, classics, anthropology, poetry, religion— that would send them out as liberally educated men and women. If I were an employer I would rather employ graduates who have this range and

curiosity than those who narrowly pursued safe subjects and high grades. I know countless students whose inquiring minds exhilarate me. I like to hear the play of their ideas. I don't know if they are getting *A*s or *C*s, and I don't care. I also like them as people. The country needs them, and they will find satisfying jobs. I tell them to relax. They can't.

20   Nor can I blame them. They live in a brutal economy. Tuition, room, and board at most private colleges now comes to at least $7,000, not counting books and fees. This might seem to suggest that the colleges are getting rich. But they are equally battered by inflation. Tuition covers only 60 percent of what it costs to educate a student, and ordinarily the remainder comes from what colleges receive in endowments, grants, and gifts. Now the remainder keeps being swallowed by the cruel costs—higher every year—of just opening the doors. Heating oil is up. Insurance is up. Postage is up. Health-premium costs are up. Everything is up. Deficits are up. We are witnessing in America the creation of a brotherhood of paupers—colleges, parents, and students, joined by the common bond of debt.

21   Today it is not unusual for a student, even if he works part time at college and full time during the summer, to accrue $5,000 in loans after four years—loans that he must start to repay within one year after graduation. Exhorted at commencement to go forth into the world, he is already behind as he goes forth. How could he not feel under pressure throughout college to prepare for this day of reckoning? I have used "he," incidentally, only for brevity. Women at Yale are under no less pressure to justify their expensive education to themselves, their parents, and society. In fact, they are probably under more pressure. For although they leave college superbly equipped to bring fresh leadership to traditionally male jobs, society hasn't yet caught up with this fact.

22   Along with economic pressure goes parental pressure. Inevitably, the two are deeply intertwined.

23   I see many students taking pre-medical courses with joyless tenacity. They go off to their labs as if they were going to the dentist. It saddens me because I know them in other corners of their life as cheerful people.

24   "Do you want to go to medical school?" I ask them.

25   "I guess so," they say, without conviction, or "Not really."

26   "Then why are you going?"

27   "Well, my parents want me to be a doctor. They're paying all this money and . . ."

28   Poor students, poor parents. They are caught in one of the oldest webs of love and duty and guilt. The parents mean well; they are trying to steer their sons and daughters toward a secure future. But the sons and daughters want to major in history or classics or philosophy—subjects with no "practical" value. Where's the payoff on the humanities? It's not easy to persuade such loving parents that the humanities do indeed pay off. The intellectual faculties developed by studying subjects like history and classics—an ability

to synthesize and relate, to weigh cause and effect, to see events in perspective—are just the faculties that make creative leaders in business or almost any general field. Still, many fathers would rather put their money on courses that point toward a specific profession—courses that are pre-law, pre-medical, pre-business, or, as I sometimes heard it put, "pre-rich."

29   But the pressure on students is severe. They are truly torn. One part of them feels obligated to fulfill their parents' expectations; after all, their parents are older and presumably wiser. Another part tells them that the expectations that are right for their parents are not right for them.

30   I know a student who wants to be an artist. She is very obviously an artist and will be a good one—she has already had several modest local exhibits. Meanwhile she is growing as a well-rounded person and taking humanistic subjects that will enrich the inner resources out of which her art will grow. But her father is strongly opposed. He thinks that an artist is a "dumb" thing to be. The student vacillates and tries to please everybody. She keeps up with her art somewhat furtively and takes some of the "dumb" courses her father wants her to take—at least they are dumb courses for her. She is a free spirit on a campus of tense students—no small achievement in itself—and she deserves to follow her muse.

31   Peer pressure and self-induced pressure are also intertwined, and they begin almost at the beginning of freshman year.

32   "I had a freshman student I'll call Linda," one dean told me, "who came in and said she was under terrible pressure because her roommate, Barbara, was much brighter and studied all the time. I couldn't tell her that Barbara had come in two hours earlier to say the same thing about Linda."

33   The story is almost funny—except that it's not. It's symptomatic of all the pressures put together. When every student thinks every other student is working harder and doing better, the only solution is to study harder still. I see students going off to the library every night after dinner and coming back when it closes at midnight. I wish they could sometimes forget about their peers and go to a movie. I hear the clacking of typewriters in the hours before dawn. I see the tension in their eyes when exams are approaching and papers are due: *"Will I get everything done?"*

34   Probably they won't. They will get sick. They will get "blocked." They will sleep. They will oversleep. They will bug out. *Hey Carlos, help!*

35   Part of the problem is that they do more than they are expected to do. A professor will assign five-page papers. Several students will start writing ten-page papers to impress him. Then more students will write ten-page papers, and a few will raise the ante to fifteen. Pity the poor student who is still just doing the assignment.

36   "Once you have twenty or thirty percent of the student population deliberately overexerting," one dean points out, "it's bad for everybody. When a teacher gets more and more effort from his class, the student who is doing

normal work can be perceived as not doing well. The tactic works, psychologically."

37 Why can't the professor just cut back and not accept longer papers? He can, and he probably will. But by then the term will be half over and the damage done. Grade fever is highly contagious and not easily reversed. Besides, the professor's main concern is with his course. He knows his students only in relation to the course and doesn't know that they are also overexerting in their other courses. Nor is it really his business. He didn't sign up for dealing with the student as a whole person and with all the emotional baggage the student brought along from home. That's what deans, masters, chaplains, and psychiatrists are for.

38 To some extent this is nothing new: a certain number of professors have always been self-contained islands of scholarship and shyness, more comfortable with books than with people. But the new pauperism has widened the gap still further, for professors who actually like to spend time with students don't have as much time to spend. They also are overexerting. If they are young, they are busy trying to publish in order not to perish, hanging by their finger nails onto a shrinking profession. If they are old and tenured, they are buried under the duties of administering departments—as departmental chairmen or members of committees—that have been thinned out by the budgetary axe.

39 Ultimately it will be the students' own business to break the circles in which they are trapped. They are too young to be prisoners of their parents' dreams and their classmates' fears. They must be jolted into believing in themselves as unique men and women who have the power to shape their own future.

40 "Violence is being done to the undergraduate experience," says Carlos Hortas. "College should be open-ended: at the end it should open many, many roads. Instead, students are choosing their goal in advance, and their choices narrow as they go along. It's almost as if they think that the country has been codified in the type of jobs that exist—that they've got to fit into certain slots. Therefore, fit into the best-paying slot.

41 "They ought to take chances. Not taking chances will lead to a life of colorless mediocrity. They'll be comfortable. But something in the spirit will be missing."

42 I have painted too drab a portrait of today's students, making them seem a solemn lot. That is only half of their story; if they were so dreary I wouldn't so thoroughly enjoy their company. The other half is that they are easy to like. They are quick to laugh and to offer friendship. They are not introverts. They are usually kind and are more considerate of one another than any student generation I have known.

43 Nor are they so obsessed with their studies that they avoid sports and extracurricular activities. On the contrary, they juggle their crowded hours to play on a variety of teams, perform with musical and dramatic groups,

and write for campus publications. But this in turn is one more cause of anxiety. There are too many choices. Academically, they have 1,300 courses to select from; outside class they have to decide how much spare time they can spare and how to spend it.

44   This means that they engage in fewer extracurricular pursuits than their predecessors did. If they want to row on the crew and play in the symphony they will eliminate one; in the '60s they would have done both. They also tend to choose activities that are self-limiting. Drama, for instance, is flourishing in all twelve of Yale's residential colleges as it never has before. Students hurl themselves into these productions—as actors, directors, carpenters, and technicians—with a dedication to create the best possible play, knowing that the day will come when the run will end and they can get back to their studies.

45   They also can't afford to be the willing slave of organizations like the *Yale Daily News.* Last spring at the one-hundredth anniversary banquet of that paper—whose past chairmen include such once and future kings as Potter Stewart, Kingman Brewster, and William F. Buckley, Jr.—much was made of the fact that the editorial staff used to be small and totally committed and that "newsies" routinely worked fifty hours a week. In effect they belonged to a club; newsies is how they defined themselves at Yale. Today's student will write one or two articles a week, when he can, and he defines himself as a student. I've never heard the word newsie except at the banquet.

46   If I have described the modern undergraduate primarily as a driven creature who is largely ignoring the blithe spirit inside who keeps trying to come out and play, it's because that's where the crunch is, not only at Yale but throughout American education. It's why I think we should all be worried about the values that are nurturing a generation so fearful of risk and so goal-obsessed at such an early age.

47   I tell students that there is no one "right" way to get ahead—that each of them is a different person, starting from a different point and bound for a different destination. I tell them that change is a tonic and that all the slots are not codified nor the frontiers closed. One of my ways of telling them is to invite men and women who have achieved success outside the academic world to come and talk informally with my students during the year. They are heads of companies or ad agencies, editors of magazines, politicians, public officials, television magnates, labor leaders, business executives, Broadway producers, artists, writers, economists, photographers, scientists, historians—a mixed bag of achievers.

48   I ask them to say a few words about how they got started. The students assume that they started in their present profession and knew all along that it was what they wanted to do. Luckily for me, most of them got into their field by a circuitous route, to their surprise, after many detours. The students are startled. They can hardly conceive of a career that was not pre-planned.

They can hardly imagine allowing the hand of God or chance to nudge them down some unforeseen trail.

Topics for Writing and Discussion

1. Zinsser begins his essay with a series of notes college students at Yale wrote to their dean. What are the common thoughts and feelings that unite these examples? How do they serve as an introduction to Zinsser's thesis?

2. What four major categories does Zinsser establish as he discusses college pressures? How does he see these categories in relationship to each other? Is each category clearly defined as separate and distinct?

3. What is Zinsser's main purpose? Does he use the categories primarily as a way of explaining the pressures? Does he see college pressures as mostly positive? Mostly negative? Inevitable? Does he hope to encourage changes on college campuses?

4. This essay was first published in 1979. Do Zinsser's categories still hold true today? Do college students face fewer pressures now? More? About the same? Have some of the 1979 pressures been replaced by new forces?

5. Write an essay classifying the primary pressures motivating people in some group other than college students (for instance, members of varsity sports teams, politicians, business executives, mothers, fathers, doctors). Explain whether you think these pressures are a positive or negative force in the lives of the individuals you are discussing.

William Golding at age 72 at his home near Salisbury, England, on the day he received the Nobel Prize for literature (AP/Wide World Photos)

Thinking as a Hobby

William Golding
(1911–   )

William Golding was educated at Marlborough
Grammar School and Brasenose College, Oxford,
England. "Thinking as a Hobby" draws its settings
from both institutions. Golding, who has worked
as a schoolteacher, is best known for his novel
Lord of the Flies (1954), a frightening story of the
cruelty and inhumanity of a group of English
schoolboys who are stranded without adults on an
island. Many of his works reflect his rejection of
society's norms and the status quo, particularly *The
Inheritors* (1955) and *Rites of Passage* (1980). A
more recent work, *Fire Down Below*, was published
in 1989. Golding has many avocations, including
archeology and classical Greek. In "Thinking as a
Hobby" he describes another favorite activity and
provides illustrations of what he classifies as grade-
three, grade-two, and grade-one thinking.

1   While I was still a boy, I came to the conclusion that there were three
grades of thinking; and since I was later to claim thinking as my hobby, I
came to an even stranger conclusion—namely, that I myself could not think
at all.

2   I must have been an unsatisfactory child for grownups to deal with. I
remember how incomprehensible they appeared to me at first, but not, of
course, how I appeared to them. It was the headmaster of my grammar
school who first brought the subject of thinking before me—though neither
in the way, nor with the result he intended. He had some statuettes in his
study. They stood on a high cupboard behind his desk. One was a lady
wearing nothing but a bath towel. She seemed frozen in an eternal panic

lest the bath towel slip down any farther; and since she had no arms, she was in an unfortunate position to pull the towel up again. Next to her, crouched the statuette of a leopard, ready to spring down at the top drawer of a filing cabinet labeled A–AH. My innocence interpreted this as the victim's last, despairing cry. Beyond the leopard was a naked, muscular gentleman, who sat, looking down, with his chin on his fist and his elbow on his knee. He seemed utterly miserable.

3   Some time later, I learned about these statuettes. The headmaster had placed them where they would face delinquent children, because they symbolized to him the whole of life. The naked lady was the Venus of Milo. She was Love. She was not worried about the towel. She was just busy being beautiful. The leopard was Nature, and he was being natural. The naked, muscular gentleman was not miserable. He was Rodin's Thinker, an image of pure thought. It is easy to buy small plaster models of what you think life is like.

4   I had better explain that I was a frequent visitor to the headmaster's study, because of the latest thing I had done or left undone. As we now say, I was not integrated. I was, if anything, disintegrated; and I was puzzled. Grown-ups never made sense. Whenever I found myself in a penal position before the headmaster's desk, with the statuettes glimmering whitely above him, I would sink my head, clasp my hands behind my back and writhe one shoe over the other.

5   The headmaster would look opaquely at me through flashing spectacles.

6   "What are we going to do with you?"

7   Well, what *were* they going to do with me? I would writhe my shoe some more and stare down at the worn rug.

8   "Look up, boy! Can't you look up?"

9   Then I would look up at the cupboard, where the naked lady was frozen in her panic and the muscular gentleman contemplated the hindquarters of the leopard in endless gloom. I had nothing to say to the headmaster. His spectacles caught the light so that you could see nothing human behind them. There was no possibility of communication.

10   "Don't you ever think at all?"

11   No, I didn't think, wasn't thinking, couldn't think—I was simply waiting in anguish for the interview to stop.

12   "Then you'd better learn—hadn't you?"

13   On one occasion the headmaster leaped to his feet, reached up and plonked Rodin's masterpiece on the desk before me.

14   "That's what a man looks like when he's really thinking."

15   I surveyed the gentleman without interest or comprehension.

16   "Go back to your class."

17   Clearly there was something missing in me. Nature had endowed the rest of the human race with a sixth sense and left me out. This must be so, I mused, on my way back to the class, since whether I had broken a window,

or failed to remember Boyle's Law, or been late for school, my teachers produced me one, adult answer: "Why can't you think?"

18 As I saw the case, I had broken the window because I had tried to hit Jack Arney with a cricket ball and missed him; I could not remember Boyle's Law because I had never bothered to learn it; and I was late for school because I preferred looking over the bridge into the river. In fact, I was wicked. Were my teachers, perhaps, so good that they could not understand the depths of my depravity? Were they clear, untormented people who could direct their every action by this mysterious business of thinking? The whole thing was incomprehensible. In my earlier years, I found even the statuette of the Thinker confusing. I did not believe any of my teachers were naked, ever. Like someone born deaf, but bitterly determined to find out about sound, I watched my teachers to find out about thought.

19 There was Mr. Houghton. He was always telling me to think. With a modest satisfaction, he would tell me that he had thought a bit himself. Then why did he spend so much time drinking? Or was there more sense in drinking than there appeared to be? But if not, and if drinking were in fact ruinous to health—and Mr. Houghton was ruined, there was no doubt about that—why was he always talking about the clean life and the virtues of fresh air? He would spread his arms wide with the action of a man who habitually spent his time striding along mountain ridges.

20 "Open air does me good, boys—I know it!"

21 Sometimes, exalted by his own oratory, he would leap from his desk and hustle us outside into a hideous wind.

22 "Now boys! Deep breaths! Feel it right down inside you—huge draughts of God's good air!"

23 He would stand before us, rejoicing in his perfect health, an open-air man. He would put his hands on his waist and take a tremendous breath. You could hear the wind, trapped in the cavern of his chest and struggling with all the unnatural impediments. His body would reel with shock and his ruined face go white at the unaccustomed visitation. He would stagger back to his desk and collapse there, useless for the rest of the morning.

24 Mr. Houghton was given to high-minded monologues about the good life, sexless and full of duty. Yet in the middle of one of these monologues, if a girl passed the window, tapping along on her neat little feet, he would interrupt his discourse, his neck would turn of itself and he would watch her out of sight. In this instance, he seemed to me ruled not by thought but by an invisible and irresistible spring in his nape.

25 His neck was an object of great interest to me. Normally it bulged a bit over his collar. But Mr. Houghton had fought in the First World War alongside both Americans and French, and had come—by who knows what illogic?— to a settled detestation of both countries. If either country happened to be prominent in current affairs, no argument could make Mr. Houghton think well of it. He would bang the desk, his neck would bulge still further and

go red. "You can say what you like," he would cry, "but I've thought about this—and I know what I think!"

26   Mr. Houghton thought with his neck.

27   There was Miss Parsons. She assured us that her dearest wish was our welfare, but I knew even then, with the mysterious clairvoyance of childhood, that what she wanted most was the husband she never got. There was Mr. Hands—and so on.

28   I have dealt at length with my teachers because this was my introduction to the nature of what is commonly called thought. Through them I discovered that thought is often full of unconscious prejudice, ignorance and hypocrisy. It will lecture on disinterested purity while its neck is being remorselessly twisted toward a skirt. Technically, it is about as proficient as most businessmen's golf, as honest as most politicians' intentions, or—to come near my own preoccupation—as coherent as most books that get written. It is what I came to call grade-three thinking, though more properly, it is feeling, rather than thought.

29   True, often there is a kind of innocence in prejudices, but in those days I viewed grade-three thinking with an intolerant contempt and an incautious mockery. I delighted to confront a pious lady who hated the Germans with the proposition that we should love our enemies. She taught me a great truth in dealing with grade-three thinkers; because of her, I no longer dismiss lightly a mental process which for nine-tenths of the population is the nearest they will ever get to thought. They have immense solidarity. We had better respect them, for we are outnumbered and surrounded. A crowd of grade-three thinkers, all shouting the same thing, all warming their hands at the fire of their own prejudices, will not thank you for pointing out the contradictions in their beliefs. Man is a gregarious animal, and enjoys agreement as cows will graze all the same way on the side of a hill.

30   Grade-two thinking is the detection of contradictions. I reached grade two when I trapped the poor, pious lady. Grade-two thinkers do not stampede easily, though often they fall into the other fault and lag behind. Grade-two thinking is a withdrawal, with eyes and ears open. It became my hobby and brought satisfaction and loneliness in either hand. For grade-two thinking destroys without having the power to create. It set me watching the crowds cheering His Majesty the King and asking myself what all the fuss was about, without giving me anything positive to put in the place of that heady patriotism. But there were compensations. To hear people justify their habit of hunting foxes and tearing them to pieces by claiming that the foxes liked it. To hear our Prime Minister talk about the great benefit we conferred on India by jailing people like Pandit Nehru and Gandhi. To hear American politicians talk about peace in one sentence and refuse to join the League of Nations in the next. Yes, there were moments of delight.

31   But I was growing toward adolescence and had to admit that Mr. Houghton was not the only one with an irresistible spring in his neck. I, too, felt the

compulsive hand of nature and began to find that pointing out contradiction could be costly as well as fun. There was Ruth, for example, a serious and attractive girl. I was an atheist at the time. Grade-two thinking is a menace to religion and knocks down sects like skittles. I put myself in a position to be converted by her with an hypocrisy worthy of grade three. She was a Methodist—or at least, her parents were, and Ruth had to follow suit. But, alas, instead of relying on the Holy Spirit to convert me, Ruth was foolish enough to open her pretty mouth in argument. She claimed that the Bible (King James Version) was literally inspired. I countered by saying that the Catholics believed in the literal inspiration of Saint Jerome's *Vulgate*, and the two books were different. Argument flagged.

32   At last she remarked that there were an awful lot of Methodists, and they couldn't be wrong, could they—not all those millions? That was too easy, said I restively (for the nearer you were to Ruth, the nicer she was to be near to) since there were more Roman Catholics than Methodists anyway; and they couldn't be wrong, could they—not all those hundreds of millions? An awful flicker of doubt appeared in her eyes. I slid my arm round her waist and murmured breathlessly that if we were counting heads, the Buddhists were the boys for my money. But Ruth had *really* wanted to do me good, because I was so nice. She fled. The combination of my arm and those countless Buddhists was too much for her.

33   That night her father visited my father and left, red-cheeked and indignant. I was given the third degree to find out what had happened. It was lucky we were both of us only fourteen. I lost Ruth and gained an undeserved reputation as a potential libertine.

34   So grade-two thinking could be dangerous. It was in this knowledge, at the age of fifteen, that I remember making a comment from the heights of grade two, on the limitations of grade three. One evening I found myself alone in the schoolhall, preparing it for a party. The door of the headmaster's study was open. I went in. The headmaster had ceased to thump Rodin's Thinker down on the desk as an example to the young. Perhaps he had not found any more candidates, but the statuettes were still there, glimmering and gathering dust on top of the cupboard. I stood on a chair and rearranged them. I stood Venus in her bath towel on the filing cabinet, so that now the top drawer caught its breath in a gasp of sexy excitement. "A-ah!" The portentous Thinker I placed on the edge of the cupboard so that he looked down at the bath towel and waited for it to slip. Grade-two thinking, though it filled life with fun and excitement, did not make for content. To find out the deficiencies of our elders bolsters the young ego but does not make for personal security. I found that grade two was not only the power to point out contradictions. It took the swimmer some distance from the shore and left him there, out of his depth. I decided that Pontius Pilate was a typical grade-two thinker. "What is truth?" he said, a very common grade-two thought, but one that is used always as the end of an argument instead of

the beginning. There is a still higher grade of thought which says, "What is truth?" and sets out to find it.

35   But these grade-one thinkers were few and far between. They did not visit my grammar school in the flesh though they were there in books. I aspired to them, partly because I was ambitious and partly because I now saw my hobby as an unsatisfactory thing if it went no further. If you set out to climb a mountain, however high you climb, you have failed if you cannot reach the top.

36   I *did* meet an undeniably grade-one thinker in my first year at Oxford. I was looking over a small bridge in Magdalen Deer Park, and a tiny mustached and hatted figure came and stood by my side. He was a German who had just fled from the Nazis to Oxford as a temporary refuge. His name was Einstein.

37   But Professor Einstein knew no English at that time and I knew only two words of German. I beamed at him, trying wordlessly to convey by my bearing all the affection and respect that the English felt for him. It is possible—and I have to make the admission—that I felt here were two grade-one thinkers standing side by side; yet I doubt if my face conveyed more than a formless awe. I would have given my Greek and Latin and French and a good slice of my English for enough German to communicate. But we were divided; he was as inscrutable as my headmaster. For perhaps five minutes we stood together on the bridge, undeniable grade-one thinker and breathless aspirant. With true greatness, Professor Einstein realized that any contact was better than none. He pointed to a trout wavering in midstream.

38   He spoke: *"Fisch."*

39   My brain reeled. Here I was, mingling with the great, and yet helpless as the veriest grade-three thinker. Desperately I sought for some sign by which I might convey that I, too, revered pure reason. I nodded vehemently. In a brilliant flash I used up half of my German vocabulary. *"Fisch. Ja. Ja."*

40   For perhaps another five minutes we stood side by side. Then Professor Einstein, his whole figure still conveying good will and amiability, drifted away out of sight.

41   I, too, would be a grade-one thinker. I was irreverent at the best of times. Political and religious systems, social customs, loyalties and traditions, they all came tumbling down like so many rotten apples off a tree. This was a fine hobby and a sensible substitute for cricket, since you could play it all the year round. I came up in the end with what must always remain the justification for grade-one thinking, its sign, seal and charter. I devised a coherent system for living. It was a moral system, which was wholly logical. Of course, as I readily admitted, conversion of the world to my way of thinking might be difficult, since my system did away with a number of trifles, such as big business, centralized government, armies, marriage. . . .

42   It was Ruth all over again. I had some very good friends who stood by me, and still do. But my acquaintances vanished, taking the girls with them.

Young women seemed oddly contented with the world as it was. They valued the meaningless ceremony with a ring. Young men, while willing to concede the chaining sordidness of marriage, were hesitant about abandoning the organizations which they hoped would give them a career. A young man on the first rung of the Royal Navy, while perfectly agreeable to doing away with big business and marriage, got as rednecked as Mr. Houghton when I proposed a world without any battleships in it.

43   Had the game gone too far? Was it a game any longer? In those prewar days, I stood to lose a great deal, for the sake of a hobby.

44   Now you are expecting me to describe how I saw the folly of my ways and came back to the warm nest, where prejudices are so often called loyalties, where pointless actions are hallowed into custom by repetition, where we are content to say we think when all we do is feel.

45   But you would be wrong. I dropped my hobby and turned professional.

46   If I were to go back to the headmaster's study and find the dusty statuettes still there, I would arrange them differently. I would dust Venus and put her aside, for I have come to love her and know her for the fair thing she is. But I would put the Thinker, sunk in his desperate thought, where there were shadows before him—and at his back, I would put the leopard, crouched and ready to spring.

Topics for Writing and Discussion

1.   Why did Golding as a boy come to the conclusion that he could not think at all? What examples does he give to explain how he reached that conclusion? What irony does an adult, reading Golding's examples, see in his claim that he could not think?

2.   Why does Golding call grade-two thinking dangerous? How does his adventure with Rodin's Thinker and Venus (paragraph 34) in the head-master's office illustrate what he believes to be one of the primary limitations of grade-two thinking?

3.   Golding describes the negative aspects of grade-three and grade-two thinking. Does he see grade-one thinking as entirely desirable? What sacrifices does grade-one thinking require? Would these sacrifices, in your opinion, be justified by a world full of Golding's grade-one thinkers?

4.   What does Golding's meeting with Einstein illustrate? Why does this meeting confirm his decision to be a grade-one thinker? How does the final paragraph, with its references to the Thinker, Venus, and the leopard, relate to Golding's decision to be a "professional"?

5.   Write an essay establishing your own "grades of thinking." Use examples from your childhood, adolescence, and adulthood to illustrate your categories.

Gilbert Highet (© NYT Pictures)

The Face in the Mirror

Gilbert Highet
(1906–1978)

Born in Scotland, classicist Gilbert Highet was educated at Glasgow University and Oxford University before coming to the United States and beginning a long tenure at Columbia University as a professor of Greek and Latin. In 1951, the same year he became a U.S. citizen, Highet received a Guggenheim fellowship. Acclaimed for his writing on classicism, including *The Classical Tradition: Greek and Roman Influences on Western Literature* (1949), he also authored *The Immortal Profession: The Joy of Teaching and Learning* (1976).

Throughout his career, Highet sought to make the classics more accessible to the lay reader. In "The Face in the Mirror," Highet classifies three types of biographies and describes how each offers insights to the reader.

1   They say that every man and every woman has one book inside him or her. Some have more, but everybody has at least one. This is a volume of autobiography. We have all been talked almost to death by bores who attached themselves to us in a club car or a ship's smoking room, and insisted on giving us a play-by-play account of their marital troubles, or their complete medical history. I once met one who carried a set of his own x-rays. Yet even these people might be interesting if they could tell the whole truth. They are boring not because they talk about themselves, but because they talk about only one aspect of themselves, that phase of their lives which fascinates and worries them personally. If they were really to tell us everything, we should listen with amazement.

2   Most of us cannot tell the whole truth, or even the important parts of the truth. This is one reason why there are not many good autobiographies.

People cannot, or will not, put down the facts. The wife of the philosopher Carlyle said that the story of her life, written down without falsification or disguise, would have been a priceless record for other women to read, but that "decency forbade her to do any such thing." Think how many millions of people have told secrets to their wives or husbands, to their psychiatrists, to their doctors, their lawyers, or their priests—secrets which they would rather die than see printed in a book and published under their own names. And the other reason for the dearth of readable autobiographies is simply that most people cannot write. Writing an interesting story, a fictional story, is difficult enough. Writing eloquently about oneself is still more difficult; it needs a style even more subtle and a finer sense of balance.

3   Apparently there are three kinds of autobiography: three different ways of telling the story of one's life. (We can leave out journals like Pepys's *Diary*, which was not meant to be published, and collections of letters, and disguised autobiographies, which so many modern novels are.)

4   The first group could all be issued under the same title. They could all be called "What I Did." They are essentially success stories. In them, a man who has achieved something of wide importance explains how he did it, what were the obstacles in his way, how they were overcome, and what was the effect on the world. Self-made men often write such books—or have such books written for them. There is a splendid one by Ben Franklin, and an equally good one by his English opposite number, William Cobbett: these are optimistic works, a good tonic for anyone who despairs of solving his own problems.

5   Sir Winston Churchill's six-volume work *The Second World War* (published by Houghton Mifflin) is really an autobiographical record. He himself says it is "the story as I knew and experienced it as Prime Minister and Minister of Defense of Great Britain." Therefore it cannot be called anything like a complete history of the war. For example, Churchill tells the story of one of the crucial events of the war, one of the crucial events of this century— the reduction of Japan to impotence and surrender by intensive bombardment culminating in what he calls the "casting" of two atomic bombs—in only eight pages, while a greater amount of wordage is devoted to a reprint of the broadcast which he made to British listeners on VE day.

6   A similar personalized history of the last twenty years is *The Secret Diary of Harold L. Ickes* (issued by Simon & Schuster). This is a view of the New Deal and of the war years, as experienced and interpreted by a single, rather lonely politician. It is not a traditional success story. Ickes was so fantastically vain and ambitious that he saw the world as a conspiracy designed to deprive him of his rights; he would scarcely have been content with anything less than the perpetual presidency of the entire solar system. Therefore he accepted, and recorded in his diary, every piece of flattery which was offered to him—however blatant or insincere—and, while freely and gladly delivering cruelly effective attacks on his rivals and enemies, he bitterly resented

any personal slight to himself. There is one very funny chapter in the latest volume, in which Ickes explains why he stopped going to the Gridiron Club dinners in Washington. At the last one he attended, a reporter dressed up as Donald Duck caricatured Secretary Ickes: "crowing like a rooster, he strutted and patted himself on the chest, and indicated by sound and action that evidently he thought that Secretary Ickes was the greatest man in the world." Ickes goes on to comment, "I have completely fooled myself if I give the impression to anyone that I am conceited and possess a feeling of superiority over other men." Obviously he did give just that impression, and every entry in his diary confirms it; but he refuses to face the fact. On the very same page he describes Governor Thomas Dewey as "a political streetwalker," and similar delicacies occur throughout the book. Still, there is no doubt that Ickes conceived of himself as a champion fighting alone against tremendous odds, and for that reason his diary is a success story.

7   One instructive contrast between the autobiographies of Churchill and Ickes is in the matter of discretion. Churchill has often been charged with talking out of turn, and dropping rash remarks to provoke the opposition, but anyone who reads his book carefully will be surprised to see how much is tactfully omitted. For example, he spends a page on describing his meeting with King Ibn-Sa'ud just after Yalta. His account is full of vivid and interesting details—such as the fact that the king's cupbearer gave Churchill a glass of water from the sacred well at Mecca, "the most delicious" (he says) "that I had ever tasted"—and probably the first such drink he had had for a very long time. It is only when we reread the episode that we realize how discreet the old statesman has been: he has not said a single word about the purpose of the meeting, and not a single word about its results, although his book purports to be a history of the war. On the other hand, Ickes seems to have attended confidential meetings of the Cabinet and of other bodies, at which data of great importance and secrecy were given out, and then to have come straight home and dictated a verbatim report to his secretaries, who then typed it up and kept it in a folder. No doubt it was relief for him to do so, and certainly it makes interesting reading now, but surely it was a shocking piece of indiscretion for a man in a position of confidence to betray everything to his employees, particularly secrets which were not his to keep or to disclose.

8   So much for the first type of autobiography: "What I Did." The second type might be called "What I Saw." Here the emphasis is not on the achievements of the narrator, but rather on the strange sights he saw and the strange experiences through which he lived. Most good books of exploration are like this. Both the book *Kon-Tiki* and the film were absorbingly interesting, not because the author was an unusual man, but because he could describe to us some unique adventures. We shall never cross New Guinea on foot, or spend a whole year alone with two companions on the Arctic ice, or climb Mount Everest; therefore we are delighted when a man who has done such

a thing can tell us about it clearly—and modestly. The greatest of all such books in the English language is probably Doughty's *Travels in Arabia Deserta*. Some good adventure autobiographies have been written by ordinary soldiers and sailors. Many of our finest descriptions of the Napoleonic wars come from such books as the *Recollections of Rifleman Harris*, and there are similar documents from the American Civil War. Such also are the pathetic and marvelous books of reminiscence written by men and women who have survived long terms in prison. It would be virtually impossible for us to tell how the German and Russian prison camps worked, if we did not possess such books as Christopher Burney's *Dungeon Democracy*, Tadeusz Wittlin's *A Reluctant Traveller in Russia*, Seweryna Szmaglewska's *Smoke Over Birkenau*, and Odd Nansen's *From Day to Day*. Finally, a great deal of social history is best conveyed through autobiography. At or near the top of the ladder there is a rather snobbish but delightfully written work by Sir Osbert Sitwell, in five volumes, which came out at intervals during the last decade, and which he himself describes as "a portrait of an age and person." At the bottom of the ladder, there is a painful but unforgettable description of the life of tramps and outcasts by George Orwell, called *Down and Out in Paris and London*. What Orwell tells us about the filth and calculated vileness of the kitchens in smart Parisian restaurants (where he himself worked as a dishwasher) is enough to sicken the strongest stomach, and I know that I personally have never enjoyed a meal in Paris since I read his book. One paragraph about the handling of food in the smart hotel kitchens ends, "Roughly speaking, the more one pays for food [in Paris], the more sweat and spittle one is obliged to eat with it." A good book of this kind has a perfectly unequaled impact: if its author can write at all, it is very hard to forget what he says.

9   Then there is a third kind of autobiography. It does not describe "What I Did," or "What I Saw," but "What I Felt," "What I Endured." These are the books of inner adventure. In them there is achievement, yes, but it is a struggle and a victory within the spirit. In them there are dangerous explorations, and the discovery of unknown worlds, but the explorer is making his way through the jungles of the soul. Such are the books of failure, disaster, and regeneration which are now so popular: for example, Lillian Roth's *I'll Cry Tomorrow*, which tells how a woman wrecked her life with drink and then rebuilt it. Such also are the books which describe one of the most dangerous of all adventures: the process of growing up. My own favorite among them is Edward Gibbon's autobiography, partly because it is unconsciously funny. More famous perhaps are the self-studies of John Stuart Mill, Herbert Spencer, and Henry Adams—all of which seem to me excruciatingly pompous and dull. There is also an exquisite little book, now out of print and very hard to procure, which tells how a little boy brought up in a sternly intellectual and narrowly religious family fought his way out and remade his character. This is *Father and Son*, by Edmund Gosse. I wish

it could be reprinted. It is both very sad and very amusing. The famous records of religious suffering and conversion could all be subtitled "What I Felt": the *Confessions* of St. Augustine, the journals of John Bunyan and of the first Quaker, George Fox. And many of the most famous autobiographers have concentrated on reporting the events which happened during their lifetime, not as objective facts, but simply as occurrences which impinged upon their own personalities: in books like the reminiscences of Benvenuto Cellini, of Rousseau, of Boswell, Yeats, and André Gide, we see the world as in an elaborate distorting mirror.

10   "What I Did," "What I Saw," "What I Felt." . . . Really, it is difficult to make a sharp division between the three types of autobiographical writing. The emphasis in one book is more toward reporting of external happenings, in another toward self-analysis, but a man can scarcely describe what he did without also letting us know what he felt and saw. Even the most egoistic of men, like St. Augustine and James Boswell, do from time to time give us valuable information about their outer as well as their inner worlds. The most interesting of these books give us something of all three kinds of experience. For a time, while we read them, it is possible to enjoy one of the rarest artistic pleasures—complete escape: escape into another sphere of action and perception. From that escape we return—with what relief!—to the real center of the universe, which is our own self.

Topics for Writing and Discussion

1. According to Highet, what are the three types of autobiography? What techniques does he use to illustrate the strengths and potential limitations of each?

2. What qualities, as Highet implies, are shared by the best autobiographies? What single characteristic prohibits the success of most would-be autobiographers?

3. What does the reader of each type of autobiography gain? From your own experience as a reader, what type of autobiography is most rewarding for you? Why?

4. If you were to write your own autobiography at this stage of your life, which of the three types would you be most likely to pursue? Explain why.

5. Consider the experiences in your life that have had a significant impact on you. Choose one of these experiences as the focus of an essay in which you examine this event from the angle you selected in question 4. Why would readers find themselves interested in this part of your autobiography?

Writing Assignments for Chapter Nine
Division and Classification

1. After reading Judith Viorst's essay "Friends, Good Friends, and Such Good Friends" and John Updike's "Three Boys," write an essay categorizing the kinds of friends you had during a specific period in your life—during part of your childhood or your first year of college, for example. Which friends were the best and why? Make your categories clear, as Viorst and Updike did, by using vivid details.

2. Think of a familiar place where a variety of people congregate—your school library, a local food co-op, a favorite nightspot, a sports or recreation area, for example—and classify the kinds of people there by contrasting their views of the place, as E. B. White does in "Three New Yorks." After you present these diverse views, your readers should have a clear sense of the place's complex personality.

3. In "College Pressures," William Zinsser describes the economic, parental, peer, and self-induced pressures he sees creating anxiety among college students today. Think about your own need to succeed, and explain the three or four main kinds of pressures you feel. Are your sources of anxiety the same as those described by Zinsser?

4. The college pressures Zinsser describes often lead students to become "stressed-out" or physically ill. Write an article for your school newspaper that identifies some good ways to cope with the stress of classes and exams. Make your suggestions concrete by illustrating them from your own experience or from that of your friends. Or, if you prefer, present one way you cope with stress (running or shopping or listening to music, perhaps) and explain the main reasons your method works for you.

5. Using William Golding's categories in "Thinking as a Hobby," write an essay in which you offer current illustrations of grade-one, -two, and -three thinking. Consider using as examples some of the popular social or political controversies or trends today.

6. Although in "The Face in the Mirror" Gilbert Highet classifies autobiographies into three categories, he ultimately concludes that the best life stories contain some elements of all three types. Think of the best au-

tobiographical book, story, essay, or film you ever found. Write a review of it for a local newspaper or magazine, making clear how it fits Highet's categories. To ensure that your readers will understand the autobiography's merit, you will have to include a number of specific references to the story, but do make your review more than mere summary.

7. Write your own autobiographical essay, but instead of narrating your life from birth to the present, pick out three noteworthy episodes that illustrate Highet's categories of "what I did," "what I saw," and "what I felt." How might these episodes be connected to give your readers a sense of your values thus far? Do these three episodes reveal your philosophy or general attitude toward living?

Chapter Ten

Cause and Effect

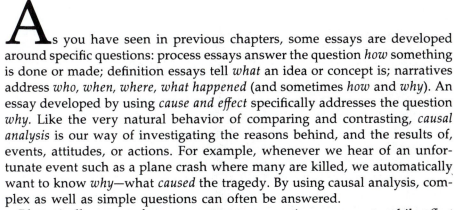

As you have seen in previous chapters, some essays are developed around specific questions: process essays answer the question *how* something is done or made; definition essays tell *what* an idea or concept is; narratives address *who, when, where, what happened* (and sometimes *how* and *why*). An essay developed by using *cause and effect* specifically addresses the question *why*. Like the very natural behavior of comparing and contrasting, *causal analysis* is our way of investigating the reasons behind, and the results of, events, attitudes, or actions. For example, whenever we hear of an unfortunate event such as a plane crash where many are killed, we automatically want to know *why*—what *caused* the tragedy. By using causal analysis, complex as well as simple questions can often be answered.

Rhetorically, *cause* often concerns reasons, actions, or events while *effect* concerns the consequences of those reasons, actions, or events manifested at some later time. Therefore by using cause-and-effect relationships between ideas, you can focus a discussion either on an analysis of the cause of something or on the outcome of something. By using causal analysis, officials could determine that faulty wing design (the cause) led to a plane crash (the effect) and further use that information to prevent a similar occurrence from happening again. Causal analysis allows you to examine a question by moving from the cause to the effect or from the effect to the cause.

Establishing cause-and-effect relationships can be a complicated endeavor, for not all causes are created equal. You must weigh the significance of the cause in its relation to the effect, and you must also determine the appropriate sequence of causes that logically leads to the effect. The first step, then, in organizing your thoughts for a cause-and-effect essay is to examine the various types of causes and how those causes relate to a given effect.

Types of Causes

There are four types of causes: necessary (or main), sufficient, contributing, and remote. A *necessary* cause is just that—*necessary* for the effect to occur. This cause *must* be present; without it the effect *will not* happen. Note, however, that it is possible (and, perhaps, probable) that the necessary cause *alone* could not produce the effect. For example, some type of fuel or energy is absolutely necessary for an automobile to operate; however, fuel or energy *alone* will not put a car in motion.

A *contributing* cause *contributes* to or *aids in bringing about* the effect. It does not work alone but is an important factor in producing the effect. For example, on December 1, 1955, when Mrs. Rosa Parks refused to relinquish her seat on a city bus in Montgomery, Alabama, to a white passenger, her action sparked (or contributed to) the Montgomery bus boycott. Her arrest for that refusal was not necessary to produce the boycott, but it contributed to the frustrations that led to the boycott. The *necessary* reason for the action, however, was the racist attitude that presumed she should give up her seat to a white person.

A *sufficient* cause *could* by itself produce an effect, but other factors might also play a role. Certainly heart disease could cause death, but the victim might also have suffered from diabetes or high blood pressure.

A *remote* cause is not an impossible or unlikely one, as the term might suggest. Instead it is a cause so far removed in time and, perhaps, distance from the sequence of occurrences that its role in producing the effect is often overlooked. Ignoring remote causes can be a serious mistake, though, for failure to recognize their importance could lead to flawed predicted outcomes or oversimplified cause-and-effect relationships. In exploring the causes of the Rosa Parks incident, you might discover that a remote cause of the white driver's ordering of Mrs. Parks to leave her seat was a long-held belief that black people were inferior to white people and thus blacks' needs were less important than whites' needs. Seeking the remote cause for an effect is, therefore, a logical way to analyze a problem, but you should be careful not to go too far afield. For instance, to argue that a man would not have had a fatal heart attack at age 40 if his mother had not allowed him to eat ice cream when he was a child is not convincing.

The Cause-Effect Chain

Exploring remote causes can often lead to a sequence of causes and effects called a *cause-and-effect chain* or a *causal chain* where Cause A produces Cause B, which in turn produces Cause C, which produces Cause D, and so on. Causal analyses of historical events often take this form; for example, one might show the connection between the Stamp Act, the Boston Tea Party, and other events leading to the American Revolution.

Writing the Cause-and-Effect Essay

The following guidelines will help you to prepare a cause-and-effect essay.

1. *Choose a subject that you can manage.*

Narrow your thesis to accommodate the scope of the assignment. If the assigned length of your essay is 500 words, don't try to discuss the causes of World War I. Volumes have been written about that conflict; it might not be possible to explain the causes of the Great War in "500 words or less."

2. *Examine the evidence on which you will base your ideas.*

Is the information you plan to use adequate? Is your own experience or expertise enough? Will research be necessary? Is your evidence logical? Accurate? Remember, any essay based on faulty evidence will be weak.

3. *Decide if you should focus on the cause or on the effect, or both.*

Ask yourself, "What exactly *is* the cause-and-effect relationship of my topic? What is my point?" Once you have answered this question, you can decide on the focus. If you decide that your essay should focus on the causes, your essay will show how X, Y, and Z caused (or will cause) some stated effect. If your essay will focus on the effects, it will show how certain results were (or will be) brought about by certain causes. Perhaps you will decide that your subject will be better served if you do both. If you choose to discuss both causes and effects, limit your topic so that your analysis will not be skimpy or underdeveloped.

4. *Use the essay's introduction to lay the foundation of your case and present a clear thesis that specifically states or strongly suggests the major idea of the essay.*

In "Politics and the English Language," for example, writer George Orwell begins his essay by setting up a problem: the decline of the English language and people's assumption that nothing can be done about it. In his second paragraph Orwell presents the main ideas of his essay. He dismisses the notion that faulty language is the product of a few bad writers and argues that it has political and economic causes and effects. According to Orwell, sloppy language is not only ugly but also "makes it easier for us to have foolish thoughts." But bad habits can be reversed, and doing so "is clearly a necessary first step toward political regeneration." Orwell then goes on to devote the rest of his well-known essay to illustrate this cause-and-effect relationship between language and thought.

5.   *Though your thesis should be clear, do not overstate your idea and run the danger of oversimplifying a possibly complex cause-and-effect relationship.*

Remember that for most subjects there may be *many* causes that often are determined by the perspective from which those causes are viewed. Furthermore, some cause-and-effect relationships just cannot be proved conclusively, especially those that predict future outcomes. Therefore, when you present your cause-and-effect ideas, avoid words that leave no room for exceptions. Words like *must, will, all* are restrictive and deny other possibilities. Instead, use words like *may, many, probably* that leave room for alternative connections between the cause and the effect.

6.   *Review the types of causes you are using to support your thesis.*

If your essay will focus on the causes of something, begin thinking about the *necessary* cause, the condition that *must* be present. Then you should distinguish between sufficient cause and contributory cause. Could one (or more) of the causes you present have created the result all by itself? Next, review the sequence of causes to see if you need to include a remote cause.

7.   *Make your analysis convincing.*

It is not enough to merely state that "X caused Y"; you must prove your case by showing the reader the steps of the causal relationship in a convincing manner. Your essay is successful when your reader can say, "Yes, I can see how and why this happened" or "I can clearly see the effects or results of this." In " 'This Is the End of the World': The Black Death," historian Barbara Tuchman, for instance, convinces her readers of the terrible effects of the plague that devastated Europe in the fourteenth century by presenting numerous statistics, chilling eyewitness reports, and vivid descriptions.

8.   *Avoid* post hoc *reasoning.*

Do not automatically assume that because A precedes B in time, A *caused* B. In other words, do not mistake coincidence for causality. For example, if you found a $100 bill lying on the ground moments after a black cat had crossed your path, it would be *post hoc* reasoning to believe that each time a black cat crossed your path you would discover a $100 bill.

Norman Cousins (Steve Shapiro/Sygma)

Pain Is Not the Ultimate Enemy

Norman Cousins
(1912–1990)

After graduating from Teachers College of
Columbia University, Norman Cousins began his
career as a journalist. He directed the *Saturday
Review* for over 30 years. During this time, he
wrote columns for the *Review* as well as hiring
other writers who, along with Cousins, determined
the direction this highly respected periodical would
take. In addition to directing the *Saturday Review*,
he published many books, including *Writing for
Love or Money* (1949), a collection of his columns,
and *Human Options* (1981), commentaries on
contemporary issues. When Cousins was diagnosed
as having a paralyzing collagen disease from which
there was little hope for recovery, he researched
his problem and decided to heal himself. He took
massive injections of vitamin C and, in addition,
surrounded himself with humor and laughter. He
described his insights about the causes of illnesses
and the effects of his self-prescribed cures in *The
Celebration of Life* (1974), *Anatomy of an Illness*
(1979), *Human Options: An Autobiographical
Notebook* (1981), and *The Healing Heart: Antidotes
to Panic and Helplessness* (1983). His last book,
Head First, was published in 1990. "Pain Is Not the
Ultimate Enemy" originally appeared in *Anatomy of
an Illness.* In this essay, Cousins describes and
evaluates some of the causes of pain and the
effects of medications traditionally recommended to
control pain. Although Cousins' analyses are
considered highly controversial by many medical
professionals, they raise intriguing questions and
offer thought-provoking answers.

A
1   mericans are probably the most pain-conscious people on the face of the earth. For years we have had it drummed into us—in print, on radio, over television, in everyday conversation—that any hint of pain is to be banished as though it were the ultimate evil. As a result, we are becoming a nation of pill-grabbers and hypochondriacs, escalating the slightest ache into a searing ordeal.

2   We know very little about pain and what we don't know makes it hurt all the more. Indeed, no form of illiteracy in the United States is so widespread or costly as ignorance about pain—what it is, what causes it, how to deal with it without panic. Almost everyone can rattle off the names of at least a dozen drugs that can deaden pain from every conceivable cause—all the way from headaches to hemorrhoids. There is far less knowledge about the fact that about 90 percent of pain is self-limiting, that it is not always an indication of poor health, and that, most frequently, it is the result of tension, stress, worry, idleness, boredom, frustration, suppressed rage, insufficient sleep, overeating, poorly balanced diet, smoking, excessive drinking, inadequate exercise, stale air, or any of the other abuses encountered by the human body in modern society.

3   The most ignored fact of all about pain is that the best way to eliminate it is to eliminate the abuse. Instead, many people reach almost instinctively for the painkillers—aspirins, barbiturates, codeines, tranquilizers, sleeping pills, and dozens of other analgesics or desensitizing drugs.

4   Most doctors are profoundly troubled over the extent to which the medical profession today is taking on the trappings of a pain-killing industry. Their offices are overloaded with people who are morbidly but mistakenly convinced that something dreadful is about to happen to them. It is all too evident that the campaign to get people to run to a doctor at the first sign of pain has boomeranged. Physicians find it difficult to give adequate attention to patients genuinely in need of expert diagnosis and treatment because their time is soaked up by people who have nothing wrong with them except a temporary indisposition or a psychogenic ache.

5   Patients tend to feel indignant and insulted if the physician tells them he can find no organic cause for the pain. They tend to interpret the term "psychogenic" to mean that they are complaining of nonexistent symptoms. They need to be educated about the fact that many forms of pain have no underlying physical cause but are the result, as mentioned earlier, of tension, stress, or hostile factors in the general environment. Sometimes a pain may be a manifestation of "conversion hysteria" . . . the name given by Jean Charcot to physical symptoms that have their origins in emotional disturbances.

6   Obviously, it is folly for an individual to ignore symptoms that could be a warning of a potentially serious illness. Some people are so terrified of getting bad news from a doctor that they allow their malaise to worsen, sometimes past the point of no return. Total neglect is not the answer to

hypochondria. The only answer has to be increased education about the way the human body works, so that more people will be able to steer an intelligent course between promiscuous pill-popping and irresponsible disregard of genuine symptoms.

7   Of all forms of pain, none is more important for the individual to understand than the "threshold" variety. Almost everyone has a telltale ache that is triggered whenever tension or fatigue reaches a certain point. It can take the form of a migraine-type headache or a squeezing pain deep in the abdomen or cramps or a pain in the lower back or even pain in the joints. The individual who has learned how to make the correlation between such threshold pains and their cause doesn't panic when they occur; he or she does something about relieving the stress and tension. Then, if the pain persists despite the absence of apparent cause, the individual will telephone the doctor.

8   If ignorance about the nature of pain is widespread, ignorance about the way pain-killing drugs work is even more so. What is not generally understood is that many of the vaunted pain-killing drugs conceal the pain without correcting the underlying condition. They deaden the mechanism in the body that alerts the brain to the fact that something may be wrong. The body can pay a high price for suppression of pain without regard to its basic cause.

9   Professional athletes are sometimes severely disadvantaged by trainers whose job it is to keep them in action. The more famous the athlete, the greater the risk that he or she may be subjected to extreme medical measures when injury strikes. The star baseball pitcher whose arm is sore because of a torn muscle or tissue damage may need sustained rest more than anything else. But his team is battling for a place in the World Series; so the trainer or team doctor, called upon to work his magic, reaches for a strong dose of butazolidine or other powerful pain suppressants. Presto, the pain disappears! The pitcher takes his place on the mound and does superbly. That could be the last game, however, in which he is able to throw a ball with full strength. The drugs didn't repair the torn muscle or cause the damaged tissue to heal. What they did was to mask the pain, enabling the pitcher to throw hard, further damaging the torn muscle. Little wonder that so many star athletes are cut down in their prime, more the victims of overzealous treatment of their injuries than of the injuries themselves.

10   The king of all painkillers, of course, is aspirin. The U.S. Food and Drug Administration permits aspirin to be sold without prescription, but the drug, contrary to popular belief, can be dangerous, and, in sustained doses, potentially lethal. Aspirin is self-administered by more people than any other drug in the world. Some people are aspirin-poppers, taking ten or more a day. What they don't know is that the smallest dose can cause internal bleeding. Even more serious perhaps is the fact that aspirin is antagonistic to collagen, which has a key role in the formation of connective tissue. Since

many forms of arthritis involve disintegration of the connective tissue, the steady use of aspirin can actually intensify the underlying arthritic condition.

11   Aspirin is not the only pain-killing drug, of course, that is known to have dangerous side effects. Dr. Daphne A. Roe, of Cornell University, at a medical meeting in New York City in 1974, presented startling evidence of a wide range of hazards associated with sedatives and other pain suppressants. Some of these drugs seriously interfere with the ability of the body to metabolize food properly, producing malnutrition. In some instances, there is also the danger of bone-marrow depression, interfering with the ability of the body to replenish its blood supply.

12   Pain-killing drugs are among the greatest advances in the history of medicine. Properly used, they can be a boon in alleviating suffering and in treating disease. But their indiscriminate and promiscuous use is making psychological cripples and chronic ailers out of millions of people. The unremitting barrage of advertising for pain-killing drugs, especially over television, has set the stage for a mass anxiety neurosis. Almost from the moment children are old enough to sit upright in front of a television screen, they are being indoctrinated into the hypochondriac's clamorous and morbid world. Little wonder so many people fear pain more than death itself.

13   It might be a good idea if concerned physicians and educators could get together to make knowledge about pain an important part of the regular school curriculum. As for the populace at large, perhaps some of the same techniques used by public-service agencies to make people cancer-conscious can be used to counteract the growing terror of pain and illness in general. People ought to know that nothing is more remarkable about the human body than its recuperative drive, given a modicum of respect. If our broadcasting stations cannot provide equal time for responses to the pain-killing advertisements, they might at least set aside a few minutes each day for common-sense remarks on the subject of pain. As for the Food and Drug Administration, it might be interesting to know why an agency that has energetically warned the American people against taking vitamins without prescriptions is doing so little to control over-the-counter sales each year of billions of pain-killing pills, some of which can do more harm than the pain they are supposed to suppress.

Topics for Writing and Discussion

1. Why does Cousins believe that Americans are highly conscious of pain? What has resulted from this awareness?

2. What does Cousins believe are the most common causes of pain in our society? How does he think this pain can best be eliminated?

3. How does Cousins use his explanations of cause and effect to appeal to his audience? For example, does he offer sound evidence? Does he

explain what most people would agree to be common experiences? Does he give reasonable credit to the medical profession for what its members have achieved?

4. What effects would Cousins like his essay to have? What changes does he recommend directly? What changes does he imply he would like to see?

5. Write an essay describing the struggle of someone you know with an addiction. Explain the causes and the most important effects.

E. M. Forster, working on the libretto of Benjamin Britten's opera Billy Budd *for the 1951 Festival of Britain (The Bettmann Archive)*

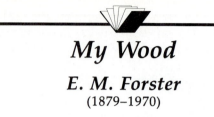

My Wood

E. M. Forster
(1879–1970)

Edward Morgan Forster was born in London and
spent his early years in England. While studying at
King's College, Cambridge, he became deeply
interested in cultures other than his own and later
traveled widely. In 1912 he sailed with two friends
to India where his observations and experiences
provided him with the materials from which he
later created his highly acclaimed novel *A Passage
to India* (1924), the book to which he refers in the
first paragraph of "My Wood." Forster also wrote
literary criticism, biographies, and essays on travel.
A collection of his essays, *Two Cheers for
Democracy*, was published in 1951. In this essay
from *Abinger Harvest* (1936), Forster explains the
effects produced by owning property. With wit and
humor, Forster suggests that purchasing land may
not bring the uncomplicated happiness one
might expect.

1   A few years ago I wrote a book which dealt in part with the difficulties
of the English in India. Feeling that they would have had no difficulties in
India themselves, the Americans read the book freely. The more they read
it the better it made them feel, and a cheque to the author was the result.
I bought a wood with the cheque. It is not a large wood—it contains scarcely
any trees, and it is intersected, blast it, by a public footpath. Still, it is the
first property that I have owned, so it is right that other people should
participate in my shame, and should ask themselves, in accents that will
vary in horror, this very important question: What is the effect of property
upon the character? Don't let's touch economics; the effect of private own-

ership upon the community as a whole is another question—a more important question, perhaps, but another one. Let's keep to psychology. If you own things, what's their effect on you? What's the effect on me of my wood?

2   In the first place, it makes me feel heavy. Property does have this effect. Property produces men of weight, and it was a man of weight who failed to get into the Kingdom of Heaven. He was not wicked, that unfortunate millionaire in the parable, he was only stout; he stuck out in front, not to mention behind, and as he wedged himself this way and that in the crystalline entrance and bruised his well-fed flanks, he saw beneath him a comparatively slim camel passing through the eye of a needle and being woven into the robe of God. The Gospels all through couple stoutness and slowness. They point out what is perfectly obvious, yet seldom realized: that if you have a lot of things you cannot move about a lot, that furniture requires dusting, dusters require servants, servants require insurance stamps, and the whole tangle of them makes you think twice before you accept an invitation to dinner or go for a bathe in the Jordan. Sometimes the Gospels proceed further and say with Tolstoy that property is sinful; they approach the difficult ground of asceticism here, where I cannot follow them. But as to the immediate effects of property on people, they just show straightforward logic. It produces men of weight. Men of weight cannot, by definition, move like the lightning from the East unto the West, and the ascent of a fourteen-stone bishop into a pulpit is thus the exact antithesis of the coming of the Son of Man. My wood makes me feel heavy.

3   In the second place, it makes me feel it ought to be larger.

4   The other day I heard a twig snap in it. I was annoyed at first, for I thought that someone was blackberrying, and depreciating the value of the undergrowth. On coming nearer, I saw it was not a man who had trodden on the twig and snapped it, but a bird, and I felt pleased. My bird. The bird was not equally pleased. Ignoring the relation between us, it took fright as soon as it saw the shape of my face, and flew straight over the boundary hedge into a field, the property of Mrs. Henessy, where it sat down with a loud squawk. It had become Mrs. Henessy's bird. Something seemed grossly amiss here, something that would not have occurred had the wood been larger. I could not afford to buy Mrs. Henessy out, I dared not murder her, and limitations of this sort beset me on every side. Ahab did not want that vineyard—he only needed it to round off his property, preparatory to plotting a new curve—and all the land around my wood has become necessary to me in order to round off the wood. A boundary protects. But—poor little thing—the boundary ought in its turn to be protected. Noises on the edge of it. Children throw stones. A little more, and then a little more, until we reach the sea. Happy Canute! Happier Alexander! And after all, why should even the world be the limit of possession? A rocket containing a Union Jack, will, it is hoped, be shortly fired at the moon. Mars. Sirius. Beyond which . . . But these immensities ended by saddening me. I could not suppose that

my wood was the destined nucleus of universal dominion—it is so very small and contains no mineral wealth beyond the blackberries. Nor was I comforted when Mrs. Henessy's bird took alarm for the second time and flew clean away from us all, under the belief that it belonged to itself.

5   In the third place, property makes its owner feel that he ought to do something to it. Yet he isn't sure what. A restlessness comes over him, a vague sense that he has a personality to express—the same sense which, without any vagueness, leads the artist to an act of creation. Sometimes I think I will cut down such trees as remain in the wood, at other times I want to fill up the gaps between them with new trees. Both impulses are pretentious and empty. They are not honest movements toward money-making or beauty. They spring from a foolish desire to express myself and from an inability to enjoy what I have got. Creation, property, enjoyment form a sinister trinity in the human mind. Creation and enjoyment are both very, very good, yet they are often unattainable without a material basis, and at such moments property pushes itself in as a substitute, saying, "Accept me instead—I'm good enough for all three." It is not enough. It is, as Shakespeare said of lust, "The expense of spirit in a waste of shame": it is "Before, a joy proposed; behind, a dream." Yet we don't know how to shun it. It is forced on us by our economic system as the alternative to starvation. It is also forced on us by an internal defect in the soul, by the feeling that in property may lie the germs of self-development and of exquisite or heroic deeds. Our life on earth is, and ought to be, material and carnal. But we have not yet learned to manage our materialism and carnality properly; they are still entangled with the desire for ownership, where (in the words of Dante) "Possession is one with loss."

6   And this brings us to our fourth and final point: the blackberries.

7   Blackberries are not plentiful in this meagre grove, but they are easily seen from the public footpath which traverses it, and all too easily gathered. Foxgloves, too—people will pull up the foxgloves, and ladies of an educational tendency even grub for toadstools to show them on the Monday in class. Other ladies, less educated, roll down the bracken in the arms of their gentlemen friends. There is paper, there are tins. Pray, does my wood belong to me or doesn't it? And, if it does, should I not own it best by allowing no one else to walk there? There is a wood near Lyme Regis, also cursed by a public footpath, where the owner has not hesitated on this point. He had built high stone walls each side of the path, and has spanned it by bridges, so that the public circulate like termites while he gorges on the blackberries unseen. He really does own his wood, this able chap. Dives in Hell did pretty well, but the gulf dividing him from Lazarus could be traversed by vision, and nothing traverses it here. And perhaps I shall come to this in time. I shall wall in and fence out until I really taste the sweets of property. Enormously stout, endlessly avaricious, pseudocreative, intensely selfish, I shall weave upon my forehead the quadruple crown of possession until

those nasty Bolshies come and take it off again and thrust me aside into the outer darkness.

Topics for Writing and Discussion

1. What are the four effects Forster describes as resulting from his purchase of the wood? Explain briefly some of the details Forster uses to explain each of these four effects.

2. In the opening section of the essay, Forster describes the response of Americans to a book he wrote. Why does he emphasize the reaction of Americans? What relationship does the opening paragraph have to the rest of the essay?

3. Forster uses many allusions (references to works or events outside the essay itself) to explain his ideas. Research several of these allusions and explain how these contribute to the central idea of the essay. (For example, in the second paragraph Forster refers to the Gospel of Matthew, 19:24, and to Leo Tolstoy's views on property.)

4. In the fifth paragraph, Forster begins with specific examples from his own wood and his response to it and ends with generalizations. As he moves from the concrete to the abstract, his tone changes. Analyze the change in tone and explain how it relates to Forster's thesis.

5. Think of something you have purchased after wanting it for a long time. In an essay explain the two or three main ways in which owning this item has affected your life.

Barbara Tuchman at home in Connecticut (© 1988 Jill Krementz)

"This Is the End of the World": The Black Death

Barbara Tuchman
(1912–1989)

After graduating from Radcliffe in 1933, Barbara
Tuchman worked for the Institute for Public
Relations. She began her career as a journalist
writing for the *Nation* and *The New Statesman*
magazines. During the Spanish Civil War and
during World War II, she served as a correspondent
for the *Nation* (London Office). Her historical
writings have been highly praised for both their
narrative power and their careful scholarship. Two
of her books have been awarded the Pulitzer Prize:
The Guns of August (1962) and *Stillwell and the
American Experiment in China* (1971). Tuchman was
a frequent contributor to such magazines as
Atlantic, American Scholar, Foreign Affairs, and
Harper's. In 1981, she collected many of her essays
and speeches in the highly regarded *Practicing
History* and in 1984 published *The March of Folly,
from Troy to Vietnam.* " 'This Is the End of the
World': The Black Death" was taken from *A
Distant Mirror* (1978). In this essay, Tuchman
explains both the causes and effects of the
devastating plague that swept through Europe in
the fourteenth century.

1 In October 1347, two months after the fall of Calais, Genoese trading
ships put into the harbor of Messina in Sicily with dead and dying men at
the oars. The ships had come from the Black Sea port of Caffa (now Feo-
dosiya) in the Crimea, where the Genoese maintained a trading post. The
diseased sailors showed strange black swellings about the size of an egg or

an apple in the armpits and groin. The swellings oozed blood and pus and were followed by spreading boils and black blotches on the skin from internal bleeding. The sick suffered severe pain and died quickly within five days of the first symptoms. As the disease spread, other symptoms of continuous fever and spitting of blood appeared instead of the swelling or buboes. These victims coughed and sweated heavily and died even more quickly, within three days or less, sometimes in 24 hours. In both types everything that issued from the body—breath, sweat, blood from the buboes and lungs, bloody urine, and blood-blackened excrement—smelled foul. Depression and despair accompanied the physical symptoms, and before the end "death is seen seated on the face."

2   The disease was bubonic plague, present in two forms: one that infected the bloodstream, causing the buboes and internal bleeding, and was spread by contact; and a second, more virulent pneumonic type that infected the lungs and was spread by respiratory infection. The presence of both at once caused the high mortality and speed of contagion. So lethal was the disease that cases were known of persons going to bed well and dying before they woke, of doctors catching the illness at a bedside and dying before the patient. So rapidly did it spread from one to another that to a French physician, Simon de Covino, it seemed as if one sick person "could infect the whole world." The malignity of the pestilence appeared more terrible because its victims knew no prevention and no remedy.

3   The physical suffering of the disease and its aspect of evil mystery were expressed in a strange Welsh lament which saw "death coming into our midst like black smoke, a plague which cuts off the young, a rootless phantom which has no mercy for fair countenance. Woe is me of the shilling in the armpit! It is seething, terrible . . . a head that gives pain and causes a loud cry . . . a painful angry knob . . . Great is its seething like a burning cinder . . . a grievous thing of ashy color." Its eruption is ugly like the "seeds of black peas, broken fragments of brittle sea-coal . . . the early ornaments of black death, cinders of the peelings of the cockle weed, a mixed multitude, a black plague like halfpence, like berries. . . ."

4   Rumors of a terrible plague supposedly arising in China and spreading through Tartary (Central Asia) to India and Persia, Mesopotamia, Syria, Egypt, and all of Asia Minor had reached Europe in 1346. They told of a death so devastating that all of India was said to be depopulated, whole territories covered by dead bodies, other areas with no one left alive. As added up by Pope Clement VI at Avignon, the total of reported dead reached 23,840,000. In the absence of a concept of contagion, no serious alarm was felt in Europe until the trading ships brought their black burden of pestilence into Messina while other infected ships from the Levant carried it to Genoa and Venice.

5   By January 1348 it penetrated France via Marseille, and North Africa via Tunis. Shipborne along coasts and navigable rivers, it spread westward from

Marseille through the ports of Languedoc to Spain and northward up the Rhône to Avignon, where it arrived in March. It reached Narbonne, Montpellier, Carcassonne, and Toulouse between February and May, and at the same time in Italy spread to Rome and Florence and their hinterlands. Between June and August it reached Bordeaux, Lyon, and Paris, spread to Burgundy and Normandy, and crossed the Channel from Normandy into southern England. From Italy during the same summer it crossed the Alps into Switzerland and reached eastward to Hungary.

6   In a given area the plague accomplished its kill within four to six months and then faded, except in the larger cities, where, rooting into the close-quartered population, it abated during the winter, only to reappear in spring and rage for another six months.

7   In 1349 it resumed in Paris, spread to Picardy, Flanders, and the Low Countries, and from England to Scotland and Ireland as well as to Norway, where a ghost ship with a cargo of wool and a dead crew drifted offshore until it ran aground near Bergen. From there the plague passed into Sweden, Denmark, Prussia, Iceland, and as far as Greenland. Leaving a strange pocket of immunity in Bohemia, and Russia unattacked until 1351, it had passed from most of Europe by mid-1350. Although the mortality rate was erratic, ranging from one fifth in some places to nine tenths or almost total elimination in others, the overall estimate of modern demographers has settled—for the area extending from India to Iceland—around the same figure expressed in Froissart's casual words: "a third of the world died." His estimate, the common one at the time, was not an inspired guess but a borrowing of St. John's figure for mortality from plague in Revelation, the favorite guide to human affairs of the Middle Ages.

8   A third of Europe would have meant about 20 million deaths. No one knows in truth how many died. Contemporary reports were an awed impression, not an accurate count. In crowded Avignon, it was said, 400 died daily; 7,000 houses emptied by death were shut up; a single graveyard received 11,000 corpses in six weeks; half the city's inhabitants reportedly died, including 9 cardinals or one third of the total, and 70 lesser prelates. Watching the endlessly passing death carts, chroniclers let normal exaggeration take wings and put the Avignon death toll at 62,000 and even at 120,000, although the city's total population was probably less than 50,000.

9   When graveyards filled up, bodies at Avignon were thrown into the Rhône until mass burial pits were dug for dumping the corpses. In London in such pits corpses piled up in layers until they overflowed. Everywhere reports speak of the sick dying too fast for the living to bury. Corpses were dragged out of homes and left in front of doorways. Morning light revealed new piles of bodies. In Florence the dead were gathered up by the Compagnia della Misericordia—founded in 1244 to care for the sick—whose members wore red robes and hoods masking the face except for the eyes. When their

efforts failed, the dead lay putrid in the streets for days at a time. When no coffins were to be had, the bodies were laid on boards, two or three at once, to be carried to graveyards or common pits. Families dumped their own relatives into the pits, or buried them so hastily and thinly "that dogs dragged them forth and devoured their bodies."

10   Amid accumulating death and fear of contagion, people died without last rites and were buried without prayers, a prospect that terrified the last hours of the stricken. A bishop in England gave permission to laymen to make confession to each other as was done by the Apostles, "or if no man is present then even to a woman," and if no priest could be found to administer extreme unction, "then faith must suffice." Clement VI found it necessary to grant remissions of sin to all who died of the plague because so many were unattended by priests. "And no bells tolled," wrote a chronicler of Siena, "and nobody wept no matter what his loss because almost everyone expected death. . . . And people said and believed, 'this is the end of the world.' "

11   In Paris, where the plague lasted through 1349, the reported death rate was 800 a day, in Pisa 500, in Vienna 500 to 600. The total dead in Paris numbered 50,000 or half the population. Florence, weakened by the famine of 1347, lost three to four fifths of its citizens, Venice two thirds, Hamburg and Bremen, though smaller in size, about the same proportion. Cities, as centers of transportation, were more likely to be affected than villages, although once a village was infected, its death rate was equally high. At Givry, a prosperous village in Burgundy of 1,200 to 1,500 people, the parish register records 615 deaths in the space of fourteen weeks, compared to an average of thirty deaths a year in the previous decade. In three villages of Cambridgeshire, manorial records show a death rate of 47 percent, 57 percent, and in one case 70 percent. When the last survivors, too few to carry on, moved away, a deserted village sank back into the wilderness and disappeared from the map altogether, leaving only a grass-covered ghostly outline to show where mortals once had lived.

12   In enclosed places such as monasteries and prisons, the infection of one person usually meant that of all, as happened in the Franciscan convents of Carcassonne and Marseille, where every inmate without exception died. Of the 140 Dominicans at Montpellier only seven survived. Petrarch's brother Gherardo, member of a Carthusian monastery, buried the prior and 34 fellow monks one by one, sometimes three a day, until he was left alone with his dog and fled to look for a place that would take him in. Watching every comrade die, men in such places could not but wonder whether the strange peril that filled the air had not been sent to exterminate the human race. In Kilkenny, Ireland, Brother John Clyn of the Friars Minor, another monk left alone among dead men, kept a record of what had happened lest "things which should be remembered perish with time and vanish from the memory of those who come after us." Sensing "the whole world, as it were,

placed within the grasp of the Evil One," and waiting for death to visit him too, he wrote, "I leave parchment to continue this work, if perchance any man survive and any of the race of Adam escape this pestilence and carry on the work which I have begun." Brother John, as noted by another hand, died of the pestilence, but he foiled oblivion.

13   The largest cities of Europe, with populations of about 100,000, were Paris and Florence, Venice and Genoa. At the next level, with more than 50,000, were Ghent and Bruges in Flanders, Milan, Bologna, Rome, Naples, and Palermo, and Cologne. London hovered below 50,000, the only city in England except York with more than 10,000. At the level of 20,000 to 50,000 were Bordeaux, Toulouse, Montpellier, Marseille, and Lyon in France, Barcelona, Seville, and Toledo in Spain, Siena, Pisa, and other secondary cities in Italy, and the Hanseatic trading cities of the Empire. The plague raged through them all, killing anywhere from one third to two thirds of their inhabitants. Italy, with a total population of 10 to 11 million, probably suffered the heaviest toll. Following the Florentine bankruptcies, the crop failures and workers' riots of 1346–47, the revolt of Cola di Rienzi that plunged Rome into anarchy, the plague came as the peak of successive calamities. As if the world were indeed in the grasp of the Evil One, its first appearance on the European mainland in January 1348 coincided with a fearsome earthquake that carved a path of wreckage from Naples up to Venice. Houses collapsed, church towers toppled, villages were crushed, and the destruction reached as far as Germany and Greece. Emotional response, dulled by horrors, underwent a kind of atrophy epitomized by the chronicler who wrote, "And in these days was burying without sorrowe and wedding without friendschippe."

14   In Siena, where more than half of the inhabitants died of the plague, work was abandoned on the great cathedral, planned to be the largest in the world, and never resumed, owing to loss of workers and master masons and "the melancholy and grief" of the survivors. The cathedral's truncated transept still stands in permanent witness to the sweep of death's scythe. Agnolo di Tura, a chronicler of Siena, recorded the fear of contagion that froze every other instinct. "Father abandoned child, wife husband, one brother another," he wrote, "for this plague seemed to strike through the breath and sight. And so they died. And no one could be found to bury the dead for money or friendship. . . . And I, Angolo di Tura, called the Fat, buried my five children with my own hands, and so did many others likewise."

15   There were many to echo his account of inhumanity and few to balance it, for the plague was not the kind of calamity that inspired mutual help. Its loathsomeness and deadliness did not herd people together in mutual distress, but only prompted their desire to escape each other. "Magistrates and notaries refused to come and make the wills of the dying," reported a Franciscan friar of Piazza in Sicily; what was worse, "even the priests did not come to hear their confessions." A clerk of the Archbishop of Canterbury

reported the same of English priests who "turned away from the care of their benefices from fear of death." Cases of parents deserting children and children their parents were reported across Europe from Scotland to Russia. The calamity chilled the hearts of men, wrote Boccaccio in his famous account of the plague in Florence that serves as introduction to the *Decameron*. "One man shunned another . . . kinsfolk held aloof, brother was forsaken by brother, oftentimes husband by wife; nay, what is more, and scarcely to be believed, fathers and mothers were found to abandon their own children to their fate, untended, unvisited as if they had been strangers." Exaggeration and literary pessimism were common in the 14th century, but the Pope's physician, Guy de Chauliac, was a sober, careful observer who reported the same phenomenon: "A father did not visit his son, nor the son his father. Charity was dead."

16   Yet not entirely. In Paris, according to the chronicler Jean de Venette, the nuns of the Hôtel Dieu or municipal hospital, "having no fear of death, tended the sick with all sweetness and humility." New nuns repeatedly took the places of those who died, until the majority "many times renewed by death now rest in peace with Christ as we may piously believe."

17   When the plague entered northern France in July 1348, it settled first in Normandy and, checked by winter, gave Picardy a deceptive interim until the next summer. Either in mourning or warning, black flags were flown from church towers of the worst-stricken villages of Normandy. "And in that time," wrote a monk of the abbey of Fourcarment, "the mortality was so great among the people of Normandy that those of Picardy mocked them." The same unneighborly reaction was reported of the Scots, separated by a winter's immunity from the English. Delighted to hear of the disease that was scourging the "southrons," they gathered forces for an invasion, "laughing at their enemies." Before they could move, the savage mortality fell upon them too, scattering some in death and the rest in panic to spread the infection as they fled.

18   In Picardy in the summer of 1349 the pestilence penetrated the castle of Coucy to kill Enguerrand's mother,[1] Catherine, and her new husband. Whether her nine-year-old son escaped by chance or was perhaps living elsewhere with one of his guardians is unrecorded. In nearby Amiens, tannery workers, responding quickly to losses in the labor force, combined to bargain for higher wages. In another place villagers were seen dancing to drums and trumpets, and on being asked the reason, answered that, seeing their neighbors die day by day while their village remained immune, they believed that they could keep the plague from entering "by the jollity that is in us. That is why we dance." Further north in Tournai on the border of

[1]To unify and personalize *A Distant Mirror*, the study of the fourteenth century from which this excerpt is taken, Tuchman shows how events affected the life of one individual, a French nobleman named Enguerrand de Coucy. [Ed. note]

Flanders, Gilles li Muisis, Abbot of St. Martin's, kept one of the epidemic's most vivid accounts. The passing bells rang all day and all night, he recorded, because sextons were anxious to obtain their fees while they could. Filled with the sound of mourning, the city became oppressed by fear, so that the authorities forbade the tolling of bells and the wearing of black and restricted funeral services to two mourners. The silencing of funeral bells and of criers' announcements of deaths was ordained by most cities. Siena imposed a fine on the wearing of mourning clothes by all except widows.

19   Flight was the chief recourse of those who could afford it or arrange it. The rich fled to their country places like Boccaccio's young patricians of Florence, who settled in a pastoral palace "removed on every side from the road" with "wells of cool water and vaults of rare wines." The urban poor died in their burrows, "and only the stench of their bodies informed neighbors of their death." That the poor were more heavily afflicted than the rich was clearly remarked at the time, in the north as in the south. A Scottish chronicler, John of Fordun, stated flatly that the pest "attacked especially the meaner sort and common people—seldom the magnates." Simon de Covino of Montpellier made the same observation. He ascribed it to the misery and want and hard lives that made the poor more susceptible, which was half the truth. Close contact and lack of sanitation was the unrecognized other half. It was noticed too that the young died in greater proportion than the old; Simon de Covino compared the disappearance of youth to the withering of flowers in the fields.

20   In the countryside peasants dropped dead on the roads, in the fields, in their houses. Survivors in growing helplessness fell into apathy, leaving ripe wheat uncut and livestock untended. Oxen and asses, sheep and goats, pigs and chickens ran wild and they too, according to local reports, succumbed to the pest. English sheep, bearers of the precious wool, died throughout the country. The chronicler Henry Knighton, canon of Leicester Abbey, reported 5,000 dead in one field alone, "their bodies so corrupted by the plague that neither beast nor bird would touch them," and spreading an appalling stench. In the Austrian Alps wolves came down to prey upon sheep and then, "as if alarmed by some invisible warning, turned and fled back into the wilderness." In remote Dalmatia bolder wolves descended upon a plague-stricken city and attacked human survivors. For want of herdsmen, cattle strayed from place to place and died in hedgerows and ditches. Dogs and cats fell like the rest.

21   The dearth of labor held a fearful prospect because the 14th century lived close to the annual harvest both for food and for next year's seed. "So few servants and laborers were left," wrote Knighton, "that no one knew where to turn for help." The sense of a vanishing future created a kind of dementia of despair. A Bavarian chronicler of Neuberg on the Danube recorded that "Men and women . . . wandered around as if mad" and let their cattle stray "because no one had any inclination to concern themselves about the fu-

ture." Fields went uncultivated, spring seed unsown. Second growth with nature's awful energy crept back over cleared land, dikes crumbled, salt water reinvaded and soured the lowlands. With so few hands remaining to restore the work of centuries, people felt, in Walsingham's words, that "the world could never again regain its former prosperity."

22   Though the death rate was higher among the anonymous poor, the known and the great died too. King Alfonso XI of Castile was the only reigning monarch killed by the pest, but his neighbor King Pedro of Aragon lost his wife, Queen Leonora, his daughter Marie, and a niece in the space of six months. John Cantacuzene, Emperor of Byzantium, lost his son. In France the lame Queen Jeanne and her daughter-in-law Bonne de Luxemburg, wife of the Dauphin, both died in 1349 in the same phase that took the life of Enguerrand's mother. Jeanne, Queen of Navarre, daughter of Louis X, was another victim. Edward III's second daughter, Joanna, who was on her way to marry Pedro, the heir of Castile, died in Bordeaux. Women appear to have been more vulnerable than men, perhaps because, being more house-bound, they were more exposed to fleas. Boccaccio's mistress Fiammetta, illegitimate daughter of the King of Naples, died, as did Laura, the beloved—whether real or fictional—of Petrarch. Reaching out to us in the future, Petrarch cried, "Oh happy posterity who will not experience such abysmal woe and will look upon our testimony as a fable."

23   In Florence Giovanni Villani, the great historian of his time, died at 68 in the midst of an unfinished sentence: ". . . *e dure questo pistolenza fino a . . .* (in the midst of this pestilence there came to an end . . .)." Siena's master painters, the brothers Ambrogio and Pietro Lorenzetti, whose names never appear after 1348, presumably perished in the plague, as did Andrea Pisano, architect and sculptor of Florence. William of Ockham and the English mystic Richard Rolle of Hampole both disappear from mention after 1349. Francisco Datini, merchant of Prato, lost both his parents and two siblings. Curious sweeps of mortality afflicted certain bodies of merchants in London. All eight wardens of the Company of Cutters, all six wardens of the Hatters, and four wardens of the Goldsmiths died before July 1350. Sir John Pulteney, master draper and four times Mayor of London, was a victim, likewise Sir John Montgomery, Governor of Calais.

24   Among the clergy and doctors the mortality was naturally high because of the nature of their professions. Out of 24 physicians in Venice, 20 were said to have lost their lives in the plague, although, according to another account, some were believed to have fled or to have shut themselves up in their houses. At Montpellier, site of the leading medieval medical school, the physician Simon de Covino reported that, despite the great number of doctors, "hardly one of them escaped." In Avignon, Guy de Chauliac con-fessed that he performed his medical visits only because he dared not stay away for fear of infamy, but "I was in continual fear." He claimed to have

contracted the disease but to have cured himself by his own treatment; if so, he was one of the few who recovered.

25 Clerical mortality varied with rank. Although the one-third toll of cardinals reflects the same proportion as the whole, this was probably due to their concentration in Avignon. In England, in strange and almost sinister procession, the Archbishop of Canterbury, John Stratford, died in August 1348, his appointed successor died in May 1349, and the next appointee three months later, all three within a year. Despite such weird vagaries, prelates in general managed to sustain a higher survival rate than the lesser clergy. Among bishops the deaths have been estimated at about one in twenty. The loss of priests, even if many avoided their fearful duty of attending the dying, was about the same as among the population as a whole.

26 Government officials, whose loss contributed to the general chaos, found, on the whole, no special shelter. In Siena four of the nine members of the governing oligarchy died, in France one third of the royal notaries, in Bristol 15 out of the 52 members of the Town Council or almost one third. Tax-collecting obviously suffered, with the result that Philip VI was unable to collect more than a fraction of the subsidy granted him by the Estates in the winter of 1347–48.

27 Lawlessness and debauchery accompanied the plague as they had during the great plague of Athens of 430 B.C., when according to Thucydides, men grew bold in the indulgence of pleasure: "For seeing how the rich died in a moment and those who had nothing immediately inherited their property, they reflected that life and riches were alike transitory and they resolved to enjoy themselves while they could." Human behavior is timeless. When St. John had his vision of plague in Revelation, he knew from some experience or race memory that those who survived "repented not of the work of their hands. . . . Neither repented they of their murders, nor of their sorceries, nor of their fornication, nor of their thefts."

Notes²

1. "Death Is Seen Seated": Simon de Covino, q. Campbell, 80.
2. "Could Infect the World": q. Gasquet, 41.
3. Welsh Lament: q. Ziegler, 190.
9. "Dogs Dragged Them Forth": Agnolo di Tura, q. Ziegler, 58.
10. "Or If No Man Is Present": Bishop of Bath and Wells, q. Ziegler, 125. "No Bells Tolled": Agnolo di Tura, q. Schevill, *Siena*, 211. The same observation was made by Gabriel de Muisis, notary of Piacenza, q. Crawfurd, 113.

²In *A Distant Mirror* Tuchman chooses to document all the sources of her information at the end of her book, rather than to use hundreds of footnotes throughout her study. For this excerpt, however, we have listed Tuchman's sources by the paragraph in which they appear in this text. A bibliography of the works cited follows these notes. [Ed. note]

11. Givry Parish Register: Renouard, III. Three Villages of Cambridgeshire: Saltmarsh.

12. Petrarch's Brother: Bishop, 273. Brother John Clyn: q. Ziegler, 195.

13. Atrophy; "and in These Days": q. Deaux, 143, citing only "an old northern chronicle."

14. Agnolo Di Tura, "Father Abandoned Child": q. Ziegler, 58.

15. "Magistrates and Notaries": q. Deaux, 49. English Priests Turned away: Ziegler, 261. Parents Deserting Children: Hecker, 30. Guy De Chauliac, "A Father": q. Gasquet, 50–51.

16. Nuns of the Hotel Dieu: *Chron. Jean de Venette*, 49.

17. Picards and Scots Mock Mortality of Neighbors: Gasquet, 53, and Ziegler, 198.

18. Catherine de Coucy: *L'Art de vérifier*, 237. Amiens Tanners: Gasquet, 57. "By the Jollity That Is in Us": *Grandes Chrons.*, VI, 486–87.

19. John of Fordun: q. Ziegler, 199. Simon de Covino on the Poor: Gasquet, 42. On Youth: Cazelles, *Peste*.

20. Knighton on Sheep: q. Ziegler, 175. Wolves of Austria and Dalmatia: ibid., 84, III. Dogs and Cats: Muisis, q. Gasquet, 44, 61.

21. Bavarian Chronicler of Neuberg: q. Ziegler, 84. Walsingham, "The World Could Never": Denifle, 273.

22. "Oh Happy Posterity": q. Ziegler, 45.

23. Giovanni Villani, "*e dure questo*": q. Snell, 334.

24. Physicians of Venice: Campbell, 98. Simon de Covino: ibid., 31. Guy de Chauliac, "I Was in Fear": q. Thompson, *Ec. and Soc.*, 379.

27. Thucydides: q. Crawfurd, 30–31.

Bibliography

L'Art de vérifier les dates des faits historiques, par un Religieux de la Congregation de St.-Maur, vol. XII. Paris, 1818.

Bishop, Morris, *Petrarch and His World.* Indiana University Press, 1963.

Campbell, Anna M., *The Black Death and Men of Learning.* Columbia University Press, 1931.

Cazelles, Raymond. "*La Peste de 1348–49 en Langue d'oil; épidémie prolitarienne et enfantine.*" *Bull. philologique et historique,* 1962, pp. 293–305.

Chronicle of Jean de Venette. Trans. Jean Birdsall. Ed. Richard A. Newhall. Columbia University Press, 1853.

Crawfurd, Raymond, *Plague and Pestilence in Literature and Art.* Oxford, 1914.

Deaux, George. *The Black Death, 1347.* London, 1969.

Denifle, Henri, *La Désolation des églises, monastères et hopitaux en France pendant la guerre de cent ans,* vol. I. Paris, 1899.

Gasquet, Francis Aidan, Abbot, *The Black Death of 1348 and 1349,* 2nd ed. London, 1908.

Grandes Chroniques de France, vol. VI (to 1380). Ed. Paulin Paris. Paris, 1838.

Hecker, J. F. C., *The Epidemics of the Middle Ages.* London, 1844.

Renouard, Yves. "*La Peste noirs de 1348–50.*" *Rev. de Paris,* March, 1950.

Saltmarsh, John, "Plague and Economic Decline in England in the Later Middle Ages," *Cambridge Historical Journal,* vol. VII, no. 1, 1941.

Schevill, Ferdinand, *Siena: The History of a Medieval Commune.* New York, 1909.

Snell, Frederick, *The Fourteenth Century*. Edinburgh, 1899.
Thompson, James Westfall, *Economic and Social History of Europe in the Later Middle Ages*. New York, 1931.
Ziegler, Philip, *The Black Death*. New York, 1969. (The best modern study.)

Topics for Writing and Discussion

1. According to Tuchman's account, where did the bubonic plague originate and how did it spread to Europe?

2. Tuchman describes a complex scene as she explains the responses of groups and of individuals to the plague. Make a list of these responses and then divide them into negative, positive, and neutral categories. How did these responses affect the spread of the plague?

3. Tuchman cites many statistics to support her ideas. How does she keep these statistics from being simply a dull list of numbers?

4. How does Tuchman use cause-and-effect structure in this essay? Does she first explain the causes of the plague and then describe its effects? Or does she describe first effects and then causes? Or is the structure more complex than either of these choices?

5. Research the primary effects of a rare but nevertheless serious medical problem and write an essay similar to Tuchman's. Try to combine statistics and facts with examples of human responses and dilemma.

Alice Stewart Trillin in New York City (© Nancy Crampton)

Of Dragons and Garden Peas

Alice Stewart Trillin
(1938–   )

Public education consultant Alice Stewart Trillin,
author of *Teaching Basic Skills in College* (1980) as
well as numerous essays, developed lung cancer in
her thirties. The cancer was successfully treated
with chemotherapy, and when Trillin delivered the
speech "Of Dragons and Garden Peas" to students
at Cornell and Albert Einstein schools of medicine,
the former college instructor had been free of
cancer for four years. First published in the *New
England Journal of Medicine* in 1981, the article
addresses a basic truth that Trillin sees as common
ground for those who have cancer and those who
are cancer-free: "We are all afraid of dying."

1   When I first realized that I might have cancer, I felt immediately that I had entered a special place, a place I came to call "The Land of the Sick People." The most disconcerting thing, however, was not that I found that place terrifying and unfamiliar, but that I found it so ordinary, so banal. I didn't feel different, didn't feel that my life had radically changed at the moment the word *cancer* became attached to it. The same rules still held. What had changed, however, was other people's perceptions of me. Unconsciously, even with a certain amount of kindness, everyone—with the single rather extraordinary exception of my husband—regarded me as someone who had been altered irrevocably. I don't want to exaggerate my feeling of alienation or to give the impression that it was in any way dramatic. I have no horror stories of the kind I read a few years ago in the *New York Times*; people didn't move their desks away from me at the office or refuse to let their children play with my children at school because they thought that cancer was catching. My friends are all too sophisticated and too sen-

sitive for that kind of behavior. Their distance from me was marked most of all by their inability to understand the ordinariness, the banality of what was happening to me. They marveled at how well I was "coping with cancer." I had become special, no longer like them. Their genuine concern for what had happened to me, and their complete separateness from it, expressed exactly what I had felt all my life about anyone I had ever known who had experienced tragedy.

2   When asked to speak to a group of doctors and medical students about what it was like to be a cancer patient, I worried for a long time about what I should say. It was a perfect opportunity—every patient's fantasy—to complain about doctors' insensitivity, nurses who couldn't draw blood properly, and perhaps even the awful food in hospitals. Or, instead, I could present myself as the good patient, full of uplifting thoughts about how much I had learned from having cancer. But, unlike many people, I had had very good experiences with doctors and hospitals. And the role of the brave patient troubled me, because I was afraid that all the brave things I said might no longer hold if I got sick again. I had to think about this a great deal during the first two years after my operation as I watched my best friend live out my own worst nightmares. She discovered that she had cancer several months after I did. Several months after that, she discovered that it had metastasized; she underwent eight operations during the next year and a half before she died. All my brave talk was tested by her illness as it has not yet been tested by mine.

3   And so I decided not to talk about the things that separate those of us who have cancer from those who do not. I decided that the only relevant thing for me to talk about was the one thing that we all have most in common. We are all afraid of dying.

4   Our fear of death makes it essential to maintain a distance between ourselves and anyone who is threatened by death. Denying our connection to the precariousness of others' lives is a way of pretending that we are immortal. We need this deception—it is one of the ways we stay sane—but we also need to be prepared for the times when it doesn't work. For doctors, who confront death when they go to work in the morning as routinely as other people deal with balance sheets and computer printouts, and for me, to whom a chest x-ray or a blood test will never again be a simple, routine procedure, it is particularly important to face the fact of death squarely, to talk about it with one another.

5   Cancer connects us to one another because having cancer is an embodiment of the existential paradox that we all experience: we feel that we are immortal, yet we know that we will die. To Tolstoy's Ivan Ilyich, the syllogism he had learned as a child, " 'Caius is a man, men are mortal, therefore Caius is mortal,' had always seemed . . . correct as applied to Caius but certainly not as applied to himself." Like Ivan Ilyich, we all construct an elaborate set of defense mechanisms to separate ourselves from Caius. To

anyone who has had cancer, these defense mechanisms become talismans that we invest with a kind of magic. These talismans are essential to our sanity, and yet they need to be examined.

6   First of all, we believe in the magic of doctors and medicine. The purpose of a talisman is to give us control over the things we are afraid of. Doctors and patients are accomplices in staging a kind of drama in which we pretend that doctors have the power to keep us well. The very best doctors—and I have had the very best—share their power with their patients and try to give us the information that we need to control our own treatment. Whenever I am threatened by panic, my doctor sits me down and tells me something concrete. He draws a picture of my lung, or my lymph nodes; he explains as well as he can how cancer cells work and what might be happening in my body. Together, we approach my disease intelligently and rationally, as a problem to be solved, an exercise in logic to be worked out. Of course, through knowledge, through medicine, through intelligence, we do have some control. But at best this control is limited, and there is always the danger that the disease I have won't behave rationally and respond to the intelligent argument we have constructed. Cancer cells, more than anything else in nature, are likely to behave irrationally. If we think that doctors and medicine can always protect us, we are in danger of losing faith in doctors and medicine when their magic doesn't work. The physician who fails to keep us well is like an unsuccessful witch doctor; we have to drive him out of the tribe and look for a more powerful kind of magic.

7   The reverse of this, of course, is that the patient becomes a kind of talisman for the doctor. Doctors defy death by keeping people alive. To a patient, it becomes immediately clear that the best way to please a doctor is to be healthy. If you can't manage that, the next best thing is to be well-behaved. (Sometimes the difference between being healthy and being well-behaved becomes blurred in a hospital, so that it almost seems as if being sick were being badly behaved.) If we get well, we help our doctors succeed; if we are sick, we have failed. Patients often say that their doctors seem angry with them when they don't respond to treatment. I think that this phenomenon is more than patients' paranoia or the result of overdeveloped medical egos. It is the fear of death again. It is necessary for doctors to become a bit angry with patients who are dying, if only as a way of separating themselves from someone in whom they have invested a good bit of time and probably a good bit of caring. We all do this to people who are sick. I can remember being terribly angry with my mother who was prematurely senile, for a long time. Somehow I needed to think that it was her fault that she was sick, because her illness frightened me so much. I was also angry with my friend who died of cancer. I felt that she had let me down, that perhaps she hadn't fought hard enough. It was important for me to find reasons for her death, to find things that she might have done to cause it, as a way of separating myself from her and as a way of thinking that I would some-

how have behaved differently, that I would somehow have been able to stay alive.

8   So, once we have recognized the limitations of the magic of doctors and medicine, where are we? We have to turn to our own magic, to our ability to "control" our bodies. For people who don't have cancer, this often takes the form of jogging and exotic diets and transcendental meditation. For people who have cancer, it takes the form of conscious development of the will to live. For a long time after I found out that I had cancer, I loved hearing stories about people who had simply decided that they would not be sick. I remember one story about a man who had a lung tumor and a wife with breast cancer and several children to support; he said, "I simply can't afford to be sick." Somehow the tumor went away. I think I suspected that there was a missing part to this story when I heard it, but there was also something that sounded right to me. I knew what he meant. I also found the fact that I had cancer unacceptable; the thought that my children might grow up without me was as ridiculous as the thought that I might forget to make appointments for their dental checkups and polio shots. I simply had to be there. Of course, doctors give a lot of credence to the power of the will over illness, but I have always suspected that the stories in medical books about this power might also have missing parts. My friend who died wanted to live more than anyone I have ever known. The talisman of will didn't work for her.

9   The need to exert some kind of control over the irrational forces that we imagine are loose in our bodies also results in what I have come to recognize as the "brave act" put on by people who have cancer. We all do it. The blood-count line at Memorial Hospital can be one of the cheeriest places in New York on certain mornings. It was on this line, during my first visit to Memorial, that a young leukemia patient in remission told me, "They treat lung cancer like the common cold around here." (Believe me, that was the cheeriest thing anyone had said to me in months.) While waiting for blood counts, I have heard stories from people with lymphoma who were given up for dead in other hospitals and who are feeling terrific. The atmosphere in that line suggests a gathering of knights who have just slain a bunch of dragons. But there are always people in the line who don't say anything at all, and I always wonder if they have at other times felt the exhilaration felt by those of us who are well. We all know, at least, that the dragons are never quite dead and might at any time be around, ready for another fight. But our brave act is important. It is one of the ways we stay alive, and it is the way that we convince those who live in "The Land of the Well People" that we aren't all that different from them.

10   As much as I rely on the talisman of the will, I know that believing in it too much can lead to another kind of deception. There has been a great deal written (mostly by psychiatrists) about why people get cancer and which

personality types are most likely to get it. Susan Sontag has pointed out that this explanation of cancer parallels the explanations for tuberculosis that were popular before the discovery of the tubercle bacillus. But it is reassuring to think that people get cancer because of their personalities, because that implies that we have some control over whether we get it. (On the other hand, if people won't give up smoking to avoid cancer, I don't see how they can be expected to change their personalities on the basis of far less compelling evidence.) The trouble with this explanation of cancer is the trouble with any talisman: it is only useful when its charms are working. If I get sick, does that mean that my will to live isn't strong enough? Is being sick a moral and psychological failure? If I feel successful, as if I had slain a dragon, because I am well, should I feel guilty, as if I have failed, if I get sick?

11   One of the ways that all of us avoid thinking about death is by concentrating on the details of our daily lives. The work that we do every day and the people we love—the fabric of our lives—convince us that we are alive and that we will stay alive. William Saroyan said in a recent book, "Why am I writing this book? To save my life, to keep from dying, of course. That is why we get up in the morning." Getting up in the morning seems particularly miraculous after having seriously considered the possibility that these mornings might be limited. A year after I had my lung removed, my doctors asked me what I cared about most. I was about to go to Nova Scotia, where we have a summer home, and where I had not been able to go the previous summer because I was having radiation treatments, and I told him that what was most important to me was garden peas. Not the peas themselves, of course, though they were particularly good that year. What was extraordinary to me after that year was that I could again think that peas were important, that I could concentrate on the details of when to plant them and how much mulch they would need instead of thinking about platelets and white cells. I cherished the privilege of thinking about trivia. Thinking about death can make the details of our lives seem unimportant, and so, paradoxically, they become a burden—too much trouble to think about. This is the real meaning of depression: feeling weighed down by the concrete, unable to make the effort to move objects around, overcome by ennui. It is the fear of death that causes that ennui, because the fear of death ties us too much to the physical. We think too much about our bodies, and our bodies become too concrete—machines not functioning properly.

12   The other difficulty with the talisman of the moment is that it is often the very preciousness of these moments that makes the thought of death so painful. As my friend got closer to death she became rather removed from those she loved the most. She seemed to have gone to some place where we couldn't reach her—to have died what doctors sometimes call a "premature death." I much preferred to think of her enjoying precious moments. I remembered the almost ritualistic way she had her hair cut and tied in

satin ribbons before brain surgery, the funny, somehow joyful afternoon that we spent trying wigs on her newly shaved head. Those moments made it seem as if it wasn't so bad to have cancer. But of course it was bad. It was unspeakably bad, and toward the end she couldn't bear to speak about it or to be too close to the people she didn't want to leave. The strength of my love for my children, my husband, my life, even my garden peas has probably been more important than anything else in keeping me alive. The intensity of this love is also what makes me so terrified of dying.

13   For many, of course, a response to the existential paradox is religion—Kierkegaard's irrational leap toward faith. It is no coincidence that such a high number of conversions take place in cancer hospitals; there is even a group of Catholic nurses in New York who are referred to by other members of their hospital staff as "the death squad." I don't mean to belittle such conversions or any help that religion can give to anyone. I am at this point in my life simply unqualified to talk about the power of this particular talisman.

14   In considering some of the talismans we all use to deny death, I don't mean to suggest that these talismans should be abandoned. However, their limits must be acknowledged. Ernest Becker, in *The Denial of Death*, says that "skepticism is a more radical experience, a more manly confrontation of potential meaninglessness than mysticism." The most important thing I know now that I didn't know four years ago is that this "potential meaninglessness" can in fact be confronted. As much as I rely on my talismans—my doctors, my will, my husband, my children, and my garden peas—I know that from time to time I will have to confront what Conrad described as "the horror." I know that we can—all of us—confront that horror and not be destroyed by it, even, to some extent, be enhanced by it. To quote Becker again: "I think that taking life seriously means something such as this: that whatever man does on this planet has to be done in the lived truth of the terror of creation, of the grotesque, of the rumble of panic underneath everything. Otherwise it is false."

15   It astonishes me that having faced the terror, we continue to live, even to live with a great deal of joy. It is commonplace for people who have cancer—particularly those who feel as well as I do—to talk about how much richer their lives are because they have confronted death. Yes, my life is very rich. I have even begun to understand that wonderful line in *King Lear*, "Ripeness is all." I suppose that becoming ripe means finding out that none of the really important questions have answers. I wish that life had devised a less terrifying, less risky way of making me ripe. But I wasn't given any choice about this.

16   William Saroyan said recently, "I'm growing old! I'm falling apart! And it's VERY INTERESTING!" I'd be willing to bet that Mr. Saroyan, like me, would much rather be young and all in one piece. But somehow his longing

for youth and wholeness doesn't destroy him or stop him from getting up in the morning and writing, as he says, to save his life. We will never kill the dragon. But each morning we confront him. Then we give our children breakfast, perhaps put a bit more mulch on the peas, and hope that we can convince the dragon to stay away for a while longer.

Topics for Writing and Discussion

1. In what way does the essay's title reflect its content and central theme?

2. What cause-and-effect relationship does Trillin explore? Is the emphasis primarily on causes or on effects?

3. Since "Of Dragons and Garden Peas" was written as an address to medical students, what is Trillin's goal? Describe the changes in tone and content that might be needed if this essay had instead been directed toward people newly diagnosed with cancer.

4. What purpose do Trillin's numerous literary allusions serve? Do her readers need to be familiar with the authors mentioned to appreciate these references?

5. Trillin notes "that having faced the terror, we continue to live, even to live with a great deal of joy," and that many cancer survivors find their lives richer after the illness. In an essay describe a time in your life when you faced a great fear and show how it affected your view of life.

How Do You Know It's Good?

Marya Mannes
(1904–   )

Marya Mannes
(NYT Pictures)

As a feature editor for *Vogue* (1933–36) and *Glamour* (1946), Marya Mannes became a well-known figure in New York journalism. In addition to writing a monthly column for the *New York Times* (1967), Mannes has authored a number of novels, including *Message from a Stranger* (1948); a compilation of essays, *More in Anger* (1958); and a study of divorce, *Uncoupling: The Art of Coming Apart* (1972). In the 1962 essay "How Do You Know It's Good?" Mannes argues for the existence of definitive standards of artistic worth.

1   Suppose there were no critics to tell us how to react to a picture, a play, or a new composition of music. Suppose we wandered innocent as the dawn into an art exhibition of unsigned paintings. By what standards, by what values would we decide whether they were good or bad, talented or un-talented, successes or failures? How can we ever know that what we think is right?

2   For the last fifteen or twenty years the fashion in criticism or appreciation of the arts has been to deny the existence of any valid criteria and to make the words "good" or "bad" irrelevant, immaterial, and inapplicable. There is no such thing, we are told, as a set of standards, first acquired through experience and knowledge and later imposed on the subject under discussion. This has been a popular approach, for it relieves the critic of the responsibility of judgment and the public of the necessity of knowledge. It pleases those resentful of disciplines, it flatters the empty-minded by calling them open-minded, it comforts the confused. Under the banner of democracy and the kind of equality which our forefathers did *not* mean, it says, in effect, "Who are you to tell us what *is* good or bad?" This is the same cry used so long and so effectively by the producers of mass media who insist that it is the public, not they, who decides what it wants to hear and see, and

that for a critic to say that *this* program is bad and *this* program is good is purely a reflection of personal taste. Nobody recently has expressed this philosophy more succinctly than Dr. Frank Stanton, the highly intelligent president of CBS television. At a hearing before the Federal Communications Commission, this phrase escaped him under questioning: "One man's mediocrity is another man's good program."

3   There is no better way of saying "No values are absolute." There is another important aspect to this philosophy of *laissez faire:* It is the fear, in all observers of all forms of art, of guessing wrong. This fear is well come by, for who has not heard of the contemporary outcries against artists who later were called great? Every age has its arbiters who do not grow with their times, who cannot tell evolution from revolution or the difference between frivolous faddism, amateurish experimentation, and profound and necessary change. Who wants to be caught *flagrante delicto* with an error of judgment as serious as this? It is far safer, and certainly easier, to look at a picture or a play or a poem and to say "This is hard to understand, but it may be good," or simply to welcome it as a new form. The word "new"—in our country especially—has magical connotations. What is new must be good; what is old is probably bad. And if a critic can describe the new in language that nobody can understand, he's safer still. If he has mastered the art of saying nothing with exquisite complexity, nobody can quote him later as saying anything.

4   But all these, I maintain, are forms of abdication from the responsibility of judgment. In creating, the artist commits himself; in appreciating, you have a commitment of your own. For after all, it is the audience which makes the arts. A climate of appreciation is essential to its flowering, and the higher the expectations of the public, the better the performance of the artist. Conversely, only a public ill-served by its critics could have accepted as art and as literature so much in these last years that has been neither. If anything goes, everything goes; and at the bottom of the junkpile lie the discarded standards too.

5   But what are these standards? How do you get them? How do you know they're the right ones? How can you make a clear pattern out of so many intangibles, including that greatest one, the very private I?

6   Well for one thing, it's fairly obvious that the more you read and see and hear, the more equipped you'll be to practice that art of association which is at the basis of all understanding and judgment. The more you live and the more you look, the more aware you are of a consistent pattern—as universal as the stars, as the tides, as breathing, as night and day—underlying everything. I would call this pattern and this rhythm an order. Not order—*an* order. Within it exists an incredible diversity of forms. Without it lies chaos—the wild cells of destruction—sickness. It is in the end up to you to distinguish between the diversity that is health and the chaos that is sickness, and you can't do this without a process of association that can link a bar of

Mozart with the corner of a Vermeer painting, or a Stravinsky score with a Picasso abstraction; or that can relate an aggressive act with a Franz Kline painting and a fit of coughing with a John Cage composition.

7   There is no accident in the fact that certain expressions of art live for all time and that others die with the moment, and although you may not always define the reasons, you can ask the questions. What does an artist say that is timeless; how does he say it? How much is fashion, how much is merely reflection? Why is Sir Walter Scott so hard to read now, and Jane Austen not? Why is baroque right for one age and too effulgent for another?

8   Can a standard of craftsmanship apply to art of all ages, or does each have its own, and different, definitions? You may have been aware, inadvertently, that craftsmanship has become a dirty word these years because, again, it implies standards—something done well or done badly. The result of this convenient avoidance is a plenitude of actors who can't project their voices, singers who can't phrase their songs, poets who can't communicate emotion, and writers who have no vocabulary—not to speak of painters who can't draw. The dogma now is that craftsmanship gets in the way of expression. You can do better if you don't know *how* you do it, let alone *what* you're doing.

9   I think it is time you helped reverse this trend by trying to rediscover craft: the command of the chosen instrument, whether it is a brush, a word, or a voice. When you begin to detect the difference between freedom and sloppiness, between serious experimentation and egotherapy, between skill and slickness, between strength and violence, you are on your way to separating the sheep from the goats, a form of segregation denied us for quite a while. All you need to restore it is a small bundle of standards and a Geiger counter that detects fraud, and we might begin our tour of the arts in an area where both are urgently needed: contemporary painting.

10   I don't know what's worse: to have to look at acres of bad art to find the little good, or to read what the critics say about it all. In no other field of expression has so much double-talk flourished, so much confusion prevailed, and so much nonsense been circulated: further evidence of the close interdependence between the arts and the critical climate they inhabit. It will be my pleasure to share with you some of this double-talk so typical of our times.

11   Item one: preface for a catalogue of an abstract painter:

12   "Time-bound meditation experiencing a life; sincere with plastic piety at the threshold of hallowed arcana; a striving for pure ideation giving shape to inner drive; formalized patterns where neural balances reach a fiction." End of quote. Know what this artist paints like now?

13   Item two: a review in the *Art News:*

14   ". . . a weird and disparate assortment of material, but the monstrosity which bloomed into his most recent cancer of aggregations is present in

some form everywhere. . . ." Then, later, "A gluttony of things and processes terminated by a glorious constipation."

15 Item three, same magazine, review of an artist who welds automobile fragments into abstract shapes:

16 "Each fragment . . . is made an extreme of human exasperation, torn at and fought all the way, and has its rightness of form as if by accident. *Any technique that requires order or discipline would just be the human ego.* No, these must be egoless, uncontrolled, undesigned and different enough to give you a bang—fifty miles an hour around a telephone pole. . . ."

17 "Any technique that requires order or discipline would just be the human ego." What does he mean—"just be"? What are they really talking about? Is this journalism? Is it criticism? Or is it that other convenient abdication from standards of performance and judgment practiced by so many artists and critics that they, like certain writers who deal only in sickness and depravity, "reflect the chaos about them"? Again, whose chaos? Whose depravity?

18 I had always thought that the prime function of art was to create order *out* of chaos—again, not the order of neatness or rigidity or convention or artifice, but the order of clarity by which one will and one vision could draw the essential truth out of apparent confusion. I still do. It is not enough to use parts of a car to convey the brutality of the machine. This is as slavishly representative, and just as easy, as arranging dried flowers under glass to convey nature.

19 Speaking of which, i.e., the use of real materials (burlap, old gloves, bottletops) in lieu of pigment, this is what one critic had to say about an exhibition of Assemblage at the Museum of Modern Art last year:

> Spotted throughout the show are indisputable works of art, accounting for a quarter or even a half of the total display. But the remainder are works of non-art, anti-art, and art substitutes that are the aesthetic counterparts of the social deficiencies that land people in the clink on charges of vagrancy. These aesthetic bankrupts . . . have no legitimate ideological roof over their heads and not the price of a square intellectual meal, much less a spiritual sandwich, in their pockets.

20 I quote these words of John Canaday of *The New York Times* as an example of the kind of criticism which puts responsibility to an intelligent public above popularity with an intellectual coterie. Canaday has the courage to say what he thinks and the capacity to say it clearly: two qualities notably absent from his profession.

Next to art, I would say that appreciation and evaluation in the field of music is the most difficult. For it is rarely possible to judge a new composition at one hearing only. What seems confusing or fragmented at first might well become clear and organic a third time. Or it might not. The only salvation here for the listener is, again, an instinct born of experience and association which allows him to separate intent from accident, design from experimentation, and pretense from conviction. Much of contemporary music is, like its sister art, merely a reflection of the composer's own fragmentation: an absorption in self and symbols at the expense of communication with others. The artist, in short, says to the public: If you don't understand this, it's because you're dumb. I maintain that you are not. You may have to go part way or even halfway to meet the artist, but if you must go the whole way, it's his fault, not yours. Hold fast to that. And remember it too when you read new poetry, that estranged sister of music.

> A multitude of causes, unknown to former times, are now acting with a combined force to blunt the discriminating powers of the mind, and, unfitting it for all voluntary exertion, to reduce it to a state of almost savage torpor. The most effective of these causes are the great national events which are daily taking place and the increasing accumulation of men in cities, where the uniformity of their occupations produces a craving for extraordinary incident, which the rapid communication of intelligence hourly gratifies. To this tendency of life and manners, the literature and theatrical exhibitions of the country have conformed themselves.

22   This startlingly applicable comment was written in the year 1800 by William Wordsworth in the preface to his "Lyrical Ballads"; and it has been cited by Edwin Muir in his recently published book "The Estate of Poetry." Muir states that poetry's effective range and influence have diminished alarmingly in the modern world. He believes in the inherent and indestructible qualities of the human mind and the great and permanent objects that act upon it, and suggests that the audience will increase when "poetry loses what obscurity is left in it by attempting greater themes, for great themes have to be stated clearly." If you keep that firmly in mind and resist, in Muir's words, "the vast dissemination of secondary objects that isolate us from the natural world," you have gone a long way toward equipping yourself for the examination of any work of art.

23   When you come to theatre, in this extremely hasty tour of the arts, you can approach it on two different levels. You can bring to it anticipation and innocence, giving yourself up, as it were, to the life on the stage and reacting to it emotionally, if the play is good, or listlessly, if the play is boring; a part of the audience organism that expresses its favor by silence or laughter and its disfavor by coughing and rustling. Or you can bring to it certain critical faculties that may heighten, rather than diminish, your enjoyment.

24   You can ask yourselves whether the actors are truly in their parts or merely projecting themselves; whether the scenery helps or hurts the mood; whether the playwright is honest with himself, his characters, and you. Somewhere along the line you can learn to distinguish between the true

creative act and the false arbitrary gesture; between fresh observation and stale cliché; between the avant-garde play that is pretentious drivel and the avant-garde play that finds new ways to say old truths.

25 Purpose and craftsmanship—end and means—these are the keys to your judgment in all the arts. What is this painter trying to say when he slashes a broad band of black across a white canvas and lets the edges dribble down? Is it a statement of violence? Is it a self-portrait? If it is *one* of these, has he made you believe it? Or is this a gesture of the ego or a form of therapy? If it shocks you, what does it shock you into?

26 And what of this tight little painting of bright flowers in a vase? Is the painter saying anything new about flowers? Is it different from a million other canvases of flowers? Has it any life, any meaning, beyond its statement? Is there any pleasure in its forms or texture? The question is not whether a thing is abstract or representational, whether it is "modern" or conventional. The question, inexorably, is whether it is good. And this is a decision which only you, on the basis of instinct, experience, and association, can make for yourself. It takes independence and courage. It involves, moreover, the risk of wrong decision and the humility, after the passage of time, of recognizing it as such. As we grow and change and learn, our attitudes can change too, and what we once thought obscure or "difficult" can later emerge as coherent and illuminating. Entrenched prejudices, obdurate opinions are as sterile as no opinions at all.

Yet standards there are, timeless as the universe itself. And when you have committed yourself to them, you have acquired a passport to that elusive but immutable realm of truth. Keep it with you in the forests of bewilderment. And never be afraid to speak up.

Topics for Writing and Discussion

1. According to Mannes, what has happened to critical "standards" in recent years, and what effects has this change had on the art community? On critics? On the general public?

2. Note that Mannes' essay was first printed in 1962. Are her claims still applicable to our culture over thirty years later? Cite examples of current art forms, and the ways they are received by the public and reviewed by critics, to support your response.

3. Review the essay and consider the point of view used by Mannes. At what point does she shift from emphasis on first person ("I") to second person ("you")? How does this shift affect the audience? What does this change tell the reader about her purpose in writing?

4. Describe Mannes' tone. Is it consistent throughout the essay?

5. Mannes concludes her essay by noting that there are standards for critical judgment and exhorts the reader to "never be afraid to speak up." Consider the standards by which you judge the artistic worth of literature, painting, theater, music, film, or other visual and performing arts. Choose one art form as your focus and narrow your subject to a particular type, genre, or style (for example, literature might be narrowed to science fiction; film might be narrowed to Westerns; painting might be narrowed to pop art, and so on). Write an essay in which you present your own definition of "quality" for the kind of art you have chosen; use sufficient examples to illustrate your definition and to convince the reader that your opinion is accurate.

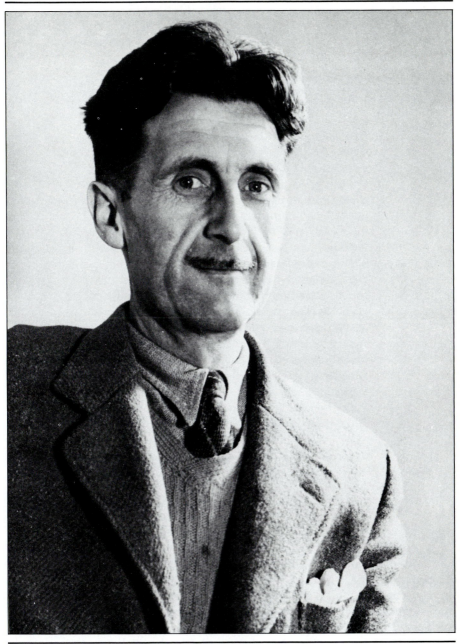

George Orwell, in an undated photograph (AP/Wide World)

Politics and the English Language

George Orwell
(1903–1950)

George Orwell, whose real name was Eric Blair, served with the Indian imperial police in Burma after finishing his school years at Eton in England. His first novel, *Burmese Days,* reflects his experiences as a police official. When he left Burma in 1927, he returned to Europe and conducted a three-year study of poverty in Paris and in London's East End. He recorded his observations in *Down and Out in Paris and London* (1933). In 1936, responding to his growing interest in socialism, he fought with the Loyalists in Spain. He is best known for *Animal Farm* (1945) and *1984* (1949), works that reflect his hatred of tyranny, his commitment to independence, and his sympathy for the oppressed. In "Politics and the English Language," taken from the collection *Shooting an Elephant and Other Essays* (1950), Orwell explores the cause-and-effect relationships among thought, language, and politics.

1   **M**ost people who bother with the matter at all would admit that the English language is in a bad way, but it is generally assumed that we cannot by conscious action do anything about it. Our civilization is decadent and our language—so the argument runs—must inevitably share in the general collapse. It follows that any struggle against the abuse of language is a sentimental archaism, like preferring candles to electric light or hansom cabs to aeroplanes. Underneath this lies the half-conscious belief that language is a natural growth and not an instrument which we shape for our own purpose.

2   Now, it is clear that the decline of a language must ultimately have political and economic causes: it is not due simply to the bad influence of this or that individual writer. But an effect can become a cause, reinforcing the original cause and producing the same effect in an intensified form, and so on indefinitely. A man may take to drink because he feels himself to be a failure, and then fail all the more completely because he drinks. It is rather the same thing that is happening to the English language. It becomes ugly and inaccurate because our thoughts are foolish, but the slovenliness of our language makes it easier for us to have foolish thoughts. The point is that the process is reversible. Modern English, especially written English, is full of bad habits which spread by imitation and which can be avoided if one is willing to take the necessary trouble. If one gets rid of these habits one can think more clearly, and to think clearly is a necessary first step toward political regeneration: so that the fight against bad English is not frivolous and is not the exclusive concern of professional writers. I will come back to this presently, and I hope that by that time the meaning of what I have said here will have become clearer. Meanwhile, here are five specimens of the English language as it is now habitually written.

3   These five passages have not been picked out because they are especially bad—I could have quoted far worse if I had chosen—but because they illustrate various of the mental vices from which we now suffer. They are a little below the average, but are fairly representative samples. I number them so that I can refer back to them when necessary:

> (1) I am not, indeed, sure whether it is not true to say that the Milton who once seemed not unlike a seventeenth-century Shelley had not become, out of an experience ever more bitter in each year, more alien [*sic*] to the founder of that Jesuit sect which nothing could induce him to tolerate.
>
> Professor Harold Laski (Essay in Freedom of Expression)

> (2) Above all, we cannot play ducks and drakes with a native battery of idioms which prescribes such egregious collocations of vocables as the Basic *put up with* for *tolerate* or *put at a loss* for *bewilder*.
>
> Professor Lancelot Hogben (Interglossa)

> (3) On the one side we have the free personality: by definition it is not neurotic, for it has neither conflict nor dream. Its desires, such as they are, are transparent, for they are just what institutional approval keeps in the forefront of consciousness; another institutional pattern would alter their number and intensity; there is little in them that is natural, irreducible, or culturally dangerous. But *on the other side*, the social bond itself is nothing but the mutual reflection of these self-secure integrities. Recall the definition of love. Is not this the very picture of a small academic? Where is there a place in this hall of mirrors for either personality or fraternity?
>
> Essay on psychology in Politics (New York)

> (4) All the "best people" from the gentlemen's clubs, and all the frantic fascist

captains, united in common hatred of Socialism and bestial horror of the rising tide of the mass revolutionary movement, have turned to acts of provocation, to foul incendiarism, to medieval legends of poisoned wells, to legalize their own destruction of proletarian organizations, and rouse the agitated petty-bourgeoisie to chauvinistic fervor on behalf of the fight against the revolutionary way out of the crisis.

Communist pamphlet

(5) If a new spirit *is* to be infused into this old country, there is one thorny and contentious reform which must be tackled, and that is the humanization and galvanization of the B.B.C. Timidity here will bespeak cancer and atrophy of the soul. The heart of Britain may be sound and of strong beat, for instance, but the British lion's roar at present is like that of Bottom in Shakespeare's *Midsummer Night's Dream*—as gentle as any sucking dove. A virile new Britain cannot continue indefinitely to be traduced in the eyes or rather ears, of the world by the effete languors of Langham Place, brazenly masquerading as "standard English." When the Voice of Britain is heard at nine o'clock, better far and infinitely less ludicrous to hear aitches honestly dropped than the present priggish, inflated, inhibited, school-ma'amish arch braying of blameless bashful mewing maidens!

Letter in *Tribune*

4   Each of these passages has faults of its own, but, quite apart from avoidable ugliness, two qualities are common to all of them. The first is staleness of imagery; the other is lack of precision. The writer either has a meaning and cannot express it, or he inadvertently says something else, or he is almost indifferent as to whether his words mean anything or not. The mixture of vagueness and sheer incompetence is the most marked characteristic of modern English prose, and especially of any kind of political writing. As soon as certain topics are raised, the concrete melts into the abstract and no one seems to think of turns of speech that are not hackneyed: prose consists less and less of *words* chosen for the sake of their meaning, and more and more of *phrases* tacked together like the sections of a prefabricated henhouse. I list below, with notes and examples, various of the tricks by means of which the work of prose-construction is habitually dodged:

Dying Metaphors

5 A newly invented metaphor assists thought by evoking a visual image, while on the other hand a metaphor which is technically "dead" (e.g., *iron resolution*) has in effect reverted to being an ordinary word and can generally

be used without loss of vividness. But in between these two classes there is a huge dump of worn-out metaphors which have lost all evocative power and are merely used because they save people the trouble of inventing phrases for themselves. Examples are: *ring the changes on, take up the cudgels for, toe the line, ride roughshod over, stand shoulder to shoulder with, play into the hands of, no axe to grind, grist to the mill, fishing in troubled waters, rift within the lute, on the order of the day, Achilles' heel, swan song, hotbed.* Many of these are used without knowledge of their meaning (what is a "rift," for instance?), and incompatible metaphors are frequently mixed, a sure sign that the writer is not interested in what he is saying. Some metaphors now current have been twisted out of their original meaning without those who use them even being aware of the fact. For example, *toe the line* is sometimes written *tow the line*. Another example is *the hammer and the anvil*, now always used with the implication that the anvil gets the worst of it. In real life it is always the anvil that breaks the hammer, never the other way about: a writer who stopped to think what he was saying would be aware of this, and would avoid perverting the original phrase.

Operators or Verbal False Limbs

6 These save the trouble of picking out appropriate verbs and nouns, and at the same time pad each sentence with extra syllables which give it an appearance of symmetry. Characteristic phrases are: *render inoperative, militate against, make contact with, be subjected to, give rise to, give grounds for, have the effect of, play a leading part (role) in, make itself felt, take effect, exhibit a tendency to, serve the purpose of, etc., etc.* The keynote is the elimination of simple verbs. Instead of being a single word, such as *break, stop, spoil, mend, kill,* a verb becomes a *phrase*, made up of a noun or adjective tacked on to some general-purpose verb such as *prove, serve, form, play, render.* In addition, the passive voice is wherever possible used in preference to the active, and noun constructions are used instead of gerunds (*by examination of* instead of *by examining*). The range of verbs is further cut down by means of the *-ize* and *de-* formation, and the banal statements are given an appearance of profundity by means of the *not un-* formation. Simple conjunctions and prepositions are replaced by such phrases as *with respect to, having regard to, the fact that, by dint of, in view of, in the interests of, on the hypothesis that;* and the ends of sentences are saved from anticlimax by such resounding commonplaces as *greatly to be desired, cannot be left out of account, a development to be expected in the near future, deserving of serious consideration, brought to a satisfactory conclusion,* and so on and so forth.

Pretentious Diction

7 Words like *phenomenon, element, individual* (as noun), *objective, categorical, effective, virtual, basic, primary, promote, constitute, exhibit, exploit, utilize,*

eliminate, liquidate, are used to dress up simple statements and give an air of scientific impartiality to biased judgments. Adjectives like *epoch-making, epic, historic, unforgettable, triumphant, age-old, inexorable, inevitable, veritable,* are used to dignify the sordid processes of international politics, while writing that aims at glorifying war usually takes on an archaic color, its characteristic words being: *realm, throne, chariot, mailed fist, trident, sword, shield, buckler, banner, jackboot, clarion.* Foreign words and expressions such as *cul de sac, ancien régime, deus ex machina, mutatis mutandis, status quo, gleich-shaltung, weltanschauung,* are used to give an air of culture and elegance. Except for the useful abbreviations *i.e., e.g.,* and *etc.,* there is no real need for any of the hundreds of foreign phrases now current in English. Bad writers, and especially scientific, political and sociological writers, are nearly always haunted by the notion that Latin or Greek words are grander than Saxon ones, and unnecessary words like *expedite, ameliorate, predict, extraneous, deracinated, clandestine, subaqueous* and hundreds of others constantly gain ground from their Anglo-Saxon opposite numbers.[1] The jargon peculiar to Marxist writing (*hyena, hangman, cannibal, petty bourgeois, these gentry, lacquey, flunkey, mad dog, White Guard,* etc.) consists largely of words and phrases translated from Russian, German, or French; but the normal way of coining a new word is to use a Latin or Greek root with the appropriate affix and, where necessary, the *-ize* formation. It is often easier to make up words of this kind (*deregionalize, impermissible, extramarital, nonfragmentatory* and so forth) than to think up the English words that will cover one's meaning. The result, in general, is an increase in slovenliness and vagueness.

Meaningless Words

8 In certain kinds of writing, particularly in art criticism and literary criticism, it is normal to come across long passages which are almost completely lacking in meaning.[2] Words like *romantic, plastic, values, human, dead, sentimental, natural, vitality,* as used in art criticism, are strictly meaningless in the sense that they not only do not point to any discoverable object, but

[1]An interesting illustration of this is the way in which the English flower names which were in use till very recently are being ousted by Greek ones, *snapdragon* becoming *antirrhinum, forget-me-not* becoming *myosotis,* etc. It is hard to see any practical reason for this change of fashion: it is probably due to an instinctive turning-away from the more homely word and a vague feeling that the Greek word is scientific.

[2]Example: "Comfort's catholicity of perception and image, strangely Whitmanesque in range, almost the exact opposite in aesthetic compulsion, continues to evoke that trembling atmospheric accumulative hinting at a cruel, an inexorably serene timelessness . . . Wrey Gardiner scores by aiming at simple bull's-eyes with precision. Only they are not so simple, and through this contended sadness runs more than the surface bitter-sweet of resignation."*(Poetry Quarterly)*

are hardly ever expected to do so by the reader. When one critic writes, "The outstanding feature of Mr. X's work is its living quality," while another writes, "The immediately striking thing about Mr. X's work is its peculiar deadness," the reader accepts this as a simple difference of opinion. If words like *black* and *white* were involved, instead of the jargon words *dead* and *living,* he would see at once that language was being used in an improper way. Many political words are similarly abused. The word *Fascism* has now no meaning except in so far as it signifies "something not desirable." The words *democracy, socialism, freedom, patriotic, realistic, justice,* have each of them several different meanings which cannot be reconciled with one another. In the case of a word like *democracy,* not only is there no agreed definition, but the attempt to make one is resisted from all sides. It is almost universally felt that when we call a country democratic we are praising it: consequently the defenders of every kind of régime claim that it is a democracy, and fear that they might have to stop using the word if it were tied down to any one meaning. Words of this kind are often used in a consciously dishonest way. That is, the person who uses them has his own private definition, but allows his hearer to think he means something quite different. Statements like *Marshall Pétain was a true patriot, The Soviet Press is the freest in the world, The Catholic Church is opposed to persecution,* are almost always made with intent to deceive. Other words used in variable meanings, in most cases more or less dishonestly, are: *class, totalitarian, science, progressive, reactionary, bourgeois, equality.*

9   Now that I have made this catalogue of swindles and perversions, let me give another example of the kind of writing that they lead to. This time it must of its nature be an imaginary one. I am going to translate a passage of good English into modern English of the worst sort. Here is a well-known verse from *Ecclesiastes:*

> I returned and saw under the sun, that the race is not to the swift, nor the battle to the strong, neither yet bread to the wise, nor yet riches to men of understanding, nor yet favour to men of skill; but time and chance happeneth to them all.

Here it is in modern English:

> Objective consideration of contemporary phenomena compels the conclusion that success or failure in competitive activities exhibits no tendency to be commensurate with innate capacity, but that a considerable element of the unpredictable must invariably be taken into account.

10   This is a parody, but not a very gross one. Exhibit (3), above, for instance, contains several patches of the same kind of English. It will be seen that I have not made a full translation. The beginning and ending of the sentence

follow the original meaning fairly closely, but in the middle the concrete illustrations—race, battle, bread—dissolve into the vague phrase "success or failure in competitive activities." This had to be so, because no modern writer of the kind I am discussing—no one capable of using phrases like "objective consideration of contemporary phenomena"—would ever tabulate his thoughts in that precise and detailed way. The whole tendency of modern prose is away from concreteness. Now analyze these two sentences a little more closely. The first contains forty-nine words but only sixty syllables, and all its words are those of everyday life. The second contains thirty-eight words of ninety syllables: eighteen of its words are from Latin roots, and one from Greek. The first sentence contains six vivid images, and only one phrase ("time and chance") that could be called vague. The second contains not a single fresh, arresting phrase, and in spite of its ninety syllables it gives only a shortened version of the meaning contained in the first. Yet without a doubt it is the second kind of sentence that is gaining ground in modern English. I do not want to exaggerate. This kind of writing is not yet universal; and outcrops of simplicity will occur here and there in the worst-written page. Still, if you or I were told to write a few lines on the uncertainty of human fortunes, we should probably come much nearer to my imaginary sentence than to the one from *Ecclesiastes*.

11   As I have tried to show, modern writing at its worst does not consist in picking out words for the sake of their meaning and inventing images in order to make the meaning clearer. It consists in gumming together long strips of words which have already been set in order by someone else, and making the results presentable by sheer humbug. The attraction of this way of writing is that it is easy. It is easier—even quicker once you have the habit—to say *In my opinion it is a not unjustifiable assumption that* than to say *I think*. If you use ready-made phrases, you not only don't have to hunt about for words; you also don't have to bother with the rhythms of your sentences, since these phrases are generally so arranged as to be more or less euphonious. When you are composing in a hurry—when you are dictating to a stenographer, for instance, or making a public speech—it is natural to fall into a pretentious, Latinized style. Tags like *a consideration which we should do well to bear in mind* or *a conclusion to which all of us would readily assent* will save many a sentence from coming down with a bump. By using stale metaphors, similes and idioms, you save much mental effort, at the cost of leaving your meaning vague, not only for your reader but for yourself. This is the significance of mixed metaphors. The sole aim of a metaphor is to call up a visual image. When these images clash—as in *The Fascist octopus has sung its swan song, the jackboot is thrown into the melting pot*—it can be taken as certain that the writer is not seeing a mental image of the objects he is naming; in other words he is not really thinking. Look again at the examples I gave at the beginning of this essay. Professor Laski (1) uses five negatives in fifty-three words. One of these is superfluous, making nonsense

of the whole passage, and in addition there is the slip *alien* for *akin,* making further nonsense, and several avoidable pieces of clumsiness which increase the general vagueness. Professor Hogben (2) plays ducks and drakes with a battery which is able to write prescriptions, and, while disapproving of the everyday phrase *put up with,* is unwilling to look *egregious* up in the dictionary and see what it means. (3), if one takes an uncharitable attitude towards it, is simply meaningless. Probably one could work out its intended meaning by reading the whole of the article in which it occurs. In (4), the writer knows more or less what he wants to say, but an accumulation of stale phrases chokes him like tea leaves blocking a sink. In (5), words and meaning have almost parted company. People who write in this manner usually have a general emotional meaning—they dislike one thing and want to express solidarity with another—but they are not interested in the detail of what they are saying. A scrupulous writer, in every sentence that he writes, will ask himself at least four questions, thus: What am I trying to say? What words will express it? What image or idiom will make it clearer? Is this image fresh enough to have an effect? And he will probably ask himself two more: Could I put it more shortly? Have I said anything that is avoidably ugly? But you are not obliged to go to all this trouble. You can shirk it by simply throwing your mind open and letting the ready-made phrases come crowding in. They will construct your sentences for you—even think your thoughts for you, to a certain extent—and at need they will perform the important service of partially concealing your meaning even from yourself. It is at this point that the special connection between politics and the debasement of language becomes clear.

12   In our times it is broadly true that political writing is bad writing. Where it is not true, it will generally be found that the writer is some kind of rebel, expressing his private opinions and not a "party line." Orthodoxy, of whatever color, seems to demand a lifeless, imitative style. The political dialects to be found in pamphlets, leading articles, manifestos, White Papers and the speeches of under-secretaries do, of course, vary from party to party, but they are all alike in that one almost never finds in them a fresh, vivid, home-made turn of speech. When one watches some tired hack on the platform mechanically repeating the familiar phrases—*bestial atrocities, iron heel, bloodstained tyranny, free peoples of the world, stand shoulder to shoulder*—one often has a curious feeling that one is not watching a live human being but some kind of dummy, a feeling which suddenly becomes stronger at moments when the light catches the speaker's spectacles and turns them into blank discs which seem to have no eyes behind them. And this is not altogether fanciful. A speaker who uses that kind of phraseology has gone some distance towards turning himself into a machine. The appropriate noises are coming out of his larynx, but his brain is not involved as it would be if he were choosing his words from himself. If the speech he is making is one that he is accustomed to make over and over again, he may be almost

unconscious of what he is saying, as one is when one utters the responses in church. And this reduced state of consciousness, if not indispensable, is at any rate favorable to political conformity.

13   In our time, political speech and writing are largely the defense of the indefensible. Things like the continuance of British rule in India, the Russian purges and deportations, the dropping of the atom bombs on Japan, can indeed be defended, but only by arguments which are too brutal for most people to face, and which do not square with the professed aims of political parties. Thus political language has to consist largely of euphemism, question-begging and sheer cloudy vagueness. Defenseless villages are bombarded from the air, the inhabitants driven out into the countryside, the cattle machine-gunned, the huts set on fire with incendiary bullets: this is called *pacification*. Millions of peasants are robbed of their farms and sent trudging along the roads with no more than they can carry: this is called *transfer of population* or *rectification of frontiers*. People are imprisoned for years without trial, or shot in the back of the neck or sent to die of scurvy in Arctic lumber camps: this is called *elimination of unreliable elements*. Such phraseology is needed if one wants to name things without calling up mental pictures of them. Consider for instance some comfortable English professor defending Russian totalitarianism. He cannot say outright, "I believe in killing off your opponents when you can get good results by doing so." Probably, therefore, he will say something like this:

14   "While freely conceding that the Soviet régime exhibits certain features which the humanitarian may be inclined to deplore, we must, I think, agree that a certain curtailment of the right to political opposition is an unavoidable concomitant of transitional periods, and that the rigors which the Russian people have been called upon to undergo have been amply justified in the sphere of concrete achievement."

15   The inflated style is itself a kind of euphemism. A mass of Latin words falls upon the facts like soft snow, blurring the outlines and covering up all the details. The great enemy of clear language is insincerity. When there is a gap between one's real and one's declared aims, one turns as it were instinctively to long words and exhausted idioms, like a cuttlefish squirting out ink. In our age there is no such thing as "keeping out of politics." All issues are political issues, and politics itself is a mass of lies, evasions, folly, hatred and schizophrenia. When the general atmosphere is bad, language must suffer. I should expect to find—this is a guess which I have not sufficient knowledge to verify—that the German, Russian and Italian languages have all deteriorated in the last ten or fifteen years, as a result of dictatorship.

16   But if thought corrupts language, language can also corrupt thought. A bad usage can spread by tradition and imitation, even among people who should and do know better. The debased language that I have been discussing is in some ways very convenient. Phrases like *a not unjustifiable assumption, leaves much to be desired, would serve no good purpose, a consid-*

eration which we should do well to bear in mind, are a continuous temptation, a packet of aspirins always at one's elbow. Look back through this essay, and for certain you will find that I have again and again committed the very faults I am protesting against. By this morning's post I have received a pamphlet dealing with conditions in Germany. The author tells me that he "felt impelled" to write it. I open it at random, and here is almost the first sentence that I see: "(The Allies) have an opportunity not only of achieving a radical transformation of Germany's social and political structure in such a way as to avoid a nationalistic reaction in Germany itself, but at the same time of laying the foundations of a co-operative and unified Europe." You see, he "feels impelled" to write—feels, presumably, that he has something new to say—and yet his words, like cavalry horses answering the bugle, group themselves automatically into the familiar dreary pattern. This invasion of one's mind by ready-made phrases *(lay the foundations, achieve a radical transformation)* can only be prevented if one is constantly on guard against them, and every such phrase anaesthetizes a portion of one's brain.

17   I said earlier that the decadence of our language is probably curable. Those who deny this would argue, if they produced an argument at all, that language merely reflects existing social conditions, and that we cannot influence its development by any direct tinkering with words and constructions. So far as the general tone or spirit of a language goes, this may be true, but it is not true in detail. Silly words and expressions have often disappeared, not through any evolutionary process but owing to the conscious action of a minority. Two recent examples were *explore every avenue* and *leave no stone unturned,* which were killed by the jeers of a few journalists. There is a long list of flyblown metaphors which could similarly be got rid of if enough people would interest themselves in the job; and it should also be possible to laugh the *not un-* formation out of existence,[3] to reduce the amount of Latin and Greek in the average sentence, to drive out foreign phrases and strayed scientific words, and, in general, to make pretentiousness unfashionable. But all these are minor points. The defense of the English language implies more than this, and perhaps it is best to start by saying what it does *not* imply.

18   To begin with it has nothing to do with archaism, with the salvaging of obsolete words and turns of speech, or with the setting up of a "standard English" which must never be departed from. On the contrary, it is especially concerned with the scrapping of every word or idiom which has outworn its usefulness. It has nothing to do with correct grammar and syntax, which are of no importance so long as one makes one's meaning clear, or with the avoidance of Americanisms, or with having what is called a "good prose style." On the other hand, it is not concerned with fake simplicity and the

[3]One can cure oneself of the *not un-* formation by memorizing this sentence: *A not unblack dog was chasing a not unsmall rabbit across a not ungreen field.*

attempt to make written English colloquial. Nor does it even imply in every case preferring the Saxon word to the Latin one, though it does imply using the fewest and shortest words that will cover one's meaning. What is above all needed is to let the meaning choose the word, and not the other way about. In prose, the worst thing one can do with words is to surrender to them. When you think of a concrete object, you think wordlessly, and then, if you want to describe the thing you have been visualizing you probably hunt about till you find the exact words that seem to fit. When you think of something abstract, you are more inclined to use words from the start, and unless you make a conscious effort to prevent it, the existing dialect will come rushing in and do the job for you, at the expense of blurring or even changing your meaning. Probably it is better to put off using words as long as possible and get one's meaning as clear as one can through pictures or sensations. Afterwards one can choose—not simply *accept*—the phrases that will best cover the meaning, and then switch round and decide what impression one's words are likely to make on another person. This last effort of the mind cuts out all stale or mixed images, all prefabricated phrases, needless repetitions, and humbug and vagueness generally. But one can often be in doubt about the effect of a word or a phrase, and one needs rules that one can rely on when instinct fails. I think the following rules will cover most cases:

(i)   Never use a metaphor, simile or other figure of speech which you are used to seeing in print.

(ii)   Never use a long word where a short one will do.

(iii)   If it is possible to cut a word out, always cut it out.

(iv)   Never use the passive where you can use the active.

(v)   Never use a foreign phrase, a scientific word or jargon word if you can think of an everyday English equivalent.

(vi)   Break any of these rules sooner than say anything outright barbarous.

These rules sound elementary, and so they are, but they demand a deep change in attitude in anyone who has grown used to writing in the style now fashionable. One could keep all of them and still write bad English, but one could not write the kind of stuff that I quoted in those five specimens at the beginning of this article.

19   I have not here been considering the literary use of language, but merely language as an instrument for expressing and not for concealing or preventing thought. Stuart Chase and others have come near to claiming that all abstract words are meaningless, and have used this as a pretext for advocating a kind of political quietism. Since you don't know what Fascism

is, how can you struggle against Fascism? One need not swallow such absurdities as this, but one ought to recognize that the present political chaos is connected with the decay of language; and that one can probably bring about some improvement by starting at the verbal end. If you simplify your English, you are freed from the worst follies of orthodoxy. You cannot speak any of the necessary dialects, and when you make a stupid remark, its stupidity will be obvious, even to yourself. Political language—and with variations this is true of all political parties, from Conservatives to Anarchists—is designed to make lies sound truthful and murder respectable, and to give an appearance of solidity to pure wind. One cannot change this all in a moment, but one can at least change one's own habits, and from time to time one can even, if one jeers loudly enough, send some worn-out and useless phrase—some *jackboot, Achilles' heel, hotbed, melting pot, acid test, veritable inferno* or other lump of verbal refuse—into the dustbin where it belongs.

Topics for Writing and Discussion

1. What does Orwell mean when he says in paragraph 2 that "an effect can become a cause, reinforcing the original cause and producing the same effect in an intensified form"? How does he illustrate this assertion? How does he apply the illustration to his beliefs concerning the decline of the English language?

2. According to Orwell, what are the four main "tricks" writers of political English use to dodge "the work of prose construction." What *is* "the work of prose construction"? Why do writers use "tricks" to keep language from doing its intended work? (See paragraphs 11 through 14.)

3. In the first part of the essay, Orwell argues that "thought corrupts language," but in paragraph 16 he turns his thesis around and proposes that "language can also corrupt thought." What does he mean by this? How can use of language affect the way a person thinks? Do you find Orwell's examples convincing?

4. What does Orwell believe must be done to cure what he sees as the decadence of the English language? Do you think he would make the same recommendations today?

5. Select a paragraph from another essay in this text that you think is clear and well written. As Orwell did with the verse from *Ecclesiastes*, rewrite the passage using as many vague, clichéd abstractions as possible. Exchange papers with a classmate and see how many of Orwell's rules you can apply to the murky prose.

Writing Assignments for Chapter Ten
Cause and Effect

1. According to Norman Cousins in "Pain Is Not the Ultimate Enemy," America is becoming a nation of "pill-grabbers and hypochondriacs." Write an essay in which you describe the effects of drug or alcohol abuse on someone you have known. You might wish to consider the effects of common over-the-counter drugs like aspirin, as Cousins did, as well as excessive use of prescription drugs or illegal narcotics.

2. Cousins faults television advertising for promoting hypochondria. Select some advertisements from popular magazines and use them in an editorial to show how drug manufacturers encourage people to pop pills for every small ache and pain.

3. In "My Wood," E. M. Forster discusses the effects of ownership. Think of your most prized material possession. What one item would you save if your house, apartment, or dorm were on fire? Write an essay that clearly explains the reasons for, or causes of, your attachment to this object.

4. Research and argue either the primary causes or effects of some well-known disaster, such as the 1919 influenza epidemic, the 1906 San Francisco earthquake, the 1929 stock-market crash, the 1986 *Challenger* explosion, or the 1991 Oakland hills' fire. Try to incorporate your facts, figures, and quotations as smoothly as Barbara Tuchman did in " 'This Is the End of the World': The Black Death." Help the reader, as she did, to experience the event you describe.

5. In "Of Dragons and Garden Peas," Alice Stewart Trillin spoke about our fear of death and what that fear sometimes causes us to do or believe. If you have ever experienced a life-threatening illness or accident, write about its effects on you. Are you different for having convinced the "dragon to stay away for a while longer"? (Or, if you prefer, write an essay explaining the effects of someone else's illness or accident on you, your family, or circle of friends.)

6. In answer to Marya Mannes' essay "How Do You Know It's Good?", write a critical review of a piece of art you consider first-rate. You may choose a painting, a piece of literature, a film, a photograph, a sculpture,

or some other artistic creation. Keep in mind Mannes' guidelines: "Purpose and craftsmanship—end and means—these are the keys to your judgment in all the arts." Show your readers clearly why you think the subject of your review is "good," avoiding the vague or pretentious language Mannes finds in reviews and quotes in her essay.

7. Using George Orwell's advice in "Politics and the English Language" as a guide, analyze a piece of ineffective writing, clearly explaining the causes and effects of its "bad habits." Do you agree that "the slovenliness of our language makes it easier for us to have foolish thoughts"?

Chapter Eleven

Persuasion and Argument

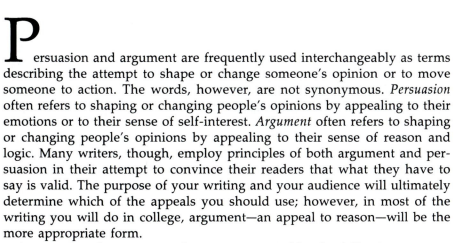

P ersuasion and argument are frequently used interchangeably as terms describing the attempt to shape or change someone's opinion or to move someone to action. The words, however, are not synonymous. *Persuasion* often refers to shaping or changing people's opinions by appealing to their emotions or to their sense of self-interest. *Argument* often refers to shaping or changing people's opinions by appealing to their sense of reason and logic. Many writers, though, employ principles of both argument and per-suasion in their attempt to convince their readers that what they have to say is valid. The purpose of your writing and your audience will ultimately determine which of the appeals you should use; however, in most of the writing you will do in college, argument—an appeal to reason—will be the more appropriate form.

As you plan the structure of your essay, consider the following:

1. *Audience.* Your audience will probably fall into one or more of these four categories:

• those who have formed opinions, hold tightly to those opinions, and are hesitant to acknowledge the validity of another view

• those who have formed opinions but realize that another view may be equally valid

- those who have not formed an opinion but are interested in learning more about the issue

- those who have not formed an opinion because they are uninterested in the issue

Once you recognize the attitudes of your audience, you can decide which methods of development—appeal to emotions, appeal to logic, or appeal to self-interest, or some combination—will be the most effective in swaying your readers to your side. To prepare your case, consider these questions:

- Does your audience *already* agree with you? If so, the presentation of your case may be primarily ceremonial, providing encouragement, reinforcement, or inspiration, like a "pep talk" or a "rallying cry" rather than a genuine attempt at persuasion. In addressing this audience, reason and logic might be couched in an appeal to the audience's emotions. (Emotional appeals often speak to people's pride, vanity, fears, prejudices, or loyalties. For instance, a candidate might stir an audience by constantly referring to his or her plan as the "American way.")

- Is your audience interested but perhaps poorly informed? If so, rely heavily on evidence and logic because this audience is looking for information upon which to *base* an opinion. It's up to you to provide that solid base.

- Is your audience neutral or ambivalent on the issue? If so, take great care in organizing your material in a logical, reasonable manner, for there may be many reasons why this audience has not formed an opinion or has developed conflicting feelings toward the issue. Give this audience solid, well-documented evidence; however, be aware that the neutrality or ambivalence may be emotionally based, so an appropriate emotional appeal might also be effective.

- Is your audience *un*interested in the issue? Unless you can establish a *strong* basis for your case that would be beneficial to the audience, you may not succeed.

- Does your audience hold a view entirely different from yours? If so, establishing your credibility as one who is an authority or as one who has done considerable research on the issue is essential, even crucial, for this audience will present the strongest resistance to persuasion. Here, it is especially necessary to state and refute opposing arguments to show your audience that you clearly understand all sides of the issue.

2.   *Topic.* Your topic should be one you really care about.

Your essay will be more convincing if the reader believes that you have a genuine interest (though not one of personal gain) in it. Your approach to the topic may be serious or humorous, but it *must* be sincere.

3. *Position.* Your position on the issue must be clearly stated.

Once you begin to write, the first and most important step is stating your position, taking a firm stand. Of course, you should come to that firm stand only *after* you have given the issue considerable thought and, if necessary, done considerable research. When you are comfortable in your own position, you will be better able to plan the strategy necessary to persuade your audience.

Once you have carefully thought about your own position, you can express that position in the form of a *thesis.* Your thesis must be one that is debatable, addressing an issue that has two or more sides.

4. *Opposition.* The next step in determining your plan of persuasion will be to decide what evidence you will need.

As you gather the material to support your own case, keep in mind that you must also deal effectively with *opposing views.* Though *refuting* or answering all arguments against your position may be impossible, certainly you must address the most obvious ones. Discover the most notable objections to your thesis and straightforwardly address them. By doing this you will go far in convincing your audience that your position is sound.

Prepare your strategy by carefully considering the kinds of evidence you will need to support your argument and watch for any fallacies you might encounter as you gather your evidence and organize your thoughts.

Types of Evidence

Evidence is the information you use to persuade your audience to accept your ideas and to agree with your position on an issue. It is also the material you must present to refute the major opposing views. So, in argumentation the judicious selection of evidence is essential.

As you consider your choice of evidence upon which to base your argument, notice the types of information at your disposal. *Facts* will provide evidence based on information whose verification is not affected by the source. No matter who says it, a fact is a fact. It is a fact, for example, that President John F. Kennedy was killed on November 22, 1963, in Dallas, Texas, while riding in a motorcade. The source of that information does not affect the truth of the information. However, even though much investigation and debate has been focused on the assassination, the question of who was ultimately responsible for the murder is, for many people, still a matter of *opinion*—that is, depending on the speaker, a lone gunman named Lee Harvey Oswald committed the crime, Oswald and another assailant were responsible, the Mafia ordered the killing, the Cuban government was involved, or perhaps some other persons or groups were part of a conspiracy. *Opinions*, then, are often based on personal feelings or beliefs or on one's interpretations of facts.

Facts are *primary* sources of information. They may be cited and documented in your essay directly or they may be presented by experts in the field of the issue you are discussing. When readers feel that the information they receive is from a knowledgeable, credible, and reliable source, they will be more likely to accept your view.

Another type of evidence is judgment. *Judgments* are secondary sources derived from the synthesizing of primary sources. The strength of judgments you might use in your argument will be largely based upon the source of the judgment. An expert in the field, one with a good reputation, could present judgments that your audience may readily accept; however, realize that judgments are interpretations. For your readers to accept the judgment, they must accept the source.

Statistics can play a role similar to that of *expert testimony* in presenting facts. They can provide solid evidence on which to base an argument, and we seem to be a society with a respect for numbers. If we hear that 99 out of 100 physicians who treat patients suffering from tension headaches recommend a particular pain reliever, we may be tempted to try that medication if we have a tension headache.

For statistics to be reliable evidence in persuasion, however, they must be unambiguous. For instance, if we hear that 10 out of 100 drivers are involved in automobile accidents each day, we may not be convinced to be more careful drivers or to take better care of our vehicles because we know so little about the accidents. However, if we are told that 10 of 100 drivers are involved in traffic accidents *because of faulty brakes*, we might be more inclined to have our car brakes checked. The statistics are more convincing because we know specifically what they address.

It also is important to use statistics from a *reliable source.* You would probably accept statistically based evidence that suggests you have your brakes checked if the report came from the National Highway Safety Committee. However, if that same information came from a spokesperson for a chain of brake and muffler shops, the evidence might be suspect.

Types of Reasoning

Two types of reasoning may be used to present an argument: inductive and deductive. In *inductive* reasoning, specific facts or individual cases or observations lead to a *general* conclusion, one that appears to be true or appears to be better than any other conclusion. In *deductive* reasoning, one begins with a *general premise* or assumption and moves to a specific conclusion. Deductive reasoning tells us that if all the premises are true, the conclusion must be true. Inductive reasoning tells us that the conclusion must be true if the evidence points to it.

Inductive Reasoning

In form, the inductive argument begins with a *hypothesis* stating the conclusion you will try to impress upon your reader. For the reader to accept your hypothesis, you must present evidence that leads directly to it; thus the reader can conclude that your hypothesis is valid.

Hypothesis: Donald is in love with Helen.

Evidence: He talks about her in glowing terms.
He often sends her flowers and candy.
He writes her love poems.
He frequently surprises her with gifts.

Conclusion: Donald is in love with Helen.

This is a simple example, but it serves to demonstrate how a hypothesis can lead to a probable conclusion (called an *inference*) if the evidence is convincing. However, if any piece of the evidence does not fit in with the hypothesis, the conclusion would be invalid.

Remember, conclusions drawn from inductive reasoning are often *probable* conclusions drawn from incomplete evidence, so the evidence you choose should be selected carefully. For example, you might believe that all Hollywood celebrities are selfish, superficial people who care only about themselves and their careers, and who are willing to do unethical, even immoral things to achieve their goal of superstardom (hypothesis). You may base your logic on the gossip found in scandal newspapers and magazines and on what you've read in some celebrity biographies (evidence). Additionally, all your friends view the "Hollywood type" in the same way. Therefore, you conclude that Hollywood personalities are vain, obnoxious, selfish people who feel no sense of loyalty or obligation to the public who pay to see their movies or buy the products they advertise, but who seek to serve themselves (conclusion). The truth is, though, you do not know any celebrities personally, and at best what you have seen or heard accounts for only a limited sample of the "celebrity" population. Thus, the specific conclusion in thinking from a limited sample to a general conclusion is called an *inductive leap*.

True, conclusions made from inductive reasoning are common; in fact, most of what we "know" is known by induction. But because induction can lead to conclusions that may not be valid, it often contributes to unfair and sometimes untrue assumptions that are made about people, places, and ideas. These assumptions can later become the basis of stereotypes, which in turn may lead to misunderstandings, misconceptions, and perhaps even distrust and hatred. Therefore, for a conclusion based on inductive reasoning to be creditable, the sample from which the conclusions are drawn must be *known*, *sufficient*, and *representative*.

A *known* sample is literally one you know, one you can examine for yourself to test its reliability. Suppose you were about to book a vacation to an exotic spot in the South Pacific—say, Fiji—and your best friend tried to dissuade you by saying that Fiji is a terrible place for a vacation because the hotels are poorly run, the people are arrogant and unfriendly, and the beaches are littered and covered with seaweed. You respond by asking the source of his information and find that he just "heard it somewhere." Your friend's conclusions about Fiji were made without a known sample, and therefore his conclusions may be invalid.

In addition to a known sample, a *sufficient* sample is also necessary to make sound judgments. Consider the following statements:

> Sure, I'm over 35; I love french fries, potato chips, and chocolate bars; my body's carrying a few extra pounds; and I smoke and drink. So what? I'll still live to be 100 because my grandfather lived to be 105, and my grandmother is now 92.

> Calculus must be a really difficult course because two of my friends who took it failed.

> A black family in the neighborhood spells trouble. My cousin has been in dispute with his black neighbors ever since they moved in.

Statements like the ones above are all founded on insufficient evidence to base a general conclusion. The truth is that many doctors maintain that diet and lifestyle *do* play a role in determining not only the quality of our life but also the probable length of our life. Though heredity is important, it is not a guarantee of a long life. Similarly, the trouble that two friends had in calculus does not indicate the course is difficult for all students. The two friends who failed may have done so for a variety of reasons. Likewise, a person's race is not an indicator of the type of neighbor that person will be. Neighborhood disputes can arise from a number of things. It is possible that the cousin's disagreement with his black neighbors stemmed from their meticulous house- and lawnkeeping habits that made the cousin's own habits seem bad in comparison.

It is in this area of induction that stereotypes leading to prejudices are born. Simplistic negative descriptions of ethnic, racial, religious, political, and other groups often come from people whose beliefs have insufficient samples as their foundations.

In addition to a known sample and a sufficient sample, one needs a representative sample before a sound conclusion can be drawn. A *representative* sample is a sample typical of the entire class of things being discussed. A city could not decide on its policy toward the treatment of the homeless by polling only those hostile to their plight. Nor could that city gauge the attitudes of its citizens toward adult entertainment by polling only the owners of adult-entertainment businesses. Such polls would be unrepresentative of the city's population. Or, if you were to discover that students at your school ranked fifth out of five schools on a standardized test given to students at the end of their sophomore year, the news would be quite distressing. But if you found out that the test from which the statistics were derived was given to only *two* students at your school and 150, 100, 230, and 89 students respectively at the other schools, any conclusions suggesting a poor quality of education at your institution would be invalid.

Sometimes, drawing conclusions from limited information is difficult to avoid. We do it every day. The important point to remember: be aware of the possible flaws in the conclusions that have been drawn.

Deductive Reasoning

The intellectual method used to come to a conclusion in deductive reasoning is the opposite of the method used in inductive reasoning. As stated before, deduction moves from *general* assumptions, called *premises,* to a *specific* conclusion about the general assumptions or to a specific application of the general assumptions. The organizational form of this type of reasoning is the *syllogism,* in which two premises are made and a conclusion is drawn from them.

For a syllogism to be useful in constructing an argument, its premises must be true; its language must be clear and unambiguous; and its form must be valid.

First, remember that your conclusion will be valid only if the premises upon which you base it are themselves valid. The classic example of a syllogism is this:

Major Premise: All men are mortal.

Minor Premise: Socrates is a man.

Conclusion: Socrates is mortal.

Another example is this:

Major Premise: All students pay tuition.

Minor Premise: Adam is a student.

Conclusion: Adam pays tuition.

Notice that the conclusion is drawn directly from the premises and depends on their accuracy for its own accuracy. Your premises will most likely be accurate if they are drawn from known, sufficient, or representative samples—the same conditions needed to draw a sound conclusion by inductive reasoning.

Now, notice what happens to the conclusion when one or both of the premises are inaccurate:

Major Premise: All Americans are wealthy and drive luxury cars.

Minor Premise: Donald is an American.

Conclusion: Donald is wealthy and drives a luxury car.

Because the major premise is not accurate, the conclusion is not necessarily valid either.

Next, the language of your premises must be clear and unambiguous if the conclusion is going to be sound. For example,

Major Premise: Only good citizens should have the right to run for office.

Minor Premise: Beth is a good citizen.

Conclusion: Beth should have the right to run for office.

Here the term "good citizen" is unclear. What constitutes a good citizen? Does Beth fit the definition? Until we know specifically how the term is used, we cannot accept the conclusion as true, that Beth should be allowed to run for office.

Finally, the structure—or form—of the syllogism must be valid. This means that 1) the subject or general topic (or condition) of the major premise must appear in the minor premise but 2) the subject or general topic (or condition) of the minor premise must not be equal to the major premise. For example,

Major Premise: All college students eat food.

Minor Premise: All criminals eat food.

Conclusion: All college students are criminals.

The problem with this syllogism is that the minor premise does not repeat the subject (college students) of the main premise. What results is an invalid— and ridiculous—conclusion.

Or consider this example:

Major Premise: Roses are flowers.

Minor Premise: Daisies are flowers.

Conclusion: Daisies are roses.

The problem with this syllogism is twofold: the term *roses* does not recur in the minor premise and daisies are not a subclass—or division—of roses. When the minor premise is revised to repeat the subject of the major premise and to be a subclass of the major premise, the conclusion becomes valid:

Major Premise:	Roses are flowers.
Minor Premise:	The American Beauty is a rose.
Conclusion:	The American Beauty is a flower.

Types of Fallacies

Fallacies are flawed statements in arguments. They may sound reasonable, but upon close scrutiny you will discover that they cannot be defended logically. Whether they are used intentionally or unintentionally, a reader's detection of these statements can cast the writer in a poor light indeed, making the writer seem ignorant or, even worse, dishonest. Often you may not recognize fallacious statements in your essay's first draft. However, when you are ready to revise, watch out for these common flaws in logic:

False Analogy.   This fallacy is based on presumption. To base an argument on analogy means to base the argument on the comparison of two things you know to be alike in certain aspects. The fallacy occurs when that analogy is presumed to extend into other aspects. For example, you might hear someone argue that today's anti-smoking laws won't work because they are just like Prohibition reforms of the 1920s. But are the programs so alike? Anti-smoking laws today have popular support as well as support from the medical profession and government health officials. Remember also that while the best of analogies may sound persuasive, they cannot *prove* anything.

Equivocation.   This fallacy occurs when you shift the meaning of a key term or terms in the midst of the argument to make your conclusion appear to follow logically from your premise. Read the following carefully:

> In the realm of human experience we all find ourselves presented with difficult choices to make. It is, then, a very human experience to make the mistake that our client did.

The use of "human experience" in the first sentence refers to the *experience* of being human. The second sentence refers to an *act* that a person committed.

Begging the Question.   This fallacy results when you present a debatable premise as if it were a fact. For example, notice this premise:

> An immoral book such as *The Adventures of Huckleberry Finn* must be removed from our school's library because it will corrupt young minds.

This statement begs the question because it presents as *fact* an idea that must be proven—that *Huckleberry Finn* is an immoral book. Such a statement cannot be used as a premise.

Post Hoc, Ergo Propter Hoc.   [After this, therefore because of this] This fallacy occurs when the writer establishes a false cause-effect relationship. The *post hoc* fallacy presumes that since one thing happened first in time, it caused the second happening. The problem with this reasoning is that it ignores some of the complex factors that actually contribute to an outcome. Using this kind of reasoning, one might conclude that finding a lucky horse-shoe in the morning caused one to win an election that afternoon.

Non Sequitur.   [It does not follow] This fallacy occurs when the writer suggests that a given fact has already led to or must eventually lead to a particular result. For example, to suggest that a famous scientist will deliver a brilliant lecture is not necessarily true. Knowing a subject well does not automatically mean one can communicate it; hence the conclusion is not necessarily valid.

Circular Argument.   In circular argument, the writer argues that something is true simply because it is true. For example, to suggest that freeways are too crowded because people drive too many cars is simply repetition. Such an argument is a dead-end topic.

Either/or Fallacy.   This fallacy assumes that an issue of argument has only two sides when it actually could have many facets. For example, if a friend told you that she failed a math examination that you considered easy, you would commit an either/or fallacy by responding, "Well, either you didn't study or you don't have an aptitude for understanding math!" Of course, either (or both) of those things might be true, but there are also several other possible reasons for her failing grade: perhaps she felt ill and found she could not concentrate on the exam; perhaps she did not finish the test (for a variety of reasons); perhaps she suffers from test anxiety and no matter how prepared she is for a test, she "freezes" whenever an exam is placed in front of her. The point is that there could be *many* other reasons why your friend failed the exam.

Argument ad Hominem.   [Argument to the man] Arguments of this type attack a person rather than an issue:

> The Governor supports raising taxes. What else would you expect from a multi-millionaire who inherited all his money?

On occasion, you may find that raising questions about a person's character is justified, that the person's character really may be one of the issues. For example, if a political candidate for a high national office belonged to a club that restricted women or minorities, one might ask if the candidate's membership might be an issue by which the person should be judged—that is, if his choice suggests a character trait or flaw that would affect his ability to function fairly in office. But *argument ad hominem* appeals only to passions and prejudices rather than to reason and logic. We often use the term "mud slinging" to describe the practice.

Similar to argument ad hominem is *argument ad populum* [Argument to the people]. Here the writer defends, "sells," or attacks an ideology, a group, or a product by asking the reader to associate one idea that appeals to people's emotions or prejudices with another idea, regardless of a logical connection. An example would be suggesting that all Southerners are racists in order to sway support away from a southern political candidate. Like *argument ad hominem,* the attack is not on the issue; instead, the reader's attention is transferred to something else, a perception about Southerners. Consider the use of pretty female models, cute animals, and American symbols in commercials for products having nothing whatsoever to do with gender, nature, or nationalism.

Still another type of "argument to-" is *argument ad verecundiam* [argument to authority]. Here the reader's attention is focused upon an authority who shares the same ideas with the writer. The reader acknowledges the authority and thus is persuaded to accept the argument. For instance, when manufacturers advertise that their product is the one most used by doctors, the idea is, "Well, if *doctors* use it, it must be good." Beware, too, the false authority. For example, do football players know any more about popcorn poppers than anyone else?

Consensus Genitum   [Consensus (agreement) of the people]. This is the concept of "going along with the crowd"; it is also called "the bandwagon." The fallacy attempts to establish that something is true or worthwhile simply because many people believe it is or because "everybody's doing it." The validity of the point to be made is based on majority vote. To argue that the speed limit along a certain stretch of road should be raised because everybody exceeds it anyway, argues the point based on *consensus genitum.*

Hasty Generalization.   This fallacy presumes that a general principle is applicable to any specific case. To assume that because Nancy lost 20 pounds in one week on an artichoke and banana diet, everyone else would also lose 20 pounds in one week on the same diet is making a hasty generalization. There are many factors that might have contributed to Nancy's dramatic weight loss, factors that might not be present in any other case.

Red Herring.   This fallacy represents a move of desperation. It occurs when the writer changes the subject to divert the reader's attention away from the issue at hand. Such a ploy is used when the writer finds that the position he or she is supporting is so weak that something is needed to obscure the issue. For example, "Yes, this man has admitted to brutally killing two people but he only turns mean when he's had too much to drink; otherwise, he is a kind, considerate, generous man who has financially supported many of the cultural endeavors of this town."

Tu Quoque.   [You're another] This fallacy occurs when you avoid the issue or hostile charge by making a similar charge against your opponent:

> Don't tell me to take better care of myself; you smoke.

> How can you tell me I need a good education when you dropped out of school in the eleventh grade?

Weaknesses in inductive reasoning or deductive reasoning or in the careless use of words usually lead to the fallacies you have read about in this chapter. Be careful when you form your argument based on syllogism, for a flawed syllogistic form will result in a false analogy. Likewise, an inductive leap can result in a *post hoc* error. Remember that if you must use a fallacy to support your argument, the argument is weak or the information from which you support the argument is insufficient. In either case, you need to reexamine your position.

Use of Other Strategies in Argument and Persuasion

Persuasion and argument may use many of the rhetorical strategies discussed earlier in this text.

Writers often include examples to *illustrate* hypotheses or premises, thereby leading the reader to accept their views. For instance, Jonathan Swift ironically proposes examples of ways children can be used to bring about prosperity in Ireland in his "A Modest Proposal." Both Thomas Jefferson and Elizabeth Cady Stanton present many examples of grievances in their respective "Declarations."

The principles of *causal analysis* also appear frequently in arguments, especially when writers are trying to convince their readers that something needs to be done to prevent or to create something in the future. Rachel Carson, for example, argues the effects of pesticides on nature in "The Obligation to Endure," and in his "I Have a Dream" speech Martin Luther King, Jr., calls for action that will assure a better future for all children, regardless of race.

Richard Rodriguez uses *narrative* techniques in "None of This Is Fair" as he recounts the story of his academic job search, a process that shaped his views on affirmative action. Virginia Woolf makes extensive use of *descriptive* details in "Professions for Women" as she confesses to a metaphorical murder, and anthropologist Margaret Mead *contrasts* the kinds of anxieties she sees to make her point in "One Vote for This Age of Anxiety."

Rhetorical strategies are seldom used in isolation, and essays of argument and persuasion may call on any or all of them to help make their positions clear and convincing. Good writers recognize and use all the tools available to them.

Rachel Carson at her home in Washington in March 1963 (AP/Wide World Photos)

The Obligation to Endure

Rachel Carson
(1907–1964)

Born in Springfield, Pennsylvania, Rachel Carson
attended Pennsylvania College for Women and
Johns Hopkins University. Following graduation,
Carson taught at the University of Maryland and
then became an aquatic biologist for the U.S. Fish
and Wildlife Service. For more than 15 years, she
continued to work for the government while
writing books that explained and analyzed aspects
of marine biology. In 1941 she published *Under the
Sea-Wind: A Naturalist's Picture of Ocean Life* and in
1945, *Fish and Shellfish of the Middle Atlantic Coast.*
These books proved her ability to write for both
lay and scientific audiences, and in 1951 she was
given the National Book Award for her highly
acclaimed *The Sea Around Us.* In the years that
followed she published several more books,
including the controversial and widely read *Silent
Spring* (1962), in which she argues against the
indiscriminate use of pesticides. "The Obligation to
Endure" first appeared as part of *Silent Spring.* In
this essay, Carson explains her reasons for urging
careful study of the threat chemical insecticides
pose to our environment.

1   The history of life on earth has been a history of interaction between
living things and their surroundings. To a large extent, the physical form
and the habits of the earth's vegetation and its animal life have been molded
by the environment. Considering the whole span of earthly time, the opposite effect, in which life actually modifies its surroundings, has been rel-

atively slight. Only within the moment of time represented by the present century has one species—man—acquired significant power to alter the nature of his world.

2   During the past quarter century this power has not only increased to one of disturbing magnitude but it has changed in character. The most alarming of all man's assaults upon the environment is the contamination of air, earth, rivers, and sea with dangerous and even lethal materials. This pollution is for the most part irrecoverable; the chain of evil it initiates not only in the world that must support life but in living tissues is for the most part irreversible. In this now universal contamination of the environment, chemicals are the sinister and little-recognized partners of radiation in changing the very nature of the world—the very nature of its life. Strontium 90, released through nuclear explosions into the air, comes to earth in rain or drifts down in fallout, lodges in soil, enters into the grass or corn or wheat grown there, and in time takes up its abode in the bones of a human being, there to remain until his death. Similarly, chemicals sprayed on croplands or forests or gardens lie long in soil, entering into living organisms, passing from one to another in a chain of poisoning and death. Or they pass mysteriously by underground streams until they emerge and, through the alchemy of air and sunlight, combine into new forms that kill vegetation, sicken cattle, and work unknown harm on those who drink from once pure wells. As Albert Schweitzer has said, "Man can hardly even recognize the devils of his own creation."

3   It took hundreds of millions of years to produce the life that now inhabits the earth—eons of time in which that developing and evolving and diversifying life reached a state of adjustment and balance with its surroundings. The environment, rigorously shaping and directing the life it supported, contained elements that were hostile as well as supporting. Certain rocks gave out dangerous radiation; even within the light of the sun, from which all life draws its energy, there were short-wave radiations with power to injure. Given time—time not in years but in millennia—life adjusts, and a balance has been reached. For time is the essential ingredient; but in the modern world there is no time.

4   The rapidity of change and the speed with which new situations are created follow the impetuous and heedless pace of man rather than the deliberate pace of nature. Radiation is no longer merely the background radiation of rocks, the bombardment of cosmic rays, the ultraviolet of the sun that have existed before there was any life on earth; radiation is now the unnatural creation of man's tampering with the atom. The chemicals to which life is asked to make its adjustment are no longer merely the calcium and silica and copper and all the rest of the minerals washed out of the rocks and carried in rivers to the sea; they are the synthetic creations of man's inventive mind, brewed in his laboratories, and having no counterparts in nature.

5   To adjust to these chemicals would require time on the scale that is nature's; it would require not merely the years of a man's life but the life of generations. And even this, were it by some miracle possible, would be futile, for the new chemicals come from our laboratories in an endless stream; almost five hundred annually find their way into actual use in the United States alone. The figure is staggering and its implications are not easily grasped—500 new chemicals to which the bodies of men and animals are required somehow to adapt each year, chemicals totally outside the limits of biologic experience.

6   Among them are many that are used in man's war against nature. Since the mid-1940's over 200 basic chemicals have been created for use in killing insects, weeds, rodents, and other organisms described in the modern vernacular as "pests"; and they are sold under several thousand different brand names.

7   These sprays, dusts, and aerosols are now applied almost universally to farms, gardens, forests, and homes—nonselective chemicals that have the power to kill every insect, the "good" and the "bad," to still the songs of birds and the leaping of fish in the streams, to coat the leaves with a deadly film, and to linger on in soil—all this though the intended target may be only a few weeds or insects. Can anyone believe it is possible to lay down such a barrage of poisons on the surface of the earth without making it unfit for all life? They should not be called "insecticides," but "biocides."

8   The whole process of spraying seems caught up in an endless spiral. Since DDT was released for civilian use, a process of escalation has been going on in which ever more toxic materials must be found. This has happened because insects, in a triumphant vindication of Darwin's principle of the survival of the fittest, have evolved super races immune to the particular insecticide used, hence a deadlier one has always to be developed—and then a deadlier one than that. It has happened also because, for reasons to be described later, destructive insects often undergo a "flareback" or resurgence, after spraying in numbers greater than before. Thus the chemical war is never won, and all life is caught in its violent crossfire.

9   Along with the possibility of the extinction of mankind by nuclear war, the central problem of our age has therefore become the contamination of man's total environment with such substances of incredible potential for harm—substances that accumulate in the tissues of plants and animals and even penetrate the germ cells to shatter or alter the very material of heredity upon which the shape of the future depends.

10 Some would-be architects of our future look toward a time when it will be possible to alter the human germ plasm by design. But we may easily be doing so now by inadvertence, for many chemicals, like radiation, bring about gene mutations. It is ironic to think that man might determine his own future by something so seemingly trivial as the choice of an insect spray.

11   All this has been risked—for what? Future historians may well be amazed by our distorted sense of proportion. How could intelligent beings seek to control a few unwanted species by a method that contaminated the entire environment and brought the threat of disease and death even to their own kind? Yet this is precisely what we have done. We have done it, moreover, for reasons that collapse the moment we examine them. We are told that the enormous and expanding use of pesticides is necessary to maintain farm production. Yet is our real problem not one of *over-production?* Our farms, despite measures to remove acreages from production and to pay farmers *not* to produce, have yielded such a staggering excess of crops that the American taxpayer in 1962 is paying out more than one billion dollars a year as the total carrying cost of the surplus-food storage program. And is the situation helped when one branch of the Agriculture Department tries to reduce production while another states, as it did in 1958, "It is believed generally that reduction of crop acreages under provisions of the Soil Bank will stimulate interest in use of chemicals to obtain maximum production on the land retained in crops."

12   All this is not to say there is no insect problem and no need of control. I am saying, rather, that control must be geared to realities, not to mythical situations, and that the methods employed must be such that they do not destroy us along with the insects.

13   The problem whose attempted solution has brought such a train of disaster in its wake is an accompaniment of our modern way of life. Long before the age of man, insects inhabited the earth—a group of extraordinarily varied and adaptable beings. Over the course of time since man's advent, a small percentage of the more than half a million species of insects have come into conflict with human welfare in two principal ways: as competitors for the food supply and as carriers of human disease.

14   Disease-carrying insects become important where human beings are crowded together, especially under conditions where sanitation is poor, as in time of natural disaster or war or in situations of extreme poverty and deprivation. Then control of some sort becomes necessary. It is a sobering fact, however, as we shall presently see, that the method of massive chemical control has had only limited success, and also threatens to worsen the very conditions it is intended to curb.

15   Under primitive agricultural conditions the farmer had few insect problems. These arose with the intensification of agriculture—the devotion of immense acreages to a single crop. Such a system set the stage for explosive increases in specific insect populations. Single-crop farming does not take advantage of the principles by which nature works; it is agriculture as an engineer might conceive it to be. Nature has introduced great variety into the landscape, but man has displayed a passion for

simplifying it. Thus he undoes the built-in checks and balances by which nature holds the species within bounds. One important natural check is a limit on the amount of suitable habitat for each species. Obviously then, an insect that lives on wheat can build up its population to much higher levels on a farm devoted to wheat than on one in which wheat is intermingled with other crops to which the insect is not adapted.

16   The same thing happens in other situations. A generation or more ago, the towns of large areas of the United States lined their streets with the noble elm tree. Now the beauty they hopefully created is threatened with complete destruction as disease sweeps through the elms, carried by a beetle that would have only limited chance to build up large populations and to spread from tree to tree if the elms were only occasional trees in a richly diversified planting.

17   Another factor in the modern insect problem is one that must be viewed against a background of geologic and human history: the spreading of thousands of different kinds of organisms from their native homes to invade new territories. This worldwide migration has been studied and graphically described by the British ecologist Charles Elton in his recent book *The Ecology of Invasions.* During the Cretaceous Period, some hundred million years ago, flooding seas cut many land bridges between continents and living things found themselves confined in what Elton calls "colossal separate nature reserves." There, isolated from others of their kind, they developed many new species. When some of the land masses were joined again, about 15 million years ago, these species began to move out into new territories—a movement that is not only still in progress but is now receiving considerable assistance from man.

18   The importation of plants is the primary agent in the modern spread of species, for animals have almost invariably gone along with the plants, quarantine being a comparatively recent and not completely effective innovation. The United States Office of Plant Introduction alone has introduced almost 200,000 species and varieties of plants from all over the world. Nearly half of the 180 or so major insect enemies of plants in the United States are accidental imports from abroad, and most of them have come as hitchhikers on plants.

19   In new territory, out of reach of the restraining hand of the natural enemies that kept down its numbers in its native land, an invading plant or animal is able to become enormously abundant. Thus it is no accident that our most troublesome insects are introduced species.

20   These invasions, both the naturally occurring and those dependent on human assistance, are likely to continue indefinitely. Quarantine and massive chemical campaigns are only extremely expensive ways of buying time. We are faced, according to Dr. Elton, "with a life-and-death need not just to find new technological means of suppressing this plant or that animal"; instead we need the basic knowledge of animal populations and

their relations to their surroundings that will "promote an even balance and damp down the explosive power of outbreaks and new invasions."

21   Much of the necessary knowledge is now available but we do not use it. We train ecologists in our universities and even employ them in our governmental agencies but we seldom take their advice. We allow the chemical death rain to fall as though there were no alternative, whereas in fact there are many, and our ingenuity could soon discover many more if given opportunity.

22   Have we fallen into a mesmerized state that makes us accept as inevitable that which is inferior or detrimental, as though having lost the will or the vision to demand that which is good? Such thinking, in the words of the ecologist Paul Shepard, "idealizes life with only its head out of water, inches above the limits of toleration of the corruption of its own environment . . . Why should we tolerate a diet of weak poisons, a home in insipid surroundings, a circle of acquaintances who are not quite our enemies, the noise of motors with just enough relief to prevent insanity? Who would want to live in a world which is just not quite fatal?"

23   Yet such a world is pressed upon us. The crusade to create a chemically sterile, insect-free world seems to have engendered a fanatic zeal on the part of many specialists and most of the so-called control agencies. On every hand there is evidence that those engaged in spraying operations exercise a ruthless power. "The regulatory entomologists . . . function as prosecutor, judge and jury, tax assessor and collector and sheriff to enforce their own orders," said Connecticut entomologist Neely Turner. The most flagrant abuses go unchecked in both state and federal agencies.

24   It is not my contention that chemical insecticides must never be used. I do contend that we have put poisonous and biologically potent chemicals indiscriminately into the hands of persons largely or wholly ignorant of their potentials for harm. We have subjected enormous numbers of people to contact with these poisons, without their consent and often without their knowledge. If the Bill of Rights contains no guarantee that a citizen shall be secure against lethal poisons distributed either by private individuals or by public officials, it is surely only because our forefathers, despite their considerable wisdom and foresight, could conceive of no such problem.

25   I contend, furthermore, that we have allowed these chemicals to be used with little or no advance investigation of their effect on soil, water, wildlife, and man himself. Future generations are unlikely to condone our lack of prudent concern for the integrity of the natural world that supports all life.

26   There is still very limited awareness of the nature of the threat. This is an era of specialists, each of whom sees his own problem and is unaware of or intolerant of the larger frame into which it fits. It is also an era dominated by industry, in which the right to make a dollar at whatever

cost is seldom challenged. When the public protests, confronted with some obvious evidence of damaging results of pesticide applications, it is fed little tranquilizing pills of half truth. We urgently need an end to these false assurances, to the sugar coating of unpalatable facts. It is the public that is being asked to assume the risks that the insect controllers calculate. The public must decide whether it wishes to continue on the present road, and it can do so only when in full possession of the facts. In the words of Jean Rostand, "The obligation to endure gives us the right to know."

Topics for Writing and Discussion

1. The essay's title is taken from a quotation by Jean Rostand and cited by Carson in the final paragraph. How do Rostand's words suggest Carson's main idea and the thesis of her argument?

2. Does Carson seem to be writing to a hostile or a friendly audience? For example, does she assume that her readers will share many of her concerns? Does she seem to blame her readers for the pollution of the environment or does she identify those who are responsible as someone other than her audience?

3. How does Carson try to convince her audience of her views? Is her approach mainly rational or mainly emotional? Or is it a combination? How does she use statistics, reference to authority, and anecdotal examples to support her ideas?

4. What changes have taken place in the manufacture and use of pesticides since Carson wrote this essay in 1962? Has the situation she describes improved or worsened? Explain the reasons for your decision.

5. Both Rachel Carson in "The Obligation to Endure" and Annie Dillard in "Writing and Vision" (Chapter Two) write about nature. Contrast the way each uses aspects of nature to fulfill the purpose of her essay. Which author is more effective in achieving her purpose? Why do you think so?

Martin Luther King, Jr., delivering his "I Have a Dream" speech at the March on Washington demonstration, August 1963 (AP/Wide World)

I Have a Dream

Martin Luther King, Jr.
(1929–1968)

Martin Luther King, Jr., was the son of a Baptist minister and at age 18 was himself ordained. He later studied at Morehouse College, Crozer Theological Seminary, Boston University, and Chicago Theological seminary. Soon after his ordination in 1947, he became involved in civil-rights actions, and in 1955 he became an acknowledged leader of the movement against segregation when he organized a successful boycott against the Montgomery, Alabama, bus system. In 1957, he founded the Southern Christian Leadership Conference and served as its first president. While holding this office, he continued to support and promote his belief in nonviolent resistance to civil-rights violations, and in 1964 King was awarded the Nobel Peace Prize. In 1968 he was assassinated in Memphis, Tennessee. Widely acclaimed for his powerful use of the English language, King's writing includes *Letter from Birmingham Jail* (1963), *Why We Can't Wait* (1964), and *Where Do We Go from Here: Chaos or Community?* (1967). On August 28, 1963, King led a march of 200,000 people to the Lincoln Memorial where he delivered his now-famous speech, "I Have a Dream," to commemorate the centennial of the Emancipation Proclamation, which declared all slaves to be free.

1   Five score years ago, a great American, in whose symbolic shadow we stand, signed the Emancipation Proclamation. This momentous decree came

as a great beacon light of hope to millions of Negro slaves who had been seared in the flames of withering injustice. It came as a joyous daybreak to end the long night of captivity.

2   But one hundred years later, we must face the tragic fact that the Negro is still not free. One hundred years later, the life of the Negro is still sadly crippled by the manacles of segregation and the chains of discrimination. One hundred years later, the Negro lives on a lonely island of poverty in the midst of a vast ocean of material prosperity. One hundred years later, the Negro is still languishing in the corners of American society and finds himself an exile in his own land. So we have come here today to dramatize an appalling condition.

3   In a sense we have come to our nation's capital to cash a check. When the architects of our republic wrote the magnificent words of the Constitution and the Declaration of Independence, they were signing a promissory note to which every American was to fall heir. This note was a promise that all men would be guaranteed the unalienable rights of life, liberty, and the pursuit of happiness.

4   It is obvious today that America has defaulted on this promissory note insofar as her citizens of color are concerned. Instead of honoring this sacred obligation, America has given the Negro people a bad check; a check which has come back marked "insufficient funds." But we refuse to believe that the bank of justice is bankrupt. We refuse to believe that there are insufficient funds in the great vaults of opportunity of this nation. So we have come to cash this check—a check that will give us upon demand the riches of freedom and the security of justice. We have also come to this hallowed spot to remind America of the fierce urgency of *now*. This is no time to engage in the luxury of cooling off or to take the tranquilizing drugs of gradualism. *Now* is the time to make real the promises of Democracy. *Now* is the time to rise from the dark and desolate valley of segregation to the sunlit path of racial justice. *Now* is the time to open the doors of opportunity to all of God's children. *Now* is the time to lift our nation from the quicksands of racial injustice to the solid rock of brotherhood.

5   It would be fatal for the nation to overlook the urgency of the moment and to underestimate the determination of the Negro. This sweltering summer of the Negro's legitimate discontent will not pass until there is an invigorating autumn of freedom and equality. 1963 is not an end, but a beginning. Those who hope that the Negro needed to blow off steam and will now be content will have a rude awakening if the nation returns to business as usual. There will be neither rest nor tranquility in America until the Negro is granted his citizenship rights. The whirlwinds of revolt will continue to shake the foundations of our nation until the bright day of justice emerges.

6   But there is something that I must say to my people who stand on the warm threshold which leads into the palace of justice. In the process of

gaining our rightful place we must not be guilty of wrongful deeds. Let us not seek to satisfy our thirst for freedom by drinking from the cup of bitterness and hatred. We must forever conduct our struggle on the high plane of dignity and discipline. We must not allow our creative protest to degenerate into physical violence. Again and again we must rise to the majestic heights of meeting physical force with soul force. The marvelous new militancy which has engulfed the Negro community must not lead us to a distrust of all white people, for many of our white brothers, as evidenced by their presence here today, have come to realize that their destiny is tied up with our destiny and their freedom is inextricably bound to our freedom. We cannot walk alone.

7   And as we walk, we must make the pledge that we shall march ahead. We cannot turn back. There are those who are asking the devotees of civil rights, "When will you be satisfied?" We can never be satisfied as long as the Negro is the victim of the unspeakable horrors of police brutality. We can never be satisfied as long as our bodies, heavy with the fatigue of travel, cannot gain lodging in the motels of the highways and the hotels of the cities. We cannot be satisfied as long as the Negro's basic mobility is from a smaller ghetto to a larger one. We can never be satisfied as long as a Negro in Mississippi cannot vote and a Negro in New York believes he has nothing for which to vote. No, no, we are not satisfied, and we will not be satisfied until justice rolls down like waters and righteousness like a mighty stream.

8   I am not unmindful that some of you have come here out of great trials and tribulations. Some of you have come fresh from narrow jail cells. Some of you have come from areas where your quest for freedom left you battered by the storms of persecution and staggered by the winds of police brutality. You have been the veterans of creative suffering. Continue to work with the faith that unearned suffering is redemptive.

9   Go back to Mississippi, go back to Alabama, go back to South Carolina, go back to Georgia, go back to Louisiana, go back to the slums and ghettos of our northern cities, knowing that somehow this situation can and will be changed. Let us not wallow in the valley of despair.

10   I say to you today, my friends, that in spite of the difficulties and frustrations of the moment I still have a dream. It is a dream deeply rooted in the American dream.

11   I have a dream that one day this nation will rise up and live out the true meaning of its creed: "We hold these truths to be self-evident; that all men are created equal."

12   I have a dream that one day on the red hills of Georgia the sons of former slaves and the sons of former slaveowners will be able to sit down together at the table of brotherhood.

13   I have a dream that one day even the state of Mississippi, a desert state sweltering with the heat of injustice and oppression, will be transformed into an oasis of freedom and justice.

14   I have a dream that my four little children will one day live in a nation where they will not be judged by the color of their skin but by the content of their character.

15   I have a dream today.

16   I have a dream that one day the state of Alabama, whose governor's lips are presently dripping with the words of interposition and nullification, will be transformed into a situation where little black boys and black girls will be able to join hands with little white boys and white girls and walk together as sisters and brothers.

17   I have a dream today.

18   I have a dream that one day every valley shall be exalted, every hill and mountain shall be made low, the rough places will be made plain, and the crooked places will be made straight, and the glory of the Lord shall be revealed, and all flesh shall see it together.

19   This is our hope. This is the faith with which I return to the South. With this faith we will be able to hew out of the mountain of despair a stone of hope. With this faith we will be able to transform the jangling discords of our nation into a beautiful symphony of brotherhood. With this faith we will be able to work together, to pray together, to struggle together, to go to jail together, to stand up for freedom together, knowing that we will be free one day.

20   This will be the day when all of God's children will be able to sing with new meaning

> My country, 'tis of thee,
> Sweet land of liberty,
> Of thee I sing:
> Land where my fathers died,
> Land of the pilgrims' pride,
> From every mountain-side
> Let freedom ring.

21   And if America is to be a great nation this must become true. So let freedom ring from the prodigious hilltops of New Hampshire. Let freedom ring from the mighty mountains of New York. Let freedom ring from the heightening Alleghenies of Pennsylvania!

22   Let freedom ring from the snowcapped Rockies of Colorado!

23   Let freedom ring from the curvaceous peaks of California!

24   But not only that; let freedom ring from Stone Mountain of Georgia!

25   Let freedom ring from Lookout Mountain of Tennessee!

26   Let freedom ring from every hill and molehill of Mississippi. From every mountainside, let freedom ring.

27   When we let freedom ring, when we let it ring from every village and every hamlet, from every state and every city, we will be able to speed up that day when all of God's children, black men and white men, Jews and

Gentiles, Protestants and Catholics, will be able to join hands and sing in the words of the old Negro spiritual, "Free at last! free at last! thank God almighty, we are free at last!"

Topics for Writing and Discussion

1. What is King's thesis? How does he establish that idea in the first four paragraphs? How does he use Lincoln's words and sentiments to lead to his own?

2. What problems and injustices suffered by African Americans does King list? How does he believe these wrongs can best be addressed? What examples does he use to inspire his audience to the actions he sees as most appropriate and most effective?

3. King's speech is rich with metaphors and allusions. Find several examples of each and explain what they contribute to the essay's thesis and how they serve to make his argument convincing.

4. Identify examples of repetition and parallel structure. How does King use these devices to emphasize his beliefs and to urge his audience to share his vision?

5. Write an argument either for or against the following proposition: the essential elements of Martin Luther King, Jr.'s dream have become reality today.

Lewis Thomas at Lincoln Center in New York City after winning a National Book Award (© 1991 by Jill Krementz)

The Health-Care System

Lewis Thomas
(1913–   )

Lewis Thomas was educated at Princeton
University and Harvard Medical School and served
as president of the Memorial Sloan-Kettering
Cancer Center for nearly twenty years. His early
writing on pathology appeared in numerous
scientific journals, and in 1971 he began
contributing a regular column, "Notes of a Biology
Watcher," to the *New England Journal of Medicine.*
Thomas won the National Book Award for Arts
and Letters for his collection of essays, *The Lives of
a Cell: Notes of a Biology Watcher* (1974). More
recent work includes *Late Night Thoughts on
Listening to Mahler's Ninth Symphony* (1983) and *Et
Cetera, Et Cetera: Notes of a Wordwatcher* (1990).
Thomas' essay "The Health-Care System"
examines the dangers of a society that promotes
the belief that we are "fundamentally fragile,
always on the verge of mortal disease" rather than
celebrating the reality of longer, healthier lifespans
than those of previous generations.

1   The health-care system of this country is a staggering enterprise, in any
sense of the adjective. Whatever the failures of distribution and lack of
coordination, it is the gigantic scale and scope of the total collective effort
that first catches the breath, and its cost. The dollar figures are almost beyond
grasping. They vary from year to year, always upward, ranging from something like $10 billion in 1950 to an estimated $140 billion in 1978, with
much more to come in the years just ahead, whenever a national health-
insurance program is installed. The official guess is that we are now investing
around 8 percent of the GNP in Health; it could soon rise to 10 or 12 percent.

2   Those are the official numbers, and only for the dollars that flow in an authorized way—for hospital charges, physician's fees, prescribed drugs, insurance premiums, the construction of facilities, research, and the like.

3   But these dollars are only part of it. Why limit the estimates to the strictly professional costs? There is another huge marketplace, in which vast sums are exchanged for items designed for the improvement of Health.

4   The television and radio industry, no small part of the national economy, feeds on Health, or, more precisely, on disease, for a large part of its sustenance. Not just the primarily medical dramas and the illness or surgical episodes threaded through many of the nonmedical stories, in which the central human dilemma is illness; almost all the commercial announcements, in an average evening, are pitches for items to restore failed health: things for stomach gas, constipation, headaches, nervousness, sleeplessness or sleepiness, arthritis, anemia, disquiet, and the despair of malodorousness, sweat, yellowed teeth, dandruff, furuncles, piles. The food industry plays the role of surrogate physician, advertising breakfast cereals as though they were tonics, vitamins, restoratives; they are now out-hawked by the specialized Health-food industry itself, with its nonpolluted, organic, "naturally" vitalizing products. Chewing gum is sold as a tooth cleanser. Vitamins have taken the place of prayer.

5   The publishing industry, hardcover, paperbacks, magazines, and all, seems to be kept alive by Health, new techniques for achieving mental health, cures for arthritis, and diets mostly for the improvement of everything.

6   The transformation of our environment has itself become an immense industry, costing rather more than the moon, in aid of Health. Pollution is supposed to be primarily a medical problem; when the television weatherman tells whether New York's air is "acceptable" or not that day, he is talking about human lungs, he believes. Pollutants which may be impairing photosynthesis by algae in the world's oceans, or destroying all the life in topsoil, or killing all the birds are being worried about lest they cause cancer in us, for heaven's sake.

7   Tennis has become more than the national sport; it is a rigorous discipline, a form of collective physiotherapy. Jogging is done by swarms of people, out onto the streets each day in underpants, moving in a stolid sort of rapid trudge, hoping by this to stay alive. Bicycles are cures. Meditation may be good for the soul but it is even better for the blood pressure.

8   As a people, we have become obsessed with Health.

9   There is something fundamentally, radically unhealthy about all this. We do not seem to be seeking more exuberance in living as much as staving off failure, putting off dying. We have lost all confidence in the human body.

10   The new consensus is that we are badly designed, intrinsically fallible, vulnerable to a host of hostile influences inside and around us, and only precariously alive. We live in danger of falling apart at any moment, and

are therefore always in need of surveillance and propping up. Without the professional attention of a health-care system, we would fall in our tracks.

11   This is a new way of looking at things, and perhaps it can only be accounted for as a manifestation of spontaneous, undirected, societal *propaganda*. We keep telling each other this sort of thing, and back it comes on television or in the weekly newsmagazines, confirming all the fears, instructing us, as in the usual final paragraph of the personal-advice columns in the daily paper, to "seek professional help." Get a checkup. Go on a diet. Meditate. Jog. Have some surgery. Take two tablets, with water. *Spring* water. If pain persists, if anomie persists, if boredom persists, see your doctor.

12   It is extraordinary that we have just now become convinced of our bad health, our constant jeopardy of disease and death, at the very time when the facts should be telling us the opposite. In a more rational world, you'd think we would be staging bicentennial ceremonies for the celebration of our general good shape. In the year 1976, out of a population of around 220 million, only 1.9 million died, or just under 1 percent, not at all a discouraging record once you accept the fact of mortality itself. The life expectancy for the whole population rose to seventy-two years, the longest stretch ever achieved in this country. Despite the persisting roster of still-unsolved major diseases—cancer, heart disease, stroke, arthritis, and the rest—most of us have a clear, unimpeded run at a longer and healthier lifetime than could have been foreseen by any earlier generation. The illnesses that plague us the most, when you count up the numbers in the U.S. Vital Statistics reports, are respiratory and gastrointestinal infections, which are, by and large, transient, reversible affairs needing not much more than Grandmother's advice for getting through safely. Thanks in great part to the improved sanitary engineering, nutrition, and housing of the past century, and in real but less part to contemporary immunization and antibiotics, we are free of the great infectious diseases, especially tuberculosis and lobar pneumonia, which used to cut us down long before our time. We are even beginning to make progress in our understanding of the mechanisms underlying the chronic illnesses still with us, and sooner or later, depending on the quality and energy of biomedical research, we will learn to cope effectively with most of these, maybe all. We will still age away and die, but the aging, and even the dying, can become a healthy process. On balance, we ought to be more pleased with ourselves than we are, and more optimistic for the future.

13   The trouble is, we are being taken in by the propaganda, and it is bad not only for the spirit of society; it will make any health-care system, no matter how large and efficient, unworkable. If people are educated to believe that they are fundamentally fragile, always on the verge of mortal disease, perpetually in the need of support by health-care professionals at every side, always dependent on an imagined discipline of "preventive" medicine, there can be no limit to the numbers of doctors' offices, clinics, and hospitals

required to meet the demand. In the end, we would all become doctors, spending our days screening each other for disease.

14   We are, in real life, a reasonably healthy people. Far from being ineptly put together, we are amazingly tough, durable organisms, full of health, ready for most contingencies. The new danger to our well-being, if we continue to listen to all the talk, is in becoming a nation of healthy hypochondriacs, living gingerly, worrying ourselves half to death.

15   And we do not have time for this sort of thing anymore, nor can we afford such a distraction from our other, considerably more urgent problems. Indeed, we should be worrying that our preoccupation with personal health may be a symptom of copping out, an excuse for running upstairs to recline on a couch, sniffing the air for contaminants, spraying the room with deodorants, while just outside, the whole of society is coming undone.

Topics for Writing and Discussion

1.   Thomas titled his essay "The Health-Care System." What "system" is he referring to? What role does the American consumer play in it?

2.   Consider Thomas' tone and word choice, particularly his use of "we." What effect does this have on his audience?

3.   Note the structure of the essay. At what point does Thomas' focus become clear? Is there one—or more than one—dominant idea that he communicates to the reader?

4.   In paragraphs 4, 7, and 11 Thomas offers a cataloguing of ills, cures, and advice. How does the mention of these specifics, rather than general description, change the impact of the essay? Which items would you add to each of these lists?

5.   Test Thomas' claim that our health paranoia is fed by mass media. Choose a popular weekly magazine to review or watch television during prime time and keep a log of the type of products you see advertised. Do your findings confirm or call into question Thomas' viewpoint? Present your findings in an essay responding to "The Health-Care System," using your own perspective to either refute Thomas or agree with, and extend, his argument.

None of This Is Fair

Richard Rodriguez
(1944–   )

Richard Rodriguez
(© Georges Borchardt, Inc.)

Richard Rodriguez is a journalist who has written for many publications, including *Time, Harpers,* and *Mother Jones.* His most recent book is *Mexico's Children* (1990). He was born in San Francisco, the son of Mexican-American immigrants, and was raised speaking only Spanish until, at the age of five, he started school. Rodriguez reacted strongly to his early school experiences and for a while refused to speak Spanish at all, learning most of what he knows of his parents' native tongue from studying Spanish as a "foreign" language in high school. He continued his education at the University of California at Berkeley where he received the Ph.D. degree in English. After receiving his doctorate, Rodriguez, as he explains in "None of This Is Fair," was deluged with job offers. He felt uncomfortable about the motives of those offering him academic positions and about the laws that may have motivated those offers. In this essay, which was later reprinted as part of his book *Hunger of Memory: The Education of Richard Rodriguez* (1982), he argues against both the assumptions and the effects of affirmative-action programs.

1   **M**y plan to become a professor of English—my ambition during long years in college at Stanford, then in graduate school at Columbia and Berkeley—was complicated by feelings of embarrassment and guilt. So many times I would see other Mexican-Americans and know we were alike only in race. And yet, simply because our race was the same, I was, during the last years of my schooling, the beneficiary of their situation. Affirmative Action programs had made it all possible. The disadvantages of others permitted my promotion; the absence of many Mexican-Americans from academic life allowed my designation as a "minority student."

2   For me opportunities had been extravagant. There were fellowships, summer research grants, and teaching assistantships. After only two years in graduate school, I was offered teaching jobs by several colleges. Invitations to Washington conferences arrived and I had the chance to travel abroad as a "Mexican-American representative." The benefits were often, however, too gaudy to please. In three published essays, in conversations with teachers, in letters to politicians and at conferences, I worried the issue of Affirmative Action. Often I proposed contradictory opinions. Though consistent was the admission that—because of an early, excellent education—I was no longer a principal victim of racism or any other social oppression. I said that but still I continued to indicate on applications for financial aid that I was a Hispanic-American. It didn't really occur to me to say anything else, or to leave the question unanswered.

3   Thus I complied with and encouraged the odd bureaucratic logic of Affirmative Action. I let government officials treat the disadvantaged condition of many Mexican-Americans with my advancement. Each fall my presence was noted by Health, Education, and Welfare department statisticians. As I pursued advanced literary studies and learned the skill of reading Spenser and Wordsworth and Empson, I would hear myself numbered among the culturally disadvantaged. Still, silent, I didn't object.

4   But the irony cut deep. And guilt would not be evaded by averting my glance when I confronted a face like my own in a crowd. By late 1975, nearing the completion of my graduate studies at Berkeley, I was so wary of the benefits of Affirmative Action that I feared my inevitable success as an applicant for a teaching position. The months of fall—traditionally that time of academic job-searching—passed without my applying to a single school. When one of my professors chanced to learn this in late November, he was astonished, then furious. He yelled at me: Did I think that because I was a minority student jobs would just come looking for me? What was I thinking? Did I realize that he and several other faculty members had already written letters on my behalf? Was I going to start acting like some other minority students he had known? They struggled for success and then, when it was almost within reach, grew strangely afraid and let it pass. Was that it? Was I determined to fail?

5   I did not respond to his questions. I didn't want to admit to him, and thus to myself, the reason I delayed.

6   I merely agreed to write to several schools. (In my letter I wrote: "I cannot claim to represent disadvantaged Mexican-Americans. The very fact that I am in a position to apply for this job should make that clear.") After two or three days, there were telegrams and phone calls, invitations to interviews, then airplane trips. A blur of faces and the murmur of their soft questions. And, over someone's shoulder, the sight of campus buildings shadowing pictures I had seen years before when I leafed through Ivy League catalogues with great expectations. At the end of each visit, interviewers would smile

and wonder if I had any questions. A few times I quietly wondered what advantage my race had given me over other applicants. But that was an impossible question for them to answer without embarrassing me. Quickly, several persons insisted that my ethnic identity had given me no more than a "foot inside the door"; at most, I had a "slight edge" over other applicants. "We just looked at your dossier with extra care and we like what we saw. There was never any question of having to alter our standards. You can be certain of that."

7   In the early part of January, offers arrived on stiffly elegant stationery. Most schools promised terms appropriate for any new assistant professor. A few made matters worse—and almost more tempting—by offering more: the use of university housing; an unusually large starting salary; a reduced teaching schedule. As the stack of letters mounted, my hesitation increased. I started calling department chairmen to ask for another week, then 10 more days—"more time to reach a decision"—to avoid the decision I would need to make.

8   At school, meantime, some students hadn't received a single job offer. One man, probably the best student in the department, did not even get a request for his dossier. He and I met outside a classroom one day and he asked about my opportunities. He seemed happy for me. Faculty members beamed. They said they had expected it. "After all, not many schools are going to pass up getting a Chicano with a Ph.D. in Renaissance literature," somebody said laughing. Friends wanted to know which of the offers I was going to accept. But I couldn't make up my mind. February came and I was running out of time and excuses. (One chairman guessed my delay was a bargaining ploy and increased his offer with each of my calls.) I had to promise a decision by the 10th; the 12th at the very latest.

9   On the 18th of February, late in the afternoon, I was in the office I shared with several other teaching assistants. Another graduate student was sitting across the room at his desk. When I got up to leave, he looked over to say in an uneventful voice that he had some big news. He had finally decided to accept a position at a faraway university. It was not a job he especially wanted, he admitted. But he had to take it because there hadn't been any other offers. He felt trapped, and depressed, since his job would separate him from his young daughter.

10   I tried to encourage him by remarking that he was lucky at least to have found a job. So many others hadn't been able to get anything. But before I finished speaking I realized that I had said the wrong thing. And I anticipated his next question.

11   "What are your plans?" he wanted to know. "Is it true you've gotten an offer from Yale?"

12   I said that it was. "Only, I still haven't made up my mind."

13   He stared at me as I put on my jacket. And smiling, then unsmiling, he asked if I knew that he too had written to Yale. In his case, however, no

one had bothered to acknowledge his letter with even a postcard. What did I think of that?

14   He gave me no time to answer.

15   "Damn!" he said sharply and his chair rasped the floor as he pushed himself back. Suddenly, it was to *me* that he was complaining. "It's just not right, Richard. None of this is fair. You've done some good work, but so have I. I'll bet our records are just about equal. But when we look for jobs this year, it's a different story. You get all of the breaks."

16   To evade his criticism, I wanted to side with him. I was about to admit the injustice of Affirmative Action. But he went on, his voice hard with accusation. "It's all very simple this year. You're a Chicano. And I am a Jew. That's the only real difference between us."

17   His words stung me: there was nothing he was telling me that I didn't know. I had admitted everything already. But to hear someone else say these things, and in such an accusing tone, was suddenly hard to take. In a deceptively calm voice, I responded that he had simplified the whole issue. The phrases came like bubbles to the tip of my tongue: "new blood"; "the importance of cultural diversity"; "the goal of racial integration." These were all the arguments I had proposed several years ago—and had long since abandoned. Of course the offers were unjustifiable. I knew that. All I was saying amounted to a frantic self-defense. I tried to find an end to a sentence. My voice faltered to a stop.

18   "Yeah, sure," he said. "I've heard all that before. Nothing you say really changes the fact that Affirmative Action is unfair. You see that, don't you? There isn't any way for me to compete with you. Once there were quotas to keep my parents out of certain schools; now there are quotas to get you in and the effect on me is the same as it was for them."

19   I listened to every word he spoke. But my mind was really on something else. I knew at that moment that I would reject all of the offers. I stood there silently surprised by what an easy conclusion it was. Having prepared for so many years to teach, having trained myself to do nothing else, I had hesitated out of practical fear. But now that it was made, the decision came with relief. I immediately knew I had made the right choice.

20   My colleague continued talking and I realized that he was simply right. Affirmative Action programs *are* unfair to white students. But as I listened to him assert his rights, I thought of the seriously disadvantaged. How different they were from white, middle-class students who come armed with the testimony of their grades and aptitude scores and self-confidence to complain about the unequal treatment they now receive. I listen to them. I do not want to be careless about what they say. Their rights are important to protect. But inevitably when I hear them or their lawyers, I think about the most seriously disadvantaged, not simply Mexican-Americans, but of all those who do not ever imagine themselves going to college or becoming doctors: white, black, brown. Always poor. Silent. They are not plaintiffs

before the court or against the misdirection of Affirmative Action. They lack the confidence (my confidence!) to assume their right to a good education. They lack the confidence and skills a good primary and secondary education provides and which are prerequisites for informed public life. They remain silent.

21 The debate drones on and surrounds them in stillness. They are distant, faraway figures like the boys I have seen peering down from freeway overpasses in some other part of town.

Topics for Writing and Discussion

1. Explain what Rodriguez means by Affirmative Action. Why does he believe that Affirmative Action represents a form of discrimination?

2. Rodriguez explains that he turned down a number of very good job offers. Why did he turn them down? Does he convince you that his reasons for refusing these positions are valid?

3. How do the two concluding paragraphs relate to the rest of Rodriguez's argument? Would the thesis of the essay be different if the final two paragraphs were omitted? Explain why or why not.

4. In some paragraphs, Rodriguez uses directly recorded conversation while in others he simply describes his discussions with others. (See, for instance, his conversation with his officemate in paragraphs 11–18 and his reported discussion with his professor in paragraph 4.) Why does he choose to use indirect quotation in some instances and direct quotation in others? What effect does each conversation have on the argument?

5. Write an argument defending or refuting the following statement: Richard Rodriguez unfairly attacks Affirmative-Action programs because he fails to consider many of the complexities of this issue.

Gore Vidal (© Nancy Crampton)

Drugs

Gore Vidal
(1925–   )

Born at the U.S. Military Academy at West Point,
the son of Luther Vidal, Director of Air Commerce
under Franklin Delano Roosevelt, and grandson of
Oklahoma Senator Thomas P. Gore, Gore Vidal
has blended writing and politics to emerge as a
distinctive voice in American literature. A
Democratic party candidate for Congress in New
York in 1960 and California in 1982, he has
written novels, plays, and screenplays as well as
essays, the form acknowledged by many critics as
his forte. Some of Vidal's best known novels are
Myra Breckinridge (1968), *Burr* (1973), *Lincoln*
(1984), and *Hollywood* (1990); essay collections
include *The Second American Revolution and Other
Essays* (1982), which was awarded the National
Book Critics' Circle Award for Criticism, and *At
Home* (1988). The following essay, originally
published in the *New York Times* in 1970, argues a
position that is attracting renewed attention as
America wages "the war on drugs" in the 1990s.

1   It is possible to stop most drug addiction in the United States within a
very short time. Simply make all drugs available and sell them at cost. Label
each drug with a precise description of what effect—good and bad—the drug
will have on the taker. This will require heroic honesty. Don't say that
marijuana is addictive or dangerous when it is neither, as millions of people
know—unlike "speed," which kills most unpleasantly, or heroin, which is
addictive and difficult to kick.

2   For the record, I have tried—once—almost every drug and liked none,

disproving the popular Fu Manchu theory that a single whiff of opium will enslave the mind. Nevertheless many drugs are bad for certain people to take and they should be told why in a sensible way.

3   Along with exhortation and warning, it might be good for our citizens to recall (or learn for the first time) that the United States was the creation of men who believed that each man has the right to do what he wants with his own life as long as he does not interfere with his neighbor's pursuit of happiness. (That his neighbor's idea of happiness is persecuting others does confuse matters a bit.)

4   This is a startling notion to the current generation of Americans. They reflect a system of public education which has made the Bill of Rights, literally, unacceptable to a majority of high school graduates (see the annual Purdue reports) who now form the "silent majority"—a phrase which that underestimated wit Richard Nixon took from Homer who used it to describe the dead.

5   Now one can hear the warning rumble begin: If everyone is allowed to take drugs everyone will and the GNP will decrease, the Commies will stop us from making everyone free, and we shall end up a race of zombies, passively murmuring "groovy" to one another. Alarming thought. Yet it seems most unlikely that any reasonably sane person will become a drug addict if he knows in advance what addiction is going to be like.

6   Is everyone reasonably sane? No. Some people will always become drug addicts just as some people will always become alcoholics, and it is just too bad. Every man, however, has the power (and should have the legal right) to kill himself if he chooses. But since most men don't, they won't be main-liners either. Nevertheless, forbidding people things they like or think they might enjoy only makes them want those things all the more. This psychological insight is, for some mysterious reason, perennially denied our governors.

7   It is a lucky thing for the American moralist that our country has always existed in a kind of time-vacuum: We have no public memory of anything that happened before last Tuesday. No one in Washington today recalls what happened during the years alcohol was forbidden to the people by a Congress that thought it had a divine mission to stamp out Demon Rum—launching, in the process, the greatest crime wave in the country's history, causing thousands of deaths from bad alcohol, and creating a general (and persisting) contempt among the citizenry for the laws of the United States.

8   The same thing is happening today. But the government has learned nothing from past attempts at prohibition, not to mention repression.

9   Last year when the supply of Mexican marijuana was slightly curtailed by the Feds, the pushers got the kids hooked on heroin and deaths increased dramatically, particularly in New York. Whose fault? Evil men like the Mafiosi? Permissive Dr. Spock? Wild-eyed Dr. Leary? No.

10   The government of the United States was responsible for those deaths. The bureaucratic machine has a vested interest in playing cops and robbers. Both the Bureau of Narcotics and the Mafia want strong laws against the sale and use of drugs because if drugs are sold at cost there would be no money in it for anyone.

11   If there was no money in it for the Mafia, there would be no friendly playground pushers, and addicts would not commit crimes to pay for the next fix. Finally, if there was no money in it, the Bureau of Narcotics would wither away, something they are not about to do without a struggle.

12   Will anything sensible be done? Of course not. The American people are as devoted to the idea of sin and its punishment as they are to making money—and fighting drugs is nearly as big a business as pushing them. Since the combination of sin and money is irresistible (particularly to the professional politician), the situation will only grow worse.

Topics for Writing and Discussion

1.   What is Vidal's solution for the drug problem in America?

2.   What strategies does Vidal use to argue his position? Are all his arguments equally persuasive? Critique what you believe are his strongest and his weakest points.

3.   How does Vidal try to refute his critics? Is he, in your opinion, successful? Why or why not?

4.   Characterize Vidal's "voice" in this essay. How might such comments as Americans "have no public memory of anything that happened before last Tuesday" and "American people are as devoted to the idea of sin and its punishment as they are to making money" affect Vidal's readers?

5.   This essay appeared as an editorial in 1970; since that time the debate has continued as drug use and drug trafficking have escalated. Write an editorial of your own, arguing for a sensible drug policy for the 1990s.

Margaret Mead in her office at the Museum of Natural History in New York City (© 1988 by Jill Krementz)

One Vote for This Age of Anxiety

Margaret Mead
(1901–1978)

Noted anthropologist Margaret Mead attended
Barnard College and Columbia University. In 1925
she went to live in the Samoan Islands where she
began her fieldwork living with and studying the
customs of its native peoples. Following her years
in Asia and the Pacific, she published three books
reporting and evaluating her experiences, *Coming of
Age in Samoa* (1928), *Growing Up in New Guinea*
(1930), and *Sex and Temperament in Three Primitive
Societies* (1935). In her later years, she turned to
the study of contemporary Western society and
published works such as *The School in American
Culture and Culture and Commitment, a Study of the
Generation Gap* (1970). In addition, she wrote a
series of essays for *Redbook* magazine. In "One
Vote for This Age of Anxiety" she argues that
anxiety, usually viewed as a negative emotion, may
in fact be a relatively desirable state of mind.

1   When critics wish to repudiate the world in which we live today, one
of their familiar ways of doing it is to castigate modern man because anxiety
is his chief problem. This, they say, in W. H. Auden's phrase, is the age of
anxiety. That is what we have arrived at with all our vaunted progress, our
great technological advances, our great wealth—everyone goes about with
a burden of anxiety so enormous that, in the end, our stomachs and our
arteries and our skins express the tension under which we live. Americans
who have lived in Europe come back to comment on our favorite farewell
which, instead of the old goodbye (God be with you), is now "Take it easy,"
each American admonishing the other not to break down from the tension
and strain of modern life.

2   Whenever an age is characterized by a phrase, it is presumably in contrast to other ages. If we are the age of anxiety, what were the other ages? And here the critics and carpers do a very amusing thing. First, they give us lists of the opposites of anxiety: security, trust, self-confidence, self-direction. Then, without much further discussion, they let us assume that other ages, other periods of history, were somehow the ages of trust or confident direction.

3   The savage who, on his South Sea island, simply sat and let breadfruit fall into his lap, the simple peasant, at one with the fields he ploughed and the beasts he tended, the craftsman busy with his tools and lost in the fulfillment of the instinct of workmanship—these are the counterimages conjured up by descriptions of the strain under which men live today. But no one who lived in those days has returned to testify how paradisiacal they really were.

4   Certainly if we observe and question the savages or simple peasants in the world today, we find something quite different. The untouched savage in the middle of New Guinea isn't anxious; he is seriously and continually *frightened*—of black magic, of enemies with spears who may kill him or his wives and children at any moment, while they stoop to drink from a spring, or climb a palm tree for a coconut. He goes warily, day and night, taut and fearful.

5   As for the peasant populations of a great part of the world, they aren't so much anxious as hungry. They aren't anxious about whether they will get a salary raise, or which of the three colleges of their choice they will be admitted to, or whether to buy a Ford or Cadillac, or whether the kind of TV set they want is too expensive. They are hungry, cold and, in many parts of the world, they dread that local warfare, bandits, political coups may endanger their homes, their meager livelihoods and their lives. But surely they are not anxious.

6   For anxiety, as we have come to use it to describe our characteristic state of mind, can be contrasted with the active fear of hunger, loss, violence and death. Anxiety is the appropriate emotion when the immediate personal terror—of a volcano, an arrow, the sorcerer's spell, a stab in the back and other calamities, all directed against one's self—disappears.

7   This is not to say that there isn't plenty to worry about in our world of today. The explosion of a bomb in the streets of a city whose name no one had ever heard before may set in motion forces which end up by ruining one's carefully planned education in law school, half a world away. But there is still not the personal, immediate, active sense of impending disaster that the savage knows. There is rather the vague anxiety, the sense that the future is unmanageable.

8   The kind of world that produces anxiety is actually a world of relative safety, a world in which no one feels that he himself is facing sudden death. Possibly sudden death may strike a certain number of unidentified other

people—but not him. The anxiety exists as an uneasy state of mind, in which one has a feeling that something unspecified and undeterminable may go wrong. If the world seems to be going well, this produces anxiety—for good times may end. If the world is going badly—it may get worse. Anxiety tends to be without locus; the anxious person doesn't know whether to blame himself or other people. He isn't sure whether it is the current year or the Administration or a change in climate or the atom bomb that is to blame for this undefined sense of unease.

9   It is clear that we have developed a society which depends on having the *right* amount of anxiety to make it work. Psychiatrists have been heard to say, "He didn't have enough anxiety to get well," indicating that, while we agree that too much anxiety is inimical to mental health, we have come to rely on anxiety to push and prod us into seeing a doctor about a symptom which may indicate cancer, into checking up on that old life-insurance policy which may have out-of-date clauses in it, into having a conference with Billy's teacher even though his report card looks all right.

10   People who are anxious enough keep their car insurance up, have the brakes checked, don't take a second drink when they have to drive, are careful where they go and with whom they drive on holidays. People who are too anxious either refuse to go into cars at all—and so complicate the ordinary course of life—or drive so tensely and overcautiously that they help cause accidents. People who aren't anxious enough take chance after chance, which increases the terrible death toll of the roads.

11   On balance, our age of anxiety represents a large advance over savage and peasant cultures. Out of a productive system of technology drawing upon enormous resources, we have created a nation in which anxiety has replaced terror and despair, for all except the severely disturbed. The specter of hunger means something only to those Americans who can identify themselves with the millions of hungry people on other continents. The specter of terror may still be roused in some by a knock at the door in a few parts of the South, or in those who have just escaped from a totalitarian regime or who have kin still behind the Curtains.

12   But in this twilight world which is neither at peace nor at war, and where there is insurance against certain immediate, downright, personal disasters, for most Americans there remains only anxiety over what may happen, might happen, could happen.

13   This is the world out of which grows the hope, for the first time in history, of a society where there will be freedom from want and freedom from fear. Our very anxiety is born of our knowledge of what is now possible for each and for all. The number of people who consult psychiatrists today is not, as is sometimes felt, a symptom of increasing mental ill health, but rather the precursor of a world in which the hope of genuine mental health will be open to everyone, a world in which no individual feels that he need be hopelessly brokenhearted, a failure, a menace to others or a traitor to himself.

14   But if, then, our anxieties are actually signs of hope, why is there such a voice of discontent abroad in the land? I think this comes perhaps because our anxiety exists without an accompanying recognition of the tragedy which will always be inherent in human life, however well we build our world. We may banish hunger, and fear of sorcery, violence or secret police; we may bring up children who have learned to trust life and who have the spontaneity and curiosity necessary to devise ways of making trips to the moon; we cannot—as we have tried to do—banish death itself.

15   Americans who stem from generations which left their old people behind and never closed their parents' eyelids in death, and who have experienced the additional distance from death provided by two world wars fought far from our shores are today pushing away from them both a recognition of death and a recognition of the tremendous significance—for the future—of the way we live our lives. Acceptance of the inevitability of death, which, when faced, can give dignity to life, and acceptance of our inescapable role in the modern world, might transmute our anxiety about making the right choices, taking the right precautions, and the right risks into the sterner stuff of responsibility, which ennobles the whole face rather than furrowing the forehead with the little anxious wrinkles of worry.

16   Worry in an empty context means that men die daily little deaths. But good anxiety—not about the things that were left undone long ago, but which return to haunt and harry men's minds, but active, vivid anxiety about what must be done and that quickly—binds men to life with an intense concern.

17   This is still a world in which too many of the wrong things happen somewhere. But this is a world in which we now have the means to make a great many more of the right things happen everywhere. For Americans, the generalization which a Swedish social scientist made about our attitudes on race relations is true in many other fields: anticipated change which we feel is right and necessary but difficult makes us unduly anxious and apprehensive, but such change, once consummated, brings a glow of relief. We are still a people who—in the literal sense—believe in making good.

Topics for Writing and Discussion

1.   Mead describes two types of anxiety in this essay. How does she differentiate between negative and positive anxiety? How does she use this contrast both to define and to argue for modern anxiety?

2.   What is Mead's view of our modern society, both in the United States and in the world? Do you share her view? Do you think circumstances have changed enough since Mead wrote this essay in 1965 to warrant revising either her evidence or her thesis?

3.   What contrast does Mead develop in paragraphs 3 through 6? How does she use this contrast to develop her argument? Where in the essay does she reintroduce the contrast?

4. What is Mead's conclusion? Do you think that her assertions in the final paragraph are adequately supported by the evidence she offers?

5. Write an essay arguing that anxiety is a positive or a negative force in your own life. Analyze the situations, events, and circumstances that cause your anxiety as part of your argument.

Flannery O'Connor in 1964 (© Leviton-Atlanta/Black Star)

Total Effect and the Eighth Grade

Flannery O'Connor
(1925–1964)

Born in Milledgeville, Georgia, Flannery O'Connor
showed an early talent for cartooning and satire.
This gift, refined and developed into wit and irony,
informs the fiction, essays, and letters she wrote as
an adult. Her writing cuts to the core of moral,
religious, and social issues; she does not suffer
fools—or foolish ideas—gladly. O'Connor attended
college in her hometown and then studied at the
University of Iowa's School for Writers. In 1951
she was diagnosed as having lupus erythematosus,
and she returned home to spend the rest of her
brief life writing highly acclaimed fiction and
essays. Her work includes *Wise Blood* (1952), *The
Violent Bear It Away* (1960), and *A Good Man Is
Hard to Find* (1955) and others. "Total Effect and
the Eighth Grade" first appeared in *The Bulletin,* a
Catholic diocesan newspaper for which O'Connor
wrote regularly. This essay, which argues against
assigning contemporary novels to high school
students, is included in a collection of O'Connor's
occasional prose, *Mystery and Manners* (1969).

1   In two recent instances in Georgia, parents have objected to their eighth-
and ninth-grade children's reading assignments in modern fiction. This
seems to happen with some regularity in cases throughout the country. The
unwitting parent picks up his child's book, glances through it, comes upon
passages of erotic detail or profanity, and takes off at once to complain to
the school board. Sometimes, as in one of the Georgia cases, the teacher is
dismissed and hackles rise in liberal circles everywhere.

2   The two cases in Georgia, which involved Steinbeck's *East of Eden* and John Hersey's *A Bell for Adano,* provoked considerable newspaper comment. One columnist, in commending the enterprise of the teachers, announced that students do not like to read the fusty works of the nineteenth century, that their attention can best be held by novels dealing with the realities of our own time, and that the Bible, too, is full of racy stories.

3   Mr. Hersey himself addressed a letter to the State School Superintendent in behalf of the teacher who had been dismissed. He pointed out that his book is not scandalous, that it attempts to convey an earnest message about the nature of democracy, and that it falls well within the limits of the principle of "total effect," that principle followed in legal cases by which a book is judged not for isolated parts but by the final effect of the whole book upon the general reader.

4   I do not want to comment on the merits of these particular cases. What concerns me is what novels ought to be assigned in the eighth and ninth grades as a matter of course, for if these cases indicate anything, they indicate the haphazard way in which fiction is approached in our high schools. Presumably there is a state reading list which contains "safe" books for teachers to assign; after that it is up to the teacher.

5   English teachers come in Good, Bad, and Indifferent, but too frequently in high schools anyone who can speak English is allowed to teach it. Since several novels can't easily be gathered into one textbook, the fiction that students are assigned depends upon their teacher's knowledge, ability, and taste: variable factors at best. More often than not, the teacher assigns what he thinks will hold the attention and interest of the students. Modern fiction will certainly hold it.

6   Ours is the first age in history which has asked the child what he would tolerate learning, but that is a part of the problem with which I am not equipped to deal. The devil of Educationism that possesses us is the kind that can be "cast out only by prayer and fasting." No one has yet come along strong enough to do it. In other ages the attention of children was held by Homer and Virgil, among others, but, by the reverse evolutionary process, that is no longer possible; our children are too stupid now to enter the past imaginatively. No one asks the student if algebra pleases him or if he finds it satisfactory that some French verbs are irregular, but if he prefers Hersey to Hawthorne, his taste must prevail.

7   I would like to put forward the proposition, repugnant to most English teachers, that fiction, if it is going to be taught in the high schools, should be taught as a subject and as a subject with a history. The total effect of a novel depends not only on its innate impact, but upon the experience, literary and otherwise, with which it is approached. No child needs to be assigned Hersey or Steinbeck until he is familiar with a certain amount of the best work of Cooper, Hawthorne, Melville, the early James, and Crane, and he

does not need to be assigned these until he has been introduced to some of the better English novelists of the eighteenth and nineteenth centuries.

8   The fact that these works do not present him with the realities of his own time is all to the good. He is surrounded by the realities of his own time, and he has no perspective whatever from which to view them. Like the college student who wrote in her paper on Lincoln that he went to the movies and got shot, many students go to college unaware that the world was not made yesterday; their studies began with the present and dipped backward occasionally when it seemed necessary or unavoidable.

9   There is much to be enjoyed in the great British novels of the nineteenth century, much that a good teacher can open up in them for the young student. There is no reason why these novels should be either too simple or too difficult for the eighth grade. For the simple, they offer simple pleasures; for the more precocious, they can be made to yield subtler ones if the teacher is up to it. Let the student discover, after reading the nineteenth-century British novel, that the nineteenth-century American novel is quite different as to its literary characteristics, and he will thereby learn something not only about these individual works but about the sea-change which a new historical situation can effect in a literary form. Let him come to modern fiction with this experience behind him, and he will be better able to see and to deal with the more complicated demands of the best twentieth-century fiction.

10   Modern fiction often looks simpler than the fiction that preceded it, but in reality it is more complex. A natural evolution has taken place. The author has for the most part absented himself from direct participation in the work and has left the reader to make his own way amid experiences dramatically rendered and symbolically ordered. The modern novelist merges the reader in the experience; he tends to raise the passions he touches upon. If he is a good novelist, he raises them to effect by their order and clarity a new experience—the total effect—which is not in itself sensuous or simply of the moment. Unless the child has had some literary experience before, he is not going to be able to resolve the immediate passions the book arouses into any true, total picture.

11   It is here the moral problem will arise. It is one thing for a child to read about adultery in the Bible or in *Anna Karenina,* and quite another for him to read about it in most modern fiction. This is not only because in both the former instances adultery is considered a sin, and in the latter, at most, an inconvenience, but because modern writing involves the reader in the action with a new degree of intensity, and literary mores now permit him to be involved in any action a human being can perform.

12   In our fractured culture, we cannot agree on morals; we cannot even agree that moral matters should come before literary ones when there is a conflict between them. All this is another reason why the high schools would do well to return to their proper business of preparing foundations. Whether

in the senior year students should be assigned modern novelists should depend both on their parents' consent and on what they have already read and understood.

13   The high-school English teacher will be fulfilling his responsibility if he furnishes the student a guided opportunity, through the best writing of the past, to come, in time, to an understanding of the best writing of the present. He will teach literature, not social studies or little lessons in democracy or the customs of many lands.

14   And if the student finds that this is not to his taste? Well, that is regrettable. Most regrettable. His taste should not be consulted; it is being formed.

Topics for Writing and Discussion

1.   O'Connor introduces her essay by giving several examples concerning the assignment of twentieth-century fiction in high school English courses. Then, in paragraph 4, she says that she does not plan to comment on the cases she has described. What is her purpose in giving these examples? How do they lead to her thesis?

2.   What groups of people and schools of thought does O'Connor blame for what she sees as the move away from teaching classic authors and their works? How does she use her attack on these groups and philosophies to advance her argument?

3.   What reasons does O'Connor give for assigning nineteenth-century novels to high school students? Do you find her arguments logically sound? Do you find them convincing?

4.   What is the moral problem O'Connor addresses in the final paragraphs of the essay? How are her convictions about the moral issue related to the thesis of her argument?

5.   Choose a controversial statement in O'Connor's essay and write an argument refuting or supporting that statement. For example, do you believe that "children are [considered] too stupid now to enter the past imaginatively?" Do you agree that in literature classes a student's "taste should not be consulted [because] it is being formed"?

Judy Brady (Courtesy of Judy Brady)

I Want a Wife

Judy Brady
(1937–   )

When Judy Brady graduated from the University of
Iowa in 1960, she wanted to continue her
education and become a university teacher. Her
male professors discouraged her from doing so.
Although Brady describes herself as a
"disenfranchised and fired housewife" rather than
a writer, she has published articles on a number of
topics including union organizing, the role of
women in society, and abortion. "I Want a Wife,"
which has come to be regarded as a classic feminist
satire, first appeared in *Ms.* magazine in 1971. In
this essay, Brady describes the "ideal" wife and,
with finely tuned irony, argues against the
repressive marriages in which some women may
find themselves.

1   I belong to that classification of people known as wives. I am A Wife.
And, not altogether incidentally, I am a mother.

2   Not too long ago a male friend of mine appeared on the scene fresh from
a recent divorce. He had one child, who is, of course, with his ex-wife. He
is looking for another wife. As I thought about him while I was ironing one
evening, it suddenly occurred to me that I, too, would like to have a wife.
Why do I want a wife?

3   I would like to go back to school so that I can become economically
independent, support myself, and, if need be, support those dependent upon
me. I want a wife who will work and send me to school. And while I am
going to school I want a wife to take care of my children. I want a wife to
keep track of the children's doctor and dentist appointments. And to keep
track of mine, too. I want a wife to make sure my children eat properly and

are kept clean. I want a wife who will wash the children's clothes and keep them mended. I want a wife who is a good nurturant attendant to my children, who arranges for their schooling, makes sure that they have an adequate social life with their peers, takes them to the park, the zoo, etc. I want a wife who takes care of the children when they are sick, a wife who arranges to be around when the children need special care, because, of course, I cannot miss classes at school. My wife must arrange to lose time at work and not lose the job. It may mean a small cut in my wife's income from time to time, but I guess I can tolerate that. Needless to say, my wife will arrange and pay for the care of the children while my wife is working.

4   I want a wife who will take care of *my* physical needs. I want a wife who will keep my house clean. A wife who will pick up after my children, a wife who will pick up after me. I want a wife who will keep my clothes clean, ironed, mended, replaced when need be, and who will see to it that my personal things are kept in their proper place so that I can find what I need the minute I need it. I want a wife who cooks the meals, a wife who is a *good* cook. I want a wife who will plan the menus, do the necessary grocery shopping, prepare the meals, serve them pleasantly, and then do the cleaning up while I do my studying. I want a wife who will care for me when I am sick and sympathize with my pain and loss of time from school. I want a wife to go along when our family takes a vacation so that someone can continue to care for me and my children when I need a rest and change of scene.

5   I want a wife who will not bother me with rambling complaints about a wife's duties. But I want a wife who will listen to me when I feel the need to explain a rather difficult point I have come across in my course of studies. And I want a wife who will type my papers for me when I have written them.

6   I want a wife who will take care of the details of my social life. When my wife and I are invited out by my friends, I want a wife who will take care of the babysitting arrangements. When I meet people at school that I like and want to entertain, I want a wife who will have the house clean, will prepare a special meal, serve it to me and my friends, and not interrupt when I talk about things that interest me and my friends. I want a wife who will have arranged that the children are fed and ready for bed before my guests arrive so that the children do not bother us. I want a wife who takes care of the needs of my guests so that they feel comfortable, who makes sure that they have an ashtray, that they are passed the hors d'oeuvres, that they are offered a second helping of the food, that their wine glasses are replenished when necessary, that their coffee is served to them as they like it. And I want a wife who knows that sometimes I need a night out by myself.

7   I want a wife who is sensitive to my sexual needs, a wife who makes love passionately and eagerly when I feel like it, a wife who makes sure that I

am satisfied. And, of course, I want a wife who will not demand sexual attention when I am not in the mood for it. I want a wife who assumes the complete responsibility for birth control, because I do not want more children. I want a wife who will remain sexually faithful to me so that I do not have to clutter up my intellectual life with jealousies. And I want a wife who understands that *my* sexual needs may entail more than strict adherence to monogamy. I must, after all, be able to relate to people as fully as possible.

8   If, by chance, I find another person more suitable as a wife than the wife I already have, I want the liberty to replace my present wife with another one. Naturally, I will expect a fresh, new life; my wife will take the children and be solely responsible for them so that I am left free.

9   When I am through with school and have a job, I want my wife to quit working and remain at home so that my wife can more fully and completely take care of a wife's duties.

10   My God, who *wouldn't* want a wife?

Topics for Writing and Discussion

1.   Read paragraphs 3 through 9 carefully and then summarize the six qualities of a wife as Brady sees them.

2.   How does Brady use these categories to argue the plight of wives? Do any of her descriptions seem fair and literal or are they all exaggerated? Are some more exaggerated than others? Do some of her descriptions of wives make you more sympathetic to her argument than do others?

3.   What event caused Brady to start thinking about a wife's duties? How does that event relate to the main idea of the essay? Where else in the essay does Brady allude to this event?

4.   How much have times (and people) changed since this essay was first published in 1971? Would most wives today assume the roles that Brady describes? Would most husbands expect their wives (or want their wives) to take on these roles? Could Brady publish this essay with no revisions and expect the same response she got in 1971? Can you suggest changes she would need to make?

5.   Write your own satiric argument explaining why you want a secretary, a mother, a husband, a younger (or older) brother or sister, a roommate, or someone else. Remember that your purpose is to reveal how difficult it is to be a secretary, husband, or mother and to argue that people's expectations for those who fill that role should be changed.

Thomas Jefferson (The Bettmann Archive)

Declaration of Independence
Thomas Jefferson
(1743–1826)

After graduating from William and Mary College, Thomas Jefferson became a lawyer. He later was elected to the Virginia House of Burgesses and, in 1775, became a delegate to the Continental Congress. Both in this capacity and as governor of Virginia, he wielded great power in forming and molding the new republic. Following the Revolutionary War, he served under Washington as secretary of state. He was subsequently elected vice-president and then third president of the United States. Jefferson, along with several other men, wrote and revised the Declaration of Independence, which was later amended by the Continental Congress and then accepted by that body on July 4, 1776. Although the document had several framers and went through many drafts, it reflects Jefferson's clear, direct style and his logical process of developing an argument.

1   When in the course of human events, it becomes necessary for one people to dissolve the political bands which have connected them with another, and to assume among the Powers of the earth, the separate and equal station to which the Laws of Nature and of Nature's God entitle them, a decent respect to the opinions of mankind requires that they should declare the causes which impel them to the separation.

2   We hold these truths to be self-evident, that all men are created equal, that they are endowed by their Creator with certain unalienable Rights, that among these are Life, Liberty, and the pursuit of Happiness. That to secure these rights, Governments are instituted among Men, deriving their just

powers from the consent of the governed. That whenever any Form of Government becomes destructive of these ends, it is the Right of the People to alter or to abolish it, and to institute a new Government, laying its foundation on such principles and organizing its powers in such form, as to them shall seem most likely to effect their Safety and Happiness. Prudence, indeed, will dictate that Governments long established should not be changed for light and transient causes; and accordingly all experience hath shown that mankind are more disposed to suffer, while evils are sufferable, than to right themselves by abolishing the forms to which they are accustomed. But when a long train of abuses and usurpations pursuing invariably the same Object evinces a design to reduce them under absolute Despotism, it is their right, it is their duty, to throw off such government, and to provide new Guards for their future security. Such has been the patient sufference of these Colonies; and such is now the necessity which constrains them to alter their former Systems of Government. The history of the present King of Great Britain is a history of repeated injuries and usurpations, all having in direct object the establishment of an absolute Tyranny over these States. To prove this, let Facts be submitted to a candid world.

3   He has refused his Assent to Laws, the most wholesome and necessary for the public good.

4   He has forbidden his Governors to pass Laws of immediate and pressing importance, unless suspended in their operation till his Assent should be obtained; and when so suspended, he has utterly neglected to attend to them.

5   He has refused to pass other Laws for the accommodation of large districts of people, unless those people would relinquish the right of Representation in the Legislature, a right inestimable to them and formidable to tyrants only.

6   He has called together legislative bodies at places unusual, uncomfortable, and distant from the depository of their Public Records, for the sole purpose of fatiguing them into compliance with his measures.

7   He has dissolved Representative Houses repeatedly, for opposing with manly firmness his invasions on the rights of the people.

8   He has refused for a long time, after such dissolutions, to cause others to be elected; whereby the Legislative Powers, incapable of Annihilation, have returned to the People at large for their exercise; the State remaining in the mean time exposed to all the dangers of invasion from without, and convulsions within.

9   He has endeavored to prevent the population of these States; for that purpose obstructing the Laws of Naturalization of Foreigners; refusing to pass others to encourage their migration hither, and raising the conditions of new Appropriations of Lands.

10   He has obstructed the Administration of Justice, by refusing his Assent to Laws for establishing Judiciary Powers.

11   He has made Judges dependent on his Will alone, for the tenure of their offices, and the amount and payment of their salaries.

12   He has erected a multitude of New Offices, and sent hither swarms of Officers to harass our People, and eat out their substance.

13   He has kept among us, in time of peace, Standing Armies without the consent of our Legislature.

14   He has affected to render the Military independent of and superior to the Civil Power.

15   He has combined with others to subject us to jurisdictions foreign to our constitution, and unacknowledged by our laws; giving his Assent to their acts of pretended Legislation:

16   For quartering large bodies of armed troops among us:

17   For protecting them, by a mock Trial, from Punishment for any Murders which they should commit on the Inhabitants of these States:

18   For cutting off our Trade with all parts of the world:

19   For imposing Taxes on us without our Consent:

20   For depriving us in many cases, of the benefits of Trial by Jury:

21   For transporting us beyond Seas to be tried for pretended offenses:

22   For abolishing the free System of English Laws in a Neighbouring Province, establishing therein an Arbitrary government, and enlarging its boundaries so as to render it at once an example and fit instrument for introducing the same absolute rule into these Colonies:

23   For taking away our Charters, abolishing our most valuable Laws, and altering fundamentally the Forms of our Governments:

24   For suspending our own Legislatures, and declaring themselves invested with Power to legislate for us in all cases whatsoever.

25   He has abdicated Government here, by declaring us out of his Protection and waging War against us.

26   He has plundered our seas, ravaged our Coasts, burnt our towns and destroyed the Lives of our people.

27   He is at this time transporting large Armies of foreign Mercenaries to compleat the works of death, desolation and tyranny, already begun with circumstances of Cruelty & perfidy scarcely paralleled in the most barbarous ages, and totally unworthy the Head of a civilized nation.

28   He has constrained our fellow Citizens taken Captive on the high Seas to bear Arms against their Country, to become the executioners of their friends and Brethren, or to fall themselves by their Hands.

29   He has excited domestic insurrections amongst us, and has endeavored to bring on the inhabitants of our frontiers, the merciless Indian Savages, whose known rule of warfare, is an undistinguished destruction of all ages, sexes and conditions.

30   In every stage of these Oppressions We Have Petitioned for Redress in the most humble terms: Our repeated petitions have been answered only

by repeated injury. A Prince, whose character is thus marked by every act which may define a Tyrant, is unfit to be the ruler of a free People.

31   Nor have We been wanting in attention to our British brethren. We have warned them from time to time of attempts by their legislature to extend an unwarrantable jurisdiction over us. We have reminded them of the circumstances of our emigration and settlement here. We have appealed to their native justice and magnanimity and we have conjured them by the ties of our common kindred to disavow these usurpations, which would inevitably interrupt our connections and correspondence. They too have been deaf to the voice of justice and of consanguinity. We must, therefore, acquiesce in the necessity, which denounces our Separation, and hold them, as we hold the rest of mankind, Enemies in War, in Peace Friends.

32   We, therefore, the Representatives of the United States of America, in General Congress, Assembled, appealing to the Supreme Judge of the world for the rectitude of our intentions, do, in the Name, and by Authority of the good People of these Colonies, solemnly publish and declare, That these United Colonies are, and of Right ought to be, Free and Independent States; that they are Absolved from all Allegiance to the British Crown, and that all political connection between them and the State of Great Britain, is and ought to be totally dissolved; and that as Free and Independent States, they have full power to levy War, conclude Peace, contract Alliances, establish Commerce, and to do all other Acts and Things which Independent States may of right do. And for the support of this Declaration, with a firm reliance on the protection of Divine Providence, we mutually pledge to each other our lives, our Fortunes and our sacred Honor.

Topics for Writing and Discussion

1.   The Declaration of Independence exemplifies the deductive argument at its best. What is the major premise of the Declaration? What is the minor premise? What is the conclusion that readers must reach if they are convinced that the major and minor premises are valid?

2.   How is the major premise supported? How is the minor premise supported? Do you find the inductive evidence for one more convincing than the assumptions that underlie the other?

3.   Describe the original audience for the Declaration. What parts of the document seem particularly aimed at special segments of that audience? Why did the framers of the Declaration need to explain in such detail their reasons for declaring independence?

4.   What is the tone of the Declaration? Examine the language used by Jefferson and the other writers of the document to determine their attitude toward the subject of independence.

5.   Write your own "Declaration of Independence" from someone or something you feel has compiled "a history of injuries" toward you. Make your case as clearly and as forcefully as did Jefferson.

Elizabeth Cady Stanton (© The Bettmann Archive)

Declaration of Sentiments and Resolutions

Elizabeth Cady Stanton
(1815–1902)

An early and powerful advocate for women's rights, Elizabeth Cady Stanton believed that American women had been forced into subordination by a culture based on the patriarchical principles of Judeo-Christian beliefs and English common law. When she married abolitionist Henry Brewer Stanton, her decision to keep her maiden name and eliminate the word "obey" from the ceremony underscored her belief that "The custom of calling women Mrs. John This or Mrs. Tom That is founded on the principle that white men are lords of us all." In addition to collaborating with Susan B. Anthony on *Revolution*, a weekly forum for discussion of women's rights, Cady Stanton wrote *The Woman's Bible* (1895) and an autobiography, *Eighty Years and More (1815–1897): Reminiscences of Elizabeth Cady Stanton* (1898). She presented the "Declaration of Sentiments and Resolutions" at the First Woman's Rights Convention, held in Seneca Falls, New York, in 1848.

1   **W**hen, in the course of human events, it becomes necessary for one portion of the family of man to assume among the people of the earth a position different from that which they have hitherto occupied, but one to which the laws of nature and of nature's God entitle them, a decent respect to the opinions of mankind requires that they should declare the causes that impel them to such a course.

2   We hold these truths to be self-evident: that all men and women are created equal; that they are endowed by their Creator with certain inalienable rights; that among these are life, liberty, and the pursuit of happiness; that to secure these rights governments are instituted, deriving their just powers from the consent of the governed. Whenever any form of government becomes destructive of these ends, it is the right of those who suffer from it to refuse allegiance to it, and to insist upon the institution of a new government, laying its foundation on such principles, and organizing its powers in such form, as to them shall seem most likely to effect their safety and happiness. Prudence, indeed, will dictate that governments long established should not be changed for light and transient causes; and accordingly all experience hath shown that mankind are more disposed to suffer, while evils are sufferable, than to right themselves by abolishing the forms to which they were accustomed. But when a long train of abuses and usurpations, pursuing invariably the same object, evinces a design to reduce them under absolute despotism, it is their duty to throw off such government, and to provide new guards for their future security. Such has been the patient sufferance of the women under this government, and such is now the necessity which constrains them to demand the equal station to which they are entitled.

3   The history of mankind is a history of repeated injuries and usurpations on the part of man toward woman, having in direct object the establishment of an absolute tyranny over her. To prove this, let facts be submitted to a candid world.

4   He has never permitted her to exercise her inalienable right to the elective franchise.

5   He has compelled her to submit to laws, in the formation of which she had no voice.

6   He has withheld from her rights which are given to the most ignorant and degraded men—both natives and foreigners.

7   Having deprived her of this first right of a citizen, the elective franchise, thereby leaving her without representation in the halls of legislation, he has oppressed her on all sides.

8   He has made her, if married, in the eye of the law, civilly dead.

9   He has taken from her all right in property, even to the wages she earns.

10   He has made her, morally, an irresponsible being, as she can commit many crimes with impunity, provided they be done in the presence of her husband. In the covenant of marriage, she is compelled to promise obedience to her husband, he becoming to all intents and purposes, her master—the law giving him power to deprive her of her liberty, and to administer chastisement.

11   He has so framed the laws of divorce, as to what shall be the proper causes, and in case of separation, to whom the guardianship of the children shall be given, as to be wholly regardless of the happiness of women—the

law, in all cases, going upon a false supposition of the supremacy of man, and giving all power into his hands.

12   After depriving her of all rights as a married woman, if single, and the owner of property, he has taxed her to support a government which recognizes her only when her property can be made profitable to it.

13   He has monopolized nearly all the profitable employments, and from those she is permitted to follow, she receives but a scanty remuneration. He closes against her all the avenues to wealth and distinction which he considers most honorable to himself. As a teacher of theology, medicine, or law, she is not known.

14   He has denied her the facilities for obtaining a thorough education, all colleges being closed against her.

15   He allows her in Church, as well as State, but a subordinate position, claiming Apostolic authority for her exclusion from the ministry, and, with some exceptions, from any public participation in the affairs of the Church.

16   He has created a false public sentiment by giving to the world a different code of morals for men and women, by which moral delinquencies which exclude women from society, are not only tolerated, but deemed of little account in man.

17   He has usurped the prerogative of Jehovah himself, claiming it as his right to assign for her a sphere of action, when that belongs to her conscience and to her God.

18   He has endeavored, in every way that he could, to destroy her confidence in her own powers, to lessen her self-respect, and to make her willing to lead a dependent and abject life.

19   Now, in view of this entire disfranchisement of one-half the people of this country, their social and religious degradation—in view of the unjust laws above mentioned, and because women do feel themselves aggrieved, oppressed, and fraudulently deprived of their most sacred rights, we insist that they have immediate admission to all the rights and privileges which belong to them as citizens of the United States.

20   In entering upon the great work before us, we anticipate no small amount of misconception, misrepresentation, and ridicule; but we shall use every instrumentality within our power to effect our object. We shall employ agents, circulate tracts, petition the State and National legislatures, and endeavor to enlist the pulpit and the press in our behalf. We hope this Convention will be followed by a series of Conventions embracing every part of this country.

21   [The following resolutions were discussed by Lucretia Mott, Thomas and Mary Ann McClintock, Amy Post, Catharine A. F. Stebbins, and others, and were adopted:]

22   Whereas, The great precept of nature is conceded to be, that "man shall pursue his own true and substantial happiness." Blackstone in his Com-

mentaries remarks, that this law of Nature being coeval with mankind, and dictated by God himself, is of course superior in obligation to any other. It is binding over all the globe, in all countries, and at all times; no human laws are of any validity if contrary to this, and such of them as are valid, derive all their force, and all their validity, and all their authority, mediately and immediately, from this original; therefore,

23   *Resolved,* That such laws as conflict, in any way, with the true and substantial happiness of woman, are contrary to the great precept of nature and of no validity, for this is "superior in obligation to any other."

24   *Resolved,* That all laws which prevent woman from occupying such a station in society as her conscience shall dictate, or which place her in a position inferior to that of man, are contrary to the great precept of nature, and therefore of no force or authority.

25   *Resolved,* That woman is man's equal—was intended to be so by the Creator, and the highest good of the race demands that she should be recognized as such.

26   *Resolved,* That the women of this country ought to be enlightened in regard to the laws under which they live, that they may no longer publish their degradation by declaring themselves satisfied with their present position, nor their ignorance, by asserting that they have all the rights they want.

27   *Resolved,* That inasmuch as man, while claiming for himself intellectual superiority, does accord to woman moral superiority, it is preeminently his duty to encourage her to speak and teach, as she has an opportunity, in all religious assemblies.

28   *Resolved,* That the same amount of virtue, delicacy, and refinement of behavior that is required of woman in the social state, should also be required of man, and the same transgressions should be visited with equal severity on both man and woman.

29   *Resolved,* That the objection of indelicacy and impropriety, which is so often brought against woman when she addresses a public audience, comes with a very ill-grace from those who encourage, by their attendance, her appearance on the stage, in the concert, or in feats of the circus.

30   *Resolved,* That woman has too long rested satisfied in the circumscribed limits which corrupt customs and a perverted application of the Scriptures have marked out for her, and that it is time she should move in the enlarged sphere which her great Creator has assigned her.

31   *Resolved,* That it is the duty of the women of this country to secure to themselves their sacred right to the elective franchise.

32   *Resolved,* That the equality of human rights results necessarily from the fact of the identity of the race in capabilities and responsibilities.

33   *Resolved, therefore,* That, being invested by the Creator with the same capabilities, and the same consciousness of responsibility for their exercise, it is demonstrably the right and duty of woman, equally with man, to promote every righteous cause by every righteous means; and especially in

regard to the great subjects of morals and religion, it is self-evidently her right to participate with her brother in teaching them, both in private and in public, by writing and by speaking, by any instrumentalities proper to be used, and in any assemblies proper to be held; and this being a self-evident truth growing out of the divinely implanted principles of human nature, any custom or authority adverse to it, whether modern or wearing the hoary sanction of antiquity, is to be regarded as a self-evident falsehood, and at war with mankind.

34   [At the last session Lucretia Mott offered and spoke to the following resolution:]

35   *Resolved,* That the speedy success of our cause depends upon the zealous and untiring efforts of both men and women, for the overthrow of the monopoly of the pulpit, and for the securing to woman an equal participation with men in the various trades, professions, and commerce.

Topics for Writing and Discussion

1. Describe Cady Stanton's tone and purpose. How are the two interrelated?

2. Given that Cady Stanton's "Declaration" was written for the First Woman's Rights Convention, in what ways is Cady Stanton's language and word choice appropriate for this specific audience? Who might Cady Stanton's larger intended audience be? Is her style equally appropriate for them?

3. Compare Cady Stanton's essay to Jefferson's "Declaration of Independence," noting key parallels and specific contrasts between the two documents. What effect does her purposeful allusion to Jefferson's "Declaration" have on the reader? What is the significance of Cady Stanton's "revision" of key words and phrases, as well as additions to and deletions from Jefferson's work?

4. In the nearly 150 years since Cady Stanton wrote, "The great precept of nature is conceded to be, that 'man shall pursue his own true and substantial happiness,' has this goal been met for all people? Describe a current group you believe has either made great gains since Cady Stanton's time, or continues to struggle against "a long train of abuses and usurpations."

5. Review Cady Stanton's "resolutions." Which of these have been achieved? Choose one resolution as the focus of an essay arguing either that the resolution has been fulfilled or that it has not. Use current events as well as your own perspective to support your stance.

Professions for Women

Virginia Woolf
(1882–1941)

*Virginia Woolf
photographed in the 30's
by Man Ray
(The Granger Collection)*

The daughter of respected biographer and
scholar Sir Leslie Stephen, Virginia Woolf read
widely in her father's library and thus attained
a thorough, although informal, education. Her
older sister, Vanessa, married art critic Clive
Bell and soon after, in 1912, Virginia Stephen
married author and publisher Leonard Woolf.
The Bells and Woolfs, together with economist
John Maynard Keynes, painter Roger Fry,
biographer Lytton Strachey, and novelist E. M.
Forster, comprised the "Bloomsbury Group."
The members of this group were committed to
excellence in literature and art and rebelled
against the traditional norms of the Victorians.
Virginia and Leonard Woolf founded the
Hogarth Press and published the innovative
novels that established Virginia Woolf as a
major literary figure. She is particularly
acclaimed for her striking use of stream of
consciousness writing and for her experimental
approach to point of view. From her first
published book, *The Voyage Out* (1915), it was
clear that her work demonstrated her
considerable intelligence; it was the novel *Mrs.
Dalloway,* (1925), however, that first indicated
her break from previous literary tradition and
her fascination with the limitations and
possibilities of time and space. In her long
essay, *A Room of One's Own* (1929), she
explored the questions and pressures faced by
women. "Professions for Women," first
delivered as a speech to the Women's Service
League in 1931 and later anthologized in *The
Death of the Moth and Other Essays,* further
confirms her concern for women and the roles
they were expected to play.

1   W hen your secretary invited me to come here, she told me that your
Society is concerned with the employment of women and she suggested
that I might tell you something about my own professional experiences. It
is true I am a woman; it is true I am employed; but what professional
experiences have I had? It is difficult to say. My profession is literature; and
in that profession there are fewer experiences for women than in any other,
with the exception of the stage—fewer, I mean, that are peculiar to women.
For the road was cut many years ago—by Fanny Burney, by Aphra Behn,
by Harriet Martineau, by Jane Austen, by George Eliot—many famous
women, and many more unknown and forgotten, have been before me,
making the path smooth, and regulating my steps. Thus, when I came to
write, there were very few material obstacles in my way. Writing was a
reputable and harmless occupation. The family peace was not broken by
the scratching of a pen. No demand was made upon the family purse. For
ten and sixpence one can buy paper enough to write all the plays of Shakespeare—if one has a mind that way. Pianos and models, Paris, Vienna and
Berlin, masters and mistresses, are not needed by a writer. The cheapness
of writing paper is, of course, the reason why women have succeeded as
writers before they have succeeded in the other professions.

2   But to tell you my story—it is a simple one. You have only got to figure
to yourselves a girl in a bedroom with a pen in her hand. She had only to
move that pen from left to right—from ten o'clock to one. Then it occurred
to her to do what is simple and cheap enough after all—to slip a few of
those pages into an envelope, fix a penny stamp in the corner, and drop the
envelope into the red box at the corner. It was thus that I became a journalist;
and my effort was rewarded on the first day of the following month—a very
glorious day it was for me—by a letter from an editor containing a cheque
for one pound ten shillings and sixpence. But to show you how little I deserve
to be called a professional woman, how little I know of the struggles and
difficulties of such lives, I have to admit that instead of spending that sum
upon bread and butter, rent, shoes and stockings, or butcher's bills, I went
out and bought a cat—a beautiful cat, a Persian cat, which very soon involved
me in bitter disputes with my neighbours.

3   What could be easier than to write articles and to buy Persian cats with
the profits? But wait a moment. Articles have to be about something. Mine,
I seem to remember, was about a novel by a famous man. And while I was
writing this review, I discovered that if I were going to review books I should
need to do battle with a certain phantom. And the phantom was a woman,
and when I came to know her better I called her after the heroine of a

famous poem, The Angel in the House*. It was she who used to come between me and my paper when I was writing reviews. It was she who bothered me and wasted my time and so tormented me that at last I killed her. You who come of a younger and happier generation may not have heard of her—you may not know what I mean by the Angel in the House. I will describe her as shortly as I can. She was intensely sympathetic. She was immensely charming. She was utterly unselfish. She excelled in the difficult arts of family life. She sacrificed herself daily. If there was chicken, she took the leg; if there was a draught she sat in it—in short she was so constituted that she never had a mind or a wish of her own, but preferred to sympathize always with the minds and wishes of others. Above all—I need not say it— she was pure. Her purity was supposed to be her chief beauty—her blushes, her great grace. In those days—the last of Queen Victoria—every house had its Angel. And when I came to write I encountered her with the very first words. The shadow of her wings fell on my page; I heard the rustling of her skirts in the room. Directly, that is to say, I took my pen in hand to review that novel by a famous man, she slipped behind me and whispered: "My dear, you are a young woman. You are writing about a book that has been written by a man. Be sympathetic; be tender; flatter; deceive; use all the arts and wiles of our sex. Never let anybody guess that you have a mind of your own. Above all, be pure." And she made as if to guide my pen. I now record the one act for which I take some credit to myself, though the credit rightly belongs to some excellent ancestors of mine who left me a certain sum of money—shall we say five hundred pounds a year?—so that it was not necessary for me to depend solely on charm for my living. I turned upon her and caught her by the throat. I did my best to kill her. My excuse, if I were to be had up in a court of law, would be that I acted in self-defence. Had I not killed her she would have killed me. She would have plucked the heart out of my writing. For, as I found, directly I put pen to paper, you cannot review even a novel without having a mind of your own, without expressing what you think to be the truth about human re- lations, morality, sex. And all these questions, according to the Angel in the House, cannot be dealt with freely and openly by women; they must charm, they must conciliate, they must—to put it bluntly—tell lies if they are to succeed. Thus, whenever I felt the shadow of her wing or the radiance of her halo upon my page, I took up the inkpot and flung it at her. She died hard. Her fictitious nature was of great assistance to her. It is far harder to kill a phantom than a reality. She was always creeping back when I thought I had despatched her. Though I flatter myself that I killed her in the end, the struggle was severe; it took much time that had better have been spent

The Angel in the House is a long poem by Coventry Patmore, which was originally published in four volumes (1854–62). He was a friend of Tennyson and his poem was very popular in the nineteenth century.

upon learning Greek grammar; or in roaming the world in search of adventures. But it was a real experience; it was an experience that was bound to befall all women writers at that time. Killing the Angel in the House was part of the occupation of a woman writer.

4   But to continue my story. The Angel was dead; what then remained? You may say that what remained was a simple and common object—a young woman in a bedroom with an inkpot. In other words, now that she had rid herself of falsehood, that young woman had only to be herself. Ah, but what is "herself"? I mean, what is a woman? I assure you, I do not know. I do not believe that you know. I do not believe that anybody can know until she has expressed herself in all the arts and professions open to human skill. That indeed is one of the reasons why I have come here—out of respect for you, who are in process of showing us by your experiments what a woman is, who are in process of providing us, by your failures and successes, with that extremely important piece of information.

5   But to continue the story of my professional experiences. I made one pound ten and six by my first review; and I bought a Persian cat with the proceeds. Then I grew ambitious. A Persian cat is all very well, I said; but a Persian cat is not enough. I must have a motor car. And it was thus that I became a novelist—for it is a very strange thing that people will give you a motor car if you will tell them a story. It is a still stranger thing that there is nothing so delightful in the world as telling stories. It is far pleasanter than writing reviews of famous novels. And yet, if I am to obey your secretary and tell you my professional experiences as a novelist, I must tell you about a very strange experience that befell me as a novelist. And to understand it you must try first to imagine a novelist's state of mind. I hope I am not giving away professional secrets if I say that a novelist's chief desire is to be as unconscious as possible. He has to induce in himself a state of perpetual lethargy. He wants life to proceed with the utmost quiet and regularity. He wants to see the same faces, to read the same books, to do the same things day after day, month after month, while he is writing, so that nothing may break the illusion in which he is living—so that nothing may disturb or disquiet the mysterious nosings about, feelings round, darts, dashes and sudden discoveries of that very shy and illusive spirit, the imagination. I suspect that this state is the same both for men and women. Be that as it may, I want you to imagine me writing a novel in a state of trance. I want you to figure to yourself a girl sitting with a pen in her hand, which for minutes, and indeed for hours, she never dips into the inkpot. The image that comes to my mind when I think of this girl is the image of a fisherman lying sunk in dreams on the verge of a deep lake with a rod held out over the water. She was letting her imagination sweep unchecked round every rock and cranny of the world that lies submerged in the depths of our unconscious being. Now came the experience, the experience that I believe to be far commoner with women writers than with men. The line raced

through the girl's fingers. Her imagination had rushed away. It had sought the pools, the depths, the dark places where the largest fish slumber. And then there was a smash. There was an explosion. There was foam and confusion. The imagination had dashed itself against something hard. The girl was roused from her dream. She was indeed in a state of the most acute and difficult distress. To speak without figure she had thought of something, something about the body, about the passions which it was unfitting for her as a woman to say. Men, her reason told her, would be shocked. The consciousness of what men will say of a woman who speaks the truth about her passions had roused her from her artist's state of unconsciousness. She could write no more. The trance was over. Her imagination could work no longer. This I believe to be a very common experience with women writers— they are impeded by the extreme conventionality of the other sex. For though men sensibly allow themselves great freedom in these respects, I doubt that they realize or can control the extreme severity with which they condemn such freedom in women.

6   These then were two very genuine experiences of my own. These were two of the adventures of my professional life. The first—killing the Angel in the House—I think I solved. She died. But the second, telling the truth about my own experiences as a body, I do not think I solved. I doubt that any woman has solved it yet. The obstacles against her are still immensely powerful—and yet they are very difficult to define. Outwardly, what is simpler than to write books? Outwardly, what obstacles are there for a woman rather than for a man? Inwardly, I think, the case is very different: she has still many ghosts to fight, many prejudices to overcome. Indeed it will be a long time still, I think, before a woman can sit down to write a book without finding a phantom to be slain, a rock to be dashed against. And if this is so in literature, the freest of all professions for women, how is it in the new professions which you are now for the first time entering?

7   Those are the questions that I should like, had I time, to ask you. And indeed, if I have laid stress upon these professional experiences of mine, it is because I believe that they are, though in different forms, yours also. Even when the path is nominally open—when there is nothing to prevent a woman from being a doctor, a lawyer, a civil servant—there are many phantoms and obstacles, as I believe, looming in her way. To discuss and define them is I think of great value and importance; for thus only can the labour be shared, the difficulties be solved. But besides this, it is necessary also to discuss the ends and the aims for which we are fighting, for which we are doing battle with these formidable obstacles. Those aims cannot be taken for granted; they must be perpetually questioned and examined. The whole position, as I see it—here in this hall surrounded by women practising for the first time in history I know not how many different professions—is one of extraordinary interest and importance. You have won rooms of your own in the house hitherto exclusively owned by men. You are able, though not

without great labour and effort, to pay the rent. You are earning your five hundred pounds a year. But this freedom is only a beginning; the room is your own, but it is still bare. It has to be furnished; it has to be decorated; it has to be shared. How are you going to furnish it, how are you going to decorate it? With whom are you going to share it, and upon what terms? These, I think are questions of the utmost importance and interest. For the first time in history you are able to ask them; for the first time you are able to decide for yourselves what the answers should be. Willingly would I stay and discuss those questions and answers—but not tonight. My time is up; and I must cease.

Topics for Writing and Discussion

1.   Woolf's essay is titled "Professions for Women." Which profession does she discuss in detail? Why does she say women have been successful in this profession before they have succeeded in other professions?

2.   What difficulties did Woolf face in following her chosen work? How does she use the figure of the Angel in the House to explain her struggles as a writer? What were the Angel's characteristics? What advice did Woolf imagine the angel giving her? How did Woolf respond to this advice? What does she mean when she says that she killed the angel?

3.   How does Woolf use the analogy of the "fisherman lying sunk in dreams" to explain another difficulty she faced? Who does the fisherman represent? The line racing through the girl's fingers? The smash? What is the "something hard" that the imagination smashes against?

4.   How does Woolf relate her own experiences as a writer to the problems faced by women entering professions traditionally considered to be male? What effects does she suggest might result from choosing these careers?

5.   Woolf uses several analogies to describe difficulties she faced in achieving success in her chosen profession. Develop your own analogy to explain a problem you (or someone you know) face or have faced in pursuing a chosen career.

Jonathan Swift, as painted by Charles Jervas, National Portrait Gallery, London (The Bettman Archive)

A Modest Proposal

Jonathan Swift
(1667–1745)

Born to English parents living in Ireland, Jonathan Swift attended Kilkenny Grammar School and Trinity College in Dublin. Following his college years, he worked as a secretary to Sir William Temple and in 1699, following Temple's death, he took holy orders in the Church of England. During his years as a secretary and later as a clergyman, he developed his talent for writing satire. One of these works, *A Tale of a Tub*, published anonymously in 1704, was a cutting attack on the divisions of Christianity. When he was recognized as the author, his opportunities for advancement in the Church were severely curtailed. He turned more and more often to his writing, using his biting wit to address English exploitation and repression of the Irish. Swift's *Drapier's Letters*, published in 1724, attacked the British for their scheme to debase Irish coinage, and in 1726, his masterpiece *Gulliver's Travels* brought before the eyes of the public the harsh tyranny of the English. Three years later, in 1729, came his powerful satire, "A Modest Proposal," which railed against the desperate living conditions of the Irish peasants.

**For Preventing the Children of
Poor People in Ireland
from Being a Burden to Their Parents
or Country,
and for Making Them Beneficial to the Public**

1   It is a melancholy object to those who walk through this great town or travel in the country, when they see the streets, the roads, and cabin doors,

crowded with beggars of the female sex, followed by three, four, or six children, all in rags and importuning every passenger for an alms. These mothers, instead of being able to work for their honest livelihood, are forced to employ all their time in strolling to beg sustenance for their helpless infants, who, as they grow up, either turn thieves for want of work, or leave their dear native country to fight for the Pretender in Spain, or sell themselves to the Barbadoes.

2   I think it is agreed by all parties that this prodigious number of children in the arms, or on the backs, or at the heels of their mothers, and frequently of their fathers, is in the present deplorable state of the kingdom a very great additional grievance; and therefore whoever could find out a fair, cheap, and easy method of making these children sound, useful members of the commonwealth would deserve so well of the public as to have his statue set up for a preserver of the nation.

3   But my intention is very far from being confined to provide only for the children of professed beggars; it is of a much greater extent, and shall take in the whole number of infants at a certain age who are born of parents in effect as little able to support them as those who demand our charity in the streets.

4   As to my own part, having turned my thoughts for many years upon this important subject, and maturely weighed the several schemes of other projectors, I have always found them grossly mistaken in their computation. It is true, a child just dropped from its dam may be supported by her milk for a solar year, with little other nourishment; at most not above the value of two schillings, which the mother may certainly get, or the value in scraps, by her lawful occupation of begging; and it is exactly at one year old that I propose to provide for them in such a manner as instead of being a charge upon their parents or the parish, or wanting food and raiment for the rest of their lives, they shall on the contrary contribute to the feeding, and partly to the clothing, of many thousands.

5   There is likewise another great advantage in my scheme, that it will prevent those voluntary abortions, and that horrid practice of women murdering their bastard children, alas, too frequent among us, sacrificing the poor innocent babes, I doubt, more to avoid the expense than the shame, which would move tears and pity in the most savage and inhuman breast.

6   The number of souls in this kingdom being usually reckoned one million and a half, of these I calculate there may be about two hundred thousand couples whose wives are breeders; from which number I subtract thirty thousand couples who are able to maintain their own children, although I apprehend there cannot be so many under the present distress of the kingdom; but this being granted, there will remain an hundred and seventy thousand breeders. I again subtract fifty thousand for those women who miscarry, or whose children die by accident or disease within the year. There only remain an hundred and twenty thousand children of poor parents

annually born. The question therefore is, how this number shall be reared and provided for, which, as I have already said, under the present situation of affairs, is utterly impossible by all the methods hitherto proposed. For we can neither employ them in handicraft nor agriculture; we neither build houses (I mean in the country) nor cultivate land. They can very seldom pick up a livelihood by stealing till they arrive at six years old, except where they are of towardly parts; although I confess they learn the rudiments much earlier, during which time they can however be looked upon only as probationers, as I have been informed by a principal gentleman in the country of Cavan, who protested to me that he never knew above one or two instances under the age of six, even in a part of the kingdom so renowned for the quickest proficiency in that art.

7   I am assured by our merchants that a boy or a girl before twelve years old is no salable commodity; and even when they come to this age, they will not yield above three pounds, or three pounds and half a crown at most on the Exchange; which cannot turn to account either to the parents or the kingdom, the charge of nutriment and rags having been at least four times that value.

8   I shall now therefore humbly propose my own thoughts, which I hope will not be liable to the least objection.

9   I have been assured by a very knowing American of my acquaintance in London, that a young healthy child well nursed is at a year old a most delicious, nourishing, and wholesome food, whether stewed, roasted, baked, or boiled; and I make no doubt that it will equally serve in a fricassee or a ragout.

10   I do therefore humbly offer it to public consideration that of the hundred and twenty thousand children, already computed, twenty thousand may be reserved for breed, whereof only one fourth part to be males, which is more than we allow to sheep, black cattle, or swine; and my reason is that these children are seldom the fruits of marriage, a circumstance not much regarded by our savages, therefore one male will be sufficient to serve four females. That the remaining hundred thousand may at a year old be offered in sale to the persons of quality and fortune through the kingdom, always advising the mother to let them suck plentifully in the last month, so as to render them plump and fat for a good table. A child will make two dishes at an entertainment for friends; and when the family dines alone, the fore or hind quarter will make a reasonable dish, and seasoned with a little pepper or salt will be very good boiled on the fourth day, especially in winter.

11   I have reckoned upon a medium that a child just born will weigh twelve pounds, and in a solar year if tolerably nursed increaseth to twenty-eight pounds.

12   I grant this food will be somewhat dear, and therefore very proper for landlords, who, as they have already devoured most of the parents, seem to have the best title to the children.

13   Infant's flesh will be in season throughout the year, but more plentiful in March, and a little before and after. For we are told by a grave author, an eminent French physician, that fish being a prolific diet, there are more children born in Roman Catholic countries about nine months after Lent, than at any other season; therefore, reckoning a year after Lent, the markets will be more glutted than usual, because the number of popish infants is at least three to one in this kingdom; and therefore it will have one other collateral advantage, by lessening the number of Papists among us.

14   I have already computed the charge of nursing a beggar's child (in which list I reckon all cottagers, laborers, and four fifths of the farmers) to be about two shillings per annum, rags included; and I believe no gentleman would repine to give ten shillings for the carcass of a good fat child, which, as I have said, will make four dishes of excellent nutritive meat, when he hath only some particular friend or his own family to dine with him. Thus the squire will learn to be a good landlord, and grow popular among the tenants; the mother will have eight shillings net profit, and be fit for work till she produces another child.

15   Those who are more thrifty (as I must confess the times require) may flay the carcass; the skin of which artificially dressed will make admirable gloves for ladies, and summer boots for fine gentlemen.

16   As to our city of Dublin, shambles may be appointed for this purpose in the most convenient parts of it, and butchers we may be assured will not be wanting; although I rather recommend buying the children alive, and dressing them hot from the knife as we do roasting pigs.

17   A very worthy person, a true lover of his country, and whose virtues I highly esteem, was lately pleased in discoursing on this matter to offer a refinement upon my scheme. He said that many gentlemen of his kingdom, having of late destroyed their deer, he conceived that the want of venison might be well supplied by the bodies of young lads and maidens, not exceeding fourteen years of age nor under twelve, so great a number of both sexes in every county being now ready to starve for want of work and service; and these to be disposed of by their parents, if alive, or otherwise by their nearest relations. But with due deference to so excellent a friend and so deserving a patriot, I cannot be altogether in his sentiments; for as to the males, my American acquaintance assured me from frequent experience that their flesh was generally tough and lean, like that of our schoolboys, by continual exercise, and their taste disagreeable; and to fatten them would not answer the charge. Then as to the females, it would, I think with humble submission, be a loss to the public, because they soon would become breeders themselves; and besides, it is not improbable that some scrupulous people might be apt to censure such a practice (although indeed very unjustly) as a little bordering upon cruelty; which, I confess, hath always been with me the strongest objection against any project, how well soever intended.

18　But in order to justify my friend, he confessed that this expedient was put into his head by the famous Psalmanazar, a native of the island Formosa, who came from thence to London above twenty years ago, and in conversation told my friend that in his country when any young person happened to be put to death, the executioner sold the carcass to the persons of quality as a prime dainty; and that in his time the body of a plump girl of fifteen, who was crucified for an attempt to poison the emperor, was sold to his Imperial Majesty's prime minister of state, and other great mandarins of the court, in joints from the gibbet, at four hundred crowns. Neither indeed can I deny that if the same use were made of several plump young girls in this town, who without one single groat to their fortunes cannot stir abroad without a chair, and appear at the playhouse and assemblies in foreign fineries which they never will pay for, the kingdom would not be the worse.

19　Some persons of a desponding spirit are in great concern about that vast number of poor people who are aged, diseased, or maimed, and I have been desired to employ my thoughts what course may be taken to ease the nation of so grievous an encumbrance. But I am not in the least pain upon that matter, because it is very well known that they are every day dying and rotting by cold and famine, and filth and vermin, as fast as can be reasonably expected. And as to the younger laborers, they are now in almost as hopeful a condition. They cannot get work, and consequently pine away for want of nourishment to a degree that if any time they are accidentally hired to common labor, they have not strength to perform it; and thus the country and themselves are happily delivered from the evils to come.

20　I have too long digressed, and therefore shall return to my subject. I think the advantages by the proposal which I have made are obvious and many, as well as of the highest importance.

21　For first, as I have already observed, it would greatly lessen the number of Papists, with whom we are yearly overrun, being the principal breeders of the nation as well as our most dangerous enemies; and who stay at home on purpose to deliver the kingdom to the Pretender, hoping to take their advantage by the absence of so many good Protestants, who have chosen rather to leave their country than to stay at home and pay tithes against their conscience to an Episcopal curate.

22　Secondly, the poorer tenants will have something valuable of their own, which by law may be made liable to distress, and help to pay their landlord's rent, their corn and cattle being already seized and money a thing unknown.

23　Thirdly, whereas the maintenance of an hundred thousand children, from two years old and upwards, cannot be computed at less than ten shillings a piece per annum, the nation's stock will be thereby increased fifty thousand pounds per annum, besides the profit of a new dish introduced to the tables of all gentlemen of fortune in the kingdom who have any refinement in taste. And the money will circulate among ourselves, the goods being entirely of our own growth and manufacture.

24   Fourthly, the constant breeders, besides the gain of eight shillings sterling per annum by the sale of their children, will be rid of the charge for maintaining them after the first year.

25   Fifthly, this food would likewise bring great custom to taverns, where the vintners will certainly be so prudent as to procure the best receipts for dressing it to perfection, and consequently have their houses frequented by all the fine gentlemen, who justly value themselves upon their knowledge in good eating; and a skillful cook, who understands how to oblige his guests, will contrive to make it as expensive as they please.

26   Sixthly, this would be a great inducement to marriage, which all wise nations have either encouraged by rewards or enforced by laws and penalties. It would increase the care and tenderness of mothers toward their children, when they were sure of a settlement for life to the poor babes, provided in some sort by the public, to their annual profit instead of expense. We should see an honest emulation among the married women, which of them could bring the fattest child to the market. Men would become as fond of their wives during the time of their pregnancy as they are now of their mares in foal, their cows in calf, or sows when they are ready to farrow; nor offer to beat or kick them (as is too frequent a practice) for fear of a miscarriage.

27   Many other advantages might be enumerated. For instance, the addition of some thousand carcasses in our exportation of barreled beef, the propagation of swine's flesh, and improvements in the art of making good bacon, so much wanted among us by the great destruction of pigs, too frequent at our tables, which are no way comparable in taste or magnificence to a well-grown, fat, yearling child, which roasted whole will make a considerable figure at a lord mayor's feast or any other public entertainment. But this and many others I omit, being studious of brevity.

28   Supposing that one thousand families in this city would be constant customers for infants' flesh, besides others who might have it at merry meetings, particularly weddings and christenings, I compute that Dublin would take off annually about twenty thousand carcasses, and the rest of the kingdom (where probably they will be sold somewhat cheaper) the remaining eighty thousand.

29   I can think of no one objection that will possibly be raised against this proposal, unless it should be urged that the number of people will be thereby much lessened in the kingdom. This I freely own, and it was indeed one principal design in offering it to the world. I desire the reader will observe, that I calculate my remedy for this one individual kingdom of Ireland and for no other that ever was, is, or I think ever can be upon earth. Therefore, let no man talk to me of other expedients: of taxing our absentees at five shillings a pound: of using neither clothes nor household furniture except what is of our own growth and manufacture: of utterly rejecting the materials and instruments that promote foreign luxury: of curing the expensiveness

of pride, vanity, idleness, and gaming in our women: of introducing a vein of parsimony, prudence, and temperance: of learning to love our country, in the want of which we differ even from Laplanders and the inhabitants of Topinamboo: of quitting our animosities and factions, nor acting any longer like the Jews, who were murdering one another at the very moment their city was taken: of being a little cautious not to sell our country and conscience for nothing: of teaching landlords to have at least one degree of mercy toward their tenants: lastly, of putting a spirit of honesty, industry, and skill into our shopkeepers; who, if a resolution could now be taken to buy only our native goods, would immediately unite to cheat and exact upon us in the price, the measure, and the goodness, nor could ever yet be brought to make one fair proposal of just dealing, though often and earnestly invited to it.

30   Therefore, I repeat, let no man talk to me of these and the like expedients, till he hath at least some glimpse of hope that there will ever be some hearty and sincere attempt to put them in practice.

31   But as to myself, having been wearied out for many years with offering vain, idle, visionary thoughts, and at length utterly despairing of success, I fortunately fell upon this proposal, which, as it is wholly new, so it hath something solid and real, of no expense and little trouble, full in our own power, and whereby we can incur no danger in disobliging England. For this kind of commodity will not bear exportation, the flesh being of too tender a consistence to admit a long continuance in salt, although perhaps I could name a country which would be glad to eat up our whole nation without it.

32   After all, I am not so violently bent upon my own opinion as to reject any offer proposed by wise men, which shall be found equally innocent, cheap, easy, and effectual. But before something of that kind shall be advanced in contradiction to my scheme, and offering a better, I desire the author or authors will be pleased maturely to consider two points. First, as things now stand, how they will be able to find food and raiment for an hundred thousand useless mouths and backs. And secondly, there being a round million of creatures in human figure throughout this kingdom, whose sole subsistence put into a common stock would leave them in debt two millions of pounds sterling, adding those who are beggars by profession to the bulk of farmers, cottagers, and laborers, with their wives and children who are beggars in effect; I desire those politicians who dislike my overture, and may perhaps be so bold to attempt an answer, that they will first ask the parents of these mortals whether they would not at this day think it a great happiness to have been sold for food at a year old in this manner I prescribe, and thereby have avoided such a perpetual scene of misfortunes as they have since gone through by the oppression of landlords, the impossibility of paying rent without money or trade, the want of common sustenance, with neither house nor clothes to cover them from the incle-

mencies of the weather, and the most inevitable prospect of entailing the like or greater miseries upon their breed forever.

33   I profess, in the sincerity of my heart, that I have not the least personal interest in endeavoring to promote this necessary work, having no other motive than the public good of my country, by advancing our trade, providing for infants, relieving the poor, and giving some pleasure to the rich. I have no children by which I can propose to get a single penny; the youngest being nine years old, and my wife past childbearing.

Topics for Writing and Discussion

1. When does it first become obvious that "A Modest Proposal" is written ironically? What hints do you have in earlier paragraphs that the proposal you are reading is not to be taken literally? Notice particularly both the denotations and connotations of words Swift chooses to describe the Irish people.

2. Swift uses the persona of a "projector" (a person who suggests plans for social or economic change) to put forth the "modest proposal." How would you characterize the projector? How do his views differ from the views of Swift? Where do you find Swift's voice (and beliefs) breaking through the voice of the persona?

3. How does Swift use statistics and other facts to promote his own argument while remaining in the character of his projector?

4. Swift condemns the English for their oppression and exploitation of the Irish, but he also condemns the Irish for certain social practices and beliefs. Analyze and give examples of his criticism of both the English and the Irish.

5. Write your own "modest proposal," adopting a persona and using irony to argue for better treatment of a particular group of people in your community or in this country.

Writing Assignments for Chapter Eleven
Argument and Persuasion

1. In a popular song of a few years ago, Joni Mitchell claimed that we'd "paved paradise and put up a parking lot." She called on farmers to put away their chemicals and "give me spots on my apples but leave me the birds and bees." Research the use of some chemical agent or food additive that you believe seriously threatens our health or environment today, and write an argumentative essay calling for its investigation or prohibition. Think of your congressional representative as your audience, and try to maintain a concerned, reasonable tone as does Rachel Carson in "The Obligation to Endure."

2. On August 28, 1963, when Martin Luther King, Jr., delivered his "I Have a Dream" speech, he faced a formidable task. He had to turn some of his audience away from anger and thoughts of violence while, at the same time, inspire them to continue the nonviolent fight for civil rights. Select a social problem that arouses controversy today and designate an audience whose sympathies are not firmly aligned with yours. Write a speech that will convince them to adopt your point of view.

3. In "The Health-Care System" Lewis Thomas declares that "we have become obsessed with Health." According to Thomas, we are worrying ourselves to death because we are "being taken in by the propaganda." Focus on some specific health issue, and write an essay arguing for or against Thomas' position that we spend too much time and energy becoming a nation of healthy hypochondriacs. For instance, is our attitude toward thinness and dieting a product of mass media? Or does Thomas overstate his case? Are jogging and bicycling more than fads of people preoccupied with disease and death?

4. Thomas argues that the health obsession he describes will make any health-care system unworkable. Research the debate on national health care currently raging in this country, and write an essay arguing for or against some specific plan or proposal you discover in your reading. What are the primary arguments for and against this plan? Who is for or against such a plan, and why? Is Thomas's complaint one of the major reasons some people oppose such a plan or proposal?

5. In "None of This Is Fair," Richard Rodriguez uses his own experience and that of his classmate to argue the disadvantages of Affirmative Action. Select a controversial law or social action and, similarly, use

your personal experience to point out one of its main strengths or weaknesses. You may wish, as Rodriguez did, to experiment with dialogue as well as narrative.

6. In his essay "Drugs" Gore Vidal calls for the truthful, not exaggerated, description of illegal drugs' effects on people, and he mentions, to establish his credibility, his own experimentation with drugs. Have you or someone you know well been adversely affected by illegal drug use? Has the experience shaped or changed your attitude toward drug sale or use? Write an essay using your experience to argue your views on the sale or use of a particular drug popular on the streets today.

7. Vidal claims that prohibition of alcohol from 1920 to 1933 and today's laws aimed at drug use are similar in their promotion of violence and crime. Research the Prohibition era in this country and write an essay that argues for or against similarities of either the problems or their solutions.

8. Several authors represented in this text write about different aspects of health care in America: Lewis Thomas in "The Health-Care System"; Norman Cousins in "Pain Is Not the Ultimate Enemy"; Alice Stewart Trillin in "Of Dragons and Garden Peas"; Gore Vidal in "Drugs." Select any two of these essays and compare/contrast their effectiveness. How do their purposes differ? Their rhetorical strategies? Which, overall, do you find more persuasive and why?

9. In her essay, "One Vote for This Age of Anxiety," Margaret Mead notes that Americans often feel anxious and apprehensive about changes that are good but difficult—then when the changes are finally made, we feel "a glow of relief." Write a persuasive essay arguing for a social or political change that you feel is difficult but right, one that our country will eventually feel good about embracing.

10. Flannery O'Connor in "Total Effect and the Eighth Grade" argues that students should read eighteenth- and nineteenth-century fiction because they need to understand the history and perspective behind modern literature if they are to receive its "total effect." Think about your own experiences with literature, and then write a letter to your local school board that supports or argues against O'Connor's suggestion that only certain seniors (with parental consent) be allowed to read modern novelists.

11. Many books have been—or continue to be—banned in parts of the United States; novels as different as *The Adventures of Huckleberry Finn*, *The Catcher in the Rye*, and *The Grapes of Wrath* have been taken off public school and community library shelves. Research the subject of contemporary book banning in this country (or in your area), and write

an editorial arguing your views as they might apply to your own community.

12.   In "I Want a Wife" Judy Brady describes the many roles a wife has often been expected to play. Using Brady's essay as your inspiration, write an essay about a role you do *not* want to play, a role that perhaps has been dictated by other people's expectations or by certain traditions or even by your family. Why do you reject this role? Do you see, as Brady did, something inherently unfair about it?

13.   Consider Martin Luther King, Jr.,'s "I Have a Dream" speech and Thomas Jefferson's "Declaration of Independence." Draft a letter King might have written to Jefferson, urging him to make important changes in the famous document. You may draw on twentieth-century events to make your arguments persuasive.

14.   In 1848 when Elizabeth Cady Stanton drafted the "Declaration of Sentiments and Resolutions," she obviously felt the original Declaration did not speak adequately to both sexes. Research one of the grievances Cady Stanton lists (for example, no right to vote, no property rights, few educational or employment opportunities) and write an editorial advocating change that might have appeared in a local newspaper in 1848. What specific arguments might Cady Stanton have offered to support any one of the "tyrannies" she mentions in her "Declaration"?

15.   As a writer, Virginia Woolf had to overcome some serious obstacles, including the Angel in the House whose "murder" she describes in "Professions for Women." Think of an obstacle that you have faced in your pursuit of an important personal or professional goal, and argue one means of conquering that problem. Consider writing your paper as an address to people who are just beginning to face the obstacle you successfully overcame.

16.   Compare and contrast Virginia Woolf's essay "Professions for Women" with her other essay in this text, "If Shakespeare Had Had a Sister." How do the two selections compare in terms of purpose, audience, organizational techniques, language, and tone? In effectiveness? If you were to select only one of these two essays to give to a friend interested in Virginia Woolf or in women's issues, which would you select? Support your answer with ample illustrations from the two essays.

17.   Choose some regulation, requirement, or plan currently in effect on your campus that you think is unwise. Using Jonathan Swift's famous essay as a model, write your own satire that acquaints your readers with this unjust or ineffective situation. Consider sending your essay to your campus or local newspaper.

Glossary of Rhetorical Terms

Ad Hominem Attack An *ad hominem* argument attacks an opponent's character rather than his or her ideas and beliefs.

Alliteration Alliteration is the repetition of the initial consonant sounds of two or more neighboring words: wild and woolly, "The Woman Warrior," tea for two.

Analogy An analogy shows a similarity between two otherwise dissimilar things. For example, music is analogous to the wind—strong and loud at some times, gentle and quiet at others. A false analogy distorts the points of similarity and results in an invalid conclusion.

Analysis Analysis breaks a subject into parts in order to clarify the whole.

Antithesis An antithesis is an idea directly opposite to the thesis of an essay.

Argument Argument is a mode of writing whose purpose is to persuade the reader to act or agree. (See Chapter 11.)

Audience Audience is the expected readership for an essay that helps to determine the writing strategy and evidence the writer will use.

Brainstorming Brainstorming means writing down anything that comes to mind in an unstructured way in order to generate ideas for writing. (See Chapter 2.)

Cause and Effect Cause and effect is a strategy of development used by a writer to explain the reasons for, or the results of, a particular action or event. (See Chapter 10.)

Characterization Characterization refers to the ways a writer depicts and develops the characters in an essay.

Chronological Order Chronological order refers to presenting the events in an essay in the same time sequence in which they occurred or are occurring.

Cliché A cliché is a trite, overused expression, such as "old as the hills" or "up the creek without a paddle."

Climactic Order Climactic order refers to arranging the parts of a composition from the least important to the most important or from smallest to largest.

Coherence Coherence is the clear and logical connection of the thesis and all parts of an essay, achieved by a logical sequence, transitions, and repetition of key words or synonyms.

599

Comparison and Contrast   Comparison and contrast is a strategy of development used by a writer to examine the similarities and differences between people, ideas, and things. (See Chapter 8.)

Connotation   Connotation refers to the feelings and memories associated with a word, such as moonlight suggesting romance and mystery. See also *Denotation*.

Controlling Idea   The controlling idea, or thesis, of an essay is the central meaning or message that the writer is trying to convey to the reader.

Deduction   Deduction is the method of logical reasoning that moves from the general to the specific, such as "All men are mortal" and "Socrates is a man" producing the conclusion "Therefore, Socrates is mortal."

Definition   Definition refers both to the explanation of the meaning of a word and the strategy of development used by a writer to explore the meaning of a word or concept in an essay. (See Chapter 6.)

Denotation   Denotation is the literal and explicit meaning of a word independent of any emotional association, such as moonlight being "the rays of light reflected by the moon." See also *Connotation*.

Description   Description is the mode of writing in which a writer uses concrete details to create a representation of what something is or appears to be. (See Chapter 4.)

Division and Classification   Division and Classification are strategies of development used to explain a general category that is sorted into smaller groups on the basis of some selected principle. (See Chapter 9.)

Essay   An essay is a short, nonfiction composition on one topic, often written from a personal point of view.

Evidence   Evidence is the material used to support an opinion, argument, or explanation.

Exposition   Exposition refers to a mode of writing that explains a subject by supplying information through the strategies of illustration, comparison and contrast, division and classification, process analysis, definition, and cause and effect.

Figurative Language   Figurative language is the use of comparisons and associations to communicate meaning and to achieve emphasis. Common figures of speech are the metaphor, simile, personification, and hyperbole.

Freewriting   Freewriting means writing down whatever thoughts occur in order to stimulate ideas and generate material for writing an essay.

Hyperbole   Hyperbole is expression that uses deliberate exaggeration rather than a literal statement to make a point: He's the most handsome man this side of the Mississippi.

Illustration Illustration is a strategy of development used by a writer to prove the validity of the thesis of an essay by supporting or clarifying it with examples. (See Chapter 7.)

Image An image is a vivid description that appeals to the reader's sense of sight, sound, smell, taste, or touch.

Induction Induction is the method of logical reasoning that derives a conclusion about an entire group by examining some of its members.

Jargon Jargon is the special vocabulary of a specific group such as doctors, film directors, or anthropologists. Jargon should be avoided when it obscures meaning or overburdens style.

Metaphor A metaphor is a figure of speech that conveys information by comparing two dissimilar things in order to show or clarify an unexpected similarity: Her eyes were stars shining in the midnight sky.

Narration Narration is a mode of writing wherein the writer tells a story or recounts events. (See Chapter 3.)

Non Sequitur A non sequitur is a logical fallacy in which the conclusion does not follow from the evidence: If one brownie tastes good, two must taste twice as good.

Paradox A paradox is an idea or statement that seems contradictory but which expresses a truth: arming for peace, spending money to make money.

Persona Persona refers to the voice and character an author creates in a piece of fiction or non-fiction.

Personification Personification is a figure of speech that assigns human characteristics to nonhuman things: The car waited patiently in the driveway. The vacuum cleaner devoured the dust.

Point of View Point of view refers to the way the narrator presents the subject in a piece of writing. Points of view for the same subject may differ, depending on the opinion of each different writer.

Process Process is a strategy of development used by a writer to trace the steps of an event or operation. (See Chapter 5.)

Purpose Purpose is the writer's reason for writing—to entertain, to explain, to win an argument, to move the audience to action.

Rhetoric Rhetoric is the study and effective use of language. The rhetorical modes (narration, description, exposition, and argument) present different organizational strategies for achieving an author's purpose in an essay.

Satire A satire is a piece of writing that may use wit, irony, and ridicule to expose the folly of its subject matter.

Simile A simile is a figure of speech in which a comparison is made between two dissimilar things by using the words *like* or *as:* as jumpy as a cat on a hot tin roof, children sprouting up like weeds.

Spatial Order   Spatial order refers to arranging details in a description so that readers can follow the eye's path.

Symbol   A symbol is an image or an object that stands for an idea or complex of ideas. An eagle may symbolize freedom; a heart may symbolize love.

Synonym   A synonym is a word with approximately the same meaning as another word: "fright" is a synonym for fear; "bravery" is a synonym for courage.

Thesis   The thesis is the central or controlling idea of an essay. The content of the essay should support and develop the thesis.

Tone   Tone refers to the general attitude of the writer toward the essay's subject or audience: The tone of the movie review was hostile.

Topic Sentence   The topic sentence is the statement of the main idea in a paragraph.

Index

A

"American Way of Death, The," 240, 241, 245–251
Analogy, 367
    false, 521
Analysis, essay, 6–12
"Angel in the House," 522
Angelou, Maya, 147, 148–158
Argument, persuasion and, 511–598. *See also* Reasoning
Argument ad hominem, 522–523
Argument ad populum, 523
Argument ad verecundiam, 523
"Art of Reading, The," 53–57
Assumptions, 515
"Attitude," 241, 253–256
Audience, 74, 241, 511–514

B

Baker, Russell, 368, 369, 375, 376–378
Baker, Sheridan, 90, 109–113
Baldwin, James, 225, 226–236
Bandwagon, 523
"Beauty: When the Other Dancer Is the Self," 135, 165–172
Begging the question, 521–522
Berke, Jacqueline, 90, 114, 115–120
Berry, Wendell, 13
"Best Refuge for Insomniacs, The," 65–71
Big Sea, The, 135
"Billy Budd," 465
"Black Men and Public Space," 87–88, 328–331
Body
    essay, 83
    of process essay, 240
Brady, Judy, 565, 566–568
Brainstorming, 76–77

Britton, Benjamin, 465
"Brown Wasps, The," 357–361
Buckley, William F., Jr., 318, 318, 321–326

C

Carson, Rachel, 524–532
Categories, establishing, 411–412
Catton, Bruce, 368, 370, 379, 380–384
Causal analysis, 455, 524
Cause-and-effect (causal) chain, 459
Cause and effect, 455–511
    types of causes, 456
Characters, 368
Ciardi, John, 279, 285–288
Circular argument, 522
Clarification, illustration and, 318
Class, 277
Classification, 279, 410
    division and, 409–453
Clustering ideas, 77–79
"College Pressures," 430–437
Comparison and contrast, 279, 367–408
Conclusion, 7, 86–88, 515
    and deductive reasoning, 516–521
    essay, 83
    and inductive reasoning, 516
    of process essay, 240–241
Consensus genitum, 523
Contrast, comparison and, 367–408
Contributing cause, 456
Cousins, Norman, 459, 460–464
Critical reading. *See* Reading, critical

D

"Declaration of Independence," 569–574
"Declaration of Sentiments and Resolutions," 575–580

"Declarations." *See "Declaration of Independence;" "Declaration of Sentiments and Resolutions"*
Deductive reasoning, 516, 519–521
Definition, 277–315
    extending, 278
    types of, 277–278
    writing, 278–280
Definition essays, 455
Description, 183–238, 279
    types of, 184
Descriptive essay, writing, 184–186
Didion, Joan, 90–91, 92–97, 279, 289–293
Differences, 367
Differentiation, 277
Dillard, Annie, 98, 99–102
Directional process essays, 239–240
"Discovering Books," 35–42
"Discrimination," 279, 307–313, 317
"Discus Thrower, The," 143–146
Division, 279
Division and classification, 409–453
Dominant impression, 184
"Drugs," 550–553

E

"Economy," 264–268
Effect
    cause and, 455–511
Eiseley, Loren, 356, 357–363
Either/or fallacy, 522
Elbow, Peter, 90, 106–108
Ellison, Ralph, 279, 306, 307–313, 317
Essay. *See also* type of essay
    analysis of, 6–12
    body of, 82, 83
    cause and effect, 455–511
    comparison/contrast, 368–408
    division or classification, 410–453
    illustration, 318–319
    process, 239–275
    revising, 88–89
    structuring, 82–88
Evidence, 515
    types of, 515–516
Examples, 279, 317, 318–319
Expert testimony, 516
Extended definition, 278
Extended illustration, 319

F

"Face in the Mirror, The," 447–451
Facts, 516
Fadiman, Clifton, 13
Fallacies, 521–524
False analogy, 521
Faulkner, William, 368
Figurative language, 7
Figures of speech, 185–186
Focus, of comparison/constrast essay, 368
Formal definition, 277–278
Forster, E. M., 465, 466–469
"Four Kinds of Reading," 49–52
"Freewriting," 106–108
"Friends, Good Friends, and Such Good Friends," 83, 420–425

G

Gansberg, Martin, 159, 160–163
Generalizations, 523
Golding, William, 438, 439–445
Goodman, Ellen, 279, 279, 282–284
"Graduation in Stamps," 148–158
"Grant and Lee: A Study in Contrasts," 370, 380–384
Grapes of Wrath, The, 183

H

Hall, Donald, 48, 49–52
"Health Care System, The," 540–543
Highet, Gilbert, 446, 447–451
"Hispanic-America culture," 279, 295–299
"How Books Helped Shape My Life," 43–47, 86–87, 317
"How Do You Know It's Good?" 490–496
How to process, as essay type, 240
Hughes, Langston, 135, 138, 139–141
Hypothesis, 515

I

Idea development, 6
"If Shakespeare Had Had a Sister," 185, 186, 213–224
"I Have a Dream" speech, 524, 534–539
"Iks, The," 368–369, 394–397
Illustration, 317–365
    extended, 319
    functions of, 317–318

Illustration essay, writing, 318–319
Impressionistic description, 184
Inductive leap, 515
Inductive reasoning, 516, 515–519
Inference, 515
Information sources, 516. *See also* Evidence
Informative process essay, 239, 240
"In Search of Our Mother's Gardens," 318.
  319, 347–355
Instructional process essay, 239
Interest, illustration and, 318
Introduction, 6
  essay, 82, 83
  to process essay, 240
"It's Failure, Not Success," 279, 282–284
"I Want a Wife," 565–568

J

Jargon, 278
"Jeaning of America, The," 240, 241,
  242–244
Jefferson, Thomas, 317, 524, 569, 570–574
Judgments, 516

K

Keillor, Garrison, 241, 252, 253–256
King, Martin Luther, Jr., 257, 258–262,
  524, 534, 535–539
Kingston, Maxine Hong, 183, 191, 192–196
Known sample, 518

L

Lin Yutang, 53–57Locale, 368
Lopez, Barry, 385, 386–392

M

MacNeil, Robert, 13, 58, 59–64
"Maker's Eye, The: Revising Your Own
  Manuscripts," 127–131
"Mankind's Better Moments," 317, 318,
  333–338
Mannes, Marya, 490–496
Mead, Margaret, 279, 300, 301–305, 524,
  553, 554–558
Metaphor, 186
Mitford, Jessica, 240, 241, 245–251
"Modest Proposal, A," 524, 588–595

Momaday, N. Scott, 185, 186, 197,
  198–203
Morrison, Toni, 81, 398, 399–406
Morrow, Lance, 13, 65–71
Murray, Donald, 13, 14, 15–16, 90,
  127–131
"My Horse," 386–392
"My Wood," 466–469

N

Narration, 135–182, 524
Narrative, writing, 136–137
Narrative essays, 455
Necessary cause, 456
Negation, 279
"New Superstitions for Old," 279,
  301–305
"None of This Is Fair," 86, 524, 545–549
Non sequitur, 522
"Nonviolent Resistance," 258–262

O

O'Connor, Flannery, 278, 368, 560,
  561–564
Objective description, 184
"Obligation to Endure, The," 524, 526–533
"Of Dragons and Garden Peas," 483–489
"Once More to the Lake," 184, 205–211
"One Vote for This Age of Anxiety," 525,
  554, 555–559
"On Keeping a Private Journal," 104–105
"On Self-Respect," 289–293
Opinion, 515
Opposition, 515
Orwell, George, 173, 174–180, 457–458,
  497, 498–509
Oxymoron, 186

P

"Pain Is Not the Ultimate Enemy,"
  460–464
Parks, Rosa, 456
Personification, 186
Persuasion, illustration and, 318
Persuasion and argument, 513–598
Planning process, 73, 74–81
Point-by-point development method, 369
Point of view, 241

"Politics and the English Language,"
    457–458, 498–509
Polls, 518–519
"Portraits of My Parents," 183, 192–196
Position, 515
Post hoc fallacy, 522
Post hoc reasoning, 458
Premises, 516, 519–521
Prereading, 4–5
Prewriting process, 73
Process, 239–275
Process analysis, 240
Process essay
    organizing, 240–241
    writing, 241–242
Process essays, 455
"Professions for Women," 581–586
Purpose
    identifying, 368
    of reading, 5
"Qualities of Good Writing, The," 115–120
Quinn, Carin, 240, 241, 242–244

R

Reading, techniques for, 16–29.
    See also Writing
Reading, critical, 3–71
    reasons for, 3–4
    writers on, 13
"Reading as a Reader," 15–29
Reasoning, types of, 516–521
Red herring, 523–524
Remote cause, 456
Representative sample, 508–519
Restrictive definition, 278
Revision process, 73, 88–89
    and structuring, 82–90
Rhetorical strategy
    argument and persuasion nd, 524
    causal analysis and, 455
    description and, 183, 184
    illustration and, 317

Rhetorical terms, glossary of, 599–602
Rodriguez, Richard, 86, 279, 294, 295–299,
    524, 544–548

S

"Salvation," 135–136, 139–141
Samples, 517–519
Scudder, Samuel H., 269, 270–274

Selzer, Richard, 142, 143–146
Shaping process, 73, 81–82
"Shooting an Elephant," 174–180
Similarities and differences, 367
Simile, 185–186
Slang, 278
"Slow Walk of Trees, A," 81, 399–406
Sources, reliable, 516
Stanton, Elizabeth Cady, 317, 524, 574,
    575–579
Staples, Brent, 87–88, 317, 327, 328–331
Statistics, 516
Steinbeck, John, 183, 186, 187, 188–190
"Stranger in the Village," 226–236
Structuring and revising process, 73, 82–90
"Style," 122–126
Style, 7
Style and mechanics, 89
Subject-by-subject development method,
    369–370
Subjective description, 184
Subjects, dividing and classifying, 409–453
Sufficient cause, 456
Sufficient sample, 508
"Sweet Devouring, A," 31–34
Swift, Jonathan, 524, 587, 588–595
Syllogism, 519–521
Synonyms, 279

T

"Take This Fish and Look At It," 269–274
Tense, 241
Term, 277
Testimony, 516
Theme, 368
Thesis, 6, 80–81, 458, 515
    examples supporting, 318–319
    reviewing, 89
Thesis plan, 82
Thesis statement, 241, 368
"Thinking as a Hobby," 439–445
"38 Who Saw Murder Didn't Call Police,"
    160–163
" 'This Is the End of the World': The Black
    Death," 87, 458, 471–481
Thomas, Lewis, 368–369, 393, 394–397,
    539, 540–543
Thoreau, Henry David, 103, 104–105, 263,
    264–268
"Three Boys," 414–418
"Three New Yorks," 427–429

Thurber, James, 317, 332, 333–338
Time sequence, 137
Title, 6
Tone, 7
Topic, 514
Topic selection, 74–76, 368
Topic sentence, 6, 83–84
"Total Effect and the Eighth Grade,"
    561–563
Transitions, 240
    devices for, 7
Trillin, Alice Stewart, 482, 483–489
Tuchman, Barbara, 87, 317, 318, 339,
    340–346, 458, 470, 471–481
Tu quoque, 524
"Turtle, The," 186, 188–190
Twain, Mark, 369, 371, 372–374
"Two Ismo's, The," 368, 369, 376–378
"Two Ways of Looking at the River," 369,
    370–374

U

"University Days," 317, 333–338
Updike, John, 413, 414–418

V

Vidal, Gore, 550, 551–553
Viorst, Judith, 13, 43–47, 83, 86–87, 317,
    419, 420–425

Voice, 7, 136

W

Walker, Alice, 135, 164, 165–172, 318, 319.
    347–355
"Way to Rainy Mountain, The," 185,
    198–203
Welty, Eudora, 30, 31–34
"What Is Happiness?" 279, 285–288
"What Shall I Write?" 109–113
Wheatly, Phillis, 319
White, E. B., 184, 204, 205–211, 426,
    427–429
"Why Don't We Complain?" 318 ,
    321–326
"Why I Write," 92–97
Woolf, Virginia, 185, 212, 213–224, 524,
    581–586
"Wordstruck," 59–64
Wright, Richard, 13, 35–42
Writers, on writing, 90–131
Writing. *See also* Reading; Reading, critical
    essay, 6–7
    of narrative, 136–137
"Writing and Vision," 99–102
Writing process, 73–131
    phases of, 73–90

Z

Zinsser, William, 121, 122–126, 430–437

Literary Credits

Maya Angelou, "Graduation in Stamps," from *I Know Why the Caged Bird Sings*. Copyright © 1969 by Maya Angelou. Reprinted by permission of Random House, Inc.

Russell Baker, "The Two Ismo's," from *The New York Times*, June 5, 1982. Copyright © 1982 by The New York Times Company. Reprinted by permission.

Sheridan Baker, "What Shall I Write?," from *The Practical Stylist*. Copyright © 1982 by Sheridan Baker. Reprinted by permission of HarperCollins Publishers.

James Baldwin, "Stranger in the Village," from *Notes of a Native Son* by James Baldwin. Copyright © 1955, renewed 1983, by James Baldwin. Reprinted by permission of Beacon Press.

Jacqueline Berke, "The Qualities of Good Writing," from *Twenty Questions for the Writer: A Rhetoric with Questions*. Copyright © 1990 by Harcourt Brace Jovanovich, Inc. Reprinted by permission of Harcourt Brace Jovanovich, Inc.

Wendell Berry, "In Defense of Literacy," from *A Continuous Harmony*. Copyright © 1972, 1970 by Wendell Berry. Reprinted by permission of Harcourt Brace Jovanovich, Inc.

William F. Buckley, Jr., "Why Don't We Complain?" Copyright © 1960 by Esquire. Renewed. Reprinted by permission of the Wallace Literary Agency.

Rachel Carson, "The Obligation to Endure," from *The Silent Spring*. Copyright © 1962 by Rachel Carson. Reprinted by permission of Houghton Mifflin Co.

Bruce Catton, "Grant and Lee: A Study in Contrasts," from *The American Story*. Copyright U.S. Capital Historical Society. All rights reserved. Used with permission.

John Ciardi, "What is Happiness?" from *Saturday Review*. Copyright © 1964 John Ciardi. Reprinted by permission of Omni International, Ltd.

Norman Cousins, "Pain Is Not the Ultimate Enemy," from *Anatomy of an Illness, As Perceived by the Patient* by Norman Cousins. Copyright © 1979 by W. W. Norton & Company, Inc. Reprinted by permission of W. W. Norton & Company, Inc.

Joan Didion, "On Self-Respect," from *Slouching Towards Bethlehem*. Copyright © 1961, 1964, 1965, 1966, 1967, 1968, by Joan Didion. Reprinted by permission of Farrar, Straus & Giroux. "Why I Write," from *Salvador*. Copyright © 1976 by Joan Didion. Reprinted by permission of Simon & Schuster, Inc.